Generalship in Ancient Greece,
Rome and Byzantium

For NCT

Generalship in Ancient Greece, Rome and Byzantium

Edited by Richard Evans and Shaun Tougher

EDINBURGH
University Press

Edinburgh University Press is one of the leading university presses in the UK. We publish academic books and journals in our selected subject areas across the humanities and social sciences, combining cutting-edge scholarship with high editorial and production values to produce academic works of lasting importance. For more information visit our website: edinburghuniversitypress.com

© editorial matter and organisation Richard Evans and Shaun Tougher, 2022
© the chapters their several authors, 2022

Edinburgh University Press Ltd
The Tun – Holyrood Road, 12(2f) Jackson's Entry, Edinburgh EH8 8PJ

Typeset in 10/14 Ehrhardt
by Cheshire Typesetting Ltd, Cuddington, Cheshire

A CIP record for this book is available from the British Library

ISBN 978 1 4744 5994 5 (hardback)
ISBN 978 1 4744 5996 9 (webready PDF)
ISBN 978 1 4744 5997 6 (epub)

The right of Richard Evans and Shaun Tougher to be identified as the editors of this work has been asserted in accordance with the Copyright, Designs and Patents Act 1988, and the Copyright and Related Rights Regulations 2003 (SI No. 2498).

Contents

Acknowledgements — vii
List of Contributors — ix
Abbreviations — xii

Introduction — 1
Richard Evans and Shaun Tougher

1. Kings, Tyrants and Bandy-Legged Men: Generalship in Archaic Greece — 6
   Cezary Kucewicz

2. Commemorating Thermopylae: The *andreia* of Glorious Defeat as a Literary Construct — 36
   Richard Evans

3. Plato on Military and Political Leadership — 52
   Nicholas Rockwell

4. Reconstructing Early Seleucid Generalship, 301–222 BC — 67
   Alex McAuley

5. Generalship and Knowledge in the Middle Roman Republic — 86
   Michael Taylor

6. Command Assessment in the *Bellum Gallicum*: Caesar and *Fortuna* — 98
   David Nolan

7. Remembering P. Quinctilius Varus: Opposing Perspectives on the Memory and Memorialisation of the Failed General in the *Annales* of Tacitus 116
   Daniel Crosby

8. Decius and the Battle near Abritus 139
   David Potter

9. Ammianus and the Heroic Mode of Generalship in the Fourth Century AD 151
   Conor Whately

10. The Fine Line between Courage and Fear in the *Vandal War* 164
    Michael Stewart

11. The Generalship of John Troglita: Art in Artifice 187
    Martine de Marre

12. The Best of Men: Cross-Cultural Command in the 630s AD 206
    Eve MacDonald

13. Tian Yue Marshals His Tropes: Public Persuasion and the Character of Military Leadership in Late Tang China 225
    David A. Graff

14. The Ideal of the Roman General in Byzantium: The Reception of Onasander's *Strategikos* in Byzantine Military Literature 242
    Philip Rance

15. Generalship and Gender in Byzantium: Non-Campaigning Emperors and Eunuch Generals in the Age of the Macedonian Dynasty 264
    Shaun Tougher

16. The Politics of War: Virtue, *Tyche*, Persuasion and the Byzantine General 284
    Dimitris Krallis

Epilogue 306
Richard Evans and Shaun Tougher

Bibliography 307
Index 351

Acknowledgements

This volume has its origins in a panel on 'The Art of Generalship: Late Antique, Byzantine, and Chinese Ideals' held at the International Medieval Congress in Leeds in 2014. For this publication the scope of the original panel was extended to encompass the ancient Graeco-Roman world. In the course of its production several debts of gratitude have been incurred. We would like to thank all the contributors to the original panel, including those who were not able to contribute to the final volume: Doug Lee, Peter Lorge, Ken Swope and Jamie Wood. We are also indebted to the many colleagues around the world who acted as readers for the individual chapters and supplied helpful and constructive feedback. In addition, we cannot thank enough Edinburgh University Press for their support and extreme patience, especially Carol Macdonald. The schedule faced of course not just the usual obstructions to finalisation experienced by academics but also the ongoing Covid pandemic. Finally, Shaun would like to thank Richard for his immense contribution to the completion of the volume; he proved as excellent and positive a co-editor as he was a colleague at Cardiff.

Richard Evans and Shaun Tougher
Pretoria and Cardiff

List of Contributors

Daniel Crosby recently completed his PhD studies at Bryn Mawr College, Philadelphia, USA. While the main focus of much of his forthcoming and ongoing research is on divination in the ancient world, he has also published on Roman prosopography (2016), on Patristics (2017) and in this volume on Tacitus and the dynamics of cultural memory.

Martine de Marre is currently Associate Professor of Ancient History in the Department of Biblical and Ancient Studies at the University of South Africa, Pretoria. Her research focuses on the socio-cultural history of Roman North Africa, especially the role of women, and the works of Augustine, Fulgentius and notably Corippus (2020).

Richard Evans taught at the University of South Africa, Pretoria, and Cardiff University, Wales. He is currently an Academic Associate in the Department of Biblical and Ancient Studies, University of South Africa. He has authored books on Gaius Marius (1994), the Roman Republic (2003), ancient Syracuse (2009 and 2016), Pergamum (2012) and ancient warfare (2010, 2013 and 2015). He has also edited or co-edited volumes on mass and elite interaction in antiquity (2017), ancient divination (2018) and piracy in ancient Greece and Rome (2020).

David A. Graff is Professor in the Department of History at Kansas State University, Manhattan, USA. Since 2017 he has held the Richard A. and Greta Bauer Pickett Chair for Exceptional Faculty. He has published widely on Chinese military history, with a particular focus on the Tang Dynasty (2002) and the comparative military practice of China and Byzantium (2016).

Dimitris Krallis is Professor at the Department of Humanities and Director of the Stavros Niarchos Foundation Centre for Hellenic Studies at Simon Fraser University, Canada. He has published on the social, political and intellectual history of the Byzantine Empire, with books on the life, work and career of Michael Attaleiates (2012 and 2019).

Cezary Kucewicz completed an MA in Ancient History at Cardiff University, Wales, and more recently his PhD at University College London, England, on Homeric warfare. He is currently a postdoctoral fellow at the University of Gdańsk, Poland, and Wolfson College, Cambridge, England. He is the author of *The Treatment of the War Dead in Archaic Athens: An Ancestral Custom* (2021).

Alex McAuley is Senior Lecturer in Hellenistic History at Cardiff University, Wales. He has published extensively on the Hellenistic period, notably on the acculturation process between Macedonians and Mesopotamian groups at the start of Seleucid rule. Royal women in the dynastic structures of the Diadochi have also been a focus of recent research.

Eve MacDonald is a Lecturer in Ancient History at Cardiff University, Wales. She is interested in the social and military history of the Sasanian period and its connections to the Byzantine and early Islamic worlds. She has published on the archaeology of the Sasanian frontiers, and on Carthage and North Africa.

David Nolan completed his PhD at the University of Tasmania, Australia. His research interests focus on Caesar's leadership in his conquest of Gaul, on the battle narrative in the *Bellum Gallicum* and on the role of the centurions (2016).

David Potter is Professor of Ancient History at the University of Michigan, Ann Arbor, USA. His research interests encompass Greek and Latin historiography, public entertainments in the Graeco-Roman world, ancient warfare, and Greek and Roman Asia Minor. His publications are many, including *Emperors of Rome* (2008), *The Roman Empire at Bay* (2014) and *The Origin of Empire* (2018).

Philip Rance obtained his PhD at St Andrews, Scotland. He has taught History and Greek Language at universities in the UK and Germany, and held numerous research fellowships in Europe. He is a Visiting Scholar at the Free University, Berlin, Germany, and a Research Fellow at the Centre for Advanced Study, Sofia, Bulgaria. He has published extensively on late antique and Byzantine history and literature.

Nicholas Rockwell is a Lecturer in Political Science and History at the University of Colorado, Denver, USA. He obtained his PhD from the University of California, Los Angeles, USA, and his MA and BA from California State University, Fresno, USA. He is the author of a monograph entitled *Thebes: A History* (2017), and is currently engaged in research towards a study of the citizen-soldier in the ancient world.

Michael Stewart is an Honorary Research Fellow in the School of History and Philosophical Inquiry at the University of Queensland, Australia. Having completed his PhD thesis in 2013 he has since published extensively, including *The Soldier's Life: Martial Virtues and Manly Romanitas in the Early Byzantine Empire* (2016).

Michael Taylor is an Assistant Professor in the History Department, State University of New York at Albany, USA. He obtained his PhD from the University of California, Berkeley, USA. He has published widely on Roman Republican warfare and political life, and is the author of *Soldiers and Silver: Mobilizing Resources in the Age of Roman Conquest* (2020).

Shaun Tougher is Professor of Late Roman and Byzantine History at Cardiff University, Wales. His numerous publications include *The Reign of Leo VI* (1997), *Julian the Apostate* (2007), *The Eunuch in Byzantine History and Society* (2008) and, most recently, *The Roman Castrati: Eunuchs in the Roman Empire* (2021).

Conor Whately is Associate Professor in Classics at the University of Winnipeg, Canada. He has written or co-edited six books. One was a co-edited volume with James Chlup on Greek and Roman military manuals (2020), one was on the Roman military in the imperial-era Balkans (2016), and two were on assorted aspects of Procopius' writing as they pertain to war and war-making (2016 and 2021). Two books are for a more general audience, one an introduction to the Roman military (2020), the other an introduction to sensory aspects of ancient warfare (2021).

Abbreviations

The following is a list of abbreviations of key journals and collections listed in the bibliography. Ancient writers and their works are generally abbreviated according to current conventions, although some contributors adopt variations. Likewise, individual contributors follow personal preference in the spelling of names and transliteration of ancient Greek. Regarding dating abbreviations, BC and AD are adopted throughout the volume.

AClass	*Acta Classica*
AFLS	*Annali della Facoltà di Lettere e Filosofia dell'Università di Siena*
AHB	*The Ancient History Bulletin*
AJP	*American Journal of Philology*
Anc. Soc.	*Ancient Society*
AnnBari	*Annali della Facoltà di Lettere e Filosofia, Università di Bari*
ANRW	*Aufstieg und Niedergang der römischen Welt*
Ant. Class.	*L'Antiquité Classique*
BCH	*Bulletin de Correspondence Hellénique*
BF	*Byzantinische Forschungen*
BMGS	*Byzantine and Modern Greek Studies*
Byz	*Byzantion*
BZ	*Byzantinische Zeitschrift*
C&M	*Classica et Mediaevalia*
CJ	*Classical Journal*
Cl. Ant.	*Classical Antiquity*
CP	*Classical Philology*
CQ	*Classical Quarterly*

CR	Classical Review
CW	Classical World
DHA	Dialogues d'Histoire Ancienne
DOP	Dumbarton Oaks Papers
EA	Epigraphica Anatolica
G&R	Greece and Rome
GRBS	Greek, Roman and Byzantine Studies
Hist.	Historia
JAH	Journal of Ancient History
JHS	Journal of Hellenic Studies
JJS	Journal of Jewish Studies
JLA	Journal of Late Antiquity
JÖB	Jahrbuch der Österreichischen Byzantinistik
JRA	Journal of Roman Archaeology
JRS	Journal of Roman Studies
MAAR	Memoirs of the American Academy in Rome
MD	Materiali e Discussioni
MH	Museum Helveticum
NC	The Numismatic Chronicle
P&P	Past and Present
PBSR	Papers of the British School at Rome
PG	Patrologia Graeca
PhW	Philologische Wochenschrift
PLLS	Papers of the Leeds Latin Seminar
RE	Paulys Real-Encyclopädie der classischen Altertumswissenschaft
REA	Revue des Études Anciennes
Rev. Ét. Grec.	Revue des Études Grecques
RhM	Rheinisches Museum
TAPA	Transactions of the American Philological Association
TM	Travaux et Mémoires
WJA	Würzburger Jahrbücher für die Altertumswissenschaft
ZPE	Zeitschrift für Papyrologie und Epigraphik

Introduction

Richard Evans and Shaun Tougher

'Tis not in mortals to command success,
But we'll do more, Sempronius; we'll deserve it.

Joseph Addison, *Cato: A Tragedy*, 1.2.43

The art of generalship or the ability of successful leadership in a military context, as Addison perceptively observed, is not at all dependent on fortune or *tyche* (meaning in reality good luck) to ensure victory. Victory might be obtained through good luck just happening,[1] but the soundest method of ensuring success relies on fastidious management in the camp and while on the march in conjunction with inspiring leadership on the field of battle. How many or how few generals in antiquity measure up to such a stringent assessment of their capabilities, their practice of the art of being a general, and so deserved the successes they obtained and their subsequent immortal fame? In the following chapters the discussion aligns to this focus. Julius Caesar, for example, makes frequent reference to 'good fortune' in his Gallic campaigns (Nolan), but he was an able if not the consummate manager of his military adventures, in Gaul, Italy, Spain and Greece in the first century BC.[2] In political life he perhaps lacked that lightness of touch which his successor Augustus, only a moderately capable military leader, possessed in abundance. Leonidas, the Spartan king

---

[1] Such as a timely thunderstorm, a dust storm or a snowstorm, or a fortuitous eclipse of the sun or moon. All these natural phenomena could affect the moods of the opposing sides in military campaigns, but could also be explained as divine intervention.

[2] His expeditions to Britain in 55 and 54 BC, however, showed the limitations of ancient access to information and the logistical difficulties relating to organising long-range seaborne expeditions.

(Evans), and the Roman emperor Decius (Potter), on the other hand, no doubt both capable soldiers, found immortality not in success, but in two of the most famous defeats in the history of the Greeks and Romans: Thermopylae in 480 BC and Abritus in AD 251 respectively.

The importance to cultures in antiquity of success in military affairs can easily be measured by noting that Homer's *Iliad*, among the earliest surviving literary evidence for the history and civilisation of the ancient Greeks, is essentially a tale in verse about the flawed leadership of the protagonists: Agamemnon, Achilles and Hector. All are active participants in the military campaigning around Troy and the battles that took place there (Kucewicz). None is the perfect general, but Alexander the Great (336–323 BC), probably the greatest warrior general of history, and the most sublime practitioner of generalship, constantly sought to emulate these mythical figures; and he was not an isolated example. On the other hand, the Roman emperor Trajan (AD 98–117), certainly regarded by the Romans as completely equal in ability to Alexander, was, very much like Caesar, a manager of his armies and not a front-line fighter. In late antiquity, the ambitious eastern campaign of emperor Julian (361–363) can be presented or even understood as a desire to follow in the footsteps of Alexander the Great and the Homeric heroes. Julian's death on the field of battle on 26 June 363 was in keeping with the by then thousand-year-old tradition of the Graeco-Roman warrior.[3] Further, he was certainly not the last, as the following discussions will illustrate. Indeed, Julian's words are as revealing as his actions. Well known for his writings as much as his political and military career, in his celebrated satire *The Caesars* – in which the gods undertake to decide who has been the best Roman emperor of all – three of the six finalists were chosen as being the most warlike: Julius Caesar, Augustus and Trajan.[4] Further, although Marcus Aurelius was selected as a philosopher,[5] and Constantine was thrown into the mix as a lover of pleasure,[6] both emperors also played a military role, and as much as Julian sought to downplay it, Constantine was a highly successful general. The one Greek figure who was allowed to be included in the competition and as one of the finalists reflects the prevalence of the military role of leaders too, for it was Alexander the Great.[7]

Homeric generalship involved conspicuous participation on the battlefield and could and did result in some of the most memorable leadership qualities displayed throughout antiquity by, for example, not only Alexander the Great, the

---

[3] Amm. Marc. 25.3.
[4] *Caesars* 317B.
[5] *Caesars* 317C.
[6] *Caesars* 317D–318A.
[7] *Caesars* 316B–D.

early Seleucids (McAuley) or Julius Caesar, but also Epaminondas of Thebes (died 362 BC), Agesilaus of Sparta (c. 400–360 BC) and Dionysius I of Syracuse (405–367 BC). It could also result in disaster, not only for Julian but also, for example, for Antigonus Monophthalmus or Pyrrhus of Epirus, both killed fighting at vital times for the fortunes of their states, in 301 BC and 272 BC respectively. Homeric generalship also belonged to an epoch in which the leader of a state was first and perhaps only a warrior, or portrayed as such: Odysseus, Ajax, even Nestor (when he was a young man). But the increasing sophistication of states and how they operated in the ancient world brought with it a change in the way military governance was conceived. Civic leadership, which required competencies across a number of vital fields from the juridical to oratorical ability for meetings of citizen assemblies, and civil administration, brought with it a diminution of the purely military career. By the fifth century BC in Athens leaders such as Miltiades, Aristides, Themistocles, Pericles and Nicias possessed as many strengths as administrators as they did as generals. Their successes in peace as in war indicate not only a wealth of talent in Athenian society, but also that those who reached the pinnacle of success were extraordinary all-rounders. From the fifth century on, there were as many generals who directed their armies from behind the front line of fighting as there were Homeric-type warrior generals on the battlefield. While in the first half of the fourth century BC the Theban leaders Pelopidas and Epaminondas were likely to face opponents such as Agesilaus of Sparta, Alexander of Pherae or Iphicrates of Athens on the front line, there were equally successful generals who saw little or no actual combat.[8] Philip II (359–336 BC), the Macedonian monarch who was father of a greater son, was highly successful in pursuit of territorial acquisitions, but he is not remembered in the same way as his warrior-king son Alexander the Great.[9]

The expansion into different areas of concern and the growing complexities of management in military affairs must have been the primary cause for writers such as Aeneas Tacticus and Xenophon in the fourth century BC to circulate reflections on how campaigns might be organised by a general, the sort of training needed to become a good commander, and the various elements of campaigns: from battlefield encounters to armies on the march, and even the preparations and techniques need to besiege or defend a city. It is evident that both the specific problems confronting

---

[8] Pelopidas was killed on the battlefield. Epaminondas and Agesilaus were active in combat well into old age. Epaminondas died at the Battle of Mantinea in 372 BC, Agesilaus while returning from serving as a mercenary in Egypt in 350 BC.

[9] Philip lost the sight of an eye at the siege of Methone, but he appears to have been at some distance from the front line when he suffered this injury. At his greatest victory, Chaeronea in 338 BC, Philip commanded the right wing but it was his son on the left wing who is recorded as being in the thick of the fighting.

generals and the wider issues of what was implicit in generalship or leadership began to be a topic of debate among intellectual circles, as can easily be gauged from the extant works of Plato and Aristotle (Rockwell), and remained so even a full millennium later in the Byzantine Empire, as reflected by such texts at the *Strategikon* ascribed to the emperor Maurice (582–602) and the *Taktika* of the emperor Leo VI (886–912) (Rance, Tougher, Krallis).

As yet there was no specialised military elite as is found today in the graduates of numerous military academies scattered around the world. The general was very much an amateur, as exemplified by the commanders of armies in the Roman Republic (Taylor), and indeed the phenomenon persisted until the First World War (1914–1918). As such these amateurs could, and often did, scale dizzy heights in their successes: Scipio Africanus at Zama in 202 BC, the younger Aemilius Paullus at Pydna in 168 BC, Gaius Marius at Vercellae in 101 BC; but they might also plumb the depths of catastrophic disasters: Gaius Flaminius at Lake Trasimene in 217 BC, the elder Aemilius Paullus at Cannae in 216 BC, or Augustus' general Quinctilius Varus at the Teutoburg Wald in AD 9 (Crosby).

By the time of the early Roman Empire, the rulers, although commanders-in-chief of their armies stationed on the far-flung frontiers, rarely ventured from the metropolis. Active generalship roles were therefore the occupation of subordinates, but victories, and by implication defeats,[10] belonged to the ruler and reflected either his glory or his lack of talent. By the mid-second century AD Roman emperors had taken to leading campaigns personally if not actually fighting in battles. Marcus Aurelius (161–180) spent much of his rule directing efforts to prevent Germanic tribes from penetrating the Roman Empire's northern borders. From the rule of Septimius Severus (193–211) onwards it again became almost a rule of thumb that the emperor was active in campaigns. Decius (249–251) was the first Roman emperor to die in battle against invaders. Further, the third century was the age of the soldier emperors, the phenomenon that many of those who became emperor had risen through the ranks of the army. This began with Maximinus Thrax (235–238) but is exemplified by the famous figure of Diocletian (284–305). This age of emperor generals included Constantine the Great (306–337), Constantius II (337–361), Julian (355–363), Valentinian I (364–375) and his brother Valens (364–378) (Whately), but the death of Theodosius I (379–395) marked a return to the figure of the non-campaigning emperor. This shift began with Theodosius' young sons and successors Arcadius (395–408) and Honorius (395–423), but is famously exemplified by Justinian I (527–565), who nevertheless presided over the reconquest of North Africa and Italy,

---

[10] Victories were often celebrated lavishly, while defeats could be blamed on the commander in the field rather than on the emperor.

reliant on generals such as the celebrated Belisarius and John Troglita (Stewart, de Marre). This trend could fluctuate; witness the campaigns of Heraclius (610–641) against both Persians and Arabs (MacDonald) and the number of non-campaigning emperors who distinguish Byzantium's Macedonian Dynasty (Tougher). Non-campaigning emperors could nonetheless lay claim to military authority and divine support for success, as well as the masculine virtue of courage, so key in the identity of the general. In Byzantium even generals who were eunuchs, such as Narses in the sixth century and Basil Lekapenos in the tenth century, could be celebrated for this quality (Tougher).

Whilst this volume focuses primarily on generalship in Greece, Rome and Byzantium, it is important to recognise that these cultures did not exist and act in a vacuum, but rather interacted with other cultures and peoples they encountered. Thus, ideas about generals and generalship could come into direct dialogue. Further, there is scope for comparative approaches. These issues are particularly foregrounded in the chapters by MacDonald and Graff. The former chapter examines narratives of 'best men' in relation to the campaigns and conflicts in the Near East in the seventh century AD, considering for instance Persian and Arab views of commanders as well as Roman/Byzantine ones. Graff's chapter takes us further east, to imperial China during the Tang Dynasty (618–907), yet still to the familiar issue of the speeches of encouragement given by generals.

Further, although this volume deals with ideals and specific aspects of generalship across an extensive chronological period, from archaic Greece through to the Byzantine Empire in the twelfth century, common themes and concerns emerge across the chapters. These include the subjects of speeches of commanders, gender (especially the virtue of courage) and cross-cultural comparisons, as already noted, but also encompass commemoration of both military victories and defeats and the intersection of the political and military roles of leaders. All these themes and concerns feature in the final chapter by Krallis, which thus serves as a fitting conclusion to the set of chapters. While the chronological span of the volume means that not every aspect of the art of generalship, and certainly not every lauded or denigrated general, receives detailed treatment, it does mean that commonalities and divergences emerge clearly and that a more holistic view of the subject is provided. We hope that this proves useful and encourages further research, shifting the focus from the study of the careers of individual generals to the ideas and ideals that underpinned them.

1 | Kings, Tyrants and Bandy-Legged Men: Generalship in Archaic Greece

Cezary Kucewicz

In 476/5 BC, an Athenian force under Cimon sailed to Thrace to recapture the city of Eion held by the Persians. After a successful battle against the enemy, Cimon besieged the city and forced the Persian general Butes, who would not surrender, to set the whole city – including his family – on fire. In the aftermath of these events, the Athenians authorised Cimon to erect three inscribed monuments at Athens to commemorate the victory. The third of them, as Aeschines and later Plutarch relate (Aeschin. 3.185; Plut. *Cim.* 7.5), evoked the timeless Athenian superiority in the art of marshalling warriors as exemplified by Menestheus, the Homeric hero who led the Athenians at Troy:

> Once from this city Menestheus, summoned to join the Atreidae,
> Led forth an army to Troy, plain beloved of the gods.
> Homer has sung of his fame, and has said that of all the mailed chieftains
> None could so shrewdly as he marshal the ranks for the fight.
> Fittingly then shall the people of Athens be honoured, and called
> Marshals and leaders of war, heroes in combat of arms.[1]

---

[1] All translations are taken from the Loeb Classical Library unless otherwise indicated. The exceptions are the *Iliad* and *Odyssey*, for which Richmond Lattimore's translations are used. This chapter is part of a postdoctoral project funded by the National Science Centre, Poland (project number 2018/28/C/HS3/00418). I am grateful for the critical insights from Bogdan Burliga, Roel Konijnendijk, Caroline Musgrove, Robin Osborne and Hans van Wees, who commented on the earlier drafts of this chapter. They are not necessarily in agreement with my views, and any remaining mistakes are entirely my own.

In the inscription Menestheus, praised in the *Iliad* for his outstanding ability in 'the arrangement in order of horses and shielded fighters' (2.554), provided an archetype of the Athenian supremacy in generalship, thus justifying their leadership in the newly formed Delian League.[2] Such evocations of the mythical heroes of the past were by no means unusual as the Homeric epics provided the classical Greeks with an inexhaustible source of wisdom and inspiration. In particular, any subjects related to war were almost inevitably set against the battle narratives of the *Iliad*, seen as an exemplar in all things military. Mentions of Homer featured prominently in discussions regarding troop arrangement, tactics, bravery, war ethics and even appropriate campaign diets, spread across a variety of classical authors and genres.[3] From the Hellenistic period onward Homeric citations formed an important part of the advice collected in the military manuals on tactics and stratagems, confirming the unquestionable authority of the *Iliad* for the Greek thinking about war.[4]

One area for which the Homeric epics supplied invaluable guidelines in the eyes of the ancient Greeks was the art of generalship. The mythical kings who fought on the plains of Troy, among whom Menestheus was just one, provided universal models on how to draw up, lead, exhort and discipline warriors, arrange army formations and set up ambushes. Such was Homer's authority that even a professional rhapsode could lay claim to a knowledge of good generalship on the sole basis of his familiarity with the *Iliad*.[5] But despite Homer's influence on the later Greeks, our understanding of the norms of generalship of the archaic period – the era in which the Homeric epics were composed – remains limited and surprisingly problematic for modern scholars tackling the subject.[6]

Greek warfare of the archaic period has traditionally been a highly contentious scholarly field, primarily due to the scarcity of contemporary written evidence for

---

[2] See also Hdt. 7.161. For more on the monument and Cimon's attempts to engage with the mythical past, see Arrington (2015) 196–204.

[3] See, for instance, Ar. *Ran.* 1034–6; Pl. *Resp.* 404B–C; Xen. *Symp.* 4.6; Arist. *Eth. Nic.* 1116A–B. For more extensive references, see Wheeler (1991) 155 n. 12; Lendon (2005) 348 n. 11.

[4] For more on the so-called Homeric *Tactica*, see Wheeler (1983) 17 n. 85, 18 n. 91; Lendon (2005) 360 n. 13.

[5] Pl. *Ion* 541A–B. According to a scholiast (Σ 21.331d), Homer provided instructions for generals (*didaskalia de strategikon*) on how to be inventive and see things quickly.

[6] The question of the historicity and date of the Homeric poems is too broad and controversial to discuss here. For the purposes of this chapter, it is enough to say that the epics reached their final written form no later than the mid-seventh century BC, but combine a number of different, and sometimes historically incompatible, elements which reflect the oral tradition behind their creation. For recent discussions on the historicity of Homeric warfare, see van Wees (2004) 249–52; Schwartz (2009) 105–15; Kagan and Viggiano (2013b) 44–9.

the practice of war. Most of the available battle accounts of archaic wars come from later sources. These, composed in very different political and military contexts, often looked back to the earlier ages of Greek warfare with nostalgia, idealising the way their predecessors conducted war. Polybius, for instance, romanticised the fairness and simplicity of the ancients, who never used deception and always declared their wars (13.3.2–6). Similar sentiments are expressed in the writings of Herodotus (7.9) and Demosthenes (9.47–52), which relate a distinct principle of fairness in Greek military conflicts. Their remarks have made a significant mark on modern studies of Greek warfare, in particular those emphasising the 'agonistic' nature of war in Greece, which stressed its rule-bound character, designed to lessen the impact of war on the Greek *poleis*.[7] The agonistic ideal has influenced nearly every aspect of our understanding of Greek warfare, including early concepts of generalship.

According to the statements of Polybius and others, early Greek wars consisted exclusively of hand-to-hand pitched battles fought in an open way; there was little room for tactical manoeuvres or ingenuity and even less for deception. This ideal of simple and predictable battles, where rival phalanxes clashed with little support from light-armed troops or cavalry, became deeply entrenched in the scholarship on Greek warfare.[8] Hoplite battles, as Victor Davis Hanson summarised, consisted of 'a brief collision of uniformly armed equals – little tactics, little strategy, little generalship'.[9] This model, according to him, dominated the armed conflicts in the Greek world throughout the archaic period until the Graeco-Persian Wars (or the Peloponnesian War), which eroded the unwritten traditional code and introduced new elements widening the scope, complexity and destructive potential of war.[10] One such innovation was the increased prominence given to strategy, tactics and deception, extending the roles of Greek generals beyond their previously basic duties of leading the phalanx in its charge. As a result, studies of Greek generalship

---

[7] The notion of Greek warfare as an *agon*, or contest, was most famously presented in a collection of essays edited by Vernant (1968). According to this study, the Greeks fought their battles more for status than survival, and followed a number of unwritten military protocols, reminiscent of medieval tournaments. Later proponents of this notion include Connor (1988); Hanson (1995); and Ober (1996) 53–7.

[8] For the early history of this ideal, see Konijnendijk (2018) 6–38.

[9] Hanson (1991b) 10. His earlier book on infantry battle in classical Greece introduces the model (1989) 19–26, 107–16.

[10] For Hanson (1995) 338, the erosion of the hoplite code came with the Graeco-Persian Wars; Ober (1991) and (1996) 63–9 saw Pericles' strategy of avoiding battle during the Peloponnesian War as decisive. Singor (2009) 599–601 dates the changes more generally to the end of the archaic period.

have usually focused on the classical and Hellenistic periods, giving little attention to the generals of the archaic era.[11]

The agonal interpretation of archaic Greek warfare has been challenged by revisionist scholars over the past two decades. Their studies have successfully shown that Greek warfare was more complex and unregulated, and that the accounts of Polybius and Demosthenes were little more than panhellenic propaganda.[12] In a similar way, the model of pitched battles fought by rival phalanxes has fallen out of favour, as numerous examples of small-scale warfare, ambushes and surprise attacks have been shown to be a common occurrence from the archaic period onward. Nevertheless, the role of generals in early Greek warfare remains largely unconsidered.

The most influential interpretation of ancient Greek generalship, including Homer and the archaic period, was proposed by Everett Wheeler. He posited a long process of transition from the Homeric/archaic warrior chieftain to the classical phalanx commander, and eventually the Hellenistic battle manager.[13] Wheeler's theory traced the development of combat leadership side by side with the evolution of the hoplite phalanx. This transition was set against two competing ideals of the warrior inherited from the Homeric poems: Achilles, who represented the traditional model of courage and martial skill; and Odysseus, the master of careful planning, trickery and ambush. The chieftains of pre-state war-bands, which dominated most of the archaic period, followed the ideal of Achilles. With the institutionalisation of citizen armies and the offices of generals (*strategoi*) in the Greek *poleis*, the art of generalship was gradually transformed as considerations of tactics, unit deployment, surprise and ambush became increasingly significant, drawing from the Homeric ideal of Odysseus. As such, Wheeler traced 'the emergence of generalship' to the period between 479 and 362 BC, giving the impression that generalship was severely limited, if not altogether non-existent, in the preceding archaic period. The model of transition from Homeric chieftain generals to the *strategoi* of the classical period features prominently in recent studies, which tend to see the Peloponnesian War as the watershed moment for Greek generalship.[14]

---

[11] See, for instance, Adcock (1957) 82–97; Pritchett (1994b) 27–144; Hamel (1998); Boëldieu-Trevet (2007); Moore (2013); Roisman (2017).

[12] Krentz (2000); (2002); Rawlings (2000); (2007); van Wees (2004); (2011); Dayton (2006); Konijnendijk (2018). For specific references to Polybius, Demosthenes and Herodotus, see Krentz (2000); van Wees (2004) 115–17; Wheeler (2007) 186–92; Konijnendijk (2016).

[13] Wheeler (1991); (2007) 213–23.

[14] 'The Emergence of Generalship, 479–362 BC' is a sub-chapter in Wheeler (2007) where he does in fact suggests a certain degree of continuity between archaic and classical concepts of generalship but does not elaborate any further on the claim. Adcock (1957) 89 suggested

The purpose of this chapter is to revisit the evidence for the ideals and practice of generalship in archaic Greece and offer a more nuanced overview of the duties of early Greek commanders. Several aspects of their craft will be considered, such as the source and extent of a general's authority; the role of generals in combat; and the use of strategy and tactics in battle. Despite the limited evidence for early battles, the poems of Homer, Tyrtaeus and Archilochus, along with the traditions associated with the tyrant Peisistratus and the Spartan king Cleomenes, all indicate that the art of generalship developed over time reflecting wider changes in the nature of Greek warfare and the organisation of early Greek armies.

Homeric Generalship

For a reader accustomed to modern military standards, the significance of a story featuring selfish leadership (Agamemnon) and gross insubordination (Achilles), placed within a context of a battlefield where larger-than-life heroes compete in individual displays of martial skill, may not fit a discourse on good generalship. An episode from the *Odyssey* illustrates the problem. After arriving at Ithaca, Odysseus first encounters the swineherd Eumaeus. Posing as the son of a Cretan nobleman, Castor, Odysseus relates a story of a raiding expedition which he claims to have led against Egypt. After gathering many warriors with daily feasts and promises of easy plunder, the expedition sails to Egypt and lands just inside the Nile, upon which the son of Castor orders his men to stay vigilant and refrain from violence:

> Then I urged my eager companions to stay where they were, there
> close to the fleet, and to guard the ships, and was urgent with them
> to send look-outs to the watching places; but they, following
> their own impulse, and giving way to marauding violence,
> suddenly began plundering the Egyptians' beautiful
> fields, and carried off the women and innocent children,
> and killed the men, and soon the outcry came to the city.
>
> (*Od.* 14.259–65)

Ignoring the orders of the expedition general, the raiding party is attacked by a substantial force of Egyptians and defeated with ease. Although fictional, the story shows that a fundamental lack of discipline and obedience characterised Homeric warriors, who ignore the orders of their commander and pursue their personal inter-

---

that the 'watershed between the older and the newer battle tactics lies in the career of Epaminondas'. See also Moore (2013) 458; Roisman (2017) 9–14.

ests instead. But while the episode demonstrates poor military organisation, it also offers important strategic advice which readers could learn from: always establish a strong, defensible position before attacking the enemy.[15] As such, it falls within a larger pattern of battle narratives in the *Iliad* and *Odyssey*, in which stories of poor leadership and insubordination are mixed with examples of exceptional generalship and sound tactical lessons.

At the head of Homeric armies stood the elite noblemen referred to in the poems as the *basileis*. The narratives focus almost exclusively on their actions at the expense of the multitude of commoners who quietly follow the *basileis* on the battlefields. As a consequence, the mechanics of their leadership over the latter are not clearly delineated in the epics, which instead depict the brave exploits of the Homeric kings.[16] Their superiority in combat is unquestionable; all notable *basileis* are presented as excellent fighters, each enjoying long episodes of outstanding martial feats (*aristeia*) featuring the mass slaughter of their enemies.[17] Martial excellence (*arete*) defined their social status and validated their right to command others. As Sarpedon, the king of the Lycians, explains to a fellow nobleman, Glaucus, the many privileges which the *basileis* enjoy in their communities are given to them because of the 'strength of valour in them, since they fight in the forefront of the Lycians' (*Il.* 12.320–1). Homeric generals were expected to excel in fighting, risk their lives in combat and lead their warriors by example; by and large, they seem to have lived up to these expectations in the poems.

Although all Homeric *basileis* were notionally equal, Agamemnon and Hector held the positions of supreme general, based on the superior size of the contingents which they commanded. The overall army structure was outlined in the so-called Catalogue of Ships, which lists twenty-nine separate contingents on the Greek side and sixteen on the Trojan side (*Il.* 2.484–877). Each contingent, comprising on average around 2,000 men, consisted of warriors drawn from specific regions and led usually by one or two named *basileis*. In combat, the regional contingents were further subdivided into smaller units, or war-bands, which formed the main organisational principle of Homeric armies. Such bands were made up of a single *basileus* – on whom the fighting usually focuses – followed by a few dozen companions and

---

[15] For more on the episode, see Rawlings (2007) 104–5. A similar story features in Odysseus' recounting of his raid on the Ciconians to Alcinous (9.39–61).

[16] On the *basileis* and their leadership in combat, see Donlan (1979); van Wees (1988); (1996) esp. 27–9; Wheeler (1991) 126–9; Lendon (2005) 20–38.

[17] Diomedes' *aristeia*, during which he even succeeds in wounding Ares, takes up most of Book 5 and continues into Book 6. Cf. Agamemnon (11.15–283) and Achilles (20.75–22.404), who are no less impressive. For a list of passages highlighting the martial superiority of Homeric *basileis*, see van Wees (1988) 21.

retainers. Loyalty within the war-bands was usually strong but its basis was not any formal obligation to obey orders; a mix of comradeship, mutual support and fear played a far more significant role.[18] And while the mechanics of leadership are often lost in the almost exclusive focus on the personal exploits of the *basileis*, it is clear that keeping discipline was an important consideration of the Homeric generals, one which – as the example of the son of Castor shows – was not always easy to uphold, as warriors were free to disobey orders or even withdraw their services.[19]

Commanders sometimes threaten to kill their men if they fail to obey orders. Agamemnon promises death to those hanging 'back by the curved ships' (*Il*. 2.392); Hector makes a similar threat to warriors holding back to gather spoils (*Il*. 15.347–51).[20] Enforcing obedience can also involve violence, illustrated by the famous case of Thersites' criticism of Agamemnon (*Il*. 2.265–9). Such instances may suggest the dominance of a coercive kind of discipline, but within the larger context of the poems these scenes are exceptional. In the highly competitive environment of Homeric societies, where social status needed to be constantly reaffirmed, any forms of aggressive behaviour invited repercussions. Coercive discipline was therefore applied mostly to the rank and file within the war-bands. Enforcing orders on fellow *basileis* could have disastrous consequences, as the conflict between Agamemnon and Achilles showcased. Respectful encouragements and exhortations are the norm.[21]

Leading men by positive exhortations is – next to martial prowess – one of the central tasks of every Homeric commander. Most exhortations aim to encourage warriors to join the fighting: 'Let us go back to the fighting wounded as we are' (*Il*. 14.128); 'do not give up, and urge on each man as you find him' (*Il*. 13.230).

---

[18] Van Wees (1988) 6 n. 23 estimates that a typical war-band consisted of around fifty warriors. Each contingent was tied by a variety of bonds, such as family, friendship, economic dependence and social deference. Elements of public organisation are also hinted at in the poem, including a fee for those who refuse to join the campaign (*Il*. 13.669–70). For recruitment and organisation of Homeric armies, see van Wees (1986); (1997) 669–73; Singor (1991) 24–33; Rawlings (2007) 31–3.

[19] Achilles provides the main example of a warrior disobeying orders and withdrawing from fighting, *Il*. 1.225–44; see also 17.154–5. The importance of comradeship and collective solidarity within Homeric armies is best illustrated by van Wees (1996) esp. 16–21.

[20] See also *Il*. 2.357–9; 12.248–50.

[21] As van Wees (1996) 27 summarises: 'those of higher status are politely asked to get a grip of themselves'; *Il*. 2.185–210, 243–69. The few verses depicting the use of coercive discipline for the rank and file may suggest that threats and physical intimidation were simply a tacit norm in Homeric warfare. Considering the elite ideology and outlook of the poems, the interactions between the *basileis* and the masses are rarely depicted, being of lesser interest to the poet and his audience. On class interactions in Homeric society, see Rose (2012) 93–165; Kucewicz (2018) 21–6.

Such appeals are plentiful throughout the *Iliad* and indicate the significance of encouragement for any Homeric general.[22] Far from relying on coercive discipline only, Homeric leadership was therefore largely egalitarian, as the commanders put themselves in the role of companions to their followers, sharing in the same dangers and supporting each other in combat. The duty of exhorting comrades was indeed extended to every member of the war-band; the *basileis* were simply more vocal than others.[23] Such personal and group exhortations, combined with occasional threats to the rank and file, meant that Homeric generals could depend upon the obedience of their warriors once the fighting started. The resulting poetic image of the Greek army advancing into battle, marching steadily 'in fear of their commanders', could easily serve as an exemplar for any ancient Greek commander turning to the *Iliad* for guidance on discipline (*Il.* 4.427–32).

Apart from leading by example and exhortation, Homeric generals were also in charge of drawing up their warriors before the engagement; the orders of the son of Castor to establish defensive positions before a raid are one example. The *Iliad* shows limited interest in the tactical handling of bodies of men, but a number of passages indicate that the ability to marshal troops was a desirable skill among the *basileis*. The standard procedure hinted at in the poem has the commander dividing his forces into smaller sections, usually led by five subcommanders specifically appointed for the task.[24] Nestor also suggests, much to the approval of Agamemnon, army organisation by tribes and phratries (*Il.* 2.362–3). His own contingent from Pylos, commanded by five named leaders, is further singled out for a specific arrangement: the best and bravest warriors are stationed at the back in order to drive forward the cowards in the centre (*Il.* 4.297–300).[25] These passages are clearly designed to highlight Nestor's superior skill in arranging men. His ability, as J. E. Lendon remarked, belonged to a set of excellences (*aretai*) which all Homeric *basileis* desired and competed for with one another.[26] But despite the praise which Nestor receives, strategic considerations were ascribed less significance than military prowess in combat. Both Agamemnon

---

[22] E.g. *Il.* 13.767; 17.117, 683.

[23] For more on coercion and exhortations in the *Iliad*, see van Wees (1996) 27–9, 69 n. 76.

[24] *Il.* 4.294–6; 12.86–7; 16.171–2. At one point, the entire Trojan army divides into 'five well-ordered battalions', *Il.*12.87. On the fivefold unit divisions in the *Iliad*, see Singor (1991) 25–6, 37–9; van Wees (1986) 291; (1997) 675. Although strategic deployment is not a feature of battles, Homer does divide the battlefield into a right, centre and left, *Il.* 13.308–9.

[25] On tribes and phratries in Homer, with specific reference to Nestor's advice, see Andrewes (1961). On the tactical benefits of deploying the bravest men in the rear of the unit in the wider context of Greek warfare, see Konijnendijk (2018) 183–5.

[26] Lendon (2005) 31–2.

and Hector are at times criticised for bad tactical choices, which seemingly takes nothing from their pre-eminence as generals.[27] It is, furthermore, revealing that neither Nestor's suggestions nor the fivefold unit subdivisions which the poem occasionally mentions are maintained in the subsequent battle narratives. Apart from showcasing the skill of the *basileus* commanding his men, they play no role in the actual fighting of the *Iliad*. This, in turn, has led scholars to suspect that such tactical and organisational considerations were relatively new at the time of the epic's final composition, introducing elements previously unfamiliar to Greek warfare.[28]

Another feature which may reflect a contemporary military development is the *Iliad*'s depiction of the effectiveness of dense formations. The majority of Homeric battle scenes are fought in predominantly open formations, which allow considerable freedom for each war-band to move around the battlefield. The fighting combined both close-range and missile warfare; occasional intensification draws more men together, usually in response to a particular crisis (e.g. protecting a fallen comrade, defending the ships etc.). Despite the general fluidity and openness of Homeric battlefields, the *Iliad* accentuates the advantages of cohesion in combat. Numerous passages mention the importance of warriors protecting one another in battle, indicating that the effectiveness of dense formation and mutual support were clearly understood by the poet (*Il.* 3.8–9; 14.368–9; 17.364–5, 721).[29] It is also striking, as Hans van Wees observed, that it is only Greek warriors who explicitly recommend such behaviour, in sharp contrast to the Trojans. The tactical advantages of disciplined warriors forming ad hoc close formations were therefore not only recognised and put to good use but could also offer a hint of the superior tactical knowledge of the Achaean generals.[30]

---

[27] *Il.* 13.726–47; 14.83–102. The military authority of the *basileis* is not, however, determined by their physical prowess. Their position is based instead on social standing within their communities, usually inherited and founded on superior wealth and numbers of followers. Courage and martial skill are certainly expected of them, but occasionally they do give in to fear and flee the battlefield, which does not undermine their authority, e.g. *Il.* 5.571–2; 8.137–56. While fleeing is equated in the *Iliad* with cowardice, e.g. 11.408, there is no expectation for warriors to fight when the odds are against them, 7.109–19. The fluid nature of the battlefield means that temporary withdrawals are common and easily rallied from. For more, see van Wees (1996) 8–10.

[28] Andrewes (1961); Wheeler (1991) 128; van Wees (1997) 691. On the historicity of Homeric warfare, see n. 6.

[29] For the military importance of the masses in Homer, see Latacz (1977); Pritchett (1985) 7–33; Raaflaub (2008).

[30] Van Wees (1996) 59–60. Greek *basileis* specifically recommend solidarity in combat, e.g. *Il.* 4.303–5 (Nestor); 13.236–8 (Thoas/Poseidon); 17.356–9 (Ajax). It is fair to note that the verses depicting the effectiveness of dense formations demonstrate predominantly the

The final aspect which contributed to the image of a good general in the epics was a combination of cunning intelligence (*metis*) and skilful craft (*techne*). These allowed the Homeric *basileis* to gain advantage over the enemy through ambushes and surprise attacks. The most famous of them was the stratagem of the Trojan Horse but the poems mention a variety of other assaults designed deliberately to catch the enemy at a disadvantage, including: ambuscades (*Il.* 1.227; 4.392; 18.513; 24.779; *Od.* 14.217–21, 469), night raids (*Il.* 10.338–497; 21.36–41), taking hidden positions (*Il.* 10.349–50; 13.276–7) or slaughtering warriors in their sleep (*Il.* 10.469–97). There is not a hint of criticism in the epics for such attacks; in fact, it is made explicit that only the bravest men can endure the physical and mental strain required for a successful ambush (*Il.* 13.276–87).[31] Accordingly, the planning and execution of surprise attacks remained the exclusive prerogative of the Homeric *basileis*. Seeking advantage at all cost, often resulting in brutal slaughter, was indeed part of the larger strategic aim behind the Greek expedition to Troy. The latter, concealed under the official banner of avenging a dishonour done to Menelaus, was the complete annihilation of the city and its entire population, spelled out at one point by Agamemnon (*Il.* 6.57–60). Such genocidal visions were admittedly not the norm in Homeric warfare, as other passages in the *Iliad* indicate, but it is clear that victory in war was complete only with considerable destruction of the enemy, a reality the Homeric generals were perfectly familiar with.[32]

To sum up, the gamut of virtues which defined Homeric generals extended well beyond their outstanding martial prowess and bravery in combat. The latter form the dominant theme of the *Iliad*'s depiction of the *basileis*, validating their excellence and social status among their followers, therefore resulting in a seemingly one-sided

greater solidarity of the Achaeans, and not necessarily any tactical acumen on the part of the generals. The latter, however, could be implied, especially when the order to maintain cohesion comes directly from the *basileus*, e.g. Nestor, Ajax. Cf. Sears (2010), who argues that dense, phalanx-like formations were successfully utilised only by the specially trained Myrmidons.

[31] Although the Greek word *strategema* appears for the first time only in Xenophon (*Mem.* 3.5.22), the extensive vocabulary associated with stratagems in Greek warfare originated in Homer and the epic tradition, as demonstrated by Wheeler (1988) 25–49. As the latter summarised (1988) 46: 'Greeks preferred to call a stratagem not *strategema*, but a trick, device, skill, wisdom, deceit, or cleverness, perhaps reflecting the epic tradition's descriptions of Odysseus upon whom the ethos of stratagem was based.' On stratagems and ambushes in Homeric warfare, see Pritchett (1974) 178; Krentz (2000) 172–4; van Wees (2004) 132; Rawlings (2007) 33–4.

[32] The norm appears to have been to kill adult men and enslave women and children, *Il.* 9.593–4. For more on the fate of prisoners in Homer, see van Wees (2011) 96–7.

image of Homeric generalship.[33] But while leading by example was a major expectation for every Homeric commander, other factors played a significant role in his craft. Firstly, the egalitarian spirit shared by all warriors impacted his authority to command. There was no clear-cut obligation for men to obey orders, which could lead to conflicts in cases where warriors disagreed with the general. This required the *basileis* to exhort, encourage and, when necessary, coerce their men into following on a constant basis, urging them to fight and protect one another. Secondly, the ability to deploy warriors and prepare basic tactical plans before battle was a clearly attested virtue, which most Homeric generals displayed, but only a few truly excelled in; the effectiveness of dense formations employed occasionally by the Achaeans stood out in particular as testament to their greater solidarity, giving some commanders a tactical advantage over less cohesive forces. Finally, cunning was highly praised, especially when used to catch the enemy off guard; surprise attacks and ambushes were common and expected of the *basileis*. All these qualities, alongside superior martial prowess, make up the ideal of Homeric generalship, which inspired countless generations of later Greeks. Its immediate influence over the generals of archaic armies is harder to determine, but a closer look at the available sources suggests that the epic standards of generalship had much in common with the realities of early Greek warfare.

Archaic Poetry

The main bulk of historical evidence for archaic warfare consists of archaeological evidence of weapons and armour, a few fragments of contemporary poetry, and some highly stylised artistic depictions on vases. Since no detailed accounts of archaic battles exist before the fifth century BC, the available sources for the study of early generalship are far more limited than those for later periods. In addition, a number of important developments in Greek warfare are traditionally ascribed to the archaic era, in particular the rise of citizen armies and the introduction of the phalanx formation. Both would have had a considerable impact on the position and duties of generals, but how and when they appeared in Greece is difficult to determine and

---

[33] The image of the Homeric generals as chieftains, whose physical leadership was all that mattered, certainly dominates the current scholarship on Greek generalship. Wheeler (1991) 126–9 concludes that: 'fighting skill and bravado constituted the warrior chieftain's two most important functions in battle'. He does, nonetheless, note the occasional concern for organisation, suspecting that it 'may demonstrate the initial stage of progress from submilitary to military combat and the beginning of transition to the classical phalanx'. Moore (2013) 457–8 offers a more limited treatment, stating that: 'generalship did not exist in any real sense' in the Homeric poems.

highly contested among scholars. Despite all this, a careful piecing together of the surviving sources, especially various fragments of early poetry, can offer valuable glimpses into the battlefield realities faced by contemporary commanders.

The earliest mention of an army general appears in the mid-seventh-century BC poetry of Archilochus of Paros, a seasoned warrior and mercenary. The iambic poems of Archilochus, performed at less formal settings such as symposia, tend to satirise the epic images of glorious battles, presenting the non-heroic side of war.[34] The surviving fragments of his songs, often purposefully rude and scandalous, bring us much closer to the mundane concerns facing contemporary warriors having to choose between glory and their own lives; or trying to distinguish true effectiveness in combat from superficial heroic appearance. In his description of an ideal general Archilochus states his preference for a level-headed man, concerned more about his men than his looks:

I have no liking for a general who is tall, walks with a swaggering gait,
takes pride in his curls, and is partly shaven.
Let mine be one who is short, has a bent look about the shins,
stands firmly on his feet, and is full of courage.

(Arch. Fr. 114)

The fragment is clearly satirical, but its immediate significance lies in the use of the term *strategos* for general; Archilochus' poem is, in fact, the first attested use of the term in Greek warfare.[35] In later times, *strategos* came to be associated with a formally defined position of military authority, most famously the public offices of ten *strategoi* from classical Athens. For Archilochus and his contemporaries, however, the term most likely signified a military leader, without any public or institutional attachments. Since the term appears only once in what is left of Archilochus' songs, it is impossible to determine the extent or grounds of the authority of the *strategoi* of his day. Furthermore, considering the rich military career of Archilochus, we cannot say with any certainty if the position he refers to was specific to a mercenary or citizen army, or indeed was a generic term applicable to any military force. But while the fragment offers little information regarding any formal basis for early generalship, it does provide the first indication of a leadership position exclusive to the realm of warfare in the Greek world. Where the battlefield authority of the Homeric

---

[34] Archilochus' military activities took place during the Parian colonisation of Thasos, where he fought many battles against local Thracian tribes. For a recent comprehensive study of Archilochus, including his relation to heroic epic, see Swift (2019) esp. 18–22.

[35] Wheeler (1991) 132.

basileis was the inseparable product of their political and social standing, the *strategoi* of Archilochus may arguably be seen as an indication of a purely military position not necessarily defined by such factors.

Archilochus presents his audience with two models of generalship. On the one hand, there is the tall and glamorous general, who takes more pride in his looks than his courage in battle; on the other, the short, 'bandy-legged' man, courageous in battle, with whom ordinary warriors can more easily identify.[36] To an extent, the contrast may be a parody of the proverbial good looks of the Homeric *basileis*. But the crucial feature singled out by Archilochus is the general's steadiness, borne out by a mixture of courage and, most likely, experience. These qualities suggest that generals of early Greek armies were expected to play a significant part in combat, reminiscent of their counterparts in the Homeric poems.[37] Alternatively, it may indicate that the distinguishing feature between good and bad *strategoi* was indeed their involvement and performance in combat. Steadiness and courage made for a general that men could place their trust and obedience in, which, in turn, may again remind us of the more personal relationships within the Homeric war-bands, based on comradeship and mutual support between the leader and his followers. By contrast, we should assume that a general's cowardice was noticeable and could lead to criticism and mockery; whether the lack of 'liking' for a cowardly *strategos*, tall or otherwise, impacted his men's loyalty or performance in battle is not clear.

The earliest conflict for which we have more concrete testimony is the Second Messenian War (c. 640–600 BC). This comes in the form of martial elegies composed by Tyrtaeus. Although Tyrtaeus' identity was disputed by ancient authors, his exhortations to his countrymen fighting the Messenians were ascribed important didactic value by later Spartan warriors, who recited his songs on campaigns (Athenaeus 14.630f). According to some traditions, Tyrtaeus served as a general in the Second Messenian War and was instrumental in the final success of the Spartans.[38] Doubtful as these traditions may be, his elegies certainly provide an insight into the warrior ethos of the period, as well as the expectations that archaic generals might have had of their warriors.

---

[36] According to Dio Chrysostom (33.17), Archilochus also envisions 'thick hair on the shins' of his ideal general. Galen (π. ἄρθρων, xviii (I) 604 (Kühn)) adds that people with bent legs are more difficult to trip up. For a commentary on the fragment, with further references, see Swift (2015) 103–4; (2019) 295–7.

[37] In Fr. 113 Archilochus mentions 'a commander (*archos*) well trained in the javelin'; the context of the fragment, which appears to offer both praise and mockery, is difficult to determine. For more, see West (1974) 129–30; Swift (2019) 294–5.

[38] Lycurg. *In Leocr.* 106; Diod. 8.27.1–2; Plut. *Apophth. Lac.* 230d; Athenaeus, 14.630f. See also Wheeler (1991) 161 n. 54.

The central themes of Tyrtaeus' poems include cohesion and solidarity among warriors engaged in hand-to-hand combat.[39] Much as in Homer, military engagements provide room for men to display their martial skill and win personal glory, but the importance of the latter is largely subsumed within the larger considerations of the well-being of the community and loyalty to fellow warriors.[40] Tyrtaeus praises the benefits of men staying close together, standing firm in the front ranks and protecting one another:

> Come, you young men, stand fast at one another's side and fight,
> and do not start shameful flight or panic,
> but make the spirit in your heart strong and valiant,
> and do not be in love with life when you are fighting men.
> (Tyrt. Fr. 10.15–18)

> Those who dare to stand fast at one another's side
> and to advance towards the front ranks in hand-to-hand conflict,
> they die in fewer numbers and they keep safe the troops behind them;
> but when men run away, all esteem is lost.
> (...)
> with foot placed alongside foot and shield pressed against shield,
> let everyone draw near, crest to crest, helmet to helmet,
> and breast to breast, and fight against a man,
> seizing the hilt of his sword or his long spear.
> (Tyrt. Fr. 11.11–14, 31–4)

> This is a common benefit for the state and all the people,
> whenever a man with firm stance among the front ranks
> never ceases to hold his ground, is utterly unmindful of shameful flight,
> risking his life and displaying a steadfast spirit,
> and standing by the man next to him speaks encouragingly.
> (Tyrt. Fr. 12.15–19)

---

[39] For more on Tyrtaeus and archaic warfare, see Wheeler (1991) 129–32; van Wees (2000) 149–54; (2004) 172–4; Rawlings (2007) 54–5; Schwartz (2009) 115–23.

[40] The motif of patriotism, although present in the Homeric epics (e.g. *Il.* 15.496–9), is less prominent than in the martial elegies of Tyrtaeus (or Callinus). For patriotism in Homer, see van Wees (1996) 14–16.

The appeals for bravery and cohesiveness among the front ranks, which dominate the overall tone of Tyrtaeus' elegies, are a clear reminder of similar messages conveyed by the Homeric generals to their warriors; the Homeric overtones are also clear in the spirit of solidarity expressed in encouraging comrades.[41] In the *Iliad* cohesive formations, as we saw, were formed only on an ad hoc basis, and we might suspect that the need to remind the warriors to stand together suggests that massed infantry formations in Tyrtaeus' era were similarly not the norm at all times; indeed, the impression given is that men needed to be constantly encouraged to hold their position. On top of this, the occasional mentions of light-armed warriors, crouching beneath the shields of the heavy-armed to hurl javelins, suggests that battle lines remained relatively open and flexible, in contrast to the later classical phalanx formations (Tyrt. Fr. 11.35–8).

One aspect which distinguishes the poems of Tyrtaeus from the battle descriptions of the *Iliad* is the importance ascribed to men keeping their ground and not turning to flee.[42] Panic and flight are repeatedly described as shameful; men who abandon their comrades are warned of losing esteem and bringing dishonour to their families. In addition, fleeing made warriors easy prey to the Messenians, who 'will kill all of the Spartans . . . fleeing in retreat' (Tyrt. Fr. 23a.20–2). The prevalence of this theme in the elegies of Tyrtaeus may therefore indicate not only that warriors were prone to run away during combat but also that commanders could do little to stop them and had no formal means to punish men for desertion and cowardice.[43] Constant exhortations to uphold an ideal of courage and patriotic duty appear to have been the only tool available to the Spartan generals of Tyrtaeus' era.

---

[41] The major fragments of Tyrtaeus (Frs 10–12) put a clear stress on the importance of cohesive formations and the spirit of solidarity; all three, however, come from the later works of Lycurgus and Stobaeus, who preserved them because of their special relevance for later audiences. Such fragments use traditional epic language and, as van Wees (2000) 149 rightly observed, 'would have been highly relevant to soldiers in a classical phalanx, and indeed this is why the main fragments survived'. The fragments preserved in papyri (e.g. Frs 19, 23–23a) convey a somewhat different image of combat, less compatible with the realities of classical phalanx warfare.

[42] On Homeric concepts of flight in archaic poetry, see Barker and Christensen (2005); Swift (2012).

[43] An instance of stationing warriors in front of a trench to prevent them from running away was, according to Eustratius' commentary on Arist. *Eth. Nic.* 3.8.5.1116a36, supposedly mentioned by Tyrtaeus as the Spartan 'manner of fighting' against the Messenians (Fr. 9). This has been associated with the so-called Battle of the Great Trench, recorded in Pausanias, 4.6.2, 17.2, which indicates that it might have been a desperate measure necessitated by the normal tendency of men to run away, familiar from Tyrtaeus' poems. For a short commentary on the fragment, see van Wees (2000) 162 n. 47.

Other fragments from Tyrtaeus demonstrate that obedience to military superiors was repeatedly mentioned and recommended by the poet. One of them, preserved on the Berlin papyrus (third century BC), has the Spartan warriors proclaiming: 'we will obey the ... of our leader(s)' (Tyrt. Fr. 19.11). Despite its lacunose nature, the explicit mention of obeying leaders (*peisometh' hegem[o*), as Wheeler observed, could imply 'a definite command system quite unlike the Homeric *basileis* and their *hetairoi*'.[44] The *hegemones* in question were most likely the Spartan kings, who stood at the head of the army and whose authority and standing derived from the gods. Obedience to the Spartan kings was indeed mentioned in Tyrtaeus' *Eunomia* (Fr. 2), albeit not in a military setting. Such a strong position of personal authority, however, must have been exceptional among the *poleis* of the archaic era.[45] And even though a definite structure of command could be echoed in the fragments of Tyrtaeus, it seems more likely that the poet's constant exhortations to warriors to stand their ground, not give in to panic, and obey their superiors reflect the weakness, or indeed the lack, of any such system, and the poet's ambition to ingrain a sense of obedience into the Spartan warriors fighting the Messenians. Whichever is the case, the fragment suggests that warriors' obedience could not be taken for granted by generals, even those with a strongly rooted position of institutional authority, in seventh-century BC Greece.

The remaining fragments of archaic poets offer little more on generals' authority or their roles in combat. The fragments do confirm, nonetheless, that concerns regarding warriors holding their position voiced by Tyrtaeus were not ungrounded. Archilochus casually recounts how he fled a battle in Thrace, throwing away his shield in the process (Fr. 5).[46] In a similar fashion, he consoles a friend who also shook his 'sturdy shield off and turned tail' by stating that 'braver men than you have given way to panics such as that' (Adesp. 38).[47] Alcaeus of Lesbos (Fr. 428a), having fought the Athenians for the control of Sigeum, mentions his loss of fine armour and

---

[44] Wheeler (1991) 132.
[45] The roles and duties of the Spartan kings on campaign are outlined in Xenophon's *Lak. Pol.* 13. How many of these go back to the archaic period is impossible to determine.
[46] The motif of 'throwing away one's shield' (*rhipsaspia*) is common in archaic poetry, exploring the theme of glorious death vs preservation of life. For more on the fragment, see Schwertfeger (1982); Anderson (2008); Swift (2015) 101–3; (2019) 212–15.
[47] The Telephus Elegy (Fr. 17a; P. Oxy LXIX 4708), first published in 2005, recounts the myth of Telephus' rout of the Achaeans, defending flight as proper in the face of divine opposition. Barker and Christensen (2005) argued that the poem celebrates flight; Swift (2012); (2019) 231–3 disagreed and suggested that Archilochus displays a more ambivalent attitude to flight in his poems.

a shield, presumably thrown away during flight.[48] He also asks the gods to gather together 'a scattered host of men, inspiring them with traditional discipline' (Alc. Fr. 382). Perhaps a deficiency of the latter was why the Mytilenaeans were ultimately defeated in the conflict. One aspect which is more conspicuous by its absence is the relative lack of any mentions of tactical considerations in archaic poetry; we do not hear of generals drawing up warriors, dividing their forces into smaller contingents or planning surprise attacks or raids.[49] The limited interest in such issues, which fell within the scope of generals' duties in the *Iliad*, may be due to the nature of our sources. Neither Tyrtaeus' exhortations to the rank and file nor Archilochus' sympotic songs were meant to contain specific tactical advice for commanders. On the other hand, the absence of tactics and strategy may indicate that they played a less significant role in early archaic warfare. Since no independent units of cavalry and heavy- or light-armed warriors featured on battlefields at this point, tactical actions would have been limited to drawing up troops and maintaining their cohesion in battle. Ambushes and raids were no doubt a constant feature of early warfare, but they need not have required any more than basic planning.[50] Gathering men together and exhorting and fighting alongside them in combat was what mattered the most for seventh-century BC generals.

All in all, archaic poetry reveals a number of themes which offer glimpses of perceptions of generalship in early archaic Greece. Archilochus' satirical remarks on his ideal *strategos* suggest that generals were expected to be steady, courageous and ready to share the dangers of combat with their men. Discipline and obedience to the general were grounded predominantly in a sense of comradeship and trust, which the commanders earned through their actions on the battlefield; apart from the Spartan kings, any sense of institutional authority behind the general's position is not explicit in the surviving fragments of early poets. Although the martial elegies of Tyrtaeus might suggest a slight shift towards an increased density of formations, cohesive bodies of mutually supportive men were not necessarily the norm; light-

---

[48] See also Hdt. 5.95.

[49] The only exceptions come from Archilochus, who mentions enemies lying in ambush (Fr. 128) and capture by encirclement (Fr. 146).

[50] On the prominence of raiding in early Greek warfare, see Jackson (1993); Kucewicz (2018) 134–6. Surprise attacks feature prominently in the heroic poems of the Epic Cycle, and stratagems and ambushes were widespread: the elaborate ploy of the Trojan Horse was covered at length in the *Little Iliad* and *Sack of Ilion*; Achilles' ambush of Troilus was related in the *Cypria*; and the Theban fifty-man ambush of Tydeus was recounted in the *Thebaid*. None of these stories, however, devote any space to tactical planning or generalship as such. For more on the episodes, see Gantz (1993) 512–13, 597–603, 635, 646–57; West (2013) 121–2, 179–81, 193–5, 203–8, 227–33.

armed mingled with the heavy-armed in the front ranks and warriors habitually threw their armour away and fled the battlefield. All this suggests that there was little to distinguish the standards of generalship of the archaic era from those of the Homeric poems. A number of developments in the structure and organisation of the Greek armies in the sixth century BC, however, meant that the position and roles of generals underwent some changes.

Citizen Armies and Generalship

The sixth century BC witnessed a gradual increase in institutionalisation of Greek armies. The exact shape of the latter is hard to ascertain, but the early signs of the process may be seen with the introduction of magistrates called polemarchs, whose responsibility would have predominantly concerned the area of war, across seventh-century BC *poleis*.[51] The extent of the changes to the organisation of public militias towards the end of the archaic period inevitably varied from one *polis* to another. Their overall aim, nonetheless, was to regulate most processes associated with service in the citizen armies, including mobilisation and unit division; and to establish more sophisticated chains of command. These processes would also have affected the position of generals, whose roles were now predominantly public.

In Athens, public war-making was presided over by the annually appointed polemarch, and built around the system of forty-eight naucraries, local administrative units led by officials known as *naukraroi* (ship captains), responsible for levying taxes in wartime, providing ships, and mobilising cavalry and, most likely, infantry.[52] The public service of the *naukraroi* in the citizen army consisted predominantly of defensive actions and only occasional offensive expeditions. Their authority to mobilise warriors and fund their activities from the 'naukraric fund' (Arist. *Ath. Pol.* 8.3) implied relatively high levels of fiscal and administrative organisation in archaic Athens; furthermore, the *naukraroi* would also have commanded the forces raised from their respective districts, under authority granted to them by the polemarch

---

[51] As discussed by Wheeler (1991) 133, 161 nos. 58–60. Examples include Athens (Arist. *Ath. Pol.* 3.2); Sparta (Xen. *Lak. Pol.* 11.4; Plut. *Lyc.* 12.3); Corinth (Nicolaus of Damascus, *FGrHist* 90 F57.5); Sicyon (*FGrHist* 105 F2).

[52] Some scholars assert that there was no public army in Athens until the reforms of Cleisthenes of 508 BC: van Effenterre (1976); Frost (1984); Pritchard (2010). Others claim that the early Athenian army was modelled on the system of four Attic *phylai*, subdivided into three *trittyes*: Andrewes (1982) 366; Siewert (1982) 154–5. As is clear from the discussion above, I maintain that the public system of naucraries was instrumental in the Athenian military organisation, as first suggested by van Wees (2013); (2018). For a fuller discussion, see Kucewicz (2018) 133–80.

and the Athenian *polis*. Attempts were also made to regulate the mobilisation processes in Athens and impose formal criteria for military service, as evidenced by the Solonian property classification system (*tele*) of 594/3 BC which imposed an obligation to serve in the citizen army on the wealthiest Athenians.[53] In addition, around the same time laws on draft evasion and desertion may have been introduced, imposing penalty measures for cowardly and disobedient warriors.[54]

The early organisation of the Spartan army is considerably harder to trace, but the first signs of institutionalisation and formal command systems also appear in the sixth century BC.[55] According to Herodotus (1.65), the Spartan military organisation in the archaic era was built on three key components: 'the sworn bands, the division of the thirty, and the communal messes'. Of particular importance for the question of military structure and obedience was the establishment of the sworn bands (*enomotiai*), the smallest unit in the regular Spartan army, introduced most likely in the mid-sixth century BC. An oath recorded on a fourth-century BC *stele* from Acharnae suggests that these units made compulsory pledges, swearing loyalty to unit commanders (*taxiarchos*, *enomotarches*), as well as obedience to the generals (*strategoi*).[56] The mention of only two levels of military unit, led respectively by a *taxiarchos* and an *enomotarches*, suggests, as Hans van Wees observed, that the oath goes back to a time when Spartan division into *morai*, *lochoi* and *pentekostys* was not yet in exist-

---

[53] For more on the military dimension of the Solonian *tele*, see Kucewicz (2018) 149–58. Some scholars argue that the Athenian army was disbanded for the duration of the tyranny of the Peisistratids, who relied on the support of mercenary troops, e.g. Frost (1984) 291–4. Our sources, however, make it clear that Peisistratus left the Athenian constitution intact and did not modify any public institutions, Hdt. 1.59; Thuc. 6.54; Arist. *Ath. Pol.* 16.2, 8. If this was the case, we should assume that the military organisation based on the naucraries and the *tele* were similarly unaffected and continued until the reforms of Cleisthenes.

[54] Aesch. 3.175–6. For a recent discussion, see van Wees (2018) 110–20.

[55] On the archaic Spartan army, see Lazenby (1985) 82–102; Trundle (2001); van Wees (2006). Early Spartan armies were most likely structured around a system based on tribes, obes and phratries, perhaps not unlike Nestor's advice to Agamemnon to arrange troops by tribes and phratries (*Il.* 2.362–3). For more, see Huxley (1962) 48–9.

[56] The oath recorded on the Acharnae *stele* is more commonly known as the Oath of Plataea, reputedly sworn by the allied Greek forces on the eve of the Battle of Plataea in 479 BC. The full text reads as follows: 'I shall fight while I am alive, and I shall not regard being alive as more important than being free. And I shall not leave my *taxiarchos* or my *enomotarches*, whether he is alive or dead. And I shall not go away unless the leaders lead us away, and I shall do whatever the generals order. And the dead among my fellow-fighters I shall bury on the spot, and unburied I shall leave no-one.' Translation from van Wees (2006). The mention of *enomotiai* in the oath suggests a Spartan origin. For more on the Acharnae *stele* and the Oath of Plataea, see van Wees (2006); Cartledge (2013).

ence, that is, the late sixth century BC.⁵⁷ The oath also contained other clauses about not fleeing the battlefield and fighting until death, which can be seen as a response to the problems faced by the generals of Tyrtaeus' era. Strong morale, combined with an official command structure based on loyalty and obedience, both of which became trademarks of the Spartan army in the classical period, was therefore a product of the late archaic era, reflecting wider processes of military institutionalisation within the Greek world.⁵⁸

The overall effect of the changes to the organisation of citizen militias would have had a significant impact on the position and authority of the generals who led them. The role of the latter was now officially granted by the *polis* and its citizens, who ascribed it considerably more authority.⁵⁹ Obedience within armies was maintained and supported by different levels of military officers as part of the more complex

---

⁵⁷ Van Wees (2006) 134–5.
⁵⁸ According to Herodotus (5.75), following the failed invasion of Attica in 506 BC the Spartans also passed a motion which forbade their kings campaigning together, in order to prevent any disagreement between them. This indicates, in turn, that Spartan kings might have shared the duties of generalship in earlier conflicts. The example of Anchimolius, who led the Spartans at Phalerum in 512 BC, shows that distinguished citizens could also act as generals of smaller task forces, Hdt. 5.63. Sealey (1974) 339 suggests that Anchimolius might have been the first Spartan navarch. Pausanias (4.7.8) also mentions Euryleon, a member of the Aigeid family, commanding the centre of a Spartan army alongside kings Theopompus and Polydorus sometime during the First Messenian War. Pausanias' account of the battle, drawn most likely from a third-century BC rhetorician, Myron, features personal involvement in combat by Theopompus and Polydorus' order to stop an enemy rout; the narrative, however, is heavily based on later conventions of hoplite battles and is therefore to be doubted.
⁵⁹ We should also suspect that archaic generals of public armies, acting on behalf of their *polis*, were in some way accountable for their actions. A possible early instance of military officials being tried and punished for misconduct might be seen in the 630s BC, when the Athenians banished the family of the Alcmeonids from the city as a result of their sacrilegious massacre of the supporters of Cylon's failed *coup d'état*, Hdt. 5.71; Thuc. 1.126. Despite some inconsistencies in the sources, we can plausibly assume that the officials in charge were the *naukraroi*, whose immediate response to the coup was to mobilise a full Athenian levy to deal with the situation. Some scrutiny could apply even to the Spartan kings; after his return from a campaign in the Argolis, Cleomenes was summoned before the ephors, who accused him of not taking the city of Argos after his major victory at Sepeia in 494 BC, Hdt. 6.82. Such early trials of army commanders, however, may have been motivated more by political and personal enmities than by genuine military factors; they are also relatively rare in our sources, especially in comparison with the trials of the generals known from the classical period. For more on the Cylonian affair, see Lavelle (2005) 36–41; Kucewicz (2018) 141–3. For more on disciplinary actions against classical Athenian *strategoi*, see Hamel (1998) 122–57.

chains of command, as well as some measures imposed to punish desertion and insubordination.[60] Maintaining discipline, which formed a key part of a general's craft in Homer and Tyrtaeus, was therefore no longer an essential duty of the *strategoi* leading the citizen armies of archaic *poleis*. The initial success of such reforms is difficult to determine, but the overall nature of Greek warfare towards the end of the archaic period underwent some noticeable changes. Citizen armies grew, formations were more cohesive, and light-armed troops and cavalry began to operate independently from the heavy-armed.[61] The battle duties of the generals reflect these wider developments, as mentions of their martial skill and courage disappear from our sources and new considerations of strategic planning and tactics are given more attention. This is particularly clear in the surviving traditions about Peisistratus and Cleomenes, the most successful generals of the period.

Peisistratus and Cleomenes

Peisistratus' early rise to political power came on the back of his achievements in the war with Megara in the 560s BC. But it was his third attempt at tyranny, established after a land battle at Pallene in 546 BC, that firmly rooted the rule of his dynasty until the expulsion of his son Hippias in 510 BC. The end of the tyranny in Athens was facilitated by another formidable general of the period, the Spartan king Cleomenes. Not unlike Peisistratus, Cleomenes was largely responsible for the political supremacy of Sparta in the Peloponnese towards the end of the archaic period. His reign witnessed a number of significant military victories, in particular the defeat of Argos at Sepeia in 494 BC. The ancient traditions associated with Peisistratus and Cleomenes present them as controversial figures: one is a tyrant, who despite his overall fairness denied the Athenians their political freedom; the other, an unscrupulous schemer, who succumbed to madness by the end of his life. Beneath these images, however, is another tradition which ascribed their success to cunning, pragmatism and an ability to deploy deception.

---

[60] Explicit instances of desertion or insubordination are rare in the sixth century BC. The example of the Athenians deserting the citizen army to join the forces of Peisistratus before the Battle of Pallene in 546 BC is less obvious, since Peisistratus himself was a former general and war hero of the Athenians (see below).

[61] The artistic evidence on Greek vases suggests that the difference between heavy-armed (single thrusting spear) and light-armed (javelins, bow) warriors was defined by the end of the seventh century BC. Light-armed troops in the form of Thracian peltasts and Scythian archers appear in Attic vase painting from c. 540 BC, perhaps indicative of their service in the Athenian army. Cavalry was certainly used by the Peisistratids, Hdt. 5.63, perhaps by the time of the Pallene campaign. For more, see Konijnendijk (2018) 96.

Despite the relatively rich historical tradition associated with Peisistratus and Cleomenes, neither of them has featured in modern studies on archaic Greek generalship. The reason for this lies primarily in the nature of the surviving sources. Herodotus, who provides our main account for their military careers, uses deceit, both military and political, as the main factor behind Peisistratus' rise to power in Athens; Cleomenes' stratagems, on the other hand, feature as part of his larger narrative explaining the madness of the Spartan king. Other accounts by Aeneas Tacticus, Frontinus and Polyaenus are usually dismissed because of their wider agendas (e.g. collecting useful military stories), late dates and reliance on biased traditions which had influenced Herodotus. Most importantly, however, the clever stratagems associated with Peisistratus and Cleomenes have been overlooked because they do not fit the traditional scholarly model of archaic warfare. The notion of generals winning battles by trickery and deceit stood against the ideal of fair hoplite combat, which, as it has been assumed, left no room for such things until at least the Peloponnesian War. However, when set against the wider Homeric ideology surrounding cunning and clever ploys in battle, it becomes clear that the stratagems ascribed to Peisistratus and Cleomenes would hardly have been meant to discredit them. These stratagems may not only survive in the historical record as cautionary tales, therefore, but instead preserve genuine historical truths about generalship.

Peisistratus' military fame began with his capture of the Megarian port of Nisaea, which ended the long-standing conflict over Eleusis and Salamis in Athens' favour.[62] Herodotus (1.59) simply states that Peisistratus, acting as the Athenian general (*strategos*) in the campaign, accomplished 'great deeds', of which the taking of Nisaea stood out.[63] The lack of further detail in Herodotus has led scholars to speculate on Peisistratus' exact achievements in the conflict. One ancient tradition, preserved by a fourth-century BC writer, Aeneas Tacticus, provides some more information. According to Aeneas, after being warned of a Megarian attack on Athenian women celebrating the Thesmophoria at Eleusis, Peisistratus set up an ambush and killed most of the invaders. He then used the enemy boats to transport Athenian troops pretending to be Megarians (and Athenian women) returning from the raid and prepared to land close to Nisaea. The Megarians, expecting their own men back with a cargo of female captives, gathered to greet them, upon which Peisistratus ordered his troops 'to disembark with daggers and stab some of the Megarians but carry off

---

[62] On the Megarian conflict, see Lavelle (2005) 30–65.
[63] Herodotus uses the title *strategos* as a generic term to denote army leadership, as he does for other non-Greek military positions, e.g. 1.162; 5.26; 6.94. The classical office of *strategos* was first introduced in Athens towards the end of the sixth century BC, *Ath. Pol.* 22.2.

to the boats as many as possible of the most distinguished of them'.[64] With their officials captured, the Megarians promptly surrendered Nisaea (*Aen. Tact.* 4.8–12).[65]

The historical value of Aeneas' account is undeniably dubious. Firstly, its similarity to a tradition ascribed to Solon, which also features a Megarian raid on Athenian women foiled by an ambush and counter-attack on Salamis, puts the authenticity of both accounts into question.[66] Secondly, it is hard to imagine that the Megarians would have surrendered their main port to a small force of Athenians in exchange for their officials. Capturing Nisaea would surely have required a much larger force in operation, and we should suspect that Peisistratus' actual offensive was carefully planned and probably involved a sizeable force.[67] A stratagem of some sort might have been employed – an element of surprise would certainly have helped the Athenian cause. But whether a trick was involved or not, Peisistratus' main achievement was the realisation of the larger strategic potential which seizing Nisaea would have for ending the drawn-out conflict. With Nisaea taken, the Megarians had to surrender. Realising where and how to strike was what brought Athenian victory, and the credit for it went entirely to Peisistratus.

The attribution of stratagems to Peisistratus was, in fact, part of a larger *topos* associated with the tyrant since Herodotus.[68] In the account of the latter, Peisistratus' use of clever ploys allowed him to trick the Athenian people twice in his early accessions to power (Hdt. 1.59–61). To some extent, the prevalence of the theme of cleverness was used by Herodotus to exonerate the Athenians from any responsibility for the tyranny.[69] But we should not assume that its significance was simply invented. Peisistratus' cunning was clearly remembered in Herodotus' and later Aeneas' time and it is unlikely that there was no ground to it. The pragmatism and strategic planning which characterised Peisistratus' military acumen featured in almost every ancient work which dealt with the tyrant, favourable to him or not. Its most outstanding example was the Battle of Pallene.

Like his offensive in the Megarian war, Peisistratus' third and final bid for power was carefully planned. After a period of exile from Athens, he gathered wealth and allies, and eventually assembled an army to force his way back. The latter consisted of warriors from Argos, Thebes and Naxos, cavalry from Eretria, and possibly a

---

[64] Translation from Whitehead (1990) 50.
[65] Frontinus (*Str.* 2.9.9) and Justin (2.8.1–5) also relate the story.
[66] Plut. *Sol.* 8.4–6; 9.2–3. For a summary of the traditions concerning Solon's attack on Salamis, see Figueira (1985) 280–5. Lavelle (2005) 271–2 n. 156 offers some speculation on the sources behind Aeneas' narrative.
[67] As argued in a lengthy study by Lavelle (2005) 30–65.
[68] E.g. Polyaen. 1.21.1–3.
[69] For more on Herodotus and his biases, see Lavelle (2005) 9–11.

contingent of light-armed Thracians.⁷⁰ Setting out from Eretria, Peisistratus' force landed at Marathon, where, as Herodotus tells us (1.62), they were joined by many Athenians 'who loved the rule of one more than freedom'. This preference for tyranny was hardly the cause for such desertions; Peisistratus' past successes and military reputation preceded him and drew men from all over Attica. Because of this, his decision to land at Marathon was probably deliberate, allowing him to strengthen morale by gathering more troops. It is equally possible that Marathon was chosen for its suitability for cavalry, which Peisistratus may have wished to rely on in his attack.⁷¹ Perhaps because of the latter, the Athenians chose not to engage his forces at Marathon and took up strong defensive positions at the sanctuary of Athena in Pallene, mustering a full citizen army and barring the way to Athens.

The actual battle, according to Herodotus, was quick and won by another stratagem. Upon receiving a favourable prophecy from his seer, Peisistratus immediately ordered his army to charge, apparently catching the Athenians by surprise. The latter, he relates, 'had at this time gone to their breakfast, and after breakfast some betook themselves to dicing and some to sleep: they were attacked by Peisistratus' men and put to flight' (Hdt. 1.63). The simple narrative attributes Peisistratus' victory to trickery and divine favour, implying that the armies hardly even came to blows. This, of course, absolved the Athenians of any accusations of cowardice; resistance was simply not possible. Other details of his narrative, however, suggest that a battle took place, as some Athenians stood their ground and died in combat (Hdt. 1.64). We can also reasonably assume that Peisistratus' initial charge did involve an element of surprise; charging an enemy in a highly defensible position would have been a risky venture and involved a prolonged period of fighting. Since there is no indication of the latter in our sources, which would surely have mentioned any valiant efforts to preserve Athens' freedom, we must suspect that either the defenders were betrayed or Peisistratus did indeed manage to catch them at a

---

⁷⁰ Hdt. 1.61; *Ath. Pol.* 15.2. Lavelle (2005) 139–42 discusses Peisistratus' army at Pallene. For more on the Peisistratid army in general, see Lavelle (1992); Singor (2000); Kucewicz (2018) 159–72.

⁷¹ Hippias advised the Persians to land at Marathon in 490 BC, 'the fittest part of Attica for horsemen to ride over' (Hdt. 6.102). Although cavalry as such does not feature at Pallene, Peisistratus' sons rode up ahead after the battle to reassure the fleeing Athenians of their safety (Hdt. 1.63). The latter episode has been interpreted as a shrewd political move aimed at facilitating Peisistratus' return to the city; it may also, however, demonstrate Peisistratus' authority and control over his army in the aftermath of battle. Massacring the defeated enemy after a victorious encounter, made all the easier for armies with a cavalry force, was a common occurrence in Greek warfare that generals could often do little about. For more on the rout in Greek warfare, see Konijnendijk (2018) 178–205.

disadvantage. Whichever was the case, Peisistratus gained the upper hand before the combat began and capitalised on it in a decisive fashion.

The Pallene campaign reinforced the image of Peisistratus as a cunning and pragmatic general, whose success was due to his careful planning and ability to exploit the weaknesses of his enemies. His landing at Marathon indicates deliberate delay to gather more warriors, bolster morale and seek terrain suitable for cavalry. His successful charge at Pallene shows the use of deception to overcome an unfavourable strategic position. Revealingly, not a single mention of Peisistratus' martial skill or involvement in actual combat has survived. Instead, it was his grasp of strategic considerations that enabled his victories and later gave him a reputation for masterful stratagems. Even Herodotus, whose democratic agenda shone through his account of the Athenian tyranny, felt obliged to mention the 'great deeds' of Peisistratus in the Megarian conflict; his narrative of Pallene, even though offering no obvious praise to Peisistratus, shows him utterly outmatching his Athenian counterparts. Strategic planning, pragmatism and an ability to use deception were what defined the generalship of Peisistratus. Similar qualities can be seen in the military career of Cleomenes of Sparta.

Cleomenes was certainly a controversial figure. His political shrewdness made him many enemies in his native Sparta; Herodotus, drawing on Spartan informants hostile to Cleomenes, described him (5.42) as 'not in his right senses, but crazy' and 'sick of madness' (6.75). In fact, Cleomenes' most impressive military victory, the defeat of the Argives at Sepeia in 494 BC, features as a part of Herodotus' wider narrative of the king's moral outrages, progressing madness and ultimate suicide. Despite a clear bias, the details which he provides for the Sepeia campaign convey a picture of a clever and ruthless general, whose methods were as brutal as they were effective.

Herodotus' account of the battle begins with a stalemate between the cautious Spartan and Argive armies, who, camped close to each other at Sepeia near Tiryns, were reluctant to initiate combat. The Argives, fearing that the Spartans might resort to trickery, decided to copy every move of their opponents, made easier as each order was announced by a Spartan crier. When Cleomenes realised what was happening, he took immediate advantage and:

> gave command that when the herald cried the signal for the men to breakfast, they should then put on their armour and attack the Argives. The Lacedaemonians performed this bidding: for when they assaulted the Argives they caught them breakfasting in obedience to the herald's signal; many of them they slew, and more by far of the Argives fled for refuge into the grove of Argus, where the Lacedaemonians encamped round and closely watched them. (Hdt. 6.78)

Cleomenes subsequently gathered some Argive deserters and ordered them to shout out the names of the men taking refuge in the sanctuary, telling them that their ransoms had been paid. Every time one of them emerged, Cleomenes had him slaughtered, killing around fifty men in this way. The Argives did not initially sense foul play, but when one of them climbed a tree to see what was happening to those who answered the call, they refused to come out. Cleomenes then set fire to the entire grove and burned the remaining Argives to death. In total, Herodotus (7.148) reports that a staggering 6,000 Argives were killed in the conflict; in the aftermath, 'Argos was so wholly widowed of her men, that their slaves took all in possession, and ruled and governed, till the sons of them that were slain came to man's estate' (Hdt. 6.83). The campaign dealt a crippling blow to a major Spartan rival for Peloponnesian hegemony; as such, it was a massive success for the Lacedaemonians.[72]

The events of the battle itself, won by Cleomenes' quick thinking in response to the movements of the Argives, serve as a clear demonstration of the importance of gaining an upper hand over the enemy before the attack. Similarly to Peisistratus' charge at Pallene, Cleomenes managed to surprise the unprepared Argives and thereby tip the scales decisively in his favour. Herodotus' narrative of misleading signals has been questioned by some scholars, primarily due to the popularity of the basic scenario in later works on military stratagems.[73] But just as in the case of Peisistratus, we should suspect that some form of trickery was used by the Spartan king. The actual events of the battle, which from the perspective of the wider narrative of Cleomenes' insanity were less important than the aftermath, suggest that there was no immediate need for Herodotus' source(s) to relate a clever strategic ploy on behalf of the mad king – unless, of course, it was widely known and remembered in Herodotus' time. Cleomenes certainly had a reputation for stratagems, and his ploy to lure out the defeated Argives from the grove of Argus was one of many which defined his career as a general. It was his actions in the aftermath of Sepeia, however,

---

[72] Lazenby (1985) 73 referred to Sepeia as 'one of the most decisive victories ever won by a hoplite army'. He also suggested, based on Herodotus' account, that Cleomenes feigned an invasion across the Erasinos before attacking by sea at Nauplion. For more on the Sepeia campaign, see Huxley (1962) 83–4; Tomlinson (1972) 93–5; Hendriks (1980); Cartledge (2002) 128–9; Nevin (2017) 113–18.

[73] Griffiths (1989) 57. Polyaenus, 1.14, describes the stratagem with specific reference to Cleomenes. A different account of the battle was related by Plutarch, *Mor.* 223a, who reports that Cleomenes made a truce with the Argives for seven days but then attacked during the night, on the premise that the oath did not include nights. Pausanias, 2.20.8–9, 3.4.1, also mentions the battle and the massacre at the grove, but no pre-battle stratagems feature in his account.

which drew condemnation from his contemporaries and contributed to his image as a madman. But did Cleomenes cross the line?

The usual accusation about Cleomenes' transgression in Sepeia concerns his treacherous slaughter of the suppliants and the sacrilegious burning of the sacred grove of Argus. The Argives, according to Herodotus (6.75), certainly saw this as his main crime and the sole reason for his last fit of madness which led to his suicide. Some modern scholars, in fact, dismiss the aftermath of Sepeia as later fabrication aimed to slander Cleomenes.[74] Such scepticism is, however, ungrounded. The outrage of the Argives at the actions of Cleomenes is understandable but, revealingly, the Spartans appear to have shown no moral qualms about the events. Upon his return to Sparta, Cleomenes was in fact summoned before the ephors, but the charge had nothing to do with killing suppliants or committing religious outrages. Instead, the king was charged with not doing *more* damage and taking the city of Argos (Hdt. 6.82). According to the Spartans, then, the brutal massacre of the Argives created the perfect opportunity to annihilate their long-standing enemy. Killing defeated warriors after battles, as van Wees argued, was seen as legitimate and sometimes even desirable in Greek warfare.[75] The aim was to defeat the enemy and deal as crippling a blow as possible, especially when the enmity between the opponents was long-standing. Cleomenes' actions were therefore those of a ruthless general exploiting his victory and scoring a major triumph for Sparta. He seized an opportunity, as Alastar Jackson concluded, 'that the Argive hoplites gave him at Sepeia, by taking refuge in the sacred grove, to burn them to death in their thousands, not the act of a madman but what today might be called a strategic necessity'.[76] His only transgression might have been in violating sacred land, but the end seems to have justified the means.[77]

In summary, the military careers of Peisistratus and Cleomenes demonstrate the importance of strategic planning and cunning for archaic generals. The accounts of

---

[74] Griffiths (1989) 57–8; Piérart (2003) 284. Others emphasise the un-Greekness of Cleomenes' actions: Tomlinson (1972) 94; Cartledge (2002) 129.

[75] Van Wees (2011) 77–98; cf. Hanson (1995) 311. The Sepeia campaign may also indicate that Spartan kings in the field acted independently of the home authorities, making their own decisions about the fate of the defeated enemy. Cleomenes' summoning before the ephors suggests that they could be accountable for their actions later. To what extent this applied to generals in other archaic *poleis* is less clear. Peisistratus' order not to rout the Athenians at Pallene (see n. 71) could be an example of a general's independent decision making, but he did not command a public army. The influence of the *demos* on the campaign decisions of the Athenian *strategoi* was certainly considerable in the classical period; for more, see Hamel (1998) 113–21.

[76] Jackson (2000) 306, quoted in Nevin (2017) 115.

[77] For a recent work on sacred spaces and military leaders, see Nevin (2017).

the battles of Pallene and Sepeia show generals actively seeking advantage before attacking the enemy. Contrary to the traditional scholarly view of archaic generalship, tricks, deception and misdirection were common tools in their craft. Considerations of terrain were also a factor. The main aim of the general was to deliver an effective and decisive blow, capable of ending a long-term conflict (Nisaea), a short-term campaign (Pallene) or, when necessary, massacring the enemy to ensure no retaliation was possible (Sepeia). The increased institutionalisation of archaic armies in the sixth century BC meant that the general's authority to command, as well as the discipline of his army, were less of a problem than they were for the commanders of seventh-century BC forces.[78] Combined with wider developments in Greek warfare of the sixth century BC, in particular the appearance of separate heavy- and light-armed infantry, alongside cavalry units, the role of strategy and tactics became increasingly important in the general's craft.[79] Finally, although mentions of the general's courage and physical prowess disappear from our sources, we should expect that once the battle started, the general's place remained among his men on the front line. His reputation and the obedience of his troops, however, no longer relied on his martial skill and performance in combat; the Homeric figures of Nestor, Menestheus and Odysseus were now the clear general's archetype.

Conclusion

The image of the archaic warrior general, who led his troops by example and could do little more than fight valiantly to influence the outcome of a battle, dominates current scholarship. The art of generalship in the archaic period, however, required significantly more from commanders than martial prowess, and its development can tell us much about the changes in the nature of warfare and army organisation

---

[78] Where the authority to command was not publicly granted, additional oaths of obedience could be introduced. During his self-imposed exile in Arcadia, as Herodotus relates, Cleomenes united the local inhabitants against Sparta and made them swear obedience to him, with the leading Arcadians swearing 'an oath of loyalty on the waters of the Styx' (6.74). Oaths designed to instil obedience to army commanders were probably sworn by the allied Greek forces during the Persian Wars (see n. 56).

[79] Apart from Hippias' use of Thessalian cavalry to rout the Spartans at Phalerum (Hdt. 5.63), we do not hear of generals making tactical use of the light-armed or cavalry units in the archaic period. This, however, may be due to a tendency in ancient sources to omit the contribution of such units in their accounts of pitched battles. According to Herodotus, 9.29, the Greek *poleis* fielded a staggering force of 69,500 light troops at Plataea in 479 BC, which suggests that such troops must have been a regular part of Greek citizen armies by the end of the archaic period. For a good discussion of the bias in our sources with regard to the light troops in Athens, see Trundle (2010) 139–47.

in early Greece. The generals of Archilochus' and Tyrtaeus' age were expected to inspire and maintain good morale in their warriors; constant exhortations were a recurring feature in early warfare, as discipline and obedience were a major issue for generals, who recognised that the cohesion and solidarity of their forces was the key to victory. The latter, nonetheless, was difficult to maintain due to limited chains of command and the fluid nature of battlefields, where light-armed warriors freely intermingled with heavy-armed. With the institutionalisation of citizen militias in the sixth century BC, the organisation and structures of Greek armies changed, reflected in new unit divisions, army officials and means to control the obedience of warriors. As a result, considerations of strategy and tactics gradually took on more significance. Depending on the operation (naval or land), the generals planned the attack, taking into account factors of terrain and enemy position; whenever possible, they attempted to incorporate elements of surprise and stratagems, aiming to maximise their side's advantage and exploit any potential weakness of the enemy before the engagement began. Notwithstanding the changes in the shape and organisation of Greek armies in the archaic era, the overall ideal of a general in the era was one of courage, pragmatism and cunning, all of which featured to a different degree across a variety of sources and genres in the period: from Homeric *basileis*, whose martial prowess and leadership, combined with their *metis* and *techne*, provided an archetype for later generations; Tyrtaeus' Spartan generals, expecting obedience and scolding shameful flight; Archilochus' bow-legged commanders, steady and full of guts; to charismatic leaders of late archaic citizen militias, whose strategic planning, ruthlessness and clever schemes gave them a reputation for masterful stratagems in later traditions.

The prevalence of these ideals beyond the archaic era suggests, in turn, significant continuities within the discourses and practices of war into the classical period. The common realities of classical Greek warfare, as argued in recent studies, feature several factors which indicate that the main duties of the generals most likely remained the same.[80] Greek wars were fought primarily by amateur citizens who lacked training and discipline and were incapable of complex formations or manoeuvres. Once the battle started, generals could do little to change their course apart from courageously leading the phalanx and making sure it did not collapse. Their efforts were, therefore, concentrated on drawing up before battle, coordinating the attacks of the phalanx, the light-armed and cavalry, and exploiting the advantages of terrain and, if possible, ambush. The ultimate aim was to break the opposing forces and inflict maximum damage while doing so; 'brutal pragmatism', as Roel Konijnendijk

---

[80] Echeverria Rey (2011); Konijnendijk (2018).

summarised, was the 'one and only rule' of warfare of the classical era.[81] Eventually, the emergence of specialised and professional troops, capable of tactical manoeuvres during battle, added new elements to the art of generalship in Greek warfare. The overall similarities, however, reveal that archaic generalship was part of a much longer heritage.

---

[81] Konijnendijk (2018) 227.

2 Commemorating Thermopylae: The *andreia* of Glorious Defeat as a Literary Construct

Richard Evans

Introduction

> For you the inhabitants of the broad plains of Sparta
> Either your great and glorious name will be destroyed by the men of Persia
> Or, if that is avoided, instead Sparta up to its frontiers will mourn for a dead king,
> A descendant of the Heraclidae.
>
> (Herodotus 7.220)

> Leonidas said that the Spartans must stay behind and not leave their defence of the 'Gates', since it was fitting that the leaders of Hellas should be prepared to die when toiling for the prize of honour. So the rest retreated at once, leaving Leonidas and his fellow citizens to perform heroic and incredible deeds. (Diodorus 11.9.1–2)[1]

At Thermopylae in early August 480 BC, after a brief stalemate lasting roughly four days (Hdt. 7.210), the Persians in the next two to three days overcame the Spartan-led defence of the narrow coastal link that joined Thessaly to Boeotia and Attica. The defenders were mostly killed but the greater part of the army of the Peloponnesian city-states, members by then of a Hellenic League, retreated in good order to the Isthmus. When news of the defeat at Thermopylae was related to the accompanying

---

[1] Diodorus' account may derive from two main sources, neither of which was Herodotus' history. For Diodorus' use of Ctesias see Green (2006) 47, but this was not necessarily at first hand since his main source for this period was surely Ephorus. Ephorus had much easier access to works composed in the fifth century BC.

fleet stationed further along the coast opposite Euboea it also retired, and the way was left open for a Persian advance into Attica and the capture of Athens, all within a fortnight. This was the darkest hour for the Greek *poleis* that had decided to oppose any form of rapprochement with the Persians and their king Xerxes: it was Hellenic independence or death. As Herodotus describes, and what is thoroughly familiar to most, the Greek fleet went on to win an unexpected victory over the Persians at Salamis. Moreover, in the next summer the combined armies of the mostly southern Greek city-states routed the Persians at Plataea. Xerxes' ambitions to extend his empire westward were ended. Thermopylae was, in practical terms, not at all a contributing factor to the victory of the Greeks over Persia: rather the opposite, since the Boeotian League, politically lukewarm to both Athens and Sparta, the leaders of the Hellenic League, turned instead to Persia for an alliance in order to save its cities from destruction.[2] However, Thermopylae served another purpose: indicating bravery in the face of adversity, selflessness for the good of fellow Greeks and a devotion to duty against all the odds. All these factors contributed to the confident mood that ushered in the Greek civilisation of the classical period.

The binding thread of the discussion in this volume is the art of the general, usually, but not exclusively, military leadership at its best. Here the discussion looks at how a failed general such as Leonidas and, for all its heroism, a defeat in battle have become celebrated almost, if not more, than the most splendid victory. Besides those mentioned already, some further reasons are offered for this perception about Thermopylae, and that its fame rather than its infamy, which has captured the imagination throughout the ages, is surely just a clever literary construct. Enough has been said of the Persian invasion of Greece of which Thermopylae was the first encounter between the warring parties;[3] and so the focus here is rather on what came next. By this is meant the process of commemoration and intentionally, or not, reinventing the event and therefore recasting history to the advantage of, initially, the losers, who later became triumphant in the conflict with Persia. Thermopylae hence became the precursor to victories and not an episode to be forgotten or minimised in the minds

---

[2] It is ironic that the Thebans then fought alongside the Persians at Plataea and as a result were heavily penalised by the Hellenic League afterwards, not least in the termination of the Boeotian League of which they were leaders. Further, this treatment deepened Thebes' resentment towards Athens and Sparta, as events in the Peloponnesian War and in the first half of the fourth century plainly illustrate, and which made mainland Greece easy prey for Macedonian imperial ambitions after 359 BC.

[3] The sea battle at Artemisium was fought almost simultaneously. Salamis followed in the next month, Plataea at the start of the following summer, Mycale towards the end of summer of 479. See de Sélincourt and Marincola (2003) 671 n. 56 for references to modern studies and analyses of the fight at Thermopylae.

of a later audience. The process of transformation occurred very rapidly, it would appear, that is if Herodotus is accurate in his summing up of the battle (7.220–34, 8.24–39), which is a problem in itself.[4] However, here it is another issue that needs to be teased out of the literary sources. This is the actual commemoration of Leonidas and Thermopylae and the authors of this episode, and to whom did it become advantageous when the reinvigorated history was circulated among its Greek audience.

An Overview of the Thermopylae Episode

The Persian army and fleet crossed the Hellespont in early summer and advanced through Thrace, pausing at Doriscus, in the vicinity of Mount Athos at Acanthus, and at Therma before advancing into Greece via Thessaly and making an encampment just to the north of Thermopylae (Hdt. 7.198–201). The Persians were opposed by a small army comprising Spartans and their Peloponnesian allies (Hdt. 7.202–3), in total about 3,100 hoplites, together with 4,100 citizen soldiers from Phocis, Locris, Malis, Thebes and Thespiae (Diod. 11.4.6).[5] In command of the army Leonidas

---

[4] Thus see van Wees (2019) 19–53.

[5] Herodotus does not mention the Helots who would have accompanied the Spartiates. They were perhaps not armed at Thermopylae, unlike at Plataea in the following year. Herodotus (7.202) provides a detailed list of those involved in the final fight: 300 Spartiates, 700 from Thespiae and 400 from Thebes, not counting at least 1,500 Helots, if there were the same number of Helots for each Spartiate as at Plataea. His claim that 4,000 Greeks died at Thermopylae (8.25) therefore seems feasible, but considering that the Thebans were not killed does leave the question of who the others were. Herodotus claims (7.206) that the force stationed at Thermopylae was merely an advance guard and that the main Greek army was to follow after the Spartans had concluded their Carneia festival and when the games at Olympia had been completed. This is not entirely convincing, since the Carneia had caused complete inaction when the Athenians had appealed to Sparta for aid just a decade earlier before Marathon. The Olympic Games took just three days to complete and was only an impediment to warfare when the festival was ongoing. The games are recorded as having taken place, with a list of winners including competitors from Chios and Thasos who were residents of the Persian Empire. Diodorus does not mention that Leonidas was to wait for reinforcements, but would the Spartans have committed their entire military capability at that juncture? There is nothing to suggest this, and it hence makes Herodotus' account less plausible and Diodorus' evidence seem more reliable. Diodorus (11.4.4–7) states that Leonidas was accompanied by 1,000 Spartans, of whom 300 were Spartiates, with another 3,000 troops from the other Greeks (from the Peloponnese), and claims that they were joined at Thermopylae by 1,000 Locrians, 1,000 Malians, nearly 1,000 Phocians and 400 Thebans. At 11.9.2 he notes that following the withdrawal ordered by Leonidas there remained just 500 including a contingent from Thespiae. Diodorus, on the other hand, has further exaggerated the glory by not mentioning the total number of Spartans including

had, however, to maintain contact with the Greek fleet, numbering 271 triremes (Hdt. 8.2) which had taken up a defensive position near Artemisium. Eurybiades, also a Spartiate, had overall command of the whole expedition (Diod. 11.4.2).[6] A simple assessment of the numbers involved in the combined Greek forces on that occasion indicates that the fleet was the greater armament. The purpose of the army at Thermopylae must have been to delay Xerxes' advance until the Greek fleet had inflicted sufficient damage to the enemy's warships for them to lose their supremacy on the sea. With that purpose achieved, the Persians would have been obliged to withdraw, as indeed was the outcome of the Greek victory at Salamis.

The defence of Thermopylae was therefore meant to be a classic holding operation, which probably ended rather more dramatically than was originally intended.[7] First of all, the point of defence was surely deliberately chosen because it reduced the numerical advantage of the enemy, which also suggests sound reconnaissance of the terrain and hence reduces the likelihood that a hidden track was left unexplored. Still the enemy's obvious superiority in numbers meant that eventually the Greeks would have to withdraw or die, and some secret mountain path was irrelevant to the battle plan. Herodotus states that Xerxes delayed because he expected the Greeks to withdraw, and only then ordered an assault on the 'Gates', where fighting took place over two consecutive days (Hdt. 7.211–12) before the Persians paused, realising that the defenders were proving more obdurate than anticipated, and could only be overcome by employing a flanking manoeuvre through the famous 'secret' mountain track. The fact that the Phocians were guarding this approach indicates that an attack from this direction was expected and it was only a matter of time before it occurred. The tale of an informer from Trachis enlivens the narrative but is perhaps an embroidered story even if preserved by both Herodotus and Diodorus (11.8.4). That the path was well known to the defenders shows that the Persian invaders, who had many Greeks in their ranks, would have been equally well informed. Xerxes had no need to listen to the supposed traitor Ephialtes of Trachis, an account which may be laced with bias.[8] It is notable that the account of the treachery in Diodorus (11.8.4–5) is given much

---

Helots and possibly *perioeci*. See Green (2006) 55 n. 28 for a discussion of the missing 700 including possible *perioeci*.

[6] Herodotus does not make this clear until the start of Book 8 and after the defeat at Thermopylae had already taken place.

[7] Thus Munro (1939) 299.

[8] At the time Trachis was a *polis* of the Malians. The Spartans refounded Trachis as Heraclea in 426, just four miles from Thermopylae, as a strategic outpost against Athens (Thuc. 3.92). A hostile tale about Trachis might not have been inappropriate if Book 7 of Herodotus' history was composed in the 420s.

less prominence than in Herodotus.⁹ The Phocian contingent at the mountain track withdrew as the Persian column approached over the mountain.¹⁰ Leonidas ordered the withdrawal of the majority of the troops, but chose to remain as did the Thespian and Theban detachments. The remaining Greeks resisted a further assault along the coastal path and during this fighting the Spartan king was killed (Hdt. 7.224). When the Persians were seen approaching from the south the Greeks – but not the Thebans – are said to have occupied a small hill behind the 'Phocian Wall'. Soon afterwards the defenders were overwhelmed (Hdt. 7.225). Herodotus states that whereas 4,000 Greeks were killed the Persians received 20,000 fatalities (Hdt. 8.24–5). He goes on to relate Xerxes' attempted ruse of concealing most of the bodies of the Persian dead in order to enhance his victory, but nobody, it appears, was hoodwinked. Herodotus states that the body of Leonidas was decapitated and that such a savage action on the order of Xerxes was uncharacteristic for a Persian, but a reflection of the hatred the one king felt for the other (Hdt. 7.238.).¹¹

Diodorus' account has notable differences in detail, not least regarding a supposed night attack on the Persian camp by the Greeks, and therefore does not rely on Herodotus. The description of the last fight is longer, with less coherence and probably rather more fictitious elements than that of Herodotus. While both historians lacked a sound understanding of military affairs, Diodorus' evidence still cannot be dismissed out of hand. He has a slightly more realistic total for an army than Herodotus. He has the Persians making camp specifically at the river Spercheius (11.5.4; cf. Hdt. 7.221), launching their assault on the Greeks from there and encountering their enemy at the narrowest point of the coastal track. He also provides (11.7.2–3) a credible enough reason for Persian frustration at being unable to advance against the Greeks, claiming that the size of the hoplite shield made

---

⁹ Diodorus neglects even to give the name of the betrayer of the Greeks, although it will also have been common knowledge.

¹⁰ Xerxes ordered a column of 20,000 troops to carry out the outflanking of the Greeks, according to Diodorus (11.8.5). Herodotus (7.215) provides no figure except that it was the Persian Immortals, a force of 10,000, although these had received severe casualties in the fighting already (Hdt. 7.211). The number given by Diodorus is probably inflated, thus noted by Green (2006) 59 n. 39 and 45 as symptomatic of ancient historiography. There were 1,000 Greeks guarding the path, so a number superior to that should be in order. In the Roman victory over Antiochus III in 191 there were 2,000 troops from the Aetolian League guarding this track, according to Appian (*Syrian Wars* 4.18) but just 600 according to Plutarch (*Cato Mai.* 13.7). These, like the Phocians before them, fled at the arrival of the enemy, in this case the elder Cato leading a part of the consular army of Manius Acilius Glabrio. For the account see Plutarch, *Cato Mai.* 13.1–7; also Evans (2011) 32–4.

¹¹ Elsewhere Xerxes' brutality and arrogance are well illustrated by Herodotus 7.38–9: the execution of Pythius' eldest son.

defence easier while the attackers with less armour, especially smaller shields, were more vulnerable targets. Herodotus, on the other hand (7.211–12), mentions the shorter and less effective spears of the Persians and some rather more improbable tactics devised by the Spartans.[12] When the Greeks learned from a deserter (Diod. 11.8.5) that the Persians were in the process of outflanking their rear, they held a council and Leonidas dismissed most of the army. Once surrounded, those who had remained with the king were killed not in close combat but from a distance with arrows and javelins (Diod. 11.10.4; cf. Hdt. 7.225). Diodorus concludes his coverage with a rhetorical digression on the extent of the bravery of the Greek dead. The discrepancies between the two main accounts of the episode do not affect the essential details.[13]

The Supernatural Elements in the Thermopylae Episode

Herodotus wrote his account of this section of the Persian Wars most probably in the 420s, which were themselves momentous years in the history of the Greek states. There can also be little doubt that with regard to historical accuracy Herodotus often leaves his reader in a quandary. For example, he states (7.228) quite clearly that the Greeks were buried where they fell in the battle, but later in Book 8 (8.25) he claims that all 4,000 fatalities were collected and buried together. The second version allows Herodotus to retell a story of Xerxes' *hubris*, but it also causes uncertainty about which of the two was correct and whether or not the historian had little more than a vague idea of precise events. In the preface to Herodotus' account of the Thermopylae episode, there is the very dubious declaration (Hdt. 7.175) that the defence of the road at Thermopylae was agreed before there was any knowledge that there was a route by which, as indeed happened, defenders might be outflanked. This claim, as already noted above, seems extraordinary considering that although the Greek mainland is mountainous and in places inaccessible, it was, by ancient standards, well populated. Moreover, through regular religious festivals and a high level of trade there was discourse between the various scattered communities. It is simply unbelievable that Themistocles, a consummate strategist, would not have

---

[12] Improbable because the apparent withdrawal and then turnabout into an attack seems designed for a more open field of battle. On the final day's fighting Herodotus states that the Spartans advanced outside their fortifications into a broader section of the path and that many Persians fell to their death into the sea (Hdt. 7.223), and so reveals that Thermopylae was not a 'pass' at all, but a coastal track, which is still easily identifiable today even though the sea at this point has retreated from its ancient coastline. For further discussion on the geographical location, see Kraft et al. (1987).

[13] See also De Bakker (2019) 54–90.

been fully aware of the lie of the land around Amphissa before he committed the warships of Athens to shadowing the army of Leonidas, on whom he had to depend to hold back the Persian advance while the Hellenic fleet saw action against the invaders.[14] Further, would the citizens of Trachis not have revealed the existence of a 'secret' path between the mountain range of Anopaea and Mount Callidromus (Plut. *Cato Mai.* 13.3–4) before the summer of 480? Perhaps what Herodotus had in mind was the introduction of some suspense into the narrative, but by doing so he allowed the incredible elements to become dominant. But these components when taken together are surely the building blocks of an elaborate construct.

These fantastical elements are best represented by the omnipresence of the supernatural throughout the narrative of Thermopylae, and easily surpass divine intervention at Marathon or the other battles of the Greek–Persian Wars. The gods, primarily Apollo through the Pythia, or the ancient heroes, Phylacus and Autonous (Hdt. 8.39), play an inordinately active role in the outcome of events in August 480. Yet there is no sceptical observation from Herodotus, who lived through an age when there was lively agnosticism and philosophical discourse on the relationship between gods and humans. This apparent descent into naive storytelling can do little to reassure the reader that the account of Thermopylae is really history, especially when oracular messages of foreboding from Delphi (Hdt. 7.220) and actual divine intervention at the oracular shrine itself (Hdt. 8.39–39) enfold the military action.

This supernatural activity is finely balanced between the positive and negative. Thus the Pythia (Hdt. 7.178) gives hope of victory to the Greeks, but deters the Argives from becoming involved (Hdt. 7.148).[15] The political sympathies of the Delphic cult, as is well recognised, were for an accommodation with Persia, and these oracles, like many, are probably inventions designed to deflect criticism of Medising. Indeed, much of the entire section in Herodotus, although nominally about Thermopylae, is essentially an apologia for Delphi.[16] The positive oracle there-

---

[14] The fleet of the Hellenic League was not simply present as a support for the army, and its role was different from that of the fleet of the Persians, which had to ferry supplies to the enormous military presence summoned into Europe by Xerxes. The Greeks must have hoped that there was a chance that if the army held the 'Gates' and the fleet could inflict considerable damage on the Persian shipping, then the enemy would withdraw. This strategy seems likely, but the failure of Leonidas to hold Thermopylae brought a rapid alteration in the Greek planning.

[15] The Greeks were advised to pray to the 'winds', who would be 'great allies'. This is meant to reflect the storms and gales which the Persian fleet encountered sailing from the Hellespont to Attica. Herodotus (7.190–1) maintains that the Persians lost 400 warships and countless merchant vessels just between Casthanaea and Cape Sepias.

[16] Munro (1939) 301; Hammond (1959) 237; Bury and Meiggs (1975) 530 n. 6.

fore receives some prominence, but is soon subsumed in the all-pervading gloom brought on by the fear of imminent conquest by a foreign power.[17] Both main powers in Greece, Athens (Hdt. 7. 140–2) and Sparta (Hdt. 7.220), were warned of destruction, but the wording of the oracles ensured that steps could be taken – the wooden walls (ships) of Athens, the loss of a Spartan king – to change the future. Hence the reader, as in poetic technique, has the future predicted from the hindsight of the future, and all turns out well, as expected, therefore, because the Athenians obey the 'true interpretation' of the 'wooden walls' and Leonidas is killed at Thermopylae.

It is not merely the frequency of oracles that punctuates the text; Herodotus also draws on what he states is evidence for the outcome of the battle at the 'Gates' provided by a mantis named Megistias, who happened to be present (Hdt. 7.221). He is said to have observed negative omens before the battle began. Since Megistias died with the Spartans, the source of this evidence supposedly corroborating the oracle came to Herodotus only second- or third-hand via descendants of the seer. And that would mean that Megistias had time to pass on this knowledge in the brief spell between his observations and the retreat of the greater part of the Greek army.[18] Regarding the giant ghostly warriors at Delphi, Herodotus claims (8.38–9) to have heard it said that the survivors of the Persian rout considered the sudden intervention of the two ancient local heroes divinely inspired. He does not claim to have heard this story from Delphi at all, nor does he voice any disbelief in the excuses offered by those apparently defeated by a small number of defenders at Apollo's shrine. The real history of this attack on Delphi, if it occurred, would probably have been interesting without the participation of magical warriors, but any such information has been completely lost. This suggests that except in Herodotus' imagination it did not exist. Diodorus (11.14.2–4) also recounts the attack on Delphi but has a more logical explanation for the defeat of the Persians, attributing it to the sudden onset of a storm that unleashed an avalanche from Mount Parnassus. This caused the attackers to retreat in confusion, and was taken as a sign from the gods perhaps,

---

[17] The whole notion of a foreign foe is quite misleading since Greeks and Persians had lived in close proximity since the fall of Croesus in c. 545 BC at least. The Persian presence in Thrace was also long-standing, and remained down to the rule of Alexander the Great. The Persian harbour at Eion in Thrace remained free of Greek control until 334.

[18] Note the parallel use (Hdt. 5.44–5) of Callias, another mantis, in the narrative and the 'evidence' obtained from this individual's descendants. Megistias chose to stay with the Spartans, but his 'only' son, who was serving as a soldier, left Thermopylae with the others. This son could have passed on what he had been told by his father to others. The role of the seer in the army is well documented. For example, Nicias, commander of the Athenians at Syracuse in 414 and 413, relied heavily on the advice of seers – too heavily, according to Thucydides (7.50).

but no apparitions were sighted. In general, moreover, oracles do not feature in Diodorus' account. In Herodotus the failed attack on Delphi concludes the episode (Hdt. 8.35–8), while Diodorus (11.14.4) has the citizens of Apollo's cult centre erect a victory trophy at the precinct of Athena Pronaea where the Persians had been repulsed. The absence of the supernatural perhaps points to one of Diodorus' main sources: the history of Ephorus, whom the later Sicilian historian perhaps viewed as a more serious historian, less prone to storytelling, But Ephorus also covered a far greater chronological span, which was of more use to the plan of Diodorus' universal history. Still, it is interesting nonetheless that a writer regarded today as an authority should be avoided, although it is worth noting that Thucydides in his few references to Thermopylae also has no mention of Herodotus.[19]

Simonides and the Workshop of Commemorative Monuments

It became a common practice from the archaic period of Greece and throughout the fifth century to celebrate the triumphs of rulers (mainly tyrants), victors in various panhellenic games and festivals, and military successes through praise poetry. The last were often inscribed on trophies or monuments at the place where the rout of the enemy began. The fame of poets such as Aeschylus, Bacchylides, Pindar and Simonides, especially, illustrates the brisk activity of this practice. The role of Simonides in the celebration of the Greek defeat at Thermopylae is of particular relevance here. At Thermopylae there was no panic-stricken rout symptomatic of an ending to a battle, but a massacre, which was not unusual in itself, but unusual in that those killed were all trapped together in a confined space; and it is probably unique that the defeated rather than the victor set up the trophy or trophies.[20] And it is Simonides who appears to be credited with a number of commemorations of this episode; however, there are some interesting issues involved in assigning such numerous creations to a single literary figure.

---

[19] Thucydides in his overview of events in Greece in Book 1 dismisses the Persian Wars in one sentence, not even mentioning the battles by name, 1.23. His history of the Peloponnesian War has no divine influence, but much of it was written at about the same time as Herodotus' Books 7–8. However, Thucydides (4.36) describes the situation of the Spartans at Pylos in 424 as being similar to that of their encirclement at Thermopylae, and considers the former a lesser affair than the latter. The outcome of Sphacteria was, however, a direct result of the outcome of Thermopylae and illustrated the weakness of the Spartan political hierarchy. Thucydides ignores the causal connection surprisingly. Thermopylae is noted elsewhere, 2.101, 3.92, but only as a geographical indicator.

[20] For unusual trophies, particularly that by the Syracusans after their decisive victory over the Athenians in 413, see Evans (2016) 213–17.

Herodotus provides three 'epitaphs' (Hdt. 7.228) in his narrative.[21] Of these monuments Herodotus actually cites Simonides as the author only of the epitaph of Megistias, although modern consensus is for Simonides as the author of all three.[22] The text of the epitaphs is as follows: (1) 'Four thousand here from Pelops' land, / against three million once did stand.' (2) 'Go tell the Spartans, you who read: / we took their orders, and here lie dead.'[23] (3) 'Here lies Megistias, who died / when the Mede passed Spercheius' tide. / A prophet; yet he scorned to save / himself, but shared the Spartans' grave.'[24] Herodotus is no help in assigning a date for the Thermopylae epitaphs or under what circumstances these commemorations were set up, which more than likely was some years after the event. In that case can Simonides have been the author of monuments built possibly several years after 479? He is considered to have been born before 550 and was already active as a poet during the tyranny of Hippias (527–510). He is known to have spent time in Syracuse during the rule of Hieron (478–467) and died in Akragas a year or two after the collapse of the Deinomenid tyranny (466/5). Is it possible to consider Simonides the author of the epitaphs in light of his, by then, advanced age, and not being resident in Greece? Moreover, his connection with Megistias is unknown, while composition of and

---

[21] Although Herodotus is the chief source for a study of Thermopylae, he was not the earliest. See the discussion by Green (2006) 41–7. It is also possible that Aeschylus inserted a mention of this event into one of his compositions, but nothing pertinent survives. His *Persae* provides a good commentary on Salamis and therefore a reference to Thermopylae is strangely missing. He fought at Marathon and like Simonides remained active throughout the Persian Wars period.

[22] There were five columnal *stelai* commemorating the 'Greek' army. These comprised commemorations of the Greeks in general, of the Spartans, of Megistias, of the Thespians and of the Opuntian Locrians; How and Wells (1912) 1.230. How and Wells, 1.231, considered Simonides 'doubtless' the author of all three cited at Hdt. 7.228; Godley (1922) 545 n. 1. Cf. Bury (1939) 492: 'one which may safely be attributed'; Lattimore (1960) 53: 'the epitaph . . . is not certainly his'.

[23] Trans. de Sélincourt and Marincola (2003) 495. Cf. Diod. 11.33.2. See Green (2006) 90–1 and n. 139, who notes that Diodorus' version of 'we took their orders' or 'did what they told us to do' is given as 'obeying their laws', which may as easily be a copyist error as that of the historian. Note Lattimore's translation (1960) 56: 'Traveler take this word to the men of Lakedaimon; we who lie buried did what they told us to do.' Diodorus' account of the Persian attack on Delphi (11.11.14) is much more believable than that of Herodotus (8.35–39). An army of 10,000 infantry was not unusual for this period; just so the Athenian army at Marathon in 490.

[24] Cf. Lattimore's (1960) 56: 'This is the grave of that Megistias, whom once the Persians / and Medes killed when they crossed the Spercheios River; / a seer who saw clearly the spirits of death advancing upon him, / yet could not bring himself to desert the Spartiate kings.'

payment for that monument, while poignant, rather lack credibility when its author was living in Sicily, old even if still vigorous, and surely in no position to supervise the construction of the *stele* and its inscription.

Diodorus (11.33.2) places the commemoration of the Greek dead at some time following the Battle of Plataea in 479; and this seems credible enough. However, earlier in his narrative Diodorus (11.11.6) also places immediately after his account of Thermopylae an encomium which he attributes to Simonides. This is not recorded by Herodotus and its authorship is open to some doubt.

> Of those who died at Thermopylai renowned is the fortune, noble the fate:
> Their grave's an altar, their memorial our mourning, their fate our praise.
> Such a shroud neither decay nor all-conquering time shall destroy.
> This sepulcher of brave men has taken the high renown of Hellas for its fellow
>   occupant, as witness
> Leonidas, Sparta's king who left behind a great memorial of valor, everlasting
>   renown.
>
> (Diod. 11.11.6 = trans. Green (2006) 63)

This additional epitaph, or perhaps a choral ode, to the Spartan dead evidently did not find a place in Herodotus' account, nor was it considered worth mentioning. Its authenticity can be questioned if it was composed for some later ceremony that took place after the hostilities had ceased. How long afterwards is the crucial point here. Pausanias (3.14.1) states that the tomb of Leonidas was situated in Sparta, and that the Spartan commander at Plataea, also named Pausanias, reburied the king's remains forty years after Thermopylae. This Pausanias died in 470, hence there is some confusion in the text: either the tomb was built in the 470s or (perhaps more likely) not completed until about 440, and the author has conflated his information.[25] There was also a *stele* listing the names of the Spartan dead (Paus.3.14.1). At Thermopylae there was another column recording the names of all 300 Spartans killed in the battle, but Pausanias states that a festival dedicated to these heroes was annually conducted at the tombs of Leonidas and Pausanias, the regent. Herodotus (7.224) claims to have learned all the names of the Spartan dead and so it is possible that he saw either the column at Thermopylae or the *stele* in Sparta.[26] If the monument at Sparta was erected in the 470s, celebrations of the Spartan dead could

---

[25] The games referred to would have been the sort of events visitors to Sparta in the second century AD, Pausanias' time, would have expected to witness. The tombs may well have been rebuilt many times.

[26] How and Wells (1912) 1.230 considered that such a *stele* belongs to the 470s.

have included an encomium written by Simonides, but if this only happened in the 440s, or later, then an encomium, if one was written at all, must have had different authorship. The tomb of Pausanias must surely belong to the 460s and may well be later than the revolt of the Messenian Helots in 464/3, following an earthquake which caused severe damage to Sparta.[27] Rebuilding and the subsequent elaboration of royal tombs might easily belong to the 450s and 440s rather than the 470s, when the Greeks were still recovering from the effects of the war with Persia. The same financial constraints would certainly be applicable to commemorative monuments in other parts of mainland Greece. Reconstruction at Athens after its sack by the Persians would alone have meant that monuments remembering the dead of Xerxes' invasion are more probably an indication of the financial security of the 440s and 430s than of the 470s. It is worth remembering that the Parthenon at Athens, itself in part a commemoration of Marathon, was not begun until 448/7 and hardly finished before the start of the war with Sparta in 431.[28] Altogether, therefore, there is more than sufficient doubt about the dates of these commemorative monuments, and so it follows that there must also be some doubt about the author or authors of preserved encomia.

It is, moreover, worth adding that Diodorus' account (11.11.1–6) following Thermopylae is highly rhetorical and elaborate, which suggests that the encomium he quotes (11.11.6) and which ends that section is also of the same inventive material.[29]

---

[27] Plutarch, *Cim.* 16.4, claims total destruction of the *polis* buildings; cf. Diod. 11.63.1 under the year 469 with the claim that there were 20,000 casualties.

[28] Plut. *Per.* 12–13. For the Parthenon, see Neils (2001) 11–31.

[29] Diodorus makes the point that this section is discursive and not central to his narrative: 'For they alone of those commemorated down the ages chose to preserve the tradition of their city-state rather than their own lives, not resentful of the fact that so great a peril hung over them, but convinced that for those who practice valor, nothing could be more desirable than exposure to contests of this kind. Moreover, anyone who argued that these men were also more responsible for achieving the freedom of the Greeks than the victors in subsequent battles against Xerxes would be in the right of it; for when the barbarians recalled their deeds, they were terror-struck, whereas the Greeks were encouraged to attempt similar acts of bravery.' Diod 11.11.4–5 = trans. Green (2006) 62–3. Green (2006) 63 n. 46, notes that Diodorus' own narrative (11.16.15–16) plainly disproves or at the very least disagrees with this assertion and hence shows a divergence in opinion among the sources. The sentiment expressed by Diodorus or his source had, however, become the acceptable version of events, certainly by the fourth century. Thus after the Battle of Leuctra in 370 the Peloponnesian League requested aid from Athens in its war against Thebes: 'Are there any others you would be happier to have as your fellow soldiers than those men whose countrymen, standing at Thermopylae, chose to die fighting rather than live and allow the barbarian into Greece?' (Xen. *Hell.* 6.5.43).

A little later in the narrative, following his account of the Greek victory at Plataea, Diodorus (11.33.2) devotes some attention to the process of commemoration.[30] He recounts and quotes the two epitaphs (1 and 2 above) given by Herodotus (7.228), but gives no indication of an author, or whether or not he was aware of an epitaph of Megistias.[31] There can be little doubt that after the victory of the magnitude that the Greeks achieved against Persia, all city-states that participated in this triumph would have set up commemorative monuments. *Stelai* would have decorated the landscape or various agoras in profusion; and the industry of commemorative epitaphs would have thrived. Most writers of these commemorations are unknown, while some few achieved fame, and, therefore, so much better that a famous praise poet be assigned to a monument in the works of later historians.

Regarding the existence of encomia or epitaphs of dubious provenance, two examples are of particular relevance here. Herodotus (9.81) provides written confirmation for the tripod and 'Serpent Column' erected at Delphi by the Hellenic League after the Battle of Plataea, which listed all or most of the *poleis* that fought against Xerxes.[32] The column was commissioned, completed and presumably set up in the 470s and the date is considered established because Pausanias, commander of the Greeks at Plataea, was instrumental in pursuing this project, and he died in 470. However, Thucydides (1.132) also notes that Pausanias ordered that an elegiac couplet should be inscribed on the 'gold' tripod celebrating his own role in the Greek triumph. This inscription was apparently removed by the Spartans, perhaps when Pausanias became *persona non grata* in the late 470s, and Thucydides very specifically describes how this verse was 'destroyed', meaning that the inscription was obliterated. Thucydides here is perhaps not reliable, for he appears to think that this inscription was on the tripod and the removal of inscriptions on bronze or gold would have caused damage to the tripod. He also appears to juxtapose removal of Pausanias' hubristic self-aggrandisement with its replacement with the listing of the city-states in the Hellenic League, again all on the tripod. Such an assessment is not correct, as Meiggs and Lewis and others have shown. No evidence of this verse has come to light, and Thucydides sadly rarely mentions a source. But, crucially, Herodotus (9.81–2) fails to note this epigram and overall portrays Pausanias in a much more favourable fashion than does Thucydides. These contrasting versions

---

[30] Compare Diod. 11.33.2, where the text is rather a repetition of 11.11 and probably indicates use of the historian's 'other' source.

[31] Megistias, like the oracles and apparitions, does not appear in Diodorus' account. Diodorus would surely have included this epitaph had he employed Herodotus' history as a vital source.

[32] See Meiggs and Lewis (1969) 57–61 for a full discussion of the column, ancient sources and major modern studies.

are incompatible and suggest the existence of two traditions, each with a different characterisation of Pausanias. Finally, neither Herodotus nor Thucydides claims to have ever seen the monument at Delphi. And so where does that leave the 'Pausanias encomium'? Pausanias was not the author and hence would have commissioned a poet – possibly another in the corpus of Simonides – and there would have been the employment of an inscriber as well. Neither is remembered, and the whole episode begins to look like invective designed to portray the character of Pausanias in a negative light. Diodorus (11.33.2) complicates the narrative even further by asserting that an encomium celebrating the victory of the Greeks which is supposed to have replaced the Pausanias encomium, but again has never been discovered, was composed by none other than Simonides. Since this elegiac couplet is unique to Diodorus' text, although it has been assigned tentatively to Simonides, it is generally considered an invention.[33] Diodorus is unlikely to have invented the couplet and so obtained the material from one of his sources, which again points to the popularity of a Simonides as a potential author of such epitaphs among later writers.

The passing of time did not dim the fame of Simonides or the popularity of attributing to his ever-growing corpus epitaphs of which he cannot possibly have been the author. Authorship by Simonides evidently conveyed a high degree of kudos, even more so than by a poet such as Aeschylus. A *stele* commemorating Megarian citizens who died in the war with Persia (*IG* 7.53 = Tod no. 20),[34] like those at Thermopylae, Delphi and many other places around Greece, is dated to the 470s. It was probably somewhat later, as the discussion above has argued. According to Todd, the original inscription on this memorial at Megara had weathered over the course of 800 years and so a certain Helladius, chief priest in the city, had the memorial reinscribed. From an inspection of the lettering and spelling on the inscription the date is assigned to the fourth to fifth centuries AD. At this juncture Simonides' name was added as author of the epitaph.

Why this attribution to Simonides of compositions about Thermopylae, Plataea and the Persian Wars in general? Simonides of Ceos was not a soldier, but a professional poet who was responsible for the epitaph for the Athenian dead at Marathon in 490.[35] But by the mid-470s he, like Aeschylus and other literary figures, was living

---

[33] Oldfather (1946) 212 n. 1; Meiggs and Lewis (1969) 60; cf. Green (2006) 90 n. 138 with less scepticism. Diodorus is incorrect in his chronology here since he claims that the Thebans surrendered only after this monument had been decided upon. No monuments can have been decided upon before the final victory at Mycale later in the year. The Greeks had pressing military matters to conclude.

[34] Tod (1946) 24: 'A slab of dark limestone'. Cf. Paus. 1.43.3.

[35] *Life of Aeschylus* 8. This epitaph for the Athenian dead at Marathon may have been composed in the 480s but equally in the great patriotic outburst following the final defeat of

in Sicily under the patronage of Hieron of Syracuse.[36] Nonetheless, Simonides' reputation and especially his connection with the epitaph at Marathon caused him to become the writer to whom such verses were necessarily attached. Thus it would appear that a cottage industry or art workshop had developed in commemorations, which has been continued well into our own times. That attributing composition to Simonides became a feature to add pedigree was almost as important as the glorification of the bravery of those commemorated. The Megarian Decree was a rewriting of history from the distant future, but the process had begun very much closer to the original event.

Conclusion

This discussion has been rather less about the 'art' of the general and rather more about the 'artifice' of those commemorating poor or inadequate generalship, specifically in this case that of Leonidas, the Spartan king, at Thermopylae. Leonidas may have been a warrior of some prowess; at least the literary tradition shows this tendency, although even this could have been mostly invention. There is little secure evidence of Leonidas' character or abilities in the way that Themistocles or Aristides have drawn the attention of ancient commentators. What stands out is that, in the absence of literary evidence, what we possess illustrates that Leonidas lacked discipline, and that his failure to maintain good communications with his superior Eurybiades, who was with the Greek fleet, and his failure to withdraw all the troops from Thermopylae when he could, were detrimental to the Greek cause. The defeat of the Greeks and the death of so many Spartiates had no effect at all on

---

Xerxes in the 470s, and hence may very well belong to a larger portfolio composed by Simonides which included a Thermopylae epitaph. See also Bury and Meiggs (1975) 161. Aeschylus left for Sicily when he failed to win the commission for the Marathon work, and is securely placed there after Plataea. Simonides also lived in Sicily from this time, both he and Aeschylus benefiting from the patronage of Hieron I. Any rivalry between the two could not have been more than a professional one, seeing that they would have spent a considerable amount of time together either in Syracuse or in Catane, the latter being the chosen residence of Hieron. It seems that the reason for Aeschylus' departure from Athens, namely that he took umbrage at losing the commission to Simonides, is more the creation of the *Life* than of history.

[36] Simonides is considered to have been present in Athens in the aftermath of the Persian defeat and hence on the spot for writing encomia, Bury (1939) 505. Plutarch (*Them*. 5.4–5) records some interaction between Themistocles and Simonides, probably to be dated to the 480s. There appears to be little concrete evidence for placing Simonides firmly in Athens after about 480, however. It would seem plausible to suggest that the poet went to Syracuse in order to escape the turmoil of the Persian invasion.

the progress of the Persians into southern Greece.[37] A tactical withdrawal would have been the more sensible move. It is notable that not a single ancient writer exposes the ineffectiveness of Leonidas' decision to remain and the lack of sound strategic planning; they rather focus on 'Homeric heroism'. Of course this heroic act and sacrifice could then be reworked in later accounts as the turning point in the fortunes of the Hellenic League. So effective has been the commemoration of what was little short of a long-term disaster for Sparta that the name Thermopylae has become synonymous with glorious defeat, and with the first round of a military contest that led ultimately to an extraordinary Greek achievement, in that a small number of city-states defeated the Persian Empire with all its huge resources. This inglorious episode arguably became more celebrated for its bravery, or *andreia*, than any of the Greek victories in the Persian Wars or probably later. To some extent this remarkable turning of history on its head can be attributed to the reputation of Simonides and the craft of Herodotus. Sparta may have suffered from the effects of this disaster; meanwhile Athens went from strength to strength, to dominate the political and cultural landscape for the next fifty years. To conclude with a reference to another inglorious military moment, this time in the history of the British Empire, namely the charge of the Light Brigade during the Battle of Balaclava in the Crimea in October 1854: in a phrase equally apposite to Thermopylae, it was 'in every sense a disaster, except the all-saving sense of immortal courage'.[38]

---

[37] The defeat at Thermopylae was in all respects a catastrophe for the unique Spartan socio-political hierarchy from which it never recovered. Three hundred Spartiates died and this casualty figure had a profoundly negative effect on the Spartan elite and its declining numbers over the next century.

[38] Feiling (1966) 910.

3 Plato on Military and Political Leadership
Nicholas Rockwell

The works of Plato provide great insight into the fundamental connection between warfare and politics in ancient Greece. Generals were often also political leaders who needed a variety of skills to have successful careers. For Plato, generals needed a thorough knowledge of military matters to effectively command soldiers in war. It was imperative that military leaders especially understand how best to deploy various units of hoplites, cavalry and light-armed troops. One passage in particular illustrates Plato's thinking on the natural progression in learning how to become a general. In the *Laches*, Plato has the Athenian general Nicias explain that 'everyone who has learned to fight in heavy armour desires learning the next thing, which is tactics; after understanding this and taking pride in it, the person rushes onto everything dealing with generalship' (182b–c; cf. *Euthyd.* 273c).[1] Most importantly for Plato, however, a great leader needed to understand all aspects of virtue, or human excellence. Besides knowledge of fighting in armour and military tactics and strategy, generals especially needed to embody the virtue of courage. As Plato has the Athenian Stranger say in the *Laws*, 'the leader of fighting men needs to be brave' (640a). For Plato, courage is one of the key components of virtue, which also includes justice, moderation and wisdom. This ideal combination is stated succinctly in the *Laws* when Plato has the Athenian Stranger say, 'justice, moderation, and wisdom coming to the same thing, along with courage are better than

---

[1] All translations are my own and based on the texts in the *Thesaurus Linguae Graecae*, with the exception of the text of the Platonic *Letters*, which is the one found in the Loeb Classical Library. Textual divisions for the works of Plutarch are also those of the Loeb Classical Library. The standard abbreviations for Plato's works and other ancient sources are those found in the fourth edition of the *Oxford Classical Dictionary*.

courage on its own' (*Leg.* 630a–b).² If a proper balance is not maintained between these distinct characteristics of virtue, each has the potential to become a destructive attribute, such as cowardice or recklessness.³ In Plato's *Laches*, in fact, it seems that moderation is the essential component for maintaining balance among the different aspects of virtue.⁴

An important question, however, was whether or not virtue could be taught. Plato seems to assume that virtue is teachable, otherwise philosophical inquiry would lack purpose and relevance for human endeavours. As Richard Kraut writes,

> Plato believes that human beings need not be put into one of two exhaustive categories: those who have perfect understanding of what is good, and those who are utterly ignorant of value. Most people, he assumes, fall somewhere between these extremes; and if someone has an unusually good understanding of value, it is appropriate – in fact, it may even be necessary – for him to try to educate those whose grasp of the good is smaller, but who are nonetheless educable.⁵

The whole reason Plato invests so much time and energy in formulating ideal institutions and practices is undoubtedly to help citizens improve themselves and live virtuous lives.

Nevertheless, acquiring the knowledge and skills necessary for virtuous living requires effort. Yet, for Plato, conventional education was not reliable because it was based on problematic traditions and texts such as the Homeric epics. Plato's critique of Homeric poetry is seen clearly in the *Ion*,⁶ which involves a private conversation Socrates has with the dialogue's eponymous character. As an accomplished rhapsode of Homeric poetry, Ion is especially proud of his abilities. At one point he makes the outrageous claim that because he is a Homeric rhapsode he would make a great general: Socrates, in fact, gets Ion to go so far as to agree that Ion himself is the best general in all of Greece because he is the most learned rhapsode of Homer's poetry (*Ion* 540d–541b). In the end, however, Socrates convinces Ion that Homer and the other poets are divinely inspired but they do not possess real knowledge. They provide only a dim reflection or imitation of knowledge. For Plato, it is imperative that political and military leaders have expert knowledge. The way they gain this knowledge is through philosophical inquiry. Much like the process of reading through a

---

² Cf. Meyer (2015) 100–3.
³ See Rowe (2018).
⁴ Stefou (2018) 47–51.
⁵ Kraut (2010) 51.
⁶ See Rijksbaron (2007) 9–14.

Platonic dialogue, which requires thinking through the dialectical arguments and discovering important truths for oneself, generals and statesmen need to engage in years of intellectual effort to be able to rule well. In fact, in one of the most famous passages in the *Republic*, Plato has Socrates say,

> until philosophers rule as kings in our cities or those we now call kings and rulers pursue philosophy legitimately and sufficiently . . . there will be no rest from evils for cities, nor do I think even for the human race. (473c–d; cf. *Resp.* 499b, 501e, 540d–e; *Leg.* 711d–712a; *Plt.* 293c)[7]

For Plato, the ultimate paragon of pursuing true knowledge was Socrates. Plato consistently presents Socrates as steadfast in seeking genuine knowledge and conducting himself according to strict moral standards. This was seen especially in the military sphere, where Socrates served as a hoplite on multiple Athenian campaigns. In the *Apology*, Plato's Socrates says the following:

> wherever someone has stationed himself believing it to be the best or has been marshalled by a commander, it is necessary to remain there to face danger, as it seems to me, giving no thought at all to death or anything else except disgrace. (*Ap.* 28d)

Just before this statement, Plato has Socrates refer to the famous scene in Homer's *Iliad* where Achilles chooses to avenge Patroclus and face certain death rather than live the life of a coward (*Il.* 18.78–104). This possibly implies that Socrates sees himself as abiding by the heroic code followed by Achilles. Yet Plato later has Socrates implicitly undermine another famous scene involving Achilles: namely, the meeting in Hades between Odysseus and Achilles in Homer's *Odyssey* (*Od.* 11.467–91). Plato makes Socrates assert,

> to fear death, gentlemen, is nothing other than to think you are wise when you are not – it is to think you know things that you do not know. For nobody knows whether or not death is the greatest of all benefits to humankind, yet they fear it as if they know for sure that it is the greatest of evils . . . since I do not have adequate knowledge of things in Hades, I therefore do not think I know. But I do know that

---

[7] There is a similar statement in the Platonic *Seventh Letter*, one of thirteen letters attributed to Plato but of uncertain authenticity: 'human races will not cease from evils until either the race of philosophers justly and truly occupy the political offices or the race of rulers in our cities, by some divine dispensation, really pursue philosophy', [Pl.] *Ep.* 7.326a–b.

it is evil and a disgrace to commit injustice and disobey a superior, whether a god or a human. (*Ap.* 29a–b)

Thus Plato has Socrates simultaneously using the Homeric tradition to support his position of heroically facing death while also undermining the very validity of that tradition. For Socrates to say 'I do not have adequate knowledge of things in Hades' raises fundamental questions about the reliability of the Homeric tradition and its usefulness for a robust epistemology.

There is also a very practical component to Socrates' message. He explains that it was essential to abide by the established military code to maintain his appointed position in combat:

> I would have done terrible things, Athenian gentlemen, if at the time when the commanders whom you elected to command me at Potidaea, Amphipolis and Delium ordered me to remain where they stationed me just like anyone else running the risk of death, but when god ordered me, as I thought and supposed, to live the life of a philosopher examining myself and others, I abandoned my post because I was terrified of death or anything else whatsoever. (*Ap.* 28d–29a)[8]

Socrates apparently believed that it was imperative for him to obey his duly elected generals rather than divine commands. Yet, in other passages, Socrates explains that throughout his life he frequently obeyed a divine voice (*Ap.* 31c–d, 40a–c).[9] This contradiction, however, is less problematic if we view Socrates as Plato's ideal moral leader who possessed true knowledge of right action at the right time in military matters. In the *Symposium*, Plato has the aristocrat Alcibiades relate how Socrates saved his life as well as his hoplite armour and weapons during the Battle of Potidaea (*Symp.* 220d–e; cf. *Leg.* 943e–945a). Alcibiades goes on to say that he told the generals that Socrates deserved a commendation for his actions in the battle: 'But the generals, who were looking at my social position, wanted to give the military decoration to me, and you [Socrates] were more eager than the generals that I receive it rather than yourself' (*Symp.* 220e). As Alcibiades makes clear earlier in his speech, Socrates placed little value on outward honours and appearances (*Symp.* 216e).[10] During the Battle of Delium later in the Peloponnesian War, Alcibiades says Socrates again displayed tremendous courage in the heat of combat. The Athenians had been routed by the Boeotians and were forced to flee the battlefield. Plato has Alcibiades assert,

---

[8] See van Wees (2004) 299 n. 10; Konijnendijk (2018) 185–6 n. 27.
[9] Cf. Slings (1994) 153–5.
[10] Cf. Rowe (1998) 205–6.

'I happened to be serving with the cavalry, and Socrates was a hoplite. After the men were already scattered, he retreated with Laches' (*Symp.* 221a; cf. *Lach.* 181b). Alcibiades then says that Socrates 'was far superior to Laches in keeping his wits about him' and carried 'himself with a swagger and glancing eyes', adding that Socrates 'was calmly looking out for friends and enemies. Even from a very great distance, it was clear he would vigorously retaliate if anyone were to attack this man. This is what saved both of them' (*Symp.* 221b; cf. Plut. *Alc.* 4–7).

According to Plato, Socrates also displayed principled moral leadership in the political arena. In the tragic aftermath of the Athenian naval victory at Arginusae near the end of the Peloponnesian War, Socrates served on the committee overseeing deliberations to decide the fate of the Athenian generals who were held responsible for not rescuing survivors from disabled ships. Eventually, the Athenians condemned the generals en masse and executed them (Xen. *Hell.* 1.7.1–34). In Plato's *Apology*, Socrates declares,

> This was illegal, as you all realised at a later time. I was the only member of the presiding committee to oppose you so that you would not do anything contrary to the laws, and I voted against it. Even though the orators were eager to prosecute me and take me away, and you were shouting and encouraging them, I thought it was more necessary for me to run the risk on the side of law and justice rather than join you in resolving to commit unjust actions, for fear of imprisonment or death. These things occurred when the city was still a democracy. (*Ap.* 32b–c)

Plato then has Socrates go on to speak about how he also stood up to the oligarchy that came to power after Athens' defeat in the Peloponnesian War. He states,

> After the oligarchy was established, the Thirty summoned me and four others to the rotunda and commanded us to bring Leon from Salamis so that he could be executed. These men were giving many such orders to many others at the time because they wanted to defile as many as possible with their guilt. Then of course I showed again, not in word but in deed, that I did not care about death whatsoever – if it were not somewhat rude to say – but rather my whole concern is not to do anything unjust or unholy. That government, even though it was very violent, did not frighten me into doing anything unjust. When we left the rotunda, the other four went to Salamis and carried off Leon, but I went home. I might have been put to death for this, if the government had not been put down soon after. (*Ap.* 32c–d)

The lawless actions of the extreme forms of democracy and oligarchy in Athens undoubtedly had a powerful impact on Plato and the development of his ideas on the necessity of stable and lawful government. Despite Plato's portrayal of Socrates as the ideal moral leader, however, there is little doubt that Socrates' self-righteous attitude and his association with anti-democratic leaders like Alcibiades and Critias were ultimately his undoing: Alcibiades was a catalyst for the oligarchic revolution in 411, and Critias was the ringleader of the Thirty Tyrants who came to power in 404.[11] Both revolutions temporarily upended Athenian democracy and were connected with wealthy aristocrats in Athens, many of whom were long-time associates of Socrates.

Although Socrates is the paragon of moral leadership in the works of Plato, it is well known that Plato places greater emphasis on political leadership and ideal constitutions throughout his dialogues. In the *Laws*, Plato has the Athenian Stranger assert,

> Among political systems there are two mothers so to speak that one could rightly say have given birth to all the others. The correct name for one is monarchy and the other is democracy – the Persians represent the classic type of the first, and we [Athenians] represent the second. Nearly all the others, as I said, have been varieties of these. Therefore, it is absolutely necessary to combine both of these if there is to be freedom and friendship with wisdom. (693d-e; cf. 756e)

Continuing in the *Laws*, the Athenian Stranger declares,

> The Persians first became free men when, during the time of Cyrus, they maintained a better balance between slavery and freedom, and they also became masters of many others. For the rulers gave the ruled a share of freedom and led them based on equality – the soldiers were friendlier to their generals and showed themselves to be eager in dangerous situations. (*Leg.* 694a–b)

This passage insists on a direct connection between political freedom and military effectiveness, which was a common assumption among Greek authors in the fifth and fourth centuries: freedom greatly increased a state's military and political power.[12] As Plato has the Athenian Stranger say about the Persians under Cyrus:

---

[11] All dates are BC. Alcibiades and Critias were close friends and associates of Socrates when they were young. Critias was also a cousin of Plato's mother Perictione, see Davies (1971) 322–35; Nails (2002) 106–13. In the Platonic *Seventh Letter*, the author claims that some members of the Thirty Tyrants were his relatives and invited him to join their oligarchic government after the overthrow of the Athenian democracy: 'But I saw how they showed men in a short time that the preceding constitution was gold', [Pl.] *Ep.* 7.324d.

[12] For example, Hdt. 5.78; [Xen.] *Ath. Pol.* 1.2; Thuc. 2.37–9; Isoc. 16.27; Dem. 60.25–6. See also Pritchard (2019).

if any of them, moreover, was wise and able to offer advice – seeing that the king was not jealous, allowed freedom of speech, and honoured those who were able to give any advice – such a person was able to show the collective strength of thinking in due moderation. In fact, at that time all their affairs advanced because of freedom, friendship and their partnership in reason. (*Leg.* 694b)[13]

It is significant that Plato allows for the possibility that non-Greeks could have moderate government based on freedom. As the founder of the Persian Empire, Cyrus was idealised by many sources.[14] However, Plato has the Athenian Stranger say that the entire enterprise of the Persian Empire was almost ruined by Cyrus' neglect of a proper upbringing for his son and successor Cambyses. The Athenian Stranger speculates that even though Cyrus was probably 'a good and patriotic general, he did not at all engage in the right education and paid no attention to household management' (*Leg.* 694c). The Athenian Stranger finally says the following about Cyrus:

he probably spent his entire life from childhood on campaign, and handed over his children for the women to raise . . . In fact, it was an effeminate upbringing for the children by royal women who had recently become wealthy, while the men were absent and occupied with wars and many dangers. (*Leg.* 694d-e)

This passage is reminiscent of Plato's *Laches*, where the son of the famous Athenian leader Aristides says that his father did not provide a good education for him because he was too busy with public affairs (179c–d, cf. 180b). Yet, even if a leader provided his son with the best possible education, it did not necessarily mean the son would be successful. In the *Meno*, Plato has Socrates explain that talented Athenian leaders like Aristides, Themistocles, Thucydides son of Melesias, and Pericles were unable to pass their virtues on to their sons despite providing them with excellent education (93c–94e).[15] In fact, Plato seems to think that such leaders were successful primarily

---

[13] For a recent discussion of this section of the *Laws* and what it tells us about Plato's ultimate views on democracy, see Sørensen (2016) 170–3.

[14] Kuhrt (2010) 70–4; Hdt. 1.95–216; Xen. *Cyr.* 3–5; Isaiah 41–2, 44–5; Ezra 6:3–5. For comparisons between the works of Plato and Xenophon as they relate to Cyrus and Persia, see Atack (2018); Tuplin (2018).

[15] Pericles' career and family life are especially interesting because he was responsible for passing a citizenship law in 451/450 that required both parents to be Athenian citizens, [Arist.] *Ath. Pol.* 26.4; Plut. *Per.* 37.2–5. After his two legitimate sons died from the plague at the beginning of the Peloponnesian War, however, he persuaded the Athenians to allow his illegitimate son Pericles, from his mistress Aspasia, to become an Athenian citizen, Plut.

because of rhetoric. In the *Gorgias*, Plato has the eponymous character declare that rhetoric in fact 'brings together and subordinates to itself practically all powers' (456a; cf. *Ion* 539e). Both Themistocles and Pericles used their extraordinary rhetorical skills to persuade the Athenians to fund public works projects that greatly increased the military and political power of the city. However, Plato has Socrates question the benefits of these projects: 'For without moderation and justice, they have filled the city with harbours, dockyards, walls, tribute payments and such nonsense' (*Grg.* 519a; cf. 455b–e, 503a–d, 515c–516e). Ultimately, Plato seems to believe that the development of Athens' powerful professional navy was disastrous because the Athenians became sailors instead of traditional hoplites. In the *Laws*, Plato has the Athenian Stranger insist that once the Athenians developed a navy they only engaged in hit-and-run tactics:

> they do not consider it disgraceful at all when they lack the courage to die waiting for their enemies to attack. On the contrary, they have plausible and well-prepared excuses when they lose their shields and weapons; they certainly get away, as they say, by non-disgraceful flights. These sayings are likely to come from heavily armed sailors: such statements are not worthy of countless commendations, but rather the opposite. One must never allow bad habits to develop, especially among the best part of the citizenry. (706c–d)

Greek triremes usually had a small contingent of ten hoplites on board, who were probably wealthier than most sailors because they could afford hoplite equipment.[16] Plato's contrast between traditional hoplites and those who served on ships conveys the idea that seafaring had a corrupting influence on society and military effectiveness. Heavily armed hoplites were supposed to stand firm and maintain their ordered ranks in the phalanx, even if that meant certain death. Naval personnel, on the other hand, could be more mobile, quickly attacking enemy territory and withdrawing as soon as defenders arrived. This contrast was certainly oversimplified, but Athenian naval strength certainly changed the nature of warfare and politics in classical Greece. And Themistocles and Pericles became symbols of these major changes in the Athenian democracy. The foundation of the Athenian fleet was in fact connected

---

Per. 36.3–5, 37.2, 37.5. The younger Pericles was one of the generals executed after the Battle of Arginusae in 406, Xen. *Hell.* 1.7.2, 1.7.34.

[16] Cf. Pritchard (2019) 42–3. For the likelihood of rowers serving as light-armed troops on expeditions, see van Wees (2004) 62–5. Cavalry and hoplite forces were generally wealthier members of Athenian society, but rowers and light-armed troops were less well off and often denigrated or left out of accounts by ancient authors who invariably came from the upper class.

directly to Themistocles, who persuaded the Athenians to build a fleet of ships when there was a major silver strike in Attica around 483.[17] This fleet proved decisive for the Greek victory in the Persian Wars, but it also meant that the Athenians no longer had to abide by the conventions of traditional hoplite warfare.[18] Pericles also played a pivotal role in Athenian military and political changes. Even though Athenian generals had to stand for election each year, Pericles dominated Athenian politics for some three decades and was elected general continuously from 443 to his death in 429.[19] And because Athenian generals came from wealthy families, elections merely reinforced entrenched social hierarchies and economic inequalities.[20]

Still, generals needed to use persuasion as much as compulsion to maintain their positions. In the *Statesman*, Plato has the Eleatic Stranger declare that generalship has affinities with 'that part of rhetoric which works in common with kingship to persuade [people] of what is just and to govern the affairs in cities together' (303e–304a; cf. *Phdr.* 269c–d). And in the *Laws*, Plato has the Athenian Stranger emphasise the importance of having preambles to laws in order to persuade citizens of the justness of legislation.[21] Nevertheless, throughout Plato's writings, it is clear that generals

---

[17] Cf. Thuc. 1.14.3, 1.93.7, 1.138.3; Plut. *Them.* 4.1–2. For details of Themistocles' background and family, see Davies (1971) 211–20; Nails (2002) 278–81. The silver mines were at Laurium in southern Attica near Cape Sunium. Significantly, Herodotus says Themistocles used persuasion to get the Athenians to build 200 ships (7.144). The author of the Aristotelian *Athenian Constitution*, however, claims Themistocles tricked the Athenians into building 100 ships, [Arist.] *Ath. Pol.* 22.7.

[18] In his biography of Themistocles, Plutarch mentions Plato's charge that Themistocles made the Athenians into sailors instead of steadfast infantrymen. He then quotes the following vivid accusation made against the statesman: 'Themistocles took away the spear and shield from the citizens and reduced the Athenian people to the rower's cushion and oar' (*Them.* 4.3). Undoubtedly, there were crucial land battles during the Persian Wars, particularly Marathon, Thermopylae and Plataea; the last was in fact the resounding Greek victory that ended the entire war in 479. Nevertheless, the size and power of the Athenian fleet allowed Athens to go on to create an Aegean-wide empire during the fifth century.

[19] Thuc. 2.22.1, 2.65.8–9; Plut. *Per.* 16.3; Rowe (1995) 238; cf. [Xen.] *Ath.* 1.3. Pericles first came to political prominence with his prosecution of Cimon in 463, [Arist.] *Ath. Pol.* 27.1; Plut. *Cim.* 14.2–4; *Per.* 10.5. Although Cimon was acquitted during this trial, he was eventually ostracised in 461, Plut. *Cim.* 15–17.2. Around the same time, Ephialtes, the leading opponent of Cimon, was murdered, leaving Pericles as the major democratic leader; cf. [Arist.] *Ath. Pol.* 25, 28.2. After Thucydides son of Melesias, Cimon's relative by marriage and successor as the main oligarchic leader, was ostracised around 443, Pericles became the undisputed leader of Athens, Plut. *Per.* 14.

[20] Cf. Pl. *Menex.* 238b–d; Hansen (1999) 272–4. For the socio-economic backgrounds of important Athenian leaders, see Davies (1971); Nails (2002).

[21] See Morrow (1960) 553–8.

and orators needed to be subordinate to kings and statesmen. In the *Euthydemus*, Plato has one of his characters declare that whenever generals 'capture some city or military camp, they hand them over to statesmen because they do not know how to use the things that they captured' (290d). Additionally, in the *Statesman*, Plato has the Eleatic Stranger explicitly say, 'we will not regard the knowledge of generals as statesmanship because it is subordinate' (305a). He goes on to state,

> It must be understood when one looks at all the kinds of knowledge discussed that none of them has proved to be statesmanship. For what is actually kingship must not engage in action, rather it must command those who have the power to act; it recognises the right and wrong time to begin and exert effort on the most important things in cities; and the others must carry out the orders given to them. (*Plt.* 305c–d; cf. 259c–d)

Plato undoubtedly has a clear hierarchy in mind. Yet there is a central paradox in Plato's *Statesman*, namely that 'wisdom can only be shown in action, but the true king does not act'.[22] Because kings and statesmen, according to Plato, were not supposed to act, they would ultimately be vulnerable to ambitious generals or orators, who had skills and knowledge that could potentially undermine the authority of hereditary or elected leaders (cf. *Leg.* 908d). Generals could use their armies to make themselves rulers without concern for established political institutions or the legal rights of individual citizens. Ideally, however, rulers would always do the right thing at the right time,[23] which would make it impossible for subordinates to overthrow kings or statesmen. Ultimately, enlightened rulers would also be above the laws. As Plato has the Eleatic Stranger declare, 'it is best that the laws not prevail, but rather the royal man who has wisdom' (*Plt.* 294a).[24]

For Plato, then, wise leadership was central to creating the best constitution. He most famously sketched an ideal city in the *Republic*. However, he also developed one in the *Laws*, where at one point the Athenian Stranger declares, 'It is most correct to describe the best constitution as well as the second and third, and having described them give the choice to each with the authority for founding a settlement' (*Leg.* 739a–b). In the ideal constitution of the *Laws*, rulers would be elected by all who currently serve or who have served in the military (*Leg.* 753b, 755b–c). Later in the dialogue, the Athenian Stranger says,

---

[22] Benardete (1986) 142.
[23] Cf. Atack (2018) 529–38.
[24] For discussion of the ideal rule of the political expert in Plato's *Statesman*, see Sørensen (2018).

> There is much deliberation about military affairs, and there are many laws based on custom: the most important thing is that no one, male or female, should ever be without a leader; nor should a person become accustomed in mind to doing anything alone and on one's own initiative at work or play. Rather, at all times in war and peace, a person should always live by looking to and following the leader, being governed by him in the smallest details: for example, when somebody gives the command, one should stand up, march, exercise, wash, eat, and wake at night to serve among the guards and messengers; and even in dangerous situations themselves, one should neither pursue someone nor yield to another without the order of the leaders. (*Leg.* 942a–c)

In all military units, but especially in the hoplite phalanx, maintaining order and group solidarity was essential to victory. And just as in the military, all citizens in the political sphere should learn to obey and give orders. The Athenian Stranger thus states,

> In a word, a person must teach the mind through habitual acts not even to think or be capable of doing anything apart from the other members of the group; but rather, one's life should always be, as much as possible, in close and common association with all. For there is not, nor will there ever be, something stronger, better or more artful in securing victory in war than this: in peacetime one must practise this right from childhood, to rule others and in turn be ruled by others. (*Leg.* 942c)

Scholars often interpret Plato's ideal city in the *Laws* as a second-best constitution compared to the one described in the *Republic*. Plato even has the Athenian Stranger say of the city being sketched in the *Laws* that 'through calculation and experience the city will appear to be governed second to the best' (*Leg.* 739a; cf. 739e). But as Malcolm Schofield notes about the *Laws*, 'its political theory is no less idealistic in its main shape and direction than the *Republic*'s'.[25]

Just as in the *Laws*, in the *Republic* Plato has Socrates suggest that rulers should come from the military class (*Resp.* 412c). Socrates further explains that 'anyone who is continually tested as a child, youth and adult and emerges undefiled should be appointed ruler of the city and guardian' (*Resp.* 413e–414a). The ideal city in the *Republic* would be divided into roughly three groups – rulers, soldiers and producers – and the leaders would lie to the citizens that they are all 'earthborn brothers' (414e). The rulers would command the soldiers in war and establish a military encampment in the city to control the population and protect against foreign enemies (*Resp.*

---

[25] Schofield (2016) 18.

415d–e). But the rulers and soldiers would not be able to own any unnecessary private property and would receive only a modest income from the other citizens; they would also live together, have communal dining halls and be forbidden to even touch gold or silver (*Resp.* 416d–e). Socrates states, 'if they themselves acquire private land, households, and money, they will be household managers and farmers instead of guardians; they will become hated despots rather than allies of the rest of the citizens' (*Resp.* 417a–b).

Significantly, one of the key differences between the ideal city in the *Laws* and the one in the *Republic* is how the state would handle land and labour. Plato has the Athenian Stranger summarise in the *Laws* many of the key proposals for the rulers and soldiers outlined in the *Republic*, most importantly that wives, children and property would be communal (*Leg.* 739c). However, land and households would not be held in common in the ideal city of the *Laws* (*Leg.* 739e–740a). Each male citizen would receive an equal plot of indivisible and inalienable land for his household, amounting to a total of 5,040 parcels of land for the entire city, with slaves and immigrants working the land (*Leg.* 737e, 740b–742a, 806d–e).[26] Schofield writes,

> The *Laws* accordingly does not postulate a guardian class whose philosophical cultivation of reason over other sources of motivation sets them apart from the rest of the population. It proposes a rather more egalitarian, if still very idealistic, social and political system – at any rate for the citizenry, whose leisure (they are debarred from commerce or artisan crafts) is to be sustained by the labours of slaves and immigrants.[27]

Nonetheless, Plato does make the Athenian Stranger say that 'anyone allotted a portion of land must consider it the common property of the city as a whole' (*Leg.* 740a; cf. 877d, 923a–b).

Without a doubt Plato's most radical proposal in both the *Republic* and the *Laws* is gender equality. Even though there are derogatory remarks about women in both works (*Resp.* 431b–c, 455c–d, 469d, 557c, 579b, 605d–e; *Leg.* 639b, 781a–d, 909e–910a, 934e–935a), Plato seems to insist on the active participation of women in warfare and politics. Thanassis Samaras convincingly argues that Plato's feminism is based on 'equality of opportunity rather than essential equality' and that 'this type of feminism is logically compatible with derogatory comments about women'.[28] Additionally, Samaras writes, 'despite its failure to endorse essential equality, the

---

[26] See Morrow (1960) 103–14.
[27] Schofield (2016) 14.
[28] Samaras (2010) 190–1.

Republic is still an exceptionally feminist work within its historical context'.[29] It is also clear in the *Laws* that women would be expected to serve in the military and hold public office, all of which would begin with educating both girls and boys. Plato has the Athenian Stranger assert,

> education must be compulsory for every man and boy as far as possible, since they belong to the city more than to their parents. For females as well, my law would have all the same provisions as for the males: it is necessary to train females equally. (*Leg.* 804d–e; cf. 813b–814c, 833c–d)

The Athenian Stranger goes on to criticise contemporary Greek practice that employs only half the population for military service (*Leg.* 804e–805b; cf. 794d–e, 806a–c). Women would train for war, but as Samaras states, 'what Plato says about the military role of women is consistent with the assumption that they will normally be used in auxiliary and defensive roles'.[30] The Athenian Stranger also says,

> Military service for a man will be from twenty to sixty years old; for a woman, whatever service seems necessary to impose for military actions – after she bears children – should be performed until the age of fifty; a practical and appropriate duty should be assigned to each and every one of them. (*Leg.* 785b; cf. 783b, 813e–814c)

Adolescent females would be expected to marry at some point between sixteen and twenty years old and would be supervised by female officials for ten years to ensure that they produced children with their husbands (*Leg.* 784a–b, 785b, 930a). At the age of forty, women would be eligible to hold public office (*Leg.* 785b; cf. 806e, 813b–c). However, it is never specified whether women would be able to hold the highest military and political offices. As Samaras correctly observes, 'In the *Laws*, Plato continues the feminist revolution in thought of the *Republic* in a way which is remarkable, but also remains incomplete.'[31] Ultimately, Plato does not work out in detail how women would be able to play an active role in the public sphere when they would not be fully liberated in the private sphere.

Much of Plato's focus in both the *Laws* and the *Republic* is on the fundamental failings of contemporary political systems, namely tyranny, oligarchy and democracy. In the *Laws*, Plato has the Athenian Stranger say,

---

[29] Samaras (2010) 186.
[30] Samaras (2010) 192.
[31] Samaras (2010) 196.

None of these is a political system: they are all most correctly described as factional states. None is a system based on the willing ruling the willing, rather the willing rules the unwilling with a certain amount of persistent force. The one who rules fears the one who is ruled; and he will never of his own accord allow the one who is ruled to become honourable, wealthy, strong, courageous or at all warlike. (832c; cf. 697c–d)

Although the absolute power of a tyrant is considered the quickest and easiest way to bring about the ideal city (*Leg.* 709e–712a), Plato's Athenian Stranger also makes the following statement:

There does not exist, my friends, a human soul whose nature would ever be able to handle absolute power among human beings while young and unaccountable. Having its mind filled with folly, the greatest disease, it becomes a hateful object to its closest friends. Once this has happened, hate quickly ruins the soul and destroys all of its power. (*Leg.* 691c–d; cf. 713c, 875a–c)[32]

This passage somewhat anticipates Lord Acton's famous saying that 'power tends to corrupt and absolute power corrupts absolutely'.[33] But political turmoil was also characteristic of oligarchic and democratic systems. In the *Republic*, Socrates asserts that an oligarchic city is really two cities: 'a city of poor men and one of rich men, living in the same place and always plotting against one another' (551d). Socrates then adds that this makes it likely oligarchic cities will not be able to wage war because their leaders will be afraid to arm the poor citizens; and they will not want to pay mercenaries because they are in love with money (*Resp.* 551e). Socrates ultimately contends that there is an inherent conflict of interest in an oligarchy. 'In such a constitution,' Socrates says, 'there is a meddling in state affairs that occurs when the same people are farmers, moneymakers and soldiers simultaneously' (*Resp.* 551e–552a; cf. 374b–d). After a while, oligarchic systems become vulnerable to revolution because the rich and their offspring become mentally and

---

[32] See also Morrow (1960) 544–5.
[33] This famous statement comes from a letter Lord Acton wrote to Bishop Creighton in 1887 in which he says historians should judge kings and popes by universal moral standards. For Lord Acton, this is especially important because he believed that leaders tend to lack legal restrictions during their lifetimes, so history needs to provide a powerful corrective to the abuse of power. In the same paragraph of the letter, Lord Acton writes that there is 'the tendency or the certainty of corruption by authority. There is no worse heresy than that the office sanctifies the holder of it. That is the point at which . . . the end learns to justify the means', Acton–Creighton Correspondence (1887) para. 24.

physically weak and lazy, having focused almost exclusively on making money. Plato has Socrates add,

> Whenever rulers and subjects are exposed to one another, whether walking on roads or during any other common undertakings, on an embassy or military campaign, as fellow sailors or soldiers, or when looking on one another amidst the same dangers: in these circumstances, poor men are in no way despised by rich men. On the contrary, the poor man – often lean and exposed to the sun – is arrayed in battle next to a wealthy man – brought up in the shade and carrying a lot of excess flesh – and sees him experiencing shortness of breath and being full of perplexity. Don't you think he considers these men to be rich through the cowardice of the poor, and one poor man says to another whenever they meet together in private: 'these men are ours, they are nothing'? (*Resp.* 556c–e)

According to Plato, after the poor overthrow the rich, they establish a democracy by exiling or killing their opponents. Then the poor 'give those that remain an equal share in the constitution and public offices, and for the most part the offices are assigned by lot' (*Resp.* 557a). Violent factional strife was a common occurrence in many Greek cities (cf. *Leg.* 636b), which is why Plato focused so much of his energy on formulating ideal cities that could potentially provide better stability, prosperity and happiness (*Resp.* 420b–c). Ideally, there would be a proper balance in both the military and political spheres so that constitutions would not be overturned or replaced without due consideration. Even though Plato envisioned statesmen or kings ruling over generals, the reality was that generals often were statesmen and kings. By examining the ways Plato writes about military and political leadership, it becomes clear he believes great leaders need to possess not only expert knowledge and practical skills but also moral excellence and profound wisdom. Even if most leaders did not possess all of these traits, there was always the possibility that under the right circumstances and the correct philosophical training rulers could become truly enlightened and create prosperous and peaceful states.

4 Reconstructing Early Seleucid Generalship, 301–222 BC

Alex McAuley

In the unique milieu of the Hellenistic world the court and the army were perhaps the two most prominent *loci* of power in which the fates of empires, dynasties and peoples were decided. But amidst abundant scholarship on both institutions there remains a tendency towards compartmentalisation: the army, unsurprisingly, is analysed while at war through a mechanical approach emphasising equipment, structure and tactics; the court, for its part, is treated as a political arena of personal competition for prestige and influence through largely pacific means.[1] In other words, a sharp divide tends to be drawn between 'the political' on the one hand and 'the military' on the other. Scholarship of the Roman Republic has long overcome this divide with an underlying awareness of the intrinsic connection between these spheres of influence and the dynamic interplay between military and political affairs.[2] The domestic battlefield of aristocratic competition shaped, and in turn was shaped by, the campaigns waged against Rome's foreign and domestic enemies; success or failure in one field determined success or failure in the other. The study

---

[1] The recent slew of monographs from Pen and Sword on various aspects of Hellenistic militaries encapsulate this compartmentalisation neatly, especially Grainger (2011), Esposito (2019) and Pietrykowski (2012). Sekunda and McBride (1994) vols 1 and 2 are a fitting example of a purely 'military' approach to Hellenistic armies, as well as Launey (1948). Bikerman (1938) and Bevan (1902) tend to treat the Seleucid court and institutions in isolation. Given the vast scholarship on Hellenistic militaries and court institutions, the references of this chapter have no pretence to comprehensiveness. Only those titles explicitly engaged with are cited. Throughout this chapter all translations of Greek and Latin are my own.

[2] On this see e.g. Beck (2009); Hölkeskamp (1993); (2004a) esp. 11–48; (2004b) esp. chs 6 and 7; (2017); Morstein-Marx (1995); Rosenstein (1990); Eckstein (1987).

of the Hellenistic world has come to this realisation only more recently, thanks in no small part to Angelos Chaniotis' 2005 *War in the Hellenistic World*, which treated its topic not through the lens of kit or strategy but through that of society and culture.[3] Despite a recent revival of interest in the enigmatic Seleucid Dynasty, however, the old dichotomy of military and political, of the army and the court, continues to persist: the mechanics of the former have been thoroughly studied since the 1970s with Bezalel Bar-Kochva's pioneering study of the Seleucid army, and the past two decades have produced abundant research on the latter, notably thanks to Laurent Capdetrey's 2007 study of Seleucid administration and Rolf Strootman's 2014 monograph *Courts and Elites in the Hellenistic Empires*.[4]

In the context of the present volume, the figure of the Seleucid general provides us with an ideal unit of analysis with which to straddle the traditional dichotomy between 'the political' and 'the military'. Particularly in the early generations of the dynasty, the military and political structures of the empire were intertwined to the point of being inseparable. In the rapidly developing ideology of Seleucid royalty and its representations in the third century BC it is easy to forget that martial prowess was the *sine qua non* of Seleucid kings, as indeed it was among their royal contemporaries. If such prowess was obligatory for the king himself, so too would it have been for his closest confidants and officials, whose political power was in turn derived from their capabilities on the battlefield. To provide us with a biographical anchor in a fairly wide-ranging examination, this chapter will take the rather shadowy figure of Alexander of Sardis as being representative of the various roles, responsibilities and expectations of generals in the Seleucid realm.[5] As I shall argue below, just enough is known of his background and career to make him a fitting *exemplum* of the concept of a 'Seleucid general' in an abstract sense. He, along with many of his fellow potentates at the height of Seleucid administration, was not merely an idle court functionary detached from reality with a lofty title, nor was he simply an eminently able and experienced military man myopically following orders received from above. Rather it is in the figure of the Seleucid general represented by Alexander of Sardis that we find the intersection of the broad strategic ideology of the Seleucid realm with its practical day-to-day administration. The general is helpful as an analytical object

---

[3] Chaniotis (2005) esp. chs 2, 6, and 7 on the ramifications of Hellenistic warfare off the battlefield.

[4] Bar-Kochva (1976); Capdetrey (2007); Strootman (2014). See also the edited volume of Erickson (2018) for a reappraisal of the first half-century of Seleucid rule; Chrubasik (2016) on usurpers in the Seleucid realm; Engels (2017).

[5] Alexander of Sardis = Grainger (1997), Alexander (O1) 75. See D'Agostini and McAuley (2012) s.v. 'Alexander of Sardis'; McAuley (2018) 48–9; D'Agostini (2013); Chrubasik (2016) 72–3; and further references below.

precisely because he was equally active within the court and in the field. To borrow the Roman idiom, he had a part to play *domi militiaeque* – at home and abroad.

The career of Alexander, as we shall see, is certainly distinct in its particulars but by no means exceptional in its broader trajectory. Considering certain aspects of Alexander's career – his background, his military experience, his practical roles and responsibilities, and his place in propagating the Seleucid ideology of empire – in the context of other men at the height of Seleucid influence shows that he had a great deal in common with his peers. But given the rich vocabulary with which Seleucid generals were described in the early generations of the dynasty, we shall begin by formulating a more precise definition of 'general' in this context. The chronological scope of this chapter (301–222 BC) is defined in relation to the traditional view that Antiochus III radically reformed the structure of the empire as a whole during his reign by formalising various aspects that had up to this point developed organically over time.[6] Accordingly, we shall focus on the concept of Seleucid generalship as it emerges in the formative early generations of the dynasty's history stretching from the campaigns of Seleucus I to the accession of Antiochus III.

At a Loss for Words: Defining the Seleucid General

In the case of generalship along with sundry other titles and designations, a great deal is either lost or distorted in the translation of ancient into modern terminology. The contemporary term 'general' is equal parts precise and normative: the identification of someone as a 'general' brings along a raft of implicit and explicit assumptions about them and the system in which they operate. 'General' is intrinsically a military designation, and assumes a rigid chain of command, precise rights and responsibilities, the insignia to mark them, and a tightly defined relationship with other designations both within an organisation and among others. Everything from one's salary, range of operations, relative autonomy and even physical appearance in uniform are governed by the rank. The term is so highly systematised in the twenty-first century that identifying a given officer as *OF-7* according to the NATO code, for instance, easily allows the recognition of one's rank across dozens of military systems. On a broader level, the title of general presumes that a clearly defined system of ranks even exists in the first place, and that these are fundamentally military designations.

---

[6] Engels (2017) 76; Carsana (1996) 57–8. Dreyer (2011) most directly elaborates this argument that Antiochus III was responsible for the reorganisation of the court, overturning the old notion that such a complex court structure was the produce of later second-century kings with diminishing power.

The early Hellenistic period was hardly so particular or fastidious in its terminology, resulting in a vast array of roles, responsibilities and titles being lumped into the contemporary designation of 'general'.[7] Translating specific ancient military ranks into modern vocabulary is a thorny enough process; the difficulty is compounded in the Seleucid instance by the fact that for much of the period under our consideration there simply was no equivalent structure of ranks. David Engels has observed that while Seleucus I was eager to create his own imitation of Alexander the Great's circle of designated *philoi*, a complex and nuanced hierarchy denoting different grades of proximity to the king does not emerge until the reign of Seleucus IV.[8] Chiara Carsana has also noted a marked shift away from appointing immediate family members to high posts and towards naming qualified officials, often non-Greek, to a more clearly defined imperial structure during the reign of Antiochus III.[9] Bar-Kochva's detailed reconstruction of the rank structure of the Seleucid army rests almost entirely on Polybius' narration of the reign of Antiochus III, along with other evidence from the 220s onwards.[10] Care must be taken, then, not to project this later system of ranks and designations onto the earlier generations of the dynasty which are the focus of our current inquiry.

How then are we to define a Seleucid general between 301 and 222 BC if a consistent military and aulic hierarchy had not yet emerged? Even *strategos*, the Greek word that we would expect to provide the most likely candidate for the Hellenistic equivalent of 'general', is slippery in its imprecision.[11] In contemporary attestations, a *strategos* could be an (elected) annual magistrate of a Greek civic community, the commander of a royal garrison in a given Seleucid city, a regional governor whose administrative role was equivalent to that of a satrap, a representative of the king on a given expedition or mission, or the commander of an independent unit in the army. The distinction between *strategoi* and other high-ranking officers – *hipparchoi*, *nauarchoi*, *chiliarchoi* – is nebulous at best.[12] Figures whom we would expect to

---

[7] Chaniotis (2005), for instance, does not provide a hard and fast definition of 'general' in the ancient context, but as elsewhere it is de facto assumed that a *strategos* is the ancient equivalent of a contemporary general officer. See especially Chaniotis (2005) 31–6 for a discussion of the civic *strategos*.

[8] Engels (2017) 76 with notes, and see Dreyer (2011) for the argument that this process began somewhat earlier.

[9] Carsana (1996); see also Istasse (2006) on non-Greek generals in the service of Seleucid kings, especially under Antiochus III.

[10] Bar-Kochva (1976) 85–93, esp. nn. 1–27.

[11] On the *strategos*, see Bikerman (1938) 65–6; Bengston (1964) 64–5; Bar-Kochva (1976) 86–91.

[12] For attestations, especially later in the Seleucid period, of officials bearing these various

be identified as *strategos* are often not explicitly referred to as such; frequently in Seleucid royal correspondence the governor, general or official in charge of a given region or locale is simply addressed by name without any further title.[13] The extrapolation of an elaborate hierarchy from such disparate attestations is tempting but futile, as is an attempt to clearly distinguish 'civic' or administrative functions from military roles. A compelling argument could be made for identifying all of the officials named above as a 'general'.

The ambiguity and indeed diversity of Seleucid generalship is precisely the point. Seleucid officials at court and abroad were not limited to one realm of responsibility throughout their careers, and a rather different way of thinking about authority and command is needed. The conclusions of Ivana Savalli-Lestrade in 1998 and Laurent Capdetrey in 2007 regarding the courtly functions of prominent officials should equally be applied beyond the palace. Savalli-Lestrade has brought to light the mobility of royal *philoi* from one function to the other, and argued that those closest to the king should be thought of as a group of trusted confidants who would be despatched on one task or another by the king, rather than as a council of functionaries with tightly defined roles.[14] In the process they could easily transition between roles that we would typically classify as either courtly or administrative. Among these trusted men of the king, Capdetrey argues that 'la notion de charge est plus pertinente que celle de fonction pour définir les domaines de compétence des agents

titles see Grainger (1997) 73–124. From among them, the nebulous distinction between *strategos* arises in the case of, for instance, Diognetos, who is identified as a *nauarchos* in Polybius 5.43 but is commanding troops on land in the same passage as he escorts Laodice III to marry Antiochus III. Diokles, a governor who commanded part of the army at Platanos in 218 (Pol. 5.69.5), is, however, identified as a *strategos*, while his contemporary Diomedon, commander of troops at Seleukeia on the Tigris, was described as an *epistates* (Pol. 5.48.12). Dionysios, the commander of Antiochus' bodyguard, is identified as *hegemon* during the siege of Sardis when he commands an assault on the city's gate (Pol. 7.16.2, 17.3, 18.1). Artaxias, however, the governor of Armenia, is identified as a *strategos*; see the attestations of him in Grainger (1997) 83. The salient point here is that many of these men seem to be performing similar functions but are identified with inconsistent terminology.

[13] The point will be developed further below in the case of Alexander of Sardis, who is not identified with a specific title but rather simply characterised by a passive participle. For other examples, see, for instance, Austin[2] no. 164, in which Antiochus' official in Ilion is addressed by the king simply as 'Meleager'. Interestingly, this same Meleager is identified by the people of Ilium as *strategos* in Austin[2] no. 165. This would seem to be a case of a local civic community identifying Meleager with the closest equivalent of their own civic magistracy (*strategos*) rather than a reflection of official Seleucid titulature. Austin[2] no. 172 is another example of a king addressing his local governor/commander simply by name, in this case 'Euphemus'.

[14] Savalli-Lestrade (1998) 362.

royaux'.¹⁵ Given this 'porosité', as Capdetrey puts it, among the administrative, courtly and military domains of the Seleucid Empire, I shall not attempt to provide a hard and fast typology of Seleucid generalship or identify a consistent vocabulary with which it is identified in the ancient tradition.¹⁶ Instead, I will identify early Seleucid generals based on the following criteria: (1) being Graeco-Macedonian men who are not from the immediate family of Alexander the Great or subsequent kings and thus cannot claim 'royal' status; (2) a close relationship, either formalised or de facto, with the king; (3) attestation of a present or past role in some form of military command; and (4) attestation of the individual as someone who was, as Capdetrey defined Seleucid *strategoi*, an agent of the king in the administration of the empire.¹⁷ We shall consider each criterion first as it relates to Alexander of Sardis, and then among other men whom we can identify as Seleucid generals.

Background, Status and Descent

As is generally the case with the officials who filled the upper ranks of the Hellenistic kingdoms, we have only scant and indirect attestation of the background, status and descent of Alexander of Sardis. Nevertheless, a broad picture can be sketched: as suggested by his name, Alexander was of Graeco-Macedonian descent and hailed from an elite, though not royal, family who had risen to prominence in Asia Minor. His father, Achaeus 'the Elder', had probably been a general who had served with distinction in the eastern campaigns of Antiochus I and was handsomely rewarded by the king with estates near Laodicea on the Lycus in Anatolia. His father remained prominent in the region and is attested in January 267 as the *kyrios tou topou*, when he seems to have exercised a fair bit of local clout.¹⁸ It is also possible that Alexander's mother was a Seleucid princess who had been given in marriage to his father as further recognition of the king's gratitude and esteem.

At any rate, Alexander of Sardis was, like many of the Macedonian dynasts, analysed in detail by Richard Billows in 1989 and 1995, neither royal nor 'common', but rather a part of the emerging military elite whose status was due on the one hand to their Graeco-Macedonian ethnicity, but on the other to their personal achievements

---

[15] Capdetrey (2007) 277.

[16] Capdetrey (2007) 288 on the porosity of administrative competencies of top officials. See also the relevant sections of Aperghis (2004) on the financial interrelation of the court and the military.

[17] Capdetrey (2007) 287.

[18] On the career of Achaeus the Elder, see McAuley (2018) 38–47. The original inscription referring to him is *I. Laodikeia am Lykos* 1, discussed by Wörrle (1975). See other citations in McAuley (2018).

in the military realm.[19] It is in figures such as him that we begin to appreciate how blurred the line between 'royalty' and 'elite' was in the early generations of the period. His sister, Laodice, was married to Antiochus II at some point before 261 BC, thus during most of his career Alexander was both the brother-in-law of the Seleucid king and a member of the extended royal family – though he himself is never identified with any royal signifiers.[20] His other sister, Antiochis, had married another member of this emerging Graeco-Macedonian elite in Anatolia: her husband was Attalus, brother of Philetaerus, who himself had ruled over Pergamon in the name of the Seleucids.[21] Alexander's brothers-in-law through his sisters' marriages were initially loyal to the Seleucids, but by the late 260s had taken on royal ambitions of their own, in one of many instances of successful and prominent generals revolting against their overlords. Unfortunately we have no attested wife or children of Alexander of Sardis, though this in and of itself is telling: although he was closely linked to the royal family, he himself did not go on to create his own dynasty. In sum, Alexander's background was Graeco-Macedonian, he spoke Greek, he was of elite but not quite royal status, and he was part of an extended Graeco-Macedonian family that had established this status through military service and imperial administration.

Alexander of Sardis was not unique in fulfilling these general characteristics of background, status and descent. Although in his case we are unusually well informed regarding his extended family, other men whom we can safely identify as early Seleucid generals also fit into the same categories. Demodamas of Miletus, whose contributions to Seleucid imperial ideology we shall discuss below, is identified as 'Demodamas, son of Aristeides' (Δημοδάμας Ἀριστείδου) in two inscriptions from Miletus.[22] This identification by patronymic in a civic inscription is telling in and of itself, as Demodamas implicitly comes from a line of citizens of this ancient Ionian city. His attestation in two such inscriptions as the man who proposed a motion

---

[19] Billows (1995) 81–107 provides a very thorough analysis of the Macedonian dynasts of Asia Minor in this period, as does Billows (1989) in the case of one family. See also his analysis of the career of Antigonos Monophthalmos, Billows (1990). On other Macedonian dynasts, see most recently Mitchell (2018).

[20] For the full citations and further discussion of the siblings of Alexander of Sardis, see McAuley (2018) 46–69; D'Agostini (2013) 97–9. On the marriage of Antiochus II to Laodice, see Porphyry F 32.6.

[21] For this marriage see Strabo 13.4.2; Hansen (1947) 28–29. Hansen (1947) remains the canonical history of the Attalids, bolstered recently by the relevant sections of Marek (2016).

[22] *I Didyma* 479 = OGIS 213 and *I Didyma* 480 = Austin² no. 51. On the descent of Demodamas, see Savalli-Lestrade (1998) 4–5; Chaniotis (2005) 64; Sherwin-White and Kuhrt (1993) 26–7. On his military career see Sherwin-White and Kuhrt (1993) 18; Robert (1984). See also Grainger (1997) 86 for his entry on Demodamas.

to the *demos* and *synedron* which was later accepted and engraved suggests that he hailed from the city's elite, a conclusion supported by the traditionally oligarchic leanings of Milteus' civic structures.[23] His local prestige is further highlighted by the fact that he is one of the three men charged with commissioning a statue that will be placed in Didyma.[24] Again, he satisfies the same criteria as Alexander of Sardis.

So too does Patrocles, another figure to whom we shall shortly turn in more detail. While there are not epigraphic *testimonia* attesting his patronymic, his patently Graeco-Macedonian name is obviously a marker of his ethnic descent.[25] This may be further assumed from the fact that he composed several works in Greek, as did Demodamas, indicating his Greek status, education, connection to literary circles and, in the early Hellenistic period at least, descent. In a similar vein, his attestation among the companions of Seleucus in Babylon in c. 312 BC probably implies that he was among the first or second generation of Graeco-Macedonian soldiers to fight in the aftermath of Alexander the Great's campaigns.[26] Megasthenes, Seleucus' ambassador to the court of Chandragupta Maurya and later author of the *Indica*, can probably be described in similar terms as well.

I refer the reader to the comprehensive prosopographies of Carsana and Grainger for attestations of Graeco-Macedonian individuals in military service of the king, but at any rate the pattern, it seems, remains consistent.[27] As Boris Dreyer has recently reiterated, the basic requirement for prominence at the Seleucid court identified by Christian Habicht in 1958 remains equally applicable today: first, at least on a de facto level, one had to either be of Graeco-Macedonian descent or speak Greek to succeed in the Seleucid court.[28] While other aspects of Seleucid administration show elements of ethnic diversity and integration, the highest ranks of its military in the first generations of the dynasty appear to have been dominated by Graeco-Macedonians and those who had adopted Graeco-Macedonian culture.[29]

---

[23] Dimitriev (2005) 67–75.

[24] See the closing lines of *I Didyma* 479 for the presence of Demodamas among the commissioners.

[25] For ancient citations and references to Patrocles, see Grainger (1997) 111 with a succinct synopsis of his career.

[26] For the first attestations of Patrocles, see Kosmin (2014) 67 and n. 59 citing BNJ 712 T2 = Plut. *Demetr.* 47.4. On Megasthenes, see also Grainger (1997) s.v. Megasthenes (p. 103), who cites Strabo 2.1.4, Athenaeus *Deip.* 153d, Arr. *Anab.* 5.6.2, *RE* 15.230–326.

[27] See Grainger's (1997) section 'Officials'; Carsana (1996) 53–60.

[28] A conclusion that is also borne out by Dreyer's observation (2011) 46 that in our prosopographical corpora, Greeks or Macedonians comprise over 90 per cent of those serving in close proximity to the Seleucid king. The original observations are discussed by Habicht (1958) as cited in Dreyer (2011).

[29] Two important caveats to this generalisation must be made here. The first is that this

Generalship, in this context, was an occupation reserved almost exclusively for those who were at least culturally Greek.

Proximity to the King

It is in the proximity of Seleucid generals to the reigning king that we find the most overlap between the aulic and military functions of these men, as the clearest indication that Seleucid generals derived their authority in no small part from proximity to the king, which was in turn strengthened by their service. As discussed above, Alexander of Sardis had quite an intimate relationship with Antiochus I and II by virtue of his family's marriage connections. While the status of generals in Hellenistic courts is often predicated on fictive kinship with the reigning monarch, in Alexander's case this family proximity was literal. As the king's cousin (to Antiochus I) and later brother-in-law (to Antiochus II) for much of his career he would have had both indirect access to the king via his sister and direct access to the king via his station. With such family connections we can presume ease of correspondence and access to the court, both of which granted a figure such as Alexander an easy route to the king's ear. For Alexander this proximity manifested itself in his identification as the intermediary between the people of the region under his charge and the king himself. An inscription from Bargylia in Caria dating to late in the reign of Antiochus I identifies him at ll. 46–8 as 'Ἀλεξάνδρωι τῶι [καταλ]ελειμμένωι ὑπὸ [τοῦ] [β]ασιλέως' – 'Alexander who has been left behind in the region by the King'.[30] The grammar of the construction captures the relationship succinctly: Alexander is the subject of the king's agency. But when the citizens of Bargylia wish to communicate something directly to the king – in this case the good judgement of Tyron – they turn to Alexander personally. He is, in a basic sense, the bridge between the on-the-ground realities of the Seleucid realm and the court, a

---

conclusion relies heavily on prosopographic data which is incomplete, and we must also bear in mind the c. 10 per cent of attested individuals in Carsana (1996) who are not of Graeco-Macedonian background. The second caveat follows on from the first: the question of name-changing has perennially made such generalisations problematic, as we are unsure how common it was for someone of a non-Greek ethnic background to either adopt a Greek name when in imperial service, or employ a Greek name in a Greek social or political context. In our prosopographic data there could thus be more individuals of a non-Greek ethnic background who are considered Greek on onomastic grounds, for lack of any further attestation. At any rate, as long as it is limited to Graeco-Macedonian culture and language, not ethnicity, I believe the generalisation stands.

[30] On this inscription see most recently D'Agostini (2013) 97, and also Merkelbach (2000) 126–8; Billows (1995) 95–7. The inscription itself is *Syll.*³ 426 = *I Iasos* 608.

mechanism which we shall explore below in greater detail with another attestation of Alexander's local role.

In the proposals he made before the citizen body of his native Miletus, Demodamas similarly emphasises his proximity to the king and his own role as an intermediary between the Milesians and the royal family. Demodamas' motion that was accepted by the citizen body in the two decrees mentioned above (*I Didyma* 479 and 480) was to praise Antiochus I, his father Seleucus and his mother Apama for their goodwill and benevolence towards the city of Miletus.[31] Demodamas stands to benefit from his proximity to the royal family in two directions: at court he will be praised for securing such honours and recognition for the royal family in the city of Miletus, while at Miletus he in turn gains civic prestige for having attracted this benefaction to the city and thereby put it on the royal map, as it were. It is noteworthy that the queen is honoured for the great goodwill and zeal (πολλὴν εὔνοιαν καὶ προ[θυμίαν]) she displayed towards the Milesian soldiers serving in her husband's army, presumably under the command of Demodamas.[32] Her civic prestige is thus derived from her involvement in military matters.[33] By the legislation he proposed as a prominent citizen of Miletus, Demodamas himself is in turn bringing the king's designated heir into the civic body of his native city: besides commanding that an equestrian statue of Antiochus I be erected at Didyma, the decree grants Antiochus *asylia* and *ateleia* in the city, meals in the Prytaneion at public expense and priority in access to the oracle, and mandates that the same privileges be granted to his descendants.[34] By essentially making Antiochus a *proxenos* of the city, Demodamas has translated his military prestige into civic prestige, which in turn gains him favour at court.[35] None of this would be possible without the close relationship between the Seleucid king and his generals.

Our other generals, Patrocles and Megasthenes, do not have such explicitly detailed attestation of their proximity to the king, but such trust is clearly evident

---

[31] See the references above to scholarly discussions of these inscriptions.

[32] Line 5 of *I Didyma* 480.

[33] On the relationship between Apama and Demodamas via Bactria/Sogdiana, see Sherwin-White and Kuhrt (1993) 25–7. For the full publication history of this decree see the notes to Austin² no. 51.

[34] These privileges are enumerated in lines 31–45 of the decree. Essentially they are the standard rights granted to *proxenoi* and *euergetai* when it comes to his legal status in the city, but the addition of an equestrian statue, meals in the Prytaneion and the religious rights granted to him are by all accounts extraordinary. The combination of these honours is all the more striking given the early Hellenistic provenance of the inscription, before such formulae became standardised in the late third/early second centuries.

[35] As Mack (2005) has made clear, the recognition of someone as *proxenos* was not entirely a retroactive honorific, but rather implied an ongoing close relationship with the city granting the honour.

in the tasks with which they were charged. After the death of Seleucus I, Patrocles was hand-picked by Antiochus I to secure Seleucid authority in Asia Minor amid the turmoil of the early years of the new king's reign. At a time of such heightened anxiety, Antiochus would only have trusted a man who was both a confidant and a capable commander, with a task that required complete assurance. This trust by Antiochus seems to have been inherited from his father: Patrocles is identified by Plutarch as 'a famously wise man, and a trusted friend of Seleucus' in whom the king had such faith that he took his advice regarding how to treat the conquered Demetrius Poliorcetes.[36] Trust, proximity to the king and expertise are also implicit in the attestation of Megasthenes as the ambassador of Seleucus I to Chandragupta Maurya's capital of Pataliputra. As with Alexander of Sardis, the relationship between Megasthenes and the king is aptly captured by Strabo's use (2.1.9) of the passive voice when describing his mission to India.[37] Each king seems to have had his own trusted retinue, as Strabo further notes that another general, Deimachos, was sent to maintain an embassy to the Mauryan court by the next generation of Seleucid royalty under Antiochus I. In both cases, their role as ambassador to another monarch is predicated on their proximity to the king and their trustworthiness.

What is noteworthy in each of the above cases is the fact that the proximity of the Seleucid generals was not always based entirely on military matters. Alexander of Sardis is attested as a local civic administrator, Demodamas as a member of the local civic elite with a direct line to the royal family, Patrocles as a court strategist, and the ambassadors Megasthenes and Deimachos as trusted representatives. And this proximity to the king is expressed not in terms of rank or hierarchy but in the vocabulary of interpersonal relationships: Alexander had been 'left behind' by his sovereign, Demodamas could communicate directly with the royal family, Patrocles was a 'trusted friend' of Seleucus, and the ambassadors had been sent by their respective overlords.[38] Though they clearly had imperial functions in their respective domains, these were understood and communicated in personal terms. But despite this personal connection, we must remember that military prowess and strategic acumen formed the practical basis of this proximity to the king.

---

[36] Plut. *Demetr.* 47.3: ἀνὴρ συνετὸς εἶναι δοκῶν καὶ Σελεύκῳ φίλος πιστός.
[37] Strabo 2.1.9: ἐπέμφθησαν μὲν γὰρ εἰς τὰ Παλίμβοθρα, ὁ μὲν Μεγασθένης πρὸς Σανδρόκοττον ὁ δὲ Δηίμαχος πρὸς Ἀλλιτροχάδην τὸν ἐκείνου υἱὸν κατὰ πρεσβείαν: 'These men were sent [by the king] to Pataliputra as ambassadors, Megasthenes to Chandragupta and Deimachos to his son Amitrochates.'
[38] See the comments of Strootman (2014) esp. parts II and III on the social dynamics of *philoi* and courtiers in the court of the king, as well as their role in the ritual and ceremonial of the court.

Military Prowess

Out of our four criteria for characterising early Seleucid generalship, military prowess is the most straightforward to identify and describe. Given the aforementioned lack of consistency in the military terminology of the early dynasty, I follow Capdetrey's argument that identifying a function of military command is more pertinent among these early generals than an explicitly attested rank. The specific equipment, duties and battlefield expectations of such commanders has been discussed by other scholars in such depth that they need not be repeated here.

Alexander of Sardis was by all accounts the chief military commander of Seleucid forces in Asia Minor. As has been most recently supported by D'Agostini, it seems a sound conclusion to identify the Alexander attested epigraphically with the satrap of Sardis mentioned by a fragment of Porphyry.[39] Virgilio has argued that the governor of Sardis under the Seleucids should best be understood as a continuation of its Achaemenid precedent.[40] The governor thus was not merely a civic official but also a prominent military commander in his own right, having charge of royal forces stationed in the region. Given the recurrent unrest in the region, the constant threat posed by Galatian tribes and other incursions from the north, this command would not have been an idle sinecure. Later in his career, Alexander of Sardis seems to have supported the rival claimant Antiochus Hierax in the so-called 'War of the Brothers'.[41] As a distinguished commander with a sizeable corps of troops at his disposal, he was by no means an insignificant ally. Finally, the military attestations of his family members are a further indirect, though nevertheless pertinent, indication of his military accomplishments.

Patrocles' military career is fairly well attested and has been most recently reconstructed by Paul Kosmin.[42] Patrocles accompanied Seleucus I in his campaign to Bactria in 312 and was then made governor of the region – as is possibly also attested in cuneiform sources.[43] At some point later, he had command of Seleucid forces in Bactria and Sogdiana, before he is attested campaigning with Seleucus I

---

[39] D'Agostini (2013) 98 and n. 46; Porphyry F 32.8.

[40] Virgilio (2003) 140–2.

[41] Porphyry F. 32.8 mentions that Hierax had the support of a general named Alexander, who by all accounts must be our Alexander here. Polyaenus (4.17) mentions that Seleucus II was supported by Andromachus, another relative of Alexander of Sardis, so a split within the family over loyalties during the 'War of the Brothers' remains likely. On this see Walbank (1957) 1.501; Schmitt (1964) 30–1; Wörrle (1975) 59–87. See also D'Agostini and McAuley (2012) s.v. 'Andromachus'.

[42] Kosmin (2014) 67–8, esp. nn. 59–64 with scholarly history.

[43] Kosmin (2014) 67 and n. 60.

against Demetrius Poliorcetes in the West of the empire.⁴⁴ Finally, as mentioned previously, Patrocles was in command of Seleucid forces in Asia Minor after the accession of Antiochus I, from where he would later set off on his famous *periplus* of the Caspian Sea. His high military authority in Asia Minor is further indicated by the fact that he sent another (subordinate) Seleucid general, Hermogenes, on a campaign against Heraclea Pontica that would ultimately prove unsuccessful.⁴⁵ Despite the lack of a specific or consistent title, it is clear that early Seleucid generals essentially held the highest military status below the king.

Attestations of the precise military roles of Demodamas of Miletus and Megasthenes are scarce compared to our preceding two examples, though adequate to identify them as military commanders. Although Demodamas' decrees in Miletus indicate that he had some relationship with the army, Pliny the Elder identifies him clearly as *Seleuci et Antiochi regum dux*, 'a commander of the kings Seleucus and Antiochus', serving in Central Asia.⁴⁶ As Kosmin has noted, the mention of both Seleucid kings implies that Demodamas was serving with the military in the Seleucid East during the co-regency of Seleucus I and Antiochus I, that is, 294/293–281 BC.⁴⁷ The timing is noteworthy given that his civic actions in Miletus date from c. 300–298, since this implies that Demodamas had served in some sort of military capacity before returning to Miletus, perhaps after the Battle of Ipsus, and then was given his Central Asian command several years later.⁴⁸ As we shall shortly discuss, he then went on to lead a Seleucid military expedition into Central Asia. The chronology and geography of Megasthenes' career remain a topic of debate, but the broad outline is unchanged in any event: he first appears as what must have been a middle-ranking officer in the service of Sibyrtius, the satrap of Arachosia from 324 to 316 who had been appointed by Alexander and retained his command for part of the turbulent decade following Alexander's death.⁴⁹ Given that Sibyrtius was a critical military player in these years, it follows logically that Megasthenes would have

---

⁴⁴ Plut. *Demetr.* 47.4; Kosmin (2014) 67 n. 62. Strabo (2.1.17), cited by Kosmin (2014) 67–8 n. 61, mentions Patrocles as 'ὁ τῶν τόπων ἡγησάμενος τούτων Πατροκλῆς', which is often somewhat mistranslated as 'governed these regions'. ἡγέομαι with a genitive object as here more specifically means 'to have military control of' or 'to command', hence it seems safe to assume that this was more of a military than an administrative posting. On his career see also Grainger (1997) 111; Memnon 227a; Diod. 19.100.5

⁴⁵ Memnon 227a; *RE* 8.862–3, cited by Grainger (1997) s.v. Hermogenes (O1) 93.

⁴⁶ Pliny, *NH* 6.16.49, discussed by Kosmin (2014) 61–2 and nn. 22–3.

⁴⁷ Kosmin (2014) 61–2.

⁴⁸ On this see Sherwin-White and Kuhrt (1993) 25–7.

⁴⁹ See Bosworth (1996) for the argument that Megasthenes only visited India once before c. 318 BC, while Kosmin (2014) 260–4 argues convincingly for the traditional chronology.

begun his career in Sibyrtius' service before, as Kosmin suspects, being retained by Seleucus as a regional governor (Arr. *Anab.* 5.6.2). In this part of the empire, governorship and military command were synonymous with one another.

For all of the importance attached to our preceding criteria of background, descent and status, as well as proximity to the king, it must be borne in mind that something like Greek descent and elite status only opened the door of influence to men such as these early Seleucid generals. It was through practical service in the field that they walked through the door and entered prominence at the court. It seems, in the early Hellenistic period at least, that military prowess could lead to courtly influence, but not the opposite. It was as a reward for meritorious service in the field that they gained proximity to the king at court, and the elite status that this entailed. All of their other realms of competence and influence flowed from their basic martial ability. But in their transition from being simply commanders in the military realm to the agents of the king outside the court, they transformed conquered place into imperial space – and it is to this ideological function of Seleucid generalship that we turn by means of conclusion.

Conclusions: Seleucid Generals as Empire Builders

The common thread that runs through the various duties of these early Seleucid generals beyond the military sphere is their role in the establishment and demarcation of the Seleucid Empire. It is thanks in no small part to them that the Seleucid Empire was given form and shape, and its place in the emerging Hellenistic *oikoumene* was delineated. It was in their capacity as the 'men of the king in the provinces', to translate Capdetrey's turn of phrase, that these generals accomplished this task of imperial consolidation; it is in this task itself in turn that we find the consolidation of the prestige and authority imparted by their background, descent, proximity to the king and experience in the military realm.

In the closing lines of the inscription *OGIS* 229 it is easy to pass over the individual named Alexander without comment and assume that he is simply a local administrative functionary, but in the context of our broader discussion of Seleucid generalship we instead see that he is playing a pivotal role in the (re-)establishment of the Seleucid Empire in Asia Minor. The rather long text of the inscription narrates a settlement negotiated between Smyrna and Magnesia after the soldiers of the latter rebelled against the king and his supporters in the former city (c. 242).[50] The soldiers at Magnesia who rebelled are to be resettled in their holdings, and the city

---

[50] *OGIS* 229 = *Staatsverträge* 492 = *Smyrna* 9 = *I Smyrna* 573. Alexander appears in lines 100–5, as discussed by D'Agostini (2013) 97, esp. nn. 42 and 43.

itself is to be absorbed into Smyrna. Alexander of Sardis is the figure who transmits the record of the pre-uprising land holdings of these soldiers to the local authorities at Smyrna. Again, he is the intermediary between the royal 'centre' and the 'periphery' of the provinces. Alexander is thus ultimately the man charged with overseeing the details of this resettlement of soldiers on their lands, and their subsequent integration into the enlarged civic community of Smyrna. Viewed in relation to broader Seleucid imperial policy this role is of capital importance: the early Seleucid kings had woven the fabric of the empire by stitching groups of veterans and other soldiers into emerging Greek civic communities throughout their domain.[51] These veterans, and the civic communities of which they were a part, were meant to provide the local manifestation of the king's power in this vast and disparate realm. By overseeing the resettlement of these soldiers who rebelled during the uncertainty of the late 240s, Alexander was not simply shuffling land holdings around. He was rather mending the tears in the imperial tapestry that had been rent by the Third Syrian War. In resettling these troops in Anatolian countryside, he was not only pacifying an unruly corner of the empire, but also reaffirming the bond between these soldiers and the Seleucid king that was represented by the *kleros* each received. As a man of military experience himself, he would have been eminently aware of the imperial ramifications of his charge in post-war Anatolia. In this local context, he was re-establishing the imperial structure that his father and family had previously been so instrumental in first erecting. His possible attestation in Porphyry as the satrap of Sardis suggests that for Alexander this role was far from instantaneous.

While Alexander and his family in Anatolia had their part to play in perpetuating the internal coherence of the empire, in their far-reaching expeditions our remaining generals established the empire in broader 'global' and 'historical' dimensions. 'In salutary contrast to the armchair scholars of Ptolemaic Alexandria,' Paul Kosmin writes, 'the Seleucid court author actively participated in the physical formation

---

[51] The role of urban foundations in securing Seleucid imperial territory and creating imperial space has been a subject of intense discussion recently. On the mechanism of city foundations in Syria and their territorial dynamics, see Grainger (1990) and the various case studies elucidated by Cohen (1978). Sherwin-White and Kuhrt (1993) 143–9 discuss the scholarly history of Seleucid city foundations. Kosmin (2014) 93–119 discusses the case study of the Seleucid colonisation of Syria in great detail, which in turn sheds light on this mechanism in Asia Minor. We should note that not all of these cities were created *ex nihilo*, but rather some were simply colonies of veterans founded in or near existing communities that were then reorganised into a Greek civic body. On this issue, see McAuley (2019) and the introduction to Cohen (1978). On the relationship between the king and the populace of a given city, see Billows (1995) 149–54; Cohen (1978) 81–5; Sherwin-White and Kuhrt (1993) 162–6.

of the empire he described.'[52] As seen in the preceding biographical reconstructions, these Seleucid court authors could equally be described as Seleucid generals. Megasthenes, Patrocles and Demodamas each situated the Seleucid Empire with regard to their various regions of influence: Megasthenes with India, Patrocles with the Caspian Sea and Demodamas in Central Asian lands. We shall consider each in turn, drawing extensively from Kosmin's work on space and ideology in the Seleucid realm.[53]

Having been exposed to the Mauryan kingdom during his military service and tenure as Seleucus' ambassador to Chandragupta, Megasthenes went on to write the *Indica*, a detailed account of the rival empire. Although the account is ostensibly about the historical trajectory of Indian society, the nascent Seleucid Empire constantly haunts the backdrop.[54] In ideological terms, Seleucus was faced with something of a problem after the Treaty of the Indus which ended the unsuccessful Seleucid invasion of Mauryan India: he had lost a major campaign, ceded territory and failed in the same expedition as Alexander.[55] Megasthenes, however, presents a very different view of India from that which traditionally prevailed in Greek literature: Chandragupta's kingdom was highly urbanised, its society highly stratified and its lands dominated by a strong monarch. It was no longer a bizarre, isolated, fantastical land of the 'other', but rather an imperial space with an urban network, a centre and periphery and natural geographical borders.[56] In the same vein, it was neither utopian nor static, but rather followed a historical trajectory familiar to Greek thought. In the very act of creating an imperial space in India that was identifiable to the Greeks, Megasthenes was acting as a Seleucid apologist who argued that the borders of the empire had been determined by the constraints of geography rather than defeat.[57] By legitimating India as a sophisticated empire with its own centre, Megasthenes was simultaneously legitimating the Seleucid Empire

---

[52] Kosmin (2014) 76.

[53] My account of the role of these Seleucid general-geographers in the delineation of imperial space and its situation in the broader geographical context of contemporary antiquity is derived from Kosmin's brilliant account of this throughout his 2014 monograph. My aim in this section is not to add further observations to Kosmin's analysis, but rather to resituate it in the biographical context of each of these authors. Comparing them to individuals like Alexander of Sardis, I would argue, reveals a coherent strategy of empire which both organises domestic imperial place and situates the broader empire as a geographic and historical space.

[54] On Megasthenes see Kosmin (2014) 32–58. On the date of the *Indica*, see also his appendix, 261–72.

[55] Kosmin (2014) 32–5 on the context of the Treaty of the Indus.

[56] Kosmin (2014) 40–50.

[57] Kosmin (2014) 39.

as a worthy contemporary. Mauryan India provided an analogy through which to consider the Seleucid Empire and situate it in a much longer, 'global' historical narrative. Through this general's description of Chandragupta's kingdom, Seleucus becomes the natural successor of the Babylonians, Achaemenids and Alexander the Great, a powerful king at the head of an empire that lies in the centre of the world rather than on its edges.[58]

Just as Megasthenes defined the Seleucid Empire's place with regard to India, Demodamas of Miletus defined its relationship with the lands of Central Asia. The Milesian general wrote an autobiographical account of his service to Antiochus I in the eastern satrapies during the early years of the king's reign which further attests to the role of Seleucid general as a demarcator of imperial space. According to Pliny the Elder, upon reaching the banks of the Iaxartes, Demodamas then crossed the river and established altars dedicated to Apollo of Didyma on the far banks.[59] In the process Demodamas was not only imitating Alexander the Great's erection of altars in far-flung corners of his campaign, he was also clearly marking the limit of the Seleucid Empire in this region. By defining its end with altars on the far bank of a river he was simultaneously marking the land up to that point as the Seleucid interior.[60] Demodamas' own account goes on to place this act on behalf of his king in a long line of precedents ranging from Dionysus and Heracles to Alexander. As Kosmin notes, this dedication to Apollo of Didyma also created a unified imperial whole: Seleucid space was now bracketed by the altars of Demodamas in the East, and the sanctuary of Apollo of Didyma in the West.[61] The general is likely to have crafted a narrative for the interior organisation of this imperial space as well: Pliny's account suggests that Demodamas presented a sequence of events in Central Asia in which Alexander the Great founded cities, which were then destroyed by nomadic tribes, only to be refounded by the newly civilising influence of Antiochus I. As Megasthenes had done with India, Demodamas defined the shape and limits of the Seleucid Empire and created a narrative of the reigning king's relationship with it.

Finally, as Demodamas worked with the land, so Patrocles with the sea. During his command in the East, Patrocles was charged by the king(s) with leading a *periplus*, an exploratory mission, around the Caspian Sea at the north-eastern border of the empire. The very fact that the Seleucid kings charged an accomplished general with

---

[58] Kosmin (2014) 50–3.

[59] Pliny, *NH* 6.20 (following Mayhoff's 1906 edition of the Latin text): *includente flumine iaxarte, quod scythae silim vocant, alexander militesque eius tanain putavere esse. transcendit eum amnem demodamas, seleuci et antiochi regum dux, quem maxime sequimur in his, arasque apollini didymaeo statuit.*

[60] Kosmin (2014) 62–3.

[61] Kosmin (2014) 63–4.

such a purely geographical exploration indicates the degree to which the military and ideological prominence of such commanders were intertwined. In this the Seleucids were also situating themselves as the latest in a long line of kings and rulers who had commanded such exploration of the territories under their control, preceded most recently by Alexander the Great's abortive naval expedition to the east.[62] Following this naval expedition Patrocles published an account of his travels, a *Periplus*, in another instance of the literary pursuits of early Seleucid generals. The *Periplus* became the standard reference work on the Caspian Sea for several centuries, and in it Patrocles defined the empire in relation to its limits in the same way as Demodamas and Megasthenes. An expedition beyond the borders of the empire in turn reinforced those borders themselves, while Patrocles' perspective on territory from the sea further strengthened the Seleucid territorial claim. But it was most of all in the liberties Patrocles took with the geographical descriptions in his *Periplus* that we find his ideological agenda. Kosmin notes that Patrocles' renaming of the Caspian Sea as the Caspian Gulf was an act of imperial repossession that created an unbounded northern maritime border to the Greek *oikoumene*.[63] There was thus nothing beyond the northern domain of the Seleucid kings. In the same vein, his mention of a planned canal linking the Black Sea and the Caspian Sea would have created a natural aquatic barrier that circumscribed all of Seleucid imperial space.[64] Just like the Hindu Kush to the east that separated the Seleucid realm from the Mauryan Empire, the empire's northern geography lent it a natural unity. The imperial project as undertaken by these generals was as viable by land as by sea.

When analysing the literary and intellectual accomplishments of men such as these it is easy to lose sight of the diversity of their service in, and contribution to, the early Seleucid realm. Beyond being authors, each was also a soldier, a commander, an administrator, a governor, a courtier and a confidant of the king. Just as their proximity to the king was contingent on their military abilities, so too did their role in the construction of Seleucid imperial space derive from this martial background and courtly prestige.[65] But the recurrent theme in the ideological realm as elsewhere is that the Seleucid general provided the bridge between the will of the king and the reality of the empire on the ground. This intermediary role necessitates trust and capability in equal measure, and we must take care not to emphasise one at the

---

[62] On the political and intellectual context of Patrocles' *periplus*, see Kosmin (2014) 67–9.

[63] On the renaming of the Caspian Sea, see Kosmin (2014) 70–1.

[64] Kosmin (2014) 73–6, noting that the Seleucids planned to complete a long-surmised plan of their Achaemenid predecessors.

[65] On the equivalent of this process of intellectual patronage and imperialism in the Ptolemaic court, see Strootman (2017).

expense of the other. Treating the realm of courtly intrigue in isolation from the administrative realities of the regional capital or the manoeuvres of the battlefield is to the detriment of our understanding of the fuller picture of Hellenistic imperialism. Given the wide range of competencies and the freedom of action enjoyed by these early Seleucid generals, it comes as little surprise that the line between loyal subordinate and usurper could be so easily crossed. It is precisely as a consequence of this that the notion of generalship and officialdom was constrained by Antiochus III in response to his own experience of the rebellion of Achaeus the Younger, among others.[66] A more strictly delineated system, with more precisely defined competencies, came to replace the more freewheeling system of the early generations of the dynasty. Perhaps it was precisely because they were afforded such a wide range of influence that these early generals remained happily loyal to the Seleucid kings in the first place.

Where are we to locate the inspiration for this multifaceted and expansive sense of generalship in the early Seleucid period? The immediate temptation is to view this as simply the natural perpetuation of a Macedonian system of *hetairoi* and *philoi* that they had inherited from Alexander the Great.[67] Intimacy and friendship with the king, the concerns of status and descent, and military prowess were certainly defining criteria there as well. But the Macedonian system was never faced with the administrative realities of such a vast and expansive empire as the Seleucid realm, and something else must have been at work. In this link between generalship and the ideology of empire we can find clear traces of Achaemenid inspiration, but the early Seleucid court lacked the ritualised complexity of the Achaemenid hierarchy.[68] The link between military prowess, elite status and civic prestige in the local realm was of course nothing new in the urban culture of the Greek *polis*, so perhaps in this we find the legacy of the political culture of the Greek mainland. As with so many other aspects of Seleucid royal ideology, the dynamic and diverse character of generalship in the early Seleucid Empire was the product of a delicate mix of tradition and innovation that was the mark of an emergent empire, not a weak one.

---

[66] On this, see D'Agostini (2014).

[67] See Hammond (2000) on the broader continuity of Macedonian institutions in the early Hellenistic period. See also Strootman (2014) 1–28 for a discussion of various precedents for the Hellenistic courts.

[68] See Llewellyn-Jones (2013) 12–41 on the relationship between the Achaemenid kings and their men at court, and 42–73 on the ritualistic and performative aspect of the court.

5 Generalship and Knowledge in the Middle Roman Republic

Michael Taylor

Amateurism and Command

As the Romans conquered the Italian peninsula and secured dominion over the entire Mediterranean, the men who led the legions were politicians, elected magistrates of the Roman people. Their time in command was short, officially a year, occasionally extended (*prorogatio*), providing limited time for on-the-job training before a replacement arrived. Most Roman generals were for all intents and purposes amateurs, often enjoying only a few months' experience commanding their army before they led it into battle for the first time.

Professional generalship, in the modern technocratic sense, was absent from the ancient world at large. There was no ancient equivalent of the specialised education modern general officers receive at various points along their careers (e.g. West Point, the US Army War College), nor were there the technocratic career paths that see modern officers hold a series of alternating command and staff positions at various echelons, working their way up the ranks from second lieutenants in charge of platoons to the ranks of general officers commanding divisions, corps and armies. But many ancient military systems had the capacity to identify men with the aptitude for generalship, and to assign them either to long-term positions or to a series of high-profile commands. Take for example the Achaemenid general Mardonius, who reorganised the Ionian cities after 494 BC, then invaded Thrace and Macedonia in 492 BC, and finally died at Plataea leading Xerxes' invasion force in 479 BC.[1] Philip II of Macedon (359–336 BC) famously quipped that he envied the Athenians for electing

---

[1] Ionian command: Hdt. 6.43.; Macedonian campaign: 6.44–5; death at Plataea: Hdt. 6.94.2.

ten generals a year, because he had only found one in his own lifetime: Parmenio.² The Seleucid king Antiochus III identified Zeuxis as a successful field commander in 221 BC, and Zeuxis was still active, thirty years later, at the Battle of Magnesia in 190 BC.³ Social status underlay these royal appointments, for Mardonius, Parmenio and Zeuxis would not have been generals had they had not also firstly been well-connected courtiers. But not every courtier was entrusted with high profile or extended commands, and those that were had proven their capacity for generalship at some point along the way.

Ancient kings often served as their own generals, and a king over a long reign could accrue extensive personal experience leading armies in the field. Alexander the Great was the exemplar over the course of his short and brutal reign, and he was closely, if sometimes clumsily, imitated by his Hellenistic successors.⁴ Most Hellenistic kings nonetheless knew their way around a camp, and often had far more experience than their Roman opponents. When Philip V encountered Titus Quinctius Flamininus at Cynoscephalae in 197 BC, Philip had been personally leading armies and fleets since 220 BC, while the campaign represented Flamininus' first major command, as he had skipped the praetorship.⁵ When Antiochus III engaged Lucius Scipio at Magnesia in 190 BC, Antiochus had also been commanding armies personally since 221 BC, and could claim a string of splendid victories from Sardis to Bactria.⁶ The campaign represented Lucius Scipio's first combat command, as he had previously served as praetor in the pacified province of Sicily.⁷ In both instances, untested Roman generals decisively defeated the battle-hardened monarchs.

Non-monarchic regimes were based on the principle of power-sharing, either across an aristocratic class or with the populace more broadly. Nonetheless, many non-monarchic regimes in the ancient Mediterranean focused military authority in the hands of a small number of proven generals. Athens, the most radical of ancient democracies, allowed the *strategoi*, the ten generals elected annually, to serve without term limits, so that men with strategic vision (e.g. Pericles) or tactical skill (e.g.

---

[2] Plut. *Apophth. Phil.* 2 = *Mor.* 177C.
[3] Zeuxis achieves royal prominence: Pol. 5.51–2; at the Battle of Magnesia: Liv. 37.41.1.
[4] On Alexander's battlefield leadership, see Ma (2013).
[5] Philip's first taste of generalship, at the age of seventeen: Pol. 4.73.5. On the career of Philip V in general, see Walbank (1940). For Flamininus, see Broughton (1951) 328.
[6] For the royal career of Antiochus the Great, see Schmitt (1964); Taylor (2013); Grainger (2015).
[7] Broughton (1951) 347, 356. For a positive view of L. Scipio's generalship at the battle, see Harl (2008).

Iphicrates) might hold the office for extended periods.⁸ Pericles held fifteen one-year generalships, although the record was held by Phocion, who served as general for forty-five annual terms.⁹

Carthage, likewise a republic with a mixed constitution much admired by Aristotle, separated military and political leadership altogether. Carthage's elected magistrates, *shophets*, served annual terms. Their responsibilities, however, seem to have been entirely civil. The position of general (*rab*), while also elected annually, could be held repeatedly for years and even decades.¹⁰ Hamilcar Barca held a nearly continuous series of commands between 245 BC and his death in 229 BC. His son-in-law Hasdrubal led Spanish armies for eight years until his death in 221 BC. And Hannibal Barca, acclaimed by the army as general upon Hasdrubal's death, served as a general for twenty years until the conclusion of the Second Punic War in 201 BC.¹¹ The Middle Republican system of briskly rotating commands was unique, not only in contrast to the Hellenistic kingdoms, but even when compared to other ancient republican city-states.

Knowledge and Generalship

The advantage of allowing generals to hold long-term commands, sometimes spanning decades, was that it facilitated experiential learning, allowing these generals to accumulate military knowledge as individuals. The taxonomy of military knowledge was diverse, but here I am going to simplify it into three basic categories:

1. *Technical knowledge*: the practical knowledge a general needed to have to command an army. This included martial skills like how to ride a horse and fight with weapons. More critical to generals were communication skills, including the ability to give a motivational speech before the battle.¹² This category also included sufficient knowledge of logistics, administration and tactics to oversee the supply, discipline and deployment of his force. For Roman generals, religious knowledge was held in particularly high cultural esteem, as the general's public capacity to maintain an appropriate relationship with the gods

---

[8] For the Athenian generalship as an institution, see Hamel (1998).
[9] Plut. *Per.* 16.3; *Phoc.* 8.1. The idea that generals were exceptions to the democratic principle that common citizens could rotate through any position of authority is preserved in the Ps. Xen. *Ath. Pol.* 1.3.
[10] Pilkington (2019) 129–30.
[11] For Hannibal's military and political career, see Hoyos (2003).
[12] Anson (2010).

was critical for morale.¹³ The forms of technical knowledge were too diverse to enumerate: even astronomical science on one occasion came in handy, when Aemilius Paullus dealt with the impact of a lunar eclipse on his superstitious troops.¹⁴

2. *Theatre-specific knowledge* about the general's immediate province, including local geography, ethnography, political landscape as well as the particular military capacities of opposing forces.
3. *Grand strategic knowledge* about the Mediterranean wide geopolitical environment. Until the pan-Mediterranean commands of Pompey the Great, the Romans had no concept of a 'commander-in-chief'.¹⁵ Generals were restricted by their *provincia*, effectively a bounded area of operation set by the senate. But within *provincia* generals often made decisions that had strategic and diplomatic ramifications well beyond their theater, while the senate as a whole engaged in the fundamentals of grand strategy, especially in the annual allotment of legions and provincial commands.¹⁶

Technical Knowledge

A Roman general was new to command, but well versed in warfare. Elite Roman men were required to serve ten campaigns before they were eligible to embark on a political career.¹⁷ Aristocrats in the Middle Republic fought primarily as cavalrymen; virtually all had participated in military operations and many had seen active combat. After five years of military service, a young aristocrat was eligible to run for military tribune. While not technically a magisterial office (it did not confer membership in the senate), military tribunes were elected by the Roman people at large in the *comitia tributa*, and the office was a critical first step up the aristocratic career ladder (*cursus honorum*). Twenty-four tribunes were elected every year, six for each of the four consular legions. Ten of these were elected from men with five years' military experience, and fourteen from men with ten years' experience.¹⁸ During

---

[13] E.g. Cic. *Nat. D.* 7: defeats attributed to improper religious practices; Pol. 10.11.7: use of religion to boost confidence.

[14] Plut. *Aem.*17.11; cf. Liv. 44.37.4–9, where a military tribune is given credit for explicating the eclipse.

[15] For Pompey's commands, see now Vervaet (2014) 216–23.

[16] Eckstein (1987) notes the wide leeway victorious generals were given to settle affairs in their provinces, despite the supervision of senatorial commissioners (*decem legati*).

[17] Pol. 6.19.3.

[18] Pol. 6.19.1. For a prosopography of military tribunes, although it is dated, see Suolahti (1955). Livy reports the first election of military tribunes in 362 BC (five years after the

particularly dangerous wars, experienced men, even of consular status, would occasionally run for what was usually a junior office, most notably Cato the Elder's service as a military tribune in the war against Antiochus III the Great (222–187 BC), four years after his consulship.[19] Military tribunes were responsible for organising the legions, and administering discipline in the camp, leading detachments and engaging in battlefield command and control. One thing, interestingly enough, that they did not do was actually exercise direct command. Military tribunes were not assigned subdivisions of the legion to command as battalion or brigade commanders, although for some operations individual tribunes (or a legate hand-picked by the general) might be given temporary control of a detachment or legionary element. Under normal circumstances, however, the six military tribunes collectively administered their legion as a college. The only two echelons of permanent direct command in the Roman army were the centurion over his century, and the *imperator* over the entire army.

With the minimum ten years' service complete, a young man would begin his political career, running for a series of civic offices. This *cursus honorum*, 'path of honours', was initially informal, so that some men skipped various junior offices on their way to the top, but the *cursus* was hardened in 180 BC with the *lex Villia Annalis*, which set minimum ages for holding the various posts.[20] The most junior elected office to make its holder eligible for enrolment into the Roman senate was the quaestorship. Quaestors might be assigned to serve as military quartermasters, therefore exposing the aristocrat to the critical complexities of military logistics and administration. Not all quaestors were assigned to armies, as two oversaw the treasury, but even this involved exposure to record keeping, accounting and other aspects of state administration.[21] The recovery from the Egadi Islands of the Roman naval rams (*rostra*, sunk in 241 BC in the last battle of the First Punic War) have revealed inscriptions reporting the quaestor's *probatio* of the ram, probably a quality-control review for either the ram or perhaps even the entire ship.[22] In this unglamorous

---

military tribunes with consular powers were abolished in favour of the modern consulship), although Clark (2016) argues that election may not have begun until 312 BC.

[19] Front. *Strat.* 2.4.4 *tribunus militum a populo factus*, although Livy, 36.17.1, erroneously believed him to be an appointed legate because of his seniority. Cf. Cic. *Sen.* 32; App. *Syr.* 18, who lists them as *chiliarchoi*, i.e. tribunes.

[20] For the development of the Middle Republican *cursus*, see Beck (2009). For the Roman constitution in general, including the offices discussed here, see Lintott (1999).

[21] For the quaestorship in the Middle Republic, see recently Prag (2014a); Pina Polo and Diaz Fernandez (2019).

[22] For the *probatio* inscriptions, see Prag (2014b), who also postulates that one aspect of the *probatio* was to confirm that the bronze issued by the treasury was utilised in the ram itself.

administrative process, the young quaestor gained experience not only in military contracting but also in naval architecture, not trivial knowledge should a later command include a war fleet.

Four men were annually elected aediles (two curule and two plebeian), who served as 'city managers' engaged in a wide variety of administrative tasks, including regulating urban markets, maintaining urban infrastructure and regulating the use of public land, especially through fines for overgrazing. These duties, which included issuing contracts, hearing cases in market disputes and supervising and coordinating the efforts of public slaves, might translate indirectly into the administrative complexities of military command. Also elected annually were ten tribunes of the plebs, who promulgated legislation before the voting assemblies and stood ready to protect the rights of common Roman citizens. This office required public-speaking abilities and interpersonal skills, especially personal and political engagement with common citizens that might also prove useful to a future general interacting with his citizen-soldiers.[23]

The first Roman echelon that we might refer to as a 'general' was the praetorship, the first office endowed with *imperium*, the legal and sacral capacity to exercise command.[24] Praetors could command small armies, usually a single legion with an allied wing, roughly 10,000–12,000 men, although not all praetorian provinces were militarised (by the second century BC the urban and peregrine praetors largely stayed in Rome to perform civil functions, while some provinces like Sicily usually had no standing armies).[25] The praetorship therefore provided command experience in lower-profile theatres (although praetors might still see significant combat, especially in Spain), even as the most dangerous and prestigious wars and campaigns were generally reserved for the consuls.

Thus, by the time a man was elected consul, through his decade of military service, his time as a military tribune and his administrative and political experience working his way up the senatorial *cursus*, he had opportunities to acquire technical knowledge relevant to a general, both as a soldier and as a civic administrator. He could ride a horse, give a speech, interact with peers and subordinates, and engage in logistical planning and fiscal accounting.

The *cursus honorum* did not necessarily train generals in grand tactics while on campaign, but one strength of the Roman army was the extent to which it developed deeply rooted standard operating procedures that did not require much input by the general to execute, once he made the decision to fight. In battle, Roman troops would automatically draw up into the chequerboard array of *triplex acies*, not because

[23] See Russell (2013) for public speaking by plebeian tribunes.
[24] For the legal and constitutional mechanics, see Vervaet (2014).
[25] For the praetorship, see Brennan (2000).

of any brilliant plan of the commander, but simply because these unique tactics were ingrained in the collective military consciousness, having evolved by trial and error.[26] Generals could make active decisions to vary this array, sometimes with great success (e.g. Scipio Africanus at Zama in 202 BC) and sometimes disastrously (Regulus at Tunis in 255 BC, Varro and Paullus at Cannae in 216 BC, both deploying their units with unusual depth).[27] But most generals simply deployed the standard *triplex acies*, in part because it required no extra mental effort on their part. The lazy option was not necessarily a bad one. Importantly, the third line of *triarii* functioned as a built-in tactical reserve. Most other generals had to make an active decision to draw up a reserve or rearguard. Many brilliant ancient generals neglected to deploy an adequate reserve force (Hannibal notably had none when his centre collapsed at Trebia and Cannae, allowing thousands of Romans to escape), whereas even the dullest Roman general enjoyed a sizeable reserve of *triarii* by default.[28]

Theatre-Specific Knowledge

If there was one major weakness to the Roman system, it was that most commanders lacked theatre-specific knowledge when they reached their command. Prorogation, the formal extension of *imperium* past the one-year tenure of office, might allow generals to accrue more in-depth knowledge of their theatre, but usually only added an additional year to the length of command. Stable theatre-specific knowledge is difficult for any armed force that must fight, sometimes unexpectedly, in various theatres. The American general Norman Schwarzkopf quipped that as a young officer he would never have imagined that he would see combat in Vietnam, Granada and Iraq.[29] But one advantage of maintaining a batch of professional generals is that some may accrue specialised knowledge in regions they have long campaigned in. For stable imperial configurations, where it was clear that certain frontiers would be long-term military zones, such expertise was both feasible and valuable. Looking back to the Achaemenids, Tissaphernes, the satrap (military governor) of Lydia for over twenty years, was clearly a 'Greek expert' with profound knowledge of the vagaries of Greek politics and the capacities of Greek forces.[30] But the Roman system of rotation did not allow commanders to develop

---

[26] On the mechanics of Roman manipular tactics, see recently Sabin (2000); Taylor (2014); (2014/15).

[27] Scipio at Zama: Pol. 15.14.3; see Taylor (2019) 324–5 for the nature of these manoeuvres. Tunis: Pol. 1.33.9. Cannae: Pol. 3.113.2–3.

[28] Pol. 18.32.2.

[29] Schwarzkopf (1992) 502–3.

[30] See recently Hyland (2018) 53–139 for Tissaphernes' interventions in Greek geopolitics.

theatre-specific expertise. Indeed, if anything, they relied on their own troops. For example, when Tiberius Sempronius Gracchus was dispatched to Spain in 179 BC he insisted that the army stay behind, even if the outgoing commander wanted to bring it back to Rome for his triumph (a compromise allowed a few selected soldiers to return home to triumph).[31] Similarly, during the start of the Third Macedonian War, as the Romans prepared for a fresh clash with a Macedonian-style army, efforts were made to recruit as many veterans as possible who had fought in the Second Macedonian and Syrian Wars, including the grizzled centurion Spurius Ligustinus, who had served in both conflicts.[32] Roman generals also relied on the local knowledge of foreign troops, *auxilia externa*, who supplemented legionary deployments. For example, Titus Quinctius Flamininus in Greece maintained a detachment of Athamanians with his army not for their fighting capacity, but rather to serve as guides through central Greece.[33] And Roman generals furthermore compensated for their lack of theatre-specific knowledge by deploying a modality of technical knowledge: the capacity to gather and process intelligence, for example Scipio's queries concerning the topography around New Carthage prior to his assault on the city.[34]

Grand Strategic Knowledge

If the brisk rotation of commanders hampered their ability to gain detailed theatre-specific knowledge, it had the advantage of giving individual commanders sweeping views of the Mediterranean. L. Aemilius Paullus, the vanquisher of Perseus the king of Macedon in 168 BC, had held *imperium* in three very different provinces: in Spain as praetor, in Liguria during his first consulship, and in Macedonia during his second consulship.[35] Critically, the Roman senate was filled with men who had served throughout Rome's empire as military tribunes, quaestors, praetors and consuls. A meeting of the senate therefore concentrated the vast if diffuse snippets of personal experience of various operational theatres of the Roman Republic under a single roof, percolating the disparate knowledge of the aristocracy in a single institutional *locus* with procedures that facilitated vigorous debate, fundamentally a form of knowledge exchange.[36] The speaking-order of the senate, while ranked by office, was

---

[31] Liv. 40.35.9–14.
[32] Liv. 42.32.4; for Spurius' career, see Cadiou (2002).
[33] Liv. 32.14.7. On foreign troops, see Prag (2007); Gauthier (2019).
[34] Pol. 10.8.3–9.1.
[35] Broughton (1951) 353, 381, 427–8.
[36] For senatorial debate and participation, see Ryan (1998).

also ranked in terms of experience: the men who had commanded armies (consular and praetorian) spoke before those who had not.

It was the senate that made the fundamental decisions that might be roughly if imperfectly described as 'grand strategy'. This included which provinces would be allotted to consular vs praetorian governors (dispatching a consul and his army automatically made the province a priority mission), as well as which active magistrates would have their commands extended. While the latter process could be viciously political (and occasionally the dispute had to be sent to the people for resolution in the event of senatorial gridlock[37]), it fundamentally involved a judgement of the capacities of the commanders and evaluation of their success to date, the sort of personnel considerations an institution spearheaded by ex-generals was well suited to undertake. Finally, and perhaps most importantly, it was the senate that determined the number of legions that would be kept under arms that year, the reinforcements that would be sent to armies in the field, the number of ships to be deployed in the fleet and (until 167 BC) the rate of citizen *tributum* necessary to pay for it all. These decisions required profound knowledge of the military needs of specific theatres, such as the manpower base of citizen and allied communities, the expected costs of military operation and the ration requirements of deployed forces. The knowledge to make these grand strategic decisions derived from the fact that the senior members of the senate had experienced the stark realities of high command, and even junior ones had toiled in support of these operations as military tribunes and quaestors.

The Romans therefore accepted generals with limited experience with generalship as they rotated through command, and virtually no theatre-specific knowledge. The benefit of this rotation was that even as new commanders had to rapidly find their footing before they too moved on, upon their return to Rome they contributed their acquired technical, tactical and theatre-specific knowledge to the greater pool of collective knowledge under the roof of the curia.

Conclusion: Knowledge and the Aristocratic Class

Military knowledge generated by rotation in command was diffused not simply through the ranks of the senate, but through the aristocratic class more broadly. Many aristocratic boys literally grew up with a general in the house. To be raised by a father who had been a general involved informal socialisation in military affairs. Cato the Elder personally taught his son to hurl a javelin, fight in armour, ride, box, swim and endure hot and cold, the sort of physical toughening a young soldier

---

[37] Day (2017).

would need to face the dangers of campaign.[38] Fathers might also advise their sons in personal comportment when they served under others, as when Cato wrote a letter to his son counselling him about his formal legal status when he chose to stay on as an observer after his legion had been discharged.[39] This is a relatively minor piece of advice, but provides a glimpse of the technical knowledge that might be transmitted privately between a father and son. Young aristocrats often engaged in their early military service under their own father's command. This fact not only marked them out as privileged young men, but also allowed them special access to the dynamics of the *praetorium* and *consilium*.[40] This was no doubt a cushy form of service (and the occasional austere general forced his son to serve in the ranks[41]), but it also was an apprenticeship for high command.

Finally, aristocratic sociability allowed for the quiet interpersonal transfer of military knowledge. L. Aemilius Paullus, for example, spoke to friends of the terrifying array of the Macedonian phalanx charging his position at Pydna, and presumably any future commanders listening would have received an informal case study in how to win a battle, including how to manage personal emotions of fear.[42] Similarly, when Paullus joked at dinner parties that the same state of mind was required to both prepare a banquet and array a battle, he hinted at the detailed preparations and logistical inputs required for a successful engagement.[43] The informal transfer of military knowledge between aristocrats provided the context for early military writings. In some instances, these may have simply been campaign memoirs, for example Scipio Africanus' letter, written to Philip V as a diplomatic courtesy but with a copy residing in family archives, which described in detail his campaign around New Carthage.[44] The first formal tactical treatise we know of, by Cato the Elder, which survives only in fragments, should be seen as an extension of these informal mechanisms for circulating military knowledge around the aristocratic class.

---

[38] Plut. *Cat. Mai.* 20.4.

[39] Cic. *Off.* 1.37.

[40] See, for example, Scipio Africanus, Pol. 10.3.4–6; Metellus Pius, Sall. *Iug.* 64.4; although Front. *Strat.* 4.1.11 suggests he was forced to serve as a common soldier; Scipio Aemilianus and Fabius Maximus Aemilianus, the biological sons of Aemilius Paullus, Plut. *Aem.* 22.3–6.

[41] Front. *Strat.* 4.1.12, for the son of Rutilius Rufus.

[42] Pol. 29.17.

[43] Plut. *Aem.* 28.9.

[44] Pol. 10.9.2. It is not impossible that the letter was captured with the Macedonian library, which Paullus donated to his sons, Plut. *Aem.* 28.11, including Scipio Aemilianus, the friend and patron to Polybius.

Other Romans seemed to accept aristocratic knowledge-transfer systems as generally effective, in a manner not dissimilar to the preference of modern American voters for Ivy League graduates or British voters for Oxbridge degrees. The routine preference of Roman voters for candidates from a small set of established families, while no doubt an ingrained deferential reflex, may also reflect popular acknowledgement that deep-rooted aristocratic families functioned as effective repositories and propagators of military and administrative know-how. And there were several obvious advantages to having an established political class widely populated with men capable of command. During the Second Punic War, the city survived not only the deaths of tens of thousands of Roman and Italian soldiers, but also the combat deaths of numerous experienced generals: C. Flaminius (cos. 217), Cn. Servilius Geminus (cos. 217), M. Atilius Regulus (suff. 217), L. Aemilius Paullus (cos. 216), L. Postumius Albinus (cos. 229), Ti. Sempronius Gracchus (cos. 215, 213), P. and Cn. Cornelius Scipio (cos. 218 and 222) and the five-time consul M. Claudius Marcellus, along with many other senators. The pool of military knowledge latent within the broader political class enabled the Romans to quickly regenerate military leadership, including the precipitous rise of the future Scipio Africanus (son of the consul of 218), who clearly knew a great deal about war, despite his limited command experience when he was elected extraordinary commander for Spain. Furthermore, an excess of competent if not inspired generals was critical for Rome's capacity to conduct simultaneous operations from the second century BC onwards throughout the Mediterranean, where intensive military operations might be conducted simultaneously in the Spains, Northern Italy and the Eastern Mediterranean.

Overall, the configuration of amateur commanders drawn from a militarised aristocratic class served the Roman state well during the Middle Republic. By the late second century BC, the system was under stress. While military deployments remained brisk, Rome fought far fewer major theatre wars by the late second century BC than it had during the ultra-violent period from 264 to 167 BC. This reduced the opportunities for members of the aristocratic class to obtain combat experience in major wars, and probably resulted in a diminution in the overall military knowledge of the *nobiles*. Starting in 112 BC, military defeats in Numidia and a dangerous *Völkerwanderung* of the Cimbri and Teutones exposed the deficiencies of a series of Roman commanders. In 107 BC, the *novus homo* Gaius Marius ran for consul on the basis of his extensive military expertise. The historian Sallust imagined a speech in which Marius lampooned the military knowledge of the *nobiles*, noting that he had learned from experience, unlike some consuls who scrambled to study Greek military manuals upon achieving election.[45] Marius' seven consulships, which allowed him to

---

[45] Sall. *Iug.* 85.10–13.

defeat the Numidian king Jugurtha and annihilate the threat posed by the Cimbri and Teutones, ushered in a new trend of important military commands concentrated upon a small stable of capable commanders.[46] The consummate generalissimo of the first century BC was Pompey the Great, who started his career as a civil war lieutenant of Marius' arch-enemy Sulla, and went on to hold commands *sine magistratu* in Spain (78–72 BC) and against the Spartacus rebels (71 BC). Following his consulship in 70 BC, he was assigned by tribunician laws two extraordinary commands, firstly against Mediterranean pirates (67 BC) and then against king Mithridates (66–62 BC).[47] Starting in 58 BC, Pompey supported the extraordinary command in Gaul for his political ally Julius Caesar, who used the opportunity to ruthlessly establish his military credentials, enrich himself and his officers, and earn the personal loyalty of his veteran army. Pompey and Caesar in the course of their extended campaigns also amassed tremendous military knowledge, which allowed both to undertake an array of complex operations, ranging from set-piece battles to amphibious landings to trench warfare.[48]

The concentration of military forces under these dynasts ultimately enabled the civil wars that destroyed the free Republic. But it also served to limit further the military knowledge of the senatorial elite, outside of the dynasts and their lieutenants. This created a vicious cycle, whereby only a handful of dynasts enjoyed the technical knowledge to engage in large-scale wars, while their monopolisation of major commands precluded other aristocrats from gaining significant command experience. A surprising number of key players in the Late Republic (Cicero, Cato the Younger, even Octavian) emerge as basically non-military figures. When the consul Gaius Claudius Marcellus presented Pompey with a sword and begged him to defend the Republic in 50 BC, he hardly seems to have considered himself competent to defend it on his own.[49] Indeed, the brittleness of the Late Republican senatorial class only casts into stark relief the benefits of the rotating commands provided to the Middle Republic. Most Middle Republican generals were far less adept than Caesar or Pompey, but frequent rotation of command during this period made the Roman governing class overall far more robust and resilient.

---

[46] For Marius' political and military career, see Evans (1994).
[47] See Seager (2002) for Pompey's career.
[48] Potter (2010).
[49] Plut. *Pomp*. 59.1; App. *BCiv*. 2.31; Dio Cass. 40.64.4.

6 Command Assessment in the *Bellum Gallicum*: Caesar and *Fortuna*

David Nolan

The *Bellum Gallicum* was the account of Caesar's campaigns in Gaul from 58 to 52 BC, in which he used a third-person style to narrate events chronologically, with little overt reflection or assessment for the audience.[1] This narrative conceit might leave a reader unsure of any underlying military principles, particularly as the work is highly self-promotional and often uses literary devices such as speeches and *exempla*. However, the work provides important information on warfare, whether that simply be through the details of historical battles or through the representation of the commanders described therein.[2] Caesar's choice of words in describing events also reveals ideals that are important for an understanding of Roman generalship. This chapter focuses on one such word, *fortuna*, and how its pattern of use gives insight into command at critical points in each campaign narrative.[3] The information conveyed can be as simple as the rating of a battle's success using *fortuna* as a qualification, or more comprehensive assessments of subordinates and enemy leaders. An

---

[1] For a rare first-person comment see Caesar, *B. Gall.* 5.54.5. On the historical events see Meier (1995) 235–315; Gelzer (1968) 102–94; Jehne (1997) 35–71; and most recently Schauer (2017) 50–78 on the background to composition. On style of narration and composition see Schauer (2017) 91–112; Riggsby (2006) 7–8; Kraus (2010) 48; Rüpke (1992) 212; Jehne (2006) 234–41; Meier (1995) 254–7.

[2] For example, see Caesar's criticism of the commander Sabinus at *B. Gall.* 5.52.6.

[3] Note that this chapter specifically addresses the *Bellum Gallicum* and not the *Bellum Civile*, as the appearance of *fortuna* is closely associated with the promotional aims of each work. See Weinstock (1971) 112, 124; Wardle (2009) 103–4. For general studies on *fortuna* see Kajanto (1981); Champeaux (1987); Arya (2002); Culham (1989); Lazarus (1978/9); Stewart (1968). On *fortuna* in Caesar, see Hall (1998); Ramage (2003); Tappan (1931); Warde Fowler (1903).

examination of *fortuna* in conjunction with the concept of *virtus* is also useful, as it qualifies the general Roman admiration for *virtus* by showing that it is an attribute that a commander relied on only when everything else had failed. *Fortuna* even highlights the matters that caused Caesar the most frustration, as is evident in Book 6, where there is a dramatic change in use as he struggled to present a campaign against an elusive enemy. Examination of these patterns and objectives that surround the use of *fortuna* in the *Bellum Gallicum* provides valuable information on Caesar's presentation of command and his ideals as a Roman general.

While there are questions over the veracity of the text, these can be addressed by recognising that an objective of the work was to promote Caesar's military competence. The question of whether Caesar was telling the truth, not only about *fortuna* but indeed regarding historical events, has been the subject of much debate. However, this chapter follows recent scholarship that recognises the work as self-promotional and highly persuasive in intent, while generally less convinced that it is full of outright fabrications.[4] Even if there are misrepresentations, Caesar's desire to promote his own military knowledge in competition with Pompey and other great commanders seems clear as he holds forth his expertise on military matters, indicating that his opinion on *fortuna* in war should at least warrant investigation.[5]

In addition, the complexities of Caesar's relationship to *fortuna* in his political life, his beliefs and even his association with *fortuna* outside of the *Bellum Gallicum* are less relevant for this exercise than the presence of the concept in the campaigns

---

[4] See Rambaud (1966); Mutschler (1975) for ideas of *déformation*; for *contra*, see Collins (1972). See also Meier (1995) 254–64; Gerlinger (2008) 23; Heubner (1974) 104; Walser (1995) 218. Kraus (2005) 103 notes the influence of Rambaud's propaganda approach on scholarship, although Riggsby (2006) 190, 207–14, notes that the idea of propaganda has fallen into disfavour. For recent analyses see Welch and Powell (1998) on aspects of Caesar's military reporting and Kraus (2009) 102, 165. See also Riggsby (2006) for self-promotion and Schauer (2017) 113–232 on the idea of reader manipulation. This study follows the view of Kraus and Schauer and does not regard the narrative as essentially tendentious regarding the historical events, and instead recognises that the selection, emphasis and presentation of information are designed to promote Caesar's aims, including his competence in the military sphere.

[5] Conley (1983) 173 notes that military narratives are fashioned around an outline of causes for the outcomes of battles and campaigns, and Burns (2003) 94 states of Caesar: 'it is always prudent to be sceptical of his theories of causation', as the facts are often presented to support Caesar's interpretation. Nevertheless, there are underlying military principles that can also be studied. On generalship see Welch (1998) 85–6; Goldsworthy (1998) 211. See also Kraus (2009) 170, who discusses Caesar's self-representation as the 'ideal general'. Campbell (1987) 19 notes the rarity of a writer with personal military experience.

described.⁶ The late Republican period saw the construction of temples and other buildings related to the divine Fortuna, and it appeared in literature associated with great generals such as Marius, Sulla and Caesar.⁷ There was political competition and an evolving relationship with Fortuna and the divine Victoria apparent on coinage from this time.⁸ Caesar himself cultivated this relationship, particularly in the *Bellum Civile*, and also in a letter to Cicero where he notes its role in public affairs.⁹ In the *Bellum Gallicum* usage can also be designed to reflect positively on Caesar, as evidenced when Vercingetorix resigns himself to Fortuna at the end of the work.¹⁰ There is an air of destiny in this statement that illustrates the use of *fortuna* for literary embellishment to indicate the complete submission of Gaul and the successful conclusion of the war.¹¹ Nevertheless this study takes a granular approach, recog-

---

⁶ This chapter refers to the concept as *fortuna*, and to Fortuna when it appears to be the divinity. Note also that the focus of much analysis has been on belief rather than literary purpose. See Champeaux (1987) 259–91. For further discussion of Caesar's beliefs and reputation, see Weinstock (1971) 121–6; Kajanto (1981) 537–8; Arya (2002) 205. See also Murphy (1986) 307–9; Wardle (2009) 100–4, 107–8, 110; Dick (1967) 238–9; Swain (1989) 510–11; Tappan (1931) 3–4, 6–8; Ramage (2003) 357; Bömer (1966) 63–85; Gelzer (1968) 176–8; Warde Fowler (1903) 153–5. See Arya (2002) 54–60 for discussion on the cult of Fortuna. On religiosity in Caesar, see Hall (1978); Wardle (2009); Weinstock (1971). As Arya (2002) 203 n. 650 notes, per Kajanto (1981) 537–8, much of the disagreement over Caesar's belief centres on the meaning of *fortuna* in the commentaries themselves.

⁷ See Sall. *B. Jug.* 93.1, 92.6 on Marius and *B. Jug.* 95.4 of Sulla's deserved good *fortuna*. See Cic. *Prov. Cons.* 35 on Caesar's fortune in Gaul. See also Arya (2002) 173, 175, 196–7, 206. For generals such as Pompey, Sulla and Caesar, see Campbell (1987) 23; Murphy (1986) 309; Tappan (1931) 3; Dick (1967) 239; Arya (2002) 180–3, 196–210. Note that Caesar also has a close association with Fortuna in Lucan, who was writing in the first century AD. See Lucan *B. Civ.* 1.84, 124, 226, 5.302, 327. The development of the relationship is apparent in Caesar eating breakfast after Pharsalus and enjoying the carnage related to his *fortuna* at *B. Civ.* 7.796.

⁸ See Crawford (1974) 734 for the coinage of P. Sepullius Macer (44 BC) with winged Victoria on one side and Fortuna on the reverse. See also ibid. 736–7, noting the coin issues for 44 BC. Also note that in 49 BC, the moneyer Q. Sicinius, a partisan of Pompey, issued a silver *denarius* with the first extant Roman numismatic depiction of any Fortuna. See Arya (2002) 157 for the relationship between *fortuna* and victory.

⁹ Cic. *ad Att* X 8b. See *B. Civ.* 3.73, where Caesar states his men should show gratitude to Fortuna, and *B. Civ.* 3.95.1, where Fortuna provides a benefice at Pharsalus.

¹⁰ *B. Gall.* 7.89.2.

¹¹ See Lucan, who uses *fortuna* of Pompey as his defeat becomes inevitable. See Lucan *B. Civ.* 7.488, 505, 646, 686. See also *B. Civ.* 3.103 of Pompey after Pharsalus. See Grillo (2011) 243 on the artificiality of the narrative; Nolan (2014) 60–5 on the literary aspects of Caesar's battles. Gotoff (1984) 5 notes the complexity of the text. Note the studies of Livy where the use both causally and for dramatic effect has been examined. See Lazarus (1978/9) 128.

nising political association and self-promotional aims but also viewing references as part of a cohesive narrative where the pattern of use reveals command concepts.

Any examination of *fortuna* is complicated by its relationship with *felicitas*; however, Caesar's manner of narration ensures that any ambiguity in terminology does not affect an understanding of generalship in the *Bellum Gallicum*. *Fortuna* was related to *felicitas*, the latter term indicating good fortune or the benevolence of the gods that could attend a good commander.[12] *Felicitas* appears in Cicero's list of good command characteristics, is evident in the epithet Sulla *Felix*, and was seen by Suetonius as an aspect of Caesar's success.[13] While *felicitas* might therefore seem a more appropriate term for a study of generalship, Caesar utilised *fortuna* almost exclusively over references to *felicitas*, the latter of which only appears three times in the *Bellum Gallicum*.[14] Caesar's selectivity in this case ensures that there is a consistency of terminology where the patterns and context of *fortuna* can be the focus for an understanding of command.

Ambiguities of meaning related to *fortuna* can be addressed by recognising the context and use on a case-by-case basis. The meaning of the word could be diverse, as it referred to ideas like wealth, the divine force or even *felicitas*; however, it is not a throwaway term.[15] Caesar had the luxury of referring to it retrospectively to promote his military competence and any references may have implications for command concepts.[16] For example, in Book 1 Caesar states that *fortuna* could abandon

---

[12] See Cic. *Pro Lege Manilia* 47 and Kajanto (1981) 523; Arya (2002) 164, 180, 197.

[13] See Cic. *Pro Lege Manilia* 28–9, 47–9, See Pliny *NH* 7.137 for the epithet *felix*. See Suet. *Caes*. 37, where Caesar's chariot axle breaks in front of the temple of Felicitas. See also Plutarch, *Caes*. 38, on Caesar crossing the Adriatic, and Dio 41.46.3. On *felicitas* and *felix* see Kajanto (1981) 523–4; Dick (1967) 237.

[14] See *B. Gall.* 4.25.3, 6.43.6, and for a direct reference to Caesar's *felicitas* see 1.40.13. By contrast, *fortuna* appears forty times.

[15] For examples of wealth, resources or the lot of a state see Caes. *B. Gall.* 1.11.6; 5.3.7; 5.43.4; 6.35.9; *B. Civ.* 2.5.4; 2.36.3; 3.81.2; Sall. *B. Cat.* 33.1; 51.4, 13; 52.12; *B. Jug.* 13.13; 14.2, 7; 18; 23.2. For Caesar's *felicitas* see Caes. *B. Gall.* 4.26.5. For outcomes see *B. Gall.* 2.16.4; 2.31.6; *B. Civ.* 2.6.2; 3.13.3. For ideas of luck or the divine see *B. Gall.* 5.34.2; 6.30.2; 6.35.2, 9; 6.37.10; 7.4.2; Sall. *B. Cat.* 10.2; 52.25; 53.13. For further examples in Sallust see characters such as Catiline, who refers to it directly at *B. Cat.* 58.21, and Jugurtha at *B. Jug.* 56.4. See also *B. Cat.* 2.6; 10.2; 16.2; 25.2; 51.25; *B. Jug.* 1.3; 85.15; 93.1; 95.4. On the meanings in Cicero, Sallust and Caesar see Kajanto (1981) 521–38.

[16] On ancient command in general, see Campbell (1987); Culham (1989); Gilliver (1999). On Caesar, see Conley (1983); Welch (1998); Goldsworthy (1998); Rosenstein (2009); Cic. *Pro Front.* 43; *De Off.* 1.108; *Pro Mur.* 22. On the date of composition see Riggsby (2006) 9–11; Kraus (2009) 159, who notes the lack of resolution on the composition date. Debate centres on whether the work was written periodically or at one time after 51 BC, both of which approaches involved composition after the yearly campaigning.

bad commanders, recognising that general poor behaviour such as criminality was a feature of bad generalship (*B. Gall.* 1.40.12).[17] By a recognition that the appearance of *fortuna* is a deliberate choice of word to support Caesar's opinions, military matters can be examined through patterns and context in which the word appears.

Analysis shows that in the *Bellum Gallicum*, *fortuna* is often used to assist in summarising or interpreting circumstances for the audience. This can be battlefield conditions, such as in Book 2 where Caesar describes a near-defeat at the hands of the Nervii in 57 BC (*B. Gall.* 2.18–27). Near the start of the passage he states that the situation was uneven across the battlefield and that fortunes would have varied outcomes (*B. Gall.* 2.22.2).[18] Coming as it does at the end of a chapter describing the dire situation the Roman army found itself in, this statement has a literary purpose in establishing tension and invoking the idea of uncertainty. However, the inclusion of *fortuna* is designed to encapsulate the inequality of circumstances and the problematic terrain on which the Roman army was forced to fight. *Fortuna* does not play a further role in the account and when the circumstances change, Caesar instead describes the specific events that brought about the Roman victory (*B. Gall.* 2.27.1). This use of *fortuna* in a summary role is often exclusive of other meanings in battle, as Caesar uses other terms to describe chance or random events. This is apparent in the two longest battles, where he uses *fors*, a diminutive of *fortuna*, to describe the location of participants and to establish an atmosphere of chaotic activity and ad hoc measures.[19] Turns of phrase such as *casu* ('by chance') or *accidit ut* ('it happened that') are also used to describe fortuitous or unfavourable events, such as a misaimed spear or an untimely attack against a camp.[20] *Fortuna* can therefore be seen to contextualise battle and is primarily included to assist in rating or summarising a situation.

Fortuna can be clear shorthand when used to qualify the outcome of a battle.[21] The term sometimes appears at or near the end of an account. It serves as a real or potential qualifier of the result, as in the otherwise outstanding success Caesar enjoyed against Ariovistus in 58 BC. In the aftermath of this battle he states of the return of a captive that *fortuna* did not take anything away from the victory through the loss of a friend, evoking a potential lessening of his pleasure had the prisoner

---

[17] *aut male re gesta fortunam defuisse aut aliquot facinore comperto avaritiam esse convictam.*

[18] *itaque in tanta rerum iniquitate fortunae quoque eventus varii sequebantur.* On the literary construction of this battle, see Nolan (2014) 66–71.

[19] See *B. Gall.* 2.21.1; 7.87.3. See also Kajanto (1981) 522.

[20] *B. Gall.* 5.39.2; 5.48.8. See also, for *casus*, 1.12.6; 2.21.6; 3.5.2; 6.37.1; for *dubium*, 6.7.6; 6.31.2; 7.80.6–7. For examples of *accidere* see 3.3.2; 3.14.5; 3.25.2; 4.29.1; 5.33.1–2; 5.39.2; 6.30.2; 7.35.2.

[21] For instances of *fortuna* appearing at or near the end of a battle see *B. Gall.* 1.53; 3.6; 5.34; 5.58; 6.42; 7.89. See also 5.44 for the anecdote of the centurions Vorenus and Pullo.

not been rescued (*B. Gall.* 1.53.6–7).²² *Fortuna* in this case is cited to evoke a potential qualification of an otherwise outstanding result. Occasionally *fortuna* is given a positive association, such as the approval of a plan by Labienus, yet it mostly points towards situations where Caesar's ideals might not be met.²³ This is more nuanced than the simple appearance of a beneficial Roman Fortuna and illustrates the difference between references in the political sphere and the minutiae of command in the *Bellum Gallicum*.²⁴ It is particularly obvious in Book 4, where Caesar describes the 55 BC invasion of Britain. At the conclusion of the landing he states that his failure to pursue the enemy was due to the absence of Roman cavalry, noting that this one thing was missing from his prior good fortune (*B. Gall.* 4.26.5).²⁵ He includes this overt qualification to recognise that an important aspect of victory was not met, that being the pursuit and slaughter of the enemy. Similar principles apply when Caesar is discussing his subordinates, as in the closing chapter of Galba's defence at Octodurus (*B. Gall.* 3.6).²⁶ This account of an assault on a Roman camp in the winter of 57–56 BC has been seen by scholars as both a criticism and approbation of the actions of Galba, given that Caesar appears reluctant to praise or criticise the commander directly.²⁷ However, at the end of the battle the statement that Galba did not want to tempt *fortuna* further suggests that his success was fortuitous, but the conduct and tactics were not necessarily to be considered doctrine (*B. Gall.* 3.6.4).²⁸ The qualification is particularly useful as it points to Caesar's opinion of a battle or aspects that confounded the objectives of a commander.

The absence of any reference to *fortuna* is also an indicator of Caesar's opinion. In his account of a battle against the Usipetes and Tencteri, fought in 55 BC, he states

---

[22] For other examples see *B. Gall.* 1.40.12; 4.26.5; 5.34.2.

[23] *B. Gall.* 5.58.6. Even in this passage *fortuna* puts an obstacle between the wishes of the commander and his objective, placing a proviso on victory. See also Welch (1998) 98–101 on Labienus. Rambaud (1966) 298 regards Caesar as generally downplaying the role of Labienus. There is often a negative association even where the context and meaning vary. See *B. Gall.* 1.32.4; 1.34.4; 1.36.3; 1.40.12; 3.6.2; 3.12.3; 4.26.5; 5.34.2; 7.1.5; 7.40.7; 7.62.8; 7.63.8; 7.89.2. Note the potential for harm at 1.53.7; 2.22.2; 2.31.6; 3.6.4; 5.55.2. For exceptions see 6.37.10; 5.58.6; 7.54.4.

[24] See Kajanto (1981) 538, who cites *B. Gall.* 6.30.2 and regards Caesar's view of *fortuna* as something that foils generals' plans. See Kajanto (1981) 521; Arya (2002) 135–6.

[25] There is also a rare use of *feliciter* and an invocation of the gods at *B. Gall.* 4.25.3, indicating how important Caesar considered this battle for his reputation. On pursuit, see Goldsworthy (1996) 166. See also Suet. *Div. Iul.* 60.

[26] For other subordinates see *B. Gall.* 5.34.2; 5.44.14; 5.58.6; 6.42.1–2.

[27] For two interpretations of Galba see Lendon (1999) 306; Welch (1998) 93.

[28] See also *B. Gall.* 3.5.2–3. The defenders sallied from the camp in a desperate measure proposed by Galba's subordinates.

that over 430,000 of the enemy were killed without a single Roman casualty (*B. Gall.* 4.15.3). While the veracity of the figures cited should be questioned, it is the absence of *fortuna* that points to a similar military principle to that expressed in the British invasion.[29] To be deemed a total success there must be a pursuit, something evident in this battle in a graphic description of cavalry used to cut down fleeing non-combatants, and a massacre that ended at the Rhine (*B. Gall.* 4.15.2–5). There is no mention of *fortuna* as the victory did not require any qualification. Other battles where Caesar enjoyed total victory follow a similar pattern, as evidenced in a battle against the Helvetii described in Book 1, and the naval victory over the Veneti in Book 3 (*B. Gall.* 1.27–9, 3.16). Both battles omit any reference to *fortuna*, as Caesar regarded the victories as complete with the total defeat of both nations.[30] There is a pattern of absence that points to Caesar's opinion of victory just as clearly as when *fortuna* appears in the text.

Patterns around the use of *fortuna* illustrate principles of Roman command, for example to show that good leadership is prioritised over ideas of courage. Ancient sources often phrased Roman attitudes in terms of a dichotomy where *virtus* overcame or opposed the influence of *fortuna* in war, and throughout the *Bellum Gallicum virtus* is certainly presented as a positive attribute.[31] However, the proximity of the two concepts suggests that Caesar regarded a reliance on courage as a feature of a desperate situation.[32] This is most apparent in the defeat of Sabinus and Cotta, a massacre that occurred in 54 BC that Caesar blames primarily on Sabinus (*B. Gall.* 5.27–37). Caesar states 'our men, deserted by their leader and *fortuna*, nevertheless placed all hope in *virtus*' (*B. Gall.* 5.34.2).[33] The *tametsi . . . tamen* clause used in this

---

[29] Apart from the size of the number cited, sources can be inconsistent. See Plutarch, *Caes.* 22, who cites 400,000, but at *Cato Min.* 51 cites 300,000.

[30] Note also the victory over the Nervii at *B. Gall.* 2.28.1–2. There is no mention of *fortuna* at the end of the battle and Caesar describes total victory through his use of *calamitatae* and *ad internecionem*.

[31] On the *virtus* vs *fortuna* dichotomy see Cic. *Tusc. Disp.* 2.30; 3.36; 5.2; 17, 25. See also Sallust *B. Jug.* 1.3; *B. Cat.* 53.3; Lucan *B. Civ.* 9.569. Weinstock (1971) 113 states that Romans never accepted the absolute rule of *fortuna* and contended that she helped the valiant. For a discussion of *virtus* and tactics in Caesar see also Lendon (1999) 306–16.

[32] Kajanto (1981) 538 notes that at *B. Civ.* 3.73.4 Caesar trusts to *virtus* to overcome *fortuna*. See Curio at Caes. *B. Civ.* 2.30.2 for the proximity of the concepts in disaster. As Krebs (2006) 132 notes, Caesar, *B. Civ.* 1.72.2–3, defines the imperator's duty as follows: *cur denique Fortunam periclitaretur? praesertim cum non minus esset imperatoris consilio superare quam gladio*. Note that the characters stress their own *virtus* over planning, even if planning and good leadership are often the real keys to success. See *B. Gall.* 1.13.4–6, 40.8–9.

[33] *nostri tametsi ab duce et a fortuna deserebantur, tamen omnem spem salutis in virtute ponebant*. On the representation of Sabinus see Powell (1998) 119.

statement shows how *fortuna* and *virtus* are concurrent with the dire nature of the situation when command has failed.[34] This is not the only instance where courage is proximate to the idea of desperation, as in the Battle of Octodurus Caesar describes the desperate sally by the besieged defenders as the placement of all hope in *virtus*, then contextualises the result as fortuitous.[35] When *fortuna* is brought into the narrative, a reliance on *virtus* is an act of desperation that can signify command failure.

This attitude is visible in the anecdote of Vorenus and Pullo, two centurions given a vignette in Book 5 during Quintus Cicero's defence of Aduatuca. Both men recklessly advanced beyond the defences, found themselves in trouble, and returned to camp only through mutual support (*B. Gall.* 5.44).[36] Caesar states at the end of this episode, 'so *fortuna* changed for each in competition and battle, so that, despite their mutual hostility, one was as help and succour to the other, and it was not possible to decide who seemed foremost in *virtus*' (*B. Gall.* 5.44.14).[37] This passage has been studied for its use of *exempla* as a judgement on the earlier failure of Sabinus and Cotta, and its implications for the behaviour of centurions.[38] It also describes an initial mistake that is corrected through acts of courage, where, importantly, there is no victor and the impersonal third-person *videretur* is used to judge *virtus*. *Fortuna* is brought into the account to support the idea that these men were reckless, and their reliance on *virtus* a last resort to escape the dangers of the situation. The proximity of the two concepts in an exemplary passage suggests that Caesar looked to *virtus* only when other means of victory had failed.

Patterns of use have further implications for understanding command responsibility, most importantly that a good general should not use unforeseen circumstances as an excuse for failure, and any relationship with *fortuna*, such as Caesar displayed in his political life, should not extend to a reliance at a practical level.[39] *Fortuna* can appear as a force in its own right when the term refers to the divine entity, and can often receive partial credit or blame for events in the *Bellum Civile*.[40] In the instances

---

[34] See also the last desperate gamble by Catiline at *B. Cat.* 58.21. See too *B. Gall.* 7.59.6, where *virtus* is a last resort.

[35] *B. Gall.* 3.5.3; 3.6.4.

[36] On the idea that the centurions are reckless, see Nolan (2016) 46–50.

[37] *sic fortuna in contentione et certamine utrumque versavit, ut alter alteri inimicus auxilio salutique esset neque diiudicari posset, uter utri virtute anteferendus videretur.*

[38] See Brown (2004) 307; Rambaud (1966) 231; Rasmussen (1963) 27–9; Nolan (2016) 51.

[39] On leadership and causality see Rey (2010) 25–8, 41. Rey notes the focus in ancient sources on moral factors.

[40] In Caesar's *Bellum Civile, fortuna* has a strong causal dimension. See *B. Civ.* 2.14.3; 2.17.4; 2.30.2; 3.10.6; 3.27.1; 3.79.3; 3.95.1. See also Sall. *B. Cat.* 10.2 on *fortuna* growing cruel towards Rome, and Lucan, *B. Civ.* 1.124; 1.135; 1.226; 2.735 for inferences of dual agency

where Caesar omits *fortuna* in the *Bellum Gallicum*, this could be understood as assigning responsibility solely to the commander and combatants. This is illustrated in Book 1, where he states that the tribe of the Boii appeared on his flank in the middle of the battle against the Helvetii (*B. Gall.* 1.25.6–7). This tribe was clearly a threat, as he moved his third line to engage it; however, the description is matter-of-fact, there is no mention of the machinations of *fortuna* and Caesar takes full credit for the remedial action.[41] This is more than self-promotion, as a responsibility to account for the unexpected is consistent across the work and apparent in the language used of other Roman commanders. In the meeting of the defenders at Octodurus, Caesar summarises the choice to stay in camp as *eventum experiri* ('to explore an outcome') and the choice to seek escape as *salutem contenderent* ('to strive for safety').[42] Whether deliberate or unconscious, this choice of language ensures that there is no reliance on luck in this decision making, even if the defenders are ultimately somewhat fortunate. This pattern of references is consistent even when Caesar suffers his personal defeat at Gergovia in 52 BC, which is blamed on the soldiery rather than any matters of chance or luck.[43] Even where *fortuna* is mentioned, its responsibility is limited, as in the defeat of Sabinus and Cotta, where it is conspicuous in its inability to save the army (*B. Gall.* 5.34.2).[44] Furthermore, there is little mention of *fortuna* even where Caesar describes tightly fought or difficult encounters, for example when he states of a battle fought by the legate Labienus that the outcome of victory was uncertain (*B. Gall.*7.62.6–7).[45] In this case the uncertain result is an *incerto . . . exitu*, as there was a risk involved. However, there is no inference that *fortuna* was involved in responsibilities or could excuse the individuals in command.

in Roman epic. For the potential to influence matters see also *B. Gall.* 1.53.7; 5.34.2; 5.58.6; 6.30.2; 6.30.4; 6.35.2; and Kajanto (1981) 538, noting that Kajanto does not regard Caesar's *fortuna* as a supernatural agent.

[41] The standards are clearly turned in response to the enemy appearance on the flank and the army is not already positioned to meet the threat. Even the main enemy force renews the fight in response to this unexpected appearance.

[42] See *B. Gall.* 3.3.3–4; 3.5.2–3. The desperate attempt to break out is described as *extremum auxilium experirentur*, not *fortunam experirentur*.

[43] For Gergovia see 7.36–7.52; 7.52.1–3; and Nolan (2014) 119–23 on blame.

[44] For the blame of Sabinus, see also *B. Gall.* 5.26–37; 5.52.4–6. See also Welch (1998) 95; Powell (1998) 117–20; Nolan (2014) 205–13.

[45] There is an interesting contrast here as Labienus takes the risk in crossing a river, but the death of the enemy leader Camulogenus is described at 7.62.8 as *eandem fortunam tulit Camulogenus*. The passage shows that even where Romans take risks, *fortuna* is associated with the enemy.

This responsibility to account for the unforeseen is complemented by an emphasis on the avoidance of risk.[46] *Fortuna* can evoke ideas of luck or chance, and as Iiro Kajanto notes, could stand for the 'incalculable' or the risks inherent in military endeavours.[47] It is therefore important that where the Roman perspective is adopted or described in the *Bellum Gallicum*, *fortuna* does not appear as a contextualising force at the start of a battle or campaign, and variations on *fortuna . . . experior* ('to essay fortune') are never applied to the Romans. For example, the overall pattern of language in the first invasion of Britain suggests a consistent desire to minimise references to the risks of the expedition, evident in the absence of *fortuna* until after the landing.[48] Instead, Caesar's desire to show his caution is conveyed through his extensive description of logistics prior to the crossing from Gaul (*B. Gall.* 4.21–2).[49] Caesar only mentions *fortuna* at an early point in an episode when he wishes to indicate the battle was not at a time or place of his choice, as is the case in the battle against the Nervii.[50] This pattern is indicative of his desire to present Roman command as generally careful and cautious, and to downplay any inference of recklessness.

Ideas of risk minimisation and remediation apply even when describing fortuitous or harmful forces such as variable weather conditions. In the *Bellum Gallicum*, Caesar echoes Polybius in assigning responsibility for anticipating the weather to the commander, who should be prepared or able to adapt as necessary.[51] In his description of the two invasions of Britain, Caesar mentions adverse weather conditions such as storms or winds that damage or blow his forces off course.[52] He makes no

---

[46] For discussion of risk-taking see Rosenstein (2009) 92–4; Culham (1989) 192; Goldsworthy (1998) 195–6, 199; (2007) 89. See also Pol. 9.12–16; Cic. *Pro Lege Manilia* 28–9 on minimising risks through preparation and knowledge. Caesar himself asks why he should make trial of *fortuna* at *B. Civ.* 1.72.2.

[47] Kajanto (1981) 522 notes this in *fortunam experiri* ('to test *fortuna*') and *fortunam temptare* ('to tempt *fortuna*') and notes at 539 that *temptare fortunam* and similar statements are 'set phrases' for chance in Livy.

[48] See Campbell (1987) 22–3, who cites Suet. *Aug.* 25. 4 on Augustus and caution. See also Welch (1998) 93 on praise for the caution of subordinates.

[49] See Goldsworthy (2007) 102, who notes the constant mention of logistics, for example *B. Gall.* 1.23; 2.10; 2.38; 4.7; 5.31; 6.10; 7.10; 7.32. See also Ramage (2003) 334 on *diligentia*.

[50] *B. Gall.* 2.22.2. See also *B. Afr.* 83.1, where Caesar was pressed into fighting by over-eager troops and used the watchword *felicitas*. This is not Caesar writing; however, the use of *felicitas* where he is reluctant to fight expresses the same ideas as the use of *fortuna* in the *Bellum Gallicum*.

[51] Polybius describes these aspects of command and how they should be foreseen at 9.12.1, 6–7; 16.2–3. See Walbank (2002) 23–4. For Caesar's belief that a commander should understand the weather see *B. Gall.* 4.23.5–6.

[52] *B. Gall.* 4.29–31, 34–6; 5.5, 10–11.

mention of *fortuna* in describing these affairs, simply describing his remedial actions. Similarly, when the weather turns to his advantage in the naval battle against the Veneti, he makes use of *subito* ('sudden') and *opportuna* ('opportune'), a recognition of the unpredictable without evoking divine or random influences (*B. Gall.* 3.15.5).[53] This is despite the immense advantage that his ships gained when the enemy was becalmed (*B. Gall.* 3.15.3–5) and is in marked contrast to the *Bellum Civile*, where *fortuna* is more influential in weather and other military matters.[54] The absence of references in the *Bellum Gallicum* suggests that in this work such things simply happen in war, are a pleasant surprise when they work in the commander's favour, or must be overcome if they work against his will.

An examination of language patterns and the absence of bestowments by *fortuna* also shows the degree to which Caesar prioritises the forcing of or capitalisation of mistakes by the enemy.[55] This approach is apparent in the campaign against the Usipetes and Tencteri in Book 4, where Caesar describes his outright joy that the enemy delivered their leaders into his hands (*B. Gall.* 4.13.4–6). He uses *opportunissime res accidit* ('a most opportune thing came about') to contextualise the unexpectedness of this move (*B. Gall.* 4.13.4). This phrase and the use of the term *gavisus* ('delighted') to show his pleasure is indicative of the fortuitousness of the enemy mistake and suggests that while unforeseen, it was not influenced by concepts of *fortuna* (*B. Gall.* 4.13.6). The idea of exploitation appears in other battles when patterns of reference are considered. In the description of a battle between Sabinus and the Venelli, the enemy and even the Roman soldiery criticise the commander for not seeking battle, ostensibly suggesting that a commander was expected to show courage and meet their enemy in open combat (*B. Gall.* 3.17). However, Caesar's language supports Sabinus' decision to trick the enemy and hold back from a direct confrontation until the enemy made a tactical error. While the Gallic leader Viridovix gave Sabinus *potestas* ('the ability') to fight, the Roman commander only acted when an *opportunitas* presented itself (*B. Gall.* 3.17.5–7; 3.18.5). Eventually the Gauls were fooled into thinking that the Roman leader had made an error and

---

[53] Note the use of *subito* at *B. Gall.* 4.28.2, and *accidit ut* at 4.29.1; also *tranquillitate consecuta* at 5.23.6. These are Caesar's concessions to the unexpected nature of weather and unusual tides.

[54] See *B. Civ.* 1.40.7, 52.3, 59.2; 2.14.3, 32.6; 3.10.3, 6, 7, 26.4, 68.1, 73, 95.1.

[55] As Gilliver (1999) 92–4 observes, because battles could be so decisive, it was considered vital to ensure circumstances were as favourable as possible. Gilliver at 120 also catalogues the kind of mistakes that might be exploited. On the Roman style of warfare, see Rosenstein (2009) 91; Gilliver (1999) 92–125. See also *B. Gall.* 1.51; 2.8–9; 3.24; 4.34; 5.49–51; 6.7–8; 6.10; 7.44.1.

they fell into Sabinus' trap.⁵⁶ The success of this ploy shows the wisdom of the subordinate's approach, and how it coincides with a command style, further enunciated by Labienus in Book 6, in which battle was preferably engaged in once the enemy made a mistake.⁵⁷ Caesar's choice of language suggests that exploitation was a normal expectation of Roman commanders and that they should not rely on luck for such opportunities.

The general principles enunciated are consistent even for exceptional adversaries. While Caesar's use of *fortuna* assists in the characterisation of his enemies, particularly the Gauls, as reckless or unreliable, there are some exceptions to this reductive view.⁵⁸ Ambiorix, the major opponent from 54 to 53 BC, is given similarities with Roman commanders in his tactics and in the way *fortuna* is absent from his representation. In the ambush of Sabinus and Cotta, Ambiorix appears to have inferior forces and there is no trope of an enemy horde to explain his victory (*B. Gall.* 5.27.4–8; 5.28.1). He uses stratagem to outwit his opponents by forcing a mistake, and shows a complete lack of error in the anticipation, provocation and execution of his victory.⁵⁹ As Caesar is careful to note, *At barbaris consilium non defuit* ('But the barbarians were not without a plan'), drawing attention to Ambiorix's foresight (*B. Gall.* 5.34.1). Another exceptional leader is Vercingetorix, the major opponent in 52 BC, who is portrayed in opposition to general Gallic leadership.⁶⁰

---

[56] Contrast the same Sabinus' utter failure to plan at 5.33.1–3.

[57] *B. Gall.* 6.8.3: *'habetis' inquit 'milites, quam petistis facultatem'*. Here Labienus uses *facultas*, not *fortuna*, of an opportunity to lure the enemy to cross a river and engage on unfavourable ground. At 6.7.4 Labienus enunciates the idea that a commander should await the enemy making a mistake, referring to the daring of the enemy as a characteristic that will enable him to prepare a ruse.

[58] Caesar characterises the Gauls as generally poorer tacticians and *fortuna* often forms part of that representation. See *B. Gall.* 4.13.3: *cognita Gallorum infirmitate*; 3.8.3: *ut sunt Gallorum subita et repentina consilia*. Variations on *experior. . . fortunam* are also exclusively applied to the enemy. The Nervii convince their allies to essay *fortuna*, the expression is used of the Aedui and Venetii, and Ariovistus and Vercingetorix both use it when talking to or describing their peers. See *B. Gall.* 1.31.14; 1.36.3; 2.16.4; 2.31.6; 3.8.4; 7.89.2. Caesar uses this type of language even in instances when the enemy are being cautious, part of a literary dichotomy between Romans and their enemies apparent in other ancient sources. See also 5.55.2; 7.4.2; 7.64.2. See Lazarus (1978/9) 129 for a discussion of Liv. 24.40–4, 30.30–1. Sallust uses it of Catiline at *B. Cat.* 57.5 when he is desperate, and of Micipsa at *B. Jug.* 7.1. It is also the language of Marius' soothsayer at *B. Jug.* 63.1. For a contrast to Caesar's own writing see *B. Civ.* 2.30.2; 3.95.1; and most importantly a speech by Caesar at 3.73. See also Hall (1998) 12, 22. This view fits with Hall's understanding of Roman *ratio*.

[59] See *B. Gall.* 5.32–4. For the battle see Powell (1998) 117–24.

[60] On the representation of Vercingetorix see Kraus (2010) 44; Jervis (2001) 167–76; and see

In the planning at the Battle of Alesia, the council of Gauls is described with the words *de exitu suarum fortunarum consultabant* ('they deliberated on the end of their fortunes') (*B. Gall.* 7.77.2).[61] While Vercingetorix was presumably a part of this council, it is important to note that the statement references *fortuna* in describing their aims as a group.[62] It is a marked contrast to the more specific reasoning assigned to Vercingetorix's planning an attack earlier in the book:

> if the [Roman] infantry bore help to their men and delayed there, they could not complete their journey. If, and he believed this would come about, they left behind their baggage and looked to their own safety, they would be stripped of both necessities and their dignity. With regard to the enemy cavalry, they need not doubt that not one of those men would dare to advance beyond the battle line. So that his men acted with more spirit, all his forces would be placed in front of the camp and strike fear in the enemy. (*B. Gall.* 7.66.4–7)[63]

Vercingetorix's tactics are explained in detail, showing that he had solid reasoning for his actions and clear objectives, as opposed to the more generalised laments of the council.[64] The contrast is so strong that when Vercingetorix seeks to dupe his fellow Gauls, he uses *fortuna* as an appeal to superstition (*B. Gall.* 7.20.6).[65] Caesar also emphasises risk minimisation as Vercingetorix' words echo his own in the *Bellum Civile* in rejecting a dependence on *fortuna*.[66] As Vercingetorix states, 'he would be content with the infantry he had held before, as he would not tempt *fortuna* or fight in open battle, but, as he had an abundance of cavalry, it was very easy to prevent the Romans from getting food and forage' (*B. Gall.* 7.64.2–3). Vercingetorix did not wish to tempt fortune by engaging in a pitched battle and is given good reason for doing so. He has a complex rationale alongside a contrast to *fortuna* to show that he

---

Le Bohec (1998b) 102 on Vercingetorix as general.

[61] Caesar also appears to be foreshadowing their defeat by referring to *fortuna* rather than just an ending or result. The speech of Critognatus that follows makes an appeal to ancient Gallic courage as part of the desperate situation.

[62] See also *B. Gall.* 7.4.2 where the older, presumably, wiser Gauls discuss their aversion to war in terms of *fortuna*. Caesar often uses *fortuna* when adopting the enemy perspective. See *B. Gall.* 3.6.2; 6.37.10; 7.89.2. The depth of the representation extends even to the words of Labienus, who frames a ruse in terms of *fortuna* so that his enemies can understand at *B. Gall.* 6.7.6.

[63] See also *B. Gall.* 7.14.7–8; 7.18.3–4.

[64] Note that this detail also creates tension as the audience envisages the success of the enemy leader.

[65] See also Labienus at *B. Gall.* 6.7.6.

[66] *B. Civ.* 1.72.2.

was an exceptional Gallic leader who generally adhered to Caesar's ideals regarding planning and the avoidance of risk.

While these principles are consistent for most of the work, Book 6 contains a striking and discordant use of *fortuna* that provides valuable insight into the aspect of war which caused Caesar the most frustration. In Book 6 he was faced with the task of describing a year in which there were no great victories or defeats, only inconclusive campaigns and defensive battles.[67] He states near the beginning of the book that the enemy leader Ambiorix had decided not to engage in battle, so the entire book is written with the knowledge that his main antagonist had deliberately avoided a confrontation (*B. Gall.* 6.5.3–4). Caesar later confirms 'There was, as we have shown above, no sure band, no town, no garrison to defend itself in arms, but the multitude was scattered in all directions' (*B. Gall.* 6.34.1–2). Here he is quite candid about the difficulties of a campaign against an enemy who refused to offer battle or a place to assault. It is not just this one opponent, as in this book he also describes an unsuccessful attempt to lure the Suebi into a confrontation (*B. Gall.* 6.10.2–3; 6.10.5). The enemy consistently refused to fight, which Caesar openly states was a problematic aspect of the campaign.

In order to create a positive account of his exploits, Caesar employs some unique methods, the most obvious being the inclusion of a long ethnographic description of the Gauls and Germani, which is clearly designed to distract from the lack of a victorious campaign narrative (*B. Gall.* 6.11–28).[68] The attempt to divert attention is evident in the structure of the episode with the Suebi, which pauses abruptly for the digression.[69] Caesar's annoyance even manifests itself through literary embellishment, such as the vicious curses which a dying king casts at Ambiorix (*B. Gall.* 6.31.5). There are various techniques on display that point to an underlying displeasure at the enemy strategy of evasion and his failure to overcome this.

---

[67] Gerrish (2018) 351 notes the difficulties Caesar faced regarding 55 and 54 BC both as commander, and later as author. This would be particularly so if Caesar wrote Book 6 at the end of the campaign year, when he was not aware of the success he would enjoy in 52 BC. See also Kraus (2010) 48 on narrative 'flags' in this book.

[68] On the description of the Gauls see Allen-Hornblower (2014) 682. As Allen-Hornblower argues, interpolation of the ethnographic passages is not likely, and the section cannot be justified on entertainment grounds alone. See also Schadee (2008) 175, who notes the positive impression made on the reader, despite the lack of any military success on Caesar's part. Burns (2003) 93, by contrast, calls the excursus a 'rhetorical pause' to reflect on what has gone before.

[69] Caesar adopts a similar technique at *B. Gall.* 5.12–14, where he inserts a description of Britain into a campaign against elusive British chariots. Note the abrupt transition of 5.14 to 5.15.

More importantly, Caesar places *fortuna* prominently throughout the book to contextualise affairs and even causation within its framework, which is a marked departure from the rest of the work.[70] *Fortuna* is normally only used for context, such as at Aduatuca in Book 5, or the first invasion of Britain.[71] In the ultimately successful campaign against the Veneti, Caesar uses the less evocative *labor* to capture short-term setbacks, and in Book 1 he only hints at blaming *fortuna* for the escape of Ariovistus.[72] This subtle inference is in dramatic contrast with the statement in Book 6 that 'As is often in all matters, so Fortuna is powerful in military affairs' (*B. Gall.* 6.30.2), a statement that echoes Sallust's references to its potency and Caesar's own references in the *Bellum Civile*.[73] For the first time in the *Bellum Gallicum*, Caesar ascribes a generalised and powerful role to *fortuna*. By understanding this usage, it is possible to determine how frustrating this inconclusive campaign was to the Roman general as he sought to explain his lack of progress.

Book 6 includes the appearance of *fortuna* in other statements regarding its influence in war, further indicating Caesar's frustration with his evasive enemy. Immediately after the ethnographic passage he contextualises the escape of Ambiorix from some scouts with the following two statements:

> As is often in all matters, so Fortuna is powerful in military affairs, for it happened by great accident that he [Basilus, the Roman Commander] came across the man himself [Ambiorix] unaware and indeed unprepared, and his approach was seen by all before rumour or a message could be borne, so it was of great fortune that with all military equipment around him seized, with carriages and horses taken he himself escaped death. (*B. Gall.* 6.30.2–3)

---

[70] For frequency see *B. Gall.* 6.7.6; 6.30.2–4; 6.35.2; 6.35.9; 6.37.10; 6.42.1. The word is used nine times in the book. Champeaux (1987) 266–7 observes the dramatic change in use of *fortuna* in Book 6 but asks if it is indicative of a change in attitude.

[71] For Aduatuca see *B. Gall.* 5.34.2; for the first invasion of Britain see 4.26.5.

[72] *B. Gall.* 3.14.1; 1.53.3–5. *Fortuna* is only mentioned in relation to a rescue, bringing it into the narrative.

[73] *multum cum in omnibus rebus, tum in re militari potest Fortuna*. *Fortuna* in Book 6 of the *Bellum Gallicum* resembles its potent form in the *Bellum Civile*, probably reflecting Caesar's greater concern with how the book would be received. On the power of *fortuna* in the *Bellum Civile* see 1.72.2, where it appears in words attributed to Caesar, and 2.32 in a speech by Curio, where it appears four times in one chapter. See also *B. Civ.* 3.10.6; 3.68.1; Sall. *B. Cat.* 8.1; *B. Jug.* 102.9.

so Fortuna was very strong both for experiencing and avoiding danger. (*B. Gall.* 6.30.4)[74]

These are strident comments about *fortuna* and its role in war, as indicated by the capitalisation in translation, repetition of the word and its relatively powerful agency.[75] Coming so soon after Caesar describes his failure to meet the Suebi in battle, and considering the lack of a positive result, it also associates *fortuna* with the general elusiveness of his enemies. There are further statements about its power, indirectly influencing an audience's understanding of the inconclusive results.[76] At one stage Caesar even uses *fortunatissimos*, the only time this superlative is used in his commentaries (*B. Gall.* 6.35.9). *Fortuna* is here at its most powerful, because Caesar's text reflects the frustration and lack of agency experienced while prosecuting and then writing about the campaign.

This use of *fortuna* also extends to the type that is fickle and wayward in its benefits, suggesting that a failure to engage the enemy was even more confounding than actual defeat, as Caesar invokes ideas of divine perversity to explain the reason for events. In the defence of Quintus Cicero's camp, which also occurs in Book 6, *fortuna* is not only influential but forms part of the following statement:

> [Caesar] judged that fortune was very powerful in the sudden approach of the enemy, even more so because the barbarians were turned from the very rampart and gates of the camp . . . The Germani, who had crossed the Rhine with the plan that they devastate Ambiorix' borders, drawn to the camp of the Romans bore the most longed for wish to Ambiorix. (*B. Gall.* 6.42.1–3)

In this passage *fortuna* is influential both in the appearance of the enemy and in the frustration of their assault.[77] However, the last sentence of the passage is critical in understanding Caesar's position. The Germani were brought over the Rhine

---

[74] *nam magno accidit casu, ut in ipsum incautum etiam atque imparatum incideret, priusque eius adventus ab omnibus videretur, quam fama ac nuntius adferretur, sic magnae fuit fortunae omni militari instrumento quod circum se habebat erepto raedis equisque comprehensis ipsum effugere mortem.* Note the use of *casus* and *accidere* at *B. Gall.* 6.30.2. Note also the use of *valeo* to indicate the strength of Fortuna at *B. Gall.* 6.30.4: *sic et ad subeundum periculum et ad vitandum multum Fortuna valuit.* See also *B. Civ.* 3.10.6–7; 3.68.1.

[75] The capitalisation suits the use of *Fortuna potest* as the subject of the sentence. See Kajanto (1981) 521. See also Powell (1998) 116, who notes too the use of *fortuna* and 'pre-emptive writing'. See also *B. Gall.* 6.43.6 and the use of *felicitas* to describe Ambiorix's escapes.

[76] See *B. Gall.* 6.35.2–5; 6.42.1.

[77] Welch (1998) 97–8 notes the bad luck of Quintus Cicero.

to assist the Romans, then brought a *beneficium* to Ambiorix by turning on their employers. There is a twisting of objectives and results in this use of *fortuna* that evokes the Greek concept of *tyche*, a generally fickle power that both gives and takes away.[78] The use of this type of *fortuna* solely in this book supports the idea that a defensive, inconclusive campaign was even more difficult to account for than a defeat, hence the assigning of responsibility to divine forces. *Fortuna* has a unique role in this book that is critical to an understanding of generalship, as it illustrates Caesar's priorities and the importance of being able to engage his enemy in a direct and conclusive confrontation.

In modern thought there is the idea that a good leader creates their own luck. This sentiment echoes contemporaries of Caesar such as Sallust and Cicero, where there is an association between *fortuna*, *felicitas* and good commanders. However, a close study of the presentation of the *Bellum Gallicum* presents a more comprehensive understanding of *fortuna*, in terms of both how it is used to assess battle, and what it reveals about generalship. Caesar was an accomplished commander and while there are artifices throughout the work, the underlying command principles should not be ignored simply because the work is primarily self-promotional, or because Caesar and other generals cultivated a relationship with the concept in their public lives. Caesar would have wanted to illustrate his correct knowledge of military principles, and as such *fortuna* plays a didactic role, more so than in the *Bellum Civile*, where it is often included to undermine his political opponents. Throughout the *Bellum Gallicum*, *fortuna* is evoked at important points in each episode to assess battle in a manner that appears deliberate due to the consistency of the approach, the ubiquity of the term in contextualising matters, and the way it amplifies and echoes the rest of the narrative. Through analysis of the patterns of use it is apparent that Caesar was highly risk-averse in prosecuting battle or in taking chances unless he could exploit an enemy mistake, and that this was a principle he expected of all good commanders, even amongst his enemies. Context also shows that the understanding of *virtus* as a defining feature of Roman warfare can be qualified to recognise that it had a subordinate role to good leadership. While *virtus* was important and an essential component of good soldiery, its proximity to *fortuna* in the text suggests that effective generalship was far more important for success, and a reliance on

---

[78] On fickle *fortuna* see Kajanto (1981) 525; Craig (1931) 108; Arya (2002) 60, 116–17, 135–6. See also Liv. 45.8.6–7, 45.40–1; Pol. 29.20–1; Plut. *Aem* 27.1–4; 36.1–4. For the appearance of *fortuna* with the characteristics of *tyche* see also Sall. *B. Cat.* 8.1; 10.2; Tac. *Hist* 4.47; Cic. *Piso* 22. For Fortuna's ultimate betrayal of Caesar in Lucan see *B. Civ.* 10.339, 525. On *tyche*, see Kajanto (1981) 525–32; Arya (2002) 117–20. See Walbank (2002) 29 on *tyche* and Polybius. See also Culham (1989) 191–2.

courage often a feature of desperate circumstances. The key observation is that the forcing of enemy mistakes while avoiding one's own errors was a critical aspect of command. When a commander is not given a chance to meet the enemy and exploit their mistakes, such as in Book 6, *fortuna* appears at its most powerful in foiling plans and frustrating objectives. Caesar's usually clear battlefield causality gives way to a martial landscape where *fortuna* is fickle, outcomes unpredictable and a commander struggles to impose their will. When contrasted to the use of *fortuna* throughout the rest of the work, this description of his inability to overcome the enemy, and the blatant reliance on divinity for context, provide crucial insights into the military mind of Caesar and how he perceived the challenges of command.

7 Remembering P. Quinctilius Varus: Opposing Perspectives on the Memory and Memorialisation of the Failed General in the *Annales* of Tacitus

Daniel Crosby

Introduction

Following the excavations at Kalkriese and then the relatively recent bimillennial, there has been a renewed interest in P. Quinctilius Varus and the disaster by which he was made infamous: the Teutoburg Forest in AD 9.[1] The question of the location of the battlefield has been taken up with a renewed interest as scholars once again tackle the fraught issue of the connections between author, text and the historical event.[2] Varus' reputation as an incompetent military commander has received a more even-handed evaluation as part of the broader question of whom or what to blame.[3] The descriptions of the battle, especially that of Tacitus, have profited from more literary studies, focusing on themes like transgression and memory.[4] Varus has even

---

[1] Schlüter et al. (1992); Schlüter (1999).

[2] In this chapter, I shall not enter into this debate, since it is not germane to my argument. However, I find the debate about the relevance of our literary sources to the question of the location of the battlefield to be a fascinating commentary on the theories that distinguish specialties within the field of Classical Studies, broadly defined. See Tönnies (1992); Gruber (2008); Wiegels (2011); Schmitzer (2011) 187–9; and especially Timpe (2012) for a review of recent scholarship on the socio-political and historical aspects of the study of the Battle of the Teutoburg Forest, along with a sober perspective on the association of the battlefield with the finds at Kalkriese, and the issues for future scholarship that have opened in the wake of the explosion of interest in the battle.

[3] Van Wickevoort-Crommelin (1999) 10; Wells (2003); Murdoch (2008); Wolters (2008) 80–4; Sommer (2009) 26–7; Eck (2010) 22. There are, however, some persistent voices who blame Varus' incompetence. See Benario (2003); Baltrusch (2012).

[4] Pagán (1999); (2002); O'Gorman (2000) 49–56; Seidman (2014).

re-entered the popular imagination in novels,[5] and he, Arminius and the battle have exercised the talents of a growing number of scholars, whose interests also lie in the reception of the classics.[6] The field is expanding to include in the conversation new kinds of evidence that promise to illuminate further the events and personalities of the past and our relation to it. Yet one element seems to remain static in scholarship. Interest in Varus is scarcely found outside of the historical event of the Teutoburg Forest – its causes, location and consequences – and his fairly well-charted political connections and military career.[7] The pool of our textual sources has appeared to many commentators as stagnant.[8] An appropriate investigation about Varus and the battle will include some combination of the standard sources – Velleius Paterculus, Tacitus, Florus and Cassius Dio – and little apart from them. There is, however, a body of evidence that remains relatively underappreciated. Scholars have belaboured the sources for the battle and Varus' role in it, but Varus is named many more times in Greek and Latin literature.

In this chapter, I take as my starting point all instances of the name of Varus in the extant writings from antiquity that relate to his defeat in Germania. Drawing on this evidence, I argue that in less than a decade after the disaster, Varus was made out to be the model of a negligent general, and that this became a tradition among all of our sources. I also show, however, that although Tacitus occasionally falls in with this tradition in his *Annales*, he uses Varus as a symbol of a profound loss to the Romans, their desire for vengeance and their reclamation of that loss. At the same time, he sets up Varus as a symbol of liberty from the German perspective. While demonstrating the presence of discrete Roman and German perspectives in Tacitus' work, I argue that we can read the account of Germanicus' wars as a battle between these two perspectives over Varus' memory set in the landscape of Germania. By way of conclusion, I suggest that Tacitus uses the lingering and ambivalent memory of Varus to underscore that the claims of the Roman conquest of Germania are specious.

---

[5] Clunn (2008); Turtledove (2009).
[6] Benario (2004); Winkler (2016).
[7] On Varus' personal background, see John (1958); (1963); Koenen (1970); Reinhold (1972); Crosby (2016).
[8] Eshel (2008) has brought to our attention some fascinating evidence for Jewish reactions to Varus' actions during his governorship in Syria (c. 6–4 BC).

The Tradition

Cassius Dio's account (56.24.3) of the many and marvellous portents that were observed and conjectured to bear upon the events of the Teutoburg Forest is suggestive of the contemporary anxiety. The earliest mention of the Battle of the Teutoburg Forest, in fact, comes from Marcus Manilius' *Astronomica* in connection with ominous comets.[9] However, our evidence for the contemporary reaction to the disaster immediately following the event centres on three individuals: Augustus, Tiberius and the rhetorician Cestius. According to our sources, Augustus wandered between grief at the loss and fear for the safety of the empire when he heard the news.[10] If Suetonius can be believed, he famously cried, 'Quinctilius Varus, give me back my legions!', and kept that day on which he heard the news as a day of mourning.[11] Certainly, the quote indicates that Augustus held his general responsible to some degree. Tiberius had a different reaction to Varus. In his biography of the future emperor, Suetonius says (*Tib.* 18) that upon his return to Germania, Tiberius confined his military operations strictly to certain best practices – soliciting feedback from his *consilium*, removing unnecessary baggage from the train, issuing orders in writing, and insisting on absolute clarity and timely communication within the chain of command. He did all of these things, we are told, in direct response to his observation that 'the Varian disaster happened by the thoughtlessness (*temeritate*) and negligence (*neglegentia*) of the general'.[12] Clearly, Tiberius understood that Varus was a bad general and a negative *exemplum* that he was resolved not to emulate. We also learn from Seneca the Elder that around the year AD 18 the rhetorician Cestius chastised the young son of Varus, following up his objection to the young man's claim with the words, 'By this same negligence (*neglegentia*) did your father destroy his army.'[13] To this remark, Seneca adds that the negligence of Varus that Cestius pointed out in his final retort was 'a matter which all condemned'. Thus, we are led to believe that by the end of the second decade so many Romans considered Varus to have been derelict in his military duties that the example of his carelessness could be applicable even to negligence in argumentation. Although Manilius and Strabo (7.1.4) could be understood as depicting Varus as a victim in their rush to blame the perfidious Germans, it would appear that the process of transforming Varus from

---

[9] Manilius, *Astr.* 1.896–903. Volk (2009) 137–61 favours an Augustan date of composition.
[10] Suet. *Aug.* 23; Cass. Dio 56.23.1–24.1. See Turner (2018) 263–5.
[11] Suet. *Aug.* 23.2: *Quintili Vare, legiones redde!*
[12] Suet. *Tib.* 18: *Varianam cladem temeritate et neglegentia ducis accidisse.*
[13] Sen. *Contr.* 1.3.10: *Cum multa dixisset, novissime adiecit rem quam omnes improbavimus: 'ista neglegentia pater tuus exercitum perdidit.' Filium obiurgabat, patri male dixit.* For the date, see John (1958) 251.

a convenient scapegoat into a literary or colloquial commonplace for incompetence had already begun in the principate of Tiberius.

As Rebecca Langlands in her recent work might put it, Varus was entering into a dynamic tradition of storytelling and reference that gives expression to communal ethical values, which she calls 'exemplary ethics'.[14] As she argues, exemplary narratives were a fundamental means within Roman culture by which people learned, debated, validated and deprecated the ethical value of actions. While the *exempla* themselves are complex, multivalent and indeterminate 'sites' of cultural memory with respect to the ethical values that they could express, in their use by speakers and writers they can be framed in such a way as to indicate a set ethical value in communication with a 'broad interpretive consensus'.[15] The sources already discussed show that Varus, his name and his actions were becoming terms in a shared moral language or a point of cultural reference that underlined a moral value determined by community consensus. This consensus focused on his negligence.[16]

The major historical authors who composed accounts of the Teutoburg Forest also drew on this commonplace. Velleius Paterculus, who wrote between AD 29 and 30, was intimately familiar with the happenings on the western frontier from his own experience there as an officer between AD 4 and 12. He provides our first characterisation of Varus.[17]

> Quinctilius Varus, who was from a family that was more famous than noble, was a man of delicate temper, mild in his manner, and as immovable in mind as in body ... Syria, which he had governed, testified that he was not a despiser of money. He entered the rich province as a poor man and left as a rich man from a poor province. When he was in command of the army in Germania, he had it in mind that men, who were possessing none of the marks of humanity except the voice and limbs and who were not able to be mastered with swords, could be softened by law.[18]

---

[14] Langlands (2018) 3–4.

[15] Langlands (2018) 59–63, 163–5. See also Roller (2018) 11–17, who frames similar observations in terms of the three cultural dimensions of *exempla*: rhetorical, ethical and historiographical.

[16] Langlands (2018) 128–30. There appears to be consensus that even the mention of a famous name would be enough to draw attention to the important associations from the cultural memory. See Langlands (2018) 30; Roller (2018) 4.

[17] Vell. 2.104.3. For the date of composition, see Sumner (1970) 284–8. Velleius (2.119.1) had planned to write a monograph on the Varian disaster, but if he ever wrote it, it does not survive.

[18] Vell. 2.117.2–4: *Varus Quintilius inlustri magis quam nobili ortus familia, vir ingenio mitis, moribus quietus, ut corpore ita animo immobilior . . . pecuniae vero quam non contemptor, Syria,*

Here we find a thoroughly negative appreciation of the general's character, and it is clear from both the extent of the digression and his aside about the necessity of explicating Varus' *persona* that the author implicates him. Varus is a delicate, avaricious, arrogant and unmilitary man, who is utterly deceived by the reality of the situation in Germania. It is no wonder that Velleius later attributes the cause of the whole disaster to his 'supreme stupidity' (*summa socordia*), 'indolence' (*marcor*) and an entire absence of 'sharpness of mind' (*acies animi*) and 'judgement of a commander' (*consilium imperatoris*).[19] Only 'seriousness' (*gravitas*) and 'goodwill' (*voluntas bona*) remain as traits to Varus' credit, but Velleius even looks askance at the honorific burial of Varus' severed head, with the words 'his head was sent to Caesar and was, nevertheless, honoured with burial in his ancestral tomb'.[20] Doubtless, the consensus is correct that the precipitous decline of the *gens Quinctilia* in the principate of Tiberius facilitated hostility towards him;[21] however, the thoroughness of Velleius' character assassination along with the clear juxtapositions of Varus with both the heroic Tiberius and the devious, but shrewd, Arminius highlight our primary observation:[22] Varus was steadily becoming the negative standard by which generals could be judged.[23]

Florus, writing in the second century AD, depicts Varus in a way quite similar to Velleius'. Although he gives at least some amount of blame to Augustus for having conceived a desire to conquer Germania (2.30.1–2), Varus gets the worst of it by far. As Florus explains, the Germans under Drusus had greater respect for the customs of the Romans than their martial prowess. This respect kept them pacified for the time being, but when Varus entered the scene, his habits and bearing tipped the scales.

> They began to hate the seething desire and haughtiness of Quinctilius Varus not at all otherwise than his rage. He had dared to conduct court and had issued decrees

---

qui praefuerat, declaravit, quam pauper divitem ingressus dives pauperem reliquit; is cum exercitui qui erat in Germania praeesset, concepit esse homines, qui nihil praeter vocem membraque haberent hominum, quique gladiis domari non poterant, posse iure mulceri. All translations are my own.

[19] Vell. 2.118.1; 2.119.2; 2.120.5.
[20] Vell. 2.119.5: *missum ad Caesarem gentilici tamen tumuli sepultura honoratum est.*
[21] Lana (1952) 110–18; Schmitzer (2000) 240–1; Lica (2001) 500.
[22] Woodman (1977) 42–3, 188–204 *passim*, rather, looks within the narrative to discover the opposition of Varus and Arminius; however, he also acknowledges the dramatic contrast between the disaster narrative and the succeeding account of Tiberius' exploits. See also Lana (1952) 110; Schmitzer (2000) 237–62; (2011) 187–9.
[23] Timpe (1970) 120–2.

without caution as though it were possible to stay the violence of barbarians with the rods of the lictor and the voice of a herald. And those who for a long time now were grieved that their swords were covered with rust and their horses were at rest, when they first saw togas and laws crueller than weapons, snatched up arms under their general Arminius. In the meantime, Varus' trust in the present peace was so great that he was not moved even when the conspiracy was betrayed to him by Segestes, who was one of their chiefs. Therefore, when he called them to the tribunal – o, the carelessness (*securitas*)![24] – they attacked him on all sides, being unprepared and fearing no such thing. The camps were taken; the three legions, overwhelmed.[25]

It must be admitted that Florus' account of the battle diverges widely from the other narratives of Velleius, Tacitus and Cassius Dio.[26] However, if we can shy away from taking too keen an interest in the issue of the factual accuracy of his account, we can find in this passage the way in which a later historian interpreted this particular event. Whereas Velleius is content to suggest a connection between Varus' character and the German insurrection, with his appraisal of Varus and the situation among the Germans, Florus draws a causal relationship between the two. Varus' greed, haughtiness and savagery prompt the tribes to polish their swords and mount their horses for the defence of their liberty, and his renowned carelessness removes the last remaining obstacle to what would happen.

Cassius Dio, writing in the early third century AD, follows Florus in citing the difference between Varus and his predecessors as a key contributing factor to the disaster

---

[24] The words *o securitas* jump off of the page, and since they stand independent from the sentence, they prove difficult to translate. Forster translates these two words as 'such was his confidence', and Jal, 'ô sécurité trompeuse'. Forster (1984) 339; Jal (1967) 69. I have chosen to lean harder on the word's connotation of 'carelessness' or 'negligence' in certain, obviously negative contexts. Note also the parallel usage at Vell. 2.118.2. Although this kind of vocative interjection is not exceptional in Florus, the phrase may require emendation to satisfy an accusative object which would otherwise need to be assumed. Korting (2017) suggests *cum ille securi ita se ad tribunal citaret*.

[25] Flor. 2.30.33–46: *Vari Quintilli libidinem ac superbiam haud secus quam saevitiam odisse coeperunt. Ausus ille agere conventum, et incautus edixerat, quasi violentiam barbarum lictoris virgis et praeconis voce posset inhibere. At illi, qui iam pridem robigine obsitos enses inertesque maererent equos, ut primum togas et saeviora armis iura viderunt, duce Armenio arma corripiunt; cum interim tanta erat Varo pacis fiducia, ut ne prodita quidem per Segesten unum principum coniuratione commoveretur. Itaque inprovidum et nihil tale metuentem ex inproviso adorti, cum ille – o securitas! – ad tribunal citaret, undique invadunt; castra rapiuntur, tres legiones opprimuntur.*

[26] Lemcke (1936), however, has demonstrated at least the possibility that Florus' account relies on that of Velleius, whereas John (1963) 933–4 suggests Livian influence.

that befell the three legions in Germania. To him, the greatest factor in the instigation of the rebellion was the speed with which Varus pressed the process of Romanisation, but Cassius Dio does give Varus his stereotypical haughtiness and greed.

> When Quinctilius Varus took command of Germania and was managing matters among them according to his office, he hastened to civilise them en masse. He ordered other things of them as though they were slaves, and he exacted money as though from subjects. They did not bear these matters patiently . . .[27]

Cassius Dio's critique of Varus is not as thinly veiled here as at least one scholar has suggested.[28] Indeed, we need not look much further to find the general's traditional negligence.

> He did not, therefore, keep his forces together, as indeed was reasonable in enemy territory . . . Being bold, therefore, not expecting anything bad, and not only disbelieving all those suspecting what was about to happen and recommending that he be careful, but also rebuking them for being agitated for no reason and for accusing those people. . . .[29]

Clearly, Cassius Dio considers the division of Varus' army to be counter to custom, and his lack of caution to be the worst kind of boldness. Indeed, if we are justified in interpreting 'those suspecting . . . and recommending' as members of his *consilium*, we would find some resonance with elements of the charge of negligent leadership levelled against C. Flaminius Nepos (cos. 223 BC), who fell before Hannibal at Lake Trasimene in 217 BC.[30] To be sure, we do not have in Cassius Dio's account the

---

[27] Cass. Dio 56.18.3: ἐπεὶ δ' ὁ Οὖαρος ὁ Κυιντίλιος τήν τε ἡγεμονίαν τῆς Γερμανίας λαβὼν καὶ τὰ παρ' ἐκείνοις ἐκ τῆς ἀρχῆς διοικῶν ἔσπευσεν αὐτοὺς ἀθροώτερον μεταστῆσαι, καὶ τά τε ἄλλα ὡς καὶ δουλεύουσί σφισιν ἐπέταττε καὶ χρήματα ὡς καὶ παρ' ὑπηκόων ἐσέπρασσεν, οὐκ ἠνέσχοντο.

[28] On Cassius Dio's characterisation of Varus' behaviour, I differ from Wolters (2008) 107, who deals with what he sees as '[d]er noch ohne jede Schmähung des Varus auskommende Bericht des Dio'. The critique is present, even if it is not as strongly pronounced as in, for example, Velleius or Florus. See Timpe (1970) 122; Swan (2004) 254.

[29] Cass. Dio 56.19.1, 3: οὔτ' οὖν τὰ στρατεύματα, ὥσπερ εἰκὸς ἦν ἐν πολεμίᾳ, συνεῖχε . . . θαρσοῦντος οὖν αὐτοῦ, καὶ μήτε τι δεινὸν προσδεχομένου, καὶ πᾶσι τοῖς τό τε γιγνόμενον ὑποτοποῦσι καὶ φυλάττεσθαί οἱ παραινοῦσιν οὐχ ὅπως ἀπιστοῦντος ἀλλὰ καὶ ἐπιτιμῶντος ὡς μάτην αὐτοῖς τε ταραττομένοις καὶ ἐκείνους διαβάλλουσιν. . . .

[30] Liv. 22.3–7. As Johnston (2008) has shown, although there was no obligation for the commander to follow the advice that he was given (the prerogative of *imperium*), it was considered necessary at least to hear that advice in the *consilium*.

depth of characterisation that we find in Velleius or Florus, but it is clear from the way he depicts the general's behaviour that his Varus is part of the same tradition. It is the man's negligence in practising proper military caution and heeding the advice of his advisors that is a major cause of the defeat, as Cassius Dio tells it.

There were other appearances of Varus in works of history and literature after AD 9. Beginning around the middle of the first century AD, a phrase employing a novel adjectival usage of Varus' name, *clades Variana* ('Varian disaster'), takes on a metonymic function, sufficient for recognisable allusion.[31] We know that there were other writers, contemporaries of Velleius Paterculus, who wrote about the *clades Variana*, but Livy was probably not among them.[32] Aufidius Bassus, the elder Pliny and a certain Albinovanus Pedo, who wrote an epic about Germanicus' campaigns, all perhaps had some cause to mention Varus in their work, but none of these texts has survived.[33] This evidence, however, offers us little helpful information about the reception of Varus.[34] It is possible that his characterisation in antiquity could have been more nuanced than it appears to us now, but the consistency of that characterisation among our extant sources is striking.[35] I draw two conclusions from this evidence. First, outside of the works of Tacitus and Josephus, whose chief historical interest was far from the northern frontiers of the empire, Varus becomes the very model of a terrible general. It is a matter of tradition that Varus is mentioned as a

---

[31] Plin. *NH* 7.150; Sen. *Mor. Epi.* 47.10; Front. *Strat.* 3.15.4; 4.7.8; Suet. *Aug.* 23.1; 49.1; *Tib.* 17.2; *Cal.* 3.2; 31.1. There is an even earlier attestation of the adjectival form 'Varian' to be found shortly after the defeat on the cenotaph of the M. Caelius, who 'fell in the Varian War' (*[ce]cidit·bello·Variano*). *CIL* XIII.8648 = *ILS* 2244. See Benario (1986).

[32] Rossbach (1889) 74; (1910a) 1396–8; (1910b) 121, who discovered a manuscript of the *Periochae* of Livy in the Bodleian Library that concluded with the words *clades Quinctilii Vari*, suggests that Livy's history concluded in Book 142 or a later one (!) with an account of the Teutoburg Forest, and Rossbach printed the words in his edition of 1910. However, Luterbacher (1910) 1186–8 objects to Rossbach's claim, since it would require the final book to cover over seventeen years of history, an exceedingly unlikely solution given that nothing at all survives of those seventeen years in that manuscript. His suggestion that the scribe probably made an error in confusing the events of 9 BC with those of AD 9 remains a more convincing solution. Klotz' suggestion (1926) 827 that Livy had juxtaposed Drusus' success in Germania with the failure of Varus saves the possibility that Livy might have mentioned the Teutoburg Forest.

[33] Vell. 2.119.1. Aufidius Bassus, Pliny and Albinovanus Pedo were among the sources available to Tacitus. See Syme (1958) 274–7.

[34] It is perhaps surprising that Varus does not appear in Valerius Maximus' compendium of *exempla*, but accounting for his absence from this text is outside the scope of this study.

[35] Here, I am not concerned with the historical accuracy of Varian negligence. Indeed, it is probable that this charge was a *topos* in discussions of failed commanders and governors. Van Wickevoort-Crommelin (1999) 2; Timpe (2012) 639.

way of assigning him blame for what happened in Germania, and his example of negligence could also be recalled meaningfully as one to be avoided and criticised in the contexts of both generalship and public debate. Second, although the Varus of the historians becomes such a negative *exemplum*, he is still distinctly flesh and blood in the sense that he thinks, acts and dies as a character in a story as it unfolds.

Tacitus' *Annales*

By comparison, the Varus of Tacitus lives a much more dynamic life than the Varus of the other historians. Clearly, Tacitus' main historical interest in the *Annales* lies in the events after AD 14, and it is partly a consequence of this fact that Varus never has real presence in the *Annales*. Instead, Varus exists only as a memory, an apparition, or a name on the lips of the characters in the history or the Tacitean narrator. Nothing compelled the historian to give an account of the defeat or even mention the general's name. Tacitus could have written about all of the events in the principate of Tiberius without reference to the *clades Variana*, but that he chose to include mentions of Varus in his work is, I claim, a meaningful decision, as is the way in which he makes them. Additionally, the frequency with which Varus' name is dropped underscores the importance that Tacitus attaches to the events in the Teutoburg Forest. Varus' name appears nineteen times between Books 1 and 2 of the *Annales*, and is, therefore, more prominent in the text than even Germanicus' lieutenant Caecina.[36] To some extent, this importance is unsurprising. The loss in Germania was such a momentous event that Tacitus names the *clades Variana* in his catalogue of slaughters at home and abroad that become the foundation for the bloody peace that he makes of the principate.[37] Indeed, the thread of the disaster extends through the conditions of service that send the northern legions clamouring for increased pay and discharge upon the death of Augustus in AD 14.[38] However, I argue that Varus holds greater importance to the work than just historical contextualisation. He becomes symbolically meaningful in the text because his name is inextricably connected with the military catastrophe in the Teutoburg Forest. In examining

---

[36] Tac. *Ann.* 1.3; 1.10; 1.43; 1.55 (2); 1.57; 1.58; 1.60 (2); 1.61 (2); 1.65 (2); 1.71; 2.7; 2.15; 2.25; 2.41; 2.45; also 12.27. By comparison, Caecina is only named seventeen times in the same span. Tac *Ann.* 1.31; 1.32; 1.37; 1.48 (2); 1.50; 1.56 (2); 1.60; 1.61; 1.63 (2); 1.64; 1.65; 1.66; 1.72; 2.6.

[37] Tac. *Ann.* 1.10: *Pacem sine dubio post haec, verum cruentam: Lollianas Varianasque cladis, interfectos Romae Varrones, Egnatios, Iullos.*

[38] Tac. *Ann.* 1.17, 31. The problem following the Varian disaster was getting free-born citizens to serve. Augustus needed to resort to compulsion and extension of service to meet the need, according to Cass. Dio 56.23.13.

the instances of Varus' name, we can observe that Tacitus depicts the Romans and Germans as engaged in an open conflict over the memory of the failed general.[39] The Romans attempt to redeem the memory of Varus by steadily recovering what he lost and claiming victory, while the Germans continue to remember how the battle really ended and prove Varus to be the ultimate symbol of their freedom. This ideological battle rages parallel to the confrontations of their military forces in the narrative and finds its fullest expression in Tacitus' account of the happenings at the Teutoburg Forest itself. There, the battlefield becomes the scene for a memorial tug of war.

To be sure, Tacitus does yield to the consensus opinion of Varus' negligence at certain points in the *Annales*. The one in the narrator's own voice comes by way of an explanation of the animosity between Arminius and Segestes, two German chieftains who were intimately involved in the events that led Varus and his legions to their end. Varus disbelieves Segestes' warnings of the impending plot.

> Arminius was the troubler of Germania. Segestes revealed to Varus often at other times and then at the last meal, after which arms were taken up, that a rebellion was prepared, and he urged Varus to arrest him [Arminius] and the other chiefs, saying that the people would not dare anything if their chiefs were removed, and that he would have time to distinguish between those at fault and those innocent. But Varus fell by fate and the force of Arminius.[40]

Here, Tacitus' depiction of Varus' heedlessness clearly falls in line with the tradition. However, we should note along with Koestermann that Tacitus, like Velleius, mitigates the blame of the apparently incautious general with the inclusion of Arminius' energies and fate as significant factors in the causal calculus.[41] One of the clearest indictments of Varus' inabilities comes through the mouth of Segestes himself (Tac. *Ann* 1.58), who claims to have been dismissed 'by the sloth of the general' (*segnitia ducis*). Tacitus gives similar words to Maroboduus, who diminishes Arminius'

---

[39] Shannon-Henderson (2019) 79–89 has already pointed out that memory is important to how the Romans and the Germans view their war during Germanicus' invasions, but her interest lies more in how Germanicus navigates the waters of the Augustan past, Tiberian present and Germanic resistance in his interpretation of signs and performance rituals.

[40] Tac. *Ann*. 1.55: *Arminius turbator Germaniae, Segestes parari rebellionem saepe alias et supremo convivio, post quod in arma itum, aperuit suasitque Varo ut se et ceteros proceres vinciret: nihil ausuram plebem principibus amotis; atque ipsi tempus fore quo crimina et innoxios discerneret. Sed Varus fato et vi Armini cecidit.*

[41] Koestermann (1963) 197. Additionally, Goodyear (1972) 1.74 detects in *fato* '[p]erhaps an echo of apologia early established in the tradition about an embarrassing disaster'.

victory by saying, 'Since by his treachery, he deceived three roaming legions and the general ignorant of the deceit . . .'.[42] Interestingly, the king of the Marcomanni disparages Arminius' accomplishment by cheapening both Varus' worth as a general and the legions' worth as an army. These are the most overt examples of the common charges levelled against Varus' military abilities. In these ways, Tacitus incorporates the standard interpretation of Varus, but the reactions that the memory of Varus evokes are presented more dynamically in his *Annales* than in other extant works.

Although the evocative properties of Varus' memory in the *Annales* are manifold, they can be neatly divided into two groups: those that produce reaction among Romans, and those that produce reaction among the Germans. On the Roman side, these reactions circle around a deeply felt loss. Through Tacitus' work we observe the process by which the Romans deal with these profound feelings of loss. One reaction that is clearly connected with the name of Varus is the desire for revenge, which becomes something of a theme for Book 1. Tacitus predicates the wars of Germanicus on retribution for the loss of Varus and his three legions. His invasions are punitive expeditions.[43]

> There was remaining no war at this time except the one against the Germans, more for the sake of removing the infamy resulting from the loss of the army with Varus than by desire of extending the empire or of some worthy prize.[44]

Tacitus carries this idea through the dramatic speech of Germanicus to his mutinous legions. 'You would have chosen a general who would let even my death go unpunished, but would avenge that of Varus and the three legions.'[45] The statement is typical of a histrionic emotionality with which Tacitus characterises Germanicus at times,[46] but it is clear that the pleading general imagines the ideal leader of these mutinous legions as one who would take them across the Rhine for their payback. Also, by placing the drama between Segestes, Arminius and Varus at the beginning of his account of Germanicus' expeditions across the Rhine, Tacitus draws an even closer connection between the events of Teutoburg Forest and the German Wars. The emphasis on revenge is indicative of a certain identification among the soldiers

---

[42] Tac. *Ann.* 2.46: *quoniam tres vagas legiones et ducem fraudis ignarum perfidia deceperit.* . . .
[43] Van Wickevoort-Crommelin (1999) 2.
[44] Tac. *Ann.* 1.3: *Bellum ea tempestate nullum nisi adversus Germanos supererat, abolendae magis infamiae ob amissum cum Quintilio Varo exercitum quam cupidine proferendi imperii aut dignum ob praemium.*
[45] Tac. *Ann.* 1.43: *Legissetis ducem, qui meam quidem mortem inpunitam sineret, Vari tamen et trium legionum ulcisceretur.*
[46] Shotter (1968).

of the northern frontier with the dead commander and his troops in a way that is markedly different from the attitudes expressed towards Varus in the rest of the tradition. Utilising this theme of revenge and strategic digression, Tacitus forges his link between defeat in battle and subsequent victory in war, which becomes ever more important as the historical narrative unfolds.

On the other end of loss is recovery. Tacitus' *Annales* put a good deal of importance on Varus as a symbol of recovery, which evokes feelings of joy. Whenever the army is able to regain what Varus lost, Tacitus takes note and mentions Varus by name specifically. In the first instance, Germanicus attacks those who were besieging Segestes, and there, the Romans find prizes of battle from the legions of Varus among them. 'Also taken were the spoils of the *clades Variana*, which had been given to many of those who were now surrendering.'[47] The Romans clearly reclaim the Varian spoils, but Tacitus makes this scene of recovery even more striking with the second clause. The very men who took the spoils from the Teutoburg Forest now hand them in surrender to Roman legionaries, who then take these relics as their own prizes. By carrying off the material rewards of the Varian tragedy, the Roman soldiers seem to begin a process of redemption, nearly replaying the defeat in reverse.[48]

The most significant relics of the Teutoburg Forest, at least to the Romans, were the legionary eagles that represented the identity of each legion, the loss of which was considered the gravest misfortune.[49] Of the three legionary eagles that were lost with Varus, Germanicus' army recovered two: that of the nineteenth legion 'lost with Varus' (*cum Varo amissam*) was recovered from the Bructeri by L. Stertinius in AD 15,[50] and another 'of a Varian legion' (*Varianae legionis*) was found in the year

---

[47] Tac. *Ann.* 1.57: *Ferebantur et spolia Varianae cladis, plerisque eorum qui tum in deditionem veniebant praedae data.*

[48] Here, I am trying to extend Pagán's (1999) excellent reading of Tacitus' ekphrasis of the battlefield as a collapse of time and space between the armies of Varus and Germanicus and the implications of Germanicus' efforts to sanitise the memory of the battle. I argue that this sanitisation was a process beginning even before Germanicus conceives a desire to visit the battlefield.

[49] The innovation of the eagle standard is traditionally attributed to the reforms of C. Marius in preparation for his northern wars (104 BC). Plin. *NH* 10.16. The anxiety felt over the loss of an eagle is underscored, for example, by a pair of scenes in Caesar's commentaries. Caes. *BG* 4.25; 5.37. The legions lost with Varus, probably numbered XVII, XVIII and XIX, were not reconstituted and the designations never used again in the Roman army. Ward's (2018) 292–5 suggestion that the imperial family needed to influence the memory of the disaster by discontinuing the legions and their designations may be partly convincing, but I argue that they are involved in influencing memory in other, more positive ways.

[50] Tac. *Ann.* 1.60: *Bructeros sua urentis expedita cum manu L. Stertinius missu Germanici fudit; interque caedem et praedam repperit undevicesimae legionis aquilam cum Varo amissam.*

AD 16 buried in a sacred grove, the location of which was betrayed by a chieftain of the Marsi.[51] We learn from Cassius Dio that P. Gabinius Secundus recaptured the final eagle with his defeat of the Chauci in the year AD 41 during the reign of Claudius,[52] and given Tacitus' interest in the Teutoburg Forest and the traditional significance of the recovery of legionary eagles in imperial propaganda,[53] we should expect that the historian had included this fact in the lost book that covered that year. The fact that this theme of recovery was important to Tacitus manifests itself even in Book 12, when in the year AD 50, P. Pomponius led a counter-assault against a group of marauding Chatti. 'Joy grew because they had after forty years redeemed from slavery some from the *clades Variana*.'[54] With the context of reclamation of Varian spoils, standards and captives, Tacitus builds around Varus a new, more positive set of associations apart from the disaster. In these passages, Varus comes to symbolise redemption. In this way, Tacitus is emphasising key features of the imperial vision of success in Germania and pointing to an attempt to recast the shame of Varus' defeat into fresh, albeit lesser, victory.[55]

The Roman redemption of Varus in the *Annales* is capped by the historian's description of Germanicus' visit to the battlefield. Following his assault on the lands of the Bructeri, Germanicus receives word that he is near to the site where 'the unburied remains of Varus and his legions' (*reliquiae Vari legionumque insepultae*)

---

[51] Tac. *Ann.* 2.25: *Ipse maioribus copiis Marsos inrumpit, quorum dux Mallovendus nuper in deditionem acceptus propinquo luco defossam Varianae legionis aquilam modico praesidio servari indicat.*

[52] Cass. Dio 60.8.7; Suet. *Claud.* 24.3.

[53] Augustus touted his recovery of the eagles (20 BC) from Crassus' defeat by the Parthians in his *Res Gestae* (5.29). The scene is also depicted on the breastplate of the Augustus of Prima Porta, and his dedication of them in the temple of Mars Ultor is commemorated with a few issues of coinage with the legends SIGNIS RECEPTIS or SIGNIS RECEPTIS PARTHICIS (reverse), Mattingly and Sydenham (1923) 63, 84, 86; Mattingly (1923) 60, 71–2, 110, pls 6.12, 9.13–14, 16.20, 17.1–2. See also below.

[54] Tac. *Ann.* 12.27: *Aucta laetitia quod quosdam e clade Variana quadragesimum post annum servitio exemerant.* Lica (2001) points out an interesting passage from Cassius Dio (56.22) in which the soldiers who were captured in the battle were ransomed from their captors but barred from entering Italy. If true, this passage would indicate a different attitude towards the veterans of Varus' army. Lica argues that this attitude is consistent with the precipitous decline of the Quinctilii in the principate of Tiberius.

[55] Timpe (2012) 648 points out that the recovery of the eagles along with the claims of a complete victory in Germania were part of the imperial message that they had avenged the loss of Varus and his legions, even if the message was ultimately unconvincing to some of the nobility.

lie.⁵⁶ He then resolves to bury the fallen soldiers and their general.⁵⁷ Thereupon the historian launches into his narrative of the battle that has been aptly described as 'oneiric'.⁵⁸ The historical issues and the literariness of the passage, with its nods to Vergil, Livy and indeed the historian's own work, are well-worn ground in scholarship.⁵⁹ One Vergilian allusion is particularly noteworthy here. Woodman has shown the words 'skulls nailed to the trunks of trees' (*truncis arborum antefixa ora*, *Annales* 1.61) to be an allusion to Vergil's 'skulls nailed to arrogant doors' (*foribusque adfixa superbis / ora*, *Aeneid* 8.196–7) and argued their imitative significance in connecting the semi-human Cacus, the thief of Hercules' cattle, to the 'semi-human barbarians who fastened Roman skulls to tree-trunks'.⁶⁰ We might press the parallel further and see in Germanicus a would-be Hercules, who intends to become, as Vergil has it, the 'greatest avenger' (*maximus ultor*, *Aeneid* 8.201) against the monster who tried to trick him and had been a bane to the people of ancient Pallantium (the future site of Rome). Indeed, as has been pointed out earlier, Tacitus and his Germanicus have already cast the invasion as a punitive expedition of revenge for the Varian disaster, and this Vergilian allusion draws a comparison that is fitting to that interpretation, although it ultimately turns out to be a foil.

Literary allusions aside, however, there is an element of Tacitus' narration that has received less attention. This moment is the culmination of the battle that Germanicus' troops have been waging over the memory of Varus. As we observed above, as Germanicus' army marches east, he systematically reverses the tragic defeat as if moving backwards in time, first recovering the spoil, then recovering the eagles, before finally recovering the battlefield itself. Now, with the battle for the memory of the *clades Variana* won, memorialisation follows. As opposed to the chaotic carnage left scattered about the field by the Germans, Germanicus and his men raise an orderly tumulus, which memorialises both of the Roman armies present there.⁶¹ At the same time, Tacitus' ekphrasis of the carnage in the Teutoburg Forest

⁵⁶ Tac. *Ann*. 1.60: *haud procul Teuroburgiensi saltu in quo reliquiae Vari legionumque insepultae dicebantur*.
⁵⁷ Tac. *Ann*. 1.61: *Igitur cupido Caesarem invadit solvendi suprema militibus ducique*.
⁵⁸ Pagán (1999) 309.
⁵⁹ Furneaux (1896) 260–2; Koestermann (1963) 210–11; Woodman (1979); (1998) 70–85; Pagán (2002). Based on the close comparisons that he finds between scenes in the *Historiae* and the *Annales*, Woodman suggests that the scenes of Germanicus' visit are entirely fabricated by the historian.
⁶⁰ Woodman (1979) 148–9.
⁶¹ The scene was justly famous and attracted the notice of Suetonius as well. Suet. *Cal*. 3.2. Östenberg (2018) 241–4 similarly thinks about Germanicus' expedition as having 'physically marched back in time' and represents the imposition of order over wildness.

becomes a monument in its own right, one that mirrors the tumulus Germanicus builds there, as Seidman argues.⁶² This scene is certainly constructed. As Nipperdey notes, Tacitus has the soldiers of Germanicus improbably follow the path of Varus' march.⁶³ The alteration of the geographic space is likely to be Tacitus' own innovation, and it more closely connects the armies of Varus and Germanicus in time, space and sympathy.⁶⁴ In one moment, while Germanicus' soldiers gaze at the field, the bones come back to life and activate the memory of their final moments, which is Tacitus' memorial. In the next moment, it is Germanicus' soldiers who are active, raising a burial mound for Varus' legionaries, who are bones once again.

Erecting a monument for the fallen soldiers may seem counterintuitive when considering the fact that the avowed purpose of the invasion was to wipe out the shame of the defeat. However, the act of raising a mound is more than just a convincing way of offering a 'resolution to the history of Varus', as Ellen O'Gorman sees it.⁶⁵ It is the monumental nature of the burial, the tumulus, to which I would like to draw attention. While the tumulus is certainly a tomb for Varus' slaughtered legions, it also memorialises the success of Germanicus and his men in mastering and civilising the messy and barbaric landscape left by the Germans. Indeed, the erection of a mound is also suggestive of victory memorials, not unlike the two that Germanicus raises later – one, a 'mound' (*aggerem*) with weapons on top 'in the manner of trophies' (*in modum tropaeorum*), and the other, a 'heap of weapons' (*congeriem armorum*) – after he defeated Arminius at Idistaviso.⁶⁶ In this moment, even if it is a burial mound, it would seem that there is a kind of victory: the Romans have taken the field of battle.⁶⁷

The monument that Germanicus builds to the memory of Varus and his legions is not the only one to be dedicated. Tacitus tells us about the triumphal arch that Tiberius dedicated 'next to the temple of Saturn because the standards lost with Varus were recovered under the leadership of Germanicus and the auspices of Tiberius'.⁶⁸ It is true that the arch is meant to be an honour for Germanicus and

---

⁶² Seidman (2014).
⁶³ Nipperdey (1884) 111.
⁶⁴ 'Time and space collapse into a point of absolute zero', Pagán (1999) 308.
⁶⁵ O'Gorman (2000) 53.
⁶⁶ Tac. *Ann.* 2.18, 2.22. Drusus is said to have memorialised his victory during his campaign in Germania in a similar manner: *Nam Marcomannorum spoliis et insignibus quendam editum tumulum in tropaei modum excoluit.* Flor. 2.30.23. On the other hand, the simple heaping of arms in memorialising victory appears to be an oddity among the Romans, and Charles-Picard (1957) 120, 318–19, citing Caes. *BG* 6.17.4 and Liv. 5.39.1, argues that Germanicus' army may have been imitating a Gallic custom.
⁶⁷ Walser (1951) 62; Pagán (1999) 314.
⁶⁸ Tac. *Ann.* 2.41: *arcus propter aedem Saturni ob recepta signa cum Varo amissa ductu Germanici,*

Tiberius, but as the words of Tacitus make plain, the arch memorialises the recovery of the eagles of Varus' legions. As a monument, then, it walks a fine line between the sadness of loss and the jubilation and triumph over recovery, just like the arch of Augustus that stood not far away.[69] The tension here, as in the case of the burial tumulus mentioned above, arises from the fact that Varus, a symbol more often recognisable for its connections with deep loss, as I have argued, is being reframed in the context of victory – in this case, even a triumphal victory. By framing Varus with these novel contexts, his defeat at the Battle of the Teutoburg Forest comes to be redeemed as much as possible.

However, Roman success was short-lived. The return of the Roman army to their camps on the Rhine ends up being more of a retreat over the muddy terrain and comes close to a recapitulation of the military disaster that they had just attempted to redeem. The landscape and climate of Germania, in general, and the Teutoburg Forest, in particular, suggested danger to more of our authorities than just Tacitus. Velleius digresses on the swamps and murky woods, Cassius Dio on the dense rain and slippery roots along the path, and Florus even says that Germania itself seemed to become more unpleasant than before the wars of Drusus.[70] Tacitus' description of Caecina's retreat to the Rhine is certainly suggestive of the narrative accounts of the Teutoburg Forest, and the fact that the story of Caecina's return follows on the heels of the vivid recollection of the destruction of Varus' legions helps underscore the comparison and contrast.[71] It is against this backdrop that Varus appears and even speaks. Caecina, whose forces are in an exceedingly vulnerable position, has a dream about Varus.

---

auspiciis Tiberii. In the extant literature, we only know about this arch from Tacitus. Its foundations were rediscovered in 1900. See Ashby (1901) 328–30. The style of the arch can be gleaned from its representation on the arch of Constantine. The event was later marked by issues of coinage which Mattingly and Sydenham (1923) 108 dated between AD 23 and 32. The obverse depicts Germanicus facing right in a quadriga and holding a staff, which is sometimes visibly topped with an eagle, below the legend GERMANICUS/CAESAR. The reverse shows Germanicus in military dress standing and facing left, holding a staff topped with an eagle, between the legend SIGNIS RECEPTIS/DEVICTIS GERM/SC. For variants and plates, see Mattingly (1923) cxlvii, 160–1, pls 30.9–10.

[69] Timpe (1968) 51–4 is certainly right to bring out the similarity of the purpose and placement of the arch of Tiberius and those of the arch of Augustus, which commemorated the recovery of the standards of Crassus' legions from Carrhae.

[70] Vell. 119.2; Cass. Dio 56.20; Flor. 2.30.27. Östenberg (2018) 241–4 analyses the motif of forests being protective for the northern tribes and resistant to the Romans in the narratives relating to the Teutoburg Forest.

[71] Tac. *Ann.* 1.63–4. See Timpe (2012) 630.

> And an ominous dream terrified the general. He seemed to discern Quinctilius Varus, covered with blood and risen from the swamps, and to hear him as though he were calling; nevertheless, he himself did not yield and pushed away the hand of the one reaching out to him.[72]

The similarity between the two battlefields makes the interaction between the two commanders all the more striking.[73] The stage has already been set for a repetition of the Teutoburg Forest, and a *clades Caeciniana* seems impending. Caecina, however, refuses to take the outstretched hand of Varus, the failed commander, and resolves to ward off the now very personal loss that Varus symbolises in his dream.

By way of transition to our consideration of the German perspective on Varus, it is worth examining the one instance in which these opposite points of view, Roman and German, run uncomfortably into each other. Tacitus tells us of a rumour about an insult to Varus' honour, and, by extension, to the Romans generally. It is taken very seriously.

> Now Stertinius, who was sent to receive in surrender Segimerus the brother of Segestes, had led him and his son into the state of the Ubii. Pardon was granted to both, easily to Segimerus, but more hesitantly to his son because it was rumoured that he had mocked the corpse of Varus.[74]

The rumour that the son of Segimerus had insulted the corpse of Varus, which recalls Tacitus' characterisation of the victory speech of Arminius just after the battle,[75] apparently caused some amount of indecision over whether to grant pardon to him. Tacitus implies that Germanicus and others felt enough of a connection with Varus to feel insulted vicariously. We have something entirely unexpected in this passage, for it provides a striking contrast to the other historians' Varus, with whom one would not, and probably should not, identify on account of his traditional and prominent character flaws. However, Varus clearly represented something com-

---

[72] Tac. *Ann.* 1.65: *Ducemque terruit dira quies: nam Quintilium Varum sanguine oblitum et paludibus emersum cernere et audire visus est velut vocantem, non tamen obsecutus et manum intendentis reppulisse.*

[73] Koestermann (1963) 220 agrees that there is a poetic analogy here between the two historical events and their respective commanders.

[74] Tac. *Ann.* 1.71: *Iam Stertinius, ad accipiendum in deditionem Segimerum fratrem Segestis praemissus, ipsum et filium eius in civitatem Vbiorum perduxerat. Data utrique venia, facile Segimero, cunctantius filio, quia Quintilii Vari corpus inlusisse dicebatur.*

[75] Tac. *Ann.* 1.61: *quo tribunali contionatus Arminius, quot patibula captivis, quae scrobes, utque signis et aquilis per superbiam inluserit.*

pletely different to the son of Segimerus. His play with the dead body after the Germans had won the battle shows that the killing of Varus was to be remembered with pride and a sense of accomplishment and superiority. This reaction to Varus openly challenges the agony of defeat and the joy of redemption that his memory evoked from the Romans, and the result is a tense situation followed by an awkward, Roman acquiescence. With the recent victories of the Romans, the power dynamic had shifted, and with it, the currency of the young man's earlier view of Varus, but his earlier perspective still has some measure of force to it: Varus was dead, but Arminius was still alive.

Tactius less frequently takes up a German perspective on Varus and the Teutoburg Forest in his *Annales*, for obvious reasons. But the historian does take a keen interest in developing this angle in a way that runs directly counter to the Roman point of view. We can observe this most clearly in the encounter between Arminius, commanding the German forces, and his now one-eyed brother Flavus, a man serving in the Roman army, as they stand on opposite sides of the river Weser in their respective camps.[76] It is no surprise, then, that Tacitus heavily utilises Arminius as a mouthpiece for the German perspective. In his speeches, Varus and the Teutoburg Forest are used as symbols of the freedom of the Germanic peoples and their military superiority. Arminius especially recalls the victory over Varus and his legions to his own soldiers to spur them on. During his altercation with Caecina, Arminius observes the legionaries struggling with their baggage and the narrowness of their route and exclaims, 'Behold, Varus and his legions are conquered by fate in the same way again!'[77] The text at this place is apparently corrupt, but we do not need to decide between variant readings to understand that Arminius is recalling the Teutoburg Forest. Clearly, he expects the same result as before. Later on, at the battle near the Weser, Arminius recalls the Varian legions again, calling those of Germanicus 'the fleetest armies of Varus who would not wage war, but would engage in mutiny'.[78] Lastly, Arminius gives another speech to his men before his battle with the forces of Maroboduus, the king of the Marcomanni, who, Arminius says, must be expelled from Germania just like Quinctilius Varus.[79] That Tacitus should

---

[76] Tac. *Ann.* 2.9–10. Compare with the speech of Calgacus at Tac. *Agr.* 29–32.

[77] Tac. *Ann.* 1.65: *En Varus eodemque iterum fato vinctae legiones!* For a summary of the debate over the syntactical oddity, see Goodyear (1972) 2.116–17.

[78] Tac. *Ann.* 2.15: *Variani exercitus fugacissimos qui ne bellum tolerarent, seditionem induerint.* Arminius' expression that the army before them was the remnants of Varus' army that had escaped need not just be literally true, as Furneaux (1896) 305; Koestermann (1963) 280; and Goodyear (1972) 2.226 suggest. Certainly, we can imagine a rhetorical, metonymic effect here such that what applies to the part can apply to the whole Roman army.

[79] Tac. *Ann.* 2.45: *haud minus infensis animis exturbandum quam Varum Quintilium interfecerint.*

put these words in the mouth of Arminius is not a surprise, since this Germanic chief had made all of his social and political capital from his victory in the Teutoburg Forest.[80] So this characterisation of Arminius makes sense historically, but Tacitus perhaps wants his reader to consider the Battle of the Teutoburg Forest, however briefly, as a positive event from the perspective of the Germanic peoples, one that confirms their superiority.[81] In this way, Varus and his eponymous disaster become symbols of Germanic freedom from oppressive, foreign control, and remained to be polished up and re-presented whenever an analogy seemed appropriate later in history.[82]

The most telling moment of German pride comes in the very next year following Germanicus' tour of the Teutoburg Forest. 'Nevertheless, they had scattered the mound that had just recently been raised for the legions of Varus and the old altar set up by Drusus.'[83] The Chatti tear down the tumulus that Germanicus and his legionaries built for the slain Varian legions in the previous year. In so doing, they return the site to a chaotic state, re-memorialising their victory and de-memorialising the victory claimed by the Romans. What we find in this important but overlooked passage is direct competition over the memorial for Varus between the Romans, whose ordered tumulus represents Roman claims on Germania as it does Germanicus' success in reclaiming the battlefield, and the Germanic tribes, whose chaotic, frightful and sacred monument dashes those claims.[84] As Agnès Rouveret shows, there is a seemingly programmatic representation of 'barbarians' perceiving monuments and other Roman buildings as symbols of their oppression in Tacitus' works.[85] Although the historian spends more time developing the memorialisation undertaken by the Romans, the Germans get the last word on the matter in this short but striking

---

[80] I cannot agree with Ash (2006) 130, who claims that Arminius' efforts to raise the ghost of Varus: 'sounds rather desperate, the cry of a leader resting on his laurels'.

[81] In addition to the above passages which name Varus specifically, Shannon-Henderson (2019) 81–2 has observed that Arminius, in his outburst following the capture of his wife, defies the power of Rome and its gods by stating the fact that the standards of three legions were still at that very time hanging in the groves of the German gods. Tac. *Ann.* 1.59.

[82] See, for example, Murdoch (2008) 155–80; Winkler (2016).

[83] Tac. *Ann.* 2.7: *Tumulum tamen nuper Varianis legionibus structum et veterem aram Druso sitam disiecerant.*

[84] Lund (2009) 279–83 makes the excellent point that Germanicus may have desecrated what was considered by the Germanic peoples in general, and the Chatti in particular, to be a sacred space. See also Shannon-Henderson (2019) 84–5.

[85] Rouveret (1991) 3060. Rouveret's (1991) 3073–7 explication of Tacitus' discussion of the hollow monuments of Domitian and their defacement provides something of a parallel to my claims about the monuments of Germanicus, although she interprets these as standing uncomplicatedly positive with respect to his memory.

digression: 'The princeps restored the altar and competed himself with the legions in games in honour of his father, but to rebuild (*iterare*) the tumulus did not seem worthwhile at all.'[86] They win the war over Varus' memory, a fact which nicely mirrors Germanicus' troubles in gaining any long-lasting purchase on Germania. In this way, the battle over the memory of Varus can be understood as an analogy for the overarching state of affairs along the Rhine. While Roman arms could press and had pressed deep into the heart of Germania, whatever they achieved was quickly nullified, and their monuments at home and abroad began to look rather specious.

Conclusion

In contrast to the relative homogeneity of the characterisation of Varus in Velleius Paterculus, Florus and Cassius Dio, whose narrations of the defeat turn Varus into a commonplace for negligence, Tacitus, I have argued, turns Varus into a symbol that he observes from two distinct angles: Roman and German. Throughout Book 1 and in parts of Book 2, these two perspectives compete with each other for legitimacy. In Tacitus' *Annales*, the war between the forces of Germanicus and the Germanic tribes often suggests a battle over the memory of Varus. The historian accomplishes this connection through frequent allusions to the objects, setting and naming of the famous disaster and failed general within his narrative. Additionally, the difference between the organised Roman tumulus and the scattered 'barbarian' dedications at the battlefield represents the same struggle over memory.

Looking beyond the *Annales* too, we find that Tacitus has even employed Varus in a similar way in his earlier work, the *Historiae*. The Batavian rebel Civilis recalls the famous defeat of the Romans:

> Recently, for certain, was slavery (*servitutem*) expelled from Germania when Quinctilius Varus was slain, and Vitellius was not the princeps who was provoked by war, but Augustus Caesar. Freedom (*libertatem*) is granted by nature even to mute animals; courage is the particular good of human beings.[87]

Importantly, Tacitus (*Germ.* 29) tells us elsewhere that the Batavi were related to the Chatti, a Germanic people who played a significant role in the Teutoburg Forest.

---

[86] Tac. *Ann.* 2.7: *Restituit aram honorique patris princeps ipse cum legionibus decucurrit; tumulum iterare haud visum.*

[87] Tac. *Hist.* 4.17: *nuper certe caeso Quintilio Varo pulsam e Germania servitutem, nec Vitellium principem sed Caesarem Augustum bello provocatum. Libertatem natura etiam mutis animalibus datam, virtutem proprium hominum bonum.*

Thus, we find Tacitus exploring the German perspective on Varus even before he began composing the *Annales*. The living general represents *servitus* in Germania, but his death ushers in the *libertas* that they once held, and that nature intended for their people. In fact, there is only one instance in which Tacitus' mention of Varus appears to go unmarked. Again in the *Historiae*, Tacitus (*Hist.* 5.9) runs through a brief history of the province of Syria up to the time of Vespasian, but Varus is only associated here with the punishment of a certain Simon, a pretender to the throne following the death of Herod. It is as if Varus, out of the context of Germania, is without any great significance for Tacitus.

I have argued that Tacitus' narrative can be read this way, but why would the historian have chosen to write this ambivalent Varus into his *Annales*? A passage from the *Germania* provides some helpful insight.

> Our city was six hundred and forty years old, when during the consulship of Caecilius Metellus and Papirius Carbo the arms of the Cimbri were first heard. From this time, if we should calculate to the time of the second consulship of emperor Trajan, all together it is nearly two hundred and ten years: for such a long time Germania is in the process of being conquered (*vincitur*). In such a long age there were many losses on each side. Not the Samnites, not the Carthaginian, not the Spains or the Gauls, not even the Parthians gave us caution more often. Indeed, the freedom of the Germans is more bitter than the kingdom of Arsaces. For what else would the East throw in our faces than the slaughter of Crassus, since the East itself was cast down under Ventidius after Pacorus was lost? But the Germans, after Carbo and Cassius and Scaurus Aurelius and Servilius Caepio and Maximus Mallius had been routed or captured, deprived the Roman people of five consular armies at once, and even Caesar, Varus and three legions with him. Not without penalty did C. Marius in Italy, or the divine Julius in Gaul, or Drusus or Nero or Germanicus strike against them in their own lands. Not long afterwards the grand threats of Gaius Caesar were made into a joke. Then there was a respite, while by leave of our discord and civil wars they brought harm to the Gallic provinces when the winter quarters of the legions were attacked, but they were pushed back. Now in most recent times they are more triumphed over than conquered.[88]

---

[88] Tac. *Germ.* 37: *sescentesimum et quadragesimum annum urbs nostra agebat, cum primum Cimbrorum audita sunt arma Caecilio Metello ac Papirio Carbone consulibus. Ex quo si ad alterum imperatoris Traiani consulatum computemus, ducenti ferme et decem anni colliguntur: tam diu Germania vincitur. medio tam longi aevi spatio multa in vicem damna. Non Samnis, non Poeni, non Hispaniae Galliaeve, ne Parthi quidem saepius admonuere: quippe regno Arsacis acrior est Germanorum libertas. Quid enim aliud nobis quam caedem Crassi, amisso et ipse Pacoro,*

In this history of Romano-Germanic relations, Tacitus throws into sharp relief the situation as he sees it. We find again the same themes that we observed above: Roman loss and thoughts of revenge, German freedom, and a stalemate. None of the generals whom Tacitus mentions as fighting against the Germans is ultimately successful. For instance, although Germanicus is praised many times for his military success in Tacitus' telling, the historian often complicates or undercuts it with scepticism towards Germanicus' achievements, character and motivations, a fact which has been given much attention in scholarship.[89] Tacitus does indicate (*Ann.* 1.55; 2.41) that Germanicus' triumph was celebrated for victory over the Germanic peoples 'all the way to the Elbe' (*usque ad Albim*), but he also says that it was decreed 'with the war still remaining' (*manente bello*) and held 'as though it were complete' (*pro confecto*). The triumph lacked the crowning achievement, too. The enemy leader, Arminius, led in procession remains a thing that Ovid (*Trist.* 4.2.31–4) only dreams about. Moreover, in the *Germania* Tacitus describes the Elbe, the boundary of Germanicus' triumph, as 'a river famous and known once upon a time; now it is only heard of'.[90] In ways like these, Tacitus sets Germanicus as the paradigm for all of the future Germanici: Gaius, Claudius, Nero, Domitian, Nerva and Trajan. All fought a war or pretended to fight a war in Germania; all failed to conquer the freedom-loving Germans completely.[91]

Ultimately, the German perspective wins the battle on both fronts in Tacitus' telling: the Roman army fails to keep a lasting foothold on the far side of the Rhine, and the Roman tumulus is levelled, never to be rebuilt. These failures cast a measure of doubt on the effectiveness of these campaigns that were celebrated with their own, now hollow, memorials at Rome. Varus' memory may have been momentarily rehabilitated by the Romans, but the troubling fact was that all the effort and death

---

infra Ventidium deiectus Oriens obiecerit? At Germani Carbone et Cassio et Scauro Aurelio et Servilio Caepione Maximoque Mallio fusis vel captis quinque simul consulares exercitus populo Romano, Varum tresque cum eo legiones etiam Caesari abstulerunt; nec impune C. Marius in Italia, divus Iulius in Gallia, Drusus ac Nero et Germanicus in suis eos sedibus perculerunt: mox ingentes C. Caesaris minae in ludibrium versae. Inde otium, donec occasione discordiae nostrae et civilium armorum expugnatis legionum hibernis etiam Gallias adfectavere, ac rursus pulsi; nam proximis temporibus triumphati magis quam victi sunt.

[89] Shotter (1968); Goodyear (1972) 1.239–41; Ross (1973); Rutland (1987); Pelling (1993); Williams (2009).

[90] Tac. *Germ.* 41.2: *flumen inclutum et notum olim; nunc tantum auditur.*

[91] Lund (1991) 1954–6 discusses the importance of the theme of *Germanorum libertas* and its struggle with Roman *imperium* in Tacitus' *Germania*, and I would extend it to the *Annales* as well.

in the German campaigns had not substantively changed the situation in Germania. By foregrounding Varus through the whole affair, Tacitus shows his scepticism over the prospect of lasting Roman influence in Germania. It is much like Varus himself: a dream, a ghost, a terrifying memory.[92]

---

[92] Varus has even re-entered the popular imagination in novels and in a 2020 Netflix mini-series entitled *Barbaren*.

8 Decius and the Battle near Abritus

David Potter

Gaius Messius Quintus Traianus Decius was the first Roman emperor to die in battle against a foreign enemy. Having seized the throne from his predecessor in AD 249, his most famous act of policy had been an edict commanding all his subjects to sacrifice for the empire's prosperity. That didn't do him much good. He fell victim to his own poor planning in an extended campaign against Gothic invaders that began in the summer of 250 and terminated in May of 251.

The events surrounding Decius' fatal encounter with Gothic invaders were once shrouded in mystery. The nearest contemporary account, that of Publius Herennius Dexippus, was known only through four fragments: one describing a failed 'Scythian' attack on Marcianopolis, another a letter of Decius to the people of Philippopolis (Plovdiv), the third recording the repulse of an attack by 'Skythai' on the same city, the fourth simply saying that Decius was killed near Abritus at a place called Forum Thembronios. A series of spectacular discoveries in the past decade have changed this picture. We now have extensive new passages of Dexippus' *Scythian Affairs* (*Skythika*), discovered in a palimpsest at Vienna, and we now know exactly where the battle was fought and by what units. The combination of Dexippus' expanded narrative with the archaeological evidence from the battle site makes it possible to reconstruct the events surrounding Decius' catastrophe with far greater probability than has hitherto been the case.

What emerges from the new material is striking evidence for Decius' strategy at the beginning of the campaign, and his response to the failure of his initial plan. There was no anticipation on Decius' part that Gothic raiders might resort to misdirection, with the result that Roman armies were in the wrong place to meet the main thrust of an invasion. A consequence of this failure was inadequate preparation to resist the raiders once they had breached the frontier. The best Decius could manage was a hasty pursuit of the raiders. The Gothic plan appears to have been to attack deeply into Roman territory, evading Roman forces where possible, and plunder as widely as possible before returning home. The success of their strategy is reflected not simply in the destruction of Decius' army, but in the widespread evidence for high-value Roman coinage minted between the reigns of Gordian III (238–244) and Decius that made its way, either as plunder or as ransom, into Gothic territory in the immediate context of this assault.[1]

Before proceeding, some background. Our main literary source, Dexippus, composed two works dealing with the events of his own time. One was the *Chronicle*, which began before the first Olympiad and extended down to AD 270.[2] This work is poorly preserved but does, through the agency of George Syncellus, offer a fractured narrative of the campaign in 250/251 as follows:

> In the reign of Decius very many of the Scythians who are called Goths crossed the Danube and overran the territory of the Romans. They besieged the Moesians who had fled into Nicopolis. Decius attacked them, as Dexippus says, and, although he killed 30,000 of them he was defeated, and as a result (also lost) the city of Philippopolis. It was taken and sacked by them and many Thracians were killed. Decius attacked the Scythians as they were returning home. He was killed at Abritus at the so-called Forum Thembronios together with his son, at night, he was the enemy of God. The Scythians returned home with many prisoners and very much plunder. The army proclaimed a man named Gallus who had been consul, along with Volusianus, son of Decius, and, according to Dexippus, they reigned for eighteen months, doing nothing worthy of note. According to others they reigned three years, to others, two years. (Fr. 17 Martin; 23 Mecella)[3]

The second work was the *Scythian Affairs*, in three books that recounted Rome's wars with Transdanubian peoples from the reign of Decius (249–251) to that of Aurelian (270–275).[4] Prior to 2010 this work was known entirely from three Byzantine works, the *Excerpts Concerning Speeches* (*Excerpta de sententiis*), the *Excerpts Concerning Stratagems* (*Excerpta de strategematis*) and the *Excerpts Concerning Embassies from Foreigners to the Romans* (*Excerpta de legationibus gentium ad Romanos*), as well as a passage from Jordanes' *Getica*, which is concerned with the early history of the Vandals. The new fragments from the Vienna palimpsest flesh out details connected

---

[1] Bursche (2013) 161–4.
[2] Janiszewski (2006) 39–59; Martin (2006) 155–61; Mecella (2013) 71–96.
[3] All translations are my own unless otherwiese stated.
[4] Janiszewski (2006) 109–13; Martin (2006) 161–3; Mecella (2013) 96–112.

with Philippopolis' capture, establishing a connection between Jordanes' account of the events in 250/251 (*Getica* 101–3) and the *Scythian Affairs* through parallels in otherwise unattested points of detail, chiefly the name of the Gothic leader, Cniva, and a Roman defeat before Philippopolis' capture.[5] This is not the defeat mentioned in the fragment quoted from George Syncellus, which we can now see is most likely the result of some confusion in the tradition whereby two battles became one. The fact there was a battle at Nicopolis that the Romans won is secured by a reference to that engagement in the letter Dexippus composed for Decius to the people of Philippopolis (Fr. 24.10 Martin; 29.10 Mecella). Jordanes described the second battle as follows:

> The emperor Decius, learning of his departure, and eager to bring aid to the city, came to Beroia, crossing the ridge of Mount Haemus. There, while he rested his tired soldiers and horses, Cniva descended upon him like a thunderbolt, destroying the Roman army and driving the emperor with the few men who were able to flee back to Oescus on the other side of the mountains in Moesia, where Gallus, the *dux limitis*, was waiting with a large band of men; collecting an army from there as well as from Oescus, he prepared himself for the conflict of the coming war. (*Get.* 102)

As we shall see, there are references to this engagement in the recently discovered material.

Later narratives of the campaign, not directly dependent upon Dexippus, appear in Zosimus' *New History* and Zonaras' *Epitome of the Histories*. They are informed by fantasies and of no value for reconstructing the campaign. Amongst other issues, they all put the battle in the wrong place: barbarian territory rather than Moesia Inferior.[6]

In 2011 Galena Radoslavova, Georgi Dzanev and Nikolay Nikolov, working out of the Historical Museum at Razgrad, Bulgaria, published the results of an extensive survey of the region around the village of Dryanovets, some fifteen kilometres north/north-west of Razgrad (ancient Abritus).[7] They established that there had once been a Roman camp 1.5 kilometres south of Dryanovets. Here they found a large coin hoard, including thirty *aurei* ranging in date from Gordian III to Decius, buried in a clay pot, as well as iron tent pegs, iron nails from shoes, a catapult arrowhead and other pieces of Roman equipment indicating the presence of three legions, numbered IV, VII and XIV. These legions would have been *legio* IV *Flavia Firma*,

---

[5] Grusková and Martin (2014); (2015); Martin and Grusková (2014) 728–54.
[6] Potter (2018) 32–5.
[7] Radoslavova et al. (2011).

based at Singidunum, *legio* VII *Claudia*, based at Viminacium, and *legio* XIV *Gemina* from Carnuntum.[8] A short distance away, at Osenets a second coin hoard was discovered, this one containing thirty *aurei* of emperors from Maximinus (235–238) to Decius along with hundreds more *antoniniani*. The two hoards presumably represent cash in the hands of senior officers at the time of the battle.[9]

None of the legions whose traces have been discovered around Dryanovets were based in Moesia Inferior, where the battle took place; *legiones* IV and VII were from the garrison of Moesia Superior and *legio* XIV from the garrison of Pannonia Superior. This fact suggests that the fragment of Dexippus' *Chronicle* which places the beginning of the invasion in Moesia Superior, where Nicopolis (modern Nicopol) is located, is correct. We may further conclude that Decius set out in pursuit of the invaders with an army drawn from the garrisons of the central Balkans.

Notably missing from the archaeological record are legions I *Italica*, XI *Claudia* and XIII *Gemina*, which formed the garrison of Moesia Inferior. There is an insignia that once decorated a *beneficiarius consularis* whom the excavators suggest served in Moesia Inferior, but there is nothing that would otherwise support this suggestion.[10] The evidence suggests, on the contrary, that Decius gave battle without the support of the provincial garrison. The governor of Moesia Inferior was Gaius Vibius Trebonianus Gallus, proclaimed emperor after Decius' death, and about whom nasty stories were told, chiefly that he had betrayed Decius in the final battle.[11] In a late version of the story he negotiated with the enemy and sent Decius into the swamp where he was killed. The existence of a rumour to this effect in the third century may appear in the *Thirteenth Sibylline Oracle*, whose author included the statement that Gallus would 'bring the disorderly races against the walls of Rome' (*Orac. Sib.* 13. 103–5). The author of the *Thirteenth Sibylline Oracle* was amongst those who didn't think highly of Gallus, whom the author thought responsible for disasters in Syria during 252 and introduced with a pun implying that he was a castrate priest of Cybele (a *gallus*).[12]

The evidence from the battle site confirms only that the garrison of Moesia Inferior was not involved in the battle. This does not prove that Gallus was a traitor, and he later went to some trouble to suggest that he was a loyal servant of his predecessor, even adopting Decius' younger son, Hostilianus, as Caesar.[13] Given the dis-

---

[8] Radoslavova et al. (2011) 28.
[9] Bursche (2013) 159–69.
[10] Radoslavova et al. (2011) 29.
[11] *PIR*^{2} T 579; Potter (2018) 33.
[12] *Orac. Sib.* 13. 103, with Potter (1990) 283–8.
[13] Gilliam (1956).

tance between Oescus, the last place we see him in a text descending from Dexippus (Jord. *Get.* 102), and Abritus, it is best to discount the story that Gallus took active steps to betray Decius. He was simply not there. After the battle at Nicopolis, Gallus was left to guard the border while Decius pursued Cniva, who commanded a Gothic force that evaded Roman defenders, moving south of the Haemus Mountains to sack Philippopolis.

Cniva was not the only invader in eastern Moesia, and we gain further insight into the situation from one of the recently published passages contained in the Vienna palimpsest where we meet a Gothic leader named Ostrogotha, who is plainly operating in a different area from Cniva. Dexippus wrote:

> When the leader of the Scythians, Ostrogotha, learned that Philippopolis had been taken, and that the Scythians were celebrating Cniva in songs, as was their ancestral custom, for his better luck and success in the war . . . They were attributing weakness and bad luck in connection with military planning to him. Regarding this as intolerable, and not making an apology in so great a matter to the army of the Scythians, (but) mobilising with speed, he marched with an army of fifty thousand men so as to attack the troops with Decius.[14]

The fact that the capture of Philippopolis is the point of comparison between the records of the two leaders perhaps indicates that Ostrogotha's failure was before a city – quite possibly Marcianopolis, whose successful defence against a Gothic force is described by Dexippus. Jordanes did say that Cniva divided his force into two parts to facilitate widespread destruction in Moesia, and the evidently subordinate position of Ostrogotha, who is described as a 'leader' (ἄρχων), as opposed to Cniva, who is a 'king' (βασιλεύς), supports this possibility, as Jana Grusková and Gunther Martin have noted.[15] The placement of the Marcianopolis fragment before two fragments dealing with Philippopolis in the Byzantine *Excerpta de strategematis* suggests it preceded Philippopolis in Dexippus' narrative. The crucial point is that while Gallus remained at Oescus there were two powerful Gothic raiding forces operating in eastern Moesia Inferior. This suggests that Decius was concerned to maintain the security of the frontier even after it had been breached.

The next significant moment is the Roman defeat before the capture of Philippopolis. The reference to this event in the Vienna palimpsest picks up from the end of the fragment just quoted for Ostrogotha's doings, while, despite what Jordanes says, excluding Decius from full participation in the event:

---

[14] *Codex Vind. Hist. gr.* 73 F 194ʳ 17–29; Grusková and Martin (2014) 4.
[15] Fr. 22 Martin; 28 Mecella with Grusková and Martin (2014) 41–2.

Decius was worried about the defeat of the relief force and the capture of Philippopolis, and, when he had gathered a force of around eighty thousand men, he wanted to renew the struggle if possible. He thought the situation was favourable – although he had lost the auxiliary force – to free the Thracian captives and prevent them from crossing to the other side. In the meantime, having encamped in the area of Haemisos, a district of Beroia, he remained within the stockade, together with his army, watching for whenever the enemy should cross over.[16]

An important further aspect of this passage is the statement that Decius was hoping to rescue the captives from Philippopolis, which should indicate that Philippopolis' capture was not distant in time from the battle near Abritus.

Other evidence that has come to light in the Vienna palimpsest shows that the defeat of the relief force took place before the attack on Philippopolis began (this does align with Jordanes). According to this material, the Goths abandoned their initial siege operation and withdrew some distance from the city. A faction within the city then sent messengers to the Goths offering to betray the city, directing them to a weak point in the defences around the stadium (this area is described with precision by Dexippus). Cniva sends a select force to fight its way into the city, which they succeed in doing by clambering over a low point in defences where the stadium forms a portion of the outer wall.[17] At this point, even as the fragment breaks off, it does look as though the city is on the verge of capture. Assuming that the city did indeed fall to the night-time attack preserved in the palimpsest, there is no room in the connected narrative between the arrival of the Goths and this attack for an account of another battle.

A further tradition known to Aurelius Victor states Lucius Priscus, who was governor of Macedonia, was proclaimed emperor by the Goths after they had ravaged much of Thrace. Jordanes is more circumspect, saying that Priscus, the *dux* who was in Philippopolis, allied himself with the barbarians so he could fight against Decius. A Philip, described as governor of the Macedonian and Thracian cities, is mentioned in Decius' letter to Philippopolis, and it would appear that Dexippus placed his act of treason in the context of the city's fall.[18] For Dexippus it is news of Philippopolis' fall that spurs Decius into action, and at this point he gives a speech rallying his forces by saying:

---

[16] *Codex Vind. Hist. gr.* 73 F. 194ʳ 29–194ᵛ 11 in Martin and Grusková (2014) 734.
[17] *Codex Vind. Hist. gr.* 73 fol. 195ʳ 1–195ᵛ 30; see Grusková and Martin (2015) 35–54.
[18] Jord. *Get.* 103; Aurel. Victor, *Caes.* 29.2; Dexippus Fr. 24.2 Martin; 29.2 Mecella, with further discussion in Mecella (2013) 334 n. 7.

it is the duty of prudent men to accept what happens, and not to lose their spirits, not being distressed by mishap on the battlefield or the capture of the Thracians, in case any of you are disheartened by these things, for each of those misfortunes offers arguments against your discouragement: the former was brought about by the treachery of the scouts, rather than by a fault of ours, and they took the Thracian town by trickery rather than strength, their attacks having failed.[19]

There is likely to be some irony here. Decius' statement that it is 'the duty of prudent men to accept what happens, and not to lose their spirits' will probably be contradicted by his own behaviour at Abritus, for Jordanes says:

he attacked the enemy, seeking either death or vengeance for his son, and coming to Abritus, a city in Moesia, he was surrounded by the Goths, making an end to his reign and his life. (*Get.* 103)

This was not the only place Dexippus would have Decius give advice that he would not follow himself.

The final act of the campaign is the battle near Abritus. Decius' death had not been acknowledged at Rome on 9 June 251; it was by 24 June. A letter of Cyprian suggests that Decius was still alive at least into April or May.[20] The evening weather at the time of Philippopolis' fall appears to have been warm enough for the Goths to encamp without needing to light fires.[21] That likewise suggests action in April rather than an earlier point in the year. If Decius was north of the Haemus range, as Jordanes says, in the area of Oescus (modern Pleven), it would not have taken him long to reach the area around Razgrad, which is just over a hundred miles to the west. The battle at Abritus can therefore be dated to mid-May.[22] The original crossing of the Gothic army into Moesia around Nicopolis was likely to have been in the summer of 250; the defeat of Decius' auxiliary force might thus fall in March, since it was not old news by the time of Philippopolis' capture. The failure of the siege of Marcianopolis might also fall in March. The targeting of Marcianopolis may have been dictated by the fact that the Roman army was known to be concentrated in the western part of the province.

---

[19] *Codex Vind. Hist. gr.* 73 F. 194^v 20–30; Martin and Grusková (2014) 735, 738.
[20] Cyprian, *Ep.*55.9, with Clarke (1980); the dates in June are provided by *CIL* 6. 31129; 36760.
[21] *Codex Vind. Hist. gr.* 73 F. 194^r 7–8 from Martin and Grusková (2014) 735.
[22] Mitthof (2019) 331.

Decius appears to have selected the area of Abritus as a location from which it would be possible to intercept both Gothic invasion forces. Given that Plovdiv is just under two hundred miles distant, and the Goths had a head start, the two groups would have arrived in the area at about the same time. Decius' decision to pursue the Goths with approximately half the army he might have employed suggests overconfidence on his part. Dexippus is quite clear that he thought the man was a fool.

The length of the missive to Philippopolis is intended to tell Dexippus' readers something about Decius.[23] The choice of a letter as the vehicle for this information reflects the way people in the Roman Empire formed opinions about their rulers. Hence Philostratus' telling complaint about Aspasius of Ravenna's production of letters, in his role as *ab epistulis Graecis* for Caracalla (211–217), that were more controversial than suitable, or less than clear, 'for whenever an emperor writes a letter, it is necessary that he be given neither to rhetorical syllogism nor to trains of reasoning, but to dignity, and he should not be obscure, since he gives voice to law, and lucidity is the interpreter of law' (Phil. *V. Soph.* 628). If Dexippus' readers read Decius' letter as an indication of his character, it would strike them that Decius was problematic and overconfident.

To begin with, Dexippus points out that the emperor is being insincere.[24] He is worried about the possibility that the local forces of the 'Thracians' will defeat the Goths on their own and be so inspired by this success that they will put up their own emperor. This can be read against Decius' own career as a usurper from the Danubian provinces. But, more importantly, it must be read against what is about to happen. The Romans have defeated the Goths near Nicopolis, but Decius appears to overstate the extent of the victory – his own claims seem to contradict themselves. On the one hand, he is slowed by the need to finish 'this part of the war'; on the other, substantial, undefeated enemy forces are operating in the area of Philippopolis (Fr. 24.3 Martin; 29.3 Mecella). This is one problem; another is his statement that the 'Thracians' are inexperienced in war, and evidently do not have any Roman troops in their company. If they are so inexperienced in war, why should they be a threat to Decius? Why did Decius appoint a man like Priscus to be their governor if he was so lacking in understanding of the military art? What in fact was the relationship between Priscus and the leaders of the 'Thracians'? Decius tells the 'Thracians' that 'rashness without planning, joined to intemperate daring is a fatal mixture' (Fr. 24.3 Martin; 29.3 Mecella) and warns of 'the man who goes insanely into danger when he might keep himself in safety' (Fr. 24.5 Martin; 29.5 Mecella). Was Decius capable of taking his own advice? Dexippus' readers know perfectly well how he died.

---

[23] Martin (2006) 179.

[24] Davenport and Mallen (2013) esp. 66.

At the end of his letter, Decius tells people not to worry about the destruction of their suburban houses, since he will make everything good when he arrives, even if they do not need his help.

> Whoever compares the safety of all to immediate annoyance should reckon that the pain does not afflict everyone, but only those who are of the upper classes, and, for those who are very wealthy, even without our help, recovery from the damage will be swift. (Fr. 24.9 Martin; 29.9 Mecella)

As the new material from the Vienna palimpsest makes plain, the city fell because of internal dissension.[25] Also, by the time the reader has arrived at the new section, they will know that Decius never came to Philippopolis, despite the claim that his arrival is imminent (Fr. 24.10 Martin; 29.10 Mecella). His relief force was defeated in battle first, and he wasn't with it (readers would thus know that to some extent he is lying). Decius' statement that 'being commanded by a general and meeting danger in common with others, both in planning and in action, is safest since it offers easy correction with the help of the man next to you' could only be read as ironic (Fr. 24.7 Martin; 29.7 Mecella).

What would good advice look like? There are clues in two other fragments of the *Scythian Affairs*. In a passage that appears to come from the introduction to the *Scythian Affairs*, Dexippus announces that one can see how great the Roman Empire is in the 'number of armies attacking it and in the courage on both sides and in the stratagems and the cleverness of the war engines and the virtue of the opponents' (Fr. 14 Martin; 15 Mecella). Here Dexippus is signalling his interest in good planning as a theme for his work. Decius offers no advice on how best to manage the situation; he just tells the 'Thracians' to stay behind their walls. Dexippus' own discussion of what counts as 'good advice' appears in a speech he delivers to the Athenians gathered outside their city, which has just been taken by the Heruli (AD 267).[26]

As the speech opens, it is clear that the Athenians are in trouble: the city has fallen, and the families of the two thousand or so men who are listening to Dexippus are hostages in the hands of the barbarians. The speaker points out that they are in a good position to avoid head-on engagements with the enemy, to harass the Heruli from ambush, to make use of their superior knowledge of the terrain. If attacked in force they should make use of their local knowledge to attack the enemy without exposing themselves to unnecessary danger. It is plain that these are no professional soldiers that the speaker addresses, and that he takes some comfort from the

---

[25] *Codex Vind. Hist. gr.* 73 fol. 195ʳ 9–11, with Martin and Grusková (2014) 735.
[26] F. 25–6 Martin; 31–2 Mecella with Martin (2006) 37–41; Millar (1969).

presence some way away of a Roman fleet. Still, they cannot await the fleet – they need to act now. In his account of the wars of the Diadochoi (the successors of Alexander the Great), Dexippus observed that prudence and hesitation are not the same thing – the one puts off action through fear, the other seizes the best idea and leaps into action. Elsewhere in the same work, Dexippus wrote that heaven comes to the aid of those who behave courageously (Frs 3d–e Martin; 3d–e Mecella). The sentiments in the history of the Diadochoi track those in the speech to the Athenians here: 'Death comes to all men, but to lose life in the struggle for one's homeland brings the most wonderful prize and undying fame' (Fr. 25.4 Martin; 31.4 Mecella), says this speaker. He believes that fortune will be on their side because his people are defending themselves against those who have attacked them, and that Fortune is a great equaliser. All of this is missing from Decius' letter. Perhaps most interestingly, in Decius' letter there is no reference to the need to put one's faith in the gods (the edict on sacrifices surely was not forgotten). The 'Thracians' are told to fear the enemy and their own inexperience, but in the siege sequence we are shown that good planning makes the 'Thracians' more than equal to their enemies. The people who are about to have a problem with the loud-mouthed, weapon-swinging, frightening barbarians of this letter are Decius and his men. Decius is confident that he will prevail; he does not need anyone's help. Decius is terribly wrong. Even without Decius, the people of Philippopolis should have been able to survive – treason was their undoing.

The letter to Philippopolis foreshadows the battle at Abritus. Jordanes says that Decius learned that his older son, Herennius Etruscus, had been killed, and then rushed into the battle where he died. Ammianus Marcellinus says Decius' body was lost in a swamp, and likewise mentions the death of Herennius Etruscus in the action (Amm. 31.5.16; 13.13). Aurelius Victor, Eutropius and the author of the *De Caesaribus* also mention the death, but they are influenced by a tradition that emerged in the Tetrarchic period that Decius died beyond the frontier of the empire.[27] The two conclusions that can be drawn from these accounts are that Herennius Etruscus died in a preliminary encounter, and that Decius led a headlong attack on the enemy in a subsequent encounter. Dexippus makes it clear that there were two Gothic forces in the area; stating that Decius had a bigger army than Ostrogotha, he implies his army would not be larger than the combined forces of the Gothic army if its divisions were roughly the same size. The criticism of Decius implicit in the letter to Philippopolis suggests that he would launch an unwise attack on his enemy, not stopping to consider inherent risks, and is stated absolutely by Jordanes (Jord. *Get.* 103). The fact that Gallus, with what appears to have been

---

[27] Potter (2018) 32–3.

about half the available army, was not present might confirm the fact that Decius underestimated his enemy.

The best evidence for what happened now comes from the battle site. Decius encamped two miles south of the modern village of Dryanovets to the west of the river Beli Lom. Assuming that the tradition that his body was lost in a marsh is true, it is likely that he advanced across the river into the area now known as the Buyuk goyal ('Big Marsh'), which would have involved his army crossing the Beli Lom.[28] The spread of weapons and coins south and west of Dryanovets shows that the army fell back across the river.[29] Dexippus' stress on caution as a quality of a good general, and on appreciation of the actual capacities of an enemy (qualities lacking in Decius), along with Jordanes' statement that he rushed into battle in a fit of passion, suggest that Decius launched an attack on Gothic forces encamped east of the Beli Lom and that his army, upon crossing the river, became somehow enmeshed in the swamp. At this point, presumably in the swamp, Decius died. The army collapsed. Men fled south and west to get away from the battlefield, though the burial of a substantial coin hoard in the camp itself suggests that an effort was made to rally there by at least some portion of the army.

'The man who trusts in reason is stronger than the man who hastens in the chariot of ignorance towards the uncertain rush of affairs' (Fr. 24 .5 Martin; 29.5 Mecella). The events of 251, as Dexippus described them, are largely a commentary on this adage, spoken but not understood by Decius. The finds near Dryanovets appear largely to confirm Dexippus' picture. They show us that Decius led a risky attack across disadvantageous terrain that ended in disaster. His earlier failure led to the devastation of a major provincial centre. The victory he claimed in the summer of 250 was insufficient to stop the raiders. Dexippus' ability to provide insight into the movements and plans of the Gothic invaders most likely stems from encounters he had with freed prisoners.[30] The text and artefact align to provide a consistent picture of the events surrounding one of the signal catastrophes in Roman history.

The foregoing reconstruction of Decius' final campaign has implications for Roman thinking about imperial defence. Even after the Gothic raiders penetrated Moesia Inferior, Decius retained the bulk of his forces along the frontier, essentially turning defence of the interior over to provincial militias. His assurance to the people of Philippopolis that he will show up to defend them is presented by Dexippus as a lie, and the fact that the detachment sent in pursuit of Cniva was made up of auxiliaries suggests that Decius was unwilling to move legions away from the frontier.

---

[28] Radoslava et al. (2011) 35.
[29] Radoslava et al. (2011) 28–9.
[30] Potter (2019).

Elsewhere Dexippus provides a picture of a provincial militia that assembled to meet the threat of a southward move by the Goths at Thermopylae.[31] There is no reference at this point to any contribution by the imperial government. It was only after Philippopolis has fallen that Decius moved south in person, and he did so with only half the available army. His priority was border security. Both he and his subjects would pay a heavy price for his misguided policy.

Decius' emphasis on border control in 250/251 was controversial, at least as far as Dexippus was concerned. Dexippus' ideal, as comes through perhaps most clearly in his own speech after the fall of Athens, and in his depiction of Aurelian spewing classic Greek rhetoric, stressed the importance of shared responsibility for common security.[32] Leaving provincials to look to their own defence once the border was breached was definitely not ideal from either a provincial or an imperial perspective. By the time Dexippus wrote *Scythian Affairs*, the consequence of leaving the defence of a part of the empire up to local forces was all too plainly obvious. Postumus' rebellion in Gaul in 260 and the emergence of the Palmyrene state in the east both arose from local initiatives in self-defence.

---

[31] *Codex Vind. Hist. gr.* 73 F. 194ʳ.1–16, with Grusková and Martin (2014) 32, 37–9.
[32] Martin (2006) 176, 196–209; see also Mecella (2006).

9 Ammianus and the Heroic Mode of Generalship in the Fourth Century AD

Conor Whately

Ammianus Marcellinus has attracted more attention than most late antique historians, and this interest has extended to everything from his value as a source for the government of the fourth-century Roman Empire to the literary artistry he evinces in his *Res Gestae*.[1] Amongst other things, Ammianus happens to be one of our most important sources for late Roman warfare, and his significance in this regard has long been recognised.[2] Though some aspects of his value as a military historian have attracted more attention than others, including Ammianus' characterisation of generals, gaps remain.[3] One issue concerns Ammianus Marcellinus' purported emphasis on the heroic general, one who led an assault, fighting from the front himself.[4] For John Keegan, Alexander the Great exemplified heroic generalship,[5] for he was a general wounded as much as if not more than his fellow soldiers.[6] After Alexander, generals in the Hellenistic and into the imperial Roman world tended to eschew hand-to-hand combat themselves, though there are exceptions.[7] By the imperial

---

[1] Lenski (2002); Kelly (2008). I would like to thank all those who read or listened to a version of this chapter, including those in the audience of the session in which it was first presented at the IMC in Leeds in 2015; Alan Ross, who read a much earlier version; the anonymous reviewer for their invaluable feedback; and Shaun Tougher for the initial and subsequent invitations. None of them can be blamed for any faults that remain.

[2] Crump (1975); Austin (1979).

[3] See, for instance, O'Brien (2013); Marcos (2015).

[4] Lendon (2005) 302.

[5] Keegan (1987).

[6] Burn (1965) 140.

[7] Wheeler (1991) 124. Several consuls died in battle, with at least one of the two, Lucius Aemilius Paullus, perishing at Cannae, for example. Later, Marcellus fought at Clastidium,

era, Ted Lendon notes that the practice had long since fallen into disuse, which made Titus' apparent employment of just such a practice in the Jewish War all the more remarkable.[8] Lendon has argued that this approach to command re-emerged from the fourth to the sixth centuries AD, with Alexander himself often held up as a model by the central figure of our discussion, Julian.[9] It is this last contention that we will focus on in this chapter: heroic generalship in Ammianus Marcellinus' *Res Gestae*. We will concentrate on open, pitched battles. After a brief introduction to Ammianus Marcellinus and his history, we look at how he characterises generals, especially the Caesar Julian at the Battle of Strasbourg in 358, and compare this with the depiction of the emperor Valens at the Battle of Adrianople in 378. Then we look briefly at generals in sieges before finishing with some comparative material. As we will see, the generals whom Ammianus holds in the highest regard are best considered Keegan's 'post-heroic' commanders, who adhere to the Odysseus ethos, not heroic generals in the mould of Alexander, who adhere to the Achilles ethos.[10]

Ammianus Marcellinus

Ammianus, who has been called the last great historian of Roman antiquity to write in Latin,[11] was a Greek speaker intimately familiar with his historiographical predecessors who wrote in both Greek and Latin.[12] Ammianus' *Res Gestae*, the last half or so of which survives, provides a detailed history of select aspects of the years AD 353–376, so covering the reigns of the emperors from Constantius II (337–361) to Valens (364–378).[13] Classical and classicising historians made war and politics the focus of most of their works, and Ammianus was no exception in this regard. Indeed, much of the research on Ammianus and his world has been concerned with these

Sulla at Rome, and Caesar against the Nervii.
[8] Josephus, *BJ* 3.324; Lendon (2005) 259–60.
[9] Lendon (2005) 302. Levithan (2013) 181 also characterises many of the actions of Gothic and Persian commanders in the sieges described by Ammianus as heroic.
[10] Keegan (1987) 311–51. For the Achilles ethos and the Odysseus ethos, see Wheeler (1991) 137. For Keegan, a post-heroic commander is one who does not act the hero (i.e. like Alexander), for a hero takes too many risks that might threaten the cause. This – a post-heroic or Odysseus-ethos general – is also the kind of general that Procopius prefers, Whately (2016) 188–95.
[11] Among others, Matthews (*OCD* entry for Ammianus Marcellinus) calls him this in the first sentence.
[12] On Ammianus' Latinity and/or Greekness see, for example, Barnes (1998); Kelly (2008); Ross (2016).
[13] See Kulikowski (2012) 79–80 and *passim*.

aspects of his work, that is, the historical aspects.[14] But the historiographical aspects have attracted attention too, from his Latinity to his allusiveness and artistry.[15] If we narrow our focus, we find that some scholars have discussed Ammianus' value as a military historian as well,[16] including related topics such as his characterisation of the late Roman military,[17] or his approach to battle description.[18]

Ammianus Marcellinus followed in the great tradition of Latin and especially Greek historians with practical experience (Thucydides, Xenophon, Polybius, Josephus, Cassius Dio). As such, Ammianus unsurprisingly devotes a lot of space to military matters, including combat. Due to increased interest in the artistry of Ammianus' narratives, scholars have been asking questions about both the literary and the historical character of Ammianus' descriptions of combat. Kagan,[19] in a detailed study of combat in Ammianus and Caesar, argued that Ammianus' vivid descriptions of combat, both battles and sieges, bore the hallmarks of Keegan's 'face-of-battle' approach to combat narrative.[20] More recent commentators have more or less accepted this interpretation,[21] which has a lot in common with John Matthews' earlier views on Ammianus' account of combat.[22] Indeed, Alan Ross has gone so far as to argue that the 'face-of-battle' approach was characteristic of late antique historiography.[23] A key aspect of this approach is an emphasis on combat from the perspective and experiences of the lower-ranking soldiery. On the face of it, this would seem to affect Ammianus' approach to generalship. Kagan,[24] following Guy Sabbah,[25] has argued that Ammianus 'does not conceive of battle as an activity over which commanders have control', a view which has a lot in common with one espoused by Phyllis Culham, who highlighted the chaos that typified all ancient combat and argued that it was too difficult to control.[26] This presents us with a problem: some have argued that fourth-century combat was filled with cases where generals exemplified, or at least tried to exemplify, the heroic leadership ideal, yet

---

[14] Lenski's book (2002) on a significant proportion of the content of the *Res Gestae*, the reign of Valens, makes admirable use of a diverse array of source material.
[15] Kelly (2008).
[16] Crump (1975); Austin (1979).
[17] Crump (1973).
[18] Kagan (2006).
[19] Kagan (2006).
[20] Keegan (1976).
[21] Levithan (2013) 174; Ross (2016) 139.
[22] Matthews (1989) 298.
[23] Ross (2015) 16–22; (2016) 140.
[24] Kagan (2006) 91.
[25] Sabbah (1978) 576.
[26] Culham (1989).

others contend that the century's most capable military historian himself seems to eschew a prominent role for commanders in battle.[27] Can we reconcile this apparent paradox? A closer look at the two most detailed battle descriptions in the *Res Gestae*, Strasbourg and Adrianople, will provide some clarity.[28]

Ammianus Marcellinus' Face of Battle

Scholars have long recognised the parallels between Strasbourg and Adrianople, at least as conceived and described by Ammianus.[29] Where Strasbourg, on the one hand, marks Julian's greatest military moment,[30] Adrianople, on the other hand, marks the opposite for Valens.[31] Both accounts are full of sensory details, details which give the battles, in part, their face-of-battle air, for they give a sense of how battle was experienced by its low-ranking participants.[32] At Strasbourg, we hear the notes of trumpeters (Amm. Marc. 16.12.7, 27, 36), the clashing of spears and shields (Amm. Marc. 16.12.13) and the *barritus* of the Roman soldiers.[33] We see the reddening of the sky (Amm. Marc. 16.12.7), the long flowing hair and madness in the eyes of the charging Germans (Amm. Marc. 16.12.36), and the purple dragon of Julian's standard (Amm. Marc. 16.12.39). We also feel the blazing heat of the sun overhead, the thirst of the soldiers (Amm. Marc. 16.12.11), and the fear the appearance of the Germanic soldiers engenders in the Roman forces (Amm. Marc. 16.12.36). These details convey something of what it felt like to be in combat and they might be attributable to Ammianus' interest in the plight of the common soldier, as Kagan implied, though there is another explanation.[34] Greek and Latin historiographical theorists emphasised sensory aspects of combat, and long ago Naudé remarked on some points of contact between Ammianus' descriptions and the prescriptions of Lucian.[35] In the eyes of a number of theorists, like Lucian, a battle was an ekphrasis, and it was incumbent upon speakers and writers to bring the thing described before the eyes of the listener/reader.[36] A sensory focus appealed to the emotions

---

[27] In favour of heroic leadership, Lendon (2005) 302). Opposed, Levithan (2013) 198–9.
[28] Note the comments of Elton (1996) 250–1.
[29] Blockley (1977) 218; Kelly (2008) 313; Ross (2016) 134–5.
[30] See Barnes (1998) 152; Ross (2016) 134; Hebblewhite (2017) 20.
[31] Cf. Lenski (2002) 337–63.
[32] Matthews (1989) 298; Kagan (2006) 81.
[33] Amm. Marc. 16.12.43; cf. the dreadful shouting of the Alamanni in a later encounter in 368 involving Valentinian at Amm. Marc. 27.10.10.
[34] Kagan (2006) 28, 69.
[35] Naudé (1958).
[36] While Lucian is a well-known satirist, many of his views on history writing echo what

of an audience, and was the means by which the thing described was brought before that audience's eyes.[37] Many of those same theorists – writers such as Dionysius of Halicarnassus, Pseudo-Hermogenes, Lucian and Libanius – emphasised the important role of the general in descriptions of combat. Lucian, for instance, in his *How to Write History*, stressed that the narrator should direct his attention to the daring deeds of the general and not of the common soldier (*Hist. Conscr.* 49). The bulk of the surviving theorists wrote in Greek and Ammianus himself was a Greek (Amm. Marc. 31.16.9). That other great late antique classicising historian, Procopius, placed a great deal of emphasis on commanders in combat.[38] There is, then, a precedent for describing battle in ancient histories with an emphasis on the experience of combat without short-changing the role of the general.

The Battle of Strasbourg and the Battle of Adrianople

The most detailed battle narrative in the *Res Gestae* is Strasbourg, and an historical overview runs something like this. The battle involved a seemingly paltry Roman force under Julian (13,000 Romans), admittedly a Caesar and not yet Augustus, up against a numerically superior – at least in Ammianus' eyes[39] – Alamannic force under Chonodomarius in north-east France (35,000 Alamanni).[40] Although the Romans suffered setbacks over the course of the battle, particularly when their cavalry withdrew in the face of an Alamannic charge, in the end the organisation and discipline of their infantry proved decisive:[41] Roman tactics coupled with superior morale won the day,[42] a point not lost on Ammianus.[43] Such an overview is based solely on Ammianus, our only detailed source for the battle. Ammianus' account, however, is far from straightforward, as commentators have long noted, and not simply because of his emphasis on the aforementioned experience of battle. For one

---

we find in other writers like Dionysius of Halicarnassus and Libanius, as I note below. On Ammianus' use of *amplificatio*, another rhetorical feature, in the preface to the battle (16.1.3), see Brodka (2009) 55; Ross (2016) 136. See too Menander, 373.9.

[37] Aelius Theon, Spengel p. 118; Pseudo-Hermogenes 10.1; Aphthonius 12.1; Nicolaus, Felten p. 68.

[38] Whately (2016).

[39] Cf. Elton (1996) 255–6; Drinkwater (2007) 237–9.

[40] Romans, Amm. Marc. 16.12.2; Alamanni, Amm. Marc. 16.12.26.

[41] Though note Matthews' caution, (1989) 298, about how the battle turned out.

[42] See too Lendon (1999) on the place of tactics and morale in ancient conceptions of combat. His more recent essays, (2017a); (2017b), focus more squarely on the common features of ancient battle descriptions.

[43] Ammianus, 16.12.21–2, for evidence of his tactical awareness. Note also the comments of Crump (1975) 88–9; Austin (1979) 150–4.

thing, Ammianus himself was not at this battle or at Adrianople, so far as we know. This means that he would not have been able to rely on personal autopsy, and instead he would have been forced to use conversations with participants (oral sources) or documentary sources, such as existed (and which he could access).[44] Scholars from Sabbah to Ross have remarked on Julian's conspicuous absence from the thick of the fighting, an intriguing conundrum. Indeed, despite the panegyrical elements to Ammianus' description of Strasbourg, unlike Libanius' shorter account of the same battle, in which the role of the army is minimised at the expense of Julian, in the *Res Gestae* Ammianus focuses squarely on the deeds of the soldiers.[45] In sum, Strasbourg is Julian's great achievement, he is heroic, yet Ammianus Marcellinus focuses on soldiers.[46] Can a heroic general be absent from the fighting in his greatest military achievement?

Julian is, of course, not absent from the battle entirely. We find him in the early stages giving a long speech to his troops on the eve of battle in which he attempts to bolster their courage, stress the safety of their current position, and encourage them to adopt a cautious approach.[47] As it turns out, his troops are not interested in caution, and instead urge Julian to engage their Germanic foes (Amm. Marc. 16.12.13). Julian's caution is a theme that has long been recognised by scholars – it is worth remembering this point, for we will return to it later.[48] Needless to say, Julian accedes to the will of his men, though also to the wishes of his fellow officers, represented by Florentius, who had advocated the very same – aggression, not caution (Amm. Marc. 16.12.14). Julian's seeming lack of authority should, perhaps, be understood not in terms of his weakness of character but rather in terms of his interest in, and understanding of, the importance of the unity of his army, a theme often overlooked in accounts of this battle, though not in this battle's parallel, Adrianople. Indeed, not much later Ammianus comments on the power of a similarly united

---

[44] See Ammianus' own comments at 15.1.1. On the hierarchy of research methods for the ancient historian, see Marincola (1997) 63–127.

[45] Lib. 18.55; Kagan (2006) 3; Ross (2016) 136–7. See too Ammianus' comments on the panegyrical quality of his writing (16.1.3).

[46] Levithan (2013) 196–204 characterises Julian's leadership during the campaign of AD 363 as similarly heroic.

[47] Amm. Marc. 16.12.9–12. See too Belisarius' speech to his troops at Callinicum as described by Procopius (*Wars* 1.18.11–12, 16–24); Whately (2016) 91.

[48] Sabbah (1978) 572–9 notes Julian's prudence, especially in relation to Chnodomarius and Constantius. Kelly (2008) 313–16 discusses how Julian's caution at Strasbourg contrasts with Valens at Adrianople. Note too Marcos (2015) 674 on Constantius II as delayer (*cunctator*) and Julian as leader (*ductor*), though Marcos (2015) 692 makes a strong case that a delayer general was suitable in particular contexts.

army in a different context, namely those forces who united under Vadomarius (Amm. Marc. 16.12.7). Just after that, Ammianus claims that all the soldiery, from the lowest to the highest in rank, agreed that this was the best time to engage the Alamanni (Amm. Marc. 16.12.18), agreement which underscores this army's unity. With matters just so, and as the battle begins, we find Julian directing men where needed, all the while moving across his lines shouting words of encouragement.[49] The phase of the battle that involves the struggles of the Roman cavalry follows, and Julian intervenes again to prevent those men and the rest of his troops from participating in a wholesale withdrawal from the field of battle by means of some decisive action and well-chosen words.[50] Although here Julian engages in the action himself, he is not fighting – only stopping the flight of his soldiers. As the fighting intensifies, Julian disappears and Ammianus returns to the sensory, emphasising the blood, gore and experience of combat (Amm. Marc. 16.12.42–54). With that, the battle draws to a close. To take stock, then, Julian's important duties in this battle as I see them include his interest in caution, his awareness of the importance of morale, his efforts to promote unity amongst his forces, his quick thinking, and his careful management of his troops before and during battle. What he has not done, as noted earlier, is perform any action that could be considered heroic in the Homeric sense – fighting from the front – implied by Lendon.

Julian's actions at Strasbourg should be contrasted with those of his successor Valens at Adrianople. In the latter instance, Valens famously fought against the Goths on a hot summer's day in August 378 (Amm. Marc. 31.12.10), after a long march and without waiting for the reinforcements coming with his nephew, the emperor Gratian, though some have argued that his impatience was dictated by necessity.[51] Valens, of course, lost his life in that battle, which has gone down as one of the most significant defeats in Roman history.[52] By the end of the battle, the eastern army might have lost as many as sixteen units, or so Dietrich Hoffman; of the fifty field units that Valens had at the start of his reign, only twenty were left following his death.[53] Yet again, Ammianus fills his account with the sensory, from the sights and sounds (Amm. Marc. 31.13.1) to horrific scenes filled with fallen and

---

[49] Amm. Marc. 16.12.28–35. In my mind this is a far more realistic depiction of a general's harangue than that alluded to above. On the reliability of battle speeches see Hansen (1993); Prichett (1994b); Whately (2015b).

[50] Amm. Marc. 16.12.38–40; cf. Amm. Marc. 16.12.41. On Ammianus' likening of Julian to Sulla, see the comments of Ross (2011) 184, and on Ammianus' *exempla* more generally Blockley (1977); Kelly (2008).

[51] Lenski (2002) 365.

[52] Lenski (1997).

[53] Hoffman (1969–70) I.457; Lenski (2002) 339.

falling Roman troops (Amm. Marc. 31.13.4–7). Like Julian, Valens is both present and absent, present in the build-up to the battle and its aftermath, but generally absent from the fighting itself. Valens, like Julian, is careful to consult his officers, though unlike Julian, he does not follow their advice – they advocated caution, he wanted to attack immediately (Amm. Marc. 31.12.4–7). When we find Valens at the end of the battle – a battle which is described in less detail than the aforementioned Strasbourg – we find some of Valens' bodyguards rushing to his side to protect their emperor, only to fail (Amm. Marc. 31.13.8–17). In the end, Valens' body was never found, and Ammianus provides two possibilities for his fate. Although even more goes unsaid in this battle than the last, it is worth highlighting a few features of Valens' performance: he was rash, he did not follow the advice of his advisors and wait for Gratian,[54] and his management of both the deployment of his troops and their morale was faulty, and all this, of course, is in direct contrast to Julian.[55] It is clear too that in Ammianus' account we find no evidence for a heroic general, at least in terms of personal participation in the fighting itself. If we accept Julian as the model general at Strasbourg, then we cannot explain Valens' shortcomings in terms of his absence from the thick of battle. Two detailed descriptions of combat, not a heroic general in sight.

Beyond Battle

The evidence from Ammianus, such as we have it then, reveals a preference for generals who were careful managers of their men, both low- and high-ranking alike, on the field of battle.[56] Furthermore, I would hazard that it is no coincidence that in those circumstances where we do find generals behaving heroically their actions tend to be ill-fated – and in the context of sieges,[57] with examples including Grumbates' son at Amida in 359, and Julian at Pirisabora in 363. A siege, of course, is a very different thing from a pitched battle, and there were good reasons for excluding them

---

[54] See Amm. Marc. 31.12.7.

[55] Ammianus highlights the long and difficult march to the battlefield on the day of the battle itself, and the deploying of the troops before they had all arrived, significant errors in judgement, Amm. Marc. 31.12.10–12. Regarding their morale, the troops were exhausted and hungry, as Ammianus himself readily admits, 31.12.13. When the soldiers turned and fled, Amm. Marc. 31.13.7, so did Valens, unlike Julian at Strasbourg, who stayed and urged his men on, as I discussed above.

[56] On the transition of commanders from warriors to battle managers in the ancient Greek world, see Wheeler (1991).

[57] See Hebblewhite (2017) 23.

from our study.⁵⁸ Besides, the quintessential heroic leaders, the Homeric warriors and Alexander the Great, achieved most of their glory in combat.⁵⁹ In the former instance, Grumbates' son perishes after he and his father rashly charge up to the walls of Amida. The defenders above spot the two, and a ballista is fired which successfully strikes and kills the young man (Amm. Marc. 19.1.7). The latter instance, part of Julian's invasion of Persia, comes after Julian has begun his assault on the city of Pirisabora and when some of the defences had been breached (Amm. Marc. 24.2.11ff.). Julian, surrounded by Roman soldiers, approached one gate in particular, was attacked, along with his men, by a number of defenders, and was ultimately forced to retreat (Amm. Marc. 24.2.14–17). It would seem, in Ammianus' eyes, that the consequences of heroic generalship could be detrimental to a general's army (loss of leader and subsequent loss of morale), though Ammianus notes that Julian had attacked from an exposed position, which is in contrast to a parallel he draws between Julian and Scipio Aemilianus (Amm. Marc. 24.2.16). In the case of Scipio Aemilianus, Ammianus says he had read that the Republican general accompanied by Polybius had undermined a gate at Carthage.⁶⁰ Scipio, however, had succeeded, though Ammianus stresses that he had had the good fortune of a protected position. This account does not survive in any source, or in any part of Polybius' *Histories*. Regardless, though Ammianus is attempting to explain away Julian's failure by recourse to the more straightforward circumstances of Scipio's success, it reads like special pleading. In that doomed Persian expedition, Julian received a letter from his prefect of Gaul, Sallustius, who pleaded with the emperor to abandon the campaign, clear evidence that there were others besides Ammianus who preferred caution (Amm. Marc. 23.5.4). The same issue doomed Valens at Adrianople: he did not exercise caution against the Goths; rather, he was hasty, both in deciding to face the enemy without Gratian's assistance and on the day itself, despite the adverse conditions (Amm. Marc. 31.12.10–11).

The case of Pirisabora brings up an important episode, namely Julian's ill-fated expedition against Persia, the epic or heroic character of which scholars have long recognised. Rowland Smith breaks down Ammianus' description of the expedition into two separate stories: Story A, which 'is the story of an expedition whose nobility the outcome could not tarnish, an epic mission conceived by a surpassingly great emperor',⁶¹ and Story B, which 'recounts a campaign always doomed to failure, and

---

⁵⁸ Levithan (2013).
⁵⁹ Wheeler (1991) 122.
⁶⁰ Cf. Rolfe (1940) 418 n. 2.
⁶¹ Smith (1999) 92.

marked out as such by signs available to Julian from the outset'.[62] It is the former, Story A, a monumentalising and epicising story of tragic glory, that is most relevant here.[63] One of the most interesting segments comes when Ammianus (24.14.6) says:

> Let the poets of old sing of Hector's battles and extol the valour of the Thessalian leader; let long ages tell of Sophanes, Aminias, Callimachus, Cynaegirus, those glorious highlights of the Medic wars: but not less distinguished was the valour of some of our soldiers on that day, as is shown by the admission of all men.[64]

Smith notes the Homeric grandeur of the leader of the expedition, Julian.[65] Indeed, we find bravery among the Roman leadership, such as the aforementioned case of Julian breaching the defences at Pirisabora almost single-handedly, or Julian fending off the attack of two defenders from Maiozamalcha (Amm. Marc. 24.2.14; 24.4.4). But most of the other examples of such heroism come from lower-ranking officers, like Macameus and Maurus.[66] Even then, those soldiers acted bravely when the Roman column was attacked; earlier, Julian had to bribe his soldiers with a hundred *denarii* each to get them to perform well (Amm. Marc. 24.3.3–9).

Fourth-Century Military Thought

The post-heroic approach to generalship (the Odysseus ethos) is not unique to Ammianus in late fourth-century/early fifth-century military thought. Ammianus' account of Strasbourg is not our only one, for we also have Libanius' even more flattering account found in his funeral oration for Julian. As in the *Res Gestae*, Libanius' Julian gives a speech to the troops, only in his case the purpose is not to temper their zeal but to rouse them to battle (Lib. *Or.* 18.53). The Julian of this battle is not actively involved in the combat: he shouts encouragement at low moments in the fighting but does not fight himself (Lib. *Or.* 18.58). Julian was a prolific author, at least by the standards of emperors, and he wrote a panegyric in honour of Constantius II. Though Julian does not discuss his performance at Strasbourg, he does discuss Constantius' apparent military exploits, and while doing so focuses on his military planning and logistical preparedness, praise Claudius Mamertinus also

---

[62] Smith (1999) 100.
[63] Smith (1999) 95.
[64] Amm. Marc. 24.6.14 (trans. Rolfe).
[65] Smith (1999) 93.
[66] Amm. Marc. 25.1.1–2. See too Ammianus' account of the men who charged out from the mine at Maiozamalcha at 24.4.21–24. Cf. Lendon (2005) 302.

gives to Julian in a different context.⁶⁷ When it does turn to combat itself, in this case against the Persians, Julian praises Constantius' skills in battle management and makes vague allusions to his bravery and fortitude.

Another obvious point of comparison is the late antique military manual of Vegetius, and Ross, following Pieter de Jonge, has looked closely at the points of contact between Ammianus and Vegetius, of which there are a few. Ross goes so far as to argue that Ammianus' general was a lot like Vegetius' model commander; at the very least, they both seem to agree on what a general should do in battle.⁶⁸ Following our line of inquiry, when it comes to battle Vegetius' various commanders, such as the first commander/general, the *primus dux*, were to direct and encourage both infantry and cavalry (Veg. *Mil.* 3.18.3), that is, not to be in the fray themselves engaged in combat. Indeed, Vegetius claims that good generals (*boni duces*) never fight in a general engagement (*publico certamine*) unless there is an opportunity, or they find themselves in dire straits (Veg. *Mil.* 3.26.31). In fact, Vegetius goes further, for the commanders who are second and third in command are also not to be actively involved: the second was to stand in the middle of the infantry line, while the third was bound to the left wing, managing its cavalry and light infantry (*Mil.* 3.18.5–8). Written a century or two later, the *Strategikon* of Maurice (2.16) advocated that commanders be posted to safe positions in combat too. That other giant of late antique historiography, Procopius, also highlighted the dangers of heroic generalship, especially in his account of the Gothic War.⁶⁹ Indeed, Sylvain Janniard, drawing on a wide body of evidence, has made a compelling argument that the preferred position of commanders in battle in late antiquity was at the rear,⁷⁰ and this as opposed to a position at the front, or to a flexible and changeable position. Even so, those commanders at the front need not have handled weapons themselves; that seems to have been the case in exceptional circumstances only.⁷¹

Conclusion

What we have found in this chapter is that an apparent paradox – face-of-battle descriptions of combat that emphasise the mass over the commander, written in an era when heroic generalship carried the day – was not a paradox at all.⁷² While

---

⁶⁷ See Jul. *Pan. Const.* 1.5B and 1.7D (his overall military 'genius'), and 1.21B–C (his organisational qualities). See also *Pan. Lat.* 3.14.1–2.
⁶⁸ Ross (2016) 146–8. See too Blockley (1977) 228.
⁶⁹ Whately (2016) 188–90.
⁷⁰ Janniard (2011) 135.
⁷¹ Janniard (2011) 134.
⁷² Note the comments of Gregory of Nazianzus on Julian (*Or.* 5.8); he sees current Roman

it is hard to argue against the impressionistic character of Ammianus' battles,[73] that does not mean we should see no role for commanders in them. At the same time, this is not exactly the Hellenistic or Homeric commander, master of trickery, troop deployment and one-on-one combat all at once.[74] Rather, the highest-ranking generals could be arrayers, even tricksters, but they were not to charge the front themselves.[75]

We close with a few comments on Julian, the so-called model general, that should make this clear. For all that Julian might have attempted to advertise his status as *commilito*,[76] in those rare instances when we do apparently find him fighting with his fellow soldiers the details are sparse or unclear, and/or the results are mixed, at best. In the battle outside Ctesiphon, for instance, Ammianus simply says that Julian acted as if a fellow soldier, *quasi conturmalis*.[77] If his fighting prowess had been so great, we might well have expected Ammianus to spend more time describing the emperor's slaying of Rome's foes himself. Instead, in his eulogy – Julian, significantly, died in battle – Ammianus notes one lone instance when the emperor managed to kill an enemy combatant, an activity that he states was beyond the bounds of the general's responsibilities (Amm. Marc. 25.4.10). Although at the end of that passage Ammianus says that Julian fought Germans and Persians while fighting at the front, the narrative he provided in earlier books is much more ambiguous about Julian's personal participation in the fighting.[78] Following the battle by the river Naarmalcha, Ammianus says Julian personally addressed many of his soldiers by name, and that he had personally seen their heroic deeds, a feat which seems unlikely if he had been in the thick of the fighting himself (Amm. Marc. 24.6.16). Thus, Ammianus' narrative did not always provide the proofs that his praise for Julian warranted, despite his own claims to the contrary.[79]

Julian did not charge boldly into the fray, that is, he was not a heroic general, a view which was very much in keeping with what we know about wider practice and thought in the late fourth century. When Julian rushed into battle rashly near the end of the campaign against Persia, he died (Amm. Marc. 25.4). In the instance

---

emperors as less heroic than ancient warriors, which contrasts, to some degree, with the views of Lendon (2005) 303, who sees the fourth century as the triumph of heroic leadership.

[73] Levithan (2013) 174.
[74] *Contra* Lendon (2005) 303.
[75] Note Wheeler's comments (1991) 123–4 on the Hellenistic general.
[76] Amm. Marc. 24.6.11; Hebblewhite (2017) 22–7.
[77] Amm. Marc. 24.6.11. See Hom. *Il.* 4.297.
[78] Note Amm. Marc. 24.3.2, for example.
[79] Amm. Marc. 16.1.2–3; Marincola (1997) 173.

where a Homeric comparison is made with Julian, it is not as a warrior like Achilles striking down opponents left and right, but in terms of his deployment of Homeric tactics (Amm. Marc. 24.6.9). Commanders did play a prominent role in Ammianus' descriptions of battle, though the praiseworthy generals we find might best fall into Keegan's 'post-heroic' mode. Julian's finer points, at least with respect to command, match best the characteristics Keegan identifies as integral in an era of 'post-heroic' command: generals who take action themselves only in select circumstances, as the examples of Julian during the Persian expedition attest.[80]

[80] Keegan (1987) 325–38.

10 The Fine Line between Courage and Fear in the *Vandal War*

Michael Stewart

The courageous man's fears are great and many.

Aristotle, *EE* 1228b[1]

The emotion of 'fear' takes centre stage in Procopius' *Vandal War*.[2] I am certainly not the first to notice this emphasis. Recent scholarship has underlined Procopius' stress on the febrile anxiety that gripped Constantinople when the emperor Justinian I (AD 527–565) announced his military expedition to recover the former Roman provinces of North Africa from the Vandals in the summer of 533.[3]

According to Procopius, the generals, who had just waged a series of hard-fought land campaigns against Persia, were reluctant to launch a sea invasion of a realm which had been out of Roman hands for over a century:

---

[1] The complete passage reads: ὥστε συμβαίνει τὸν ἀνδρεῖον μεγάλους φόβους καὶ πολλοὺς ποιεῖσθαι.

[2] Procopius' vocabulary for 'fear' and 'terror' consists of three primary word groups, based on the nouns φόβος, ὀρρωδία and δέος. In ancient Greek, δέος typically refers to future or possible danger, while φόβος represents the fear that seizes one when danger is clear and present. The study of emotions has become a valuable methodological tool for modern scholars studying the thought-worlds behind classical and late antique literature. For a range of recent examples, see Nussbaum (1994); Shivola and Engberg-Pederson (1998); Desmond (2006); Sidwell and Dzino (2010). For the emotions of important personalities as a vital factor in determining the historical process in the writings of Procopius, see Brodka (2004) 71.

[3] See, for example, Anagnostakis (2014); Kaldellis (2016); Whately (2016); Sarris (2017) 239; Ross (2017) 78.

Each of the generals, supposing that he himself would command the army, was in terror (κατωρρώδει) and dread (ἀπώκνει) at the greatness of the danger, if it should be necessary for him – assuming he survived the perils of the sea – to encamp in enemy land and, using his ships as a base, to engage in a war against a kingdom both large and formidable. (*Wars* 3.10.4)[4]

The memory of a botched military expedition in 468 against the Vandals had clearly left its mark on the Roman psyche.[5] This defeat had seen a formidable Roman naval force destroyed by Vandal fireships just off the shores of North Africa and had left both halves of the empire's pride dented and their finances in tatters.[6] Yet Procopius reports that the Roman generals were too frightened to speak up. Only the praetorian prefect John the Cappadocian, a man generally denigrated by the historian, had the nerve to warn the emperor about the financial and political ramifications of such a venture. Heeding John's advice, Justinian relented and temporarily abandoned his plan.[7]

It took a religious vision to change the devout emperor's mind.[8] Procopius describes how a visiting bishop related to the emperor a dream where God commanded the bishop to remind Justinian that 'after undertaking the task of protecting Christians in Libya from tyrants', the emperor 'for no good reason had become afraid (κατωρρώδησε)'. God, the bishop reassured the emperor, would be fighting

---

[4] With some exceptions and modifications, translations from the *Wars* are from Kaldellis (2014) while the translations from Maurice's *Strategikon* derive from Dennis (1984). All translations are my own.
[5] Parnell (2017) 61–2 discusses the impact on Procopius of lingering fears of 'barbarians' in mid-sixth-century Byzantium.
[6] John Lydus, *De Mag.* 3.43–4, and Candidus, Fr. 2, highlight the ongoing financial ramifications of the defeat.
[7] For elements of John's speech, which recall Herodotus' depiction of Artabanus' attempt to dissuade Xerxes from invading Greece, see Evans (1971) 85–6; Kaldellis (2004) 180; Zali (2016) 93–5. According to Procopius, *Wars* 3.9.8–14, and John Malalas, 18.57, Gelimer's dethronement of his cousin Hilderic (523–530) provided Justinian with his *casus belli*. We find further emphasis on Justinian's need to protect orthodox Christians in North Africa from persecution, *Cod. Iust.* 1.27.1–4.
[8] A contemporary African source, Victor Tonnensis, *chron.* s.a. 534, offers another version of the religious vision. He explains that the fifth-century bishop Laetus, who had been executed by the Vandal king Huneric in 479, appeared to Justinian in a vision, which inspired the emperor to launch his campaign. Countering older scholarship, most scholars now believe that the religious rhetoric surrounding the campaign only developed after the Romans achieved their surprisingly quick and easy victory. See, for example, Cameron (1993) 108; Conant (2012) 306–9.

on Justinian's side 'and make him master of Libya'. With his confidence restored, Justinian assembled his armada with Belisarius in command and his staff secretary Procopius by his side when the Byzantine fleet set sail at the close of June 533 (*Wars* 3.10.13–20).[9]

Since Procopius probably included Belisarius among this group of jittery generals, some have seen it as an implicit criticism of Belisarius.[10] For these revisionists it offers evidence of Procopius' opposition to Justinian's campaigns in the west from the start and indicates that the historian was no sycophant of Belisarius even at this early stage.[11] Yet there are grounds for caution. In this chapter I will suggest that such views simplify the role that the multifaceted Greek emotion of fear plays in Procopius. When we pay special attention to the *Vandal War*'s structure and composition a more complex picture appears. Far from just a negative trait, for Procopius 'rational fear' – in multiple contexts – functions as an essential tool of sound generalship. Moreover, the episodes concerning fear in the *Vandal War* offer far more than hollow rhetoric; Procopius' recurrent discussions on fear follow closely the advice found in Byzantine military practices and manuals.[12] While ostensibly a history of Justinian's military campaigns in the east and the west, the *Wars* also offered future political and military leaders practical and anecdotal instruction (*Wars* 1.1.2).[13] So while Procopius' emphasis on fear stems partly from his reliance on Thucydides as a historiographical model,[14] it served too a utilitarian purpose of offering a moral evaluation of the North African campaign.[15] Let us begin, then, by making some general observations on the role of fear in some sixth-century sources.[16]

---

[9] On the probability that the fleet left at the end of June rather than the middle, see Dijkstra and Greatrex (2009) 259 n. 113.

[10] Kaldellis (2004) 176–7; followed by Anagnostakis (2014) 79–94.

[11] Whately (2016) 33 summarises ancient and modern historiography on Procopius' nuanced treatment of Belisarius in his writings.

[12] This is not to downplay the role that fear plays throughout the *Wars*. The emotion stands out particularly in Book 3 and the early parts of Book 4. For 'fear' elsewhere in the *Wars*, see Whately (2016) 87–8, 97–9.

[13] For members of the bureaucracy, educated elite and the officer class as the primary audience for the *Wars*, see Kaegi (1990) 66; Treadgold (2007) 189; Whately (2016) 5; Zali (2016) 119.

[14] On fear as a crucial element of historical causation in Thucydides, see Romilly (1956) 119–27; Hunter (1982) 33; Luginbill (1999); Desmond (2006).

[15] Whately (2016) 6–20 examines the modern debates concerning the extent to which Procopius' narrative reflects actual combat and that to which it adheres to literary conventions.

[16] I have primarily limited my discussion on parallels in the *Wars* with maxims in the *Strategikon*, since it reflects contemporary (if cavalry-centric) military policies, rather than the sometimes anachronistic suggestions of a military manual such as Vegetius' probably

Military Maxims

First the bad.[17] In battle, fear leads to panic, which invariably leads to defeat. Little wonder, then, that late antique military planners strove to limit their own fears, while simultaneously maximising their enemies' terrors. There were many ways to achieve these aims. With some qualifications, armies were encouraged to shout and make noise to rattle their enemies. The *Strategikon* ascribed to Maurice proclaims, 'An army which shouts its war cries good and loud can strike terror into the enemy.'[18] The mid-sixth-century polymath Agathias describes a Roman army stealthily sneaking behind their enemy and startling them with 'a loud and piercing war cry'. The Romans then easily routed the enemy, who were 'beside themselves with fear (τοῦ δέους)'.[19] Certain tactics and strategies, such as the bait-and-switch tactics favoured by the Hunnic cavalry and adopted by the Romans, functioned to induce a state of panic in their foes (Agathias, *Histories* 1.22.1).

The propensity for soldiers' fear to quickly degrade an army's fighting capabilities meant that a successful general needed to constantly monitor his men's fear levels before, during and after battle. Speeches offered generals one avenue to achieve this goal. The mid-sixth-century *Anonymous Dialogue on Political Science* (4.1) advises prospective generals to 'make your speeches both concise and military in style, so far as audibility and circumstances permit'. Depending on the mood of his army, a set speech could either boost their courage by easing their trepidation or regulate their ardour by implanting a bit of 'needed' fear. The *Strategikon* highlights the practical importance of speeches, commenting that 'the general who possesses some skill in public speaking is able, as in the past, to rouse the weak-hearted (δειλιῶντας) to battle and restore proper contentment to a defeated army'.[20] 'Defeated troops', the author of the *Strategikon* maintained in another maxim, 'should not be allowed to fall into despair, but they should be dealt with by stirring hope' (*Strategikon* 8.1.14). Procopius too shows how one could deliver pre-battle speeches to manipulate an

---

late fourth-century Latin *Epitoma rei militaris*. For further elucidation on the purpose and audience of these military manuals, see Whately (2015a) 249–61. On some of the similarities and differences between Procopian combat and the views expressed in the *Strategikon*, see Rance (2005) 429–33.

[17] Williams (1998) 57, 78–9 touches on some of the differences between 'positive' and 'negative' fear in Thucydides.

[18] *Strategikon* 8.2.46. For further ancient examples on the use of battlefield acoustics to terrify one's foes, see Lenski (2007) 233–4.

[19] Agathias, *Histories* 5.2.2; cf. *Wars* 4.3.13.

[20] *Strategikon* 8.2.74: I have changed the translator Dennis' 'courage' for 'εὐκόλως συμφοράς' to 'proper contentment'.

army's teetering emotions. Before a naval encounter in the *Gothic War*, Procopius has a pair of Roman commanders in a pre-battle speech purposely frighten their men by explaining to them that even if they decided to behave in a cowardly fashion during the coming battle, there would be little chance of escape, since the Goths controlled land and sea (*Wars* 8.23.14–22). Although Procopius' fondness for set speeches stems from his literary role model Thucydides,[21] we can see from the examples above that we should not discount their significance in either the narrative or actual Byzantine warfare.[22] Even though the *Wars*' speeches were no doubt embellished, and in some cases perhaps made up, Procopius probably based them on actual battle speeches he had written for Belisarius or those he had heard in person.[23]

Regulating their men's fear during the chaos of battle was another vital duty for generals.[24] Although Procopius, at times, chastised Belisarius for fighting on the front lines,[25] the *Wars* contains several instances where a general's ability to monitor his men's fear during battle contributes to a victory. For example, at the Battle of Mammes in 534, the Roman general Solomon changes tactics during a cavalry charge when he has his men dismount and fight on foot after he notices the Roman soldiers and their horses are terrified of the Berber camels. This shift in tactics allows his men to recoup their courage, which leads to a notable victory for the Romans.[26] Conversely, after the Gothic king Totila turns tail at the fateful Battle of Busta Gallorum, it proves devastating to the Gothic cause, on the one hand, in the psychological damage it inflicts on the remaining Gothic soldiers, and on the other, in the practical loss of their commander, who can no longer massage his soldiers' fears (*Wars* 8.32.22–36). Overconfident troops could be just as dangerous as frightened troops, as when Belisarius' failure to quash his men's eagerness for battle before the Battle of Callincium in 531 contributes to a Roman defeat (*Wars* 1.18.19–26; cf. 5.28.1–14).

A successful Roman general needed to provoke fear both in the enemy and in his own men.[27] When dealing with insubordinate soldiers the *Strategikon* advised using punishments to swiftly restore order and thus avoid insurrection:

---

[21] The emotion of fear plays an important part in Thucydides' set speeches too. As Desmond avers (2006) 362, the battle speeches in Book 1 'play largely upon Athenian and especially Spartan fear'.

[22] See further Lee (forthcoming) on the use of pre-battle speeches in both a literary and a practical sense.

[23] Treadgold (2007) 179.

[24] *Strategikon* 7, *Points to be Observed on the Day of Battle*, 1.

[25] See, for instance, *Wars* 5.18.5.

[26] For Procopius' admiration of Solomon, see Kaldellis (2004) 189; Stewart (2017a) 41.

[27] The *Strategikon* 8.2.35 cautions generals not to be too harsh in their treatment of subordinates, since 'Fear (Φόβος) leads to great hatred.'

By being just in punishing offenders the general should instill fear (φοβερόόν). At the very first sign of a disciplinary problem he should take action to end it and not delay in dealing with it until it grows more serious. The general is successful when his men regard him as unshakeable and just. (*Strategikon* 8.1.3)

A general's reputation, moreover, could strike such fear into the enemy that they might capitulate before a sword had been drawn. For example, Procopius notes that the Moors' failure to ally with the Vandals against the Byzantines was out of 'fear' of Belisarius (*Wars* 4.8.11–17). Only once Belisarius leaves North Africa do the Moors recover their nerve and attack the Romans, which, as we see in Book 4, undermines many of the Romans' earlier accomplishments.[28]

Lastly, as Byzantine war manuals constantly stress, a general had to fear all the unknowns before, during and after battle. This fear could either prove overwhelming or spur a general to victory. Motivated by fear, a vigilant general sweated the details; such thoroughness often made the difference in battles between evenly matched sides. On this point, the *Strategikon* comments 'that a general who takes nothing for granted is secure in war'.[29] This conviction underscores why we should not take Procopius' depiction of Belisarius' near-constant fretting before and after battles as criticism, as some modern scholars do; in fact we shall see that Procopius portrays rational fear as a positive emotion. Let us now examine more closely how fear shapes the *Vandal War*.

Fifth-Century Roman Failures

Procopius opens Book 3 by trying to explain the Vandals' triumphs and the Romans' crushing defeats during the fifth century.[30] The move away from soldier emperors after the death of Theodosius I (379–396) plays an integral part in Procopius' explanation of later Roman decline. According to Procopius, the Eastern emperors Honorius (395–423) and Valentinian III (425–455) had lacked the martial qualities necessary to intimidate barbarian peoples. Consequently, the 'Gothic nations', which, for Procopius, included the Goths, Visigoths, Vandals and Gepids, ran amok and seized their lands (*Wars* 3.2.25–6). As time passed the situation became dire.

---

[28] For 'the Moors rather than Vandals' representing a greater threat to the East Romans, see Conant (2012) 255. On the Moors' inroads onto Vandal lands in Mauretania and southern Numidia in the early sixth century, see Modéran (2003b).

[29] *Strategikon* 8.2.47; 8.2.7, 56, 65, 78; cf. Thuc. 2.11.4.

[30] On the three failed fifth-century efforts, in 441, 460 and 468, to retake Roman North Africa, see McEvoy (2014).

Taking advantage of the political chaos in Rome in the aftermath of Valentinian's assassination on 16 March 455, the Vandals sacked Rome just over two months later.[31] During their fourteen-day rampage, they destroyed and looted property, stripping the ancient capital of many of its treasures, such as the riches seized by Titus from the Jewish population of Jerusalem when the future emperor sacked that city in AD 70. The Vandals also gathered an impressive haul of human booty. A number of Roman aristocrats, including Valentinian's widow and daughters, were abducted and taken back to Carthage.[32] This included Eudocia (439–c. 466/474), who would go on to marry Geiseric's son Huneric (477–484) and give birth to the future Vandal king Hilderic (523–530).[33] Blame for the debacle was placed firmly at the feet of the feeble and 'effeminate' Valentinian III for inverting the expected gender role of a manly and protective Roman *pater familias*.[34] The sack of Rome by the Vandals, for Procopius, stood as a key moment in the 'fall' of the West.[35]

Yet the story is not one of pure linear Roman decline; in Procopius' view, under a series of soldier emperors, the military capabilities of the Romans improved somewhat. Despite their setbacks at the hands of the Vandals, Procopius praises fulsomely the West Roman emperor Majorian (457–461) and the East Roman emperor Leo I (457–474) for at least standing up to the Vandals and each becoming, to borrow the historian's description of Majorian, 'an object of fear (φοβερός) to his enemies'.[36] While Procopius provides a muddled account of Majorian's reign and the soldier emperor's aborted attempt to invade Vandal Africa in 460, he offers a more accurate and detailed vision of Leo I and the West Roman emperor Anthemius' (467–472) ambitious joint campaign against the Vandals in 468.[37] The Romans' shattering defeat in 468 provides the cipher for understanding Belisarius' unexpected victory

---

[31] Cf. Priscus, Fr. 30.

[32] Procopius adheres to the rumour found in other eastern sources (Priscus, Fr. 30; Marcellinus *Chron.* s.a. 455.3) that, seeking to avoid a marriage with the new Roman emperor Petronius Maximus, Valentinian III's widow Licinia Eudoxia had summoned Geiseric to Rome. For a recent account of the sack and its impact on the senatorial elite, see Salzman (2017).

[33] Hilderic's overthrow by his cousin Gelimer (only related through Geiseric's line) in 530, in Procopius' telling, would play a significant part in Justinian's subsequent decision to invade North Africa. Conant (2012) 313–14 suggests that Gelimer's usurpation genuinely upset Justinian, who had known Hilderic since the early 520s and had developed a close political relationship with the Vandal king based on the latter's conciliatory position towards Orthodox North Africans and hostile stance against Ostrogothic Italy.

[34] *Wars* 3.3.10–12; cf. Cassiodorus, *Variae* 11.1.9–10.

[35] This view echoes Justinianic propaganda; see, for example, *Cod. Iust.* 1.27.1.6–7.

[36] *Wars* 3.7.14. On Procopius' admiration of for Majorian as a soldier emperor, see Börm (2015) 308–9.

[37] On the disaster, Courtois (1955) 201–2.

in 533; the two campaigns have been rightly designated as mirror images of each other.[38]

In contrast to what Procopius describes as Belisarius' modest force of around 18,000 fighting men, he portrays Leo's expedition as a much larger-scale affair with up to 100,000 soldiers (*Wars* 3.6.1–24). Combining forces from the West and the East, Leo and his high command organised a three-pronged operation that approached Vandalic North Africa by land and sea. A formerly independent Roman warlord, Marcellinus, took Sardinia from the Vandals.[39] Meanwhile, the commander and future emperor Basiliscus (475–476) sailed the bulk of the East Roman fleet just south of Carthage to Mercurium, where they prepared to assault the Vandal capital; lastly, a smaller fleet led by the Eastern *comes rei militaris* Heracleius successfully occupied the Vandal stronghold of Tripolis. Heracleius and his army then marched towards Carthage to link up with Basiliscus' troops when they arrived in Vandal North Africa. Procopius remarks that in the face of such overwhelming strength even the formidable Vandal king Geiseric considered surrendering, 'So overcome was Geiseric with awe of Leo as an invincible emperor' (*Wars* 3.1.2; 3.6.11). However, Basiliscus, through either treachery or cowardice, delayed attacking Carthage, thereby granting Geiseric the opportunity to launch his fireships.[40] Even then, Procopius hints that if the craven Basiliscus had not abandoned his men to return to Constantinople, the Romans might still have won the day. The tale of Basiliscus' failure thus serves as an internal *exemplum* with which to compare the actions and manly characters of the *Vandal War*'s two main protagonists, Belisarius and Gelimer.[41] It is against this backdrop that Procopius introduces his episode on Justinian's controversial decision to invade Vandalic North Africa.

The Launch

So we can see that Procopius has already shown the reader that the atmosphere of fear which gripped the capital in the summer of 533, while understandable, was based on a largely false premise of Vandal military superiority.[42] Although Procopius includes himself among those stifled by fear when war was first declared,

---

[38] Kaldellis (2004) 179; Wood (2011) 431; Whately (2016) 131.
[39] The circumstances and dates of this joint expedition are disputed and in need of a reappraisal; I largely follow Merrills and Miles' reconstruction (2010) 121–3.
[40] Merrills (2017) 505 adds: 'Geiseric was fully aware of the fear in which he was viewed and presented himself as an instrument of divine vengeance.'
[41] Whately (2016) 157.
[42] Those of us who lived through the trepidation in the lead-up to the first Iraq War in 1990 can appreciate that a perceived military threat may not be commensurate with reality.

he makes it clear that he was among the first to discover that such fears were misguided. He inserts himself into the story to reveal that he had a prophetic dream, which made him eager to go on the campaign since it forecast that the Romans would emerge triumphant.[43] Though recent scholarship has pointed out this dream's possible subversive political messages,[44] like Averil Cameron I am inclined to take it at face value.[45] It is just one of many places where Procopius grants himself foresight that others in the *Wars* besides Belisarius mostly lack.[46]

For our purpose, it is surely significant that fear plays a didactic role during the Romans' arduous three-month journey to North Africa, where everything that could go wrong did go wrong. I would suggest that besides his educational purpose, Procopius describes accurately the fear enveloping the East Romans, which nearly undid the campaign even before the imperial forces had set foot on African soil. In the narrative, Belisarius is the most important character. Procopius' retelling of the first stages of the Vandalic campaign indeed offers a blueprint for how an exemplary general like Belisarius could transform terror into courage and turn impending defeat into triumph.[47]

From the outset, Procopius projects an image of Belisarius as a modifying influence over his unruly, heterogeneous forces.[48] Fear represents one of Belisarius' strongest tools against indiscipline. We see an example of this when, stalled by a lack of wind, the fleet anchors at Abydos in the Hellespont for four days. With his army's morale and discipline deteriorating, one of Belisarius' first acts after the fleet makes landfall is to execute two Hun soldiers who had murdered a colleague in a drunken dispute. Rejecting the Huns' pleas that Roman law did not apply to them as allies, he crucifies the two Huns in plain view of his expeditionary force.[49] To elucidate

---

[43] Conor Whately (personal communication) reminded me just how prevalent the big dream was in ancient historiography dealing with major impending military operations; for instance, Xerxes' dream in Herodotus, 7.11–19. Livy, 21.22.6–9, too has Hannibal have a dream before his march to Italy, and of course there are Lactantius' *De Mort. Pers.* 44.4–6 and Eusebius' *Vita Constantini* 1.28–30 recounting Constantine's famous dream before the Battle of Milvian Bridge.

[44] Compare with Kaldellis (2016); Anagnostakis (2014) 24.

[45] Cameron (1985) 173, 186; cf. Wood (2011). Williams (1998) 57 reveals how for Thucydides' 'fear in a positive sense is . . . equated with foresight'.

[46] Procopius and Belisarius' unique prescience displayed throughout the *Wars* is discussed by Van Nuffelen (2017) 47, 49, 51, 54.

[47] For Procopius' notions on the proper truthfulness in historical writing, see Treadgold (2017) 277–92.

[48] Wood (2011) 434–5.

[49] Compare with Procopius' depiction, *Wars* 7.8. 12–25, of the Gothic king Totila's just execution of two fellow Goths for raping an Italo-Roman woman.

Belisarius' reasoning, Procopius has the commander deliver an impassioned speech to his men, in which Belisarius declares that there can be no victory without maintaining the proper balance between courage and justice.[50] The driving theme of justice becomes particularly important once the army lands in North Africa, since in Procopius' view the Romans will only gain the Libyans and God's support if they treat the natives justly.[51] Procopius then inserts a third factor, noting that when the soldiers gazed upon the two impaled men 'a great fear (δέος) washed over them', and straight away the army's discipline improved.[52] Matters, however, grew graver for the Romans after they took again to the sea. The penny-pinching praetorian prefect John, had provisioned the ships with tainted water and bread, and disease quickly spread throughout the Roman army. Barely staving off disaster, due in large part to the sage actions of his wife Antonina in storing some untainted water, Belisarius and his bedraggled force manage to finally dock in Ostrogothic Sicily.[53]

The foreboding ghosts of earlier naval defeats at the hands of the Vandals continue to haunt the Romans. Like any good general, Belisarius fretted about his lack of reliable intelligence on the Vandals, and especially their awareness of his impending attack. Procopius once again inserts himself into the narrative, explaining that Belisarius had sent him to seek out the necessary intelligence on the Vandals. Procopius then fortunately stumbles upon a childhood friend involved in the shipping business in Syracuse; the friend, whose slave had just returned from Carthage, assures Procopius that since the Vandal fleet was busy crushing an insurrection in Sardinia, they remained completely unaware of the East Roman attack force.[54] Reassured, Belisarius and Procopius head more confidently to North Africa.

Back at sea, Belisarius mulls over with his officers an invasion strategy that would surprise the Vandals and at the same time alleviate his soldiers' dual terror of the ocean and the Vandals.[55] As he does frequently in the *Wars*, Procopius crafts a pair

---

[50] For the nexus between morality and success in Procopius, see Meier (1999) 187.

[51] The necessity to treat the newly conquered North Africans justly is a primary theme in Justinianic legislation; see, for example, *Cod. Iust.* 1.27.1.15–16; 1.27.2.11.

[52] *Wars* 3.12.7–22. On the military maxims used in Belisarius' speech, see Whately (2016) 146.

[53] For the free passage and aid that the Goths provided to the Byzantine army in Sicily, see *Wars* 5.2.22–4.

[54] Merrills (2017) 501–2 posits that the merchant's knowledge about the Vandalic navy's whereabouts and the North African regime's awareness of the impending invasion were linked with his membership in a regional merchant sailing community.

[55] Dimitris Krallis discusses this same speech in his chapter in this volume, along with the vital place of such deliberations amongst the officer corps within the Roman and Byzantine military traditions.

of set speeches, which frame the debate and foreshadow coming events. Tracing Basiliscus' earlier route and strategy, the admiral Archelaus argues that since Gelimer and the Vandals were preoccupied in Sardinia, it would be better if the fleet headed straight to Carthage, where there was a safe harbour just south of the city that could be used as a secure base from which to swiftly capture the Vandals' capital.

Ever the cautious calculator, Belisarius rejects this strategy, as Procopius presents it, not so much because Basiliscus had previously failed using a similar plan, but because of his soldiers' terror of staying on the ships, which Belisarius foresaw would cripple his strike force if a storm struck or the Vandal forces met them before they disembarked. Belisarius' more prudent strategy called instead for most of his men to land at Caput Vada 240 kilometres south of Carthage, whilst the ships, with a contingent of bowmen, would shadow Belisarius' advance north. This strategy also shared several of the benefits espoused in the *Strategikon* (7.11): it had the element of surprise, split up potentially mutinous troops, and allowed Belisarius the necessary time to galvanise his men's courage.

Belisarius wins the debate, and the Roman soldiers take their first hesitant steps onto Vandal territory. Their unmolested landing does little to quash their terror, however. Once again, Procopius shifts his focus to fear's positive side. Spurred on by a combination of Belisarius' exhortations and their 'fear' (φόβου) of being left exposed to the enemy, the troops frantically make camp and while digging a trench miraculously strike water.[56] Procopius says that he told Belisarius at the time that this served as a further sign God had preordained their victory (*Wars* 3.15.35). Whichever way one chooses to interpret the theological implications of this episode, Procopius clearly expected his reader to admire Belisarius' deft manipulation of his men's fears to his advantage.[57]

Indiscipline amongst the Roman force reared its head again, so Belisarius censored his soldiers, this time for stealing fruit from the local Libyan orchards. Betraying Procopius' fondness for connected narrative flow, this incident prepares the reader for the East Romans' first contact with the native Libyans, whom Procopius labels 'Romans of old'.[58] After marching to the outskirts of the unwalled coastal city of Syllectus, Belisarius attempts to coax the locals to support the Roman cause. In this instance, Procopius provides us with evidence of the conciliatory tone and style of

---

[56] Wood (2011) 434–47 scrutinises instances of miraculous intervention and Providence in the *Wars*. See also Zali (2016) 92–100.

[57] Treadgold (2007) 177; Wood (2011) 36–7. Compare, however, with Kaldellis (2004) 180–3, who denies that Procopius sincerely believed in the miracle. I agree, however, with Brodka's recent assertion (2018) 260 that in Procopius' world view piety is admired, not mocked.

[58] The extent to which the Vandals, Libyans and Moors kept distinct identities as depicted by Procopius is doubtful; on these ethnonyms, see Conant (2012); Kaldellis (2016) 21.

Justinian's ideological offensive; it was indeed important that the character of the invasion be defined as a liberation movement. In a letter read out to the Libyans, the emperor explicitly promises the locals that the Byzantines are not making war on the Vandals – and thus breaking the treaty signed in the previous century with Geiseric – but merely punishing the usurper Gelimer, who had wrongfully overthrown the rightful Vandal *rex*.[59] Not daring to publish the letter openly, the local Libyan leaders rebuff Belisarius' overtures; fear of the Vandals at this stage exceeded the Libyans' fear of the strangers from Constantinople.[60]

Notably lacking the foresight and readiness of Belisarius, Gelimer finally learns of the Romans' impending attack.[61] After executing his royal rivals, Gelimer launches what Procopius concludes should have been a devastating and decisive counter-attack. Procopius reveals here that Geiseric's victory in 468 played a vital role in the Vandals' historical memory. Brimming with confidence, they scorned the impending invasion, declaring that the Romans would meet 'a similar fate to those whom the Vandals had defeated consistently during the fifth century'.[62] Yet much had changed since the Vandals last faced the East Romans in battle seventy years earlier. Procopius in fact consistently undermines the historiographical 'myth' of Vandalic invincibility; as we will learn, their decades of living the 'soft life' in civilised luxury had undermined the Vandals' martial spirit,[63] while, to borrow the words of Phillip Wood, 'the Romans had been hardened by fighting the Persians'.[64] At this point, each side possessed a distorted image of the other.

The narrative that follows has rightly been described as one of the most complex and asymmetric in the *Wars*.[65] To put it simply, during the crucial opening stages,

---

[59] Compare with *Novel* 78.4.1, of 539.
[60] Conant (2012) 316–23 contends that those described by Procopius as the Libyans appear to have been hostile to the East Romans, who differed from them linguistically and theologically. Yet, as Merrills and Miles (2010) 230 point out, Procopius and the Syrian historian Zacharias the Rhetor, his contemporary, tell us that North African nobles from both inside and outside the Vandalic kingdom had encouraged Justinian, in the years leading up to the campaign, to remove Gelimer.
[61] As Desmond highlights (2006) 358–9 Thucydides criticised leaders or generals whose 'fearless confidence' led them to a 'fatal neglect of the many dangers at home and abroad'.
[62] *Wars* 3.24.4–5. Procopius' depiction of the Vandals' overconfidence bears similarities with Thucydides' description 5.91; 5.97; 5.105; 5.111 of the Athenians' bravado and contempt for their enemies before the disastrous Sicilian expedition.
[63] *Wars* 4.6.5–13. In the Roman literary tradition, civilisation and wealth often led to softness, which, in turn, effeminised men; on this trope see Williams (2010) 153.
[64] Wood (2011). For the Persians' superior fighting capabilities in comparison with other non-Roman peoples such as the Vandals and the Goths, see Börm (2016) 620.
[65] Ross (2017) 83–5.

a combination of God, *tyche* (fortune/chance), Vandal missteps and Belisarius' competent generalship – highlighted by his wise decision to divide his army – preserves the East Romans from annihilation.[66] Misfortune and poor generalship afflict the Vandals during the first skirmishes of the opening battle, when Belisarius sends out his cavalry to probe the Vandals' vanguard.[67] Misjudging his arrival at Ad Decimum, Gelimer's brother Ammatas falls prey to a Roman ambush led by the general John the Armenian, which sees Ammatas killed and his force wiped out. Gelimer's nephew Gibamundus compounds the disaster. Here, fear of the unknown turns the tide of battle.[68] In this instance, however, the emotion works to the Romans' advantage. Having never laid eyes upon a Hun, Gibamundus and his 2,000 men panic when they meet the fearsome 'barbarians' and are easily cut down by the Roman allies:

> And since they (the Vandals) had never experienced a battle with the Massagetae (Huns), but heard that the nation was very warlike, they were for this reason very terrified (κατωρρωδῆσαι) of the danger ... and the Vandals did not withstand them, but breaking their ranks, they were all disgracefully destroyed. (*Wars* 3.18.17–19)

Nevertheless, Procopius reveals that the Vandals still held the upper hand; in fact, the bulk of the Vandals' elite fighters remained safely under Gelimer's command. Procopius declares that Gelimer allowed an easy victory to slip through his fingers when, not pushing his advantage and attacking the Romans, he halted instead to mourn his dead brother.

It is against the backdrop of this mayhem that the narrative returns to Belisarius, who is ignorant of this scenario. In this instance, Belisarius cannot rely on the meticulous planning and foresight that have guided him so far, but only upon his personal merits. When the Vandals gain the high ground, the panic-stricken Romans are nearly overrun; only Belisarius' arrival averts disaster. The Romans' position, however, remains exceptionally tenuous. Yet, offering a contrast to Gelimer's ill-advised conduct here and in subsequent battles, Belisarius stands firm in the midst of his men's panicked retreat: appealing to their honour, he converts their fear to courage (*Wars* 3.19.30–33). Employing a strong moralising undertone, Procopius draws attention to Belisarius' concern for the larger military cause, while also stress-

---

[66] On the Herodotean parallels in Procopius' notions on causation, see Zali (2016) 92–100.
[67] Rance (2005) 432 n. 30.
[68] Fear of the 'exotic barbarian' was a trope in Roman sources; see the comments of Conor Whately on Amm. Marc. 16.12.36 in his chapter in this volume.

ing Gelimer's personal focus on his brother's death. Fortune favours the brave, and so instead of scurrying away to fight another day, the unwavering Belisarius rallies his men and charges the Vandals, thereby raising up a large cloud of drifting dust that gives the impression of a much larger Roman force.[69] The temporarily leaderless Vandals, by contrast, collapse into disorder. Considering the battle to be over, the complacent Vandal cavalry dismount, inspecting the battlefield while Gelimer arranges his brother's funeral rites. 'Unprepared to face the onslaught of the Romans', the Vandals wilt under the force of the Romans' charge, and flee 'not to Carthage nor to Byzacium, whence they had come, but to the Plain of Bulla and the road leading into Numidia' (*Wars* 3.19.31–3). Continuing to preach moderation towards the Libyans and cautious of Vandal counter-attacks, Belisarius on 14 September enters Carthage unhindered.

Procopius ponders the reasons for Gelimer's failures with a typical rhetorical flourish:

> I am unable to say what came over Gelimer that, with victory in his hands, he willingly conceded it to the enemy, unless one ought to refer foolish actions also to God . . . I do not think that even Belisarius would have withstood him, and our cause would have been utterly and completely lost, so numerous appeared the force of Vandals and so great the fear (δέος) they inspired in the Romans. (*Wars* 3.19.25)

So we can see that a combination of luck, God and men's fear and courage plays a part in the unexpected Roman victory.[70] By halting to mourn his brother, Gelimer 'blunted the edge of his victory', and his best opportunity to defeat the East Romans evaporates. As with Basiliscus' infamous retreat in 468, Gelimer's bad luck, private concerns and failure to adapt to the vagaries of battle turn what should have been a victory into a defeat. Moreover, as the reader has learned throughout the narrative, other factors were in play. Belisarius' heroic fortitude contributed heavily to the Roman victory. Fortune was often connected to opportunity and daring deeds during the shifting tides of battle.[71] One senses that Procopius would have nodded his head in agreement with the *Strategikon*'s advice (8.2.31) to generals to 'Take your

---

[69] On the need for successful generals to be lucky, see *Strategikon* 8.2.94: Εὐτυχὴς στρατηγός τοῦ γενναίου μᾶλλον τοῖς κοινοῖς ἐστιν ὠφελιμώτερος. See also Krallis in this volume.

[70] Cameron (1985) 174 believes that Procopius emphasises here 'the hand of God'. Kaldellis (2004) 173, on the other hand, highlights the role of *tyche*. Both, in my view, underplay the connection Procopius makes between courage and Providence and/or chance, on which see Murray (2017). See also Krallis in his chapter in this volume on the intimate connection between virtue and *tyche* in Byzantine ideals of generalship.

[71] Murray (2017) 110–11.

time in planning, but when you have made your decision be fast in putting it into action. In war opportunity is fleeting and cannot be put off at all.'

The defeat was a serious blow to the confidence and prestige of the Vandals. By the close of Book 3 we find Gelimer utterly despondent. With the Vandals' hold on North Africa rapidly collapsing, Gelimer dispatches a much-cited letter to his brother Tzazo in Sardinia, in which he mulls over some reasons for the Vandals' lamentable fate:

> It was not, I think, Godas who caused the island to revolt from us, but some bane from Heaven (οὐρανοῦ) which fell upon the Vandals. For by depriving us of you and the best of the Vandals, it has stripped all the good things from the house of Geiseric at a stroke. It was not to recover the island for us that you sailed from here, but so that Justinian might be master of Libya. What Chance (τύχη) had decided upon previously it is now possible to know from the outcome. When Belisarius came against us with a small army, valour (ἀρετή) instantly departed from the Vandals, taking good fortune (ἀγαθὴν τύχην) with it.[72]

Gelimer's recollection of the Vandals' downfall exposes a part of a broader Procopian theme. By explicitly linking Providence and fortune to military valour, Procopius probably expected his audience to cross-reference his earlier digression on the plight of the unmanly fifth-century West Romans, whose inability to match the martial acumen of the barbarians had resulted in God and fortune deserting their cause.[73] Now instead of Valentinian III's family being led into captivity after Geiseric's sack of Rome in 455, it was the wives and children of the Vandals who had fallen into enemy hands.[74]

Upon learning of the disaster, Tzazo departs from Sardinia with his fleet. Curiously not using his navy to attack the Byzantines in Carthage, he instead abandons the ships and marches overland with his army to join up with Gelimer on the Plain of Bulla. The two brothers embrace, aware that the Vandals' hold on North Africa is on a razor's edge.

---

[72] For the complete letter: *Wars* 3.25.10–18.

[73] On free will and fate in the *Wars*, see Brodka (2004) 40–3, 57–8. Compare with Kaldellis (2004) 173–221; Zali (2016) 89–100.

[74] For some divergent modern opinions about how we should translate *daimonion* in this passage here and elsewhere, see Treadgold (2007) 211 n. 134; Kaldellis (2016) 15; Murray (2017) 107.

Tricamarum

'Fear' continues to loom large in Procopius' account of the lead-up to the final major battle between the Romans and the Vandals. Book 4 opens with Gelimer and his reinvigorated army on the outskirts of Carthage. Belisarius stays ensconced with his army within the city, unwilling to meet the Vandals in open combat until he shores up the city's neglected defences. Gelimer pins much of his hope for victory on his spy network's ability to undermine the Romans' hold on Carthage, through a combination of provoking 'treason' amongst the native Carthaginians and using fear to drive a wedge between the Romans and their 'reluctant' allies, the Huns and Arian Christian soldiers.[75] According to Procopius, the Huns 'feared (δεδιέναι) that if the Vandals were vanquished', the Romans would never let them return home with their war spoils.[76] Playing upon these fears, the Vandals convinced the Huns to betray the Romans. Luckily for the Romans, the ever-suspicious Belisarius hears rumours of these plots. Using the recommended carrot-and-stick approach advocated in military handbooks for dealing with potential treason (*Strategikon* 8.2.35), he counters the Vandals' subterfuge. First, he impales a suspected Carthaginian spy on a hill before the city. This has an immediate effect on those Carthaginians contemplating resistance. In Procopius' own words, 'the others came to feel a sort of irresistible fear (δέος) and refrained from attempts at treason' (*Wars* 4.1.8). Belisarius does not rely only upon fear and violence to control his men. Instead of punishing them for their planned betrayal, Belisarius showers the Huns with gifts and pledges that he will allow them to return to their homelands once they have helped him to defeat the Vandals; he coaxes the Huns to reveal their planned treason, and once they come clean, makes them reaffirm their oaths to him and the Roman cause.[77] With the immediate dangers of rebellion quashed and Carthage's defences repaired, Belisarius readies his army to attack.

Procopius then crafts three set speeches, one each by Belisarius, Gelimer and Tzazo. Belisarius' battle speech focuses on buttressing the new-found confidence his men had gained in the aftermath of their victory at Ad Decimum.[78] He tells his soldiers that this victory offers proof of their superior courage. To bring about the final collapse of Vandal rule in North Africa, they only have to maintain this valour

---

[75] On Procopius' depiction and reaction to Vandal Arianism, see Cameron (1985) 175–7.

[76] *Wars* 4.1. For Procopius' stress on the importance of 'native soil' for Romans and non-Romans in the *Wars*, see Sarris (2017).

[77] On the importance of such oaths in solidifying soldiers' loyalty within the late Roman military, see Hebblewhite (2017) 159–64.

[78] Whately (2016) 135; Kaldellis (2004) 195.

and self-assurance. Once again, he stresses that the Vandals' numerical and physical superiority would mean little in the forthcoming clash. Differentiating innate physical courage from cultivated spiritual courage, Belisarius declares that war 'is decided not by numbers of men nor their bodily size, but by the valour that is in the soul'. While appreciating that luck had contributed to their victory at Ad Decimum, he implies that actions on the battlefield could also shape one's fate. Belisarius' confidence springs as much from Vandal incompetence as from Roman prowess: 'For I know well', the general continues,

> that terror (ὀρρωδία) and the memory of misfortunes have taken hold of the enemy and compel them to become less brave, for the one fills them with fear (δεδιττομένη) because of what has already happened, the other brushes aside their hope of success.[79]

Continuing, Belisarius rejects the contention by some of his men that the Vandals will act more courageously than they had at Ad Decimum since they are now fighting to protect their wealth and loved ones. By instructing his men to 'go against the enemy with great contempt', Belisarius breaks with his usual cautious approach found during his earlier exhortations, when his men trembled with fear at the very thought of facing the Vandals (*Wars* 4.1.13–25).

The reader is privy to other details. We know that the Romans had only obtained their courage after nearly succumbing to the fears that had haunted them throughout the campaign. Their mental state before the Battle of Ad Decimum, in fact, mirrored Belisarius' description of the Vandals' current emotional state. Yes, random chance and God had played a role in the Roman victory, but this is not the whole story. Though Procopius does not mention it, we know that Belisarius' courageous and erudite generalship had contributed heavily to the Roman victory. Belisarius concludes his speech by predicting that with both the cavalry and infantry under his direct command, the Romans will easily defeat the Vandals and bring the war to a close. Such sentiments underscore the vital role late antique intellectuals believed a general played in battle; as the *Strategikon* (8.2.68) puts it, 'it is better to have an army of deer commanded by a lion than an army of lions commanded by a deer'.

On the Vandal side, with the arrival of his brother and his reinforcements, as Procopius presents it, Gelimer's mood brightens. Exploiting fear to motivate his men to deeds of courage, Gelimer forewarns his army that their families and pos-

---

[79] *Wars* 4.1.17–18. Here I have used (and slightly adapted) Dewing's rather than Kaldellis' translation because it better captures the causative relationship between ὀρρωδία and δεδιττομένη.

sessions will fall captive to the Romans if they do not defeat them in battle. Adding further shame to his future conduct, Procopius has Gelimer proclaim:

> Our fear (φόβος) is not for our bodies, nor is our danger death, but how not to be defeated by the enemy. For if we lose the victory, death will be to our advantage ... When a man is ashamed of disgrace, he need never fear danger.

He then tells his men to forget about their earlier defeats, contradicting Belisarius, by suggesting that the tides of fortune shifted arbitrarily. Gelimer closes by boasting that the Vandals' superior 'manliness' (ἀνδρείῳ) and large numbers will lead to victory (*Wars* 4.2.17). Those familiar with Roman military maxims would have known that Gelimer's sudden optimism was ill-founded. With its clear emphasis on God and sound generalship as the key factors behind a victory, the *Strategikon* specifically rejects such views:

> A ship cannot cross the sea without a helmsman, nor can one defeat an enemy without tactics and strategy. With these and the aid of God it is possible to overcome not only an enemy of equal strength but even one with superior numbers. For it is not true, as some inexperienced people believe, that battles are decided by courage (θράσους) and number of troops, but, along with God's favour (εὐμενείας Θεοῦ), by tactics and generalship (τάξεώς τε καὶ στρατηγίας), and our concern should be with these rather than wasting our time mobilizing large numbers of men. (*Strategikon* 8 Prologue)

Tzazo's speech is brief and to the point. Addressing his soldiers, whom he had just led to victory in Sardinia, he declares confidently that they will be more valorous than the recently defeated Vandals. Defeat at the hands of the Romans he warns, however, would erase any memory of their victory over Godas. Urging his men to summon God, he instructs them to set an example for the Vandals led by Gelimer.

Let us close by skipping ahead to what Procopius describes as the pivotal moment during the next Battle of Tricamarum, when, after Tzazo's manly death in battle,[80] Gelimer's moment of reckoning arrives:

> Gelimer, realizing that Belisarius was coming against him immediately with his infantry and the rest of his army, without saying anything or giving any command

---

[80] Procopius, *Wars* 4.3.14–15, constrasts 'the manly courage of Tzazo and his men' (τῶν δὲ βαρβάρων ἀνδρείως) in facing the furious Roman attack with Gelimer's disgraceful cowardice when facing his own doom.

leaped upon his horse and fled onto the road to Numidia. His kinsmen and a few of his servants followed him, stunned (καταπεπληγμένοι), keeping quiet about what was taking place. (*Wars* 4.3.20–1)

Why did Gelimer bolt during the height of the battle? Nuances of meaning can be tweaked this way and that, but the reader is left suspecting that the Vandal king's nerve had deserted him at this most meaningful moment. By facing his death manfully, Tzazo lives up to the words in his pre-battle speech. Gelimer's withdrawal only stalls his inevitable capture. Even more, it disgraces a general who had counselled his men before the battle to prove their manly courage by facing even defeat courageously and 'not bring shame upon the legacy of Geiseric' (*Wars* 4.3.22). Whereas Procopius did occasionally approve of a general's prudent retreat to live to fight another day, the result here for the Vandals was a catastrophic defeat from which they never recovered.[81]

Even after the Romans' decisive victory, Belisarius, following military maxims on wise generalship, continued to fret.[82] He feared that his men's insatiable hunger for plunder would give the remaining Vandals the opportunity to launch what might be a devastating counter-attack. Luckily for the Romans, the now leaderless Vandals were too befuddled to take advantage of the moment. According to Procopius, the threat to the Roman cause nevertheless remained all too real. It was not, however, the Vandals whom Belisarius needed to cow, but undisciplined soldiers with the imperial force:

> For neither did fear (φόβος) of the enemy nor their respect for Belisarius occur to them, nor indeed anything else at all except for desire for spoils and, being over-mastered by this, they came to disregard of everything else. (*Wars* 4.4.5)

It was only on the next day that Belisarius managed to reassert some control over his troops and marshal enough men to pursue Gelimer. Suspiciously supplying balance to his account, Procopius blames Gelimer's escape to Mount Papua, in Numidia, on Belisarius pausing his pursuit of the Vandal king to mourn the accidental death of the man in charge of his personal household, John the Armenian.[83] The delay

---

[81] For example: *Wars* 6.23.29–33. For Procopius' endorsement of retreat under certain circumstances, see Kaegi (1990) 65.

[82] *Strategikon* 8.1.32: 'After a victory we must not become careless but be on our guard all the more against surprise attacks by the vanquished.'

[83] *Wars* 4.4.14–24. Belisarius' drunken guardsman Uliaris accidentally killed John when the former attempted to shoot a bird with his bow, but instead hit John. Uliaris was the same officer whom Procopius blamed, *Wars* 3.19.24, for the Roman retreat at the Battle of Ad Decimum.

provided crucial breathing space for Gelimer. One at once recalls Gelimer's blunder when he paused to mourn his brother at Ad Decimum. Nevertheless, to read this incident as a harsh criticism of Belisarius is, I contend, to misread Procopius' larger intent.[84] Prefiguring deep fissures within the imperial forces in the second half of Book 4, Procopius blames Gelimer's escape and John's unfortunate death on a faction of undisciplined soldiers within the East Roman army. Belisarius' 'mistake' also serves to balance the scales of fortune. Yet, whereas Gelimer succumbs to his misfortune by fleeing, by keeping his cool in the face of adversity Belisarius quickly overcomes his bad luck. Gelimer's freedom indeed proves illusory.[85] Belisarius quickly tightens the noose on the Vandal king's neck by sending a contingent of soldiers to surround Gelimer's mountain fortress. Procopius relates that, after three months on the mountain top, Gelimer, racked by the dual fear of watching his young relatives starve to death and facing the inevitable storming of his stronghold, surrenders meekly to Belisarius' men (*Wars* 4.7.1–9).

Even though scholars have rightly detected sincere pathos in Procopius' depiction of Gelimer and the Vandals' downfall,[86] we should not conclude that he did not perceive Gelimer's capture and the Vandals' defeat to be a good thing. Among other things, Procopius' intent in his account of Gelimer and the Vandals may have been a literary one. Reverses are yet another theme which Procopius borrowed from his classical predecessors.[87] With Gelimer and the Vandals' shocking defeat, the tale begun in Book 3 has come full circle; it inverts both the sack of Rome in 455 and the calamitous naval campaign in 468.[88] His sympathetic sketch of the Vandals' plight likewise resembles his subsequent portrait of the suffering of the non-martial Italo-Romans at the hands of the Goths and the East Romans during the two-decade Gothic War in Italy. Without swords in their hands to defend themselves, whole peoples became highly vulnerable to more martial societies.[89] Moreover, the contention

---

[84] Kaldellis (2004) 186. This is not to claim that Belisarius' conduct was ideal. In fact, *Strategikon* 7: *On the Day of Battle*, 12: *After a Victory*, specifically admonishes generals who did not follow up promptly on a victory, claiming, 'as in hunting, a near-miss is still a complete miss'. It also highlights the need in the aftermath of a victory for 'maintaining good order among the soldiers'.

[85] Procopius' description of the gradual metamorphosis of Gelimer and the Vandals' confidence and fearlessness into despair and terror echoes Thucydides' account of the emotional transformation of the Athenians in 415 during their defeat and later withdrawal from Sicily; for a discussion of these passages from Thucydides, see Desmond (2006) 369.

[86] Cameron (1985) 141; Kaldellis (2004) 184–8; Pazdernik (2006) 176–82.

[87] As Zali points out (2016) 93, Procopius' 'preoccupation with the theme of reversal offers a marked affinity with Herodotus'.

[88] Whitby (2017) 36.

[89] Stewart (2017b).

that the defeat of the Vandals led to a protective, if metaphorical, 'enslavement' of the Libyans under the just yoke of Roman imperial rule represents a common leitmotif in Justinianic propaganda.[90] Adding to these points, Peter Van Nuffelen has spotted perceptively that once Gelimer forsakes his men at Tricamarum, he loses his narratorial voice and thus his ability to shape events: 'As long as Gelimer speaks, he can exhort his soldiers and issue orders, he is capable of having an influence on the course of events. Mute, he becomes the mere plaything of others.'[91] Gelimer's faulty generalship and enervated conduct at key points in the campaign contribute heavily to the Vandals' utter destruction. Procopius' description of a bewildered Gelimer marching downtrodden and locked in chains alongside his family through the streets of Constantinople during the Roman triumphal parade sears these lessons into the reader's mind.

Conclusion

Hence, I find Procopius' depiction of Gelimer to be less sympathetic than some.[92] As in the *Strategikon*, successful generals in the *Wars* had to control their own and their men's fear, be prepared for defeat and adapt to *tyche*'s entanglements. Gelimer fails on all fronts. He leaves his cities without walls, neglects to predict Belisarius' southern approach, underestimates his opponents and twice deserts his men when they need him most. In sharp contrast to Belisarius, he never tests his luck when the tides of fortune turn against him; instead, as with Basiliscus in 468, he cravenly flees.

The *topos* of fear remains a driving force throughout. I believe that the prominence of fear in the structure of the *Vandal War* was a conscious decision on Procopius' part, much more than mere garnish absorbed thoughtlessly from his classical models. The first half of the *Vandal War* is fundamentally a story about the value of rational fear and the dangers of overconfidence during the shifting fortunes of a military campaign. Procopius associates Gelimer's incompetence as a leader with the Vandal king's inability to, at first, experience rational fear when Belisarius' army approaches his realm, and next when he does not manage the emotion during the heat of battle. I contend, therefore, that the Roman victory over the Vandals was not 'due to dumb luck', as supposed by Anthony Kaldellis,[93] but

---

[90] For example, Paul the Silentiary, *Description of the Hagia Sophia* 15, 230.
[91] Van Nuffelen (2017) 48.
[92] For example, Cameron (1985) 147; Kaldellis (2004) 187; Pazdernik (2006) 205–6; Wood (2011) 443–5.
[93] Kaldellis (2004) 184.

determined in large part by Procopius' belief in moral differences between Gelimer and Belisarius.[94]

With his portrait of Belisarius, Procopius illuminates an ideal of generalship that was difficult for others, Roman and non-Roman, to match. The remainder of Book 4, after Belisarius departs from North Africa, paints a far gloomier picture of the return to Roman rule. Indeed, his lurid invective, the *Secret History*, is even more fervid, with Procopius' denunciations of Justinian's conduct of the military campaigns and criticisms of Belisarius.[95] It is tempting, but misleading, to conclude on the basis of this evidence that Procopius had turned against Belisarius or rejected the justice of the Romans' reoccupation of the lost African territories. When reading the *Wars*, we should not rely primarily on the criticisms, while ignoring the praise. I concur with a scholar's recent assessment that the *Wars* 'is, in fact, much more open-ended than we may be willing to admit'.[96] In my reading, Procopius laments the messy process behind the reintegration of Vandalic North Africa back into the empire, not the justice of the Roman cause. Moreover, since for Procopius virtue-based generalship contributes heavily to victories, it follows logically that a general's moral shortcomings contribute to defeats. Certainly, we should not underestimate the role that generalship plays in Procopius' vision of the Romans' triumphs over first the Vandals and then the Moors. As with another writer associated with Justinian's regime – the North African court rhetorician Corippus – for Procopius, virtuous generalship would play a significant role in returning Vandalic Africa to the Roman fold, while internal bickering, avarice, unmanly cowardice, intolerance and unjust behaviour by the Roman soldiery would lead to chaos and insurrection.

Some readers may be uncomfortable with my approach to Procopius. On the one hand, some may suggest that Procopius buried his intended meanings beneath his literary surface – safely concealed for those with the intellect to uncover the 'real' truths. On the other hand, others may lament what they see as Procopius' naive political analysis and his clichéd images and rhetorical *topoi* of fear. To do so in both instances, I would argue, is to discount the primary purpose of historical writing in the later Roman Empire and Byzantium. As Leonora Neville has recently remarked,

---

[94] Treadgold (2007) 181. Procopius, *Wars* 4.7.20–1, gives special credit for the victory over the Vandals to Belisarius' cavalry.

[95] For example, Kaldellis (2004); Sarris (2006) 5–10. On the heated debates surrounding the composition and purpose of *Secret History*, and the extent to which it expresses the historian's 'true' views, see Signes Codoñer (2003); Börm (2015). For Procopius' opinion in the *Secret History* that Belisarius' moral failures and unmanning at the hands of his wife Antonina had contributed to his military failures in Italy and Persia in the 540s, see Stewart (2015) 14–16.

[96] Van Nuffelen (2017) 52; cf. Cameron (2017) 16.

'Our desires and expectations for good history' differed from the Byzantines'. Consequently, what some modern Byzantinists consider as pointless *topoi* or mere surface rhetoric designed to appease the ruling clique instead offer critical insights into why and how Byzantines wrote and read histories. Neville continues:

> Historians told their audiences who they should admire and emulate, and whose behaviors they should avoid. They were bound to speak truth without favor or hatred, but they did so with the explicit purpose of presenting models of behavior. In deciding which deeds to commemorate and how to present them, historians became arbiters of morality and character, as well as success and failure.[97]

Even though Neville's analysis concentrates on Middle Byzantine historians, I believe that her conclusions are applicable to Early Byzantine historians like Procopius.

It is hardly surprising that in a history dedicated to recounting truthfully events Procopius had witnessed and the conduct of individuals he had known, the *Wars* bespeaks the shifting fortunes of battle, human transience and proper and improper conduct on both sides. While variable *tyche* and rare divine Providence play their part in shaping events, human free will is, for Procopius, the fundamental historical principle behind the Romans' unexpected victory over the Vandals. Though far from perfect, Belisarius' ability to master the emotion of fear enabled the East Romans to achieve a stunning success. By fearing neither too much nor too little, in the *Vandal War* Belisarius stands as a model *andreios* general and man.

---

[97] Neville (2016) 269–70.

11 The Generalship of John Troglita: Art in Artifice

Martine de Marre

Introduction

John Troglita is not a particularly well-known figure from the ancient world, and many consider Belisarius to have been the last general of renown in late antiquity.[1] But fame is not necessarily the only measure of quality.[2] We first hear mention of John serving under Belisarius during the Vandalic War (533–534), and then under Germanus and Solomon, fighting the African tribes.[3] From 541 to 545/546, Justinian appointed him as *dux Mesopotamiae* on the eastern border against the Sassanids. In 546 John Troglita was reassigned as *magister militum Africae* to quell the insurrections in the African territories, which he accomplished. His career was therefore successful enough for him to be re-employed in a number of different contexts, and he was responsible for successfully concluding the campaign against the African tribes – so one must wonder why he does not get more recognition in the ancient sources. Can this be attributed to his style of generalship, or to other factors? And to what extent are the majority of modern scholars justified in referring to him as a competent general, but not especially brilliant?

---

[1] The name Troglita is noted by Jordanes, *Romana* 385. Procopius refers to him as Ἰωάννην τὸν Πάππου ἀδελφὸν ('John, the brother of Pappus'). Further discussion on his origins in Modéran (2003a) 3866–70; Tret'yakova (2019) 38. He will be referred to in this chapter as 'John'.

[2] On the artifice of those commemorating weak generalship, see for example the chapter by Richard Evans in this volume.

[3] On the African tribes, Smith (2003); Richardot (2009) 129–40; Modéran (2003b). To distinguish the African allies from the enemy tribes, Corippus refers to the former as Maures, whereas the enemy are the Syrtes.

The Sources

Our two main sources for John's generalship are the works of Procopius of Caesarea and Flavius Cresconius Corippus, both contemporaries of the events they describe.[4] Both focus on three major battles in John's campaign in 547 (possibly concluding in 548), of which John lost the second but was ultimately victorious in the third. The account of Procopius comes at the end of his two books on the Vandalic War. Throughout, he presents examples of good and bad generalship,[5] in line with the didactic nature of his work (*Wars* 1.1.2), but his description of John's campaign is too brief to be included in this binary.[6] But where Procopius devotes very little attention to John, his strategic skills or his leadership, Corippus gives full rein to a heroic portrait of this military leader in his epic poem.[7]

From the perspective of today's ancient historian both these resources therefore have clear shortcomings from the outset. The aim here is to arrive at a balanced assessment of John's generalship, between the heroic general that Corippus describes and a mere footnote to Justinian's African campaigns, as Procopius would have it.

Procopius is generally considered the best and most trustworthy of the historians of Justinian's reign.[8] The historiographer himself informs us that he was appointed as a legal advisor (assessor or ξυμβούλος) to Belisarius (*Wars* 1.12.24), and for the wars in Africa he accompanied first Belisarius and then Solomon. He claims to have witnessed most of the events he describes (*Wars* 1.1.4), but left Africa in 536.[9] On

---

[4] All references to these authors in this chapter are to Procopius' *Wars* (primarily Books 3 and 4) and to the *Iohannis* of Corippus, unless otherwise stated. There are only three brief references to John in other ancient texts. Of these Jordanes' is the longest, giving a short report on John, and that he was 'working successfully' (*feliciter degens*) in the African province (*Romana* 385). Marcellinus Comes simply notes that John was appointed (*Chron.* Migne, *PL* 51, 547), and in the eighth century, Paulus Diaconus (*Hist. Lang.* 1.25) awards brief praise, summing up Justinian's entire African campaign only through a reference to John, 'a man of wonderful courage' (*per Iohannem exconsulem mirabili virtute*).

[5] Whately (2016) 4. There seem to be few narrative strategies in Procopius' account of John's struggle against the African tribes, and John does not accord with a stereotypical model of the 'good general', like Belisarius or Solomon, or the 'bad general', like Sergius: Cameron (1985) 230; Wood (2011) 424.

[6] Whately (2016) 2–5.

[7] There has been some debate as to whether this poem is an epic, a panegyric or even hagiographical, discussed in detail by Zarini (2003).

[8] Whately (2013) 131.

[9] Procopius is thought to have still been in Africa when he recorded extreme weather in 535 and 536, but thereafter joined Belisarius in Sicily. We have no information on whether Procopius returned to Africa at any point after 536, Evans (1970) 221.

the whole, scholars comment favourably on Procopius' knowledge and coverage of military matters and engagements.[10] But the reliability of his work has also been questioned, since, after all, we know that Procopius' work was a carefully crafted piece of literature, not a collection of historical data.[11] As one of the classicising historians, his work is strongly influenced by traditions in the historiographical genre which shaped his historical narrative, which may also account for his brevity on John.[12]

Our second contemporary account, the *Iohannis* or *De Bellis Libycis* by Corippus, is an epic poem extolling John's activities against the African tribes in 4,670 hexameter lines.[13] This work has received a mixed reception among historians, since on the one hand it relies heavily on the epic tradition and is essentially a panegyric praising its Aeneas, John, while on the other hand it does contain a great deal of detail which is missing from Procopius' account of John's campaign. It must also be said that it corroborates every aspect of the latter's account.[14] It is likely that Corippus was an eyewitness (or had access to eyewitness accounts) for most of the events which he writes about, and he was probably involved when Carthage was besieged by the Laguatan alliance of African tribes.[15] His use of names and places indicates someone

---

[10] Whately (2016) 150–1. On military intelligence, supplies, tactics, Howard-Johnston (2002); Colvin (2013) 573–98; on technical issues, Turquois (2015) 225–31.

[11] Schindler (2007) 227–309. Whately (2016) 115–57 on the literary *topoi* in the Vandalic Wars in particular. Conant (2012) 252–73 on the limitations of Procopius' evidence on the African tribes.

[12] Cresci (2001) 61–77. In praising the eunuch general Solomon, for example, Procopius compares him directly to Thucydides' Pericles; Kaldellis (2004) 189.

[13] Procopius' *Wars* is thought to have been published around 550 and his *Buildings* started around 558; Evans (1970) 222–3. Most scholars see the epic as slightly earlier than Procopius' account; Cameron (1985) 123; Kaldellis (2004) 271 nn. 138 and 141. Part of the epic was recited in Carthage to celebrate the Byzantine victory, at some point between 549 and 555; Hofmann (1989) 362 n. 7. Gärtner (2008) 72–3 has suggested that Corippus may have been aware of an earlier draft of Procopius' work on the wars in Africa, but this is convincingly refuted by Riedlberger (2010a) 15–27.

[14] On Corippus' sources and panegyric style, see Tommasi Moreschini (2001) 11–43. Many historians today use the epic to flesh out their descriptions of the turbulence in Africa as the forces of Justinian attempted to regain the African provinces as part of this emperor's Grand Strategy. For example, Cameron (1982) 38–9; (1985) 183; Mattingly (1994) 38–9; Whately (2013) 131; Merrills and Miles (2010) 129, 228, 253–4; De Marre (2018) 162–3. Shea (1998) 20 on reliable and less reliable aspects, along with detailed commentaries on specific books by Goldlust (2017); Riedlberger (2010a); Gärtner (2008); Tommasi Moreschini (2001); Zarini (2003).

[15] Shea (1998) 3; Mattingly (2008) 4314–18.

familiar with the terrain, its peoples and tribal affiliations.[16] Of Corippus himself we know nothing outside his two panegyrical works.[17] His knowledge of military matters from the *Iohannis* appears to be rather erratic. Some of the tactics described can be aligned with strategic advice in the military manuals of Vegetius and Maurice,[18] but otherwise the poet's text reveals no consistent insight into the manoeuvres of combat. Thus, where information is given, it is often incidental, and its significance is not always understood by the poet. The poet's attempts to gloss over deficiencies in John's generalship are also fairly transparent – in one instance, for example, he relates how John attempted to bring his standards together in order to join battle, and excuses his failure to do so by saying that God was not yet ready to grant John his great victory (7.314–15). Corippus overtly praises the skill of John as a general but whether this is consistently demonstrated in the description of events needs some closer examination.

Another aspect that we should not lose sight of is that both Corippus and Procopius were writing their accounts to further their own interests – Corippus went on to a court appointment, and Procopius' fortune was linked to that of Belisarius and his own court favour.[19] This seems clear in the case of Corippus, but we should not underestimate the influence of Procopius' context in determining the value of his account of John, despite his declaration at the beginning the *Wars* (1.1.5) that he will recount the events without fear or favour.

Generalship: The Criteria

John may be the hero of Corippus' epic, but the question we ask here is this: is he portrayed as a good general? Generalship encompasses both the office and the person of a commander.[20] As far as the information around personal character is concerned

---

[16] Merrills (2019) 1–11.

[17] In the *Matritensis* of the ninth to eleventh centuries (10029) Corippus is identified as a *grammaticus Afer* living in the vicinity of Carthage. He is considered to be the same Corippus who went on to a court appointment and penned the panegyric *In laudem Iustini Augusti Minoris*, Cameron (1980) 534–5; *PLRE* 395–527:329.

[18] Riedlberger (2010a) 248, particularly regarding military nomenclature and praxis. Maurice's *Strategikon*, thought to have been written around 600, is largely a compendium of existing material familiar to the Roman army in the East, Rance (2017c) 218.

[19] Corippus states at *praef.* 29–30 that he hopes his epic will win the favour of the Byzantine leaders in Africa, Cameron (1980) 534–9; Shea (1998) 3. Hofmann (1989) 362 suggests that John may even have commissioned the poem himself.

[20] Rance (2017c) 218–19 – this is the essential focus of the *Strategikon* of Maurice. Both ancient and modern writers see *strategica* as essentially tied up with generalship, Whately (2015a) 251.

– physical, moral and intellectual attributes – Corippus tends to veer towards heroic stereotypes and his text is not very useful to us.[21] On the other hand, there are those characteristics of generalship which involve professional capacity – experience, knowledge, tactical decisions on deployment or military movements and so on. Here Corippus, broadly corroborated by Procopius, is of more value to us.

Late strategic works laid emphasis on the art of picking one's battles, of deception and simulation, the importance of ensuring proper supplies and the prescribed functions and behaviour of officers and soldiers. But if we are examining the art of generalship then the general in question had to display something more than mere competence, or someone following a manual. It is also not only about winning battles – it is about how this is accomplished. He in fact had to demonstrate that he had flair, display a certain individuality, and adapt to and overcome setbacks and fresh problems.

Scholars have commented generally or in passing on John's capabilities as these have been transmitted by either or both of these two texts. Alan Cameron, for example, observes that Corippus' epic concerned the 'able but not especially distinguished general John Troglita', whereas J. B. Bury, on the other hand, placed John alongside Belisarius and Solomon as 'the third hero of the Imperial reoccupation of Africa'.[22] In exploring John's generalship in greater depth, we aim to arrive at a more definitive conclusion on John's contribution to the historical record.

The Context of Military Action in Africa

In 533 Justinian dispatched his general Belisarius to drive out the Vandals in Africa and establish peaceful alliances with individual African tribes (*Wars* 3.25.7). Belisarius was able to accomplish the former within less than a year, but in 534 he departed and Solomon (under whom John served, *Ioh.* 3.291–304) took over the African command. Solomon was, however, forced to flee when the soldiers at Carthage mutinied under the rebel leader Stotzas (*Wars* 4.15–17). Belisarius returned in 536 and defeated the rebels, but after his departure for Sicily, Stotzas and the Numidian soldiers rose in revolt. Justinian sent out a relative, Germanus, who defeated and executed the conspirators, and won over the remaining rebels. Corippus tells us (3.318) that John fought under Germanus at Scalae Veteres, an account which he embeds in some epic *topoi*,[23] presumably to avoid what Procopius

---

[21] Cameron (1984) 167–84.
[22] Mango (1991) 25–6; Cameron (2001) 28; Bury (1958) 147; Raven (1969) 219; Lee (2005) 122; Whitby (2007) 336; Conant (2012) 224; Leone (2007) 28–9.
[23] The concluding sentence to John's action with his 'mighty sword' is 'Cellas Vatari looked

tells us: that John and his forces could not hold their own against the enemy and fled in confusion (*Wars* 4.17.16–17). In 539/540 Solomon returned to campaign against the Berbers (*Wars* 4.19.1), in which he had some initial successes against Iaudas. The execution of seventy-nine Laguatan chiefs in 543 (*Wars* 4.21.2–11), however, only exacerbated the problem. A large-scale revolt broke out, co-opting other African tribes in Tripolitania under the command of Antalas. Solomon was killed at Tebesta in 544 in a skirmish against the Tripolitanian tribes (*Wars* 4.21–4; *Ioh.* 3.391–4.218) and his nephew, Sergius, the new *dux* of Tripolitania, proved wholly incapable of stemming the revolt. Areobindus was then appointed to a military command. In 546, the *dux* of Numidia, Gantharith, led a revolt against him, but was soon despatched by Justinian's general, Artabanes, who shortly afterwards asked Justinian to recall him to Constantinople (*Wars* 4.2.44). The situation required a military leader who could deal with the African insurrections as well as pacify his own rebellious troops. John, experienced in battle and familiar with the African context, was chosen by Justinian to regain the African territory for the Byzantine Empire (*Wars* 4.28.45; *Ioh.* 1.55–124) and became the new *magister militum Africae* (*Wars* 4.28.45; Jord. *Rom.* 385).[24] John's knowledge of the enemy was considered of great value – the *Strategikon* is the first work of military strategy that takes different types of enemies into account, rather than advising against a generic 'enemy', and was in line with the contemporary emphasis on controlling the costs of direct warfare.[25] Artifice in outwitting the enemy would prove to be more important than brute force. John was briefed at Constantinople and set out by ship for Africa.

John's Strategy: *cautosque . . . audacesque simul*

Although Corippus spends several poetic passages describing the turmoil of John's state of mind as he considered his strategic options, there are not many indications of his actual strategy in this process.[26] From his actions, however, we can discern something of John's thinking.[27] At the end of 546, for example, he first landed at a beach before entering the port at Carthage, surprising the enemy, who immedi-

---

upon you with a wondrous love, in much the same way as Autenti had looked upon you as you cut down its cruel enemies' (*Ioh.* 3.318–19).

[24] More detail in Evans (1996) 133–6, 151–3, 169–71; Modéran (2003a); (2003b) 'Premiere partie' of the online text.

[25] Whitby (2007) 313–14; Maur. *Strat.*6.1–5.

[26] *Ioh.* 2.288–94; 3.1–7; 6.232–5; 7.20–1; 8.286–91.

[27] As quoted in the heading of this section, *cautosque . . . audacesque simul* ('cautious while also bold'), *Ioh.* 1.561–2.

ately sought refuge in the mountains.[28] It seems to have been important to John to seize the initiative, rather than simply react to the tactics of the African alliance. Upon landing in Carthage John also went straight into action, leading his troops to Antonia Castra in Byzacium, where they pitched their camp.[29] Presumably this rapid advance was a show of strength to either intimidate or provoke confrontation with the enemy. It seems that initially he hoped to bring the Africans to agree to his terms (2.342–416; 4.287–337), but following Antalas' rejection of the conditions, John ordered his men to prepare for battle (4.304–92, 454–6).[30] John's strategy from then on was characterised by a dogged and unrelenting pursuit, regularly basing his camp in the enemy's proximity, and attempting to bring about a confrontation with the enemy on a terrain of his choosing.[31]

The tribes did not fight in formation, as the Byzantine armies were more accustomed to doing (2.179).[32] They fought in smaller units which had greater fluidity and unpredictability, and could withdraw to inaccessible areas which made them difficult to defeat.[33] After their first rout, for example, the remainder of the African tribes retreated to the mountains, and within a few months a new alliance had begun harassing cities west of Tripoli, even threatening Carthage (*Wars* 4.28.49).[34] In addressing his captains, therefore, John advised extreme caution, instructing them to be wary of the high likelihood of ambush (1.521–78).[35] To be alert and ready for action at a moment's notice was also essential. This is the reason for John's instruction not to let the horses graze too far when they pitch camp on the Fields of Cato,

---

[28] Richardot (2009) 149.

[29] Procopius, *Wars* 4.28.46: 'And this John, upon arriving in Libya speedily [ἐπεὶ τάχιστα ἐν Λιβύῃ ἐγένετο] had an engagement with Antalas and the Moors in Byzacium.' Shea (1998) 58 n. 47 argues that at least two months passed between John's arrival and the first campaign. In Corippus, Book 1 is largely devoted to John's voyage from Constantinople, but also covers the march of the army to Antonia Castra at 1.417–65.

[30] The enemy's harsh rejection of all the terms also neatly justifies their domination in the poet's eyes. See also Gärtner (2008) 66–96 for Corippus' characterisation of the enemy leader, Antalas, as further justification for war.

[31] In an involved metaphor Corippus implies that it was John's aim to 'taunt' or 'challenge' (*vocant*) the enemy (1.430–9).

[32] John's soldiers were not, it seems, very keen to fight a guerrilla-type war or engage in dense vegetation (2.191–5). Likewise, Antalas and his army were unwilling, as John had predicted, to engage John's forces 'out in the field' (4.623–6).

[33] Maur. *Strat.* 11.4.3–7; 51–68; Whitby (2007) 315.

[34] Shea (1998) 58 n. 47 on the interval.

[35] See Book 4 of Maurice's *Strategikon* on the value of ambushes in this period, particularly when the enemy was superior in number.

to be able to proceed swiftly on to battle.[36] If the maxim for any general was that nothing should be left to chance,[37] Corippus' John is made to place the emphasis of his plan of campaign on minimising risk.

Strategically John was more focused on conflict terrain and less on siege warfare (in either direction).[38] The African encampments were fortified by walls and trenches, within which barriers of animals were tied together, making an assault more difficult as men and terrified animals became entangled (*Ioh.* 4.597–602; *Wars* 3.8.25–6). Taking the enemy camp would therefore result initially from direct assault. Only in the final clash does John surreptitiously blockade the enemy camp, described by Corippus in Book 8. On that occasion Corippus praises John for choosing the right course of action, and he reveals his plan to his lieutenants – by blockading the enemy this would force them to leave the camp and confront John's army on the open plain.

John's awareness that they were vastly outnumbered by their enemy is also clear from the outset.[39] Winning and retaining the support of the African allies would therefore be of crucial importance in the struggle. Most of the African troops – both enemy and allied – were lightly armed cavalry.[40] But although Corippus spends some time praising the military prowess of the different forces, he does not indicate John's awareness of these differentiations, or that John's strategy was adjusted to the varying types of assault. We are only told the positions of the various commanders and their units, nothing about the reasoning behind it or how they were to be utilised.

While John's strategy was adapted according to the developments in the conflict, this broad plan of action drove his forces towards success, and when neglected led to failure, as will be discussed in more detail below.

Preparation: From Reconnaisance to Prayer

While swiftness of attack could be an advantage, it almost goes without saying that for any general heading into a conflict area, careful preparation of whatever resources were to hand was advocated.[41] In Procopius' *Wars*, proper planning is seen as a

---

[36] Maurice advises similarly about grazing animals (*Strat.* 9.3.106–17). Riedlberger (2010a) 248; Zarini (2003) 282.
[37] Maur. *Strat.* 8.2.63.
[38] Procopius is sceptical of the Africans' experience in poliorcetics (*Wars* 4.22.20).
[39] *Ioh.* 1.482–3; 8.384–5; Procopius, *Wars* 4.10.7; 4.11.23; 4.12.13; 4.17.8.
[40] John also brought with him more heavily armed cavalry. Corippus describes the Lagouatan fighting style in 2.150–5, and the different strengths of the various tribal contingents, e.g. the Frexes fought with infantry and swift light cavalry (2.45–47), while the Silcadinet were efficient in ambushing their enemy (2.52–3).
[41] Maurice advises (8.1.7) 'It is safer and more advantageous to overcome the enemy by plan-

cornerstone of good generalship,[42] and Corippus sometimes ascribes such prudence to John, although often at moments when the author seems to feel that some explanation for hesitation or slower action is needed.[43]

Corippus (1.125–6) mentions that John's ships were stocked at Constantinople with supplies, arms and men so that at Carthage John was able to reorganise the troops and reinforce them with the soldiers he had brought with him, mainly cavalry (archers and cataphracts).[44] Such preparations were of course fairly routine. Upon arrival a well-prepared general also had to make use of reconnaissance and information-gathering, particularly when in enemy terrain.[45] Apart from intelligence on the whereabouts of the enemy, reconnaissance could identify future problems like difficulties in terrain. At the start of the war, the local contingents had the advantage here. From Antonia Castra, for example, John sent out an advance party to choose the best route for the army's progress (2.188–91), but although this action was sound and necessary, the men were ambushed and had to be rescued by their commander leading a cavalry unit (2.188–234, 243–67). Within months John had various individuals who reported to him on enemy movements (6.222–7, 448–9, 528–30), and the Africans lost some of their advantage. One of these scouting parties also managed to capture four of the enemy, who revealed the intention to lure John and his army into the desert, as a result of which John was able to adjust his own strategy of unrelenting pursuit.[46]

Nevertheless, unforeseen eventualities, like bad weather or adverse winds, could also derail well-laid plans, and these tested the abilities of the commander in his ability to recover and adjust his tactics.[47] To counteract unexpected eventualities,

---

ning and generalship than by sheer force; in the one case the results are achieved without loss to oneself, while in the other some price has to be paid.'

[42] Procopius says that his work will be useful to others (also a Thucydidean theme), specifically for those who *plan* (βουλευομένοις), so that the outcome may be certain (*Wars* 1.1.2).

[43] For example: 'And surely his sober wisdom would be better able to conquer the tribes than armed might' (8.6–7).

[44] Tret'yakova (2019) 40 describes as catastrophic the preceding military situation, where the troops were blockaded in the main cities by the Africans.

[45] Most scholars hold the opinion that the empire excelled in providing logistical support, Whitby (2007) 324. Keeping the legions supplied with food and protecting the supply routes was but one aspect of this, e.g. *Wars* 3.13.12–20. On the importance of reconnaissance, Maur. *Strat.* 9.3–4.

[46] Corippus does not disguise, however, that this was the initiative of John's captain, Caecilides.

[47] As in one case, where unfavourable winds would not allow John to send for supplies (*Ioh.* 6.282–8). Whitby (2011) 524–5 on various other logistical problems in late antiquity. Both our authors use Tyche or divine Providence to explain events they see as being beyond

piety and prayer were also considered essential ingredients in the warfare of late antiquity.[48] According to Maurice's *Strategikon* (2.18.13–23), preparation for battle in the form of prayer and supplication, including on the day of the battle itself, was a necessary ritual to ensure victory.[49] The piety of generals in particular was believed to contribute to eventual victory.[50] Corippus also enlarges on this theme, describing how John prayed before their first battle (4.269–85), and also before the final engagement (8.341–53), shedding tears. This was aimed at not only guaranteeing success in the forthcoming battle, but also ensuring that those who died had been purified by the tears and blessings. As Paul Stephenson has observed, the belief was that the more purifying tears were shed before the battle, the less blood would be spilled later.[51] On a more pragmatic level, Christianity not only served to create unity among the soldiery, but also created a higher purpose and therefore a bond of loyalty to commander and emperor.[52] Some scholars have credited John (like the more famous Narses) with a reputation for piety based on Corippus' extensive attention to this aspect.[53] Since this was clearly expected of generals, this is probably a true reflection of the events, even if expressed in epic style.

Logistics: Organising Support and Supplies

The African tribes under Ifisdaias and Coutzinas (*Wars* 4.28.50) had previously allied themselves with the Byzantine Empire (*Ioh.* 4.472–563), and they also pledged to support John. In the first two battles the majority of the commanders listed under John's leadership were therefore part of the imperial army.[54] But in the final battle, John had increased his allies to include also the troops of Iaudas and Bezina (7.262–80; 8.370–7).[55] Corippus' figures for the allies in the final battle may be inflated, but

---

human control. Thus, says Corippus, when the Byzantines suffer initial reverses, *sed dispar fortuna regit* ('an uneven fortune rules battle') (5.60), Edmunds (1975); Cameron (1985) 118–19; Kaldellis (2004) 188.

[48] Whately (2016) 134.

[49] This constitutes one of the most noticeable differences with earlier Roman authors like Vegetius.

[50] Whitby (2007) 339.

[51] Stephenson (2012) 27.

[52] Whitby (2011) 528.

[53] John's piety, Whitby (2007) 339. For Narses see for instance Tougher (2021) 119–35.

[54] Most of the commanders under John seem to have been men of Balkan, eastern and Italic origin, and three (Pudentius, John the elder and Liberatus Caecilides) were probably of Romano-African extraction, Conant (2012) 258.

[55] African numbers in the final battle: 30,000 for Coutzinas, 100,000 for Ifisdaias and 12,000 for Iaudas, but probably exaggerated by the poet, Richardot (2009) 157.

they probably reflect the reality that by this time the allies formed a larger portion of John's army than his own troops.[56]

Maintaining good relations with and between the allies was vital, since unstable alliances between the tribes and the provincial or rebel leaders were recorded for the period just before John's arrival (*Wars* 4.25–7). John also successfully arranged for the reconciliation of two quarrelling confederates, Coutzinas and Ifisdaias. In the account of Corippus, the constancy of the allies is much praised and John is reciprocally loyal to them.[57] John's interaction with the tribes with whom they were not at war is likewise revealed as politically astute and leaving little to chance, as can be seen when he negotiates a safe passage for his troops through the land of the Astrices (6.391–436) by dissimulation, taking hostages and paying bribes.

Insofar as supplies are concerned, the *Iohannis* reveals that John was mostly successful in ensuring provisions for his troops, from instructing them to pitch their camp close to water (2.287) at Antonia Castra to arranging provisions from Carthage while they are in the fortified city of Laribus (7.110–149). But there are occasions when these arrangements are not sufficient. The African tribes attempted to weaken and exhaust the enemy by laying waste the countryside and luring John's forces into the desert (2.1–3; 6.279–95; 7.304–9). In John's army's first venture into the desert, the water and food prove to be inadequate and they are forced to withdraw. Conversely, preventing access to adequate food and water was also a tactic used by John against the enemy, as when he first tried to prevent them from getting access to the river and later blockaded their camp (6.437–92; 8.164–79), so that hunger would drive them out into the open.

Advice and Advisors

In the epic narrative, John consults his senior lieutenants, as we are told was his custom (6.236–8), while in front of his troops he controls himself and keeps 'his cares pressed in his heart' (7.135). On the surface, this seems to be 'the very model of a modern major-general'.[58] However, a commander needs to be able to discern good advice from bad and apply self-control without fail. Corippus' John does not follow the model of Procopius' ideal general, Belisarius, as a leader who takes advice

---

[56] Many of the other captains, with names such as Putzintulus or Sinduit, have been onomastically identified as non-African, Riedlberger (2010a) 343; (2010b) 255.

[57] For example, in the final battle in Book 8, the Lagouatan launched two surprise attacks, one directly against John's troops (which was successfully driven off), and the second against Coutzinas and his forces, where John came to their aid (8.457–78).

[58] Lyrics from Gilbert and Sullivan's 1879 comic opera *The Pirates of Penzance*, Act 1.

while yet retaining his authority.[59] Before the first battle John takes counsel with his lieutenant, Ricinarius, and follows his advice to send emissaries to the enemy. However, in the second battle, John allows his own misgivings (6.238–54) to be overborne by the persuasions of his subordinates. As a consequence, they are defeated (6.478–81). This version of events is no doubt the poet's attempt to exonerate John from responsibility for the loss, displaying his wisdom and foresight. However, Corippus' version also displays him vacillating before his staff, hardly a sign of good leadership and casting some doubt on his ability to take decisive action. If this episode is indeed a poetic creation, we could acquit John of a lack of authority, and since John's overall strategy was one of dogged pursuit and swift attack, it is possible that going into battle was his own decision. In this case, then, John made a bad tactical decision which actually went against his earlier cautionary warnings. Either way, the loss seems to have been the result of poor generalship.

After their defeat, John and his remaining forces retreated to the small city of Iunci. In the epic John informs Ricinarius that he means to make a swift counter-attack, while the enemy believed him to be in retreat (7.44–7), but Ricinarius advises him to first gather his scattered forces, build up their strength and make further treaties with other tribes, and John follows his advice. However, since others were not privy to these discussions, and consultation and taking advice are a common stylistic feature in epic, it is likely that this is just an opportunity for the poet to voice the issues.[60] This does John no harm as an epic hero but does not stand him in particularly good stead as a historical figure and general, since his own tactics are outdone by those of others.

In his recovery after their defeat, however, Corippus' hero shows courage, resolution and determination, and we are informed that 'no commander was ever able to resume fierce combat after being forced to make a tactical retreat with the speed of John' (7.75–7). Although we would expect this of the hero, the recovery and the swiftness of these events are confirmed by Procopius (*Wars* 4.28.50–1) and shine a more positive light on John's generalship.

---

[59] Whately (2015a) 259.

[60] In the epic tradition advice to the hero is often imparted by divine beings (for example, Nestor's role as advisor in the *Iliad*, and Hermes advising Odysseus before he meets Circe in the *Odyssey*), but more historical epics use other characters in this role, e.g. Silius Italicus' Massinissa as Scipio's advisor.

Deployment, Discipline and God

In the accounts of the three battles Procopius is too concise for us to reconstruct anything of deployment and tactics, while Corippus is heavily invested in descriptions of individual unit commanders and single-combat accounts in the epic tradition.[61] Corippus does, however, provide us with three different styles of deployment: in the first battle, John balanced the wings of his cavalry and infantry forces,[62] and set up his own standards in the centre, where he could best regulate tactical deployment (4.564–9). The majority of the units (when detail is given) seem to be infantry phalanxes, but cavalry is described in the fighting itself (5.81–3), harrying the fleeing enemy, until finally the fortifications of the enemy are breached, and there is hand-to-hand engagement with the Laguatan soldiers. They are victorious and take back the standards lost by Solomon at Cillium in 544 (*Wars* 4.28.46; *Ioh.* 5.510–12).

In the second battle, John had Coutzinas' cavalry on the right flank, himself and the infantry phalanxes in the centre, and the cavalry with Putzintulus, Geisirith and Sinduit[63] on the left flank with their archers (6.521–2). John also used allied cavalry in the role of κούρσορες, probably because they were more familiar with the terrain,[64] but even they were unable to avoid being ambushed in the dense vegetation, which, in Corippus' account, impeded both weaponry and cavalry manoeuvres, and the army's discipline fell to pieces. Corippus (6.497–773) describes how they were forced to retreat first to Iunci, and from there to Laribus. The encounter at Marta in 547 was a disaster for John and he lost many men in the engagement, as Procopius (*Wars* 4.28.48–9) confirms.

In the final battle the army is placed on two lines of combat: the first with Coutzinas' forces and the cavalry of Putzintulus and Geisirith, while the second contained the soldiers of Ifisdaias, Sinduit and Fronimuth (8.370–7). This time the enemy was routed and decisively defeated.

Even though John's skill in deployment is praised (4.477), where they are victorious the poet's conclusion is a simplistic one – that John's forces were victorious

---

[61] Gärtner (2008) 33–40.
[62] The lack of attention to the infantry in the *Strategikon* has been read to mean that this was not in need of advice or improvement, rather than that contemporary strategy favoured cavalry over infantry, Whitby (2011) 522.
[63] Sinduit is probably Germanic, but see n. 54.
[64] Maurice prescribes to the cavalry tactical roles of κούρσορες (those who ride on ahead and fight at the front) and δηφένσορες (the reserve force which follows at the rear), *Strat.* 1.3.26–30; 2.3; 3.5–10; 6.1–3; 7.B.16.3–5. Rance (2017c) 242 on the variant definitions of these forces in Maurice.

Morale and Mutiny

Inspiring confidence in their general and in themselves is one of the arts of generalship. At 1.447–51, for example, Corippus mentions how the commander continually encouraged his men: before the battle at Antonia Castra with tales of old battles, 'praising the work of war' (*Martis laudaret opus*), and 'rousing their excited minds to battle, which set them afire and made them staunch (*firmat*)' (4.404–6). Much of this encouragement is given in direct speech. The speeches in the poem are of course a generic type of motivation rather than a literal reflection of what was said.[65] Common themes are the righteousness of their cause, the support of God, and their resolution in combat (4.407–56) before battle, while in conflict John appeals to the soldiers' patriotism and honour (5.90–8), and the promise of spoils (5.408–13). These seem to be routine motivations for soldiers. Following the high losses and low morale after their defeat in the second battle, John's speech (7.262–80) displays the entire battery of motivational *topoi*, but this time he also gives them encouraging news about their allies, an important addition in view of their depleted forces (7.118–28). John's final advice in Book 8 is also much more pragmatic, since he gives his soldiers sound guidance on the most important avenues to safety.

John is described as riding among the troops (4.564–9) and fighting at their centre (4.477). But in reality, fighting and personal bravery on the battlefield were not required for a commander.[66] John was accompanied by his armour-bearers, but risked exposure when they fell, as at 6.670–3, and would have left the army leaderless had he been killed.[67]

But the courage of a commander was also a great inspiration to soldiers, as is claimed throughout the epic, (for example at 5.421, where John says 'each soldier may do in confidence and after my example what he sees me doing in combat', or at 6.630, 'Let each man do as he sees me do'). A general's presence could check retreat and renew attack (5.277–80; 6.633). The motivational factor was stronger than the contribution a general could make on the battlefield with his sword.[68]

---

[65] But since it is hardly likely that a general would send his troops into action without encouraging rhetoric, it is likely that his speeches contained these motivational *topoi*.

[66] Whitby (2007) 335; Maur. *Strat.* Book 7.

[67] The chaos which ensued when an army lost its commander is described by Corippus in the case of John's predecessor, Solomon: 'at that point, every semblance of order disappeared' (3.441).

[68] Richardot (2009) 154.

On a few occasions, however, John is not heeded by his men, and faces mutinies among the soldiers.[69] Discipline of their motley armies was a recurring problem which beset many commanders in late antiquity.[70] The first sedition is the result of pursuing the Africans into the desert. John's army lost many of its horses, and this disaster on top of deprivations of water and food gave impetus to a rising mutiny. John took his army to a water source, but when he tried to have sustenance procured by ship, a south wind prevented them from setting sail (6.386–8). Corippus describes (6.408–11) how the demoralised army broke into revolt, but John calmed them with the help of Ricinarius.

Another mutiny arose (8.50–163) as a result of John's waiting tactics, which were interpreted as a reluctance to fight.[71] When the mutiny was reported to John, Corippus says that he 'was for a moment uncertain what to do' (8.110), but the description which follows is one of an angry general who speaks forthrightly to the rebels, and, Corippus says, 'He had in fact no less power than Caesar had to terrify the Romans with his words of contempt when a rebellion threatened' (8.149–50).[72] He threatens them with the African allied soldiers, until eventually the ringleaders are given up and put to death.

John's dealings with the mutinies are therefore projected as firm and authoritative, but without the cruelty or the concomitant men's fear of their general portrayed by Lucan in the case of Caesar (*Pharsalia* 5).[73]

Artifice: To Outwit, Outlast and Outplay

As Doug Lee has noted, in summing up the wars against the African tribes, after Solomon's death it was only through the 'energetic efforts' of the new general, John Troglita, that the imperial forces managed to contain the tribes' insurrections,[74] and

---

[69] Maurice criticises the lack of training and military discipline of both generals and soldiers (*Strat*. Pr. 10–14), but as Rance (2017c) 224 points out, this was something of a *topos* for military treatises.

[70] The importance of imposing discipline on one's army is, unsurprisingly, emphasised by Maurice (*Strat*. 8. A.3, 30, 8. B.19, 27, 99), but seems to have been difficult to maintain consistently, Whitby (2011) 523–4; Bury (1958) 142; Wood (2011) 424; Cameron (1985) 186–7.

[71] Tret'yakova (2019) 42. The mutinies described by Corippus bear stylistic similarities to those in Lucan, Riedlberger (2010a) 146–8.

[72] Kaufmann (2017) 160 discusses possible intertextuality here, but despite rhetorical strategies similar to Lucan's Caesar, the comparison with Caesar is otherwise not flattering to John and is not sustained in the poem.

[73] Kaufmann (2017) 160.

[74] Lee (2013) 289.

Philippe Richardot likewise commends John as a 'général énergique', particularly in recovering after defeat.[75] Energy is certainly a desirable quality, but, as has already been mentioned, the warfare of late antiquity emphasised saving manpower. Hence the importance of guile and deception as skills which a good general should be able to deploy.

As it happened, both sides made use of deception and dissembling as part of their tactical armoury to outwit the enemy.[76] There are a number of minor incidents, for example when the soldiers mutiny during John's negotiation to pass through the land of the Astrices (6.408–11) and John tells their ambassadors that the clamour outside is evidence of his soldiers' eagerness for war (6.423–4) – a deception which (together with hostages and bribes) succeeded, since the Astrices concluded a treaty with the Byzantines.

As mentioned above, a commander's skill of anticipation was enhanced by a knowledge of the terrain, and this also applied to using the desert to exhaust the enemy. Here the Lagouatan initially had the upper hand and deceived John, since by fleeing into the desert they lured the imperial army to move away from its supply bases through devastated territory, which exhausted and demoralised them (7.302–6).[77] But the capture of the four Lagouatan soldiers by Caecilides revealed their strategy (7.374–5, 524–30). John's countermove was to cease pursuit and set up camp near Iunci on the open plains, which would give their forces the advantage (8.23–4). This location (otherwise unknown) also enabled him to receive fresh supplies brought to the nearby harbour of Lariscus (8.20–1, 41–7).

John next set up camp on a plain called the Fields of Cato where Corippus presents his best demonstration of the art of patience and guile. John soon became aware that the enemy tribes were experiencing water and food shortages. He therefore blockaded their camp and restrained his men from venturing forth.[78] The hungry enemy, also misunderstanding the Byzantines' inaction as a reluctance to attack, eventually risked battle on the open plain (8.164–79). They struck on a holy day (presumably a Sunday), hoping to catch John's forces unawares, engaged in religious rituals (8.254–5). But John and his second-in-command, Ricinarius, had anticipated

---

[75] Richardot (2009) 156.

[76] Blunt off-the-field tactics such as taking hostages and bribery were also effectively employed, e.g. John's arrest of the Lagouatan emissaries (*Ioh.* 1.498–500) at Antonia Castra, and the taking of hostages and paying of bribes in John's treaty with the Astrices at *Ioh.* 6.430–2.

[77] Tret'yakova (2019) 42. The desert wind also affected the Africans as they penetrated the desert. Richardot (2009) 157 attributes this to their numbers, which may have been too great for the oases.

[78] Also advocated in Maurice, *Strat.* 8.2.28.

this thinking and performed their devotions at dawn (thereby complying with the ideal expressed in the *Strategikon* (8.1.39), that generals should ensure readiness for battle on all days, including holy days).[79] In this game of move and countermove, therefore, John fared well and was rewarded by final success.

Loss of Life, Looting and Destruction

Ideally the art of generalship would also include minimal loss of life, not only among his own soldiers but also among the local population. In a number of instances, we are told of John's concern for the local population, his desire to 'aid the wretched land' (1.441–3) and 'the very captive people for whom he had taken up arms' (2.295). Although this is likely to be part and parcel of John's character as pious, he did remain in Africa, directing his efforts to rebuilding the provinces, so it is possible that he may have been concerned, even if from a purely pragmatic perspective, with the fate of the African provinces. In an earlier instance concerning Belisarius, Procopius informs us that this general restrained his troops from plundering since this did not prepare the way for governing a territory afterwards (*Wars* 3.16.2–8).[80] John likewise limited looting to the defeated enemy camp. His attitude to the enemy, however, was merciless, and Corippus does not disguise that John's army in conquest did not spare even the enemy's women and children (5.477–92).

Rebuilding and Administration

Procopius divulges how, in the spring of 548, the Byzantines engaged in battle and 'unexpectedly' (παραδόξου) routed the enemy (*Wars* 4.28.51), and thus John brought the African campaign to a close.[81] Corippus conveys how John personally slew his Turnus, the enemy leader, Carcasan, in epic combat. While Carcasan may not literally have died at John's hand, other sources confirm that seventeen of the African leaders were killed (*Ioh.* 8.627–36; *Wars* 4.28.50–1; 8.17.21; Jord. *Rom.* 385; Paul. Diac. *Hist. Lang.* 1.25). The territories of Numidia, Byzacena and Tripolitania

---

[79] Riedlberger (2010a) 242. On the need for swiftly being able to mobilise against a highly mobile enemy in late antiquity, Rance (2017c) 245.

[80] Nevertheless, large-scale military action was a strain on the empire's financial resources and also on the ability of commanders to move their forces without looting the surrounding countryside and villages, Whitby (2011) 524.

[81] Stephenson (2012) 27. Marcellinus Comes (*Chron.* Migne, *PL* 51, AC 551) implies that John was only finally victorious in 551, but Procopius and Corippus have the earlier date of 549, Shea (1998) 16.

were once again under Byzantine control. John became a *patricius*, and he remained in command in Africa for at least another four years.[82]

Scholars have commented on the fact that in Procopius, John's campaigns were 'appended as an afterthought', or that his account is 'positive but far from exuberant',[83] and Procopius is indeed very pessimistic regarding the fate of Africa.[84] Nevertheless, John brought to an end a war that had dragged on since 536, and none of the other ancient authors, however brief, have anything but praise for his military contribution.[85] John was able to secure peace for the region for some fifteen years, even sending a fleet to aid Justinian in Sardinia and Corsica in 551 (*Wars* 8.24.33–7), and despite Procopius' glum outlook for Africa, relative economic prosperity returned during the second half of the sixth century.[86]

As to why Procopius spends so little time on John, the first reason is surely that the historian was not an eyewitness to the conclusion of the conquest of the region. Moreover, Belisarius had been his Pericles against the Vandals, as Solomon had been against the Africans. The brevity of his discussion of John and the final campaign in Africa is therefore not due to the latter's poor generalship as such.

ab armis arte ductis?

So, ultimately, was the successful conclusion of the African campaign due to the excellence of its general?[87] Much of what we are told about John's generalship is not particularly striking or unusual. What we can reconstruct of his strategies and tactics seems to follow routine military operations of the period, even though, compared with other generals in the African war, John fares relatively well against Belisarius, Solomon, Germanus and certainly Sergius, if generalship is measured in successes.[88]

---

[82] *Patricius*, Jordanes (*Romana* 384–5); Marcell. Comes (*Chron* AC 551). John was still in charge of Africa at the end of 551, and possibly early 552 (Procopius, *Wars* 8.24–37).

[83] Treadgold (2007) 199; Cameron (1985) 179; Conant (2012) 224.

[84] Wood (2011) 424; Cameron (1985) 186–7. Procopius' negativity regarding Africa, particularly as expressed in the *Secret History*, and in the concluding sentence to the Vandal Wars: 'Thus it came to pass that those of the Libyans who survived, few as they were in number and exceedingly poor [ὀλίγοις τε καὶ λίαν πτωχοῖς οὖσιν], at last and after great toil [μόλις ἡσυχίαν] found some peace' (4.28.52), further discussion in Ure (1951) 32.

[85] See n. 4 above.

[86] Evans (1996) 171.

[87] As quoted in the heading, '*ab armis arte ductis*, 'thanks to the skill of the general', *Ioh.* 8.174–5.

[88] Sergius, Areobindus and Artabanes served for less than a year, Germanus served for three years, and Solomon served two military terms of two years and six years, Conant (2012) 287–8.

But John's success in the wars against the Africans did not come without a price. It took him two years to achieve, and the loss of many men on the battlefield. His losses, whether he listened to bad advice or followed the wrong course on his own, were due to miscalculation on his part. On the other hand, he galvanised the local forces, no doubt demoralised after years of being confined to the cities, won additional allies and after a resounding defeat turned matters around, and, against all odds, had enough authority in the army to suppress the mutinies and lead his forces to ultimate victory. He was also able to successfully adapt his strategy on the basis of the latest intelligence, as after the capture of the Laguatan soldiers. Lastly, he was sensible enough not to attempt further conquest of new areas to add to the empire, as Solomon had done. However, the problem was never permanently solved, and the African tribes represented a far more enduring threat than the Vandals had ever done.[89]

---

[89] Cameron (1993) 116.

12 The Best of Men: Cross-Cultural Command in the 630s AD

Eve MacDonald

The Middle Persian and Zoroastrian texts of the Sasanian period clearly define the role of a military commander: 'the duty of the warrior is to strike the enemy and to hold their own country and land secure and tranquil', says the text known as the *Spirit of Wisdom*.[1] By the third decade of the seventh century AD, the military elite who commanded the Sasanian armies were failing in respect of these stated aims. All-out war between the armies of the Sasanian king Khusro II and the Byzantine emperors raged for twenty-six years (602–628) early in the century, and resulted in the Sasanian military elite not keeping their lands secure or tranquil while internal conflict and civil war wracked the empire.[2] In the decade that followed the peace of 628, both the Sasanian and Byzantine Empires would be defeated in a succession of pivotal battles against the armies of the Rashidun caliphate.[3] The results of these battles in the 630s would be the complete disappearance

---

[1] Dādestān ī Mēnōg ī Xrad (Q.30.9–10), thought to date originally to the sixth century AD (or even as late as the eighth). Translation here is from Tafazzoli (2000) 3, and on the background, see Boyce (1968) 54.

[2] For background to this period see Kaegi (2003) on Heraclius; Baca-Winters (2018) for Khusro Parvez. Both books look at them as men of their times. Especially relevant here is Pourshariati (2008), who discusses the events and source material in detail for this period; Daryaee (2009) for the society and culture of Sasanian Iran; Farrokh (2017) on the Sasanian military; Greatrex and Lieu (2002) on Rome and Persian wars; Dignas and Winter (2007), who provide excellent background and source material for Romano-Sasanian wars. Howard-Johnston (2000) in the *Encyclopædia Iranica* is a very useful overview.

[3] There is an enormous bibliography for these events, and key publications consulted here include Donner (1981); (1998); Kennedy (2001); (2007); el-Hibri (2010); Howard-Johnston (2010); Morony (2012); (2013); Crone (2008).

of the Sasanians and a significant and lasting reduction in the territory of the Byzantines.

The memory of the battles between the Arab Muslim armies of the caliph Umar and the forces of the Byzantine and the Sasanian Empires in the years c. 636–638 looms large in our perception and understanding of the period.[4] The Arab victories in the 630s helped to shape the memory and narrative construction of the empires that came before and the realities of those that followed on from these events. This is also true in the portrayal of the generals in command of the armies that fought these battles. The complex stories of these men cannot be reduced to a simple binary of winner or loser, heroic or villainous, good or bad. On the field of battle were the 'best of men', who are remembered as the epitome of masculinity in their own cultures. They were military commanders in societies whose military was the governing elite. These were also men whose actions in command turned the tide of history. The memory of them is embedded in the later narrative accounts, and examining these portrayals helps to illuminate the social complexity of the times. This memory also provides a view of the competing interests that were involved in the creation of the legacy of these fields of battle.

This chapter deals specifically with memory of the men who commanded armies in the key battles of al-Yarmūk (636) and al-Qādessiyah (637/638).[5] Al-Yarmūk took place along the eponymous river, a tributary of the river Jordan in a still-contested corner of the world south-east of the Golan Heights and north-west of the

---

[4] The exact dates for the battles vary across these two years. Kennedy (2007) 107–15 thinks both could have taken place in 636; Howard-Johnston (2010) 464–70 puts al-Yarmūk in the early months of 636 and al-Qādessiyah on 6 January 638. Morony (2012) 209 dates al-Qādessiyah to June 637. The scholarship that attempts to assess the reasons and implication of these years is dense. Donner (1981) 3–9 provides an overview of the shifting scholarly attitudes towards the early Islamic conquests over the nineteenth and twentieth centuries. El-Hibri (2010) 1–25 in the introduction to his book on the Rashidun Caliphate assesses the Muslim historiography of the period. Howard-Johnston (2010) 436–81 provides an essential guide to the events and to the historians for the period. The term 'Byzantine' is used conventionally whilst acknowledging the issues around the Roman/Byzantine label for the period. See Kennedy (2001) on the armies of the Arabs; also Edwell et al. (2015) for a recent assessment of the background to the conflicts.

[5] Howard-Johnston (2010) 212 outlines some of the confusion in transmission to later sources on al-Yarmūk. Key dates and sources are contradictory and there are many battles fought across these years. Kaegi (1992) 112–46 is the standard account which Nicolle (2006) follows in the study of al-Yarmūk, published in the Osprey series of battle narratives and assessments. Kennedy (2001) covers the armies of the caliphs and their battles. The Sasanian perspective on this battle is discussed in Pourshariati (2008) 232–6; Morony (2013); Farrokh (2017) on the Sasanian military.

ancient city of Busra, a borderland today where Syria, Jordan and Israel meet. The battle was drawn out, lasting almost a week and involving attacks and counters on both sides. The celebrated commander Khālid ibn al-Walīd eventually trapped the Byzantine army and separated the cavalry from infantry. The result was a total rout. The Byzantine emperor Heraclius (610–641), directing events from his capital at Antioch, witnessed the loss of the whole of the Levant and Syria to the Arab armies in the aftermath.[6]

For the Sasanian Empire, the Battle of al-Qādessiyah was equally strategic in location and even more disastrous in outcome. The field of battle lay to the south-west of the key city of al-Ḥīrah, a frontier town that controlled the borderland between the fertile lowlands of the Tigris and the Arabian Desert, now in modern Iraq. At al-Qādessiyah, the Sasanian army faced a numerically inferior Arab force commanded by Sa'd ibn Abī Waqqās. The Sasanian army brought to the field full imperial pomp and grandeur with thirty elephants led by the royal standard of the empire. After a long period of skirmishing and negotiations, the final battle is said to have lasted three days and ended with the Sasanian commander, and many others of the leading elite, dead on the field. Like the Byzantine emperor, the Sasanian king of kings, Yazdgerd III, had not led his army into battle but remained in the relative safety of Ctesiphon, the winter capital of the empire (also Veh-Ardashir/ al-Madā'in).[7] The Sasanian defeat at al-Qādessiyah left the road towards the winter capital open to the conquering armies, and Ctesiphon would soon fall.[8]

---

[6] Kennedy (2007) 66–97 for a narrative of events. See Woods' appraisal (2007) of the role of the plague in the 'so-called battle of Yarmūk'. Kaegi (1992) 112–46 provides a detailed account; Kennedy (2001) 5–6 points out that the distinct topography of al-Yarmūk has allowed for a more specific reconstruction than many other battles in the period. As emperor, Heraclius is the most well known of the Byzantine commanders, but he was not at the battle and his propagandists, like the author George of Pisidia, focus on the earlier victories in the wars against the Byzantines rather than the disaster of al-Yarmūk. See Whitby (1998) on George of Pisidia's characterisation of Heraclius at war.

[7] How much actual control Yazdgerd III had of the empire in 636 is debated; with coins minted in the names of a number of different kings at the time the situation was far from clear. See Tyler-Smith (2000) 140, who notes only the regions of Pars, Khuzistan and Sagistan are known to have struck coins in Yazdgerd's name. For a concise outline of events, see Morony (2012) 208–11; Kennedy (2007) 169–99 for the conquest of Iran. For the increasing militarisation in Sasanian society after the reforms of Khosrow I, see Daryaee (2015).

[8] Yazdgerd would battle on for another fifteen years until his death at Merv in 651. Savant (2013) writes an intriguing account of the Arabic memory of the Sasanian capital city, how it was considered the ancient city, symbolic of the tradition of power in the pre-Islamic period. See Kennedy (2007) 108–16 for the narrative and issues of date.

Although the Arab Muslim campaigns of conquest were decades long, these two battles remain iconic in the memory of the dramatic shift of power that occurred across the Near East and Mediterranean as old empires fell and a new power was created.[9] The stories of the commanders who fought these battles are told for us in an array of extant sources, many fragmentary and deriving from a multitude of cultures and divergent literary traditions. These traditions reflect the make-up of the armies that fought, the soldiers on the ground and the ethnicity of the commanders. This was an ancient world war and those who remembered these crucial years tell us about them in epic form in Arabic, Armenian, Greek, Middle Persian and Syriac.[10]

The men in command, although often defined by religion in our sources, were in no way clearly divided along ethnic grounds in the sides they fought on. We find, for example, Christian Caucasians – in this case meaning Armenians and Albanians – commanding armies on both the Byzantine and Sasanian sides of the war. The Muslim Arab armies were united by the new religion of Islam but their commanders were of different tribal and regional backgrounds, and many local groups and units of command switched sides in the process of fighting. Especially notable were the elite units of the Sasanian army, reported to have switched sides around the time of al-Qādessiyah in return for land and salaries, according to the Arabic historian al-Balādhurī.[11] Religious identities do underlie the portrayal of command in this period, however, be it the memory of the warrior in the Zoroastrian tradition, the Christian warrior saint or the Arab Muslim heroes who vanquished both.[12] Key here is that reflected in these different religious traditions are common ideals of command that helped to define elite masculinity in the seventh century.[13]

---

[9] The narrative aspect of the stories from the Arab sources and their constructions have been long identified as literary invention and constructions. Studies used here include el-Hibri (2010); Donner (1998); Robinson (2003); and articles such as Khalek (2010) and Bray (2010).

[10] For the key studies on the seventh-century sources see Howard-Johnston (2010). The articles in Cameron (1995) set out the background to the different armies and traditions discussed here. See n. 9 for studies of the Arabic historiography.

[11] See al-Balādurī Futūḥ, 280.

[12] As noted by Fowden (1999) 3: 'divine defense went hand in hand with arms and walls' and underlies all these portrayals. Khalek (2010) explores the Byzantine hagiographical *topoi* among the description of the companions of the Prophet in some Arabic texts.

[13] For the Byzantine tradition of the 'warrior saint', see Walter (2003) esp. 266–70 on the beginnings of the cult; also Fowden (1999), who traces the influence of St Sergius of Rusafa on the warrior traditions in both the Byzantine and Sasanian narratives and the cross-cultural reasons for this. See Whitby (1998) 263 on Heraclius as the ideal Christian warrior in George of Pisidia and the critical subtext of the author.

This chapter also aims to explore the identity and representation of some of the diverse commanders from the seventh century who are repeatedly included as part of the long memory of the battles. In the memory of the men and the events that shaped these narratives we attempt to track the notion of an elite masculinity that developed around cultural, religious and ethnic identities in the centuries that followed. In trying to understand, moreover, the memory of the 'best men' across different traditions we can see how they reflect aspects of specific cultural identity in the Near East and western Asia, and the broadly consistent portrayals around ideal masculinity. Underlying this are aspects of an intercultural narrative that sustains the literary constructions of command on all sides. A comparison across the Byzantine, Persianate and Arabic commanders presents both a conception of heroised military leadership in the seventh century, and a glimpse into the complexity of the multi-ethnic and multilingual society that embodied the late antique world on the cusp of the early Middle Ages.[14]

The depiction of command and commanders here is focused on the way the narrative reflects the memory of the victorious and the defeated. Although it is traditional in battle narratives that the victors have the final say, the processes of memory of these events saw many eloquent bards who were invested in creating new epic traditions relying heavily on established narrative traditions of warriors and command to tell their stories.[15] The intention of this chapter is not to describe the events as they unfolded across 636–638, but to focus on a few key players who have lived on in the cultural memory of the battles in different traditions.

---

[14] For the sources and literary traditions there is a wide divergence in the processes of memory and the perseverance of orality that would have been especially influential. The Persian tradition in relation to military and command is discussed in Farrokh (2017) xi–xxiii. This merges into the early Arabic historiography, which is clearly detailed by Robinson (2003) 18–38, and is especially relevant for this period. For the merging of historiographical traditions, see articles in Papaconstantinou (2010) esp. Bray and Khalek. For the impact of hagiographical material and panegyric see Walter (2003); Whitby (1998).

[15] Essential here for the Arabic historiography is Donner (1998). See also el-Hibri (2010) on the use of parable in the stories of the Rashidun caliphs. Also of interest here is Khalek (2010) on hagiography and the construction of the companions of the Prophet. Nicolle (2006) 17 makes the point that it would be normal to know more about the victors than the vanquished in epic battles like these but that the inverse is true around al-Yarmūk especially.

Rostam: The Ideal Iranian

Many great generals and commanders fought in these two conclusive battles, and those who were defending and those attacking represented the cream of the Byzantine, Sasanian and Arab military. Of them all, it is perhaps the Sasanian general Rostam and the memory of him that are most clearly articulated and well preserved in the widest array of sources.[16] Although defeated and killed on the field of battle, he is remembered as the 'best of men'. The story of Rostam is told in the tenth-century epic the *Shahnameh* (Šāh-nāma), known as the *Book of Kings*. The best-known version of this epic was written down by the Samamid court poet Abolqasem Ferdowsi.[17] It was created three centuries after the events discussed, during a period in the Iranian Persian world when the society of the Sasanians, last of the pre-Islamic dynasties of ancient Iran, was celebrated, revered and mythologised.[18] The second half of the *Shahnameh* is comprised of stories of the Sasanian Dynasty, and these were packaged up in the medieval period by poets like Ferdowsi who used a whole range of sources to tell their stories. These sources included long traditions of oral histories and a multitude of written material that have enshrined the memory of the last great dynasty of ancient Iranian kings.[19]

The memories of the general Rostam are preserved in the final chapters of the epic tale. Rostam belonged to the Ispahbudhān family, who, in the final throes of the Sasanian Dynasty, were the power behind the throne of the last king of kings, Yazdgerd III.[20] His very name was shared with the legendary Iranic-Saka hero who had from Parthian times been syncretised with the figure of Herakles and played a key role in Zoroastrian myth.[21] Rostam is depicted as a 'kind and just man'. Commanding in the name of the king, he led the Sasanian armies against the Arabs who were advancing on the Sasanian capital Ctesiphon. Rostam's deeds are remembered in this mythic vein: as that of the last great Sasanian warrior, who embodied

---

[16] Lewental's (2017) study of Rostam and survey of his sources has been immensely helpful here and the idea for this chapter came after reading this fascinating study.

[17] For Ferdowsi and the Samamid court and Persian revival see Davis (1992); (2016) 13–37.

[18] The translations from the *Shahnameh* used in this chapter are from Dick Davis' Penguin edition (2016).

[19] Background to the Islamic conquest of Iran, see Morony (2013); Daryaee (2009) on the society of Sasanian Iran; Pourshairati (2008) for the events at the end of the dynasty. The sources for the Shahnameh are discussed in Davis (1996).

[20] For the history of Rostam and his brother Farrukhzād in the narrative, see Pourshariati (2008) 229–34. For his reputation and memory, Lewental (2017).

[21] For the role of Iranic-Saka heroes in the Parthian tradition, see Rose (2011) 76–7.

the memory of ancient, pre-Islamic Iranian masculinity, and as the commander who stood bravely against the Arab armies.

In the *Shahnameh*, the key players on the field of battle at al-Qādessiyah are described in a premonition recounted by this wise but ultimately doomed general, who is credited with the perceptive abilities to read the omens and understand astrology. Rostam knows 'this battle will turn out unfavourably' and, contemplating defeat and destruction, he writes a lament in a letter to his brother Farrukhzād:

> But for the Persians I will weep, and for
> The House of Sasan ruined by this war:
> Alas for their great crown and throne, for all
> The royal splendour destined now to fall
> To be fragmented by the Arabs' might;
> The stars decree for us defeat and flight.[22]

The armies of the old dynasty are doomed, a force that can no longer protect its lands, despite the nobility and wisdom of its commander. Ferdowsi's Rostam rails against his enemies, putting these words in the mouths of those who died on the field:

> Who are these upstarts who have dared to stray
> Across Mazanderan's and Persia's borders?

What is captured here is the tenth-century sense of distain that the Persian Muslim elites may have felt about the centuries of Arab power they had endured, and the way that the Samamid world in which Ferdowsi lived remembered the Arabs as 'upstarts'.[23] This may have also been the view in the seventh century, for the peoples of the Arabian Peninsula had, for so long, been the vassals and soldiers for hire in the wars of the Sasanians and the Roman/Byzantine Empires. If a colonial view of their former vassals still persisted centuries after the fall, the moral lessons are encoded in the scholar and universal historian al-Tabarī's (tenth-century) work that focuses on the decline and decay in the Sasanian state.[24] Rostam's story in the *Shahnameh* may have derived from a lament that was sung not long after the battle, possibly in the interim years between the conquest of the Sasanian Empire that followed on from

---

[22] This translation is by Dick Davis (2016). See Kennedy (2007) 110 on the lament of Rostam.

[23] Davis (1992) looks closely at the sources, cycles and subtext of the *Shahnameh*.

[24] El-Hibri (2010) 99 on the moral lessons encoded in the depiction of the Sasanian state, with the exception of Rostam, in the narratives leading up to the battle.

al-Qādessiyah and the death of the last Sasanian king, Yazdgerd III, at Merv in 651. The narrative, when stripped back to its essentials, Gershon Lewental notes, leaves the reader with the impression that Rostam at the Battle of al-Qādessiyah is largely a romantic, literary creation.[25]

Nonetheless, we also know that the Sasanian general Rostam was a member of the ruling elite, one of a handful of families who had governed and ruled the Sasanian Empire for centuries. He was Rostam b. Farrokh-Hormozd, Khorasani in origin and family.[26] The construction of his character is infused with *hunar* ('valour'), which was considered the most noble of all traits in the Middle Persian texts.[27] Valour in the Middle Persian tradition combined traits that included 'skill in the affairs of war, bravery and manliness'.[28] The role of Rostam as depicted in the *Shahnameh* is firmly embedded in the Middle Persian Avestan texts that set out the function of the warrior in society with great clarity. He embodies the archetypal leader of the societies of the Iranian heartland that had existed for centuries.

In the *Pahlavi Rivāyat*, which is a kind of question-and-answer religious text about how to live well within Zoroastrian traditions, there is a step-by-step approach about what to do when 'non-Iranian enemies come to the land of Iran'. The warriors must, in the *Rivāyat*, go towards the invading enemy and engage with them in combat, even if they are killed. For the 'warrior who does not do battle and who flees is *margazān*' – which in Middle Persian means committing a sin punishable by death. The warrior who goes to battle, however, and who is killed, is 'blessed'.[29] Rostam's death in defence of the realm on the field of battle at al-Qādessiyah allows him to retain his status as the ideal of the great Sassanian warrior, and even in defeat he becomes a mythical and a national hero, remembered by both the Persian and the early Arabic sources which sought to create the story of the conquests. In a letter written to the Arab commander before the battle as constructed in Ferdowsi's text, Rostam is named 'the benevolent and foremost warrior of the world', while the Arab commander 'seeks war and has made the world a dark and narrow place'.[30]

---

[25] Lewental (2017) 224.

[26] See Lewental (2017) 223–4 for an introduction to Rostam. Pourshariati (2008) 104–18 reconstructs the family narrative.

[27] See Taffazoli (2000) 1–17 for the role of warriors in Sasanian society.

[28] Here see Tafazzoli (2000) 3.

[29] This translation and text from the *Pahlavi Rivāyat* is taken from Tafazzoli (2000) 4 and the text used for the *Rivāyat* here is from Williams (1990) 2.34. The memory of the society that is embedded in these texts was already one of longing and memory for a lost world, as they were thought to have been written down in the late Sasanian or early Islamic period, as noted by Daryaee (2013) 91–3.

[30] Davis (2016) 946 for the translation.

The heroic Rostam, then, looms large over the memory of the battle just as the Sasanians do over the early Islamic Near East. The narrative constructions of him as an ideal man of the Iranian world are both in harmony and contrasting with the traditions and intentions of our sources.[31] There are Arabic historians who wrote of this commander and his stand as the battle itself. So closely linked is al-Qādessiyah to Rostam that it is referred to as 'the Battle of Rostam' or even the 'Battle-Day of Rostam' in al-Ṭabarī's universal history.[32] This last stand of Rostam, although not the final, final days of the Sasanian Empire, was the last moment of their claim to rule a 'world empire'. Pourshariati has noted it was the 'end of Sasanian history' in a narrative sense as recognised by the post-antique authors of their history, both Persian and Arab.[33] Therefore the idealisation of the man who stood against the Arab armies and died that day embodied all that had been lost about the Sasanians.[34] Rostam's portrayal worked for both the winners and the losers in their memory of the epic battle. A great victory is made greater when a great enemy is defeated. Lewental has recently argued for the preservation of the idealised identity of the Sasanian elite male in this figure, the role of the commander, the pious, and the construction of an epic but fallen hero all rolled into Rostam.[35]

Rostam was among the many *asbārān* at al-Qādessiyah, the elite Sasanian warriors who rode on horseback.[36] Al-Ṭabarī describes the role as that of a man who 'carries a spear, wears a coat of mail, brandishes a sword and sits firmly on the back of his horse', but the term evolves into the Arabic *asāwira* as the name given by the Iranians to 'a brave, heroic and famous man'.[37] For the Arab sources, the memory of an elite

---

[31] This juxtaposition in the Persian and Arabic memory is discussed by Lewental (2017) 233–6.

[32] Al-Ṭabarī 1.2472. Not all sources present Rostam with a noble death; Lewental (2017) 227–9 surveys the traditions and notes that some remember a less than elegant end, including the suggestion in Faravashi (1971) 481 that Rostam was killed by his own troops. 'Waqaʿat Rustam' in Ḥamzeh Eṣfahānī, *Hamzae Ispahanensis annalium libri* 10.1.152.

[33] Pourshariati (2008) 228–34, who also points out that it seems to have been a wake-up call to the Sasanian military, who proceeded to take the fight more seriously in the aftermath; see also here el-Hibri (2010) 100 on the way the narrative turns after Rostam's death.

[34] This is in contrast to Yazdgerd, who flees the Arab armies and eventually dies ignobly at Merv. See Sebēos (163.29–164–6), whose version of these events may have been transmitted through oral history, according to Howard-Johnston (2010) 83.

[35] See Lewenthal (2017).

[36] See Zakeri (1995) 112–64 on the *asbārān* and p. 57 for clarification of the meaning and spelling of the word as it evolved over Achaemenid to New Persian. See also here Farrokh (2017) 72–119 for a detailed study of the elite Sasanian cavalry, their weapons and identities.

[37] Farrokh (2017) 73–119, where he outlines the definitions, details and evidence; he emphasises that the term is specific to elite cavalry and uses the equivalent 'knights'. See also

Iranian cavalryman like Rostam reflects the processes of their growing identity and self-definition in the face of the absorption of other cultures, myths and memories through conquest.

The Armenian history attributed to Sebēos (written in the mid-seventh century) claims that the 'army of the Medes' that was under Rostam's command at al-Qādessiyah numbered 80,000 armed men.[38] Al-Tabarī constructs the defeat of this substantial force in moral terms and blames the poor judgement of the Sasanian king, demonstrated by his abusive and disrespectful behaviour towards the Arab ambassadors in the run-up to the battle.[39] Yazdgerd is reported to have told the ambassador, al-Mughīra b. Zurāra, that the Arabs represented 'the weakest, most wretched and most miserable of people' in the Persian view.[40] The disdain for the Arabs expressed by Yazdgerd here is used to condemn the king as weak, corrupt and out of touch. Al-Tabarī's tale of the Sasanian reflections on Arab society relates to the pre-Islamic society and shows how the Sasanian king is out of touch with the realities of the new Arab Muslim world. The strength and power of their new belief elevates the Arab Muslim soldiers above the disdain of a king who would soon lose his entire kingdom.

The epic framework for the battle and the commanders suited all sides. The Iranian memory of their once great empire and the nobility of Rostam coincides with the medieval Muslim historians' memory of their own fight as underdogs. Theirs, in al-Tabarī's view, was a moral victory. The rise of Islam and conquest of the Sasanian

---

Bosworth (1987) on the *asāwira* in the Iranian tradition. See Zakeri (1995) 58–9 n. 211 especially for the reference here and translations. Zakeri argues for the formal transformation in the idea of horsemen to heroic men being connected to the reforms of Khosrow I Anūshirwān, although it could be argued that it can be traced back through to Achaemenid times. Kennedy (2001) 5 n. 26 implies Zakeri exaggerates this aspect of their role. There is a common view of cavalry and its relation to masculinities that pervades all the armies of the day. See McDonnell (2006) 216–17 for equestrian valour in the Roman Republican tradition; Elton (2007) for a study of the cavalry in the late Roman period; Parnell (2017) and Stewart (2016a) on the Byzantine traditions of *virtus* and manliness.

[38] Sebēos 137, trans. Thomson in Thomson et al. (1999) 98, and see Greenwood (2002) on the apocalyptic aspect of Sebēos' history, which plays into the history of the battles and potentially the Sasanian origins for much of the information. This may then be reflecting Sasanian numbers.

[39] See al-Tabarī 1 2241–2. In his book on the Rashidun caliphs, el-Hibri (2010) notes that the scenes between the commanders before the Battle of al-Qādessiyah are built up to reflect the eternal stand-off between Moses and the pharaoh from the Hebrew Bible.

[40] Translation here from el-Hibri (2010) 99 n. 59, who notes the response from the ambassador is to agree that they 'once were those people but now things had changed with the appearance of the Prophet and the new religion'.

Empire become an inevitability in history, and the elevation of the figure of Rostam allows for the heroic aspects of Persian masculinity to be remembered and emulated in the early centuries of the Arab empires. This would become even more important when the Arab armies' successes led to many conversions in and around the crucial battles, with elite units of the Sasanian army switching sides. The Arab Muslim story of al-Qādessiyah and Rostam was also part of the elite Iranian story. A shared elite masculine identity became a means by which the memory of these events could be articulated in the aftermath of the battle and in the construction of a new state and power that incorporates the old elite.[41]

Identity through Command: The Caucasus

The cultural impact of the Sasanian elite male and construction of a heroic identity had a broad influence beyond the Iranian and Arab worlds. The region of the Caucasus had played a pivotal role in the history of the Iranian empires (i.e. Parthian and Sasanian) and their relationship with the Roman/Byzantine Empires for centuries. This is closely reflected in the narratives of the battles of the 630s and in the identity of the Caucasian commanders who fought for both Byzantine and Sasanian interests. The long history of Armenia as a buffer between the two great eastern and western empires, and their role as the continuers of the Arsacid/Parthian Dynasty into the fifth century AD, form a basis for the process of cultural differentiation taking place over this period.[42] Armenian and Albanian memories of command and the battles that preceded the fall of the Sasanians and the defeat of the Byzantines provide a distinct view of these events. These narratives are preserved through the lens of growing national identities as the deeds of the elite men in command become a component of their self-definition.[43] The historical narratives that remember the seventh-century conflicts and main characters reflect a shifting sense of identity, both religious and cultural, in the battles against the Arabs.[44]

---

[41] Here see Zakeri (1995) on the conversion and role of Sasanian soldiers in the early Islamic period in Iran, and also see Crone (1998) 1–19, who argues against some of the assumptions made in Zakeri's discussions, and looks closely at the complexity around the Iranian and Arab identities in the Abbasid period, and the continued identity of Zoroastrian Iranians in the politics of the Abbasids.

[42] See here Greenwood (2019) on Armenia as contested space.

[43] The ancient kingdom of Albania is situated in Azerbaijan, Russian Dagestan and eastern Georgia today. For the Sasanian echoes in Armenian history see Greenwood (2002), who presents Sebēos' history in its Armenian context.

[44] Evidence from Sebēos and the tenth-century Movsēs Daskhurants'i are especially relevant here. Chaumont (1985) on Albania in an Iranian context with bibliography, and also useful

Caucasian commanders were far from liminal figures in the landscape of battle and played significant roles at both the battles of al-Yarmūk and al-Qādessiyah. In the Armenian and Albanian sources, these home-grown commanders carry Iranian names but are reflected through Christian paradigms, especially emphasising the events in a biblical context.[45] The process illustrates the cross-cultural development of political and religious identities alongside a 'national' coming of age in the face of Sasanian and Byzantine power, and Arab invasions.[46] An insight into how ideal masculinity frames the developing Albanian identity comes via the heroic prince Juanšēr, who fought as a lieutenant for the Sasanians and, like Rostam, despite losing at al-Qādessiyah remained celebrated for his heroic efforts.

The Albanian history of Movsēs Daskhurants'i names the participants in the battle on the Sasanian side as 'the generals and princes, lords and indigenous nobles of the various regions subject to the kingdom of Persia who were recruited to march against the foreign foe'.[47] This idea reiterates the Zoroastrian expression of the duties of a warrior to protect his lands and also reflects the pan-regional call to his vassals made by the Sasanian king in the face of this external threat. Daskhurants'i goes on to describe that 'at the time of these events, Varaz-Grigor, prince of Albania, being himself a noble of the family of Artasir, saw his second son Juanšēr to be brave, dignified and well-formed'. The 'national' history of the Albanians celebrates the young prince as a heroic warrior descended from Iranian nobility. Not only was he 'liked by all' but he was 'swift to strike as an eagle' and 'skilled in the art of war'. The proud prince approached the field of battle as a newly appointed *sparapet* (field-marshal) expecting to 'trample the southerners underfoot'.[48] Elite Albanian

---

is Bosworth (1986) on the region's evolution to the Arabic Arān. For Armenia see Garsoïan (1985) in the history of Armenia between Byzantine and Sasanian power; and also Garsoïan (1998) 96–7 on the Armenian integration into the Byzantine Empire, which also reflects on the Iranian cultural underpinning of elite Armenian men through onomastic processes.

[45] The discussion in Garsoïan (1998) 96–7, although referring to Armenia, outlines the nuanced portrayal of Iranian-named commanders serving the Byzantine emperor and argues that cultural affiliation and religious observance were blended, and we can make similar assumptions here with Albanian identities.

[46] See here the discussion by Andrews (2013), who focuses on the sixth century as the crucial period for a growing Armenian identity in the face of religious and military conflict on all fronts. Greenwood (2019) explores the idea of Armenian space in late antiquity and notes this was a shifting and malleable concept, in no way static, as part of the processes developing an identity. See Reza (2014) esp. 35–9, 84–94, on the development of Caucasian Albania.

[47] Trans. Dowsett (1961).

[48] See Daskhurants'i 2.18–28. The total numbers in the battle in this Albanian text are recorded as 50,000 Sasanian/Persian vs 30,000 'sons of Hagar'. These are much smaller numbers than al-Balādhurī records of al-Yarmūk when he notes that Heraclius' army of

warriors were all cavalry officers and characterised in the same heroic vein as the Sasanians, with the added layer of their Christian belief guiding their actions in the manner of Byzantine elite warriors.[49] Juanšēr survived al-Qādessiyah and went on to fight for seven more years against the Arabs, each battle inflicting severe wounds on the prince, who never falters. He is divinely protected, with each step guided by 'the hand of Christ'. The evolution of Juanšēr in the narrative parallels that of his nation, as he moves from vassal prince to key instrument in the establishment of an independent Albanian kingdom that goes on to seek an alliance with the Byzantine emperor Constans II (641–668).[50] Juanšēr's elite masculinity embodies the heroic identity of the best of men from both Iranian and Byzantine traditions, and through his trials by combat he becomes a symbol of his homeland.

A contemporary of the young heroic Albanian Juanšēr was the older and more established Armenian Byzantine general Vahān. As the commander of Byzantine forces at al-Yarmūk he was second in power in the region. Vahān's reputation in the sources is contradictory.[51] He was placed in charge of the army after the emperor Heraclius' brother was removed from the position.[52] In the Arab narrative of al-Yarmūk, Vahān is constructed as a positive force. Morally upright, he is reported to have distanced himself from the behaviour of other Byzantine commanders who are accused of mistreatment of locals in Syria, including rape and appropriation of land, in the lead-up to al-Yarmūk.[53] The Arabic historians excuse Vahān, and separate him from his colleagues; he is considered more noble and his conduct more

---

Greeks, Syrians, Mesopotamians and Armenians numbered 200,000 (section 135, Hitti (1916/1924) 207). The numbers in the hundreds of thousands are in no way feasible.

[49] See Stewart (2016a) 133–66 for the construction of Christian manliness and the legacy of a masculine identity developed in the period of Theodosius II.

[50] The role of the elite men of the Caucasus in the Sasanian military is briefly outlined in Farrouk (2017) 20–1 and in more detail in pp. 72–119.

[51] For Vahān/Bāhān's complex representation and use as a foil see Khalek (2010) 120–2. See Haldon (2014b) on the organisation of the Byzantine army from c. 600 onwards. Kaegi (1992) covers the events and details. The Arab view of the Byzantine commanders is discussed in el Cheikh (2004).

[52] Theophanes, *Chronographia* AM 6125, notes that Vahān is placed alongside Heraclius' treasurer (*sakellarios*) Theodore Trithurious in command; see Kaegi (1992) 100. When Heraclius placed Theodore Trithourios in command of the armies of Syria in the lead-up to the battle, the assumption of power by this state treasurer implies that Heraclius wanted to reassure his soldiers they would be paid for their endeavours. The discussion in Kaegi (1992) 35–9 picks up on the payment in kind or land for soldiers' employ and the need to ensure cash payment here in the defence of the Levant.

[53] Here reported in Al-Azdi, *Kitāb al-futūḥ al-shām*, and discussed in el Cheikh (2004) 37–9. The lack of detail about other commanders in the Byzantine forces is notable.

righteous. In contrast, Vahān is labelled as treasonous by the Byzantines and is held responsible for the defeat by the Arab armies at al-Yarmūk.[54] The Arab sources are much more generous and consider him an exemplary enemy, while the other Byzantine commanders on the ground behave like barbarians.

The inconsistencies of the portrayal of Vahān perhaps reflect a diminished Byzantine Empire after Yarmûk that necessitated a repositioning of the story from the Byzantine perspective. There is a largely discounted report that Vahān's troops declared him emperor on the field of battle at al-Yarmūk, but this has generally been dismissed as a Byzantine attempt to blame the 'untrustworthy' Armenian for their defeat. The characterisation of the Armenians as 'crafty and deceitful' permeates descriptions by Byzantine authors, as noted by Nina Garsoïan, who cites a multitude of sources reflecting the underlying polemic of later doctrinal battles.[55] The Byzantine memory of the catastrophic defeats in the Levant diminished the role played by the emperor Heraclius (and his family), thus reflecting the selective memory of the dynasty. Walter Kaegi has argued that in the Byzantine tales of al-Yarmūk and the disarray of the army it was convenient to place the blame at the feet of Armenian commander Vahān.[56]

Armenian commanders and their role in the relationship between the two great powers in the seventh century were integral to the memory of the epic battles. It is in the career of an Armenian general, Smbat Bagratuni (died 617), who had served in both the Byzantine and Sasanian armies just a few decades earlier, that we can see how command, masculinity and loyalties were being constructed as local identity and geopolitical struggles unfolded. Ideal masculinity in the Armenian identity was, as in Sasanian, Byzantine and early Arabic traditions, tied to both combat and religious piety. Smbat embodied the role of the pious warlord as an ideal of manhood that prevailed.[57] The Armenian history attributed to Sebēos is our main source for the story, which seems to stem from a heroic account of Smbat's life and illustrates how the ideals of masculinity were represented in the Armenian world.[58] Smbat's strength,

---

[54] It is interesting that Sebēos' cryptic account, 135–7, omits any mention of Vahān but does discuss the Armenian commanders at al-Qādessiyah.

[55] See Garsoïan (1998) 65–7.

[56] See Kaegi (1992) 120, 186–7, 237, and also Lewental (2017) n. 78; Nicolle (2006) looks at the battle specifically. El Cheikh (2004) 39.

[57] Here see the traditions in Byzantine military as described by Stewart (2016a); Kuefler (2001) 105–24, especially on the 'soldiers of Christ'; McDonnell's study (2006) on Roman manliness and its evolution from Republic to empire also contains much of use.

[58] Sebēos' identity and the family are discussed in Soultanian (2009) 43–8, and McDonough (2016) nuances the figure of Smbat in the political fragmentation of the Sasanian state in the late sixth and early seventh centuries.

prowess and piety resulted in honours being bestowed upon him by the Sasanian king. These virtues were universal, and also played a part in the creation of the identity of an idealised Armenian masculinity in Sebēos' history.[59] In the celebration of this famous commander, who fought bravely and successfully for the greater powers, we have an illustration of the way that acquiring the role of command and trust of those evolves into a kind of validation of a local elite identity. In the seventh century, in the aftermath of the failed or diminished power of the emperor and king of kings, the elite men of the Caucasus who fought with them had long afterlives as symbols of a nascent national identity in their home regions.[60]

The Conquerors: Brave and Strong

The Arabic historian Ibn A´tham recounts the pre al-Yarmūk visit of the commander Khālid b. al-Walīd to the Armenian commander of the Byzantine forces, Vahān. Full imperial splendour was on display for the Arab Khālid as he approached Vahān, who had ten rows of iron-masked soldiers in columns to the right and left. The Byzantine commander sat on a golden throne surrounded by trappings of the wealth and splendour of the empire.[61] The narrative emphasises that the noble Khālid was in no way swayed by all the grandeur on display and dismissed any man who needed imperial splendour as a disguise. Khālid is remembered as the ideal Arab military man, unimpressed by displays of wealth and pomp, a man of the people, egalitarian in approach, who is also considered one of the great strategic generals of the campaigns. In the memory of the Arab conquests, he became a symbol for a new kind of egalitarianism in the Arab Muslim armies in the face of the perceived imperial despotism of the Byzantines.[62]

---

[59] See Soultanian (2009) 43–8 on the Bagratuni family in the Armenian history of Sebēos and the debate around the career of the Smbat Bagratunis and identities of Smbat, son of Manuel, and the Sasanian Marzpan Smbat Khosrow Shum. Soultanian (2009) 46 argues that they are not the same man, and the various interpretations are outlined by McDonough (2016) in his study of Smbat. McDonough also discusses the political implications of Smbat's significant role in Sasanian politics. Passages in Sebēos 27–8, 40–1, 48, 53, 86–7, 92.

[60] See Andrews (2013) 29–41 for the developments in the sixth century of Armenian identity, and Garsoïan (1998) for the cultural negotiations between Armenia and Byzantium. There is an interesting comparison to be made with the study of colonial identities developing through soldiers fighting for the imperial powers in the First World War and the impact on national identities in India, Australia, New Zealand and Canada.

[61] Ibn A´tham Kitāb al-futūḥ, 1: 239–40, 177 with translation here from el Cheikh (2004) 153–4 n. 34.

[62] Discussion in el Cheikh (2004) 36–9. Interesting parallels with the evolution of Roman

It has been acknowledged that the traditional rhetoric of these battles preserved in the Arabic sources looks back to the men who fought them with romantic idealism. The diverse set of sources were mostly written well after the victories, during the consolidation of the new Arab empire of the Abbasids and a great flowering of Arabic literature in the ninth century.[63] The memory of Khālid was employed by later Arab historians to emphasise a past before the caliphate had been corrupted by wealth, power and civil war.[64] In this way, Khālid represents the ideal of the *futūḥ* commanders, the best of the Arab Muslim warriors.[65] The processes of memory that preserved these events would have been held largely in oral epic traditions that became wrapped in the creation of identities of a distant past.

The Arabic commanders on the fields of battle were the unqualified victors in these clashes and remained the last real men standing. Their opponents were portrayed as corrupted old powers whose commanders might have some virtues but who were out of sync with the new men who had embraced a new religious identity. The Arab soldiers are characterised as brave, able to withstand huge hardships, tireless and almost above suffering. Al-Tabarī's recorded memories of the battle emphasise the endurance and hardship. On the night of al-Qādessiyah the commander, al-Qa'qā, walked among his troops encouraging them 'because victory comes with endurance' and to 'prefer endurance to fear'.[66] The Arab soldiers endured, suffered and persisted in battle and for this, they were victorious. Suffering is exemplified in another passage in al-Tabarī that records the soldier who almost does not notice that he has left a leg on the field of battle. Aspects of this model of hardship and suffering in the construction of an idealised masculinity have been viewed as an appropriation

---

masculinity in the late Republic as described by McDonnell (2006) 292 in his chapter on '*virtus* contested'.

[63] Hassan (2016) looks at this notion of longing for a purer past in the tradition of Arab and Turkish historiography.

[64] An interesting comparison could be made with the way Livy (and other Roman historians, such as Sallust) constructs the stories of the Middle Roman Republic from the principate of Augustus, especially Livy's third decade and the role of Scipio Africanus.

[65] See Kennedy (2001) 1–17 for the commanders and battles. Kennedy (2007) 12–33 outlines the processes of memory here. See el-Hibri (2010) on the literary constructions; Donner (1998) 282 on the process of identity construction. See Robinson (2003) 10–11 on the creation of the story rather than the actual facts themselves being a key notion. Kaegi (1992) 18 notes that the *futūḥ* narrative in the Arabic sources is also apparent in the Byzantine writer Theophanes' interpretation of events.

[66] A time-honoured tradition going back to the Hellenistic period (trans Friedmann 1992). See also Cubit (2010) 5 for the way the biblical and Christian traditions were used to construct identities and create moral tales of the men of the conquests. See the details in al-Tabarī (I.2335–6).

of the Christian model of the ascetic soldier saint from the Byzantine tradition.[67] It is worth emphasising the shared cultural heritage and traditions in which the commanders of the Arab armies were defined, taking aspects of both the Christian Byzantine and Zoroastrian Persian ideal soldiers into their identity creation. In the Arab narratives, this kind of comparison of cultural typologies could be used to advance their commanders as examples of good and bad men with their idealised behaviours.

The Arab soldiers were skilled as fighters and had a deep understanding of the military tactics of their opponents, having fought for and against them for the decades previous to the conquests. When Sebēos notes that 'all of the leading nobles' on the Sasanian side were killed on the field at al-Qādessiyah, some scholars believe this reflects an intentional targeting of the leadership of Rostam's army, whose factionalism had plagued the state through the previous decades of civil war.[68] The Arab commanders are thought to have understood the tribal/regional aspect of Rostam's army especially, and that those who were fighting for their own families and lands rather than any strong loyalty to a weak king were liable to abandon the fight if their leadership was eradicated.[69]

If Khālid was an ideal man among the Arab commanders, then there is the intriguing figure of the Arab Christian leader Jabala, who becomes a foil to this. When al-Balādhurī writes of al-Yarmūk, he talks of the Arabs of Syria who fought with the Byzantines of the Lakhm and Judhâm tribes under the leadership of Jabala ibn al-Ayham al-Ghassānī.[70] Jabala had once been a client king of the Byzantine emperor and came from a long line of Jafnid Arab leaders. He evolves to become a focus of memory and identity in the narratives of the battle and is characterised as the 'last Arab king'. He was a Muslim apostate, a Christian Arab who converted to Islam, who then returns to Christianity and fights on the side of the Byzantines at

---

[67] Khalek (2010) looks at the variant depictions and regional depictions and emphasises the shared narrative traditions. See also Fowden (1999) on St Sergius' role in the Roman and Persian traditions, and Walter (2003) on the warrior saint in the Byzantine tradition.

[68] Sebēos, trans. Thomson in Thomson et al. (1999) 137. See Pourshariati (2008) 232–3, who gives a particularly incisive account, based on al-Tabarī and Sebēos, but see also Kennedy (2001) 2–5; Howard-Johnston (2010) 461–74; el-Hibri (2010) 84–100, who looks closely at the narrative construction and themes of these events in the context of the caliph Umar's rule.

[69] See the discussion in Landau-Tasseron (1995) for a useful breakdown of the pre-Islamic sources and the army of the Arabs pre-conquest.

[70] For the depiction of Jabala in the early Arabic sources see Bray (2010), who assesses the role of the 'king' as a literary figure. See also the *Kitāb Futūḥ al-buldān* (section 135) – written by Aḥmad b. Yaḥyā al-Balādhurī (died c. AD 892).

al-Yarmūk. In the same way that Rostam embodies the identity of a lost masculinity in the shape of the last Sasanian warrior, Jabala is defined as the last stand of the old guard of the Arab pre-Islamic kings who give way to a new world, a new order and a new religion.[71]

Jabala and his followers were elite horsemen and his inability to accept the egalitarianism of Islam is provided as the reason he returned to the Christian Byzantine side. He had stubbornly refused to change his ways and remained elitist and arrogant; he would not call any man his master and was also notable for his love of wine, his dancing girls and songs. Julia Bray's article on Jabala outlines how both Byzantine and Arabic sources employ him in many different narratives.[72] Like the Armenian Vahān, Jabala is swayed by the luxurious temptations of the old empires, and his revelling in them illustrates how he had become an important marker that defined a lost, elite Arab identity.[73] In a world of such complexity, the depictions of Jabala's elite Arab, pre-Muslim masculinity becomes a typology of the past that is employed across many contexts. In that way he becomes a symbol of loss to the Byzantines and of the past to the Arabs, and like all our commanders he embodied aspects of both the victors and the defeated in Syria.

Conclusions

This selective survey of a few of the masculine identities of the commanders that fought the battles of al-Yarmūk and al-Qādessiyah provides an overview of the memory of the men who were sung about and lamented across the multiple traditions that remembered their stories. The memory of the great conquests and battles that shaped the new Islamic caliphate was a fundamental part of the discourse and narrative that created the early Islamic worlds across the Near East and Central Asia, Egypt and North Africa, Spain, Sicily and beyond.[74] The men who fought these battles were heroic and legendary, they were written about as parables, they were brave and sometimes misguided in a shifting environment that witnessed old traditions giving way to a new world order. In many ways, there is a convergence of

---

[71] See Bray (2010) 174. The article outlines, and also provides a non-exhaustive list of, the source mentions of Jabala.

[72] Bray (2010) 189–92 provides the examples and translations here from Ibn Qutayba, Al-Zubayr ibn Bakkār, al-Balādurī.

[73] Bray (2010) 183.

[74] The fluidity of the memory of the early caliphate and the Abbasid Empire that followed is discussed in Hassan (2016), and while not directly related to the subject matter here, it is a diachronic approach to assessing memory and power in a post-Abbasid world that serves as a useful comparison and methodology.

traditional depictions of battle heroes across cultures that becomes most apparent in their stories. The men are characterised in the time-honoured terms of the brave and strong, heroic demigods much like the legendary figures who travelled across thousands of years and infused the Iranian, Graeco-Roman and Semitic myths and stories of the Near East. These old-school heroic men had evolved to become both pious and warlike; in fact the two attributes are remembered as essential to the descriptions of positive masculinity in the seventh-century world of war.[75] Shifting identities and monotheistic traditions of the men and their memory played a part in the creation of national self-representations across the post-antique Near East; this is especially true in the Caucasus kingdoms and in the way the Arab Muslim armies embraced their stories and integrated these into the traditions of the worlds they conquered. Therefore, through these tales of elite masculinity on the fields of battle, we glimpse the long and complex processes of memory and the formation of identity. Whether it is the death of the noble Rostam or the uncorrupted Khālid, the lost king Jabala or the new young hero Juanšēr, a typology of male identity was consolidated in the memory of these years of both victory and defeat.

---

[75] Canepa's (2009) study of the co-dependent representation of the Byzantine emperor and Sasanian king of kings and their ideologies of power and kingship explores the continuities and contested areas that must have been reflected in broader society. What is interesting here is how the ruling monarchs are largely missing from the narrative and it is the men in command who are the focus.

13 Tian Yue Marshals His Tropes: Public Persuasion and the Character of Military Leadership in Late Tang China

David A. Graff

In some martial cultures, public speaking in the form of the rousing pep talk or pre-battle exhortation had a prominent place. Thucydides' history of the Peloponnesian War is peppered with commanders' speeches delivered just before leading their troops into combat, a tradition that was still alive and well when Alexander the Great campaigned against the Persian Empire.[1] Although Thucydides' speeches should not be taken as the *ipsissima verba* of the speakers, they do make it clear that the Greeks considered oratory appropriate and even necessary to the occasion. A first glance at the so-called 'Confucian Classics' would seem to suggest that the pre-battle speech was also a standard fixture of traditional Chinese warfare. The *Book of Documents* (*Shu jing*) includes several martial harangues (*shi* 誓) attributed to ancient rulers, among them the speech that King Wu, the founder of the Zhou Dynasty, purportedly delivered to his army just before his decisive victory over the last Shang king at the Battle of Muye in or around 1045 BC.[2] Yet in the end, the dominant military tradition that emerged from the Warring States period (453–221 BC) placed little reliance upon oratorical performance and emotional appeals to the rank and file. Sunzi's *Art of War* (*Sunzi bingfa*), the most influential of the military writings passed down from that time, advises the general to distance himself from his troops; he is not to share his plans with them, and he is supposed to motivate his men not by haranguing them and making demands but by placing them in desperate situations where they must conquer or die.[3]

---

[1] For just a few examples, see Thuc. 2.87–9; 4.10; 4.92. Alexander's oratory is discussed in Keegan (1987) 54–9.
[2] Karlgren (1950) 28–9.
[3] Wu Jiulong et al. (1990) 79, 202.

This is not to say that Sunzi's highly prescriptive text can be taken as fully representative of Chinese military practice. It is not difficult to find examples of generals who did give speeches or pep talks to their men. In AD 538, for example, the Western Wei general Wang Xiong defended the prefectural city of Huazhou against an Eastern Wei siege at a time when it appeared that the regime he served was on the brink of collapse. Summoning both soldiers and civilians to the city gate, Wang delivered the following speech:

> Rumour has it that the Son of Heaven has been defeated, and we don't know whether there will be good or bad fortune. You people have been alarming one another, and everyone is of a different mind. I, Wang Xiong, have been entrusted with this place, and I am willing to give my life to requite [the ruler's] favour. If you people have a different plan, you can come over here and be killed [by me]. Those who insist on fearing that Huazhou will fall shall of course be allowed to leave the city. If there are those who are loyal and sincere and capable of being of one heart and one mind with me, then we can hold out firmly together![4]

We are told that the soldiers and people were moved by Wang's sincerity, and there was no more thought of disloyalty. Huazhou did not fall, and the Western Wei (later Northern Zhou) regime that Wang served went on to survive for another four decades.[5]

In the summer of 583, not long after the Northern Zhou had been superseded by the Sui Dynasty, the Sui general Li Chong found himself surrounded in the north-eastern frontier town of Shacheng by a superior force of Türks. With his army, originally 3,000 strong, reduced to barely a hundred men after an unsuccessful sortie, Li addressed the desperate survivors:

> I, Chong, am a fellow who has lost his army, a crime for which I deserve death. Today, I will give my life as an apology to the state. After you have seen that I am dead, you may surrender to the enemy and then seek an opportunity to scatter and flee, exerting yourselves to return to your homeland. If you encounter [our] most revered [emperor], tell him what I have said.[6]

---

[4] All translations are my own.

[5] The most complete version of Wang's harangue is in Du You (1988) ch. 151, p. 3870. An abridged and slightly different version can be found in Sima Guang (1956) (hereafter *ZZTJ*) ch. 158, p. 4897. Wang Xiong's biography in Linghu Defen (1971) ch. 18, p. 292, mentions the siege but does not include the speech. Instead a different *topos* is deployed, with Wang delivering a defiant speech to the Eastern Wei leader (and some of the language from that speech reappears in the *Tong dian* and *Zizhi tongjian* speeches).

[6] Wei Zheng (1973) ch. 37, p. 1123. With only very slight differences, the same speech appears in *ZZTJ* ch. 175, p. 5466.

Thirty-five years later, the authority of the Sui Dynasty was collapsing amid a welter of peasant rebellions and defections by the dynasty's own generals. At dawn on 6 October 618, the soldiers of Wang Shichong, a nominal Sui general turned de facto warlord, were in a desperate situation, with the Luo River at their backs and the much larger army of rival warlord Li Mi occupying the heights of Mangshan in front of them. Under these circumstances, Wang Shichong is also reported to have felt the need to address the men under his command:

> This day's battle is not simply a contest that will determine victory or defeat; whether we live or die depends on this one action. If we win, it goes without saying that we will have wealth and honour; if we lose, not one of us will get away with his life. We are fighting not only on behalf of the state, but for our very lives. It is appropriate that each of you should do your utmost![7]

Speeches such as those delivered by Wang Xiong, Li Chong and Wang Shichong were, however, the exception rather than the rule, and they appear to have been more likely to occur in the most desperate circumstances rather than more routine situations.

During the Tang Dynasty (618–907), a general named Tian Yue found himself in similarly desperate straits. Tian was the military governor (*jiedushi*) of Wei-Bo, one of several autonomous provinces in the north-eastern part of the Tang realm that rebelled against imperial authority in the early 780s. At the beginning of 782, Wei-Bo's main field army, led by Tian Yue himself, was shattered by forces loyal to the Tang court at the Battle of the Huan River. Tian fled back to his headquarters at the prefectural city of Weizhou and delivered a dramatic speech to the assembled soldiers and commoners that persuaded them to rally around him in spite of his failures and resist a prolonged siege by the imperial armies. His unusual resort to public oratory occurred under conditions that were arguably typical of such 'command performances' from the sixth to the ninth centuries AD, if not throughout the entire two-thousand-year history of imperial China. Rather than being a routine procedure or the first choice of the commander when all was going well, the address to the masses was the desperate expedient of a (nearly) beaten man, a last throw of the dice to avert complete and irrevocable disaster. It was also a ploy more likely to be adopted by upstarts, rebels, fugitive rulers and any others who were not well

---

[7] *ZZTJ* ch. 186, p. 5811. The translation is taken from Mair et al. (2005) 303. This speech is not included in any of Wang Shichong's biographies: Wei Zheng (1973) ch. 85, pp. 1894–8; Liu Xu (1975) ch. 54, pp. 2227–34 (hereafter *JTS*); Ouyang Xiu and Song Qi (1975) ch. 85, pp. 3689–96 (hereafter *XTS*).

positioned to benefit from established patterns of ritual legitimacy. It was usually accompanied by some sort of material inducement, revealing a tacit underlying assumption that words alone were not sufficient to achieve the desired result. And it was a mode of leadership behaviour that was gaining currency amid the chaotic military politics of late Tang China.

This chapter will explore these themes primarily through a detailed examination of Tian Yue's case. In order to locate this single instance within a broader pattern of thought and behaviour, and to identify what elements of Tian's performance may have been new or unique, it will first offer brief accounts of two additional episodes, both involving rulers, that took place well before he delivered his speech at Weizhou.

At the end of AD 576 the Northern Qi Dynasty, based at the city of Ye in southern Hebei, was in terminal crisis. After having battled the rival Northern Zhou regime for several decades over control of north China, Qi now confronted an invasion of unprecedented strength and ferocity led by the vigorous young Zhou ruler. Qi's main stronghold, the garrison city of Taiyuan, had already fallen to the invaders when the Qi emperor Gao Wei was persuaded by his advisors to deliver a speech in order to inspire the soldiers who had been gathered for the defence of Ye. Gao, then twenty years old, was by all accounts one of China's less impressive rulers.[8] His speech was handed to him by his advisors, who also urged him to accompany his words with copious tears in order to elicit the soldiers' sympathy. When he went out to address the troops, however, the Qi ruler delivered a stunningly poor performance: he forgot what he was supposed to say and then burst out laughing, leading the fighting men to have second thoughts about their commitment to the Qi regime. Nor were material inducements on offer to redeem this signal failure of imperial oratory. Gao Wei had earlier been 'displeased' when it was suggested that he should bring out his palace treasures as rewards to encourage the soldiers. Ye soon fell to the Zhou forces, and less than a year after his botched attempt at oral persuasion Gao Wei was put to death by the victors.[9]

In contrast to Gao Wei, whose performance provides an object lesson in how not to win hearts and minds, Li Longji, the Tang emperor known posthumously as Xuanzong, hit just the right note when it became necessary for him to make a personal appeal to the disgruntled guardsmen in his entourage. In the midsummer of 756, the advance of An Lushan's rebel armies compelled the seventy-year-old emperor to flee his capital, Chang'an. At the Mawei post station about twenty-five miles west of the capital, Xuanzong's guards mutinied, murdering the chief minister

[8] *ZZTJ* ch. 172, p. 5339; Pearce (1987) 707–13.
[9] The episode of Gao Wei's speech is described in *ZZTJ* ch. 172, pp. 5365–6, and by Li Baiyao (1972) ch. 8, p. 110. For the Qi ruler's fate, see Pearce (1987) 712–13.

whom they blamed for their misfortune and forcing the execution of the emperor's favourite concubine, who happened to be a cousin of the chief minister.[10] This sacrifice alone was not enough to bring the soldiers back under control. Three days later, when the imperial party reached Fufeng Commandery, some sixty-seven miles further to the west, seditious talk again spread through the camp and the guard commanders were unable to control their men.[11] One source of disagreement was the group's ultimate destination, but there were also much deeper grievances. The guardsmen were a relatively privileged class of soldiers who were almost never called upon to serve in the field, but now not only had they been turned out of their homes but they had even had to leave their families behind in the capital – at the mercy of the approaching rebel forces.[12]

Although Xuanzong was known for his love of military glory, it had been achieved vicariously through the actions of his frontier generals.[13] The only time he had led armed men in dangerous circumstances was as a young prince, during the palace coup in 710 that had paved his way to the imperial throne. Now, however, the septuagenarian fugitive rose to the occasion. Taking advantage of the arrival of a large shipment of tribute silk from Sichuan that was passing through Fufeng en route to the capital, Xuanzong had the silk spread out, asked the officers and men in to see the display, and then addressed them himself, thanking them for their service and inviting them to divide the silk among themselves and then stay or go as they saw fit. This grand gesture produced the desired effect: the soldiers reportedly bowed their heads and tearfully proclaimed their willingness to follow the emperor 'in life or death'.[14] From this time onward, we are told, the seditious talk 'diminished somewhat'.[15] The emperor and his retinue continued southward to reach the safe haven of Chengdu, the administrative centre of distant Sichuan, on 28 August 756.

Although Xuanzong had fallen a long way by 18 July, the day he delivered his speech at Fufeng, and had been stripped by circumstances of much of his ritual dignity,[16] he must still have been able to draw upon a substantial residue of imperial legitimacy. One of the strongest of the Tang rulers, he had already occupied the

---

[10] *ZZTJ* ch. 218, pp. 6971–4; translated in Kroll (1985) 34–53.
[11] *JTS* ch. 9, p. 233, and ch. 108, p. 3277; *ZZTJ* ch. 218, p. 6976.
[12] For the composition and character of these guard units, see Wang Pu (1990) ch. 72, p. 1293; *XTS* ch. 50, pp. 1326–7; Hamaguchi Shigekuni (1930) 1255–95, 1439–1507; Gu Jiguang (1962) 242–3.
[13] See, for example, Du You (1988) ch. 148, p. 3780.
[14] *ZZTJ* ch. 218, pp. 6976–7.
[15] *JTS* ch. 9, p. 233.
[16] On this point, see Kroll (1985) 27 and *passim*.

throne for forty-four years, presiding over the pinnacle of the dynasty's power, prosperity and cultural efflorescence.

Our third speaker, Tian Yue, enjoyed no such advantages when he stood before the assembled soldiery a quarter of a century later. He did not come from a line of rulers; instead, his family had served 'for generations' as junior officers in the Tang's north-eastern frontier armies. Yue had lost his father at a very early age, and his mother was soon remarried to a soldier of the Pinglu army. When the An Lushan rebellion erupted on the north-eastern frontier at the end of 755, the Pinglu troops remained loyal to the imperial court and were eventually relocated across the Bohai Gulf to Shandong, with dependants such as Yue and his mother in tow. The boy's fortunes changed suddenly when, at the age of twelve, he entered the household of his uncle Tian Chengsi, who had recently been made prefect of Weizhou and given military authority over several other nearby prefectures.[17]

Tian Chengsi had fought for An Lushan and his successors, and by 762 he had emerged as one of the main commanders on the rebel side. Instead of being a reward for loyal service to the Tang court, his appointment to Weizhou was in fact a bribe to persuade him to end his resistance to imperial authority and thereby bring the rebellion – which had already dragged on for eight years – to an earlier conclusion than would otherwise have been possible.[18] And Weizhou was a significant prize. Located just north of the Yellow River and athwart the northern extension of the Grand Canal (Yongji ju), it had fertile, low-lying and well-watered farmland and was an important centre of handicraft silk production.[19] It was probably the most populous prefecture in all of the Hebei region, which stretched northward from the Yellow River to the vicinity of today's Beijing.[20] Shortly before the outbreak of the An Lushan rebellion, Weizhou and the neighbouring prefectures of Bo, Cang, Ying and De, which also fell within Tian Chengsi's purview as military governor (*jiedushi*) of Wei-Bo, had a combined registered population of approximately 510,000 households – or 3.67 million individuals.[21] From this resource base, which was probably

---

[17] This paragraph is based on Tian Yue's biography in *XTS* ch. 210, pp. 5926–7, plus Tian Chengsi's biographies in *JTS* ch. 141, p. 3837, and *XTS* ch. 210, p. 5923.

[18] See the commentary on the 'pacification' of the rebel leaders in Peterson (1966) 31–5, 49–50, 54.

[19] Mao Hanguang (1990) 328–9.

[20] *JTS* ch. 39 gives population figures for the Hebei prefectures during the Tianbao period (AD 742–755); at that time, Weizhou clearly had the largest registered population.

[21] These figures are based on *JTS* ch. 39, pp. 1493, 1496, 1507, 1509, 1513. The same numbers appear in *XTS* ch. 39, pp. 1011, 1017–18, 1020, with only one minor discrepancy that is clearly the result of scribal error.

not dramatically reduced by the events of 755–762, Tian was able to raise an army that was reported to be 100,000 strong.[22]

Not content with his original assignment, in 775 Tian Chengsi took advantage of the death of his western neighbour Xue Song, military governor of Xiang-Wey, to invade and annexe Xue's prefectures of Xiang, Wey, Bei, Ming and Ci.[23] This predatory move brought both gains and losses as the Tang court ordered several other provincial armies to counter-attack. When the dust settled and Tian began to negotiate his return to the court's good graces early in 776, he retained Xiang, Wey and most of Ming – but had lost Cang, Ying and De to various neighbours. Undaunted by this (at best) partial success, he sent troops south of the Yellow River to raid Huazhou later the same year, and then dispatched a much larger force to support a mutiny in the government army at Bianzhou, on the Grand Canal in northern Henan.[24]

Tian Chengsi's nephew Tian Yue had a leading role in these adventures. As a young boy, Yue had already impressed his uncle with his respectful demeanour; as he grew to manhood, 'he was agile and fierce, and was outstanding in the army for his skill at fighting'.[25] Tian Chengsi gave Yue important responsibilities, initially entrusting him to relay orders and commands from the military governor's headquarters and eventually making him commander (*bingmashi*) of Wei-Bo's 'central army' (*zhongjun*). It was in his capacity as a Wei-Bo field commander that the twenty-four-year-old Tian Yue was sent with another general to attack Cizhou, one of Xue Song's former possessions, in the late autumn of 775. His battlefield performance, however, was not impressive: he was badly defeated by forces loyal to the Tang court, reportedly losing 9,000 men dead and another 2,300 captured (including his fellow general), plus 1,000 horses and 200,000 items of equipment. A subsequent night attack on Yue's camp cost him another 500 men and 5,000 pieces of equipment.[26] Tian Chengsi's confidence in his nephew was apparently unshaken. A year later, he put Yue in command of the army he sent to support the Bianzhou

---

[22] *JTS* ch. 141, p. 3838. With regard to the impact of the An Lushan rebellion on the population of this area, see Peterson (1966) 47.

[23] This episode is described in *JTS* ch. 11, pp. 301, 306–8; *XTS* ch. 210, p. 5923; *ZZTJ* ch. 225, pp. 7228–37. 'Wey' should properly be rendered as 'Wei' in Pinyin; the variant spelling is adopted here to distinguish between the prefectures of 魏 (Wei) and 衛 (also Wei, but here rendered as Wey).

[24] *ZZTJ* ch. 225, pp. 7238–9; *JTS* ch. 11, pp. 309–10; ch. 141, p. 3839; *XTS* ch. 210, p. 5923. There is some disagreement as to whether 5,000 or 30,000 men were sent to Bianzhou.

[25] *XTS* ch. 210, pp. 5926–7.

[26] *XTS* ch. 210, p. 5923, which claims that Yue's army was originally only 10,000 strong. Also see *ZZTJ* ch. 225, pp. 7231–2.

mutineers. Yue won an initial victory over Tang provincial forces at Kuangcheng and advanced to camp a short distance from the north wall of Bianzhou – but his camp was then overrun by a surprise attack and the Wei-Bo army collapsed without putting up much of a fight. Yue managed to escape, but his losses were again immense.[27]

Amazingly, the uncle's confidence in his nephew remained unshaken. When Tian Chengsi was dying in 779, he named Yue to succeed him as military governor, passing over his own sons (all eleven of them) and instructing them to support their cousin's leadership.[28] Given Yue's record of defeat, why did Tian Chengsi consider him to be so talented? Yue was outstanding for his physical strength and courage, but his biography in the *New History of the Tang Dynasty* (*Xin Tangshu*) observes that 'he was wildly obstinate and short on plans, eager to do battle but repeatedly defeated'.[29] Another passage in the same text, however, indicates that he did have a certain effectiveness as a leader: 'He was crafty and merciless, and good at trickery. He put on a superficial display of righteousness, made light of wealth and emphasised giving to gain a good reputation, so the men all adhered to him.'[30] These qualities were on display early in 780, when the newly enthroned emperor Dezong sent out commissioners to reinvigorate tax collection from the provinces and downsize the armies of the military governors. Tian Yue, with an army said to number 70,000, was ordered to return 40,000 men to farming. He responded by gathering the officers and men who were to be discharged and addressing them as follows:

> You all have been in the army for a long time; you each have a father and mother, wife and children. Now that you have been dismissed by the commissioner, how will you be able to obtain clothing and food for your upkeep?

His speech reportedly moved the soldiers to tears, and Yue then brought out 'his family wealth and silk clothing' and distributed it to them. From this time on, we are told, the fighting men of Wei-Bo felt indebted to Yue and resented the Tang court.[31]

---

[27] *ZZTJ* ch. 225, p. 7239. According to *XTS* ch. 210, p. 5923, Yue lost 'several tens of thousands' out of an army that began the campaign 30,000 strong.
[28] *JTS* ch. 141, p. 3840; *XTS* ch. 210, p. 5927.
[29] *XTS* ch. 210, p. 5932.
[30] *XTS* ch. 210, p. 5927.
[31] *JTS* ch. 141, p. 3841; also see *ZZTJ* ch. 226, p. 7277; *XTS* ch. 210, p. 5927. The last of these sources reports that after his distribution of largesse, Tian Yue ordered the men to return to their units. Peterson (1966) 83 draws the plausible inference that those who had been dismissed were now reinstated.

Tian Yue had the good fortune to inherit his position while the old emperor Daizong, whose general policy had been to accommodate the more autonomous of the military governors, was still alive. Daizong's heir Dezong, who came to the throne in the summer of 779, had very different ideas and sought to reassert imperial authority against these overmighty subjects. The dispatch of finance commissioners to look into tax collection (and, on occasion, demand that provincial armies be reduced in size) was an opening salvo. The death of the military governor of Chengde, Wei-Bo's northern neighbour, early in 781 provided an even better opportunity for imperial assertiveness when Li Weiyue was denied permission to succeed his father as military governor. Since the rulers of the three north-eastern provinces of Chengde, Wei-Bo and Pinglu (in today's Shandong) had earlier made a pact to uphold one another's claims to hereditary succession, which they understood to be a core element of their de facto autonomy, the court's new-found intransigence meant war. In the fifth lunar month of 781, the three provinces moved into open rebellion.[32] Tian Yue's contribution to the war effort was to invade the same prefectures and counties of south-western Hebei, now belonging to the Zhaoyi military province, that his uncle had failed to annex five years earlier. Against the advice of one of his most experienced generals, Yue attacked the main walled towns and became bogged down in two prolonged sieges – further substantiating the biographer's claim that he was 'wildly obstinate and short on plans'.[33]

While Wei-Bo's army hammered at the walls of Xingzhou and Linming, a coalition of loyalist armies gathered in Shanxi to the west. Descending the Huguan pass through the Taihang Mountains, they overwhelmed a covering force and went on to attack Yue and his main army five days later at Linming. Wei-Bo's leader once again suffered a severe defeat, this time with the loss of 10,000 men, and retreated under cover of darkness.[34] Yue took up a defensive position along the Zhang River to the east, but was forced to fall back again to the Huan River after the Tang army manoeuvred around his defences. The main government commander, Ma Sui, built three bridges across the Huan and tried to provoke a battle, but his opponent now held his troops back and refused to cooperate. Running short of provisions, Ma tried a new approach and launched his army towards Weizhou – Yue's capital and a place he had no choice but to protect – during the first month of 782. Yue crossed the Huan bridges and rushed in pursuit of the government army, precipitating a see-saw battle that ended in the collapse and rout of the Wei-Bo field army (which

---

[32] *ZZTJ* ch. 226, pp. 7291–3, 7295, 7299.
[33] *XTS* ch. 210, pp. 5927–8; *ZZTJ* ch. 226, pp. 7299–300.
[34] *ZZTJ* ch. 227, pp. 7305–6. The sources quoted by Sima Guang disagree as to whether these actions occurred in the seventh or the eleventh lunar month of 781.

included substantial allied contingents from Chengde and Pinglu). When the fugitives reached the bridges and found that they had been burned by a small contingent that Ma Sui had left behind in concealment, Yue's army disintegrated completely:

> those who plunged into the water and drowned were more than could be counted; more than twenty thousand heads were taken, and more than three thousand men taken captive; corpses pillowed on one another for a distance of over thirty *li*.[35]

Gathering a small party of his surviving soldiers, Tian Yue fled back to Weizhou.[36] He arrived outside the city's southern wall during the night. The general who controlled the gates at first refused him entry – expecting, we are told, that the government forces would soon arrive – but was obliged to open the gate with the coming of daylight. Yue executed his untrustworthy subordinate and prepared to defend the city, but conditions inside the walls were not promising: there were no more than a few thousand soldiers left in the city, and 'the wails of the kinsmen of the dead filled the streets'.[37] Mounted on his horse and grasping a sabre, Yue stationed himself before the gate of his headquarters, assembled all of the soldiers (*junshi*) and townspeople (*baixing*), and addressed them with tears streaming down his face:

> I have relied upon my uncle's inheritance, and for a long time I worked together with you gentlemen in the same cause. Now that defeats and losses are coming one after another, I don't dare to expect that I will come out of this alive. But the reason that I firmly resist the punishment of Heaven is especially because in the days when the two magnates of Zi-Qing [Pinglu] and Heng-Ji [Chengde] were still alive they acted as guarantors for me at the former emperor's court, and only then did I obtain the succession. Now it is reported that the two commanders have passed away and their children seek to inherit, and because I was unable to repay them efficaciously in kind, it reached the point where I had to mobilise troops. Now our battalions have been beaten and destroyed, and the soldiers and people are in great

---

[35] *ZZTJ* ch. 227, pp. 7313–14; also see *JTS* ch. 134, pp. 3693–4. A *li* is about one-third of a mile. Tian Yue had entered the battle with upwards of 30,000 men, including 10,000 from Pinglu, 3,000 from Chengde and some 20,000 of his own Wei-Bo troops (*ZZTJ* ch. 227, p. 7306). The annals in both of the Tang dynastic histories give the *gengxu* day of the intercalary first month as the date of the battle, corresponding to 15 March 782 (Julian). If this is correct, Yue's speech at Weizhou took place on 16 March.

[36] The sources disagree over the numbers. Sima Guang gives Yue 'a thousand or more' followers, *ZZTJ* ch. 227, p. 7314, whereas his *Xin Tangshu* biography allows him no more than a few dozen 'stalwart cavalrymen', *XTS* ch. 210, p. 5928.

[37] *ZZTJ* ch. 227, p. 7315.

distress – all of this is my crime! For the sake of my mother I cannot cut my own throat, but you gentlemen should cut off my head to earn merit and honours, and not die together with me![38]

It is highly unlikely that these were the exact words Tian Yue uttered. There are at least three differently worded versions of his speech: the one in the *Old History of the Tang Dynasty* (*Jiu Tangshu*, compiled between 941 and 945), almost certainly the earliest of the three, is translated above; the other two can be found in Ouyang Xiu's *New History of the Tang Dynasty* (completed in 1060) and Sima Guang's *Comprehensive Mirror for Aid in Government* (*Zizhi tongjian*, completed in 1084).[39] It would surely have been presented with less literary polish, in a more direct way and in the vernacular idiom of that place and time – and who would have been there to record it at the moment it was delivered, anyway?[40] It is much more plausible that it is an embellished reconstruction of the gist of Yue's remarks, as remembered by one or more of his listeners and reported to the court long after the fact. What is most certain is that it reflects what the official historians believed a man like Tian Yue would have uttered under those circumstances. At an even more basic level, its presence in his biography also suggests that both the historians and their assumed audience found an emotional appeal to the mob an appropriate and even expected response for a provincial military man in desperate straits.

Although there are a number of superficial differences among the three versions of Yue's speech – in the *Comprehensive Mirror*, for example, he begins with self-deprecating stock phrases and makes it clear that his mother is elderly – all of them include the same essential points. There is the nod to Tian Chengsi's legacy, the assertion that Yue has taken up arms out of righteousness to repay his debt to Pinglu

---

[38] *JTS* ch. 141, p. 3842.
[39] For the *Jiu Tangshu* version, see n. 37 above. For the other versions, see *XTS* ch. 210, p. 5928; *ZZTJ* ch. 227, p. 7315.
[40] And this, in turn, raises the troublesome question of the sources for Tian Yue's biography. Most official biographies were based on the 'accounts of conduct' (*xing zhuang*) that relatives and former subordinates of the deceased submitted to the Department of Merit Assessments, which were then forwarded to the Historiography Office of the Tang government. These usually eulogistic compositions were incorporated into the 'veritable record' (*shi lu*) that was compiled for each reign, and from there they made their way into the dynastic history. When Yue died, however, he was not exactly in the good graces of either the Tang court or his own successor in Wei-Bo (who had in fact assassinated him and slaughtered his closest associates). His biographies portray him in a negative light and appear to be based on second-hand reports received in the capital rather than a formal 'account of conduct'. For the sources and composition of Tang biographies, see Twitchett (1992) ch. 8.

and Chengde, the acknowledgement of his failures and the resulting losses, and the offer to sacrifice his own life for the benefit of his followers. Yue's biographies in the two Tang dynastic histories also have him allude to shared experiences and his sense of comradeship with the troops, an element missing from Sima Guang's version.

In all three accounts Yue throws himself down onto the ground, moving the crowd to pity him. The *Old History of the Tang Dynasty* puts the following words in the mouth of a man who steps forward to lift Yue up: 'We have long received blessings from your lordship, and we can't bear to hear this. Right now, the masses of the soldiers and the people are still capable of fighting another battle, with life or death to be decided by it.' Wiping away tears, Yue replies, 'You gentlemen will not suffer your downfall because of me; you are still willing to be of one heart [with me]. If I die, how could I forget your generous intentions even when I am beneath the ground?'[41] In all three accounts, he then cuts off a lock of his hair as a pledge and the officers and men respond by doing the same, swearing to be as brothers. The *Comprehensive Mirror* and the *New History of the Tang Dynasty* add that he brought out the contents of his headquarters storehouse, extorted additional contributions from the city's wealthiest households, and bestowed all this upon the soldiers as a reward. With this, according to Sima Guang, 'the hearts of the masses were for the first time settled'.[42]

With the city of Weizhou – if not all of Wei-Bo's outlying garrisons – now firmly behind him, Yue was able to withstand a siege by the government armies that lasted from the second month to the fifth month of 782.[43] He was saved by one of the several major reversals that occurred during the course of the war, when the Youzhou military governor Zhu Tao, who began the conflict on the side of the Tang court, took his province over to the rebel side. Zhu led his formidable army southward and, joined by forces from Chengde, attacked the Tang army and broke its grip on Weizhou. The rebel coalition of Youzhou, Wei-Bo, Chengde and Pinglu held firm for more than a year, then shattered under the pressure of Zhu Tao's ambitions, which began to appear to the other governors as more of a threat than those of Dezong. In the tenth month of 783, Zhu Tao's brother Zhu Ci emerged as the leader of a military revolt that had seized control of the Tang capital Chang'an, and by the beginning of the following year Tao was preparing to march southward through Hebei with a huge army to assist his brother. He expected the other governors to

---

[41] *JTS* ch. 141, p. 3842. The other versions differ slightly in wording, but the import is the same: *XTS* ch. 210, p. 5928; *ZZTJ* ch. 227, p. 7315.

[42] *ZZTJ* ch. 227, p. 7315. Also see *XTS* ch. 210, p. 5298.

[43] *ZZTJ* ch. 227, pp. 7315–20, 7325, 7330–1. The commanders of Wei-Bo's outlying garrisons at Bozhou, Mingzhou and Changqiao all defected to the government side.

join this campaign and accept his orders, but Tian Yue, whose territory lay directly in his path, resisted – in part because he and most of the other governors had now been offered pardons by the hard-pressed imperial court. Zhu Tao responded by occupying much of Wei-Bo's territory and placing Weizhou itself under threat for several months beginning in the first month of 784.

It was during this period, when he was negotiating with the Tang court but still menaced by Zhu Tao, that Tian Yue's luck finally ran out. On the night of 26 March 784, Yue's twenty-year-old cousin Tian Xu, one of Tian Chengsi's sons, led a small party of armed men into Yue's bedchamber when the military governor was sleeping after a drinking party with the Tang court's envoy. Xu harboured grudges because he had earlier been subjected to corporal punishment, and because of Yue's general policy of frugality towards the members of the Tian family, but he was spurred to action at this moment because he had just struck out in anger and killed one of his kinsmen. Xu and his followers now murdered Tian Yue and several other relatives, including Yue's wife and mother. Apparently improvising his plan as he went along, Xu next cut down several of his cousin's officers after luring them into the headquarters compound on the pretext that Yue had summoned them to a meeting. He then rushed out of the compound and announced that the military governor had been assassinated – and by none other than the officer who happened to be guarding the gate! A mob obligingly gathered and tore the unfortunate officer to pieces almost immediately (suggesting, incidentally, that Tian Yue had been held in high regard by the soldiers and townspeople to the very end). Before long, however, other commanders loyal to Yue arrived and began to get the troops under control.[44] The time had come for Tian Xu, cornered and desperate, to make a speech of his own:

> I am the son of the former lord. All of you gentlemen received favours from the former lord. If you can set me up, a troop commissioner will be rewarded with two thousand strings of cash, a senior officer (*da jiang*) half of that, all the way down to the common soldiers – each man will be rewarded with a hundred strings of cash. I will exhaust both public and private resources to get this done within five days.[45]

Xu's appeal had the desired effect. The crowd turned upon Yue's supporters, and in due course Tian Xu was confirmed by the imperial court as military governor

---

[44] The narrative in this paragraph follows *ZZTJ* ch. 230, p. 7413. For other accounts of Tian Xu's coup that differ in some details, see *XTS*, ch. 210, p. 5932; *JTS* ch. 141, pp. 3845–6.
[45] *ZZTJ* ch. 230, p. 7413.

of Wei-Bo. He continued in office until 796, when he died, apparently of natural causes, at the age of thirty-two.[46]

Writing about China's earliest imperial dynasties and their pre-imperial precursors, Michael Loewe has called attention to a political tradition that privileged written communication and the practice of oral persuasion behind closed doors, allowing little scope for the exercise of public oratory. This was 'a tradition whereby arguments on the highest matters of state were presented face to face in the secluded safety of audience with a monarch. Neither in pre-imperial nor in early imperial times was there opportunity for the practice of oratory or public declamation either to advance or to denounce a proposed measure of state, as was seen in the assemblies of Athens and in the debates of Rome's senate. Chinese officials were not called upon to defend their decisions in public; nor was there any semblance of following the will expressed by a large number of people.'[47]

The case of Tian Yue suggests that in Tang times, at least, there existed an alternative leadership style that allowed for extemporised public speech, often under conditions of extreme stress and danger, where the response of the audience could be literally a matter of life or death for the speaker. There is reason to think of it as part of a sort of 'little tradition' at variance with the 'great tradition' of imperial court politics as described by Michael Loewe. Although occasionally resorted to by emperors *in extremis*, such as Xuanzong and Gao Wei, it was by no means part of the usual or normative repertoire of imperial government, which relied mainly upon hierarchical authority, ritual correctness and traditional symbols of legitimacy.[48] The speakers are most often military men – generals, military governors, even rebels against the imperial court – and their listeners invariably consist of humble folk such as soldiers, low-ranking officers and ordinary commoners. The Fengxiang military governor, for example, addressed his men to confirm their loyalty after Dezong had been driven from Chang'an by mutinous soldiers in 783.[49] There was a speech by the provost marshal of Bin-Ning to bring mutinous soldiers there back under control

---

[46] *JTS* ch. 141, p. 3846; *XTS* ch. 210, p. 5932; *ZZTJ* ch. 235, p. 7571.

[47] Loewe (2006) 187.

[48] The *Jiu Tangshu* records a speech that Dezong made to soldiers leaving to fight the rebellious Hebei governors in 781; the style is, however, highly formal and even ritualistic, and although the soldiers were reportedly moved to tears this was by no means a 'high-stakes' performance (*JTS* ch. 144, p. 3195). It is also worth noting that such imperial speeches were far from routine: when the Jingyuan army was leaving Chang'an for the front in the tenth month of 783, it was not addressed by Dezong. The soldiers went on to mutiny and drive the emperor from the capital, though the issue was skimpy material rewards rather than the lack of an imperial performance. See *ZZTJ* ch. 228, pp. 7351–3.

[49] *JTS* ch. 140, p. 3822.

in 788, and a speech by a frontier general trying to cajole his recalcitrant and ill-paid troops into combat against the Tibetans in the early ninth century.[50] There was a speech by a Zhaoyi officer that persuaded the army not to defy the imperial court by installing the son of the deceased military governor as his successor, and a speech (accompanied by cash gifts) made by the Chengde military governor to persuade his subordinates to allow him to take up a new appointment in a different province.[51] There was even an occasion when the defender of a city besieged by rebel armies addressed the garrison and made the gesture of offering up his 'cherished daughter' (*ai nü*) to the soldiers in lieu of pay so as to strengthen their morale.[52]

As should be evident from these examples, the majority of such performances recorded in the Tang histories involve loyal officers expressing impeccably loyal sentiments. This is in keeping with the general bias of the historiographical process, which was controlled by scholar-officials in the service of the imperial court. Rebels and other troublemakers could not be left out of the account entirely, however. In addition to the speeches attributed to Tian Yue and Tian Xu, there are a few other cases, such as the successful appeal (complete with cash offer) made by the mutinous officer and would-be military governor Li Wanrong to a thousand soldiers of the Bianzhou army in 793.[53] Given their inability to avail themselves of the usual court-centred legitimising mechanisms (most obviously imperial appointments to office), rebel leaders must have been especially prone to fall back on public performance and emotional appeals to the soldiery as a substitute. Tian Yue's speech, which appears as something of an outlier in the Tang historical record, may well be one of the few surviving specimens of a type of oral performance that was actually quite common in late Tang provincial politics but was largely excluded from the record by the processes and biases of official, court-centred historiography.

Regardless of whether they were rebels or loyalists, late Tang military leaders were encouraged to appeal to the crowd because the opinions of ordinary soldiers mattered far more than they had in earlier times. This was due to long-term changes in the conditions and character of military service that reached their culminating point in the years after the An Lushan rebellion (AD 755–763). In earlier times, military service had been part-time, temporary or sporadic; many if not all soldiers had devoted more of their time to farming than to soldiering, and their military role was

---

[50] *JTS* ch. 144, pp. 3919–20; ch. 161, pp. 4221–2.
[51] *JTS* ch. 132, p. 3651; ch. 142, p. 3883.
[52] *ZZTJ* ch. 227, p. 7305. This episode is supposed to have occurred during Tian Yue's siege of Linming in 781.
[53] *JTS* ch. 145, p. 3933. For other examples of problematic military governors addressing or manipulating audiences of soldiers, see *JTS* ch. 124, p. 3538; ch. 145, p. 3951.

not their only or even their primary identity. By Dezong's time, however, soldiers (and their families) had come to form distinct communities whose members relied entirely on military service for their social status and their livelihood.

Men usually became soldiers through voluntary enlistment, with military service appealing especially to the landless, bankrupt and destitute elements of the Tang population. Once a man had enlisted, he would most likely spend the rest of his life in the army and might remain on the roster even after he had become too old or infirm for active service. Some units even took on a heredity character as sons followed fathers into the ranks; when a man was killed in battle his son or brother might claim the privilege of inheriting his military status and emoluments. During his years of service, the soldier depended on the pay he received from his commander to sustain both himself and his family. His compensation package included grain rations for himself and his dependants and enough silk or hemp cloth to provide him with outfits of spring and winter clothing, and there might also be allowances of salt, wine, soy sauce and vinegar.[54] Bonuses of various sorts were also expected: for soldiers setting out on campaign, for those who were victorious in battle, and on the occasion of a major holiday (such as the Spring Festival) or the installation of a new military governor. Commanders who wanted to ensure the loyalty of their men were careful to provide generously, and those who did not paid the price. In 799, when Lu Changyuan took over as acting military governor of the Xuanwu army at Bianzhou, he refused to distribute the customary gift of silk and hemp cloth; already unpopular as a strict disciplinarian, Lu was killed, sliced up and eaten by the enraged soldiery.[55] A modern Chinese historian has counted ninety-nine instances of mutiny in the late Tang provincial armies, with financial matters the single most common cause of discontent.[56] This phenomenon goes a long way towards explaining the employment of concrete, material inducements in almost every successful public appeal to the troops.

By the last decades of the eighth century, soldiers and their families had become a sort of privileged and parasitic caste with a keen sense of their own collective interests. Those interests included the continuation of material benefits at or above the customary level, the adoption by their commanders of a rather lax approach to military discipline, and the guarantee that they and their kin would never be deprived of the military status that brought them so many benefits and privileges. Also very much in evidence was a fierce determination to protect those interests by any means necessary, including violence, mutiny and outright rebellion against the throne.

---

[54] Zhang Guogang (1987) 100, 106–7.
[55] *JTS* ch. 145, pp. 3937–8.
[56] Zhang Guogang (1987) 106; also see Wang Shounan (1968) 228.

Leaders of all political stripes had to take this development into account and adjust their behaviour accordingly. Military upstarts such as Tian Yue, challenged by their conspicuous lack of traditionally sanctioned legitimacy, could not rely solely on time-honoured styles of generalship and top-down imperial and patriarchal modes of authority, but found it necessary to appeal directly to their followers by stressing such things as long-standing emotional bonds, hardships shared and overcome, reciprocal obligations and mutual self-interest. That leaders found it necessary to justify themselves in this way is something unusual in the political history of imperial China that warrants further investigation.

14 The Ideal of the Roman General in Byzantium: The Reception of Onasander's *Strategikos* in Byzantine Military Literature

Philip Rance

Byzantium was heir to a tradition of Greek/Graeco-Roman military literature stretching back to the fourth century BC.[1] This expansive genre, ranging from general compendia to specialised monographs, encompassed prescriptive tactical handbooks, technological blueprints for siege machinery, collections of exemplary historical stratagems and maxims, and didactic manuals for gentlemen who aspired to be generals. Diversity of content, style, language and approach reflects differences of authorship, audience and literary-cultural milieu. Byzantine reception of this military-literary heritage and its inherently intellectual approach to war fostered two complementary strands of scholarship – the collection, copying, editing and adaptation of surviving texts from classical antiquity and the composition of numerous new treatises.[2] The genre seemingly flourished in the sixth/early seventh and especially late ninth/tenth centuries, coinciding with major shifts in Byzantine strategic priorities, though the intervening 'Dark Age' was perhaps less barren than is conventionally assumed.[3] Ancient treatises exercised fluctuating and multifaceted

---

[1] I thank Shaun Tougher (Cardiff) for his original invitation to write this chapter (2014). Further research was undertaken during my tenure of a Herzog-Ernst-Stipendium (Thyssen Stiftung) at the Forschungsbibliothek Gotha der Universität Erfurt (2017). I am grateful to Kai Brodersen (Erfurt) for discussions and an advanced copy of his German translation (2018), and to Georgios Chatzelis (Thessaloniki) for kindly sharing his research (forthcoming) in advance of publication.

[2] Overviews of Byzantine military literature: Dain and de Foucault (1967), though partly obsolete, remains fundamental; Hunger (1978) 2.323–40; Dagron and Mihăescu (1986) 139–60; Loreto (1995); McGeer (2008b); Cosentino (2009); Mecella (2009); Luttwak (2011) 239–65 (to be read with caution); Sullivan (2010); Rance (2017a); (2018).

[3] Rance (2017a) 291–7.

influences – practical, educational, literary, lexical, ethical – on Byzantine military culture, and variously shaped and reflected the schooling, tastes, ethos and identities of an educated officer class, military aristocracy and even civilian elites. In addition, from the tenth century, military books written by ancient Roman authors and/or for Roman emperors played a rhetorical role in the self-conscious military-literary 'renaissance' and imperial resurgence of contemporary *Rhomaioi*.

Unsurprisingly, among Byzantine readers, writers and editor-copyists certain ancient military works became more popular and influential than others, with some attaining canonical status. Relative popularity or influence may be variously gauged in terms of manuscript tradition; explicit citations and references; editorial interest evidenced by recensions and interpolations; textual adaptations such as excerpts and paraphrases; and intertextual impact as models for the form, language and/or content of Byzantine compositions. To judge by these criteria, the three most authoritative, often-read and fashionable military 'classics' were Onasander's *Strategikos* (AD 49–57/58), a military-ethical treatise on the qualities, background and conduct of an ideal Roman general; Aelian's *Taktikē Theoria* (c. 106–113), a schematic exposition of the structures, deployment and manoeuvres of an arithmetically idealised Hellenistic army; and Polyaenus' *Strategemata* or *Strategika* (c. 161–163), an excerptive compilation of historical ruses and aphorisms. Among military-technological treatises a clear favourite is less easily discerned, though Apollodorus' *Poliorketika* (c. 101–102) seemingly enjoyed the fullest *Nachleben*.[4] While scholarship has extensively addressed the late antique/Byzantine reception of Aelian and Polyaenus,[5] Onasander's contribution, though widely acknowledged, lacks comprehensive, detailed or recent inquiry. This chapter aims to investigate how Onasander's *Strategikos* was transmitted and read in Byzantium, to chart successive modifications to his text and to evaluate its influence on Byzantine writing, from the sixth to eleventh centuries. Clarification of Onasander's Byzantine audience(s) and literary-cultural milieu(x) permits some observations on the enduring popularity, authority and relevance of his treatise. Limitations of space and, in some respects, of prior scholarly groundwork allow a preliminary survey and provisional conclusions. Full exploitation of the evidence must await a later occasion.

---

[4] Blyth (1992); Sullivan (2000) esp. 4–8, 20–1, 172–7, 190–1, 210–22; Whitehead (2010) 17–18, 28–34.

[5] Aelian: Dain (1946) 129–51; Zuckerman (1990) 217–19; (1994) 385–9; Rance (2007b) 703–4, 717–19; (2017a) 299–300; (2018) 260–2, 268–74; (forthcoming); Dennis (2010) 669; Haldon (2014a) 45–9. Polyaenus: Schindler (1973) 187–225; Krentz and Wheeler (1994) 1.xvi–xxiii; Eramo (2008) 141–5; Dennis (2010) 671 (with caution); Wheeler (2012).

Onasander's *Strategikos*

In the mid-first century AD, a Greek writer named Onasander wrote a handbook on generalship, conventionally entitled *Strategikos*, which he addressed to ex-consul Quintus Veranius, sometime between his consulate (49) and death as governor of Britannia (57/58). The text reveals little about Onasander and external evidence is slim. The *Suda*, a tenth-century Byzantine encyclopedia, contains a biobibliographical entry on a 'Platonic philosopher' of this name, to whom it ascribes at least one military treatise (and possibly two) and a now-lost commentary on Plato's *Republic*.[6] Whether or not the author of the *Strategikos* is correctly identified as an exponent of Middle Platonism, he evidently enjoyed or sought the friendship and/or patronage of a distinguished Roman magistrate and military commander. The Doric form Onasander (older scholarship preferred Attic/Koine Onesander or probably spurious Onosander) prompts conjecture that their association may date to Veranius' governorship of Lycia (43–48).[7] While Onasander's treatise has rarely lacked editorial interest since the mid-fifteenth century, a new, comprehensive critical edition would be welcomed.[8]

All manuscript prototypes transmit the title Στρατηγικός, apparently '[Book] of/for the General(s)', which appears to be authorial or at least ancient, though later editorial labelling cannot be entirely excluded.[9] While formally addressing Veranius, Onasander hopes to edify and entertain a wider audience of senatorial aristocrats (pr.1–2): 'a schooling for good generals and a delight for old commanders under the *Pax Augusta*' (pr.4). Onasander claims no originality and freely admits military

---

[6] *Suda* o 386, where variant editing of transmitted τακτικὰ περὶ στρατηγημάτων can yield one military work (Τακτικὰ [ἢ] Περὶ στρατηγημάτων) or two (Τακτικά, Περὶ στρατηγημάτων). See Köchly and Rüstow (1853–5) 2.1, 84; Oldfather et al. (1923) 343; Petrocelli (2008) 6–7; Rance (2017b) 20 n. 33, 22 n. 40, 23–2.

[7] Date, authorship and context: Oldfather et al. (1923) 343–9; Dain (1930) 137–44; Daly and Oldfather (1939); Bayer (1947); Ambaglio (1981) 353–4; Le Bohec (1998a); Galimberti (2002); Schellenberg (2007); Petrocelli (2008) 5–8; Brodersen (2018) 8–12.

[8] The most often-cited edition is Oldfather et al. (1923) 368–527, frequently reprinted but far from satisfactory. The text relies on Köchly (1860) for some collations and, especially, editorial emendations. See criticisms in Dain (1930) 125–32; also Lowe (1927) 29–40. The rare and seldom-cited edition of Korzenszky and Vári (1935) integrates additional textual witnesses identified by Dain (1930) and clarifies their interrelationships. Subsequent emendations: Darkó (1936); Lammert (1938); Peters (1972) 259–70; Lucarini (2010); Brodersen (2018) 151–4. Commentaries: Peters (1972) 88–245; Petrocelli (2008) 127–273; Barral (2010).

[9] [Λόγος] Στρατηγικός is supported by Onas. pr.1; Leo, *Taktika* 14.98. See Oldfather et al. (1923) 343; Dain (1930) 174; Galimberti (2002) 143; Petrocelli (2008) 127–9.

inexperience, yet, he opines, his treatise will prove valuable inasmuch as he has compiled 'precepts of generalship', and endeavoured to abstract their inherent practical wisdom, on the basis of actual exploits of men who made Rome great (pr.3, 7–10). Onasander thus shared the cognitive horizons of most extant Graeco-Roman tacticians, few of whom possessed first-hand experience of warfare, still less of command.[10] In the absence of *exempla* or historical references, however, Onasander's sources and alleged abstractive methodology remain obscure. The *Strategikos* essentially offers a wide-ranging evaluation of the requisite qualities, temperament and conduct of an ideal general, wherein Onasander esteems virtuous character, moral upbringing, innate wisdom and divine favour over technical knowledge or professional training. Although specific affinities with Platonic writings are lacking,[11] Onasander's analysis is notable for its interest in ethical dimensions and modern-seeming insights into martial values, psychology and morale. A moral-philosophical sensibility is most evident in his consideration of the justice of conflict.[12] Accordingly, the *Strategikos* is often characterised as a timeless rhetorical-didactic treatise addressed to well-born aspirants to high command, rather than a specimen of scientific-technical writing reflective of contemporary military concerns.

The received text comprises forty-two unequal chapters, though the chapter-numbering and headings transmitted in one manuscript tradition are later interpolations (see below). Following general remarks, Onasander proceeds in a logical sequence consistent with the likely course of a campaign: appointing a general and his staff (1–3); motives and justifications for war (4–5); marches, training, encampments, logistics (6–10.B); pre-battle: intelligence, security, planning, morale (10.B–14); battle: deployments and manoeuvres (15–22); battle: motivation, communication, the general's role (23–33); post-battle: awards, booty, burial, truces (34–7); and siegecraft (38–42). Onasander's professed intention to discuss the essence of Roman warfare (pr.1–5, 7–8) sits awkwardly with his assemblage of generalities – even banalities – appropriate to most armies of most eras. Furthermore, in presenting ostensibly 'Roman' military principles, he draws on classical Greek models, especially Thucydides and Xenophon, though his debts are typically literary, stylistic and verbal rather than technical.[13] Onasander's acquaintance with military-scientific literature has been suggested but falls short of demonstration.[14] He hints at familiarity with instructional monographs on other gentlemanly pursuits – equestrianism,

---

[10] Rance (2017b) 39–40 with bibliography.
[11] Köchly and Rüstow (1853–5) 2.1, 84–5; Oldfather et al. (1923) 343–5.
[12] Gilliver (1996); Chlup (2014).
[13] Peters (1972) 25–74, 84–7; Ambaglio (1981) 357–65; Ercolani (1997).
[14] Ambaglio (1981) 362–5; Whitehead (2016) 18–19.

hunting, fishing, farming (pr.1), which perhaps furnished conceptual exemplars. Despite Onasander's predilection for 'classics' of the fourth century BC, there is nothing in the *Strategikos* that is obviously anachronistic or inappropriate to Roman warfare in the first century AD, while some passages imply awareness of Roman practices.[15] In accordance with a scholarly tendency to investigate Graeco-Roman military theoreticians as representatives of their literary-cultural environments, recent studies of the *Strategikos* discern a subtle ideological subtext of a broader intellectual dialogue that sought to accommodate Greek culture within the early Roman Empire, whereby Onasander anticipates intellectual and belletristic currents of the Second Sophistic. Onasander clearly intended his work to be a practical handbook, but one that implicitly asserts Greek antecedents to Roman military success.[16] Owing to Onasander's abstractive generality, culturally diverse readers, from late antiquity to early modern Europe, found his prescriptions widely applicable. Correspondingly, among Graeco-Roman military treatises, Onasander's *Strategikos* has proved the most easily integrated into historical scholarship on Roman warfare, though few studies seek to contextualise his precepts in relation to specific characteristics of Roman generalship and military culture.[17]

Roman and Late Antique Reception

Contemporary responses to Onasander's *Strategikos* are not recorded and its reception by later Roman readers has left little trace. Older *Quellenforschungen* inferred that Frontinus, coincidentally one of Veranius' successors as governor of Britannia (73/74–76/77), possibly utilised the *Strategikos* when writing his own now-lost military treatise, of which only the illustrative appendix, the so-called *Strategemata* (c. 84–96), survives. This hypothesis depends on a nexus of formal and contentual parallels: first, between Onasander's *Strategikos* and Frontinus' *Strategemata*; second, between Onasander's *Strategikos* and Vegetius' *Epitoma rei militaris* (383–450), most plausibly explained by positing Vegetius' intermediate use of Frontinus' lost theoretical work, which he names as a source, rather than Vegetius' direct knowledge of the *Strategikos*, given his apparent unfamiliarity with Greek sources.[18]

---

[15] E.g. Onas. 6: *agmen quadratum*; 8: encampment procedures; 19: manipular tactics; 20: *testudo*. See Oldfather et al. (1923) 349–51; Ambaglio (1981) 367–8; Rance (2000) 241–2; Schellenberg (2007) 187–91; Petrocelli (2008) 175–6, 186–9, 195, 224–2.

[16] Ambaglio (1981) 375–7; Smith (1998); Meißner (1999) 189–91; Galimberti (2002) 144–53; Formisano (2011) 44–50. Alternatively, Le Bohec (1998a) 174–9 discerns a socio-political agenda.

[17] E.g. Smith (1998) 158–64; Gilliver (1999); Galimberti (2002) 144–52.

[18] Evidence and bibliography: Milner (1996) xxi–xxiii.

Late antique citations imply awareness of – if not conversance with – Onasander's *Strategikos*. John the Lydian, a bureaucrat and antiquary writing in the 550s–560s, included Onasander in a catalogue of ancient Greek and Roman military authorities, whom he ostensibly cites as 'witnesses' to the Latin terms *adorator* and *veteranus*. Aside from the demonstrable unreliability of John's citations elsewhere, none of the extant Greek authors listed – Onasander, Aelian, Arrian, Aeneas, Apollodorus – employs either term or, on chronological and/or stylistic grounds, could be expected to have done so. All that can be said with confidence is that John knew of a military writer named Onasander.[19] Similarly, if, as seems likely, the *Suda*'s entry on Onasander derives from an abridged version of Hesychius of Miletus' now-lost *Onomatologos*, a sixth-century handbook on Greek secular authors, no particular significance should be attached to Onasander's inclusion among over 800 literary figures, while Hesychius in turn probably reproduced this information from older compendia.[20] Although these meagre *testimonia* hardly demonstrate contemporary popularity, the subsequent manuscript transmission (examined below) suggests that Onasander's *Strategikos* was held in higher regard in late antiquity.

Maurice's *Strategikon*

The *Strategikon*, a comprehensive military treatise compiled in the 590s by, for or in the name of the emperor Maurice (582–602), became a foundational text of Byzantine military science.[21] Its unprecedented vernacular idiom, semi-barbarised institutional jargon, technical content and documentary source materials are consistent with the author's professed intention to eschew stylistic proprieties and write a non-literary handbook comprehensible to senior army officers (pr.21–31). Nevertheless, his familiarity with classical military writing is manifest in self-conscious comparisons to 'the Ancients', adherence to rhetorical conventions of the genre, and conceptual, structural and/or linguistic parallelism.[22] Among those classical authors whose influence is discernible, Onasander has long attracted the most attention. Nicolas Rigault first adduced textual affinities between the two works in his *editio princeps* of Onasander's *Strategikos* (1598–9).[23] Some eighteenth-century commentators, apparently unacquainted with Maurice's text, even branded him a mere plagiarist, a view

---

[19] J. Lyd. *De mag.* 1.47, with Rance (2017a) 301.
[20] Treadgold (2007) 273–8; Costa (2010).
[21] Edition: Dennis (1981). Recent bibliography: Rance (2017c). New English translation and commentary: Rance (forthcoming).
[22] Rance (2017c) with extensive bibliography.
[23] Rigaltius [Rigault] (1598–9) 2.13, 17, 47, 51, 58–9, 89.

uncritically reiterated in standard reference works.[24] While subsequent scholarship periodically drew isolated comparisons,[25] only Vladimir Kučma undertook a detailed study.[26] The subject calls for cautious analysis: some of the numerous points of resemblance signalled by Kučma concern *topoi* of Graeco-Roman military wisdom, where similarity of content, without verbal parallels, cannot guarantee intertextuality. More specifically, Kučma cites extensively from *Strategikon* Book 8,[27] but does not appreciate that this assemblage of maxims and mostly commonplace material comprises two pre-existing collections, which were incorporated into the *Strategikon* with minimal, if any, revision.[28] Accordingly, even where Onasander's influence in Book 8 is demonstrable, albeit in fewer cases than Kučma's less exacting criteria allow,[29] such parallels are more likely to reflect the editorial preferences of the original compiler(s).

There can be no doubt, however, that Maurice had first-hand acquaintance with Onasander's *Strategikos*. No other Greek-language treatise available in the 590s offered such a wide-ranging treatment of warfare. In particular, Onasander alone discussed topics that Maurice deemed important, notably the nature of command, logistics, reconnaissance, field operations and morale. A crucial difference defines their intended audiences. Onasander addresses the *Strategikos* to readers 'who are not inexperienced in generalship', as his own literary-theoretical adjunct to their practical attainments (pr.2). He aims to distil 'guiding principles of generalship' rather than explain institutions or technical procedures; regarding battle formations, for example, he will 'present a summary' of common features, assuming that 'the general will know the variations for particular occasions' (15). In this respect, Onasander conforms to Maurice's prefatorial characterisation of 'Ancients' who wrote military treatises 'for informed and experienced readers'. Maurice, in contrast, wishes to treat precisely those rudimentary matters and mundane minutiae that previous writings typically omitted (pr.17–27). Maurice therefore found in Onasander's *Strategikos* a thoughtful delineation of the elements of generalship, which primarily assisted him in framing an agenda and arranging material, rather than as a source of technical data.

---

[24] E.g. Zur-Lauben (1757) 8–9; Schwebel (1761) xiii (unpag.); subsequently e.g. Smith (1849) 3.31.

[25] Tsybyshev (1903) footnotes *passim*; Oldfather et al. (1923) 352; Lammert (1938) 883; Rance (1994) 96–102. A textual connection is inferred by Peters (1972) 254; Hunger (1978) 2.329–30; Petrocelli (2008) 17–18.

[26] Kučma (1982–6).

[27] Kučma (1982–6) 2.23–4, 30–1.

[28] Detailed analysis in Rance (forthcoming).

[29] E.g. Maurice 8.A.1 (= Onas. 42.2), A.4 (1.4); B.15 (9.2–3), B.29 (10.9), B.35 (2.2 + 1.10), B.36 (37), B.77 (42.6), B.91 (27).

Given the titular similarity of Στρατηγικός and Στρατηγικόν (or perhaps more correctly Στρατηγικά), it is tempting to view Onasander as Maurice's main literary-conceptual model.[30] In any case, despite differences of objective, audience and idiom, Onasander's imprint is evident in structure and content. Structurally, Maurice broadly adheres to Onasander's arrangement and orientation, charting the course of a generic campaign from the perspective of a commander-in-chief. Specifically, Maurice's preface sequentially replicates features of Onasander's preface and initial chapters. First, following a preamble, Maurice (pr.36–49) exhorts the general to secure God's favour (εὐμένεια) and affirms the significance of divine Providence (πρόνοια) in all human endeavours, not least warfare. This finds a direct counterpart in Onasander's prefatorial remarks (pr.5–6) concerning the workings of divine Fortune (Τύχη) in war. To illustrate his point, Maurice (pr.42–9) likens an experienced general to an expert helmsman, inasmuch as, for all his expertise, the general is as unsuccessful without God's favour as the helmsman without favourable winds. Maurice lifted this maritime simile from a later section of Onasander's work, adapting it to his more fatalistic outlook.[31] Second, Maurice summarises (pr.50–69) the qualities of an ideal general. This list draws on Onasander's lengthier treatment 'On choosing a general' (Περὶ αἱρέσεως στρατηγοῦ) immediately after his preface (1.1–2.1), where essentially the same virtues occur – prudence, composure, accessibility, vigilance, perseverance, sartorial restraint and temperate behaviour. Onasander discusses other aspects of a general's background – wealth, ancestry, age and family; these Maurice omits, perhaps because they no longer reflected contemporary cultural imperatives. Third, Maurice (pr.59–69) concludes his preface with a passage enjoining even-handedness in dealing with subordinates' misconduct, as excessive leniency and severity are respective causes of contempt and hatred. This topic, rather too specific for a general preface, again replicates the corresponding development of Onasander's discourse (2.2). Similar parallelism in arrangement of material may be discerned elsewhere.[32]

In terms of content, Onasander's summary of general principles often prompts or informs Maurice's more technical treatment.[33] For example, both authors prescribe conceptually similar marching procedures, including the passage of defiles and difficult terrain. Maurice's discussion (9.2.33–43, 4.50–61) is longer and amplified

---

[30] Evidence for the title of Maurice's treatise: Rance (forthcoming).

[31] Maurice employs the helmsman simile twice: pr.42–49; 7.pr.4–5; Onasander thrice: 4.5, 32.9–10, 33.2. Onasander was possibly inspired by Xen. *Mem.* 1.7.3 and/or Plato, *Epin.* 975E–976B; see Petrocelli (2008) 164–5; Wheeler (2010) 20.

[32] E.g. both authors begin their discussions of siegecraft with warnings about camp security: Onas. 40.1–2; Maurice 10.1.4–8.

[33] Kučma (1982–6) 3.109–10, 113–14, 117. Detailed linguistic parallels: Rance (forthcoming).

with practical detail, but retains vestigial traces of Onasander's vocabulary (Onas. 6.5–8, 7.1–2). Maurice's remarks on logistics, especially protective measures for foraging parties (9.3.50–61), closely correspond to Onasander's (10.7–8). Maurice's recommendations concerning hygiene in encampments (12.B.22.59–64) follow Onasander's (8.2–9.1) in language and content. Maurice's remarks on ambushes and night attacks (2.5; 9.2) echo Onasander's briefer treatment (22). Maurice proposes staging large-scale simulated combat to habituate troops to battlefield conditions (12.B.17.1–13), a passage that resembles Onasander's recommendation of mock battles (10.4–6), which he in turn modelled on Xenophon's *Cyropaedia* (2.3.17–18).[34] In other cases, similarities in content are general and verbal parallels slight, but cumulatively they indicate Maurice's reading of Onasander.[35] Maurice also employs comparative imagery otherwise found only in Onasander's *Strategikos*: in addition to the aforementioned simile of the helmsman, Maurice (4.5.34–36) borrows Onasander's conception of the general as a wrestler (42.6), who dodges and feigns before delivering the killer-blow.

In some instances, specificity of content, combined with pervasive linguistic correspondence, betrays where Maurice reproduced procedural data from Onasander.[36] Maurice (7.A.5; 7.B.6.4; 9.3.31–4) selectively paraphrases Onasander's advice on treatment of captives (14.3–4), granting the fallen proper burial (36.1) and interrogation of deserters (10.[7].15). Maurice's recommendation (10.1.32–42) that forces besieging a city adopt a twenty-four-hour rota to exhaust its defenders is inspired by Onasander's detailed proposal (42.7–13).[37] Passages of this type, exhibiting more specific textual dependence, are few, however, and Maurice typically selected and modified material with a view to contemporary utility: for example, a similar system of continuous work-shifts reportedly facilitated the Roman capture of a Persian fortress in Arzanene in 587.[38] Furthermore, Maurice occasionally contradicts his ancient model. Onasander writes (28–9) that the Roman battle-line should overawe opponents by speedily advancing with raucous battle-cries and highly polished weaponry; Maurice prohibits shouting or noise of any kind during the advance (2.18; 12.B.14.2–5, 17.40–3), and, contrary to 'the common assumption', prefers to camouflage metal equipment lest its glint alert the enemy to Roman movements

---

[34] Rance (2000) 235–44.
[35] See also: logistics: Onas. 6.10–13; Maurice 1.9.12–15, 47–56; 9.1.40–43; marching formations: Onas. 6; Maurice 12.B.18–20; reserves: Onas. 21.1–2, 22.1–2; Maurice 2.1.1–56 (also noted by Tsybyshev (1903) n. 40); camp guards: Onas. 31; Maurice 7.B.9; a general's role in combat: Onas. 33; Maurice 2.16.
[36] Linguistic parallels: Rance (forthcoming).
[37] Kučma (1982–6) 3.119; Whitehead (2016) 356.
[38] Theoph. Sim. 2.18.5–6.

(7.B.15). Leo VI later remarked upon the disagreement of the two authors on this point.[39]

Just as Onasander's work was more varied than other Greek-language military treatises, Maurice's relationship to Onasander is more multifaceted and subtle than the term 'source' might ordinarily imply. The *Strategikos* primarily offered a literary-conceptual model of how to write a treatise, whereby Onasander's influence is most apparent in Maurice's scope, selection and arrangement, and especially in his preface. Although Maurice's exposition of timelessness precepts or long-standing Roman military practices is sometimes indebted to Onasander for wording and substance, linguistic similarities typically represent an unintended lexical residue rather than intentional mimesis, while Maurice's concern for contemporary utility constrained mechanical or large-scale replication of procedural content.

Middle Byzantine Reception: Manuscript Transmission and Textual Evolution

Middle Byzantine scribes seemingly had at their disposal more copies of Onasander's *Strategikos* than of other Greek/Graeco-Roman military treatises. Only Aelian's *Taktikē Theoria* boasts a more extensive tradition. The relative prevalence of ancient military authors in Byzantine codices is not purely a consequence of chance survival, but reflects also the choices of editor-copyists and tastes of patron-readers. Today Onasander's text is transmitted in five manuscript prototypes and indirectly via several derivative tenth-century works. All witnesses belong to one of three recensions.[40] The conventionally termed first or 'authentic' recension, representing a version of the text closest to the archetype, is uniquely witnessed by *Mediceo-Laurentianus gr*. LV–4 (= M), a large, collective codex of Greek, Graeco-Roman and Byzantine military literature, produced in the Great Palace in c. 950 and reflecting the literary-'encyclopaedic' programme of Constantine VII (913–959). In M (198^r–215^v [200^r–217^v]), Onasander's work occurs within an apparently recent corpus of mostly ancient tactical authors.[41] The second or 'interpolated' recension, characterised by late antique editorial interventions, is principally witnessed by three inter-related eleventh-century codices copied in an unidentified monastic scriptorium

---

[39] Leo, *Taktika* 14.98 contrasts the method that 'Onasander ... prescribes' with 'what has been said by more recent authors', Leo's usual anonymised mode of referencing Maurice. See Tsybyshev (1903) n. 118.

[40] Dain (1930) 15–47, 145–57, posthumously summarised in Dain and de Foucault (1967) 327–8, corrected and supplemented in Korzenszky (1932); (1935); with fuller argumentation in Korzenszky and Vári (1935) v–xix.

[41] Rance (2017a) 302–7 with bibliography.

in Constantinople. Their hyparchetype was an assemblage of Graeco-Roman and Byzantine tactical-poliorcetic works, compiled c. 980–1000, probably in connection with court-centred book production. Two, *Vaticanus gr.* 1164 (V) and *Parisinus gr.* 2442 (P), date to c. 1020, the third, *Neapolitanus gr.* 284 (III C 26) (N), to c. 1040. Although their stemmatic relationship has been disputed, prevailing opinion classifies V and P as siblings, and N as an apograph of V, and thus a primary witness where V is lacunose.[42] Another, at least partial witness to the 'interpolated' recension is preserved in *Ambrosianus gr.* 139 (B 119 sup.) (= A), produced in court circles in c. 959. Although a tenth-century paraphrase of Onasander's *Strategikos*, the text is of editorial value insofar as the paraphrast used a second-recension exemplar that was earlier and less corrupt than VNP (see below).[43] Furthermore, unrecognised by previous studies, the compiler of the *Sylloge Tacticorum*, a largely derivative compendium written c. 920s–940s (see below), also drew material from Onasander's treatise via a second-recension manuscript, and thus offers the earliest, albeit indirect, testimony to this textual tradition.[44] To judge by extant witnesses, therefore, the second recension, representing a late antique/Byzantine 'vulgate', became a widely circulated form of Onasander's *Strategikos*. Finally, scholarship has long identified a 'third' recension, of which no manuscripts survive, but derivative writings of Leo VI (886–912) bear indirect witness to its text (see below).[45]

Of greater significance than the number of manuscript prototypes, none predating the mid-tenth century, is information they furnish regarding the majuscule or uncial tradition of a text prior to its transliteration into minuscule, typically c. 850–c. 950, as evidenced by scribal errors arising from a misreading of majuscule script.[46] By way of comparison: four ancient military treatises – Aeneas, Asclepiodotus and Arrian's two works – are uniquely preserved via M. Codicological and textual analysis demonstrates that, in each case, the copyist mechanically transcribed into minuscule

---

[42] Rance (2017a) 298–9, 324–5 with bibliography.

[43] For A's stemmatic affiliation: Vári (1917–22) 1.xxix–xxxiii; Korzenszky and Vári (1935) v–xix; Mazzucchi (1978) 285–90; (1982) 280–2; Rance (2007b) 733–5; (2008) 126–7; (forthcoming); *contra* Dennis (1981) 39–41; (2010) xi–xii.

[44] According to the stemma codicum in Korzenszky and Vári (1935) xvii, the compiler of the *Sylloge* used a third-recension manuscript of Onasander's work, as had Leo when compiling his *Taktika*. Their own apparatus criticus, however, registers common readings in the *Sylloge* and second-recension VP against first- and third-recension witnesses. I plan to examine this question in a separate study. Likewise Rance (forthcoming) identifies the compiler's use of a second-recension exemplar of Maurice's *Strategikon*.

[45] Dain (1930) 151–4; Korzenszky and Vári (1935) v–xix; Rance (2017a) 295–7.

[46] E.g. Dain (1946) 119–22; Dennis (1981) 31–8; Rance (2007b) 736–7; (2017a) 296–7, 308–10; (2017b) 31–4.

a majuscule exemplar, which was evidently ancient and sometimes gravely defective, but nonetheless seemingly the sole or best copy available to this well-resourced, court-sponsored project. There is no indication that, for centuries, these texts had attracted editorial attention or fresh transcriptions that might signal readers' interest.[47] In contrast, the three recensions of the *Strategikos* each descend from a different majuscule ancestor; that is to say, Onasander's text was transliterated into minuscule at least three times, presumably in separate locations and by unconnected scribes. These circumstances attest a much more ample majuscule tradition across the literary-cultural 'Dark Age' (c. 640–c. 780) and, by extension, imply Onasander's prior popularity in late antiquity. Furthermore, Onasander's *Strategikos* shares this tripartite manuscript tradition with Aelian's *Taktikē Theoria* and Maurice's *Strategikon*, the two other military treatises best represented in tenth-/eleventh-century codices, indicative of their partly conjoined transmission.[48] The sequential arrangement of Aelian–Onasander–Maurice in witnesses to the 'interpolated' recension suggests that these three texts were previously bound into a small corpus, between the early seventh and mid-/late ninth centuries.[49] This trio also became the main sources for Leo's *Taktika* (c. 905) and thus, likewise in the 'third' recension, may have come into Leo's hands as a pre-assembled collection (see below).

The 'interpolated' recensions of Aelian, Onasander and Maurice are characterised by modifications and supplements affecting the text and/or its paratextual apparatus. Interpolations are less evident in Onasander's text, but editorial interventions are demonstrable. In the 'authentic' recension (M), although spacings and/or rubrication mark chapter divisions, there is no trace of numbering or (sub)headings. In contrast, both these features occur in the 'interpolated' recension (VNPA), sometimes within the text, but mostly as marginal notation. Moreover, some chapter headings contain eccentric lexical and syntactical usages, including vocabulary unattested before late antiquity: τὰ ἄπληκτα (9), σφενδονιστής (17), ἐγκρύμματα (22).[50] The chronology of this editorial activity is a complex question, though the dating of surviving manuscripts is less significant than the textual traditions they preserve. The 'interpolated' recensions of Aelian's and Maurice's

---

[47] Rance (2017a) 302–11; (2017b) 24–6, 32–4, with bibliography.

[48] Aelian: Dain (1946) 61–127, 134–47, 153–240. Maurice: Dennis (1981) 19–24, 28–41, with modifications to Dennis' stemma in Rance (2007b) 733–4; (2008) 126–7, and at length in Rance (forthcoming).

[49] Codices VNP: Dain (1930) 15–18, 167–9; (1946) 122–6, 204–7; Rance (2017a) 296–7. The same corpus is partly traceable in A, now initially mutilated and disarranged: Dain (1930) 38–40; Mazzucchi (1978) 312, 315 (fasc. 16).

[50] Dain (1930) 19, 24, 32, 41–2; Petrocelli (2008) 137–8; Rance (2017a) 307–8. Strangely Lowe (1927) omits – and neglects to report – marginal headings in A.

texts demonstrably predate transliteration into minuscule (c. 850–c. 900).[51] It seems reasonable to assume, given their conjoined transmission in this recension, that this was also the case with Onasander's work. Accordingly, unlike other specimens of the genre, these three treatises appear to have attracted editorial interest during the 'Dark Age'.[52]

Textual Adaptations: The Ambrosian Paraphrase

Ambrosianus gr. 139 (A) was previously mentioned as a partial but authoritative witness to the 'interpolated' recension, predating VNP.[53] Parchment quality, scriptorial elegance, ornamentation and orthographic correctness locate A in the high-level book production of court circles. One defining peculiarity is that almost all of the ancient military texts assembled in A, including Onasander's *Strategikos*, have been paraphrased into tenth-century Greek. Each paraphrase is unique to A.[54] Carlo Mazzucchi persuasively argued that a single expert editor-paraphrast prepared A using materials in the library of Constantine VII, around 959, at the direction of Basil Lekapenos, Constantine's brother-in-law and *parakoimomenos*, with a view to promoting Basil's candidacy for a military command. Basil's patronage of scholarship and involvement in Constantine's literary projects is well documented.[55] In its preserved state, A begins with the paraphrase of Onasander. Owing to initial mutilation, the text has lost its first third and starts mid-sentence at 10.(10).26, while surviving folios (1r–5av, 104r–113r) are disarranged.[56] Although awaiting detailed inquiry, the paraphrasis uniformly renders Onasander's Atticising idiom into Byzantine Koine, updating syntax, phraseology and vocabulary, substituting or adding synonyms, and simplifying sentence structures.[57] Studies of other paraphrases in A point to

---

[51] Aelian: Dain (1946) 61–115, 188–202. Maurice: Dennis (1981) 33–4, 41; additional remarks in Rance (forthcoming).

[52] Rance (2017a) 291–2, 296–7.

[53] See collated readings in Lowe (1927) 30–40, but with now obsolete analysis.

[54] Martini and Bassi (1906) 1.157–60 (with errors). See selectively Dain (1930) 36–42 (partly erroneous); Mazzucchi (1978) 276–84, 310–16; Dennis (1981) 21–2, 39–40; Cosentino (2000) 245–8; (2001); Leoni (2003) xviii–xxviii; Rance (2007b) 733–6; (2017a) 297–8; Bevilacqua (2013).

[55] Mazzucchi (1978) 267–82, 292–306; summarised by Leoni (2003) xviii–xx; supplemented by Cosentino (2000) 243–6; Bevilacqua (2013). On Basil see also the chapter by Shaun Tougher in this volume.

[56] Editions: Lowe (1927) 5–28; Korzenszky and Vári (1935), below apparatus criticus; also specimen texts (10.26–11.3, 11.6) in Dain (1930) 145–51, 153, seemingly unaware of Lowe.

[57] Preliminary observations in Lowe (1927) 3–4, 30–1; Dain (1930) 39–42, 147–51.

consistency in paraphrastic method.⁵⁸ It seems obvious that the editor-paraphrast aimed to facilitate contemporary readers' comprehension, but questions of purpose and audience remained unresolved. Unaware of the codex's compositional history and studying the paraphrase of Onasander in isolation, Clarence Lowe projected an audience of army officers and administrators, educated but lacking the requisite literary culture to read Onasander's original with ease.⁵⁹ If this were the case, why did the editor-paraphrast also produce, for example, a complete paraphrase of Maurice's *Strategikon* (114ʳ–124ᵛ + 96ʳ–103ᵛ + 18ʳ–91ᵛ + 331ᵛ–332ᵛ), a text expressly written in non-literary, jargon-laden Koine comprehensible to army officers? Do the paraphrases in A respond to broader literary-cultural developments or merely the requirements of a specific patron? There is no evidence that A was copied or obtainable outside a court environment, nor any reason to assume that, from the tenth century, Onasander's *Strategikos* was more frequently read in paraphrase. On the contrary, the fact that a second-recension text of Onasander – the base-text of the paraphrase – was subsequently reproduced in VNP in the 1020s–1040s, suggests that the existence of a paraphrase did not diminish interest in the original.

Tenth-Century Byzantine Military Literature

The late ninth/tenth century witnessed a well-documented florescence of Byzantine military writing and book production, reflecting broader enthusiasm for the literature and literary-artistic forms of the past, and coinciding with a gradual strategic reorientation towards offensive operations in Byzantine–Arab conflicts. One component of this military-literary 'renaissance' was the previously discussed assemblage and incorporation of surviving ancient texts in collective codices, mostly at or in association with the imperial court. Another aspect was the composition of new treatises, many of which, in various ways, drew on that textual heritage.⁶⁰

Leo VI's *Taktika*, a bookish and largely retrospective compilation composed c. 905, is essentially a reconfiguration of Maurice's *Strategikon*, updated and supplemented with new material and modified excerpts from ancient authors, chiefly Onasander and Aelian.⁶¹ As previously discussed, codicological and textual criteria suggest that Leo utilised a pre-assembled corpus of Aelian–Onasander–Maurice,

---

⁵⁸ De Foucault (1949) 13–66; Cosentino (2001); Leoni (2003), with remarks in Rance (2007b) 734–5.
⁵⁹ Lowe (1927) 3–4.
⁶⁰ Rance (2017a) 294–9, with bibliography.
⁶¹ Edition: Dennis (2010), though in several respects uncompleted Vári (1917–22), to *Taktika* 14.38, remains superior. Commentary: Haldon (2014a). Additional remarks: Rance (2017a) 294–7, 322. On Leo VI's *Taktika* see also the chapter by Tougher in this volume.

transmitted in a third-recension exemplar. In one early manuscript of the *Taktika*, tenth-/eleventh-century *Vindobonensis phil. gr.* 275 (fol. 1ʳ), marginal annotation identifies Onasander among Leo's sources.[62] Leo once cites 'Onasander himself', perhaps assuming readers' familiarity, when contrasting divergent opinions in older literature.[63] Another, anonymised citation could not be more vague: 'one of the ancients once said'.[64] Yet Leo freely borrowed from Onasander's *Strategikos* without indication of provenance: although a comprehensive study is lacking, extracts ranging from single paragraphs to entire sections have been detected in eight of Leo's twenty books or 'Constitutions' (2, 4, 7, 9, 11, 14, 16, 20). The distribution of Onasander-derived material throughout the *Taktika*, broadly replicating its original arrangement in the *Strategikos*, suggests that Leo perused Onasander's text, excerpting passages he considered useful and inserting them into a base-text supplied by Maurice's *Strategikon*.[65] As Maurice had already drawn on Onasander's *Strategikos*, some passages entered Leo's *Taktika* twice, both indirectly via Maurice's text and directly via Leo's own reading of Onasander.[66] In some sections, Leo reproduces Onasander's text largely in its original sequence. Most strikingly, the first half of Constitution 2 (2.1–17, 19) reprises, step by step, Onasander's initial consideration of the qualities of an ideal general (1.1–14, 17–25, 2.1–2).[67] Similarly, almost the entirety of Constitution 16 (16.1–5, 7–15), devoted to post-battle procedures, replicates Onasander's discourse (34–7). Other sections Leo fashioned using an intricate cut-and-paste technique: for example, *Taktika* 9.1–2, 22–40, concerning marches, comprises non-sequential excerpts from Onasander: 6.10, 6.13, 6.11–13, 10.7, 6.14–7.2, 6.1–9. This method results in another form of duplication: Leo's 9.2 and 9.24

---

[62] Vári (1898) 66–8; (1917–22) 1.xxxiii n. 1; Dennis (2010) 7 n. 4.

[63] Leo, *Taktika* 14.98 (= Onas. 28).

[64] Leo, *Taktika* 16.14 (= Onas. 36.6).

[65] Leo, *Taktika* 2.1–17, 19 (= Onas. 1.1–14, 17–25, 2.1–2); 4.3–4 (= 2.3, 2.5–3.3); 7.2, 7–14 (= 9.2, 10.1.1–6); 9.1–2, 22–4, 26–40 (= 6.1–8, 6.10–7.2, 10.7); 11.2–5 (= 8.1–9.2); 14.98 (= 28); 16.1–5, 7–15 (= 34–37); 20.153 (= 33.1), 169 (= 4.1), 191 (= 34.1–3). See Vári (1917–22) 1.xxxiii, with parallel passages juxtaposed at 16–32, 50–3, 135–7, 142–7, 208–9, 222–35, 281–4. The index fontium in Dennis (2010) 671 is neither exhaustive nor reliable, especially regarding alleged parallels in Leo, *Taktika* 20. *Contra* Dennis (2010) 28–9, *Taktika* 2.18 derives not from Onasander but from *Hypotheseis* (alias *Excerpta Polyaeni*) pref. (Melber 431.2–15), see Vári (1917–22) 1.29–31; Dain (1937) 45 n. 1. Discussion of selected passages: Vári (1898) 56–9; Dain (1930) 151–4; Rance (2000) 240–4; Haldon (2014a) 45; Riedel (2018) 62–3, 75–9 (in parts inaccurate).

[66] E.g. Leo, *Taktika* 14.31 and 16.11 (concerning burial of the fallen) both originate from Onasander 36.1, the former via Maurice 7.B.6, the latter directly.

[67] Vári (1917–22) 1.16–32; Dain (1937) 41–4.

both reproduce Onasander's 6.13.[68] Overall, Leo adapts the style and language of his model, including substitution or addition of contemporary *termini technici*, and often reconfigures Onasander's impersonal mode into first-person plural directives addressed to a second-person singular general. Frequently Leo more faithfully preserves Onasander's wording than does the Ambrosian paraphrast.[69]

The *Sylloge Tacticorum*, an anonymous compendium of 102 chapters dated to the 920s–940s, is a curious melange of variously modified extracts from classical and Byzantine military literature, combining critiques of ancient practices with prescriptions for contemporary operations against unspecified opponents, presumably Arabs.[70] Although often transposed and largely recast in a somewhat inconsistent classicising idiom, constituent chapters bear the imprint of their diverse sources.[71] The author extensively excerpted and creatively adapted Onasander's *Strategikos*. Most prominently, he not only began his treatise by reprising Onasander's criteria for an ideal general, but also chose to exploit Onasander's text directly and often near-verbatim rather than reproduce this material second-hand and pre-paraphrased from Leo's *Taktika*, which was otherwise one of his main sources.[72] In other instances, however, in the absence of detailed analysis, the precise nature of textual dependence and authorial methodology, ranging from excerption (direct or indirect) to conceptual and/or linguistic borrowings, awaits definition.[73]

Finally, Onasander's influence extended to Nikephoros Ouranos' *Taktika*, the latest and longest extant representative of this genre. Compiled c. 1000 by a distinguished general, courtier and man of letters, this vast, mostly derivative compendium of 178 chapters incorporates material from numerous ancient and Byzantine military treatises, directly or via intermediary texts. The absence of a full critical edition hinders comprehensive investigation.[74] Ouranos' *Taktika* begins with

---

[68] Vári (1917–22) 1.208–9, 222–35.
[69] Insertion of terminology: e.g. Leo, *Taktika* 4.3 (= Onas. 2.3); 9.27 (= 7.1). Juxtaposed samples of the three versions (Onasander's original text, Ambrosian Paraphrase and Leo's *Taktika*): Lowe (1927) 30–1; Dain (1930) 152–4. See also Dain (1937) 41–4.
[70] Edition: Dain (1938). English translation: Chatzelis and Harris (2017). Studies: Chatzelis (2019) with bibliography.
[71] Extant sources/influences are catalogued in Chatzelis and Harris (2017) 120–50. Discussion of sources: Dain (1946) 130–3; Mecella (2009) 99–101, 107–12; Rance (2017a) 338–56; Chatzelis (2019) 29–36.
[72] Dain (1930) 154–7; (1931) 340–1; (1937) 41–4, 53–4.
[73] Chatzelis and Harris (2017) 120–4 list textual parallels with Onasander. Discussion of selected Onasander-derived/influenced passages: Chatzelis (2019) 35–6, 73–4; (forthcoming). General remarks on the compiler's methodology: Mecella (2009) 101; Rance (2017a) 341–2.
[74] Dain (1937) supplemented and/or modified by Dain (1946) 147–50; McGeer (1991); (1995)

another reworking of Onasander's now-familiar preliminary assessment of a general's requisite qualities (*Strategikos* 1–2). Ouranos imported this content second-hand via a later (so-called 'Ambrosian') recension of Leo's *Taktika*, which Ouranos paraphrased, almost in its entirety, as the first fifty-five chapters of his treatise. As Ouranos omitted Leo's proemium and first constitution, this Onasander-derived section of Leo's second constitution (2.1–19) became the opening to Ouranos' work, that is to say, his paraphrase of Leo's paraphrase of Onasander.[75] In a subsequent section, however, it seems that Ouranos also directly utilised Onasander's treatise. *Taktika* 56–62 comprises Ouranos' revision of the complete text of Nikephoros II Phokas' tactical manual, conventionally styled *Praecepta Militaria*, composed in the 960s. There follows a miscellaneous but largely self-contained suite of chapters (63–74), of unequal length, treating diverse aspects of combat operations; some reflect Ouranos' first-hand experience or knowledge of current procedures (63–5), others reprise military literature, both ancient and recent. This intricate patchwork of influences appears to be Ouranos' own 'appendix' to Phokas' manual.[76] Several chapters are, wholly or partly, inspired by or adapted from – but not paraphrases of – Onasander's *Strategikos*, with occasional admixture from other sources and/or Ouranos' observations; detailed analysis must await another occasion.[77] For the sake of completion, one could note that a small amount of ultimately Onasander-derived material may have passed into Kekaumenos' '*Strategikon*' (or *Consilia et Narrationes*), dated c. 1075–8, mostly probably via Leo's *Taktika* or a related intermediate source(s).[78]

79–86; Mecella (2009) 101–11; Rance (2017a) 338–56, 360–3. Biography of Nikephoros Ouranos: McGeer (1991) 129–31. A critical edition of the complete text is in preparation by the present author.

[75] Dain (1937) 19–21, 40–6, with preliminary sample text at 42–3. The relevant section of Ouranos' *Taktika* is unpublished; I consulted the sole witness *Constantinopolitanus gr.* (TSMK Gİ) 36, paginated 17–26. I thank Zeynep Çelik Atbaş and Ramazan Aktemur at the Topkapı Sarayı Müzesi Kütüphanesi for their assistance.

[76] McGeer (1991) 131–4, correcting Dain (1937) 21, 47–51, 128 (summarised in De Foucault (1973) 282–3). In contrast to McGeer, I affiliate chapters 66–74 with the second section of Ouranos' *Taktika* (thus 56–74) rather than with the third section (75–175), on the basis of content, arrangement and source material.

[77] Edition: De Foucault (1973) 286–311, though see Rance (2018) 276 for new fragments since identified in *Vindobonensis phil. gr.* 120 (46^r–47^v) + 112 (9^{r-v}). Dain (1937) 21, 50 correctly discerned the influence of Onas. 22–3 in Ouranos 72–4; see general remarks by McGeer (1991) 132. My preliminary investigation identifies e.g. Onas. 10.(4).12 > Ouranos 69.1; Onas. 10.(6).14 > Ouranos 70; Onas. 21.3 > Ouranos 71.

[78] Roueché (2002) 120–2 for references and discussion.

Popularity and Readership

While the foregoing criteria affirm the enduring currency and influence of the *Strategikos* as a military 'classic', the number and identity of Onasander's Byzantine readers can only be surmised. Excepting universal constraints of cost and literacy, little can be said with confidence regarding the consumers of military treatises in any period of Greek, Roman or Byzantine history. Recent studies have sought, with varying success, to elucidate literary, educational and socio-cultural contexts in which such works were written, copied and read, beyond purely military dimensions.[79] It is generally agreed – and unremarkable – that different texts or sub-genres variously appealed to interconnected 'military' and/or 'civilian' elites, but diversity across the genre cautions against generalisations. In particular, difficulties in defining a Byzantine 'officer class', in terms of common background, identity and ethos, complicate efforts to trace the ownership and circulation of military-scientific literature, especially when the codicological evidence rarely leaves the orbit of the imperial court.

Although interpretations must remain largely impressionistic, the reception of Onasander's *Strategikos* by Byzantine military writers offers potential clues to what aspects might have attracted its Byzantine readers, military or otherwise, at least compared to other fashionable ancient military authorities. One distinctive feature is how successive Byzantine authors chose to (re)visit Onasander's original text, even when they had access to recent adaptations and/or derivative treatises, thereby incorporating Onasander-derived material both directly and through intermediary sources. Whether or not Leo VI recognised Onasander's prior influence in Maurice's *Strategikon*, in his *Taktika* (c. 905) Leo extensively supplemented Maurice's base-text with his own selection of excerpts from Onasander's work. Subsequently, though Leo's *Taktika* became a source for the *Sylloge Tacticorum* (c. 920s–c. 940s), its compiler preferred to read Onasander's text first-hand and make new selective adaptations, including passages Leo had already excerpted. In turn, Nikephoros Ouranos, in compiling his *Taktika* (c. 1000), imported extensive Onasander-derived material through his adaptation of Leo's work, but again also resorted to Onasander's treatise directly for additional content. A similar pattern emerges in the reception of Aelian's *Taktikē Theoria*, in which arcane terminology and complex tactical exposition sustained the significance of the direct textual tradition. In the case of Polyaenus, in contrast, adaptation seemingly led to the redundancy and near-disappearance of the original text. The many extant

---

[79] E.g. McGeer (1995) 191–4; Roueché (2009); Whately (2015a); Rance (2017a) 290–300; (2017b) 37–40; (2018); Chatzelis (2019) 88–98.

and posited Byzantine reworkings of Polyaenus' *Strategemata* sequentially descend from a single paraphrased and thematically rearranged abridgement, the *Hypotheseis* (c. 600–c. 850). None of the successive author-compilers ever consulted Polyaenus' original, which ultimately survived via a tenuous and peripheral manuscript tradition.[80] Recurrent reversion to the authorial text points to Onasander's manifold value as a conceptual model, linguistic exemplar and/or source of content. Although such textual dependence is easily encapsulated as '(classical/literary) mimesis' or 'antiquarianism', intertextual variety and complexity demand definitional precision. Where the compiler of the *Sylloge Tacticorum* chose to preserve Onasander's wording, in preference to more radical paraphrasis (as Leo or Ouranos), this 'imitation' can be variously interpreted: an author-specific literary allusion, ingrained rhetorical-compositional training and/or broader stylistic-linguistic aspirations to affect antique authority. Correspondingly, apparent 'antiquarianism' of method need not entail antiquarian objectives, inasmuch as actual continuities between ancient and medieval warfare permitted tradition-conscious Byzantine authors to reprise much older material without necessarily compromising practical utility.[81]

The most influential section of Onasander's *Strategikos* was his initial chapter 'On choosing a general', which shaped the preface and agenda of Maurice's *Strategikon* and, by the tenth century, was an almost obligatory ingredient of Byzantine military compendia. Commencing such works with this 'checklist' of essential and desirable qualities became as much a rhetorical-didactic strategy as an index of contemporary educational ideals. Its more pervasive influence awaits further study.[82] This development also reinforces an impression, already apparent in Maurice's methodology, that Onasander's *Strategikos* was most valuable as a literary-conceptual model, especially for formal elements such as prefaces and opening chapters/sections, where even authors who expressly disavowed belletristic ambitions made an effort to adhere to literary-stylistic conventions. The same Byzantine writers, however, were equally interested in other sections of Onasander's treatise, concerning diverse operational procedures, which they differently selected and modified, ranging from light paraphrasis to free adaptation. Like Maurice in the 590s, tenth-century authors found in the *Strategikos* wide-ranging content mostly without parallel in classical Greek military writing. Similarly, Onasander's unique emphasis on religious

---

[80] Schindler (1973) 205–25; Rance (2017b) 25–6, 35–6; (2018) 272–4.

[81] Chatzelis (2019) 27–9, 88–92; see generally Rance (2017c) esp. 226–37.

[82] Krentz and Wheeler (1994) xx–xxi; Antonopoulou (1994); Taragna (2004) 799–801. Besides preceding examples, Dain (1937) 45 n. 1, 73 n. 2 discerns Onasander's formal influence in *Hypotheseis*, pref. (Melber 431–2). See also Haldon (1990) 54, 179 (likening Text C 8–19 to Onas. pr.7–10).

observance and ethical guidance potentially cohered with Middle Byzantine martial attitudes, once references to pagan rites and divination were expunged and remarks on divine assistance Christianised. This process began in Maurice's preface, where he not only substitutes 'God's favour' or 'Providence' for Onasander's 'Fortune' (*Tyche*), but also inverts his model's religious-philosophical outlook: whereas for Onasander generalship, rather than Fortune alone, determines success or failure (pr.5–6; cf. 32.9–10), for Maurice even the ablest general, without divine favour, will find talent unavailing (pr.36–49).[83] But it was Leo, through similar manipulation of Onasander's text and creative admixture of scriptural sources, who was largely responsible for systematising notions of the ideal Christian general.[84] The *Sylloge Tacticorum* similarly invests Onasander-derived material with Christian nuances.[85]

For their Byzantine readers Graeco-Roman military 'classics' combined intrinsic literary appeal and antique cachet. They furnished military aristocrats and army officers with a conceptual framework and elevated vocabulary in which to intellectualise professional experience, while the ability to read and cite classical authorities – in short, to recall what 'Onasander himself' says (Leo, *Taktika* 14.98) – became a measure of a soldier's schooling and socio-cultural standing.[86] Civilian readers are plausibly conjectured, especially of works with historical-narrative content, such as Polyaenus' *Strategemata* and its numerous descendants, though presumably few relished the monographic technical minutiae of many Byzantine treatises. The production of the Ambrosian paraphrases, even if restricted to a court milieu, evinces interest in content above stylistic-linguistic considerations, with implications for readers' educational backgrounds. Compared to other Graeco-Roman military writers, Onasander primarily presented general – arguably immutable – principles rather than period-specific procedures and catered to a taste for ethical edification above and beyond practical utility. Both harshly condemned and excessively praised by modern critics, the abstractive generality and broad applicability of Onasander's precepts in large part account for the perennial appeal of the *Strategikos*, beyond Byzantium and into the early modern era. Two features may have especially attracted high-level Byzantine readers. First, Onasander's preliminary evaluation of ideal moral and personal qualities, whether read in the first or tenth century, transcends the context of selecting a commander-in-chief and promotes a broader aristocratic *paideia*. Specifically, Onasander's timeless prescription of virtues, temperament and

---

[83] Further commentary in Rance (forthcoming).
[84] Dain (1930) 154; Strano (2013); Riedel (2018) 74–94.
[85] Chatzelis (2019) 73–4; (forthcoming).
[86] Kaegi (1983) 20–1; McGeer (1995) 191–4; Rance (2017a) 291–4; Chatzelis (2019) 27–9, 88–92.

conduct conforms to Middle Byzantine tastes for moralising florilegia and parainetic literature, which encouraged readers to cultivate the character and values of idealised leadership.[87] Second, though Onasander's Byzantine readers may have abhorred references to arcane beliefs and practices, his overarching emphasis on propitiating divine or preternatural forces, even without Byzantine editors' Christianising interventions, was broadly transferable to Byzantine ideals of divinely sanctioned war on behalf of Orthodox Christendom. Accordingly, Onasander's manual offered an imitable antique model of self-conscious generalship and a mirror of contemporary martial ethos.

Finally, it is possible that *romanitas* was a factor in Onasander's reception. The slow dawning of an era of Byzantine victories and (re)conquest, from the 920s, heightened awareness of past glories of ancient *Rhomaioi* to whose military traditions Byzantium laid claim. Without entering ongoing discussions of 'Romanness' in Byzantine identity(ies), it must suffice here to note explicit comparisons in tenth-/eleventh-century historical literature, which may signal forms of military-cultural identification beyond mere panegyrical *topos*. Byzantine commanders are likened to Roman precursors: for his eastern conquests of c. 926–944 John Kourkouas 'assumed the appearance and name of another Trajan or Belisarius', as subsequently Romanos III (1028–1034) hoped to imitate 'those Trajans and Hadrians and, still further back, the likes of Augustus and Caesar'.[88] Public celebrations of victories in Constantinople, for example by Basil I in 873 or John Tzimiskes in 971, are overtly or allusively equated to triumphs once conducted in Old Rome.[89] Graeco-Roman military texts inspired similar historical-rhetorical posturing. Michael Psellos praises *caesar* John Doukas (died c. 1088) because

> in matters relating to generalship (στρατηγίαν), he has attained a knowledge of that science comparable to those ancient and much-sung Caesars, and all the daring deeds and accomplishments of those Hadrians and Trajans and men of the same company, not spontaneously, nor by chance, but from books on tactics and generalship and siegecraft (ἀπὸ τῶν τακτικῶν βιβλίων καὶ στρατηγικῶν

---

[87] Roueché (2002); (2003); (2009); Holmes (2010); Strano (2013); Rance (2018) 258–60; Chatzelis (2019) 100–1; and now esp. Chatzelis (forthcoming) on these literary-cultural and educational dimensions.

[88] Theophanes Continuatus 6.40, Bekker (1838) 427.12–19; Psellos, *Chronographia* 3.8, Renauld (1926–8) 1.37.15–22.

[89] Basil I: Theophanes Continuatus 5.40, Ševčenko (2011) 146.46/148.56; John Tzimiskes: Skylitzes, *Synopsis Historion*, Thurn (1973) 310.55–7 (cf. Plut. *Cam.* 7.1); Leo the Deacon 9.12, Hase (1828) 158.6–7. See McCormick (1986) 131–88.

καὶ πολιορκητικῶν) and from what the likes of Aelian and Apollodorus have written.⁹⁰

Psellos here singles out two classical works, Aelian's *Taktikē Theoria* and Apollodorus' *Poliorketika*, highly regarded representatives of their respective sub-fields, tactics and siegecraft. Both treatises were originally addressed to Trajan (98–117), though textual corruption and/or editorial guesswork left Byzantine readers unsure in either case whether the addressee was Trajan or his successor Hadrian (117–138).[91] Given this context, Psellos' conjunction of two named military 'classics' and rhetorically pluralised 'Hadrians and Trajans' implies that such Roman and/or imperial associations mattered. Certainly, those ancient military texts that became fashionable in Byzantium all boasted Roman credentials and/or authorial dedications to the incumbent emperor(s), but the correlation is less straightforward. For example, Polyaenus dedicated his *Strategemata* (c. 161–163) to co-emperors Marcus Aurelius and Lucius Verus on the eve of a Roman–Parthian war, yet these details were omitted from its principle late antique/Byzantine adaptation, the *Hypotheseis*, and thereafter played no part in its nonetheless prolific reception.[92] In contrast, although the case of Arrian's *Technē Taktikē* (136/137) is uncertain, a probable (now-lost) dedication to Hadrian seems not to have enhanced its esteem among Byzantine readers.[93] Onasander's *Strategikos* obviously lacks an imperial dedicand and it seems unlikely that Byzantine readers would have known or discovered who Quintus Veranius was. Nevertheless, Onasander's opening statement proclaims the particular propriety of addressing a work of military theory 'to Romans and especially to those Romans who have attained the senatorial aristocracy' (pr.1); he 'will consider especially the valour of Romans' and their unsurpassed dominion (pr.4) and assemble precepts derived 'entirely from deeds and genuine conflicts conducted especially by Romans' and from which 'the entire primacy of the Romans, in race and valour, up to the present, derives' (pr.7–8). No other classical military treatise is framed in such unambiguously and exclusively Roman terms, and, even if the text may ultimately lack Roman specificity, it is hard to imagine a preface more likely to appeal to tradition-conscious, literary-minded and patriotic *Rhomaioi* on the Bosporus.

---

[90] Psellos, *Chronographia* 7 (Michael VII) §16, Renauld (1926–8) 2.181.8–16 (my translation). See also Rance (2018) 269–72; Trombley and Tougher (2019) 186.

[91] Aelian: Dain (1946) 15–21. Apollodorus: Sullivan (2000) 155; Whitehead (2010) 19–23.

[92] Date and dedication: Wheeler (2010) 8–17. See *Hypotheseis* pref. (Melber 431–2).

[93] Date and dedication: Wheeler (1978); Devine (1993) 315–16; Bosworth (1993) 253–62; Meißner (1999) 250–5. Byzantine reception: Förster (1877) 450–71; Dain (1946) 134–47; Roos and Wirth (1968) 2.xxiv–xxv; Rance (2007a); Haldon (2014a) 47–50. I plan a comprehensive study.

15   Generalship and Gender in Byzantium: Non-Campaigning Emperors and Eunuch Generals in the Age of the Macedonian Dynasty

Shaun Tougher

Introduction

During the period when the Byzantine Empire was ruled by the 'Macedonian Dynasty' it experienced an age of recovery and reconquest. On its western, northern, eastern and southern borders the empire witnessed successful campaigns and conquests, including the recovery of Crete in 961 and the annexation of Bulgaria in 1018.[1] Notably in the same period there was a revival in the literature of military science, leading to the writing of several significant manuals on tactics and strategy in the tenth century.[2] Thus, generalship in the age of the Macedonian Dynasty offers a rich field of study, reflected by the increasing number of books and articles on the subject.[3] The focus of this chapter is on particularly arresting aspects of generalship in the period, namely the facts that several emperors of the Macedonian Dynasty were not active commanders themselves and among the generals whose careers distinguish the period there are several who were eunuchs. These aspects are united by the theme of gender: how was the status of emperors as men affected by the fact that they did not play an active military role (so important a feature of the promotion of imperial regimes) and how was the gender identity of eunuch generals perceived? The chapter addresses each aspect in turn, drawing on the rich diversity of sources, especially histories and military manuals but also material evidence such as reliquaries and manuscripts. It will be seen that non-campaigning emperors could present themselves as military authorities with a claim to the virtue of courage and

---

[1] See for instance Kaldellis (2017a) 21–152; Whittow (1996) 310–90.
[2] See for instance Sullivan (2010) 151–60.
[3] See below for details.

could value a personal active role, and that eunuchs could also lay claim to traditional masculine virtues and be considered successful men. In Byzantium generalship is a vital role to consider in relation to all emperors and in relation to the eunuchs who characterise the existence of the empire.

Non-Campaigning Emperors

The Macedonian Dynasty was one of the longest-lived dynasties in Byzantine history.[4] It was founded in 867 by Basil 'the Macedonian', who came to power through the patronage and then assassination of his predecessor the emperor Michael III (842–867), and lasted until the death of its last representative, the empress nun Theodora, Basil I's great-great-great-granddaughter, in 1056. Although the empire witnessed territorial expansion under this dynasty, most of its members did not take to the field themselves. Leo VI (886–912), Alexander (912–913), Constantine VII (913–959) and Romanos II (959–963) did not campaign in person. Less surprisingly, neither did the last two representatives of the dynasty, the empress Zoe (1028–1050) and her sister Theodora (1055–1056). Thus, Basil I (867–886) himself and his great-great-grandson Basil II (976–1025) stand as exceptions; Basil II's brother Constantine VIII (1025–1028) seems to have seen some limited action early in his brother's reign but did not take the field during his sole reign.[5] As for those men who became emperors through association with the Macedonian Dynasty, only the generals Nikephoros II Phokas (963–969) and John I Tzimiskes (969–976) maintained an active military role during their reigns; although Romanos I Lekapenos (920–944) had been an admiral he did not campaign during his reign. Romanos III Argyros (1028–1034), Michael IV (1034–1041) and Michael V (1041–1042) did not take the field, and Constantine IX Monomachos (1042–1055) had a minimal role.[6]

Of these non-campaigning Macedonian rulers perhaps the most arresting is Leo VI, the son and heir of Basil I.[7] This is partly because his lack of embracing of an active military role marks him out not just from his own father Basil but from all Byzantine emperors as far back as Heraclius (610–641). It seems that Leo was partly inspired by an earlier model of emperorship, for after the death of Theodosius I (379–395) emperors no longer campaigned in person until the reign of Maurice

---

[4] See for instance Tougher (2013).
[5] See Tougher (2013) 316–17. This was at the Battle of Abydos in 989, against the rebel Bardas Phokas.
[6] Romanos III Argyros, Michael IV and Constantine IX Monomachos were all husbands of the empress Zoe, while Michael V was her adopted son. On Constantine IX's minimal activity, see Trombley and Tougher (2019) 181, 183.
[7] For Leo VI see especially Tougher (1997) with Antonopoulou (2017).

(582–602), and then only regularly from the reign of Heraclius onwards.[8] Indeed, the emperor so central to the history of the Byzantine Empire, as a Christian and as the founder of Constantinople, Constantine I (306–337), was a highly active and successful general.[9] Conversely, one of the other most famous emperors, Justinian I (527–565), did not campaign in person at all, even though his reign is famed for the series of wars and the reconquest of the West that distinguishes it.[10] Indeed, it appears that Leo was looking to the example of Justinian I in particular for his concept of the nature of the role of the emperor: as a city-based, God-favoured font of authority.[11] This meant of course that the emperor was then dependent upon his generals for any military success, and his relationship with them had to be carefully managed, as any victories achieved could contribute to their own status and reputation rather than the emperor's. This is usefully illustrated by the example of Justinian I and his famous general Belisarius; the emperor allowed Belisarius a triumph for the recapture of North Africa but made clear that the general was his agent and subordinate.[12]

Another reason why Leo's non-campaigning identity is arresting is that he nevertheless played a vital part in the revival of the literature of military manuals in the tenth century, if not indeed being critical in this development. Leo wrote one of the most famous and substantial Byzantine military manuals, the *Taktika*.[13] This has been dated to the second half of his reign, seemingly being finalised in the first decade of the tenth century. It consists of twenty 'Constitutions' on various subjects, topped and tailed by a prologue and epilogue. It was followed by a slew of other military manuals, including the *Compilation of Tactics* (*Sylloge Tacticorum*, now dated to the reign of Romanos I Lekapenos), the *On Skirmishing* (elaborated for Nikephoros II Phokas from his own draft), and the *Taktika* of Nikephoros Ouranos (an exten-

---

[8] It is notable that even the general Tiberius did not campaign in person when he succeeded Justin II in 578. Phokas (602–610) seems not to have gone on campaign as emperor.
[9] Oddly, this is an aspect of Constantine not often analysed in the many monographs on him. For some brief comment see Hebblewhite (2017) 16. Constantine followed in the wake of the phenomenon of the third-century 'soldier emperors', from Maximinus Thrax (235–238) onwards and including Diocletian (284–305) himself; see for instance Hebblewhite (2017) 8–32.
[10] For Justinian see for instance Heather (2018).
[11] See Tougher (1998).
[12] See for example Procopius, *Wars* 4.9.1–14. Notably Justinian did not award Belisarius a triumph for the recapture of Ravenna in 540: Procopius, *Wars* 7.1.1–3. For Belisarius see also the chapter by Michael Stewart in this volume.
[13] For text and translation of Leo's *Taktika* see Dennis (2014) with commentary by Haldon (2014a). For the *Taktika* see now also Riedel (2018) esp. 32–94.

sive compilation written by one of Basil II's leading generals).[14] Leo's treatise was indebted in particular to the *Strategikon* attributed to the emperor Maurice, but also to other military literature, such as the *On Generalship* (*Strategikos*) of Onasander, the *Taktika* of Aelian and the *Stratagems* of Polyaenus.[15] Thus the antiquarian nature of Leo's project has been much discussed, but its contemporary significance and relevance have been recognised too.[16] As John Haldon has observed, Leo's text has a wider remit than the *Strategikon*, aiming to provide 'a more comprehensive manual for generals'.[17]

Leo's *Taktika* is especially interesting to consider in relation to generals, both the nature of his relationship with them and Byzantine ideals of generalship. Ideals concerning the general are addressed in particular in Constitution 2, 'About the Qualities Required in the General', though of course it is a recurring issue in the text.[18] To the modern eye what may surprise is that the moral character of the general seems more valued than his practical abilities. The general should be a highly virtuous man: self-controlled, frugal, noble in soul, not avaricious, admirable, of good reputation and pious. Practical abilities do surface too, however. The general should be intelligent, be sharp-witted, have practical wisdom, be an effective speaker, be able to endure toil, have courage and strength, not be impulsive, and be just but be able to inspire fear. Issues of identity also arise. The general should be neither too young nor too old, ideally be a father though this is not essential, not be involved in business, and in relation to class does not have to be noble or wealthy. As is recognised, the ideals of the general in Leo's *Taktika* are of ancient origin, drawn primarily from Onasander's *On Generalship*, which was also used by the *Strategikon* of Maurice.[19] However, this did not necessarily make them antiquarian or anachronistic; it is clear that these ideals did affect how generals were perceived and written about in historiography.[20] In relation to the heavy emphasis on virtue, this does reflect how individuals were assessed in the Roman Empire and Byzantium, witness for instance how emperors were praised in panegyrics; in his advice on writing a *basilikos logos* Menander Rhetor asserts that the emperor's deeds are categorised by the four

---

[14] For the *Sylloge Tacticorum* see Chatzelis and Harris (2017); Chatzelis (2019). For *On Skirmishing* see Dennis (1985) 137–239; Dagron and Mihăescu (1986). For the *Taktika* of Ouranos see McGeer (2008a) esp. 66–167.

[15] For the *Strategikon* of Maurice see Dennis (1984). For Leo's debt to it and other military manuals see Haldon (2014a) 39–54. See also the chapter by Philip Rance in this volume.

[16] See also Tougher (1997) 168–72, 181–3.

[17] Haldon (2014a) 73.

[18] Dennis (2014) 16–37 with Haldon (2014a) 131–4.

[19] Haldon (2014a) 131. See also the chapter by Rance in this volume.

[20] See for instance Chatzelis (2019) 100–3, and the chapter by Dimitris Krallis in this volume.

cardinal virtues: courage, justice, temperance and wisdom.[21] What is clear is that generals were expected to be more than active soldiers; they had to be leaders of men too. Indeed, they could even be expected to avoid the turmoil of battle to keep themselves safe as the brains of an army. Courage and physical strength are valued, but not at the expense of intelligence. As Leo says in Constitution 1, 'About Tactics and the General', 'It is characteristic of the general that he be superior to all under his command in practical wisdom, bravery (ἀνδρία), righteousness, and discretion.'[22]

This meant that a non-campaigning emperor such as Leo could still pose as the supreme commander and advisor of his generals. Indeed, Leo may have been led to write the *Taktika* because of a desire to be seen as an authority on military affairs since he did not take the field in person, though it was characteristic of him to claim authority in various spheres of emperorship, including legislation and religion too.[23] In the sphere of military leadership, Leo sets out his concept in the Prologue of the *Taktika*.[24] Asserting that there had been a loss of knowledge about military tactics and strategy, he acts in order to restore it. He writes the *Taktika* for his 'subcommanders' thus putting himself in the position of supreme general, a position he makes explicit in Constitution 1.[25] The emperor is the supreme authority, after whom come the generals, appointed by the emperor himself. Leo also makes clear that God is the ultimate authority, but even this enhances the status of the emperor given his especially close association with Him. Leo's conception of his intimate relationship with his generals is also reflected by the text when he moves beyond ideals and provides specific examples. It is well known that in the Byzantine Empire in the ninth and tenth centuries there emerge leading generals from families who now had surnames.[26] Prominent in the reign of Leo were for instance Nikephoros Phokas, the grandfather of the famous tenth-century commander and emperor Nikephoros II Phokas (963–969), and Andronikos Doukas and his son Constantine Doukas.[27] Nikephoros Phokas the Elder appears in the *Taktika* several times. In Constitution 11, 'About Camps', Leo recalls a successful stratagem of 'our general' Nikephoros when he was 'plundering enemy territory' in Syria (after Nikephoros' return from

---

[21] Menander Rhetor 2.1–2.373.7–8, ed. and trans. Russell and Wilson (1981) 84–5.
[22] *Taktika* 1.11, trans. Dennis (2014) 15. On the importance of combining courage and wisdom see also Lauxtermann (1998) 368–9 on the testimony of John Geometres in the late tenth century.
[23] See for instance Magdalino (2013) esp. 189–90.
[24] Dennis (2014) 2–11.
[25] Dennis (2014) 12–15.
[26] See for instance Leidholm (2019) 3–5; Kaldellis (2017a) 13–18.
[27] See Tougher (1997) 203–18.

Italy in 886 and before 895).[28] This campaign is also mentioned in Constitution 17, 'About Surprise Attacks', and specifies that Nikephoros pillaged Tarsus and Cilicia while the enemy emir raided Cappadocia.[29] An earlier campaign of Nikephoros in Lombard Italy (in Calabria in 885, in the reign of Basil I) is mentioned in Constitution 15, 'About Besieging a City'.[30] Leo also attributes the invention of a bladed tripod to Nikephoros, in the context of conflict with Bulgaria (in 895).[31] Further, Leo may allude to Nikephoros in Constitution 20, 'Concise Sayings', when he remarks that generals 'trace their lineage from a tribe or family not only illustrious in their victories, but in all their actions even to the point that their very name signifies victory'.[32] Thus Nikephoros is mentioned in relation to three different arenas of conflict, and as a general to admire and imitate, one close to the emperor himself. It is possible that Nikephoros was even a source for Leo.[33]

Leo's son Constantine VII was also keen to lay claim to military authority and emphasise his relationship with his generals. Among the numerous texts associated with him and produced during his reign, several show especial concern with military affairs. The *Excerpta* project begun under Constantine reveals an evident interest in warfare, including such titles as *On Victory* and *On Battles*.[34] In the Leipzig manuscript of the famous *Book of Ceremonies* are preserved three treatises on imperial military expeditions (texts A, B and C).[35] Of these the longest and most significant is C, entitled *On What Should be Observed When the Great and High Emperor of the Romans Goes on Campaign*.[36] Like the more famous *De Administrando Imperio*, this was written in the name of Constantine and addressed to his son and heir Romanos II.[37] It has been dated to just before 958, when Romanos was a young man (he was born c. 938). Like Leo, Constantine emphasises the value of knowledge, and courage (εὐτολμίας) in warfare is identified as being of prime value.[38] Although Constantine did not campaign in person, the text emphasises the intimate relationship of the emperor with his troops when he goes out on expedition. The text

[28] *Taktika* 11.21, trans. Dennis (2014) 203–5 with Haldon (2014a) 254, 379.
[29] *Taktika* 17.65, Dennis (2014) 418–19.
[30] *Taktika* 15.32, Dennis (2014) 366–7 with Haldon (2014a) 301.
[31] *Taktika* 11.22, Dennis (2014) 202–5 with Haldon (2014a) 254–5.
[32] *Taktika* 20.137, trans. Dennis (2014) 583 with Haldon (2014a) 432.
[33] Haldon (2014a) 55, 384.
[34] See Németh (2018) esp. 58, 189–93.
[35] See Haldon (1990).
[36] For text, translation and commentary, see Haldon (1990) 94–151, 176–293.
[37] For the *De Administrando Imperio* see Moravcsik and Jenkins (1967) with Jenkins (ed.) (1962).
[38] Haldon (1990) 94–5, 132–3.

records exchanges between the emperor and his soldiers, and the relationship is characterised as one between a father and his children.[39] He is presented as asking after their wives, described as his daughters-in-law, and their children. When he addresses the tagmatic and thematic troops, he also bids them 'Strive, soldiers of Christ and my children, so that in time of need you will show your nobility of spirit (γενναιότητα) and your bravery (ἀνδρείαν), as well as your true devotion and love for God and our majesty.'[40] Of particular value for analysing the nature of Constantine's relationship with his troops are two harangues preserved in his name.[41] As Eric McGeer observes, 'The ability to rouse the courage of their soldiers with the spoken word ranked high among the desirable attributes of Byzantine generals',[42] and in his harangues Constantine takes on this role. Both harangues relate to eastern campaigns undertaken by the Byzantines: the first is dated to 950 (after military successes of Leo Phokas the *strategos* of Cappadocia) or 952–953 (after the Battle of Germanikeia) and the second to 958. In the first harangue Constantine addresses issues of gender, noting the courage of the Byzantine troops, likening the enemy troops to feeble women, and commenting on the fear and cowardice of their leader Sayf al-Dawla, the Hamdanid emir of Aleppo. Constantine also emphasises the correct religious belief of the Byzantine troops as Christians, and thus the fact that they have Christ on their side. He makes clear too that he knows of the actions of the soldiers through his agents who report to him, and through whom he can communicate with them. Further, the emperor holds out the prospect of rewards for his troops. The second harangue is even more revealing of Constantine's conception of his relationship with his troops. Significantly, as McGeer makes clear, it is located in a different historical context, when Byzantium had gone on a determined offensive against Sayf, Nikephoros Phokas the Younger replacing his father Bardas Phokas (son of Nikephoros Phokas the Elder) as supreme commander in 955, and the generals John Tzimiskes the *strategos* of Mesopotamia and Basil the *parakoimomenos* (Constantine's brother-in-law) just about to capture Samosata and defeat Sayf in 958.[43] The emperor casts himself as the instructor of his soldiers in the art of war, enhancing and instilling courage. He is the supreme commander, the generals being his servants 'distinguished by wisdom and experience', and once again he is

---

[39] Haldon (1990) 122–3, 124–5, with commentary at 242–3.
[40] Trans. Haldon (1990) 125.
[41] See Ahrweiler (1967) for the first harangue, Vári (1908) for the second harangue, and also McGeer (2003), who provides translations of the harangues at 117–20, 127–34. For further comment on them see also Markopoulos (2012); Wander (2012) 99–102; Riedel (2016).
[42] McGeer (2003) 112.
[43] See further comment below.

the father of his soldiers.⁴⁴ Remarkably, he denigrates the successes of Byzantine soldiers on previous campaigns (thus including the recipients of his first harangue), asserting that these were accidental victories and raising the accusation of cowardice against some soldiers, with the efforts of the truly brave having been obscured. The critical role of the support of Christ and the connection between Christianity and success are emphasised once again, with the emperor sending his troops holy water drawn from the relics of the Passion of Christ (including fragments of the Cross), and appealing to the intercession of the Mother of God, the angels, the saints, clergy and monks. This is also well reflected by the cross-shaped setting for relics of the True Cross produced for Constantine and his son Romanos; contained within the later Limburg Reliquary, the cross itself has been dated to 945–959.⁴⁵ An inscription on the back of the cross makes clear the association of the Cross with military victory:

> On the one hand, God stretched out his hands upon the wood
> gushing forth through it the energies of life.
> On the other hand, Constantine and Romanos the despots
> with the synthesis of radiant stones and pearls
> displayed this same thing full of wonder.
> And on the one hand, Christ with this formerly smashed the gates of Hades
> giving new life to the dead.
> On the other hand, the crown-wearers having now adorned this
> crush with it the temerities of the barbarians.⁴⁶

Thus both Leo and Constantine were able to pose as supreme commander of the army and as agents of courage and success for their soldiers, even though they did not take the field in person. However, this is not to say that they did not value an active military role. In the first harangue Constantine declares that he yearns to participate in person, stating

> I would much prefer to don my breastplate and put my helmet on my head, to brandish my spear in my right hand and to hear the trumpet calling us to battle,

---

[44] McGeer (2003) 128.

[45] For the cross reliquary contained within the Limburg Reliquary, see especially Hostetler (2012); Pentcheva (2007) esp. 110–113. See further comment on the Limburg Reliquary below.

[46] Trans. Hostetler (2012) 8. For Constantine's broad interest in relics see Markopoulos (2012) 55 n. 85.

than to put on the crown and the purple, to wield the sceptre, and to hear the imperial acclamations.[47]

In the second harangue this seems to have become a much more concrete plan, Constantine announcing that he is going to join them in person and bring his son Romanos with him too. He tells them 'with God's approval and sanction, I have prepared and readied myself to accompany you on campaign and to be convinced by my own eyes of what in times past I used to learn and hear by report', and asks them 'If, then, there is any longing in you to see us and our son as your fellow cavalrymen, fellow infantrymen, and comrades in arms, confirm this longing now by your very deeds.'[48] The very fact that Constantine composed for his son a treatise on imperial military expeditions seems to indicate his thinking too. In addition, the *Excerpta* itself included a title *On Leading the Army*.[49] As for Leo, despite his evident lack of personal experience, in the *Taktika* he does lay claim to some direct knowledge.[50] Further, the origins of Constantine's treatise for Romanos on imperial expeditions was in fact – as he records – a project Leo had set for the *magistros* Leo Katakylas (probably Leo's general Leo Katakalon) to compose guidance on such expeditions.[51] Thus Leo himself may have visualised going on campaign in person, or together with his son Constantine, or was even laying a path for Constantine to follow. Since Constantine was born in 905 and Leo died in 912, there was not the opportunity for the two to go on campaign together. Equally, Constantine's plans to go on campaign with Romanos were cut short by Constantine's death in 959, and Romanos did not long survive his father, dying in 963. Circumstances could thus also play a part in whether an emperor did undertake an active military role. This is clearly seen in the case of Leo, for he only became the heir apparent to Basil I in 879 when Basil's eldest son Constantine died, and then Leo seems to have been confined by Basil for three years (883–886) anyway, on suspicion of plotting against him. The case of Basil I's lost heir Constantine is significant too, for Basil had taken him on campaign, in 878 it seems. On this episode the *Life of Basil* comments

---

[47] Trans. McGeer (2003) 119–20.
[48] Trans. McGeer (2003) 130.
[49] Németh (2018) 191.
[50] *Taktika*, Prologue 6, Dennis (2014) 6–7. Here Leo copies the *Strategikon* of Maurice: Haldon (2014a) 125.
[51] Text C, ed. and trans. Haldon (1990) 94–7 lines 24–39. On Leo Katakylas, see Haldon (1990) 180–1; Tougher (1997) 80–1, 85–6, 168, 179.

taking along his eldest son Constantine, [Basil] set out with him against Syria, so as to give that cub of noble race a taste for slaying the enemy and to be himself his teacher in tactics and manly valor in the face of peril.[52]

This episode highlights of course the fact that the dynasty-founder Basil did go on campaign in person when he was emperor. The active military role of Basil is a key part of the praise of the emperor in the *Life of Basil*, written for Basil's grandson Constantine VII in the mid-tenth century.[53] Turning to this subject, the *Life* declares

> [n]ow that domestic affairs were running well for the emperor and in accordance with his pious goals pleasing to God, his deep solicitude for the state as a whole summoned him to foreign campaigns, so that he might by his own efforts, courage (ἀνδρείᾳ), and excellence extend the boundaries of his realm, force out his foes, and drive them far off.[54]

It continues that Basil trained new recruits, then embarked on campaign with them, during which he led an attack on Melitene (in 873), displaying his bravery (ἀνδρείαν).[55] The *Life* also details his personal role in the campaign of 878.[56] Basil I's military role had been emphasised too by Leo VI in his *Taktika*, for he refers to him twice. In relation to the campaign of 878, Leo recalls Basil's role in ensuring the safe crossing of the river Paradeisos,[57] and he asserts that Basil trained the recently converted Slavs 'to take part in warfare against those nations warring against the Romans'.[58] Given that Leo rarely refers to specific people in the *Taktika*, the mentions of Basil, like those of Nikephoros Phokas the Elder, take on particular significance, and it is possible that Leo had even heard of these instances from Basil himself.[59] Basil too was keen to promote his image as a militarily active emperor; witness the fact that he staged triumphs in Constantinople after the cam-

---

[52] *Life of Basil* 46, trans. Ševčenko (2011) 165.
[53] See Ševčenko (2011).
[54] *Life of Basil* 36, trans. Ševčenko (2011) 133. The focus is kept on military affairs until chapter 43, and then from chapter 46 to chapter 71.
[55] *Life of Basil* 40, Ševčenko (2011) 145. Basil had also helped his soldiers build a bridge over the Euphrates, displaying his exceptional strength.
[56] *Life of Basil* 46-9. The narrative includes a prophecy that Adata would fall not to Basil but to a Constantine. Basil thinks that this might be his son Constantine, but is assured it is another, whom we are told was Constantine VII himself: *Life of Basil* 48.
[57] *Taktika* 9.14.
[58] *Taktika* 18.95, trans. Dennis (2014) 471.
[59] See Haldon (2014a) 54, 55, 85.

paigns of 873 and 878, as the *Life of Basil* attests.[60] Of the triumph of 873 it relates that

> amply rewarding all the troops under his command and bestowing upon each of his bravest soldiers a prize befitting that soldier's valor, [Basil] returned to the capital with many spoils and wreaths of victory. He entered through the Golden Gate, as ancient emperors of the most glorious Rome had done upon their triumphal returns; received the cheers of victory and shouts of acclamations from the people; and, just as he was after the campaign, he straightaway betook himself to the great temple of the Wisdom of God, to offer prayers and give due thanks. And crowned with the garland of victory by the patriarch of that time, he returned to the palace.[61]

While the *Life of Basil* treats the triumph of 878 with much more brevity, it is described in detail in *On What Should Be Observed When the Great and High Emperor of the Romans Goes on Campaign*.[62] The celebrations for the triumph of Basil and his son Constantine featured the acclamations 'Glory to God, who returns our own Lords to us victorious! Glory to God who exalts you, autocrats of the Romans! Glory to you, All-Holy Trinity, that we see our own Lords victorious! Welcome as conquerors, most courageous (ἀνδριώτατοι) Lords!'[63]

Thus Basil I and his son Constantine played an active military role, unlike Leo VI, Alexander, Constantine VII and Romanos II. More fascinating yet is the fact that Basil II (976–1025), Romanos II's eldest son, re-embraced an active military role.[64] While Macedonian emperors had come to depend on their generals to lead and fight their campaigns, Basil II returned to the field, in the context of the civil wars that dogged his early reign (in the shape of Bardas Phokas and Bardas Skleros) and then more famously in his protracted Bulgarian campaigns. It may be that the generals-turned-emperors Nikephoros II Phokas (963–969) and John I Tzimiskes (969–976) had set a powerful example of militarily active emperors, or perhaps Basil II and/or his advisors had realised that the emperor needed to be an active general to reclaim the role from powerful generals. Either way, Basil II remade the role his own, epitomised by the familiar image of him from the Venice Psalter: the emperor triumphant in military garb and holding spear and sword, sanctioned by God, flanked by busts of six military saints, and with subjects or defeated enemies

[60] *Life of Basil* 40 and 49. On the triumphs of Basil, see McCormick (1986) 155–7.
[61] *Life of Basil* 40, trans. Ševčenko (2011) 147–9.
[62] Haldon (1990) 140–7 (Text C, lines 724–807) with commentary at 268–85.
[63] Trans. Haldon (1990) 143.
[64] See also Trombley and Tougher (2019) esp. 181–2.

prostrate at his feet.⁶⁵ Also telling is that Basil II chose to be buried not in the mausoleum of Constantine the Great at Holy Apostles with most of his Macedonian predecessors, but in the church of St John the Evangelist at the Hebdomon.⁶⁶ The Hebdomon was associated with military success, as the starting point for triumphal entries into Constantinople. Basil's military role is emphasised in the tomb's verse epitaph:

> Other past emperors
> previously designated for themselves other burial places.
> But I Basil, born in the purple chamber,
> place my tomb on the site of the Hebdomon [Palace]
> and take sabbath's rest from the endless toils
> which I satisfied in wars and which I endured.
> For nobody saw my spear at rest,⁶⁷
> from when the Emperor of Heaven called me
> to the rulership of this great empire on earth,
> but I kept vigilant through the whole span of my life
> guarding the children of New Rome
> marching bravely (ἀνδρικῶς) to the West,
> and as far as the very frontiers of the East.
> The Persians and Scythians bear witness to this
> and along with them Abasgos, Ismael, Araps, Iber.
> And now, good man, looking upon this tomb
> reward it with prayers in return for my campaigns.⁶⁸

Thus of ruling members of the Macedonian Dynasty only Basil I and Basil II played an active military role, and of the emperors who ruled because of marrying into the

---

⁶⁵ For the Psalter of Basil II (Marcianus gr. 17), see Cutler (1976–7); Spatharakis (1976) 20–6. An accompanying iambic poem also describes the image, and refers to the victories of the emperor. Basil II is associated as well with another famous manuscript, the so-called Menologion of Basil II (Vaticanus Graecus 1613): see for instance Ševčenko (1962). The manuscript seems to be missing a full-page miniature depicting Basil II with Christ, but includes a dedicatory poem which describes Basil as 'excelling . . . in victories' and aided in battle by the sainted agents of God depicted in the manuscript: see Ševčenko (1962) 272–3. I will discuss the Menologion and its dynastic significance elsewhere.

⁶⁶ On Basil's tomb, see Stephenson (2005).

⁶⁷ Kaldellis (2017a) 120 uses this line as the heading of a chapter on Basil II (and for another chapter also the line 'guarding the children of New Rome': 103).

⁶⁸ Trans. Stephenson (2005) 230–1 with text in n. 17.

imperial family only Nikephoros II Phokas and John I Tzimiskes – both previously generals – played a significant military role. Nevertheless the dynasty maintained itself in power, not least as it could still claim military authority as divinely supported, and it only expired due to the lack of an heir.

Eunuch Generals

The other arresting aspect of generalship in the Macedonian period this chapter addresses is that of eunuch generals.[69] This was not a unique aspect of eunuchs in the Macedonian period, for it was a role eunuchs had played in the empire since the Grand Chamberlain Eutropius had campaigned against the Huns in the late fourth century, though it seems to have taken off significantly in the sixth century as epitomised by the career of Narses, another leading chamberlain who acquired a military role, and who ended up trumping Belisarius and defeating the Ostrogoths in Italy.[70] However, under the Macedonian Dynasty there are some notable cases of eunuch generals, and this chapter focuses especially on that of Basil Lekapenos. Evidently being a castrated male was not a bar to military command, and successful military eunuchs could be praised for their masculine virtues.

An illuminating text for considering attitudes to eunuch generals (and generals and generalship in general) in the time of the Macedonian Dynasty is the *History* written by Leo the Deacon, one of the palace clergy under Basil II.[71] Dating towards the end of the tenth century, Leo's *History* recorded the reigns of Romanos II, Nikephoros II Phokas and John I Tzimiskes, and provided brief glimpses of the reign of Basil II too. Leo can draw a gender contrast between court eunuchs and generals such as Nikephoros Phokas the Younger. For instance, he presents the eunuch Joseph Bringas (associated with Romanos II and his widow Theophano) as a villain who sought to neutralise the general Nikephoros Phokas.[72] While Leo himself does not directly deploy anti-eunuch rhetoric against Joseph, he has other characters do it, especially John Tzimiskes. Attempting to rouse his uncle Nikephoros against Bringas, John directly comments on the fact that Bringas is a eunuch, contrasting the effeminate Joseph with the martial and heroic Phokas:

---

[69] For eunuchs in Byzantium, see especially Ringrose (2003); Tougher (2008); Messis (2014). For eunuchs in the Macedonian period specifically, see Tougher (2018).

[70] For a survey of military eunuchs in Byzantium see Guilland (1943) 205–14. For Narses, see Tougher (2021) 119–35, 172–80; Brodka (2018); Stewart (2015); Fauber (1990).

[71] For Leo and his *History*, see Talbot and Sullivan (2005).

[72] Leo the Deacon 2.11.

[To think of] your labors and battles and prowess, while the [dastardly deed] is planned by an effeminate fellow (παρ᾽ ἀνδραρίου), whose very sex is doubtful, an artificial woman who knows nothing except what goes on in the women's quarters (ἀμφιβόλου τε καὶ ἀνάνδρου, καὶ γυναίου τεχνητοῦ)!

Let us rather act gallantly and courageously, so that Joseph, and anyone else who thinks like him, may realize that they are not contending with delicate and sheltered women, but with men possessed of invincible strength, who are feared and admired by barbarians.

I think it is wrong, nay intolerable, for Roman generals to be led and to be dragged by the nose, hither and thither, like slaves, by a wretched eunuch (τομίου οἰκτροῦ) from the wastes of Paphlagonia, who has insinuated himself into political power.[73]

This echoes Leo's direct verdict on another eunuch, Constantine Gongylios, who did play a military role; Leo says the eunuch's Cretan expedition in 949 failed 'on account of the cowardice (ἀνανδρίᾳ) and lack of experience of the commander, who was a eunuch of the bedchamber, an effeminate fellow (ἀνδραρίου σκιατραφοῦς) from Paphlagonia . . . the entire . . . army . . . was cut to pieces by the barbarians'.[74] In these cases the contrast between masculine warriors and effeminate palace staff is all too clear. But it is important to grasp that in the case of Joseph Bringas, Leo is putting words in Tzimiskes' mouth, and that there is also a literary model at play; the sixth-century historian Agathias discusses reaction to Narses in similar terms. When Agathias remarks upon Narses' good qualities in the context of his activities as a general in Italy he observes that 'These . . . were all the more remarkable in a eunuch (τομίας) and in one who had been brought up in the soft and comfortable atmosphere of the imperial court.'[75] Agathias also has the Alamanni leaders Leutharis and Butilinus comment on Narses that 'they were surprised at the Goths being so terrified of a puny little man, a eunuch of the bedchamber (ἀνδράριόν τι θαλαμηπόλον σκιατραφές), used to a soft and sedentary existence, and with nothing masculine about him'.[76] But the point is that they are wrong-footed, that a eunuch

---

[73] Leo the Deacon 3.3, trans. Talbot and Sullivan (2005) 90. See also the comments of Talbot and Sullivan (2005) 30 on Leo the Deacon on eunuchs.
[74] Leo the Deacon 1.2, trans. Talbot and Sullivan (2005) 59–60.
[75] Agathias, *History* 1.16.1–2, ed. Keydell (1967) 30, trans. Frendo (1975) 24. Agathias continues 'The fact is that the nobility of soul cannot fail to make its mark, no matter what obstacles are put in its path.'
[76] Agathias, *History* 1.7.8, trans. Frendo (1975) 16.

can be a successful general. Leo himself demonstrates this in his depiction of the eunuch general Peter 'Phokas'.

Peter was a eunuch of Nikephoros Phokas who was made stratopedarch by him, and went on to serve under John I Tzimiskes as well as Basil II, being killed in battle against Bardas Skleros in 976.[77] In relation to Peter's role in the capture of Antioch in 969, Leo remarks that 'the *patrikios* and *stratopedarches* Peter [was] a eunuch, but still extremely active and robust (ῥέκτην δὲ τὴν ἄλλως καὶ ῥωμαλεώτατον)'.[78] He also relates that Peter was one of the generals sent against the Rus by John Tzimiskes in 970,[79] and records a previous episode to demonstrate Peter's military ability: Peter had been made stratopedarch by Nikephoros Phokas

> because of his inherent valor and heroic feats in battle (τὰ κατὰ τοὺς πολέμους ἀνδραγαθήματα), for it is said that once, when the Scythians were raiding Thrace, it came about that Peter, although a eunuch (καίτοι τομίαν ὄντα), met them in pitched battle with the corps that was following him.

Peter then faced the Rus commander in one-to-one combat, each on horseback: 'Peter, filled with inconceivable valor and spirit (ἀλκῆς καὶ μένους), impetuously urged his horse on with his spurs, and, after brandishing his spear mightily, thrust it with both hands at the Scythian's chest.' The spear went right through the enemy commander, killing him, so that 'the Scythians turned to flight, amazed at this novel and strange sight'. Thus there is encountered the view that eunuchs can make good generals; in spite of being eunuchs they can overcome their perceived limitations and prove themselves successful in the role.[80]

Another successful eunuch general in the Macedonian period is Basil Lekapenos. Also known as Basil the *parakoimomenos*, this eunuch is one of the most interesting of the court eunuchs under the Macedonian Dynasty, if not of the whole history of the Byzantine Empire.[81] Bastard son of Romanos Lekapenos, Basil's career and authority lasted for several decades. Although prominent under Constantine VII (he was *protovestiarios* then *parakoimomenos*), Basil became even more so when he supported Nikephoros Phokas' seizure of imperial power in 963, against the opposition

---

[77] Leo the Deacon 5.4, 6.11, 10.7. See also Talbot and Sullivan (2005) 132–3 n. 41.

[78] Leo the Deacon 5.4, trans. Talbot and Sullivan (2005) 132.

[79] Leo the Deacon 6.11, trans. Talbot and Sullivan (2005) 158.

[80] Markopoulos (2004b) 14–16 emphasises Leo's negative attitude towards eunuchs at the expense of the more positive views expressed in the history, arguing that the 'exceptions . . . merely serve to underline the negative rule' (16).

[81] For Basil, see especially Brokkaar (1972); Lauxtermann (1998) 373–8; Wander (2012) 93–132; Angelidi (2013); Németh (2018) 36–46.

of the eunuch Joseph Bringas.⁸² Raising men and supplies for Nikephoros Phokas in Constantinople, Basil ensured his success.⁸³ Such was Nikephoros Phokas' gratitude to Basil that he created a new title for him, that of *proedros* (often interpreted as meaning 'President of the Senate').⁸⁴ Basil retained his position and office under John Tzimiskes. When John Tzimiskes himself died in 976, Basil in effect ruled for the young co-emperors Basil II and Constantine VIII, until being pushed out of power and exiled by his eponymous great-nephew in 985. Basil's power and status are also reflected by his famous role as patron; for instance, he was responsible for a 'monastery . . . manuscripts, chalices, patens and rings'.⁸⁵

During his career Basil played a military role. In the reign of Constantine VII he led an expedition to the eastern frontier in 958 (sent out to reinforce the army, which was under the command of John Tzimiskes); Samosata was besieged and captured and then a victory was won in battle.⁸⁶ Later, in the reign of John Tzimiskes, Basil was put in charge of the siege machinery by the emperor on a campaign against the Rus in Bulgaria in 971.⁸⁷ The campaign of 958 was particularly notable, for it was celebrated with a triumph in the hippodrome, a very public recognition of the part played by a eunuch general.⁸⁸ It seems that Basil himself was keen to promote his image as a successful general, as well as demonstrating interest in military matters generally; witness the existence of a manual on naval warfare (the *Naumachika*) which was commissioned by him.⁸⁹ Not only has this been dated to the period from late 958 to late 959 (Basil is identified as *patrikios* and *parakoimomenos*), soon after Basil's celebrated success on the eastern frontier, but also it lauds him as essentially the best general ever. The anonymous author addresses Basil as follows:

---

[82] For Joseph Bringas, see for instance Markopoulos (2004c).
[83] *Book of Ceremonies* 1.96, and Leo the Deacon 3.7.
[84] Leo the Deacon 3.8.
[85] Pentcheva (2007) 114 n. 20. On Basil as patron, see also Németh (2018) 40–2; Angelidi (2013) 20–6; Bevilacqua (2012); Wander (2012) 96–105; Lauxtermann (2003) 162–5; Ross (1958).
[86] Theophanes Continuatus 6.44, and Yahya ibn Sa'id of Antioch, *History*, ed. and French trans. Kratchkovsky and Vasiliev (1924) 775. See also Brokkaar (1972) 214; Wander (2012) 101–2; Angelidi (2013) 15; Kaldellis (2017a) 28; Theotokis (2018) 255. On Yahya ibn Sa'id, see Holmes (2005) 38. On Basil's eastern campaigning see also the remark of Skylitzes, *Synopsis Historion*, Reign of John I Tzimiskes, 1, ed. Thurn (1973) 284.2–9.
[87] Leo the Deacon 8.4.
[88] For the triumph see McCormick (1986) 166.
[89] For this *Naumachika* see Pryor and Jeffreys (2006) 183–6, 521–45 (edition and translation). It survives (incomplete) in one tenth-century manuscript, Biblioteca Ambrosiana MS. B 119-sup. [gr. 139], folios 339r–342v; for further comment on the manuscript see below.

You permit me to express my youthful exuberance on these matters, you most eminent *strategos*, adorned with great endeavours, the valiant attendant of our valiant emperor, the sure and brave servant of a sure and brave [lord] (τοῦ ἀνδρείου ἀνδρεῖος), you who by conflicts on land have gladdened the emperors themselves, feeling secure, and have demonstrated that their every subject is full of peace and joy, you who have humbled and brought low the valiant deeds (ἀνδραγαθήματα) of all other [men] both who live now and were born in former times, you who will show, if ever there should be need, that [deeds] at sea are equal to those on land.[90]

Basil is praised for his bravery, as is the non-campaigning emperor Constantine VII himself, and in addition the author anticipates the future success of the eunuch in naval conflict. The dedicatory poem at the start of the text also celebrates the military expertise and success of Basil, and is more explicit about what naval campaign he might undertake. It runs:

Having been instructed in the outstanding works of the wisdom of the Ausonians
and in files and phalanxes and unbroken battle-lines
of close-massed hoplites, indeed of mighty chariot marshals,
in the pages of history by well-born kings,
having been shown to be the all-supreme leader of the Ausonians' army,
having defeated Chambdan, you despoil the Arab race,
and if ever you wish to learn about swift-moving ships
so that, far from war at sea, you may recall doughty deeds,
gaze with your eyes, best [of men], on all the thoughts [contained] duly
in this book and cast them within your mind.
Then indeed, Basil, you will sack the plain of Crete
and destroy the race of great-hearted Carthaginians.[91]

The expedition to recapture Crete was launched in 960 and its objective successfully achieved in 961, but it was led by Nikephoros Phokas rather than Basil.[92] Perhaps Basil had hoped to lead the expedition, but circumstances changed after the

---

[90] Preface 4, trans. Pryor and Jeffreys (2006) 525. See also Wander (2012) 129; Messis (2014) 211.

[91] Trans. Pryor and Jeffreys (2006) 523. See also Messis (2014) 210–11; Mazzucchi (1978) 302.

[92] The Byzantines had been attempting to recover Crete since its loss in the early ninth century; under the Macedonians there occurred an expedition led by Himerios in 911 and the failed campaign of the eunuch Constantine Gongylios in 949: see Pryor and Jeffreys (2006) 46–7, 63, 71.

death of Constantine VII, for his heir Romanos II favoured the court eunuch Joseph Bringas. Nevertheless, the poem is testimony to the military image Basil fostered of himself, and of his further military aspirations. Marc Lauxtermann even comments that Basil 'is portrayed . . . as if he were the emperor, and his valour, wisdom and military experience are represented as virtues that are truly imperial'.[93] Certainly Basil's own name is echoed in the term for kings. Further, Charis Messis observes that the Preface of the text identifies Basil as the perfect man.[94] There is no need, however, to accept Steven Wander's argument that the description of Basil as 'manly' supports the case that he was a postpubertal eunuch; it was perfectly possible for Byzantines to ascribe masculine virtues to eunuchs, as seen for instance in the cases of Narses and Peter 'Phokas'.[95]

Basil's interest in military matters is reflected not just by the *Naumachika* alone, but by the manuscript which preserves it; this may date to the year 958/959, and seems to have been produced for him. It is a major collection of military works (Philip Rance has described it as 'one of the most important manuscript prototypes of the tradition of Greek tactical writing'), and it includes not only the very harangues of Constantine VII discussed above, but also versions of Leo VI's *Taktika* and *Naumachika*.[96] Other manuscripts associated with Basil also reflect his interest in military matters. The main surviving manuscript of the *Books of Ceremonies* (the Leipzig manuscript, which dates to the reign of Nikephoros II Phokas) may have been produced at the direction of Basil Lekapenos himself,[97] and it is this manuscript which includes the treatises on imperial military expeditions referred to above. It has been suggested that Basil was also involved in the *Excerpta* project, which has such a pronounced interest in military affairs.[98] Further, Wander has argued that it was Basil who commissioned the Joshua Roll (Biblioteca Apostolica Vaticana, Pal. gr. 431), an intriguing manuscript which illustrated the Old Testament Book of Joshua, which focuses heavily on the successful military campaigns of Joshua the leader of the Israelites; the scroll may even have copied drawings for a triumphal

---

[93] Lauxtermann (2003) 322. See also Wander (2012) 103.
[94] Messis (2014) 210–12.
[95] Wander (2012) 110–11.
[96] See in particular Mazzucchi (1978) esp. 282–4; Németh (2018) 42–5; Angelidi (2013) 15–16; Bevilacqua (2013); Wander (2012) 101–3; Pryor and Jeffreys (2006) 183–6; Rance (2007b) 733–6; McGeer (2003) 112–13. See also the chapter by Rance in this volume.
[97] See Featherstone (2004). This manuscript includes an account of how Nikephoros Phokas became emperor (1.96) which mentions the role of Basil, and also a description of the promotion of a *proedros* (1.97), which appears to be Basil himself given the dating of the manuscript; this was a position created for Basil by Nikephoros Phokas when he was emperor.
[98] Németh (2018) 23, 36–7.

column.⁹⁹ An artefact that Basil definitely commissioned was the box to contain the cross reliquary of Constantine VII and Romanos II which was discussed above. This is the famous Limburg Reliquary, which was also designed to contain other relics within compartments inside the box.¹⁰⁰ Basil, identified as *proedros*, is named in the inscription on the rim of the box, which has been dated to 968 at the earliest, as one of the containers holds hair of John the Baptist which had been recovered by Nikephoros II Phokas in 968 (or possibly by John I Tzimiskes in 975); the terminal date of the box is 985, the year Basil fell from favour with his great-nephew Basil II. Given the association of the Cross and other relics with military victories, it is likely that Basil was thus appropriating their power for himself. It has been suggested that the box was taken on campaign.¹⁰¹ It is even possible that the cross of Constantine and Romanos was associated with the successes of Basil on the eastern frontier.

Thus under the Macedonian Dynasty the Byzantine practice of appointing eunuchs to military commands continued, with some notable cases distinguishing the tenth century in particular – Peter 'Phokas' and Basil the *parakoimomenos*. These cases allow it to be seen that successful eunuch generals could be praised for their masculine virtues, though examples of unsuccessful eunuch generals could be criticised for perceived eunuch weaknesses. Thus they were gendered according to their performance in their roles, just like non-eunuch men.

Conclusion

Among the qualities desired in a general by the Byzantines, courage/bravery is prominent, drawing on long-established ideals and highlighting that gender is relevant to generalship. Nevertheless, both non-campaigning emperors and eunuch generals could lay claim to this virtue too. Emperors could claim expertise in it and the ability to foster it in their generals and soldiers, given their very position as emperor and their intimate association with God, the agent of victory. Eunuch generals could also claim it and be praised for it, if they were successful in the role, in spite of the negative views of eunuch gender identity that could exist in Byzantium. The Macedonian Dynasty was distinguished by both the number of non-campaigning rulers within it and the notably successful eunuch generals under it. Despite the dynasty-founder Basil I having gone on campaign, the only other emperor of

---

⁹⁹ Wander (2012) esp. 93–132. See, however, the comments of Németh (2018) 41 n. 91.
¹⁰⁰ See for instance Pentcheva (2007); Ševčenko (1994).
¹⁰¹ Ševčenko (1994) 292–4. She suggests Basil made the box for John I Tzimiskes for use on a joint military campaign. See also Wander (2012) 101–2.

his family who did was the celebrated Basil II.[102] However, another member of the dynasty did achieve a significant military role: Basil the *parakoimomenos*. As the half-brother of the empress Helena, wife of Constantine VII, Basil was the uncle of Romanos II and great-uncle of Basil II, and as has been seen he could even be understood to be a de facto emperor. Indeed, perhaps for Basil II it was the eunuch Basil the *parakoimomenos* who served as a model of a militarily active member of the family; both were certainly celebrated for their generalship.

---

[102] Constantine the son of Basil I and Constantine VIII both had limited experience of campaigning and in very specific circumstances: the former when he was the heir apparent of his father, and the latter when he was co-emperor of his brother and in the context of civil war.

16 The Politics of War: Virtue, *Tyche*, Persuasion and the Byzantine General

Dimitris Krallis

Βουλή μὲν ἄρχει, χείρ δ'ἐπεξεργάζεται.[1]

In an important book on elite Middle Byzantine army units, an eminent scholar noted that:

> Not only do armed forces reflect in general the social order of the state which maintains them – in terms of the social origins of officers, methods of recruitment and promotion, *qualities* required for admittance to the officer ranks and so forth; they constitute a discrete group within their own society and to this extent develop distinct, institutionalized patterns of behaviour and related attitudes.[2]

This excerpt outlines a central tension present in the study of professional armies; namely their existence in a tight but also potentially antagonistic relationship with the society that engendered them. Armies reflect society and at the same time exist apart from it by virtue of the institutional, fiscal, cultural and other arrangements that constitute them.[3] In laying out this tension, John Haldon also helps set up a central question that underpins this chapter. If the army was indeed a society apart, born nevertheless of Byzantium, were some of the general's qualities as a leader of men rooted in society itself as a whole? Was the portrait of the commander in fact

---

[1] 'The council orders, but the hand executes' (my translation). Eustathios of Thessalonike, *Orations* 286, probably citing Ion of Chios, Fr. 63.3, Snell (1971) 113 = (107 Blum).
[2] Haldon (1984) 85. Italics mine.
[3] Elton (1997) 42–50 on critiques of soldiers by civilians that may reinforce a sense of 'apartness'.

one of a man who straddled civilian life and army camp?[4] Furthermore, if, as seen in tactical manuals, orations and histories alike, skills in oratory and persuasiveness were desirable qualities for a general, what can we say not only about the nature of the marching *civitas* that was the Byzantine army, but also about the interpenetration of civilian and military life?[5]

The Mirage of the Heroic General and the Trope of the Cautious Commander

What, then, would be the *qualities* expected of a Byzantine general? How are we to approach our sources and the portraits they paint of medieval Roman commanders? Is there a consistent set of attributes expected of leaders of martial men or do we see variation? We will see here that the answer to these questions is not straightforward. In some texts, to be sure, the heroic commander reigns supreme. Take for example this eleventh-century account:

> Michael filled that entire battlefield with the bodies of the slain, as no one struck by his hand was able to avert death. The foes kept coming against him in serried phalanxes, attempting to pierce his body from all sides with the tips of their swords, but none managed to unseat him from his horse, for he cut through their spears and pikes with his sword, throwing his enemies to the ground. Some lost their head and arm to a single one of his blows, others he cut in half, and some he cut into pieces, destroying and terrorizing them with a huge variety of wounds. But the Bulgarians, whose innumerable host could not be reduced to a mere number, surrounded him like the waters of a boundless sea and strove to drown him and

---

[4] In the modern era Samuel P. Huntington's 'control' theory, as articulated in his *The Soldier and the State* (1957), framed civil–military relations with an emphasis on the army's necessary 'apartness'. In 'Civilian Control of the Military: A Theoretical Statement' (1956) 380–1, Huntington described civil–military relations in the following manner: 'It is altogether mistaken to ask where the Army stands. The Army does what it is ordered to do, and that's all there is to it.' For a reaffirmation of the Huntington thesis, with a useful presentation of critical scholarship, see Travis (2017) 395–414; Kaegi (1981) 3–4 on the very same question with applications to Byzantium. It will emerge from this chapter that such notions of apartness are by no means applicable to the Byzantine era.

[5] The impact of ideas of military virtue and manliness on more general, society-wide models of masculinity – as presented by Stewart (2016b) 11–44 – is evidence of such interpenetration. For challenges to the idea that late antique Roman society became increasingly demilitarised, Stewart (2016b) 16–17.

drag him to the bottomless abyss, the blows from their spears and other weapons of war continuously assailing him like waves.[6]

This tableau of heroism and military virtue showcases highly individualistic martial behaviour and is not unlike Western European accounts of knightly deeds.[7] Drawn from Michael Attaleiates' *History*, it describes the warlike exploits of a Byzantine commander. A century later, another historian, Niketas Choniates, had the following to report on the battlefield activities of emperor Manuel I Komnenos (1143–1180):

> Then a certain Hungarian, a giant in size, with a manly and desperate courage, broke out of the crowd and challenged the emperor full force. The latter, standing his ground, plunged his sword into the giant's eye and killed him. Taking many captives, as well as much material wealth, the emperor returned to the queen of cities.[8]

Or on another occasion: 'The Emperor dashed two knights to the ground at the same time; brandishing his lance, he charged the one, and the force of the thrust threw both opponents down.'[9] Byzantine historical texts are by no means the sole purveyors of such passages. The *Epic of Digenis*, for one, to cite the famous twelfth-century example of high-octane heroics, offers rather similar examples of warrior élan, while panegyric poems and court rhetoric also focused on heroism as they built portraits of Roman virtue.[10] What, then, are we to make of such imagery? On each occasion the heroes were commanders of the empire's forces, whether actual or fictional. Manuel Komnenos, like for that matter his father John (1118–1143) and grandfather Alexios (1081–1118), was in fact what we would today call the commander-in-chief. Can we, however, treat such *exempla* of heroism as prescriptive? Did they amount to anything more than literary flourish?[11]

---

[6] Kaldellis and Krallis (2012) 420 for the Greek, 421 for the translation. Henceforth 'Attal.' will refer to the Greek text and translation by Kaldellis and Krallis.

[7] Haidu (2004) 41–7 for the Western medieval exaltation of high-octane, violent (and extortionate) heroism.

[8] Nik. Chon. *Historia*, Reign of Manuel Komnenos Book 2, ed. van Dieten (1975) 92.54–93.59, trans. Magoulias (1984) 54.

[9] Nik. Chon. *Historia*, Reign of Manuel Komnenos Book 3, ed. van Dieten (1975) 110.89–91, trans. Magoulias (1984) 62.

[10] Theodore Prodromos, *Historical Poems* 3–6 for the Komnenian martial élan as reflected in poems and panegyrics dedicated to John Komnenos.

[11] Neville (2012) for the heroic élan of the Komnenian aristocracy in both its Roman and Homeric dimensions; Magdalino (1993) 419–20 on the supercharged martial image of

Were we to base our views of Byzantine generalship on such accounts alone we would, indeed, be getting a partial story. For every reference to martial heroics in the sources there is one that focuses on prudence, caution, good planning and what François Jullien described as the oblique approach.[12] We thus read in the sixth-century *Strategikon* – a text often attributed to the emperor Maurice and read by erudite Byzantines in the ensuing centuries[13] – that 'the state benefits more from a lucky general than from a brave one. The first achieves his results with little effort, whereas the other does so with some risk.'[14] Furthermore, 'senior officers should be stationed in safe places, so that they do not dash forward and fall in battle',[15] while 'the general should not himself join the actual fighting'.[16] This emphasis on the vulnerability of the commander and the need to protect him is paired in the *Strategikon* with extensive references on planning and deliberation. We therefore read that: 'long and careful deliberation promises great safety in war, whereas hasty and impetuous generals usually commit serious blunders'.[17] Four and a half centuries later the leonine and, up to that point, wildly successful George Maniakes died on the front ranks of his rebel army, falling prey to a cautious, lucky eunuch, only to confirm the ancient maxim.[18] It is exactly the form of caution advocated by the

---

John Komnenos in panegyrics and orations of the twelfth century. Magdalino notes an emphasis on *andreia* over *phronesis*, a celebration of the spilling of enemy blood. That said, a broader question to consider might be this: is the martial commander – one who participates actively in warfare – the same as the rash, heroic commander, who rushes into battle, remaining in the thick of it? Is Scipio, as described by Polybius, 31.25, martial or heroic? Can we distinguish between the two? Eustathios of Thessalonike clearly did when he juxtaposed Alexander the Great's rash (and almost lethal) scaling of city walls to Manuel Komnenos' careful support of the scaling ladders, and guidance of his troops at the siege of Zeugminon, as we see in Eustathios of Thessalonike, *Orations*, ed. Wirth (1999) 267.

[12] Jullien (2004a); (2004b) for obliqueness and efficacy in Chinese thought, with reference to strategy and in comparison and sometimes juxtaposition with 'Western' modes of knowing and doing; Graff (2011/12) 157–8 for parallel readings of the development of Chinese and Byzantine tactics; Kaldellis (2017a) xxvii on Byzantium as a peaceful polity; Eustathios of Thessalonike, *Orations*, ed. Wirth (1999) 234 for a fascinating, idealised description of Asia Minor in the era before 1071, as a utopian realm of peace.

[13] On the reception of the *Strategikon*, see, for example, Pérez Martín (2002) liii discussing the case of Attaleiates. On the *Strategikon* see also the chapter by Philip Rance in this volume.

[14] *Strategikon* 7.2 Maxim 94, trans. Dennis (1984) 91.

[15] *Strategikon* 2.16, Dennis (1984) 32.

[16] *Strategikon* 7.B.1, Dennis (1984) 69.

[17] *Strategikon* 8.2 Maxim 68, Dennis (1984) 88.

[18] Attal. 30–1 for text and translation; Psellos, *Chronographia* 6.77 [Renauld v.2 2] Maniakes as lion and hurricane; 6.84–85 [Renauld v.2 5–6] for his end. See Andriollo (2017) 1–12 for the function of a heroic portrait in Byzantine politics.

Strategikon that brings us before yet another relic of both Byzantine and military studies, the association of decisive battle with the West and the concomitant identification of practices of oblique warfare with the East.[19]

How, then, do heroism and caution conspire to constitute Byzantine military virtue, and what may be the elements that tip the balance in favour of one or the other? That Byzantine tactical manuals drew from late antique models such as the *Strategikon* and the works of writers ranging from Aelian to Onasander is certainly not a novel observation, as becomes evident in the apparatus criticus and commentaries on the latest translation of Leo VI's tenth-century *Taktika*. Here I suggest that what is often treated as antiquarian borrowing, must be seen as evidence of continuities in military thinking that went past drills and battlefield mechanics to imbue society's and certainly the elite's conception of warfare and command of operations.[20] Such continuities must be followed through a variety of texts. In this chapter, tactical manuals, histories and rhetorical texts are used interchangeably, not out of disregard of meaningful generic distinctions, but rather because the appearance of similar attitudes, tropes and ideas across prescriptive, descriptive/analytical and idealist texts suggests that those very ideas had broader valence.

In recent years, innovative work began to re-evaluate the nature and ideological import of Roman institutions, traditions, modes of sociability and governance in Byzantium.[21] While Byzantine history is no longer treated as a cabinet of oriental curiosities and Voltairian abominations, only recently have medieval *Rhomaioi* started morphing on the pages of contemporary work into citizens of a living, changing and

---

[19] See Hanson (2009) for straight-up battle; Luttwak (2011) for obliqueness; for Leo VI's *Taktika* see Dennis (2010) and chapters by Rance and Shaun Tougher in this volume. On the oblique approach as discussed by Byzantine thinkers, see Leo VI, *Taktika* 12.108. For a Byzantine critique of this very approach see *Strategikon* 11.2. See Dennis (1984) 116, where Scythians are presented as people who 'prefer to prevail over their enemies not so much by force, as by deceit, surprise attacks, and cutting off supplies'.

[20] On a modern, utilitarian take on Byzantine antiquarianism, see Dickey (2017) 61–2 on classical texts as linguistic and rhetorical training fields for Byzantine bureaucrats. For the antiquarianism of the *Taktika* see Dennis (2010) ix: 'But the Byzantines were not interested in original compilations, they revered the antiquity of the ancient'; Haldon (2014a) 3 for a sceptical take on previous scholarship emphasising the antiquarian nature of Leo's *Taktika*.

[21] See Kaldellis (2015) for the nature of Byzantine politics and (2007) for Roman ethnicity; Kaldellis (2012) 387–404; Krallis (2018) 11–38 for Roman identity and political agency in Byzantium's rural areas; Stouraitis (2014) 175–220 seeking to counter Kaldellis on Roman political identity; Kaldellis (2017b) 173–210 for a convincing point-by-point response to Stouraitis' critique; Haldon (2015) for a critical eye on Kaldellis' positions on identity and ethnicity in Byzantium.

vibrant Roman polity.²² A community of Romans drawing on an ever-adapting body of Roman political traditions can be mapped on a Graeco-Roman literary production that challenges traditional modes of philological and literary periodisation.²³ It is no longer possible to treat the *Rhomaioi* as stale imitators of a past constructed through the distorting mirror of a literary tradition much copied and little understood.²⁴

The Problem of *tyche*

With this in mind, I approach the interplay of virtue, fortune and persuasion as they appear in writings about generalship. Put simply, in this chapter I suggest that the tactical manuals produced in Byzantium and the historical narratives of Byzantine historians converge in their accounts of well-conceived and well-executed military and political action. Such convergence was not, I think, unrelated to enduring Graeco-Roman conceptions of fortune and virtue.²⁵ But what did the resilience of such ideas across centuries, despite cultural transformations presumably brought forth by the advent of Christianity, actually mean for our understanding of the ways Byzantine commanders led their armies? In seeking to address this question, I open with the concept of fortune and lay out evidence for its continuous and rather streamlined use in the context of military thinking from antiquity to the Middle Ages. Then I discuss what, I think, are the implications of this continued deployment of *tyche* in Greek, Roman and Byzantine texts. Finally, in the second part of the chapter, I look at the demands that such a pragmatic deployment of *tyche* placed upon Byzantine conceptions of military virtue. In doing so I note that military and political virtue cannot easily be separated – yet another element of continuity from antiquity to the Byzantine Middle Ages. The army camp and the city may not, after all, be set against one another.

I open with the following passages on *tyche* as a way to introduce the problems associated with the use of this multivalent word. Two individuals are discussed here,

---

[22] Voltaire, *Le pyrrhonism de l'histoire*, chapter 15: *Des contes absurdes intitulés 'histoire' depuis tacite* = Moland (1879) 5.27, 264; Lecky (1886) 13–14 for a potent example of post-Enlightenment anti-Byzantinism.

[23] Kaldellis and Siniossoglou (2017), 23–4 on intellectual continuities spanning centuries and defying attempts at periodisation and historical contextualisation.

[24] Mango (1965) 29–43; (1975). Wilson (1983) 198 describes Eustathios of Thessalonike's access to lost texts and sensitivity to Homeric poetry, noting in characteristic Byzantinist tone: 'the first of these merits is not his own and the second may owe more to his sources than we are now able to discern. Taken together they cannot outweigh the fault of verbosity.'

[25] For a Byzantine historian's engagement with Polybius, see Krallis (2012) 52–69, 192–205.

Romanos IV Diogenes (1068–1071) and Nikephoros Botaneiates (1078–1081)), both army commanders and emperors of the eleventh century. Let us look at the passages in question from Michael Attaleiates' *History* in paratactic manner, beginning with the following lines:

> But one from among the nobility rose up . . . in order to raise up the fallen <u>fortunes</u> of the Romans, for the state was not being <u>governed rationally</u>.[26]

The term *tyche* marks here the state of the Roman polity, and its use helps the reader associate a well-run state with reasoned governance. Notably, Attaleiates also places this line of thinking in the mind of the *strategos* Romanos Diogenes, thus directly linking the realm of war with the Romans' well-being and their quest for peace and prosperity; a linkage we see clearly expressed a century later in a series of Eustathios of Thessalonike's orations to emperor Manuel Komnenos.[27]

In the next passage we move to the battlefield of Manzikert, where we see that:

> The enemy, who were stationed on the hills, saw the sudden mis<u>fortune</u> that befell the Romans, told the sultan what was going on, and insisted that he wheel about.[28]

On this occasion *mis*fortune is once again associated with someone's state of being. The *mis*fortune in question outlines a dangerous battlefield situation. The narrative in which this passage is couched leaves no doubt that the Romans' misfortune was purely the result of human actions. In short, fortune (*tyche*) had little to do with the Romans' misfortune (*atychema*). This line of thought may also be traced in the following snippet from Attaleiates, where we read that:

> to appoint <u>a man who, with</u> <u>judgment</u>, courage, love of honor, and a compassionate soul, <u>would</u> be able to topple the tyrants on the one hand and on the other to <u>return the fortunes of the Romans to a happier state</u>.[29]

---

[26] Attal. 176–7 for Greek text: ἀλλ' ὡς τὰς τύχας ἀνορθῶσαι τῶν ἤδη πεσόντων Ῥωμαίων, ὅτι μὴ κατὰ λόγον εἶχε τὰ πράγματα and for the translation cited here.

[27] Eustathios of Thessalonike, *Orations* 204: Manuel toils in order to bring peace to his subjects; 207 Eustathios takes his audience around the empire in all the areas where Manuel has toiled on behalf of his subjects; 216 Manuel 'laboured on our behalf'; 265 Manuel with outstretched arms protects the people; 289 Manuel toiling with myriad state concerns.

[28] Attal. 292–3 for the Greek with the translation cited above: Τῶν δ' ἐναντίων οἱ ἐπὶ λόφων ἱστάμενοι, τὸ τῶν Ῥωμαίων ἰδόντες ἐξαίφνης ἀτύχημα, τῷ σουλτάνῳ καταγγέλλουσι τὸ γενόμενον καὶ τὴν ἐπιστροφὴν αὐτῷ κατεπείγουσιν.

[29] Attal. 384–7 for the Greek: ἅμα δὲ καὶ τὰς τύχας τῶν Ῥωμαίων πρὸς τὸ εὐθυμότερον

The association of the well-being (the fortunes) of the Romans with judgement, in Attaleiates' discussion of Nikephoros Botaneiates, mirrors this author's excursus on the history of the Republic, where we read:

> Thus did the generals of old respect the future and its twists of fortune (*tychas*), and showed such great concern for their own country.[30]

Concern and care for one's country were what, according to the *History*, ancient generals showed when thinking about the twists of fortune that the future held for them.[31] In the eyes of Attaleiates' social and intellectual peers, the connection between politics and war was clear. Michael Psellos openly discussed the political role of the elected consuls in ancient Roman affairs, while Attaleiates himself explained that it was public opinion which brought Romanos Diogenes to power.[32] In our concluding *tyche*-related excerpt we turn to the *History*'s encomiastic remarks about Nikephoros Botaneiates, where Attaleiates notes that:

> The emperor was superior to everyone else at restoring fortunes, offering solace to those who had suffered misfortune, and bringing men who had lost their status back to the honor that befitted them and a level that suited their position.[33]

Once more *tyche* is deployed in a passage focused on the state of the Roman union. If we thus look at the passages cited here, we note a fascinating slippage in the use of the term that may also be found in other Byzantine sources: *tyche*, more often than not, bore a double meaning. At times it denoted fortune in the ancient sense of the word – a capricious and neutral force – yet it also rather often became a stand-in for the state of one's being: what we would translate as: 'my sort', or 'my lot'. Now this 'lot' could be good or bad, though histories and chronicles brimmed

---

ἐπαναγαγεῖν φρονήσει καὶ γενναιότητι καὶ φιλοτίμῳ καὶ φιλοίκτῳ ψυχῇ and for the translation cited here.

[30] Attal. 398–9: Οὕτως οἱ παλαιοὶ στρατηγοὶ τὰς τοῦ μέλλοντος εὐλαβοῦντο τύχας καὶ τοσαύτην φροντίδα ὑπὲρ τῆς σφῶν πατρίδος ἐτίθεντο and for the translation in the body of the text.

[31] Attal.. 352ff. for Greek and for the translation on the Romans of old.

[32] Attal. 184–5 for Greek and translation; Psellos, *Historia Syntomos* 11.20–4 on Roman consuls.

[33] Attal. 552–3 for the Greek: Ἄριστος ὢν ὁ βασιλεὺς εἴπερ τις ἕτερος τύχας ἀνορθῶσαι καὶ παρηγορίαν ἐμποιῆσαι τῷ δυστυχήματι καὶ ἀδοξήσαντας ἀνθρώπους εἰς εὐδοξίαν συμφέρουσαν καὶ πρόσφορον τῇ καταστάσει τούτων ἀνενεγκεῖν and the translation cited above.

with disasters and failure. Much of history writing, after all, was supposed to be didactic and recorded attempts, both successful and less so, to avoid mishaps.[34] The texts cited here, in particular, speak of a restoration of fortunes, suggesting that there was something to be restored. Thus even when *tyche* appears in its original meaning as personified uncertainty, it is nevertheless discussed alongside issues of leadership, which in war are often linked to questions of military virtue. As noted by Leo VI in the *Taktika*, a commander should always be mindful and prepare for 'the second fortune'.[35] In the passages cited here, supernatural causation may be paid lip service but is fundamentally inessential in Attaleiates' conception of history. Barring the occasional pious disclaimer, Byzantine historians preferred to focus on human actions, remaining very much in line with Polybius' dictum according to which the gods and gods' children do not belong in real history. The Megalopolitan also averred that only those historians who cannot trace a proper causal chain introduce into history gods and their offspring.[36] Byzantine historians appeared more or less to agree.

Authors of a pronounced Christian bent were naturally troubled by such secular readings of fortune. Some forty years ago, Glenn Chesnut showed how writers like the fifth-century church historian Socrates Christianised the pagan and in effect secular concept of *tyche* in their use of *kairos*.[37] Marginalia on the manuscripts of the *Wars* record a similar distaste among the pious for Procopius' deployment of *tyche*.[38] This tension is not limited to late antique writing and persists in the Middle Byzantine era, when the eleventh-century works of Psellos and Attaleiates are good examples of a long-standing practice that intentionally confuses fortune with the divine, thus eschewing potential critiques on the part of the pious.[39]

If, however, the Byzantine conception of *tyche*, of *kairos* and, in general, of history's curveballs presents us with evidence of continuities which span the porous boundaries that divide antiquity from the Middle Ages, then perhaps conceptions of virtue, both military and, I would argue, political need to be examined in the context of a similar longue durée.[40] How, then, does one best handle fortune and the

---

[34] Attal. 8–9 for text and translation of the proem.
[35] Leo VI, *Taktika* 13.7.
[36] Polyb. 3.47.8–9: θεοὺς καὶ θεῶν παῖδας εἰς πραγματικὴν ἱστορίαν παρεισάγουσιν.
[37] Chesnut (1975) 161–6.
[38] Kaldellis (2004) 174.
[39] Krallis (2012) 174–89 on causation in Attaleiates; Kaldellis (2017c) 1–22 for arguments that relate to causation, the divine and fortune.
[40] The study of the army's history in the longue durée is, in a manner of speaking, authorised by the works of Byzantinists, who have looked at this institution by using the widest of lenses. Haldon (1984); Kaegi (1981); Treadgold (1995). In recent years Kaldellis' work

instability inherent in human affairs?[41] As noted above, the tactical manuals make it clear that the front lines of an unstable battlefield, where even virtuous and truly brave men can succumb to the lucky strike of a barely trained opponent, were not the place for a commander to display virtue.[42] The affairs of the polity – because let us remember that war is not a good in and of itself; it is the deadly serious business of protecting the polity – those affairs then clearly called for more than raw courage and reckless fighting spirit. A closer study of not only those same tactical manuals but also the historical tradition with which they were in dialogue reveals one fascinating aspect of the commander's virtue: the ability to convince and be convinced by his subordinates.

The Army as a Community of Armed Romans

The subordinates in question were soldiers. Those soldiers were sometimes foreign mercenaries but, at least in the period before the Komnenoi, they were more often than not Romans with roots in the lands of Romania and families living in the territory they were called to defend.[43] In recent work, Haldon emphatically explained that 'provincial soldiers were conscious enough of matters that seemed to them relevant to their own situation and to that of the empire as a whole, to make their views known'.[44] In doing so, he highlighted the role of soldiers as bearers of political identities by explaining that men 'recruited from particular localities served in units based in the area and thus tended to share loyalties and political and other views'.[45] The tight relationship that these warriors developed with the broader community of the Romans may also be seen in the way in which commanders were supposed to raise their troops' morale, according to the *Strategikon*. Here the leader of the army is advised to speak to his men of victories by Roman units in far-off

---

on Roman identity and politics in the *Byzantine Republic* has sought wider vistas in its periodisation.
[41] Eustathios of Thessalonike discussed Alexios Komnenos' adaptive leadership in his 1179 Autumn Oration to Manuel Komnenos. Eustathios of Thessalonike, *Orations* 241–2 for Alexios as an effective manager of misfortune.
[42] On the place of the commander in the battlefield see nn 14–16 above.
[43] Haldon (2015) 150 on the autochthonous nature of Roman soldiers in the Middle Byzantine era; Kaegi (1981) 30 and throughout on the diverse political opinions held by different army units and their commanders.
[44] Haldon (2015) 151; Krallis (2018) 28ff. on the embedding of armies in Byzantium's rural world; Kaegi (1981) 34–5 on soldiers seeking to protect their distinct interest and express their political views.
[45] Haldon (2015) 149.

battlefields, however fictitious those may have been, in order to bolster their desire to engage the enemy. Far from being narrowly focused on regional self-interest, Roman armies were apparently able to imagine themselves members of a larger family that spanned the empire's lands.[46] This was also the message of Syrianos' treatise on military oratory, where we read that a commander would be able to rouse his soldiers by pointing out the bonds of ethnicity, homeland and religion that they all shared.[47]

This association of soldiers with the larger polity they defended has a long history in Roman texts, both ancient and medieval, and explains the image that emerges from them of the army commander as a man of politics, a Polybian *pragmatikos aner*, at ease among soldiers and civilians alike.[48] It is, after all, in the *Histories* where we first encounter a description of the Roman camp as a town: 'The entire camp thus forms a square, and the way in which the streets are laid out and its general arrangement give it the appearance of a town.'[49] On his part, Livy relates, by way of the celebrated second-century BC Roman general Aemilius Paullus' speechifying, that 'a camp is the shelter of the victor, the refuge of the vanquished . . . this dwelling is the soldier's second homeland; for each, the rampart serves as his city walls, and his tent is his hearth and home'.[50] According to Virgil, this city was itself modelled on an army camp, as Aeneas 'marks out the walls with a shallow trench and builds the place and girds the first home on the shore in the manner of the camps with battlements and a rampart'.[51] The Polybian image of the army as a *civitas* under arms endured among Roman thinkers. From the very opening of the Byzantine era, Vegetius in the late fourth or fifth century notes that the Romans 'seem to carry with them everywhere a walled city'.[52] Eight hundred years later, after the sack of Constantinople by the warriors of the Fourth Crusade in 1204, George Akropolites echoed Vegetius when he described Theodore Laskaris' 'habit to ride out around twilight and pass

---

[46] *Strategikon* 8.1.12, trans. Dennis (1984) 80.

[47] Eramo (2010) 47–51 [Book 9.1–Book 13]; Rance (2007b) 701–37 on the dating of the text to the ninth century.

[48] Polyb. 12.28.3–6 for a corollary to Polybius' man of action, the *pragmatike historia*, which only a *pragmatikos aner*, a man actively engaged in politics and war, can really write; Walbank (1972) 66–96 for a discussion of *pragmatike historia*.

[49] Polyb. 6.31.10.

[50] Livy 44.39.4–5, trans. Keitel (2012) 42. In this piece Elizabeth Keitel notes that the parallel between camps and cities that may be followed in passages in Virgil's *Aeneid*, and Livy could be seen as a way to emphasise the importance of civil strife and the blending of violence and politics.

[51] Virgil, *Aen.* 7.157–159, trans. Keitel (2012) 41.

[52] Veg. *Mil.* 1.21.2.

through the entire camp and to go up and survey the whole army – which he used to call a city on the move'.[53]

Given this bleeding of civilian language into military parlance and vice versa, it is not surprising that we find ample material on the political predilections of medieval Roman soldiery. In the *Strategikon*'s discussion of foreign nations, their customs and way of life, the author presents the empire's enemies as photonegatives of the Roman political community.[54] What, then, can we glean about the Romans and their soldiers as politically conscious individuals from the following lines?

> These nations have a monarchical form of government and their rulers subject them to cruel punishments for their mistakes. Governed not by love but by fear, they steadfastly bear labors and hardships.[55]

How were Romans to interpret such ethnographic emphasis on cruel monarchy? Were the Romans not members of a monarchic polity? What does such a statement tell us about the world view of the soldiers whom commanders led to battle? The advice that the author of the *Strategikon* offers to Roman generals suggests a possible answer to this question. In discussing the general's management of his soldiers, the sixth-century writer notes that, unlike Scythian leaders, commanders should be just and 'even-tempered',[56] as punishment that is understood to be proportionate to the crime, 'for reasonable men, is not punishment but correction'.[57]

Roman campaign armies were therefore not constituted of bloodthirsty, burly, brave men – though many such men surely served under Roman pennons – but of reasoning individuals, who had to be treated with justice and managed through the appointment of 'intelligent and competent officers . . . over them'.[58] Reasoning and intelligence are also emphasised when the author of the *Strategikon* explains why battle should not be sought too soon after the army's defeat at the hands of the enemy.[59] We thus read that: 'soldiers as a whole, are unable to grasp the reason

---

[53] George Akropolites, *History* 63, trans. Macrides (2007) 305.
[54] See Kaldellis (2013) 82–7 on ethnography in Maurice and Leo VI's work.
[55] *Strategikon* 11.2, trans. Dennis (1984) 116.
[56] *Strategikon* Proem, Dennis (1984) 9.
[57] *Strategikon* Proem, Dennis (1984) 10.
[58] *Strategikon* 1.4, Dennis (1984) 16.
[59] Such deliberation was essential as ancient armies often balked in the face of battle. Reticence would often express itself in pre-battle or mid-campaign 'strikes', described as mutinies by some scholars. On this, see Carney (1996) 19–20 for a critical stance on the use of the term 'mutiny' that seems to recognise the need of ancient commanders to take soldiers' concerns seriously.

for deliberately going back into fighting'.[60] It is for this that our strategist suggests that the general should 'display a fatherly affection towards them' and 'always make sure to give advice and discuss essential matters with them in person'. This would at times entail a certain degree of fraternising, as seen in Herodian, who notes that Maximinus Thrax (235–238) 'did not confine himself only to teaching them what to do but also took the lead in all the tasks'. So much so that Maximinus was considered a fellow soldier (συστρατιώτης) and a camp mate (σύσκηνος).[61] Either way, whether through fatherly affection or instruction and even fraternising and the sharing of soldierly burdens, the general proved successful when 'his men regard him as unshakeable and just'.[62]

It is with this in mind that rebels like Thomas the so-called Slav (ninth century) were at times forced to adjust their campaign goals to the demands and expectations of their Roman soldiers.[63] The Continuator of Theophanes in fact notes the impact of battle fatigue and concerns about the well-being of their families on army morale. Skylitzes, on the other hand, explains that a rebel's forces could in fact tire of fighting fellow Romans.[64] Those very same soldiers could engage in deeply political discourse at the most inconvenient of times. In August 1057 by the city of Nicaea in Bithynia two armies prepared for battle. The first was loyal to emperor Michael VI Stratiotikos (1056–1057) and the second to Isaac Komnenos. Before the chaos of battle erupted, however, the troops of the opposing armies met in the fields and debated politics, seeking to convince their fellow Romans.[65]

Skylitzes describes those informal discussions as civil and peaceful.[66] They were, nevertheless, a threat to the two commanders' grip over their armies. Maintaining control of their forces demanded clear demarcating lines, respect for the chain of command and a clear desire to fight for the ultimate goal. To once more harden opinion, the commanders needed to convince their soldiers of the desirability of war. Skylitzes tells us that both commanders dispatched eloquent men who deployed rhetoric to convince their soldiers that fratricidal bloodletting was in effect the way forward. What we note in stories such as this is the importance of debate and persuasion in the eyes of Byzantine commanders and writers. The business of war was not

---

[60] *Strategikon* 7.11, Dennis (1984) 72.
[61] Herodian, 6.8.2, 6.8.4.
[62] *Strategikon* 8.1, Dennis (1984) 79.
[63] Theophanes Continuatus 2.18; Skylitzes, *Synopsis Historion*, Reign of Michael II, 12, ed. Thurn (1973) 39.26–8.
[64] Skylitzes, *Synopsis Historion*, Reign of Michael II, 12, ed. Thurn (1973) 39.
[65] Skylitzes, *Synopsis Historion*, Reign of Michael VI, 9, ed. Thurn (1973) 493–4.
[66] An ancient Roman equivalent may be found in Caesar's *B. Civ.* 1.74.4, where soldiers in the Caesarean and Pompeian armies fraternise before their respective army camps.

simply the purview of burly men with a desire to kill – it was a process of negotiation and debate that put on display the intensely political nature of the Roman polity.

The General as Orator and Manager

Such debate could best be won through effective rhetoric. This, some Byzantines argued, was already well known in the time of Homer, who spoke of Achilles' rage but also of his eloquence, the gift of his teachers Chiron, Peleus and Phoenix.[67] The Byzantines were clearly aware of such connections and often cast the general as an orator in their writings. This is seen early in the pages of Leo VI's *Taktika* where we read that 'to be capable in speaking and in addressing a crowd, is, I think, of the greatest benefit to the army'.[68] We can trace the more proximate Roman roots of Leo's thinking in Syrianos' ninth-century *Rhetorica Militaris*. In this work we read that the general must be an effective orator, who should be able to bolster his soldiers' morale before battle.[69] The Continuator of Theophanes in the tenth century set deliberation and debate at the very centre of a series of battlefield scenes from the ninth century. In his account of the reign of Theophilos (829–842), we thus read that while campaigning in Asia Minor, the emperor found himself on a tight spot. His reaction was not Herculean heroics. He did not, like George Maniakes, Romanos Diogenes and Manuel Komnenos, rush to the front lines to rally the troops. Rather he invited his commanders to the imperial tent for deliberation on the action to be followed.[70] Our source explains that in the course of the ensuing meeting distinct opinions were heard and debated.[71] A few years later, Theophilos' son Michael III (842–867) finds himself in similar dire straits and, this time, *demands* that his commanders speak up.[72] We may ponder the reasons behind such imperial practice. Was it that the emperor did not know what to do in a time of crisis? Was this form of consultation normal deference to real military expertise? Or was it perhaps something much more political in nature? Do we in fact see here the emperor

---

[67] Hunter (2017) 28 citing Eustathios of Thessalonike, *in Il.* 1362.46.
[68] *Taktika* 2.12.
[69] Eramo (2010) 37 [Book 1.1]. It would not be fruitful to plunge into the debate on the place of speeches in the battlefield. For a summation of the arguments regarding the audibility of battlefield orations see Anson (2010) 304–18; for doubts as to the veracity of speech accounts see Hansen (1993) 161–80.
[70] See Constantine VII, *On What Should Be Observed When the Great and High Emperor of the Romans Goes on Campaign*, Haldon (1990) 104 (Text C, lines 164–77), for a space clearly designed for entertaining the numerous people who would attend a *consilium*.
[71] Theophanes Continuatus 3.31.
[72] Theophanes Continuatus 4.24.

sharing with his commanders the responsibility for the chosen course of action by democratising the means by which decisions were to be made? Either way, what is described in these passages is not dissimilar to what we read in Michael Attaleiates' account of Romanos Diogenes' 1069 campaign in Asia Minor. On this occasion the emperor asked members of his army staff and the attending army judges for their opinion regarding the year's campaign. Attaleiates describes the scene thus:

> The other judges . . . all approved the decision, which had been made, whereas I alone stood there in silence. The emperor, carefully observing how quiet I was, demanded that I speak and asked me for my view about these matters. At first I dissimulated by appearing unable to say anything that would differ from the majority opinion or to prevail over that opinion, even if I were to attempt it; in any case, I would surely be overturned as the vote of the majority always prevails. Persistently and without relenting the emperor kept urging me to say what I thought without fear, calling on God as my witness. Changing my stance, I immediately made it clear right from the outset that this plan did not please me.[73]

This account, more detailed than that of the Continuator, places emphasis on deliberative processes, consensus building, discourse and persuasion. Romanos' tent – and we must remember that Romanos was emperor – is not a place where imperial power is celebrated. It is rather a miniature assembly open to debate. While it is tempting to treat Attaleiates' vignette as a self-serving set piece, it is important to note that such deliberations had ample precedent, as seen in Procopius' numerous accounts of debate and speech-giving among the armies of Belisarius. Most importantly, deliberation was in fact mandated by the military manuals, which on different occasions demand that the commander of the army assemble his staff and listen to expert opinion. In that, the manuals do not seem to stray far from what we read about battlefield deliberation and speeches in the work of Caesar. Scholars in fact note that though Caesar did not openly distinguish phases of deliberation and debate in his narrative, his reader may follow such processes in his presentation of the army's preparation for battle.[74] First, before deploying the battle line, he summoned a council[75] or even an assembly.[76] Then, once the line had been formed he moved up and down it

---

[73] Attal. 236–7 for text and translation.
[74] Anson (2010) 315–16.
[75] *B. Gall.* 1.40; 3.3; 5.28.2–30.3; 6.7.4, 8; 7.60.1; *B. Civ.* 1.19.1; 1.67.1; 1.73.1; 1.78.2; 2.30.1–31.8; 2.38.1; 3.86.1–87.7.
[76] *B. Gall.* 5.49.4; 6.8.3–4; 7.40.4; 7.52.1–53.1; *B. Civ.* 1.7; 1.19.1; 1.20.1–3; 2.32; 3.6.1; 3.41.5; 3.73.2–6; 3.76.2; 3.80.6; 3.82.1; 3.84.1; 3.85.4.

exhorting his troops unit by unit.[77] Caesar's council was rooted in ancient Roman military tradition.[78] According to Rosemary Moore:

> The *consilium* was a meeting of officers, often including centurions, led by the commander. Doubtless its exact character changed depending on the commander, but in Caesar's commentaries it conveyed command decisions, and, more importantly, an opportunity to deliberate the best plan of action. In this way a relatively inexperienced commander could draw on the collective experience of his subordinates.[79]

It was also a way for the commander, himself a man with roots among the Roman elite, to consult his upper-class tribunes and, in doing so, draw them into the process of decision making.[80] Processes of consensus building, so essential in Roman politics, were thus replicated in the *consilium*.[81] Despite fundamental changes in the governing practices of the Roman polity, from the age of Caesar to that of Romanos Diogenes, Byzantine historiography and military manuals appear to keep this very same tradition alive.

Byzantine generalship, as envisaged by both historians (ancient and medieval) and tactical writers, was a process whereby *tyche* was managed from the sidelines. Here the general is not the Homeric warrior of the passage of Attaleiates provided near the beginning of this chapter but rather an observer and planner, positioned in a protected segment of the army formation. But before one can even appropriately plan a course of action, processes of deliberation had to be undertaken, through which buy-in was achieved. Here lay an opportunity to draw officers and their soldiers into the logic of a proposed plan. The *Strategikon* suggests that the commander 'should deliberate about his most serious problems and carry out what was decided with as

---

[77] *B. Gall.* 2.21.1–4; 2.25.1; 7.17.4; *B. Civ.* 1.76.1; 2.41.2.
[78] How ancient, is of course debatable. Moore (2013) 463 notes that similar processes of advice procurement and discussion emerged in the time of Philip II of Macedon and Alexander the Great, as their armies developed into complex fighting machines made of distinct fighting units with different competences and roles on the battlefield. If that had indeed been the origin of deliberative processes in the army and not some transference of urban assembly politics in the realm of war, then *consilia* would probably have emerged at the time of the Punic Wars, when Rome for the first time had to conduct complex enough operations to require such coordination among the officer class.
[79] Moore (2013) 468.
[80] Such 'drawing in' of the officer corps and soldiers was essential given that victory often relied on counterintuitive *mechanemata* (tricks and stratagems), as explained by Eramo (2016) 81–91.
[81] Ando (2010) 202ff. for ideas of consensus, with emphasis on the monarchic uses of consensus.

little delay and risk as possible'.[82] In fact 'for what should be done [he should] seek the advice of many'.[83] Furthermore, 'discuss essential matters' with the soldiers 'in person', since they are, after all, rational beings open to persuasion.[84] This is how Leo VI describes such processes in the *Taktika*:

> You should not only at other times, but also in that hour when combat is imminent, not neglect to enter into consultation. Especially at that time, call together the tourmarchs under your command and anyone else you regard as shrewd and thoughtful and seek advice on what ought to be done at that time. In this way you must make your plans regarding battle.[85]

The reason for such deliberations is given in another section of the *Taktika*, where Leo explains that the high-ranking and other officers participating in such meetings should 'somehow share in [the commander's] decision'. He also explains: 'one man ... should certainly not limit himself to his own opinion' and concludes that a 'decision that has the additional testimony of many others is reliable and may be presented without uncertainty'.[86]

This is well illustrated in a telling piece from Procopius' *Wars*. In Book 3.15.18–19, Belisarius addresses the officers under his command at the tail end of a meeting where decisions were to be made in anticipation of disembarkation in Africa. Having listened to the various arguments presented by his subordinates, Belisarius, about whom Procopius specifically notes that he had been granted emperor-like authority for the campaign in question,[87] addresses the following words to his peers:

> Let no one of you, fellow officers, think that my words are those of an arbiter, nor that they are spoken last so that it becomes necessary for all to obey them, whatever they may be. I have heard what seems best to each of you. It is now proper for me also to lay before you what I think so that we can jointly chose the better course.[88]

Belisarius' subordinates are fellow officers and their opinions are appropriately heard, as the assembly of officers together comes to the best possible decision for the army. Similar processes of deliberation are on display in other parts of Procopius'

---

[82] *Strategikon* Proem, Dennis (1984) 9. Similarly in Leo VI, *Taktika* 3.1.
[83] *Strategikon* 8B Maxim 23, Dennis (1984) 85.
[84] *Strategikon* 8A Maxim 1, Dennis (1984) 79.
[85] *Taktika* 13.9.
[86] *Taktika* 4.4.
[87] *Wars* 3.11.20, Kaldellis (2014) 170.
[88] Kaldellis (2014) 177.

work. In Book 2.19.6, Belisarius assembles his officers and lays out his vision of what should happen. Right in the middle of his speech he notes: 'stupid daring leads to destruction, but discreet hesitation always saves those who adhere to it'.[89] The very notion of rash heroism is challenged in his exhortation to the army's ranking officers. At the end of the event, after everyone felt that what Belisarius said was well spoken, they proceeded to directly implement his plan. During the same campaign, when things fail to turn out as Belisarius would have wanted due to the actions of a Roman ally, a new meeting is called where Belisarius' arguments are picked apart by opposing members of the commander's council. Here John and Nicetas outlined a different vision of the campaign and won over other officers and the army, who became vocal, demanding that new marching orders be issued. Under the circumstances, the generalissimo could not but assent.

Theophylact Simocatta presents an argument, not dissimilar from Belisarius', in his discussion of a pre-battle muster that took place somewhere in the Balkans late in the sixth century. Here we encounter Comentiolus, who is preparing the army under his command for battle. In the *History* we therefore read: 'On the following day he gathered the cavalry and infantry, summoned an assembly, and exhorted the meeting not to show their backs to the barbarians, but to place everything second to courage.' Comentiolus' pep talk to the rank and file did not remain unchallenged. It was countered by one of the army tribunes, who stood up in the middle of the assembly and remarked: 'However much cowardice is reproached, recklessness in contrast is equally reprehensible. Hesitation is the most exalted mark of intellect, when it does not shame good counsel but puts prudence in good order.' The tribune then noted that the soldiers should question the commander's sway over them, suggesting that his trustworthiness unduly influenced their understanding of the situation. He explained: 'trustworthiness is an autocratic quality', which 'steers its audience exactly where it wishes'. Continuing along those lines, he averred that the soldiers should consider the tactical situation, since 'events are not the slaves of panegyrics'.[90] The debate went on and Theophylact makes it clear to the reader that he did not appreciate the tribune's line of argument, much as it was fully in line with the diktats of the *Strategikon*. The affair was settled when a veteran soldier raised his voice, asked for permission to speak, and offered a rebuttal that opened with the following lines:

> Did you realize that you were pouring forth disgraceful words in the presence of men? Or do you not see an assembly of Roman people, proud of their zeal, vigorous

---

[89] As also seen in *Strategikon* 8 Maxim 68, Dennis (1984) 88.
[90] Theophylact Simocatta 2.12.11–2.13.8 for this set of arguments, trans. Whitby and Whitby (1988) 61. Whitby translates ἀξιοπιστία as trustworthiness: 2.13.4–5.

in arms, knowledgeable in their experience of danger and providence for future advantage?[91]

This is not the end of the veteran's argument but makes a good starting point for us to consider this late antique debate. Beginning from the very end, we note that the pre-battle speeches and consultation described by Theophylact point towards something larger than a regular *consilium*. The author casts the event in political terms by having a veteran address his fellow soldiers as an assembly of Romans. In that context all earlier discussion of persuasion, debate and rhetoric is imbued with distinctly political hues. When set against the veteran's guts-and-glory push for action, the tribune's speech reads like a clear call for careful examination of facts, prudent deliberation and cautious action. To his mind the commander, Comentiolus, had abused two essential elements of his authority. First he deployed rhetoric to twist facts – 'events are not the slaves of panegyrics', the tribune notes. Then the commander proceeded to bolster his rhetoric with 'trustworthiness', which he had no doubt built over years of campaigning with his soldiers. In either case, in the tribune's eyes, the commander had used oratory and charisma to appeal to emotion rather than reason. The tribune therefore called upon the assembled soldiers to use reason and reject their commander's orders. Set in a martial context, this is no casual military debate. It is rather a discussion of truth, emotion, fortune and expedience that would not have been out of place in a Platonic dialogue about a sophist's twisting of reality.

For all that Theophylact openly sides with the grizzled veteran and his brave call for battle, we nevertheless have every reason to suspect that he cast a sceptical eye upon battlefield oratory, debates, and their combined effects on decision making and the performance of Roman arms. The same army, stirred into action by the veteran's speech, bungles its attack on the Avar horde on the very next page.[92] And yet, even though the deliberative process failed to produce positive battlefield results on this one occasion, Roman armies remained spaces of discussion and debate well into the so-called Dark Ages and the Middle Byzantine era. So much so that when in the *History* Michael Attaleiates composed the portrait of an eleventh-century aristocratic warrior, he reminded his readers of the intricate link between the political and military realms and offered a compelling image of affable urbanity:

No one ever saw Michael Botaneiates behave arrogantly towards another citizen, look down his nose at anyone, remain aloof from the normal company and gath-

---

[91] Theophylact Simocatta 2.13.15–2.14.3, Whitby and Whitby (1988) 62–3.
[92] Theophylact Simocatta 2.15.3–13, Whitby and Whitby (1988) 64–5.

erings of the citizens, or lack urbanity, a noble bearing, a calm demeanor, and the gracious smile that was part of his nature. Thus he was regarded by all people as a great marvel, worthy of adoration, for inasmuch as he was invincible, spirited, and stunning in his momentum when it came to military contests, so much more was he pleasant, gentle, and affectionate towards the people of Byzantion in times of leisure, when he was, as they say, 'off duty', and spent time in the Imperial City. He liked urbane conversation, made friends with those who had a sense of humor, and thought it unworthy to be addressed by any name other than the one he derived from the City. It is for this reason that he was exceedingly loved by everyone and was both called and known to be a benefit for all, a feast of all good things and an object of universal praise, an incomparable soldier and inimitable citizen.[93]

It was in the city, the place of easy sociability and deliberation, that the commander developed those skills essential for running the army.[94] Even Achilles, as we saw, built his power of persuasion in peacetime under the tutelage of Chiron, Peleus and Phoenix. Those very skills, normally associated with urban life, are therefore deployed at numerous moments of deliberation and planning in the army camp. The Continuator of Theophanes in fact notes that affability and humour were virtues that endeared a commander to his soldiers.[95] Deliberation and planning aimed at minimising the impact of the unexpected on the outcome of battle, through the familiarisation of all parties involved with the proposed course of action. In a way, then, the Byzantine commander was very much the consummate *pragmatikos aner*, the man of action of Polybius' political philosophy, a manager of people and fortune, a rational agent rather at odds with the images of chaotic, violent exuberance cited at the opening of this chapter.

The city itself, however, sometimes became a battlefield, as in the case of sieges. In that context, civic and army politics merged into one. A fascinating set of vignettes that put into stark relief our discussion of the commander's political virtue may be found in Eustathios' account of the sack of Thessalonike. His portrait of David Komnenos qualifies as a photonegative of all that has been related in the *Strategikon* and in the work of historians like Attaleiates on the matter of the commander's political virtue. We therefore read that:

---

[93] Attal. 428–31 for Greek text and translation; A bit more than two centuries later, George of Cyprus cast Michael Palaiologos as a balanced mix of martial vigour, heroism, reasoned planning and consultative decision-making skills: *PG* 142, col. 362.
[94] Krallis (2017b) for the urbane general.
[95] Theophanes Continuatus 2.11.

If anyone found that anything else needful was lacking and told him of it, then this man of silence became a voice to be heard afar, and he threatened beatings, decapitations, blindings and impalements if they did not cease their chattering . . . One man indeed, who was by no means a commoner, had his head broken after being struck about the face with a staff, because he complained about the unsatisfactory manner in which the defense was being conducted; and none of the onlookers dared say a word. The soldiers, although they were accustomed to frank and open speech, heard only one thing . . .: that when they had been assigned to a position, they must confine their exertions to that point alone and pay no attention to events elsewhere, unless they wished to suffer for it.[96]

This passage reveals a number of unspoken Byzantine assumptions about the management and waging of war. David Komnenos, the man responsible for the defence of the empire's second-largest city, is not an isolated figure at the top of a military hierarchy. He is accessible and the men under him assume that they *must* approach him with important information regarding the siege. Furthermore, his outbursts of violence towards those very men are seen as aberrant. They also appear to take place before others, suggesting a broader audience for the commander's meetings with his staff. More importantly, the idea that a commander would not be open to critique and advice is clearly marked as outrageous. Eustathios notes that 'the soldiers . . . were accustomed to frank and open speech', so much so that they were shocked by David Komnenos' violent reactions to their customary frankness. The commander, whom Eustathios charges with treason for his dereliction of proper supervisory duties, is a photonegative not only of both the urbane Botaneiates, who charmed soldiers and civilians alike, but also of emperors Theophilos, Michael III and Romanos Diogenes, who sought, demanded even, advice from their officers.[97]

With this focus on proper deliberation as a means by which to manage fortune, we pick up the thread of recent analysis that has sought to redefine the Byzantine polity along Graeco-Roman and even Republican lines.[98] The army and its commanders, not only in the work of the historians but also in the tactical manuals, are not a fighting Jerusalem but rather the armed version of the politically active community of Romans.[99] Much as Constantinople and its monumental landscape were the

---

[96] Eustathios of Thessalonike, *The Capture of Thessalonike*, ed. and trans. Melville-Jones (2017) 76.5–14, 77.
[97] Eustathios of Thessalonike, *The Capture of Thessalonike*, Melville-Jones (2017) 74.26–8.
[98] Kaldellis (2015); Krallis (2017a) 421–50; (2018) 11–38.
[99] Theophanes, *Chronographia* AM 6114, trans. Mango and Scott (1997) 439, on an image of the army as a congregation around its priest; Stouraitis (2011) 13–14 for bibliography that covers the discussion regarding Byzantine approaches to holy war. Also Stouraitis (2011)

stage on which an emperor sought to convince his people of the soundness of his policies, remaining under constant scrutiny for the length of his reign, so was the camp a space for deliberation (*boulē*) – which Leo's *Taktika* defines as 'consultation on what is to be done or not to be done' – about the better management of fortune's challenges.[100] In the context of such analysis, the Christian verbiage of military manuals and historical narratives must be treated much as Polybius treated calls for piety among the Romans: as utilitarian ceremony geared towards the cohesion of the *res publica*.[101]

We may therefore return to the earlier passage from Attaleiates according to which Romanos' task was to 'return the fortunes of the Romans to a happier state'.[102] Romanos sought to take hold of Roman affairs so that their fortunes – their state of being – would improve. His intervention in Roman politics was not linked to his piety or even his *tyche* (fortune). He expected to achieve his goals through dedication and bravery, but also through meticulous planning and deliberation. His task was therefore by any account eminently political. In the end, as Attaleiates notes, his defeat – the result of in-battle treason on the part of a prominent Roman commander – was also the result of politics. Clearly some among the Roman camp were not thrilled with the way Romanos' management of Roman fortunes was bound to affect their own.[103] Romanos predated Clausewitz, so could not benefit from the latter's insights, yet should not have been too surprised by the turn of events. In the end, the politics of war was very much an extension of Roman politics.

---

22 for the religious overlay upon secular state concerns: 'the religious element in Byzantine warfare functions as an ideological amplifier of the ethical legitimation of an ideologically "restrained war action" that was motivated and justified by a rational cause, with rational goals thus assimilating to the life-affirming character of modern "just war" conceptions'.

[100] *Taktika* 3.2.

[101] Krallis (2012) 199–205 on the political expediency behind proper religious observance; Polyb. 3.112–6–9 on Roman care for proper religious practice; 6.4.5 on how the ideal political system, whichever its form, is grounded in respect for custom and the gods; 21.13.10–13 on Scipio Africanus' meticulous performance of religious rite; Ando (2008) 1–18 on religious orthopraxy; Whittow (1996) 47 for Christianity as a 'useful morale booster', but one element in a complex Roman identity.

[102] Attal. 386–7 for the Greek: ἅμα δὲ καὶ τὰς τύχας τῶν Ῥωμαίων πρὸς τὸ εὐθυμότερον ἐπαναγαγεῖν φρονήσει καὶ γενναιότητι καὶ φιλοτίμῳ καὶ φιλοίκτῳ ψυχῇ, and for a translation.

[103] Attal. 292–3 for Greek text with translation.

Epilogue

Richard Evans and Shaun Tougher

There are many examples of good and poor generalship in antiquity and a relatively large corpus of literary evidence to show how the art of this leadership role evolved. In this volume a small but representative snapshot of these military leaders, their campaigns and their successes and failures has been presented, as have the works of poets, philosophers, historians and other writers who both commented on the conduct of military leadership and brought into existence its theoretical principles.

Arrian's summary of Alexander the Great's character and abilities suitably closes his history of the Macedonian king's campaigns in Asia. This eulogy serves as an appropriate conclusion, for it is not just a verdict on Alexander but a template for all for the art of generalship.

> In appearance Alexander was particularly handsome, extremely diligent, very clever and brave; and passionate in the pursuit not only of honours but also of dangers, and highly sensitive about religious matters. While he exercised great self-control when it came to bodily pleasures, when it came to those of the mind he was singularly voracious. He possessed a remarkable understanding for the correct course to take even when it was otherwise uncertain, and when all became clear most successful in his reckoning of the likelihoods. He was extremely astute in the organisation, equipping and arming of an army, in encouraging his soldiers to be positive and removing any fears they may have had because Alexander himself had no fears.[1]

---

[1] Arrian 7.28.1–2, adapted from Iliff Robson (1933) 297. See also de Sélincourt and Hamilton (1971) 395–6; Brunt (1983) 297–9.

Bibliography

Acton–Creighton Correspondence 1887. 'Letter I: Cannes, 5 April 1887.' https://oll.libertyfund.org/titles/2254.
Adcock, F. E. 1957. *The Greek and Macedonian Art of War*. Berkeley.
Aerts, W. J. 1990. *Michaelis Pselli Historia Syntomos*. Berlin.
Ahl, M. F. 1976. *Lucan, An Introduction*. Ithaca. 1976.
Ahrweiler, H. 1967. 'Un discours inédit de Constantin VII Porphyrogénète.' *TM* 2, 393–404.
Allen-Hornblower, E. 2014. 'Beasts and Barbarians in Caesar's *Bellum Gallicum* 6.21–8.' *CQ* 64, 682–93.
Ambaglio, D. 1981. 'Il trattato "Sul comandante" di Onasandro.' *Athenaeum* 59, 353–77.
Anagnostakis, I. 2014. 'Procopius's Dream Before the Campaign Against Libya: A Reading of *Wars* 3.12.1–5.' In C. Angelidi and G. Calofonos (eds) *Dreaming in Byzantium and Beyond*. Burlington. 79–94.
Anderson, C. A. 2008. 'Archilochus, his Lost Shield, and the Heroic Ideal.' *Phoenix* 62, 255–60.
Ando, C. 2008. 'Religion, Law, and Knowledge in Classical Rome.' In C. Ando (ed.) *The Matter of the Gods: Religion and the Roman Empire*. Berkeley. 1–18.
Ando, C. 2010. '"A Dwelling beyond Violence": On the Uses and Disadvantages of History for Contemporary Republicans.' *History of Political Thought* 31, 183–220.
Andrewes, A. 1961. 'Phratries in Homer.' *Hermes* 89, 129–40.
Andrewes, A. 1982. 'The Growth of the Athenian State.' In J. Boardman and N. G. L. Hammond (eds) *The Cambridge Ancient History*. Vol. 3. Cambridge. 360–91.
Andrews, T. 2013. 'Identity, Philosophy, and the Problem of Armenian History in

the Sixth Century.' In P. Wood (ed.) *History and Identity in the Late Antique Near East*. Oxford. 29–41.

Andriollo, L. 2017. 'Le charme du rebelle malheureux: Georges Maniakès dans les sources grecques du XIe siècle.' In B. Caseau, V. Prigent and A. Sopracasa (eds) *Οὗ δῶρόν εἰμι τὰς γραφὰς βλέπων νόει: Mélanges Jean-Claude Cheynet* [*TM* 21.1]. Paris. 1–12.

Angelidi, C. 2013. 'Basile Lacapène: "Deux ou trois choses que je sais de lui".' In C. Gastgeber et al. (eds) *Pour l'amour de Byzance: Hommage à Paolo Odorico*. Frankfurt. 11–26.

Anson, E. 2010. 'The General's Pre-Battle Exhortation in Graeco-Roman Warfare.' *G&R* 57, 304–318.

Antonopoulou, I. 1994. 'Les manuels militaires byzantins: La version byzantine d'un "chef romain".' *Byzantiaka* 14, 95–105.

Antonopoulou, T. 2017. 'Emperor Leo VI the Wise and the "First Byzantine Humanism": On the Quest for Renovation and Cultural Syntheses.' *TM* 21, 187–233.

Aperghis, G. G. 2004. *The Seleukid Royal Economy: The Finances and Financial Administration of the Seleukid Empire*. Cambridge.

Arrington, N. T. 2015. *Ashes, Images, and Memories: The Presence of the War Dead in Fifth-Century Athens*. Oxford.

Arya, D. A. 2002. *The Goddess Fortuna in Imperial Rome: Cult, Art, Text*. Austin.

Ash, R. 2006. *Tacitus*. London.

Ashby Jr, T. 1901. 'Recent Excavations in Rome.' *CR* 15, 328–30.

Astin, A. E. 1967. *Scipio Aemilianus*. Oxford.

Astin, A. E. 1978. *Cato the Censor*. Oxford.

Atack, C. 2018. 'Plato's *Statesman* and Xenophon's Cyrus.' In G. Danzig, D. Johnson and D. Morrison (eds) *Plato and Xenophon: Comparative Studies*. Leiden. 510–43.

Austin, N. J. E. 1979. *Ammianus on Warfare*. Brussels.

Baca-Winters, K. 2018. *Xusro Parvez, King of Kings of the Sasanian Empire (570–628 CE)*. Piscataway.

Baltrusch, E. 2012. 'P. Quinctilius Varus und die *Bella Variana*.' In E. Baltrusch, M. Hegewisch, M. Meyer, U. Puschner and C. Wendt (eds) *2000 Jahre Varusschlacht: Geschichte – Archäologie – Legenden*. Berlin. 117–34.

Barker, E. T. E. and J. P. Christensen 2005. 'Flight Club: The New Archilochus Fragment and its Resonance with Homeric Epic.' *MD* 57, 9–41.

Bar-Kochva, B. 1976. *The Seleucid Army*. Oxford.

Barnes, T. D. 1998. *Ammianus Marcellinus and the Representation of Historical Reality*. Ithaca.

Barral, P.-E. 2010. *Onosander: Le général d'armée: Introduction, traduction, commentaireii*. PhD thesis, Paris EPHE.

Bayer, E. 1947. 'Onasandros: Die Entstehungszeit des *Strategikos*.' *WJA* 2, 86–90.

Beck, H. 2009. *Karriere und Hierarchie: Die römische Aristokratie und die Anfänge des cursus honorum in der mittleren Republik*. Berlin.

Bekker, I. 1838. *Theophanes Continuatus, Ioannes Cameniata, Symeon Magister, Georgius Continuatus*. Bonn.

Bell, P. 2009. *Three Political Voices from the Age of Justinian*: Agapetus, Advice to the Emperor, Dialogue on Political Science, Paul the Silentiary, Description of Hagia Sophia. Liverpool.

Benardete, S. 1986. *Plato's Statesman: Part III of The Being of the Beautiful*. Chicago.

Benario, H. W. 1986. 'Bellum Varianum.' *Hist*. 35, 114–15.

Benario, H. W. 2003. 'Teutoburg.' *CW* 96, 397–406.

Benario, H. W. 2004. 'Arminius into Hermann: History into Legend.' *G&R* 51, 83–94.

Bengston, H. 1964. *Die Strategie in der hellenistischen Zeit: Ein Beitrag zum antiken Staatsrecht*. 2 vols. Munich.

Bevan, E. 1902. *The House of Seleucus*. London.

Bevilacqua, L. 2012. 'Basilio "parakoimomenos", l'aristocrazia e la passione per le arti sotto i Macedoni.' In A. Acconcia Longo, G. Cavallo, A. Guiglia and A. Iacobini (eds) *La sapienza bizantina: Un secolo di ricerche sulla civiltà di Bisanzio all'Università di Roma*. Rome. 183–202.

Bevilacqua, L. 2013. 'Basilio *parakoimomenos* e i manoscritti miniati: Impronte di colore nell'Ambrosiano B 119 sup.' In A. Rigo, A. Babuin and M. Trizio (eds) *Vie per Bisanzio: Atti del VII Congresso nazionale dell'Associazione Italiana di Studi Bizantini*. Bari. 1013–30.

Bikerman, E. 1938. *Institutions des Séleucides*. Paris.

Billows, R. 1989. 'The Case of the Macedonian Eupolemos in Karia.' *Cl. Ant*. 8, 173–206.

Billows, R. 1990. *Antigonus the One-Eyed and the Creation of the Hellenistic State*. Berkeley.

Billows, R. 1995. *Kings and Colonists: Aspects of Macedonian Imperialism*. London.

Bjornlie, M. S. 2013. *Politics and Tradition between Rome, Ravenna and Constantinople: A Study of Cassiodorus and the Variae, 527–554*. Cambridge.

Bleckmann, B. 1992. *Die Reichkrise des III. Jahrhunderts in der spätantiken und byzantinischen Geschichtsschreibung: Untersuchungen zu den nachdionischen Quellen der Chronik des Johannes Zonaras*. Munich.

Blockley, R. 1977. 'Ammianus Marcellinus on the Battle of Strasburg: Art and Analysis in the History.' *Phoenix* 31, 218–31.

Blyth, P. H. 1992. 'Apollodorus of Damascus and the *Poliorcetica*.' *GRBS* 33, 127–58.
Bobonich, C. (ed.) 2010. *Plato's Laws: A Critical Guide*. Cambridge.
Boëldieu-Trevet, J. 2007. *Commander dans le monde grec au Ve siècle avant notre ère*. Besançon.
Bömer, F. 1966. 'Caesar und sein Glück.' *Gymnasium* 73, 63–85.
Börm, H. 2007. *Prokop und die Perser: Untersuchungen zu den römisch-sasanidischen Kontakten in der ausgehenden Spätantike*. Stuttgart.
Börm, H. 2015. 'Procopius, his Predecessors, and the Genesis of the *Anecdota*.' In H. Börm (ed.) *Antimonarchic Discourse in Antiquity*. Stuttgart. 305–45.
Börm, H. 2016. 'A Threat or a Blessing? The Sassanians in Roman History.' In C. Binder, H. Börm and A. Luther (eds) *Diwan: Studies in the History and Culture of the Ancient Near East and the Eastern Mediterranean*. Duisburg. 615–46.
Bossi, B. and T. M. Robinson (eds) 2018. *Plato's Statesman Revisited*. Berlin.
Bosworth, A. B. 1993. 'Arrian and Rome: The Minor Works.' *ANRW* 2.34, 226–75.
Bosworth, B. 1996. 'The Historical Setting of Megasthenes' *Indica*.' *CP* 91, 113–27.
Bosworth, C. 1986. 'Arrān.' In *Encyclopædia Iranica*. Vol. 2.5. 520–2. http://www.iranicaonline.org/articles/arran-a-region.
Bosworth, C. 1987. 'Aasāwera.' In *Encyclopædia Iranica*. Vol. 2.7. 706–7. http://www.iranicaonline.org/articles/asawera-arabic-broken-plural-form-the-variant-asawirat-also-occurs-in-yaqubi-p.
Boyce, M. 1968. 'Middle Persian Literature.' In I. Gershevitch, M. Boyce, O. Hansen, B. Spuler and M. J. Dresden *Iranian Studies: Handbook of Oriental Studies 1: The Near and Middle East*. 31–66.
Bray, J. 2010. 'Christian King, Muslim Apostate: Depictions of Jabala Ibn Al-Ayham in Early Arabic Sources.' In A. Papaconstantinou (ed.) *Writing 'True Stories': Historians and Hagiographers in the Late Antique and Medieval Near East*. Cultural Encounters in Late Antiquity and the Middle Ages, 9. Turnhout. 175–204.
Brennan, T. C. 2000. *The Praetorship in the Roman Republic*. 2 vols. Oxford.
Brodersen, K. 2018. *Onasandros: Gute Führung/Strategikos*. Wiesbaden.
Brodka, D. 2004. *Die Geschichtsphilosophie in der spätantiken Historiographie: Studien zu Prokopios von Kaisareia, Agathias von Myrina und Theophylaktos Simokattes*. Frankfurt.
Brodka, D. 2009. *Ammianus Marcellinus: Studien zum Geschichtsdenken im vierten Jahrhundert n. Chr*. Krakow.
Brodka, D. 2018. *Narses: Politik, Krieg und Historiographie im 6. Jahrhundert n. Chr*. Berlin.
Brokkaar, W. G. 1972. 'Basil Lacapenus: Byzantium in the Tenth Century.' In

W. F. Bakker, A. F. Van Gemert and W. J. Aerts (eds) *Studia Byzantina et neo-hellenica Neerlandica*. Leiden. 199–234.

Broughton, T. R. S. 1951. *The Magistrates of the Roman Republic*. Vol 1. New York.

Brown, R. 2004. '"*Virtus Consili Expers*": An Interpretation of the Centurions' Contest in Caesar, *De Bello Gallico* 5, 44.' *Hermes* 132, 292–308.

Brunt, P. A. 1971. *Italian Manpower*. Oxford.

Brunt, P. A. 1983. *Arrian: Anabasis of Alexander and Indica*. Vol. 2. Cambridge, MA.

Burke, J. 2017. 'Nikephoros Phokas as Superhero.' In A. Brown and B. Neil (eds) *Byzantine Culture in Translation*. Leiden. 95–114.

Burn, A. R. 1965. 'The Generalship of Alexander.' *G&R* 12, 140–54.

Burns, T. S. 2003. *Rome and the Barbarians, 100 B.C.–A.D. 400*. Baltimore.

Bursche, A. 2013. 'The Battle of Abritus, the Imperial Treasury and Aurei in Barbaricum.' *NC* 173, 151–170.

Bury, J. B. 1939. 'Greek Literature from the Eighth Century to the Persian Wars.' In J. B. Bury, S. A. Cook and F. E. Adcock (eds) *The Cambridge Ancient History*. Vol. 4. Cambridge. 469–521.

Bury, J. B. 1958. *History of the Later Roman Empire, from the Death of Theodosius to the Death of Justinian*. 2nd edn. New York.

Bury, J. B. and R. Meiggs 1975. *A History of Greece*. 4th edn. London.

Cadiou, F. 2002. 'A propos du service militaire dans l'armée romaine au IIe siècle av. J.-C.: Le cas de Spurius Ligustinus (Tite-Live, 42, 34).' In P. DeFosse (ed.) *Hommages à Carl Deroux, II: Prose et linguistique, Médecine*. Brussels. 76–90.

Cameron, Alan 2001. 'Wandering Poets: A Literary Movement in Byzantine Egypt.' In G. Nagy (ed.) *Greek Literature in the Byzantine Period: Greek Literature*. New York. 14–55.

Cameron, A. 1980. 'The Career of Corippus Again.' *CQ* 30, 534–9.

Cameron, A. 1982. 'Byzantine Africa: The Literary Evidence'. In J. Humphrey (ed.) *Excavations at Carthage VII*. Ann Arbor. 29–62.

Cameron, A. 1984. 'Corippus' *Iohannis*: Epic of Byzantine Africa.' *PLLS* 4, 167–80.

Cameron, A. 1985. *Procopius and the Sixth Century*. Berkeley.

Cameron, A. 1993 [repr. 2003]. *The Mediterranean World in Late Antiquity, AD 395–600*. London.

Cameron, A. (ed.) 1995. *The Byzantine and Early Islamic Near East, III: States, Resources and Armies*. Princeton.

Cameron, A. 2017. 'Writing about Procopius Then and Now.' In C. Lillington-Martin and E. Turquois (eds) *Procopius of Caesarea: Literary and Historical Interpretations*. London. 13–25.

Campbell, D. A. 1982. *Greek Lyric Poetry*. London.

Campbell, J. B. 1987. 'Teach Yourself How to Be a General.' *JRS* 77, 13–29.

Canepa, M. 2009. *The Two Eyes of the Earth: Art and Ritual of Kingship Between Roman and Sasanian Iran*. Berkeley.

Capdetrey, L. 2007. *Le pouvoir séleucide: Territoire, administration, et finances d'un royaume hellénistique*. Rennes.

Carney, E. 1996. 'Macedonians and Mutiny: Discipline and Indiscipline in the Army of Philip and Alexander.' *CP* 91, 19–44.

Carsana, C. 1996. *Le dirigenze cittadine nello stato seleucidico*. Como.

Cartledge, P. 2002. *Sparta and Lakonia: A Regional History 1300 to 362 BC*. 2nd edn. Abingdon.

Cartledge, P. 2013. *After Thermopylae: The Oath of Plataea and the End of the Graeco-Persian Wars*. Oxford.

Champeaux, J. 1987. *Fortuna: Le culte de la fortune à Rome et dans le monde romain des origins à la mort de César, II: Les transformations de Fortuna sous la république*. Paris.

Chaniotis, A. 2005. *War in the Hellenistic World*. Oxford.

Charles-Picard, G. 1957. *Les trophées romains: Contribution à l'histoire de la religion et de l'art triomphal de Rome*. Paris.

Chatzelis, G. 2019. *Byzantine Military Manuals as Literary Works and Practical Handbooks: The Case of the Tenth-Century Sylloge Tacticorum*. London.

Chatzelis, G. (forthcoming). 'The Ideal General and the Impact of Onasander and Rhetoric on Middle Byzantine Military Manuals.' In D. Dimitrijević, A. Elaković-Nenadović and J. Šijković (eds) *Reshaping the Classical Tradition in Byzantine Texts and Contexts*. Belgrade.

Chatzelis, G. and J. Harris 2017. *A Tenth-Century Byzantine Military Manual: The Sylloge Tacticorum*. London.

Chaumont, M. 1985. 'Albania.' In *Encyclopædia Iranica*. Vol. 1.8. 806–10. http://www.iranicaonline.org/articles/albania-iranian-aran-arm.

Cherry, K. M. 2012. *Plato, Aristotle, and the Purpose of Politics*. Cambridge.

Chesnut, G. F. 1975. 'Kairos and Cosmic Sympathy in the Church Historian Socrates Scholasticus.' *Church History* 44, 161–6.

Chlup, J. 2014. 'Just War in Onasander's ΣΤΡΑΤΗΓΙΚΟΣ.' *JAH* 2, 37–63.

Chrubasik, B. 2016. *Kings and Usurpers in the Seleukid Empire: The Men Who Would Be King*. Oxford.

Clark, J. 2014. *Triumph in Defeat: Military Loss and the Roman Republic*. Oxford.

Clark, J. 2016. 'Were Tribuni Militum First Elected in 362 or 311 BCE?' *Hist.* 65, 275–97.

Clarke, G. 1980. 'Dating the Death of the Emperor Decius.' *ZPE* 37, 114–16.

Clunn, T. 2008. *Quest for the Lost Roman Legions: Discovering the Varus Battlefield*. New York.

Cohen, G. M. 1978. *The Seleucid Colonies: Studies in Founding, Administration, and Organization*. Wiesbaden.

Collins, H. J. 1972. 'Caesar as a Political Propagandist.' *ANRW* 1.1, 922–66.

Colvin, I. 2013. 'Reporting Battles and Understanding Campaigns in Procopius and Agathias: Classicising Historians' Use of Archived Documents as Sources.' In A. Sarantis and N. Christie (eds) *War and Warfare in Late Antiquity: Current Perspectives*. Leiden. 571–98.

Conant, J. 2012. *Staying Roman: Conquest and Identity in Africa and the Mediterranean, 439–700*. Cambridge.

Conley, F. D. 1983. 'Causes of Roman Victory Presented in the *Bellum Gallicum*: Caesar the Commander vs. Other Factors.' *Helion* 10, 173–86.

Connor, WR. 1988. 'Early Greek Warfare as Symbolic Expression.' *P&P* 119, 3–29.

Cooper, J. M. 1997. *Plato: Complete Works*. Indianapolis.

Cosentino, S. 2000. 'The Syrianos' Strategikon: A 9th-Century Source?' *Bizantinistica: Rivista di Studi Bizantini e Slavi* 2, 243–80.

Cosentino, S. 2001. 'Per una nuova edizione dei *Naumachica* ambrosiani: Il *De fluminibus traiciendis* (*Strat.* XII.B.21).' *Bizantinistica: Rivista di Studi Bizantini e Slavi* 3, 63–107, tables i–vi.

Cosentino, S. 2009. 'Writing about War in Byzantium.' *Revista de História das Ideias* 30, 83–99.

Costa, V. 2010. 'Esichio di Mileto, Johannes Flach e le fonti biografiche della *Suda*.' In G. Vanotti (ed.) *Il lessico Suda e gli storici greci in frammenti: Atti Dell'incontro Internazionale*. Rome. 43–55.

Courtois, C. 1955. *Les Vandales et l'Afrique*. Paris.

Craig, D. J. 1931. 'The General Reflection in Caesar's Commentaries.' *CR* 45, 107–10.

Crawford, H. M. 1974. *Roman Republican Coinage*. 2 vols. Cambridge.

Cresci, L. R. 2001. 'Procopio al confine tra due tradizioni storiografiche.' *Rivista di Filologia e di Istruzione Classica* 129, 61–77.

Crone, P. 1998. 'The Abbāsid Abnā' and the Sāsānid Cavalrymen.' *Journal of the Royal Asiatic Society* 8, 1–19.

Crone, P. 1999. 'The Early Islamic World.' In K. Raaflaub and N. Rosenstein (eds) *War and Society in the Ancient and Medieval Worlds*. Cambridge, MA. 309–32.

Crone, P. 2008. *From Arabian Tribes to Islamic Empire: Army, State and Society in the Near East c. 600–850*. Aldershot.

Crosby, D. J. 2016. 'The Case of Another Son of P. Quinctilius Varus: A Re-Examination of the Textual and Scholarly Traditions around Joseph. BJ 2.68 and AJ 17.288.' *JAH* 4, 113–29.
Crump, G. A. 1973. 'Ammianus and the Late Roman Army.' *Hist.* 22, 91–103.
Crump, G. A. 1975. *Ammianus Marcellinus as a Military Historian*. Wiesbaden.
Cubit, C. 2010. 'Introduction: Writing True Stories: A View from the West.' In A. Papaconstantinou (ed.) *Writing 'True Stories': Historians and Hagiographers in the Late Antique and Medieval Near East*. Cultural Encounters in Late Antiquity and the Middle Ages. Vol. 9. Turnhout. 1–12.
Culham, P. 1989. 'Chance, Command, and Chaos in Ancient Military Engagements.' *World Futures* 27, 191–205.
Cutler, A. 1976–7. 'The Psalter of Basil II.' Art. III in *Arte Veneta* 30–1, 9–19, 9–15. Repr. in A. Cutler 1992. *Imagery and Ideology in Byzantine Art*. Aldershot.
D'Agostini, M. 2013. 'La strutturazione del potere seleucidico in Anatolia: Il caso di Acheo il Vecchio e Alessandro di Sardi.' *Erga/Logoi* 1, 87–106.
D'Agostini, M. 2014. 'The Shade of Andromache: Laodike of Sardis between Homer and Polybios.' *AHB* 28, 37–60.
D'Agostini, M. and A. McAuley 2012. 'The House of Achaeus.' In A. McAuley (ed.) *The Genealogy of the Seleucids*. Digital Publication through McGill University and the University of Edinburgh, http://www.seleucid-genealogy.com/Achaeus.html.
Dagron, G. and H. Mihăescu 1986. *Le traité sur la guérilla (De velitatione) de l'empereur Nicéphore Phocas (963–969)*. Paris.
Dain, A. 1930. *Les manuscrits d'Onésandros*. Paris.
Dain, A. 1931. 'Les cinq adaptations byzantines des "Stratagèmes" de Polyen.' *REA* 33, 321–45.
Dain, A. 1937. *La 'Tactique' de Nicéphore Ouranos*. Paris.
Dain A. 1938. *Sylloge tacticorum quae olim inedita Leonis tactica dicebatur*. Paris.
Dain, A. 1946. *Histoire du texte d'Élien le Tacticien des origines à la fin du Moyen Âge*. Paris.
Dain, A. and J.-A. de Foucault 1967. 'Les stratégistes byzantins.' *TM* 2, 317–92.
Daly, L. W. and W. A. Oldfather 1939. 'Onasander.' *RE* 18.1, 403–5.
Danzig, G., D. Johnson and D. Morrison (eds) 2018. *Plato and Xenophon: Comparative Studies*. Leiden.
Darkó, E. [J.] 1936. 'Bibliographische Notizen: Korzenszky and Vári 1935.' *BZ* 36, 542–4.
Daryaee, T. 2009. *Sasanian Persia: The Rise and Fall of an Empire*. London.
Daryaee, T. 2010. 'The Fall of the Sasanian Empire to the Arab Muslims: From Two Centuries of Silence to Decline and Fall of the Sasanian Empire: The Partho-

Sasanian Confederacy and the Arab Conquest of Iran.' *Journal of Persianate Studies* 3, 239–54.
Daryaee, T. 2013. 'Marriage, Property and Conversion among the Zoroastrians: From Late Sasanian to Islamic Iran.' *Journal of Persianate Studies* 6, 91–100.
Daryaee, T. 2015. 'Wahrām Čōbēn the Rebel General and the Militarization of the Sasanian Empire.' In A. Krasnowolska and R. Rusek-Kowalska (eds) *Studies on the Iranian World I*. Krakow. 193–202.
Davenport, C. and C. Mallen 2013. 'Dexippus' Letter of Decius: Context and Interpretation.' *MH* 70, 57–73.
Davies, J. K. 1971. *Athenian Propertied Families, 600–300 B.C.* Oxford.
Davis, D. 1992. *Epic and Sedition: The Case of Ferdowsi's Shahnameh*. Washington, DC. Repr. 2006.
Davis, D. 1996. 'The Problem of Ferdowsi's Sources.' *Journal of the American Oriental Society* 116, 48–57.
Davis, D. 2016. *Ferdowsi, Abū ol Qāsem, The Shahnameh = Shahnameh: The Persian Book of Kings*. New York.
Day, S. 2017. 'The People's Role in Allocating Provincial Commands in the Middle Roman Republic.' *JRS* 107, 1–26.
Dayton, J. C. 2006. *The Athletes of War: An Evaluation of the Agonistic Elements in Greek Warfare*. Toronto.
De Bakker, M. 2019. 'A Narratological Comparison of Herodotus and Diodorus on Thermopylae.' In L. W. Van Gils, I. R. F. De Jong and C. H. M. Kroon (eds) *Textual Strategies in Ancient War Narrative: Thermopylae, Cannae and Beyond*. Leiden. 54–90.
De Blois, L., J. Bons, T. Kessels and D. Schenkeveld (eds) 2017. *The Statesman in Plutarch's Works, II: The Statesman in Plutarch's Greek and Roman Lives*. Leiden.
De Boor, C. 1883. *Theophanis Chronographia*. 2 vols. Leipzig,
De Foucault, J.-A. 1949. *Strategemata*. Paris.
De Foucault, J.-A. 1973. 'Douze chapitres inédits de la *Tactique* de Nicéphore Ouranos.' *TM* 5, 281–312.
De Marre, M. 2018. 'One Oracle Too Many? Corippus and Procopius on Female Prophecy in North African Divination.' In R. J. Evans (ed.) *Prophets and Profits: Ancient Divination and its Reception*. London. 162–82.
De Sélincourt, A. (trans.) and J. R. Hamilton (ed.) 1971. *Arrian: The Campaigns of Alexander*. Harmondsworth.
De Sélincourt, A. (trans.) and J. Marincola (ed.) 2003. *Herodotus: The Histories*. Harmondsworth.
Dennis, G. T. 1981. *Das Strategikon des Maurikios*. Vienna.

Dennis, G. T. 1984. *Maurice's Strategikon: Handbook of Byzantine Military Strategy*. Philadelphia.
Dennis, G. T. 1985. *Three Byzantine Military Treatises*. Washington, DC.
Dennis G. T. 2010. *The Taktika of Leo VI*. Washington, DC.
Dennis, G. T. 2014. *The Taktika of Leo VI: Text, Translation and Commentary*. Rev. edn. Washington, DC.
Desmond, W. 2006. 'Lessons of Fear: A Reading of Thucydides.' *CP* 101, 359–79.
Devine, A. M. 1993. 'Arrian's "Tactica".' *ANRW* 2.34.1, 312–37.
Dewing, H. B. 2014. *The Wars of Justinian: Prokopios*. Rev. and modernized with an introduction and notes by A. Kaldellis. Indianapolis.
Dick, F. B. 1967. '*Fatum* and *Fortuna* in Lucan's *Bellum Civile*.' *CP* 62, 235–42.
Dickey, E. 2017. 'Classical Scholarship: The Byzantine Contribution.' In A. Kaldellis and N. Siniossoglou (eds) *The Cambridge Intellectual History of Byzantium*. Cambridge. 61–78.
Diehl, C. 1896. *L'Afrique byzantine. histoire de la domination byzantine en Afrique (533–709)*. Paris.
Dignas, B. and E. Winter 2007. *Rome and Persia in Late Antiquity: Neighbours and Rivals*. Cambridge.
Dijkstra, J. and G. Greatrex 2009. 'Patriarchs and Politics in Constantinople in the Reign of Anastasius (with a Reedition of *O. Mon. Epiph. 59*).' *Millennium* 6, 223–64.
Dimitriev, S. 2005. *City Government in Hellenistic and Roman Asia Minor*. Oxford.
Donlan, W. 1979. 'The Structure of Authority in the *Iliad*.' *Arethusa* 12, 51–70.
Donner, F. 1981. *The Early Islamic Conquests*. Princeton.
Donner, F. 1995. 'Centralized Authority and Military Autonomy in the Early Islamic Conquests.' In A. Cameron (ed.) *The Byzantine and Early Islamic Near East, III: States, Resources and Armies*. Princeton. 337–60.
Donner, F. 1998. *Narratives of Islamic Origins: The Beginnings of Arabic Historical Writing*. Studies in Late Antiquity and Early Islam 14. Princeton.
Dowsett, C. J. F. (trans.) 1961. *The History of the Caucasian Albanians by Movsēs Dasxuranci*. London.
Dreyer, B. 2011. 'How to Become a Relative of the King: Careers and Hierarchy at the Court of Antiochus III.' *AJP* 132, 45–7.
Drinkwater, J. F. 2007. *The Alamanni and Rome 213–496*. Oxford.
Drogula, F. 2015. *Commanders and Command in the Roman Republic and Early Empire*. Chapel Hill.
Du You. 1988. *Tong dian*. Beijing.
Echeverria Rey, F. 2011. '*Taktikè technè*: The Neglected Element in Classical Hoplite Battles.' *Ancient Society* 41, 45–82.

Eck, W. 2010. 'P. Quinctilius Varus, siene senatorische Laufbahn und sein Handeln in Germanien.' In T. Capelle (ed.) *Imperium: Varus und seine Zeit: Beiträge zum internationalen Kolloquium des LWL-Römermuseums am 28. und 29. April 2008 in Münster*. Münster. 13–28.

Eckstein, A. M. 1987. *Senate and General: Individual Decision Making and Roman Foreign Relations, 264–194 B.C.* Berkeley.

Eckstein, A. M. 1995. *Moral Vision in the Histories of Polybius*. Berkeley.

Edmunds, L. 1975. *Chance and Intelligence in Thucydides*. Cambridge.

Edwell, P. et al. 2015. 'Arabs in Conflict between Rome and Persia, AD 491–630.' In G. Fisher (ed.) *Arabs and Empires before Islam*. Oxford. 214–75.

El Cheikh, N. 2004. *Byzantium Viewed by the Arabs*. Cambridge, MA.

El-Hibri, T. 2010. *Parable and Politics in Early Islamic History*. New York.

Elton, H. 1996. *Warfare in Roman Europe, AD 350–425*. Oxford.

Elton, H. 1997. 'Off the Battlefield: The Civilian's View of Late Roman Soldiers.' *Expedition* 10, 42–50.

Elton, H. 2007. 'Cavalry in Late Roman Warfare.' In A. Lewin and P. Pellegrini (eds) *The Late Roman Army in the Near East from Diocletian to the Arab Conquest*. Oxford. 377–82.

Engels, D. 2017. *Benefactors, Kings, Rulers: Studies on the Seleukid Empire between East and West*. Leuven.

Eramo, I. 2008. 'Omero e i Maccabei: Nella biblioteca di Siriano Μάγιστρος.' *AnnBari* 51, 123–47.

Eramo, I. 2010. *Syrianos Magistros: Rhetorica Militaris/Siriano: Discorsi di Guerra*. Bari.

Eramo, I. 2016. '*Mechanemata*: Mind-Machines in War.' In V. Ilari (ed.) *Future Wars: Storia della dystopia militare*. Milan. 81–91.

Ercolani, L. 1997. 'La lingua di Onasandro: Richerche sugli ἅπαξ λεγόμενα.' *AFLS* 18, 43–53.

Erickson, K. (ed.) 2018. *The Seleucid Empire, 281–222 BC: War within the Family*. Swansea.

Eshel, H. 2008. 'Publius Quinctilius Varus in Jewish Sources.' *JJS* 59, 112–19.

Esposito, G. 2019. *Armies of the Hellenistic States 323 BC–AD 30: History, Organization & Equipment*. Barnsley.

Evans, J. A. S. 1970. 'Justinian and the Historian Procopius.' *G&R* 17, 218–23.

Evans, J. A. S. 1971. 'Christianity and Paganism in Procopius of Caesarea.' *GRBS* 12, 81–100.

Evans, J. A. S. 1996. *The Age of Justinian: The Circumstances of Imperial Power*. London.

Evans, R. 1994. *Gaius Marius: A Political Biography*. Pretoria.

Evans, R. 2011. *Roman Conquests: Asia Minor, Syria and Armenia*. Barnsley.

Evans, R. 2016. *Ancient Syracuse: From Foundation to Fourth Century Collapse*. London.

Faravashi, B. 1971. 'Les causes de la chute des Sassanides.' In *Atti del Convegno Internazionale sul Tema: La Persia nel Medioevo*. Problemi Attuali di Scienza e di Cultura 160. Rome. 477–84.

Farrokh, K. 2017. *The Armies of Ancient Persia: The Sasanians*. Barnsley.

Fauber, L. H. 1990. *Narses: Hammer of the Goths*. Gloucester.

Featherstone, J. M. and J. Signes-Codoñer 2015. *Chronographiae quae Theophanis continuati nomine fertur libri I–IV*. Berlin.

Featherstone, M. 2004. 'Further Remarks on the *De Cerimoniis*.' *BZ* 97, 113–21.

Feiling, K. 1966. *A History of England*. London.

Ferdowsi, A. ol Q. 1838. *Le livre des rois par Abou'lkasim Firdousi, publié, traduit et commenté par Jules Mohl*. Paris. Repr. 1976.

Figueira, T. J. 1985. 'Chronological Table: Archaic Megara, 800–500 BC.' In T. J. Figueira and G. Nagy (eds) *Theognis of Megara: Poetry and the Polis*. Baltimore. 261–303.

Flower, M. A. 1998. 'Simonides, Ephorus, and Herodotus on the Battle of Thermopylae.' *CQ* 48, 365–79.

Formisano, M. 2011. 'The *Strategikós* of Onasander: Taking Military Texts Seriously.' *Technai* 2, 39–52.

Forster, E. S. 1984. *Florus: Epitome of Roman History*. Cambridge, MA.

Förster, R. 1877. 'Studien zu den griechischen Taktikern.' *Hermes* 12, 426–71.

Fotiou, A. 1988. 'Recruitment Shortages in Sixth-Century Byzantium.' *Byz* 58, 65–77.

Fowden, E. 1999. *The Barbarian Plain: Saint Sergius between Rome and Iran*. Transformation of the Classical Heritage 28. Berkeley.

Frendo, J. D. 1975. *Agathias: The Histories*. Berlin.

Friedmann, Y. 1992. *The History of al-Ṭabarī, XII: The Battle of al-Qādisiyyah and the Conquest of Syria and Palestine (AD 635–637/AH 14–15)*. Albany.

Frost, F. J. 1984. 'The Athenian Military before Cleisthenes.' *Hist.* 33, 283–94.

Frye, R. 1975. *The Golden Age of Persia*. London.

Furneaux, H. 1896. *P. Cornelii Taciti annalium ab excessu divi Augusti libri*. 2nd edn. London.

Galimberti, A. 2002. 'Lo *Strategikòs* di Onasandro.' In M. Sordi (ed.) *Guerra e diritto nel mondo greco e romano*. Milan. 141–53.

Gantz, T. 1993. *Early Greek Myth: A Guide to Literary and Artistic Sources*. Baltimore.

Gardner, J. F. 1974. *Leadership and the Cult of Personality*. London.

Garsoïan, N. 1985. *Armenia between Byzantium and the Sasanians*. London.

Garsoïan, N. 1998. 'The Problem of Armenian Integration into the Byzantine Empire.' In H. Ahrweiler and A. Laiou (eds) *Studies on the Internal Diaspora of the Byzantine Empire*. Washington, DC. 53–124.

Gärtner, T. 2008. *Untersuchungen zur Gestaltung und zum historischen Stoff der 'Johannis' Coripps*. Berlin.

Gauthier, F. 2019. 'Auxiliaries and War-Financing in the Roman Republic.' *JAH* 7, 251–68.

Gelzer, M. 1968. *Caesar: Politician and Statesman*. Trans. P. Needham. Oxford.

Gerlinger, S. 2008. *Römische Schlachtenrhetorik: Unglaubwürdige Elemente in Schlachtendarstellungen, speziell bei Caesar, Sallust und Tacitus*. Heidelberg.

Gerrish, J. 2018. 'Heroic Resonances in Caesar's *Bellum Gallicum* 5.' *CW* 111, 351–70.

Gilliam, J. F. 1956. 'Trebonianus Gallus and the Decii: III et I cos.' In *Studi in onore di Aristide Calderini e Roberto Paribeni*. Milan. 305–11.

Gilliver, C. M. 1996. 'The Roman Army and Morality in War.' In A. B. Lloyd (ed.) *Battle in Antiquity*. London. 219–38.

Gilliver, C. M. 1999. *The Roman Art of War*. Stroud.

Gilliver, C. M. 2007. 'Battle.' In P. Sabin, H. Van Wees and M. Whitby (eds) *The Cambridge History of Greek and Roman Warfare, II: Rome from the Late Republic to the Late Empire*. Cambridge. 122–57.

Godley, A. D. 1922. *Herodotus*. Vol. 3. Cambridge, MA.

Goldlust, B. 2017. *Corippe, Johannide, Livre 4: Introduction, édition critique, traduction et commentaire*. Paris.

Goldsworthy, A. 1996. *The Roman Army at War 100 BC to AD 200*. Oxford.

Goldsworthy, A. 1998. 'Instinctive Genius: The Depiction of Caesar the General.' In K. Welch and A. Powell (eds) *Julius Caesar as Artful Reporter: The War Commentaries as Political Instruments*. Swansea. 193–219.

Goldsworthy, A. 2007. 'War.' In P. Sabin, H. Van Wees and M. Whitby (eds) *The Cambridge History of Greek and Roman Warfare, II: Rome from the Late Republic to the Late Empire*. Cambridge. 76–121.

Goodyear, F. R. D. 1972. *The Annals of Tacitus: Books 1–6*. 2 vols. Cambridge.

Gotoff, H. C. 1984. 'Towards a Practical Criticism of Caesar's Prose Style.' *Illinois Classical Studies* 9, 1–18.

Graff, D. A. 2011/12. 'China, Byzantium and the Shadow of the Steppe.' *DOP* 65/6, 157–68.

Grainger, J. D. 1990. *The Cities of Seleukid Syria*. Oxford.

Grainger, J. D. 1997. *A Seleukid Prosopography and Gazetteer*. Leiden.

Grainger, J. D. 2011. *Hellenistic and Roman Naval Warfare*. Barnsley.

Grainger, J. D. 2015. *The Seleukid Empire of Antiochus III: 223–187 BC*. Barnsley.

Greatrex, G. and S. N. C. Lieu 2002. *The Roman Eastern Frontier and the Persian Wars AD 363–628: A Narrative Sourcebook*. London.

Green, P. 2006. *Diodorus Siculus: Books 11–12.37.1: Greek History, 480–431 BC: The Alternative Version*. Austin.

Greenwood, T. 2002. 'Sasanian Echoes and Apocalyptic Expectations: A Re-Evaluation of the Armenian History Attributed to Sebeos.' *Le Museon* 115, 323–97.

Greenwood, T. 2019. 'Armenian Space in Late Antiquity.' In P. Van Nuffelen (ed.) *Historiography and Space in Late Antiquity*. Cambridge. 57–85.

Griffiths, A. 1989. 'Was Kleomenes Mad?' In A. Powell (ed.) *Classical Sparta: Techniques Behind her Success*. London. 51–78.

Grillo, L. 2011. '*Scibam ipse de me*: The Personality of the Narrator in Caesar's *Bellum Civile*.' *AJP* 132, 243–71.

Gruber, J. 2008. 'Tacitus und der Ort der Varus-Schlacht: Vom Zeugniswert der literarischen Quellen.' *Gymnasium* 115, 453–67.

Gruen, E. 1995. 'The "Fall" of the Scipios.' In I. Malkin and Z.W. Rubinsohn (eds) *Leaders and Masses in the Roman World*. Leiden. 59–90.

Grusková, J. and G. Martin 2014. 'Eine neues Textstück aus den "Scythica Vindobanensia" zu der Ereignissen nach der Eroberung von Philippopolis.' *Tyche* 29, 29–43.

Grusková, J. and G. Martin 2015. 'Zum Angriff der Goten unter Kniva auf eine thrakische Stadt (*Scythica Vindobonensia*, f. 195v).' *Tyche* 30, 35–54.

Gu Jiguang. 1962. *Fubing zhidu kaoshi*. Shanghai.

Guilland, R. 1943. 'Les eunuques dans l'empire byzantin: Étude de titulature et de prosopographie byzantines.' *Revue des Études Byzantines* 1, 197–238.

Gyselen, R. 1989. *La géographie administrative de l'Empire Sassanide: Les témoignages sigillographiques*. Vol. 1. Paris.

Habicht, C. 1958. 'Die herrschende Gesellschaft in den hellenistischen Monarchien.' *Vierteljahresschrift für Sozial- und Wirtschaftsgeschichte* 45, 1–16.

Haidu, P. 2004. *The Subject Medieval and Modern: Text and Governance in the Middle Ages*. Stanford.

Haldon, J. F. 1984. *Byzantine Praetorians: An Administrative, Institutional and Social Survey of the Opsikion and Tagmata, c. 580–900*. Bonn.

Haldon, J. F. 1990. *Constantine Porphyrogenitus: Three Treatises on Imperial Military Expeditions*. Vienna.

Haldon, J. F. 1995 'Seventh-Century Continuities: The Anjād and the "Thematic Myth".' In A. Cameron (ed.) *The Byzantine and Early Islamic Near East, III: States, Resources and Armies*. Studies in Late Antiquity and Early Islam, 1. Princeton. 379–423.

Haldon, J. F. 2014a. *A Critical Commentary on the Taktika of Leo VI*. Washington, DC.

Haldon, J. F. 2014b. *Byzantium at War: AD 600–1453*. Oxford.

Haldon, J. F. 2015. *The Empire that Would Not Die: The Paradox of Eastern Roman Survival, 640–740*. Cambridge, MA.

Hall, L. G. M. 1998. '*Ratio* and *Romanitas* in the *Bellum Gallicum*.' In K. Welch and A. Powell (eds) *Julius Caesar as Artful Reporter: The War Commentaries as Political Instruments*. Swansea. 11–43.

Hamaguchi Shigekuni. 1930. 'Fuhei seido yori shin heisei e.' *Shigaku zasshi* 41, 1255–95, 1439–1507.

Hamel, D. 1998. *Athenian Generals: Military Authority in the Classical Period*. Leiden.

Hammond, N. G. L. 1959. *A History of Greece to 322 B.C.* Oxford.

Hammond, N. G. L. 2000. 'The Continuity of Macedonian Institutions and the Macedonian Kingdoms of the Hellenistic Era.' *Hist*. 49, 141–60.

Hansen, E. V. 1947. *The Attalids of Pergamon*. Ithaca.

Hansen, M. H. 1993. 'The Battle Exhortation in Ancient Historiography: Fact or Fiction?' *Hist*. 42, 161–80.

Hansen, M. H. 1999. *The Athenian Democracy in the Age of Demosthenes: Structure, Principles, and Ideology*. Norman.

Hanson, V. D. 1989 [2009]. *The Western Way of War: Infantry Battle in Classical Greece*. London and Berkeley.

Hanson, V. D. (ed.) 1991a. *Hoplites: The Classical Greek Battle Experience*. London.

Hanson, V. D. 1991b. 'The Ideology of Hoplite Battle, Ancient and Modern.' In V. D. Hanson (ed.) *Hoplites: The Classical Greek Battle Experience*. London. 3–11.

Hanson, V. D. 1995. *The Other Greeks: The Family Farm and the Agrarian Roots of Western Civilization*. New York.

Harl, K. 2008. 'Legion over Phalanx: The Battle of Magnesia, 190 B.C.' In T. Howe and J. Reames (eds) *Macedonian Legacies: Studies in Ancient Macedonian History and Culture in Honor of Eugene N. Borza*. Regina. 257–79.

Hase, C. B. 1828. *Leonis diaconi Caloënsis Historiae libri decem*. Bonn.

Hassan, M. 2016. *Longing for the Lost Caliphate: A Transregional History*. Princeton.

Heather, P. 2018. *Rome Resurgent: War and Empire in the Age of Justinian*. Oxford.

Hebblewhite, M. 2017. *The Emperor and the Army in the Later Roman Empire, AD 235–395*. London.

Heisenberg, A. and P. Wirth. (eds) 1978. *Georgii Akropolitae Opera*. 2 vols. Stuttgart.

Hendriks, I. H. M. 1980. 'The Battle of Sepeia.' *Mnemosyne* 33, 340–6.

Heubner, F. 1974. '*Das Feinbeld in Caesars Bellum Gallicum*.' *Klio* 56, 103–82.

Hitti, P. K. 1916/1924. *Kitāb Futūḥ al-buldān, written by Aḥmad b. Yaḥyā al-Balādhurī*. Studies in History, Economics and Public Law 163. 2 vols. New York.

Hoffman, D. 1969–70. *Das spätromische Bewegungsheer und die Notitia Dignitatum*. 2 vols. Düsseldorf.

Hofmann, H. 1989. 'Corippus as a Patristic Author?' *Vigiliae Christianae* 43, 361–77.

Hölkeskamp, K.-J. 1993. 'Conquest, Competition and Consensus: Roman Expansion in Italy and the Rise of the "Nobilitas".' *Hist.* 42, 12–39.

Hölkeskamp, K.-J. 2004a. *Senatus populusque romanus: Die politische Kultur der Republik: Dimensionen und Deutungen*. Stuttgart.

Hölkeskamp, K.-J. 2004b. *Republik: Die politische Kultur des antiken Rom und die Forschung der letzten Jahrzehnte*. Munich.

Hölkeskamp, K.-J. 2017. *Libera res publica: Die politische Kultur des antiken Rom: Positionen und Perspektiven*. Stuttgart.

Holmes, C. 2005. *Basil II and the Governance of Empire (976–1025)*. Oxford.

Holmes, C. 2010. 'Byzantine Political Culture and Compilation Literature in the Tenth and Eleventh Centuries: Some Preliminary Inquiries.' *DOP* 64, 55–80.

Hörandner, W. 1974. *Theodoros Prodromos: Historische Gedichte*. Wiener Byzantinistische Studien, 11. Vienna.

Hostetler, B. 2012. 'The Limburg Staurotheke: A Reassessment.' *Athanor* 30, 7–13.

How, W. W. and J. Wells. 1912. *A Commentary on Herodotus*. 2 vols. Oxford.

Howard-Johnston, J. 1995. 'The Two Great Powers in Late Antiquity: A Comparison.' In A. Cameron (ed.) *The Byzantine and Early Islamic Near East, III: States, Resources and Armies*. Studies in Late Antiquity and Early Islam, 1. Princeton. 157–226.

Howard-Johnston, J. 2000. 'Ḵosrow II.' In *Encyclopædia Iranica*. http://www.iranicaonline.org/articles/asawera-arabic-broken-plural-form-the-variant-asawirat-also-occurs-in-yaqubi-p.

Howard-Johnston, J. 2002. 'The Education and Expertise of Procopius.' *Antiquité Tardive* 8, 19–30.

Howard-Johnston, J. 2010. *Witnesses to a World Crisis: Historians and Histories of the Middle East in the Seventh Century*. Oxford.

Hoyos, D. 2003. *Hannibal's Dynasty*. London.

Hunger, H. 1978. *Die hochsprachliche profaner Literatur der Byzantiner*. Handbuch der Altertumswissenschaft, 12.5. 2 vols. Munich.

Hunter, R. 2017. 'Eustathian Moments: Reading Eustathius' Commentaries.' In F. Pontani, V. Katsaros and V. Sarris (eds) *Reading Eustathios of Thessalonike*. Berlin. 9–75.

Hunter, V. 1982. *Past and Process in Thucydides*. Princeton.

Huntington, S. P. 1956. 'Civilian Control of the Military: A Theoretical Statement.'

In H. Eulau, S. J. Eldersveld and M. Janowitz (eds) *Political Behavior*. Glencoe. 380–1.

Huntington, S. P. 1957. *The Soldier and the State: The Theory and Politics of Civil–Military Relations*. Cambridge, MA.

Huxley, G. L. 1962. *Early Sparta*. London.

Hyland, J. 2018. *Persian Interventions: The Achaemenid Empire, Athens and Sparta, 45–386 BCE*. Baltimore.

Iliff Robson, E. (1933). *Arrian*. Vol. 2. London and New York.

Istasse, N. 2006. 'Experts "barbares" dans le monde politique sélucude.' In J.-C. Couvenhes and B. Legras (eds) *Transferts culturels et politiques dans le monde hellénistique*. Paris. 53–80.

Jackson, A. 1993. 'War and Raids for Booty in the World of Odysseus.' In J. Rich and G. Shipley (eds) *War and Society in the Greek World*. London. 64–76.

Jackson, A. 2000. 'Argos' Victory over Corinth.' *ZPE* 132, 295–311.

Jal, P. 1967. *Florus: Œuvres*. Vol. 2. Paris.

Janiszewski, P. 2006. *The Missing Link: Greek Pagan Historiography in the Second Half of the Third Century and in the Fourth Century A.D.* Trans. D. Dzierzbicka. Warsaw.

Janniard, S. 2011. *Les transformations de l'armée romano-byzantine (iiie–vie siècles apr. J.-C.): Le paradigme de la bataille rangée*. PhD thesis, L'Atelier du Centre de Recherches Historiques.

Jehne, M. 1997. *Caesar*. Munich.

Jehne, M. 2006. 'Caesars Gallischer Krieg: Text und Tat.' In E. Stein-Hölkeskamp and K.-J. Hölkeskamp (eds) *Erinnerungsorte Orte der Antike: Die römische Welt*. Munich. 234–41.

Jenkins, R. J. H. (ed.) 1962. *Constantine Porphyrogenitus: De Administrando Imperio: A Commentary*. London.

Jervis, A. 2001. *Gallia Scripta: Images of Gauls and Romans in Caesar's Bellum Gallicum*. Philadelphia.

John, W. 1958. 'Zu den Familienverhältnissen des P. Quinctilius Varus.' *Hermes* 86, 251–5.

John, W. 1963. '(20) P. Quinctilius Varus.' *RE* 24, 907–84.

Johnston, P. D. 2008. *The Military Consilium in Republican Rome*. Piscataway.

Jullien, F. 2004a. *Detour and Access: Strategies of Meaning in China and Greece*. New York.

Jullien, F. 2004b. *A Treatise on Efficacy: Between Western and Chinese Thinking*. Honolulu.

Kaegi, W. E. 1981. *Byzantine Military Unrest 471–843: An Interpretation*. Amsterdam.

Kaegi, W. E. 1983. *Some Thoughts on Byzantine Military Strategy*. Brookline. Repr. in J. Haldon (ed.) 2007. *Byzantine Warfare*. Aldershot. 250–68.

Kaegi, W. E. 1990. 'Procopius the Military Historian.' *BF* 15, 53–85.

Kaegi, W. E. 1992. *Byzantium and the Early Islamic Conquest*. Cambridge.

Kaegi, W. E. 2003. *Heraclius: Emperor of Byzantium*. Cambridge.

Kagan, D. and G. F. Viggiano (eds) 2013a. *Men of Bronze: Hoplite Warfare in Ancient Greece*. Princeton.

Kagan, D. and G. F. Viggiano 2013b. 'The Hoplite Debate.' In D. Kagan and G. F. Viggiano (eds) *Men of Bronze: Hoplite Warfare in Ancient Greece*. Princeton. 1–56.

Kagan, K. 2006. *The Eye of Command*. Ann Arbor.

Kajanto, I. 1981. '*Fortuna*.' *ANRW* 2.17.1, 502–58.

Kaldellis, A. 2004. *Procopius of Caesarea: Tyranny, History and Philosophy at the End of Antiquity*. Philadelphia.

Kaldellis, A. 2007. *Hellenism in Byzantium: The Transformations of Greek Identity and the Reception of the Classical Tradition*. Cambridge.

Kaldellis, A. 2010. 'Procopius' *Persian War*: A Thematic and Literary Analysis.' In R. Macrides (ed.) *History as Literature in Byzantium*. London. 253–74.

Kaldellis, A. 2012. 'From Rome to New Rome, From Empire to Nation State: Reopening the Question of Byzantium's Roman Identity.' In L. Grig and G. Kelly (eds) *Two Romes: Rome and Constantinople in Late Antiquity*. Oxford. 387–404.

Kaldellis, A. 2013. *Ethnography after Antiquity: Foreign Lands and Peoples in Byzantine Literature*. Philadelphia.

Kaldellis, A. 2014. *The Wars of Justinian: Prokopios*. Trans. H. B. Dewing. Rev. and modernized with introduction and notes A. Kaldellis. Indianapolis.

Kaldellis, A. 2015. *The Byzantine Republic: People and Power in New Rome*. Cambridge, MA.

Kaldellis, A. 2016. 'Procopius's *Vandal War*: Thematic Trajectories and Hidden Transcripts.' In S. Stevens and J. Conant (eds) *North Africa under Byzantium and Early Islam*. Washington, DC. 13–21.

Kaldellis, A. 2017a. *Streams of Gold, Rivers of Blood: The Rise and Fall of Byzantium, 955 A.D. to the First Crusade*. Oxford.

Kaldellis, A. 2017b. 'The Social Scope of Roman Identity in Byzantium: An Evidence-Based Approach.' *Byzantina Symmeikta* 27, 173–210.

Kaldellis, A. 2017c. 'A Byzantine Argument for the Equivalence of All Religions: Michael Attaleiates on Ancient and Modern Romans.' *International Journal of the Classical Tradition* 14, 1–22.

Kaldellis, A. and D. Krallis 2012. *Michael Attaleiates: The History*. Washington, DC.

Kaldellis, A. and N. Siniossoglou. 2017. 'Introduction.' In A. Kaldellis and N. Siniossoglou (eds) *The Cambridge Intellectual History of Byzantium*. Cambridge. 1–26.
Karlgren, B. 1950. *The Book of Documents*. Stockholm.
Kaufmann, H. 2017. 'Intertextuality in Late Latin Poetry.' In J. Elsner and J. Hernández Lobato (eds) *The Poetics of Late Latin Literature*. Oxford. 149–75.
Keaveney, A. 2005. *Sulla: The Last Republican*. London.
Keegan, J. 1976. *The Face of Battle*. London.
Keegan, J. 1987. *The Mask of Command*. London.
Keitel, E. 2012. 'The Camp and the City in Caesar's *De Bello Gallico* and *De Bello Civili*.' *The Classical Outlook* 89, 40–3.
Kelly, G. 2008. *Ammianus Marcellinus: The Allusive Historian*. Oxford.
Kennedy, H. 1995. 'The Financing of the Military in the Early Islamic State.' In A. Cameron (ed.) *The Byzantine and Early Islamic Near East, III: States, Resources and Armies*. Princeton. 361–78.
Kennedy, H. 2001. *The Armies of the Caliphs: Military and Society in the Early Islamic State*. London.
Kennedy, H. 2007. *The Great Arab Conquests: How the Spread of Islam Changed the World We Live In*. London.
Kennedy, H. 2011. 'Great Estates and Elite Lifestyles in the Fertile Crescent from Byzantium and Sasanian Iran to Islam.' In A. Fuess and J.-P. Hartung (eds) *Court Cultures in the Muslim World*. London. 54–79.
Kennet, D. 2007. 'The Decline of Eastern Arabia in the Sasanian Period.' *Arabian Archaeology and Epigraphy* 18, 86–122.
Keppie, L. 1984. *The Making of the Roman Army*. London.
Keydell, R. 1967. *Agathiae Myrinaei Historiarum Libri Quinque*. Berlin.
Khalek, N. 2010. '"He Was Tall and Slender, and his Virtues Were Numerous": Byzantine Hagiographical Topoi and the Companions of Muhammad in Al-Azdi's Futuh al-Sham.' In A. Papaconstantinou (ed.) *Writing 'True Stories': Historians and Hagiographers in the Late Antique and Medieval Near East*. Cultural Encounters in Late Antiquity and the Middle Ages, 9. Turnhout. 105–23.
Klotz, R. 1926. '(9) T. Livius.' *RE* 13.1, 816–52.
Köchly, A. [H.] 1860. *Ονοσάνδρου Στρατηγικός: Onosandri de imperatoris officio liber*. Leipzig.
Köchly, H. and W. Rüstow 1853–5. *Griechische Kriegsschriftsteller*. 3 vols. Leipzig. Repr. 1969. Onasbrück.
Koenen, L. 1970. 'Die "Laudatio Funebris" des Augustus für Agrippa auf einem neuen Papyrus.' *ZPE* 5, 217–84.
Koestermann, E. C. 1963. *Cornelius Tacitus: Annalen*. Vol. 1. Heidelberg.

Konijnendijk, R. 2016. 'Mardonius' Senseless Greeks.' *CQ* 66, 1–12.
Konijnendijk, R. 2018. *Classical Greek Tactics: A Cultural History*. Leiden.
Korting, G. 2017. *Varus' Untergang: Textkritische Anmerkungen zu Florus 2,30,34 b.* Heidelberg.
Korzenszky, E. 1932. 'Rezension: Dain 1930.' *PhW* 52, 1–8.
Korzenszky, E. 1935. 'Besprechungen: J.-R. Vieillefond 1932.' *BZ* 35, 145–9.
Korzenszky, E. and R. Vári 1935. *Onasandri Strategicus*. Sylloge Tacticorum Graecorum, 1. Budapest.
Kosmin, P. 2014. *The Land of the Elephant Kings*. Cambridge, MA.
Kraft, J. C., G. Rapp, G. J. Szemler, C. Tziavos and E. W. Kase. 1987. 'The Pass at Thermopylae, Greece.' *Journal of Field Archaeology* 14, 181–98.
Krallis, D. 2012. *Michael Attaleiates and the Politics of Imperial Decline in Eleventh Century Byzantium*. Tempe.
Krallis, D. 2017a. 'Historians, Politics, and the *Polis* in the Eleventh and Twelfth Centuries.' In J.-C. Cheynet and B. Flusin (eds) *Autour du 'Premier humanisme byzantin' et des 'Cinq études sur le XIe siècle', quarante ans après Paul Lemerle* [*TM* 21/2]. Paris. 421–50.
Krallis, D. 2017b. 'Urbane Warriors: Smoothing out Tensions between Soldiers and Civilians in Attaleiates' Encomium to Emperor Nikephoros III Botaneiates.' In M. Lauxtermann and M. Whittow (eds), *Being in Between: Byzantium in the Eleventh Century*. London. 154–68.
Krallis, D. 2018. 'Popular Political Agency in Byzantium's Village and Towns,' *Byzantina Symmeikta* 2, 11–38.
Kratchkovsky, I. and A. Vasiliev 1924. 'Histoire de Yahya ibn Sa'id d'Antioche.' *Patrologia Orientalis* 18, 701–833.
Kraus, C. S. 2005. 'Hair, Hegemony and Historiography: Caesar's Style and its Earliest Critics.' In T. Reinhardt, M. Lapidge and J. N. Adams (eds) *Aspects of the Language of Latin Prose*. Oxford. 97–115.
Kraus, C. S. 2009. '*Bellum Gallicum*.' In M. Griffin (ed.) *A Companion to Julius Caesar*. Chichester. 159–74.
Kraus, C. S. 2010. 'Divide and Conquer: Caesar *De Bello Gallico* 7.' In C. S. Kraus, J. Marincola and C. Pelling (eds) *Ancient Historiography and its Contexts: Studies in Honour of A. J. Woodman*. Oxford. 41–59.
Kraut, R. 2010. 'Ordinary Virtue from the *Phaedo* to the *Laws*.' In C. Bobonich (ed.) *Plato's Laws: A Critical Guide*. Cambridge. 51–70.
Krebs, C. B. 2006. '"Imaginary Geography" in Caesar's *Bellum Gallicum*.' *AJP* 127, 111–36.
Krentz, P. 2000. 'Deception in Archaic and Classical Warfare.' In H. Van Wees (ed.) *War and Violence in Ancient Greece*. London. 167–200.

Krentz, P. 2002. 'Fighting by the Rules: The Invention of the Hoplite Agôn.' *Hesperia* 71, 23–39.

Krentz, P. and E. L. Wheeler 1994. *Polyaenus: Stratagems of War*. 2 vols. Chicago.

Kroll, P. W. 1985. 'The Flight from the Capital and the Death of Precious Consort Yang.' *T'ang Studies* 3, 34–53.

Kucewicz, C. 2018. *Ancestral Custom? The Treatment of the War Dead in Archaic Athens*. PhD thesis, University College London.

Kučma, V. V. 1982–86. '"Стратегикос" Онасандра и "Стратегикон Маврикия": Опыт сравнительной характеристики.' *Vizantijskij Vremennik* I, 43, 35–53; II, 45, 20–34; III, 46, 109–23. Repr. in V. V. Kučma 2001. *Военная Организация Византийской Империи*. St Petersburg. 139–207.

Kuefler, M. 2001. *The Manly Eunuch: Masculinity, Gender Ambiguity and Christian Ideology in Late Antiquity*. Chicago.

Kuhrt, A. 2010. *The Persian Empire: A Corpus of Sources from the Achaemenid Period*. London.

Kulikowski, M. 2012. 'Coded Polemic in Ammianus 31 and the Date and Place of its Composition.' *JRS* 102, 79–102.

Lammert, F. 1938. 'Rezension: Korzenszky and Vári 1935.' *PhW* 58, 881–3.

Lana, I. 1952. *Velleio Patercolo o della propaganda*. Turin.

Landau-Tasseron, E. 1995. 'Features of the Pre-Conquest Muslim Army in the Time of Muḥammad.' In A. Cameron (ed.) *The Byzantine and Early Islamic Near East, III: States, Resources and Armies*. Princeton. 299–336.

Langlands, R. 2018. *Exemplary Ethics in Ancient Rome*. Cambridge.

Latacz, J. 1977. *Kampfparänese, Kampfdarstellung und Kampfwirklichkeit in der Ilias, bei Kallinos und Tyrtaios*. Munich.

Lattimore, R. 1960. *Greek Lyrics*. Chicago.

Launey, M. 1948. *Recherches sur les armées hellénistiques*. Paris.

Lauxtermann, M. D. 1998. 'John Geometres: Poet and Soldier.' *Byz* 68, 356–80.

Lauxtermann, M. D. 2003. *Byzantine Poetry from Pisides to Geometres: Texts and Contexts*. Vol. 1. Vienna.

Lavelle, B. M. 1992. 'Herodotos, Skythian Archers and the *Doryphoroi* of the Peisistratids.' *Klio* 74, 78–97.

Lavelle, B. M. 2005. *Fame, Money, and Power: The Rise of Peisistratos and 'Democratic' Tyranny at Athens*. Ann Arbor.

Lazarus, F. M. 1978/9. '*Fortuna* and Rhetorical Structure in Livy.' *CJ* 74, 128–31.

Lazenby, J. F. 1985. *The Spartan Army*. Mechanicsburg.

Le Bohec, Y. 1998a. 'Que voulait Onesandros?' In Y. Burnand, Y. Le Bohec and J.-P. Martin (eds) *Claude de Lyon, empereur romain: Actes du Colloque Paris-Nancy-Lyon, Nov. 1992*. Paris. 169–79.

Le Bohec, Y. 1998b. 'Vercingetorix.' *Rivista Storica dell'Antichità* 28, 85–120.

Lecky, W. E. H. 1886. *A History of European Morals from Augustus to Charlemagne.* Vol. 2. London.

Lee, A. D. 2005. 'The Empire at War.' In M. Maas (ed.) *The Cambridge Companion to the Age of Justinian.* Cambridge. 113–33.

Lee, A. D. 2013. *From Rome to Byzantium, AD 363 to 565: The Transformation of Ancient Rome.* Edinburgh.

Lee, A. D. (forthcoming). 'The Rhetoric of Generalship in Late Antiquity.'

Leidholm, N. 2019. *Elite Byzantine Kinship, ca. 950–1204: Blood, Reputation, and the Genos.* Leeds.

Lemcke, G. 1936. *Die Varusschlacht: Eine Quellenuntersuchung zum Bericht des Florus.* Hamburg.

Lendon, J. E. 1999. 'The Rhetoric of Combat: Greek Military Theory and Roman Culture in Julius Caesar's Battle Descriptions.' *Cl. Ant.* 18, 273–329.

Lendon, J. E. 2005. *Soldiers and Ghosts: A History of Battle in Classical Antiquity.* New Haven.

Lendon, J. E. 2017a. 'Battle Description in the Ancient Historians, Part I: Structure, Array, and Fighting.' *G&R* 64, 39–64.

Lendon, J. E. 2017b. 'Battle Description in the Ancient Historians, Part II: Speeches, Results, and Sea Battles.' *G&R* 64, 145–67.

Lenski, N. E. 1997. '*Initium mali Romano imperio*: Contemporary Reactions to the Battle of Adrianople.' *TAPA* 127, 129–68.

Lenski, N. E. 2002. *Failure of Empire.* Berkeley.

Lenski, N. E. 2007. 'Two Sieges of Amida (AD 359 and 502–503) and the Experience of Combat in the Late Roman East.' In A. S. Lewin, P. Pellegrini, Z. T. Fiema and S. Janniard (eds) *The Late Roman Army in the Near East from Diocletian to the Arab Conquest: Proceedings of a Colloquium held at Potenza, Acerenza and Matera, Italy.* Oxford. 219–36.

Leone, A. 2007. *Changing Townscapes in North Africa from Late Antiquity to the Arab Conquest.* Bari.

Leoni, B. 2003. *La Parafrasi Ambrosiana dello Strategicon di Maurizio: L'arte della guerra a Bisanzio.* Milan.

Levithan, J. 2013. *Roman Siege Warfare.* Ann Arbor.

Lewental, D. G. 2017. 'The Death of Rostam: Literary Representations of Iranian Identity in Early Islam.' *Iranian Studies* 50, 223–45.

Li Baiyao. 1972. *Bei Qi shu.* Beijing.

Lica, V. 2001. '"Clades Variana" and "Postliminium".' *Hist.* 50, 496–501.

Lillington-Martin, C. 2017. 'Procopius, πάρεδρος/Quaestor, *Codex Justinianus*, I.27 and Belisarius' Strategy in the Mediterranean.' In C. Lillington-Martin and

E. Turquois (eds) *Procopius of Caesarea: Literary and Historical Interpretations*. London. 157–85.
Linderski, J. 1990. 'Roman Officers in the Year of Pydna.' *AJP* 111, 53–71.
Linghu Defen 1971. *Zhou shu*. Beijing.
Lintott, A. 1999. *The Constitution of the Roman Republic*. Oxford.
Liu Xu 1975. *Jiu Tangshu*. Beijing.
Llewellyn-Jones, L. 2013. *King and Court in Ancient Persia 559–331 BCE*. Edinburgh.
Loewe, M. 2006. *The Government of the Qin and Han Empires, 221 BCE–220 CE*. Indianapolis.
Loreto, L. 1995. 'Il generale e la biblioteca: La trattatistica militare greca da Democrito di Abdera ad Alessio I Comneno.' In G. Cambiano, L. Canfora and D. Lanza (eds) *Lo spazio letterario della Grecia antica* II. Vol. II. Rome. 563–89.
Lowe, C. 1927. *A Byzantine Paraphrase of Onasander*. St Louis.
Lucarini, C. M. 2010. 'Ad Onasandri Strategicum.' *MH* 67, 222–7.
Luginbill, R. 1999. *Thucydides on War and National Character*. Boulder.
Lund, A. 1991. 'Versuch einer Gesamtinterpretation der "Germania" des Tacitus, mit einem Anhang: Zu Entstehung und Geschichte des Namens und Begriffs "Germani".' *ANRW* 2.33.3, 1858–1988.
Lund, A. 2009. 'Zur Deutung der Taciteischen Darstellung des Orts der Varus-Schlacht.' *Gymnasium* 116, 275–83.
Luterbacher. F. 1910. 'Review of O. Rossbach (ed.), *T. Livi Periochae omnium Librorum*.' *Berliner Philologische Wochenschrift* 30, 1186–93.
Luttwak, E. N. 2011. *The Grand Strategy of the Byzantine Empire*. Cambridge, MA.
Ma, J. 2013. 'Alexander's Decision-Making as Historical Problem.' *Revue des Études Militaires Anciennes* 6, 113–25.
McAuley, A. 2018. 'The House of Achaios: Reconstructing an Early Client Dynasty in Seleukid Anatolia.' In K. Erickson (ed.) *The Seleukid Empire 281–222 BC: War within the Family*. Swansea. 37–58.
McAuley, A. 2019. '*Terra cognita sed vacua?* (Re-)Appropriating Territory through Hellenistic City Foundations.' In R. Evans and M. de Marre (eds) *Piracy, Pillage, and Plunder in Antiquity: Appropriation and the Ancient World*. London. 60–83.
McCormick, M. 1986. *Eternal Victory: Triumphal Rulership in Late Antiquity, Byzantium and the Early Medieval West*. Cambridge.
McDonnell, M. 2006. *Roman Manliness: Virtus and the Roman Republic*. Cambridge.
McDonough, S. 2013. 'Military and Society in Sasanian Iran.' In B. Campbell and L. A. Tritle (eds) *The Oxford Handbook of Warfare in the Classical World*. Oxford. 605–8.
McDonough, S. 2016. 'The "Warrior of the Lords": Smbat Bagratuni at the Center and Periphery of Late Sasanian Iran.' *Iranian Studies* 49, 233–45.

McEvoy, M. A. 2014. 'Between the Old Rome and the New: Imperial Co-operation ca. 400–500 CE.' In D. Dzino and K. Parry (eds) *Byzantium, its Neighbours and it Cultures*. Brisbane. 245–67.

McGeer, E. 1991. 'Tradition and Reality in the *Taktika* of Nikephoros Ouranos.' *DOP* 45, 129–40.

McGeer, E. 1995. *Sowing the Dragon's Teeth: Byzantine Warfare in the Tenth Century*. Washington, DC.

McGeer, E. 2003. 'Two Military Orations of Constantine VII.' In J.W. Nesbitt (ed.) *Byzantine Authors: Literary Activities and Preoccupations*. Leiden. 111–35.

McGeer, E. 2008a. *Sowing the Dragon's Teeth: Byzantine Warfare in the Tenth Century*. Washington, DC.

McGeer, E. 2008b. 'Military Texts.' In E. Jeffreys, J. Haldon and R. Cormack (eds) *The Oxford Handbook of Byzantine Studies*. Oxford. 907–14.

Mack, W. 2005. *Proxeny and Polis*. Oxford.

Macrides, R. 2007. *George Akropolites: The History*. Oxford.

Magdalino, P. 1993. *The Empire of Manuel I Komnenos, 1143–1180*. Cambridge.

Magdalino, P. 2013. 'Knowledge in Authority and Authorised History: The Imperial Intellectual Programme of Leo VI and Constantine VII.' In P. Armstrong (ed.) *Authority in Byzantium*. Farnham. 187–209.

Magoulias, H. J. 1984. *O City of Byzantium: Annals of Niketas Choniates*. Detroit.

Mair, V. et al. (eds) 2005. *Hawai'i Reader in Traditional Chinese Culture*. Honolulu.

Mango, C. A. 1965. 'Byzantinism and Romantic Hellenism.' *Journal of the Warburg and Courtauld Institutes* 28, 29–43.

Mango, C. A. 1975. *Byzantine Literature as a Distorting Mirror: An Inaugural Lecture Delivered Before the University of Oxford on 21 May 1974*. Oxford.

Mango, C. A. 1991. *La civiltà bizantina*. Bari.

Mango, C. A. and R. Scott 1997. *The Chronicle of Theophanes Confessor: Byzantine and Near Eastern History, AD 284–813*. Oxford.

Mao Hanguang 1990. 'Wei-Bo er bai nian shi lun.' In Mao Hanguang (ed.) *Zhongguo zhonggu zhengzhi shi lun*. Taipei. 323–90.

Marcos, M. 2015. 'A Tale of Two Commanders: Ammianus Marcellinus on the Campaigns of Constantius II and Julian on the Northern Frontiers.' *AJP* 136, 669–708.

Marek, C. 2016. *In the Land of a Thousand Gods: A History of Asia Minor in the Ancient World*. Princeton.

Marincola, J. 1997. *Authority and Tradition in Ancient Historiography*. Cambridge.

Markopoulos, A. 2004a. *History and Literature of Byzantium in the 9th–10th Centuries*. Aldershot and Burlington.

Markopoulos, A. 2004b. 'Gender Issues in Leo the Deacon.' In A. Markopoulos

History and Literature of Byzantium in the 9th–10th Centuries. Aldershot and Burlington . Ch. XXIII.
Markopoulos, A. 2004c. 'Joseph Bringas: Prosopographical Problems and Ideological Trends.' In A. Markopoulos *History and Literature of Byzantium in the 9th–10th Centuries.* Aldershot and Burlington. Ch. IV.
Markopoulos, A. 2012. 'The Ideology of War in the Military Harangues of Constantine VII Porphyrogennetos.' In J. Koder and I. Stouraitis (eds) *Byzantine War Ideology between Roman Imperial Concept and Christian Religion.* Vienna. 47–56.
Martin, G. 2006. *Dexipp von Athen: Edition, Übersetzung und begleitende Studien.* Tübingen.
Martin, G. and J. Grusková 2014. '"Scythica Vindobonensia" by Dexippus (?): New Fragments on Decius' Gothic Wars.' *GRBS* 54, 728–54.
Martini, A. [E.] and D. Bassi 1906. *Catalogus codicum graecorum Bibliothecae Ambrosianae.* 2 vols. Milan.
Matthews, J. F. 1989. *The Roman Empire of Ammianus.* London.
Matthews, J. F. 2015. 'Ammianus Marcellinus.' In *Oxford Classical Dictionary Online.* https://oxfordre.com/classics/view/10.1093/acrefore/9780199381135.001.0001/acrefore-9780199381135-e-361?product=orecla.
Mattingly, D. J. 1994. *Tripolitania.* Ann Arbor.
Mattingly, D. J. 2008. 'Laguatan.' *Encyclopédie Berbère* 28–9, 4314–18.
Mattingly, H. 1923. *Coins of the Roman Empire in the British Museum.* Vol. 1. London.
Mattingly, H. and E. A. Sydenham. 1923. *The Roman Imperial Coinage.* Vol. 1. London.
Mazzucchi, C. M. 1978. 'Dagli anni di Basilio Parakimomenos (cod. Ambr. B 119 sup.).' *Aevum* 52, 267–316.
Mazzucchi, C. M. 1982. 'Recensioni: Dennis and Gamillscheg 1981.' *Aevum* 56, 280–2.
Mecella, L. 2006. 'Πάντα μὲν ἦν ἄναρχά τε καὶ ἀβοήθητα: Le città dell'Oriente romano e le invasioni barbariche del III secolo d.c.' *Mediterraneo Antico: Economie, Società, Culture* 9, 241–66.
Mecella, L. 2009. 'Die Überlieferung der Kestoi des Julius Africanus in den byzantinischen Textsammlungen zur Militärtechnik.' In M. Wallraff and L. Mecella (eds) *Die Kestoi des Julius Africanus und ihre Überlieferung.* Berlin. 85–144.
Mecella, L. 2013. *Dexippo di Atene: Testimonianze e Frammenti.* Rome.
Meier, C. 1995. *Caesar.* Trans. D. McLintock. London.
Meier, M. 1999. 'Beobachtungen zu den sogenannten Pestschilderungen bei Thukydides II 47–54 und bei Prokop, *Bell. Pers.* II 22–23.' *Tyche* 14, 177–210.

Meiggs, R. and D. Lewis 1969. *A Selection of Greek Historical Inscriptions to the End of the Fifth Century B.C.* Oxford.

Meißner, B. 1999. *Die technologische Fachliteratur der Antike: Struktur, Überlieferung und Wirkung technischen Wissens in der Antike (ca. 400 v. Chr.–ca. 500 n. Chr.).* Berlin.

Melville-Jones, J. R. 2017. *Eustathios of Thessaloniki: The Capture of Thessaloniki.* Leiden.

Merkelbach, R. 2000. 'Wer war Alexandros, zu dem Asoka eine Gesandtschaft geschickt hat?' *EA* 32, 126–8.

Merrills, A. H. 2017. 'Rome and the Vandals.' In P. de Souza, P. Arnaud and C. Buchet (eds) *The Sea in History, I: The Ancient World.* Woodbridge. 496–507.

Merrills, A. H. 2019. 'Corippus' Triumphal Ethnography: Another Look at Iohannis II.28–161.' *Libyan Studies* 50, 1–11.

Merrills, A. H. and R. Miles 2010. *The Vandals.* Oxford.

Messis, C. 2014. *Les eunuques à Byzance, entre réalité et imaginaire.* Paris.

Meyer, S. S. 2015. *Plato: Laws 1 and 2.* Oxford.

Migne, J.-P. 1857–66. *Patrologia Graeca, 142: Georgios of Cyprus.* Paris.

Millar, F. 1969. 'P. Herennius Dexippus: The Greek World and the Third Century Invasions.' *JRS* 59, 12–29. Repr. in H. M. Cotton and G. M. Rodgers (eds) 2004. *Rome, the Greek World and the East, 2: Government, Society and Culture in the Roman Empire.* Chapel Hill. 3–22.

Milner, N. P. 1996. *Vegetius: Epitome of Military Science.* 2nd edn. Liverpool.

Mitchell, S. 2018. 'Dispelling Seleukid Phantoms: Macedonians in Western Asia Minor from Alexander to the Attalids.' In K. Erickson (ed.) *The Seleukid Empire 281–222 BC: War within the Family.* Swansea. 1–10.

Mitthof, F. 2019. 'Bemerkungen zu Kaiser Decius und seinem Gotenkrieg 250–251 n. Chr.' In F. Mitthof et al. (eds) *Empire in Crisis: Gothic Invasions and Roman Historiography.* Vienna. 311–36.

Modéran, Y. 2003a. 'Jean Troglita.' *Encyclopédie Berbère* 25, 3866–70.

Modéran, Y. 2003b. *Les Maures et l'Afrique romaine, IVe–VIIe siècle.* Rome. https://books.openedition.org/efr/1395?lang=en.

Moffatt, A. and M. Tall 2012. *Constantine Porphyrogennetos: The Book of Ceremonies.* 2 vols. Canberra.

Moland, L. 1879. *Œuvres complètes de Voltaire, 5.27: Le pyrrhonism de l'histoire.* Paris.

Molyneux, J. H. 1992. *Simonides: A Historical Study.* Wauconda.

Moore, R. 2013. 'Generalship: Leadership and Command.' In B. Campbell and L. A. Tritle (eds) *The Oxford Handbook of Warfare in the Classical World.* Vol. 2. Oxford. 457–73.

Moravcsik, G.. and R. J. H. Jenkins 1967. *Constantine Porphyrogenitus: De Administrando Imperio*. Washington, DC.

Morony, M. 2001. 'The Late Sasanian Economic Impact on the Arabian Peninsula.' *Nāme-ye Irān-e Bāstān* 1, 25–37.

Morony, M. 2004. 'Economic Boundaries? Late Antiquity and Early Islam.' *Journal of the Economic and Social History of the Orient* 47, 166–94.

Morony, M. 2012. 'Iran in the Early Islamic Period.' In T. Daryaee (ed.) *The Oxford Handbook of Iranian History*. Oxford. 208–26.

Morony, M. 2013. 'The Islamic Conquest of Sasanian Iran.' In D. T. Potts (ed.) *The Oxford Handbook of Ancient Iran*. Oxford. 975–86.

Morrow, G. R. 1960. *Plato's Cretan City: A Historical Interpretation of the Laws*. Princeton.

Morstein-Marx, R. 1995. *Hegemony to Empire: The Development of the Roman Imperium in the East from 148 to 62 BC*. Berkeley.

Munro, J. A. R. 1939. 'Xerxes' Invasion of Greece.' In J. B. Bury, S. A. Cook and F. E. Adcock (eds) *The Cambridge Ancient History*. Vol. 4. Cambridge. 268–316.

Murdoch, A. 2008. *Rome's Greatest Defeat: Massacre in the Teutoburg Forest*. Stroud.

Murphy, P. R. 1986. 'Caesar's Continuators and Caesar's *Felicitas*.' *CW* 79, 307–17.

Murray, J. 2017. 'Procopius and Boethius: Christian Philosophy in the Persian Wars.' In C. Lillington-Martin and E. Turquois (eds) *Procopius of Caesarea: Literary and Historical Interpretations*. London. 104–19.

Mutschler, F.-H. 1975. *Erzählstil und Propaganda in Caesars Kommentarien*. Heidelberg.

Nails, D. 2002. *The People of Plato: A Prosopography of Plato and Other Socratics*. Indianapolis.

Naudé, C. P. T. 1958. 'Battles and Sieges in Ammianus Marcellinus.' *AClass* 1, 92–105.

Neils, J. 2001. *The Parthenon Frieze*. Cambridge.

Németh, A. 2018. *The Excerpta Constantiniana and the Byzantine Appropriation of the Past*. Cambridge.

Neville, L. 2012. *Heroes and Romans in Twelfth-Century Byzantium: The Material for History of Nikephoros Bryennios*. Cambridge.

Neville, L. 2016. 'Why Did the Byzantines Write History?' In S. Marjanović-Dušanić (ed.) *Proceedings of the 23rd International Congress of Byzantine Studies: Plenary Papers*. Belgrade. 265–76.

Nevin, S. 2017. *Military Leaders and Sacred Space in Classical Greek Warfare: Temples, Sanctuaries and Conflict in Antiquity*. London.

Nicolle, D. 2006. *Yarmuk AD 636: The Muslim Conquest of Syria*. Oxford.

Nipperdey, K. 1884. *Cornelius Tacitus*. 8th edn. Vol. 1. Berlin.
Nolan, D. J. 2014. *The Role of Battle Narrative in the Bellum Gallicum*. PhD thesis, University of Tasmania.
Nolan, D. J. 2016. 'Caesar's *Exempla* and the Role of Centurions in Battle.' In J. Armstrong (ed.) *Circum Mare: Themes in Ancient Warfare*. Leiden. 34–62.
Nussbaum, M. C. 1994. *The Therapy of Desire: Theory and Desire in Hellenistic Ethics*. Princeton.
Ober, J. 1991. 'Hoplites and Obstacles.' In V. D. Hanson (ed.) *Hoplites: The Classical Greek Battle Experience*. New York. 173–96.
Ober, J. 1996. *The Athenian Revolution: Essays on Ancient Greek Democracy and Political Theory*. Princeton.
O'Brien, P. 2013. 'Vetranio's Revenge? The Rhetorical Prowess of Ammianus' Constantius.' *DHA* supp. 8, 221–58.
O'Gorman, E. 2000. *Irony and Misreading in the Annals of Tacitus*. Cambridge.
Oldfather, C. H. 1946. *Diodorus Siculus: Books IX–XII.40*. Cambridge, MA.
Oldfather, W. A. (et al. = The Illinois Greek Club) 1923. *Aeneas Tacticus, Asclepiodotus, Onasander*. Cambridge, MA.
Östenberg, I. 2018. 'Defeated by the Forest, the Pass, the Wind: Nature as an Enemy of Rome.' In J. H. Clark and B. Turner (eds) *Brill's Companion to Military Defeat in Ancient Mediterranean Society*. Leiden. 240–61.
Ouyang Xiu and Song Qi 1975. *Xin Tangshu*. Beijing.
Pagán, V. E. 1999. 'Beyond Teutoburg: Transgression and Transformation in Tacitus *Annales* 1.61–62.' *CP* 94, 302–20.
Pagán, V. E. 2002. 'Actium and Teutoburg: Augustan Victory and Defeat in Vergil and Tacitus.' In D. S. Levene and D. P. Nelis (eds) *Clio and the Poets: Augustan Poetry and the Traditions of Ancient Historiography*. Leiden. 45–60.
Papaconstantinou, A. (ed.) 2010. *Writing 'True Stories': Historians and Hagiographers in the Late Antique and Medieval Near East*. Cultural Encounters in Late Antiquity and the Middle Ages, 9. Turnhout.
Parnell, D. A. 2017. *Justinian's Men: Careers and Relationships of Byzantine Army Officers, 518–610*. London.
Patkanov, K. P 1866. *Essai d'une histoire de la dynastie des Sassanides, d'après les renseignements fournis par les historiens arméniens*. Trans. É. Prud'homme. Paris.
Pazdernik, C. 2006. 'Xenophon's *Hellenica* in Procopius' *Wars*: Pharnabazus and Belisarius.' *GRBS* 46, 175–206.
Pearce, S. A. 1987. *The Yü-wen Regime in Sixth-Century China*. PhD thesis, Princeton University.
Pelliccia, H. 2009. 'Simonides, Pindar and Bacchylides.' In F. Budelmann (ed.) *The Cambridge Companion to Greek Lyric*. Cambridge. 240–62.

Pelling, C. 1993. 'Tacitus and Germanicus.' In T. J. Luce and A. J. Woodman (eds) *Tacitus and the Tacitean Tradition*. Princeton. 59–85.

Pentcheva, B. V. 2007. 'Containers of Power: Eunuchs and Reliquaries in Byzantium.' *Res* 51, 109–20.

Pérez Martín, I. 2002. *Miguel Ataliates, Historia: Introducción, edición, traducción y comentario*. Madrid

Peters, W. 1972. *Untersuchungen zu Onasander*. Bonn.

Peterson, C. A. 1966. *The Autonomy of the Northeastern Provinces in the Period Following the An Lu-shan Rebellion*. PhD thesis, Columbia University.

Petrocelli, C. 2008. *Onasandro, Il generale: Manuale per l'esercizio del comando*. Bari.

Pfeilschifter, R. 2007. 'The Allies in the Republican Army and the Romanisation of Italy.' In R. Roth and J. Keller (eds) *Roman by Integration: Dimensions of Group Identity in Material Culture and Text*. Portsmouth. 27–42.

Piérart, M. 2003. 'The Common Oracle of the Milesians and the Argives (Hdt. 6.19 and 77).' In P. Derow and R. Parker (eds) *Herodotus and his World: Essays from a Conference in Memory of George Forrest*. Oxford. 275–96.

Pietrykowski, J. 2012. *Great Battles of the Hellenistic World*. Barnsley.

Pilkington, N. 2019. *The Carthaginian Empire: 550–202 BCE*. Lanham.

Pina Polo, F. and A. Diaz Fernandez 2019. *The Quaestorship in the Roman Republic*. Berlin.

Potter, D. S. 1990. *Prophecy and History in the Crisis of the Roman Empire: An Historical Commentary on the Thirteenth Sibylline Oracle*. Oxford.

Potter, D. S. 2010. 'Caesar and the Helvetians.' In G. Fagan and M. Trundle (eds) *New Perspectives on Ancient Warfare*. Leiden. 305–29.

Potter, D. S. 2018. 'Decius and Valerian.' In D. W. P. Burgersdijk and A. J. Ross (eds) *Imagining Emperors in the Later Roman Empire*. Leiden. 18–38.

Potter, D. S. 2019. 'Dexippus' Gothic Anthropology.' In F. Mitthof et al. (eds) *Empire in Crisis: Gothic Invasions and Roman Historiography*. Vienna. 357–68.

Pourshariati, P. 2008. *The Decline and Fall of the Sasanian Empire: The Sasanian–Parthian Confederacy and the Arab Conquest of Iran*. London.

Powell, A. 1998. 'Julius Caesar and the Presentation of Massacre.' In K. Welch and A. Powell (eds) *Julius Caesar as Artful Reporter: The War Commentaries as Political Instruments*. Swansea. 111–38.

Prag, J. 2007. '*Auxilia* and *Gymnasia*: A Sicilian Model of Roman Imperialism.' *JRS* 97, 68–100.

Prag, J. 2014a. 'The Quaestorship in the Third and Second Centuries B.C.' In J. Dubouloz, S. Pittia and G. Sabatini (eds) *L'imperium romanum en perspective*. Besançon. 193–209.

Prag, J. 2014b. 'Bronze Rostra from the Egadi Islands of NW Sicily: The Latin Inscriptions.' *JRA* 27, 33–59.

Pritchard, D. M. 2010. 'The Symbiosis between Democracy and War: The Case of Ancient Athens.' In D. M. Pritchard (ed.) *War, Democracy and Culture in Classical Athens*. Cambridge. 1–62.

Pritchard, D. M. 2019. *Athenian Democracy at War*. Cambridge.

Pritchett, W. K. 1974. *The Greek State at War: Part II*. Berkeley.

Pritchett, W. K. 1985. *The Greek State at War: Part IV*. Berkeley.

Pritchett, W. K. 1994a. *Essays in Greek History*. Amsterdam.

Pritchett, W. K. 1994b. 'The General's Exhortation in Greek Warfare.' In W. K. Pritchett *Essays in Greek History*. Amsterdam. 27–109.

Pryor, J. H. and E. M. Jeffreys 2006. *The Age of the ΔΡΟΜΩΝ: The Byzantine Navy ca 500–1204*. Leiden.

Raaflaub, K. A. 2008. 'Homeric Warriors and Battles: Trying to Resolve Old Problems.' *CW* 101, 469–183.

Radoslavova, G., G. Dzanev and N. Nikolov 2011. 'The Battle at Abritus in AD 251: Written Sources, Archaeological and Numismatic Data.' *Archaeologia Bulgarica* 15, 23–46.

Ramage, E. S. 2003. 'Aspects of Propaganda in the *De Bello Gallico*: Caesar's Virtues and Attributes.' *Athenaeum* 91, 331–72.

Rambaud, M. 1966. *L'art de la déformation historique dans les commentaires de César*. Paris.

Rance, P. 1994. *Tactics and Tactica in the Sixth Century: Tradition and Originality*. PhD thesis, University of St Andrews.

Rance, P. 2000. '*Simulacra pugnae*: The Literary and Historical Tradition of Mock Battles in the Roman and Early Byzantine Army.' *GRBS* 41, 223–75.

Rance, P. 2005. 'Narses and the Battle of Taginae (Busta Gallorum) 552: Procopius and Sixth-Century Warfare.' *Hist.* 54, 424–72.

Rance, P. 2007a. 'The *Etymologicum Magnum* and the "Fragment of Urbicius".' *GRBS* 47, 193–224.

Rance, P. 2007b. 'The Date of the Military Compendium of Syrianus Magister (Formerly the Sixth-Century Anonymus Byzantinus.' *BZ* 100, 701–37.

Rance, P. 2008. '*Noumera* or *mounera*: A Parallel Philological Problem in *De Cerimoniis* and Maurice's *Strategikon*.' *JÖB* 58, 121–9.

Rance, P. 2017a. 'The Reception of Aineias' *Poliorketika* in Byzantine Military Literature.' In M. Pretzler and N. Barley (eds) *A Companion to Aineias Tacticus*. Leiden. 290–373.

Rance, P. 2017b. 'Introduction.' In P. Rance and N. V. Sekunda (eds) *Greek Taktika: Ancient Military Writing and its Heritage*. Gdańsk. 9–64.

Rance, P. 2017c. 'Maurice's *Strategicon* and "The Ancients": The Late Antique Reception of Aelian and Arrian.' In P. Rance and N. V. Sekunda (eds) *Greek Taktika: Ancient Military Writing and its Heritage*. Gdańsk. 217–55.

Rance, P. 2018. 'Late Byzantine Elites and Military Literature: Authors, Readers and Manuscripts (11th–15th Centuries).' In G. Theotokis and A. Yıldız (eds) *A Military History of the Mediterranean Sea: Aspects of War, Diplomacy and Military Elites*. Leiden. 255–86.

Rance, P. (forthcoming). *The Roman Art of War in Late Antiquity: The Strategikon of the Emperor Maurice: A Translation with Commentary and Textual Studies*. London.

Rasmussen, D. 1963. *Caesars Commentarii: Stil und Stilwandel am Beispiel der Direkten Rede*. Göttingen.

Raven, S. 1969. *Rome in Africa*. London.

Rawlings, L. 2000. 'Alternative Agonies: Hoplite Martial and Combat Experiences Beyond the Phalanx.' In H. van Wees (ed.) *War and Violence in Ancient Greece*. London. 233–59.

Rawlings, L. 2007. *The Ancient Greeks at War*. Manchester.

Rawson, E. 1971. 'The Literary Sources for the Pre-Marian Army.' *PBSR* 39, 13–31.

Reeve, M. D. 2004. *Vegetius: Epitoma Rei Militaris*. Oxford.

Reinhold, M. 1972. 'Marcus Agrippa's Son-in-Law P. Quinctilius Varus.' *CP* 67, 119–21.

Reinsch, D. R., A. Kambylis and F. Kolovou (eds) 2001. *Annae Comnenae Alexias*. Berlin.

Renauld, É. 1926–8. *Psellos: Chronographie ou histoire d'un siècle de Byzance (976–1077)*. 2 vols. Paris.

Rey, F. E. 2010. 'Weapons, Technological Determinism and Ancient Warfare.' In G. Fagan and M. Trundle (eds) *New Perspectives on Ancient Warfare*. Leiden. 21–56.

Reza, E. 2014. *Azerbaijan and Aran (Caucasian Albania)*. Notes and trans. A. Ghazarians. London.

Richardot, P. 2009. 'La pacification de l'Afrique byzantine 534–546.' *Stratégique* 1–4.93–6, 129–58.

Ridley, R. T. 1975. 'Was Scipio Africanus at Cannae?' *Latomus* 34, 161–5.

Riedel, M. L. D. 2016. 'Biblical Echoes in Two Byzantine Military Speeches.' *BMGS* 40, 207–22.

Riedel, M. L. D. 2018. *Leo VI and the Transformation of Byzantine Christian Identity: Writings of an Unexpected Emperor*. Cambridge.

Riedlberger, P. 2010a. *Philologischer, historischer und liturgischer Kommentar zum*

8. Buch der Johannis des Goripp. Nebst kritischer Edition und Übersetzung. Groningen.

Riedlberger, P. 2010b. 'Recherches onomastiques relatives à la composition ethnique du personnel militaire en Afrique byzantine (546–548)'. In H. Börm and J. Wiesehöfer (eds) *Commutatio et Contentio: Studies in the Late Roman, Sasanian, and Early Islamic Near East*. Düsseldorf. 254–71

Rigaltius [Rigault], N. 1598–9. Ὀνοσάνδρου Στρατηγικός, *Onosandri Strategicus sive de imperatoris institutione . . . Latine interpretatione et notis illustravit*. Paris. Repr. 1600. Heidelberg.

Riggsby, A. M. 2006. *Caesar in Gaul and Rome: War in Words*. Austin.

Rijksbaron, A. 2007. *Plato: Ion, Or: On the Iliad*. Leiden.

Ringrose, K. M. 2003. *The Perfect Servant: Eunuchs and the Social Construction of Gender in Byzantium*. Chicago.

Robert, L. 1984. 'Documents d'Asie Mineure.' *BCH* 108, 457–532.

Robinson, C. 2003. *Islamic Historiography*. Cambridge.

Roisman, J. 2017. *The Classical Art of Command: Eight Greek Generals Who Shaped the History of Warfare*. Oxford.

Rolfe, J. C. 1940. *Ammianus Marcellinus*. Vol. 2. Cambridge, MA.

Roller, M. B. 2018. *Models from the Past in Roman Culture: A World of Exempla*. Cambridge.

Romano, R. (trans.) 1999. *La satira bizantina dei secoli XI–XV* [Anonymous, *Timarion*]. Turin.

Romilly, J. 1956. 'La crainte dans l'oeuvre de Thucydide.' *C&M* 17, 117–29.

Roos, A. G. and G. Wirth (eds) 1968. *Flavii Arriani quae exstant omnia*. Leipzig. 2 vols. Repr. 2002.

Rose, J. 2011. *Zoroastrianism: An Introduction*. London.

Rose, P. W. 2012. *Class in Archaic Greece*. Cambridge.

Rosenstein, N. S. 1986. '"*Imperatores Victi*": The Case of C. Hostilius Mancinus.' *Cl. Ant.* 5, 230–52.

Rosenstein, N. S. 1990. *Imperatores Victi: Military Defeat and Aristocratic Competition in the Middle and Late Republic*. Berkeley.

Rosenstein, N. S. 2009. 'General and Imperialist.' In M. Griffin (ed.) *A Companion to Julius Caesar*. Chichester. 85–99.

Rosenstein, N. S. 2012. *Rome and the Mediterranean 290 to 146 BC*. Edinburgh.

Ross, A. J. 2011. '*Inter Quos Ego Quoque Eram*': Authorship and Participation in Ammianus Marcellinus. PhD thesis, University of Oxford.

Ross, A. J. 2015. '"Syene as Face of Battle": Heliodorus and Late Antique Historiography.' *Ancient Narrative* 12, 1–26.

Ross, A. J. 2016. *Ammianus' Julian: Narrative and Genre in the Res Gestae*. Oxford.

Ross, A. J. 2017. 'Narrator and Participant in Procopius' *Wars*.' In C. Lillington-Martin and E. Turquois (eds) *Procopius of Caesarea: Literary and Historical Interpretations*. London. 73–90.
Ross, D. O. 1973. 'The Tacitean Germanicus.' *Yale Classical Studies* 23, 209–27.
Ross, M. 1958. 'Basil the Proedros Patron of the Arts.' *Archaeology* 11, 271–5.
Rossbach, O. 1889. 'Die handschriftliche Ueberlieferung der *Periochae* des Livius.' *RhM* 44, 65–103.
Rossbach, O. 1910a. 'Der Schluß des Geschichtswerkes des Livius.' *Berliner Philologische Wochenschrift* 30, 1396–8.
Rossbach, O. 1910b. *T. Livi Periochae omnium librorum*. Leipzig.
Roueché, C. 2002. 'The Literary Background of Kekaumenos.' In C. Holmes and J. Waring (eds) *Literacy, Education and Manuscript Transmission in Byzantium and Beyond*. Leiden. 111–38.
Roueché, C. 2003. 'The Rhetoric of Kekaumenos.' In E. Jeffreys (ed.) *Rhetoric in Byzantium*. Aldershot. 23–37.
Roueché, C. 2009. 'The Place of Kekaumenos in the Admonitory Tradition.' In P. Odorico (ed.) *L'éducation au gouvernment et à la vie: La tradition des 'règles de vie' de l'antiquité au Moyen-Âge: Actes du Colloque Internationale, Pise, 18 et 19 mars 2005*. Paris. 129–44.
Rouveret, A. 1991. 'Tacite et les monuments.' *ANRW* 2.33.4, 3051–99.
Rowe, C. 1995. *Plato: Statesman*. Warminster.
Rowe, C. 1998. *Plato: Symposium*. Warminster.
Rowe, C. 2018. '"Moderation" and Courage in Plato's *Politicus* (305e–311c).' In B. Bossi and T. M. Robinson (eds) *Plato's Statesman Revisited*. Berlin. 309–26.
Rüpke, J. 1992. 'Wer las Caesars *bella* als *commentarii*?' *Gymnasium* 99, 201–26.
Russell, A. 2013. 'Speech, Competition and Collaboration; Tribunician Politics and the Development of Popular Ideology.' In C. Steel and H. van der Blom (eds) *Community and Communication: Oratory and Politics in Republican Rome*. Oxford. 101–15.
Russell, D. A. and N. G. Wilson 1981. *Menander Rhetor*. Oxford.
Rutland, L. W. 1987. 'The Tacitean Germanicus: Suggestions for a Re-evaluation.' *RhM* 130, 153–64.
Ryan, F. X. 1998. *Rank and Participation in the Republican Senate*. Stuttgart.
Sabbah, G. 1978. *La méthode d'Ammien Marcellin*. Paris.
Sabin, P. 2000. 'The Face of Roman Battle.' *JRS* 90, 1–17.
Sabin, P., H. Van Wees and M. Whitby (eds) 2007. *The Cambridge History of Greek and Roman Warfare, I: Greece, the Hellenistic World and the Rise of Rome*. Cambridge.

Salzman, M. R. 2017. 'Emperors and Elites in Rome after the Vandal Sack of 455.' *Antiquité Tardive* 25, 243–62.

Samaras, T. 2010. 'Family and the Question of Women in the *Laws*.' In C. Bobonich (ed.) *Plato's Laws: A Critical Guide*. Cambridge. 172–96.

Sarris, P. 2006. *Economy and Society in the Age of Justinian*. Cambridge.

Sarris, P. 2017. 'Landownership and Rural Society in the Writings of Procopius.' In C. Lillington-Martin and E. Turquois (eds) *Procopius of Caesarea: Literary and Historical Interpretations*. London. 238–50.

Savalli-Lestrade, I. 1998. *Les philoi royaux dans l'Asie hellénistique*. Geneva.

Savant, S. 2013. 'Forgetting Ctesiphon: Iran's Pre-Islamic Past, c. 800–1100.' In P. Wood (ed.) *History and Identity in the Late Antique Near East*. Oxford. 169–86.

Schadee, H. 2008. 'Caesar's Construction of Northern Europe: Inquiry, Contact and Corruption in *De Bello Gallico*.' *CQ* 58, 158–80.

Schauer, M. 2017. *Der Gallische Krieg: Geschichte und Täuschung in Caesars Meisterwerk*. Munich.

Schellenberg, H. M. 2007. 'Einige Bemerkungen zum *Strategikos* des Onasandros.' In L. de Blois and E. Lo Cascio (eds) *The Impact of the Roman Army (200 BC–AD 476): Economic, Social, Political, Religious and Cultural Aspects: Proceedings of the Sixth Workshop of the International Network 'Impact of Empire', Capri, March 29–April 2, 2005*. Leiden. 181–91.

Schindler, C. 2007. 'Spätantike Geschichtsschreibung als heroische Epik: Die Maurenkriege des Johannes Troglita und ei Iohannis des Falvius Cresconius Corippus.' In D. Brodka and M. Stachura (eds) *Continuity and Change: Studies in Late Antique Historiography*. *Electrum* 13. 181–92.

Schindler, F. 1973. *Die Überlieferung der Stratagemata des Polyainos*. Österreichische Akademie der Wissenschaften phil.-hist. Klasse Sitzungsberichte, 284.1. Vienna.

Schlüter, W. 1999. 'The Battle of the Teutoburg Forest: Archaeological Research at Kalkriese near Osnabrück.' *JRA* 32 (supp.), 125–59.

Schlüter, W. et al. 1992. 'Archäologische Zeugnisse zur Varusschlacht? Die Untersuchungen in der Kalkrieser-Niederwedder Senke bei Osnabrück.' *Germania* 70, 307–402.

Schmitt, H. 1964. *Untersuchungen zur Geschichte Antiochos des Grossen und seiner Zeit*. Wiesbaden.

Schmitzer, U. 2000. *Velleius Paterculus und das Interesse an der Geschichte im Zeitalter des Tiberius*. Heidelberg.

Schmitzer, U. 2011. 'Roman Values in Velleius.' In E. Cowan (ed.) *Velleius Paterculus: Making History*. Swansea. 177–202.

Schofield, M. 2016. *Plato: Laws*. Trans. T. Griffith. Cambridge.

Schwarzkopf, H. N. 1992. *It Doesn't Take a Hero: The Autobiography of H. Norman Schwarzkopf*. New York.
Schwartz, A. 2009. *Reinstating the Hoplite: Arms, Armour and Phalanx Fighting in Archaic and Classical Greece*. Stuttgart.
Schwebel, N. 1761. Ὀνοσάνδρου Στρατηγικός, *Onosandri Strategicus sive de Imperatoris Institutione liber . . . Una cum versione Gallica liberi Baronis de Zur-Lauben ad calcem libri adjecta*. Nuremberg.
Schwertfeger, T. 1982. 'Der Schild des Archilochos.' *Chiron* 12, 253–80.
Seager, R. 2002. *Pompey: A Political Biography*. 2nd edn. London.
Sealey, B. R. 1974. 'Die spartanische Nauarchie.' *Klio* 58, 335–58.
Sears, M. 2010. 'Warrior Ants: Elite Troops in the *Iliad*.' *CW* 103, 139–55.
Seidman, J. 2014. 'Remembering the Teutoburg Forest: *Monvmenta* in *Annals* 1.61.' *Ramus* 43, 94–114.
Sekunda, N. and A. McBride 1994. *Seleucid and Ptolemaic Reformed Armies*. 2 vols. Montvert.
Ševčenko, I. 1962. 'The Illuminators of the Menologium of Basil II.' *DOP* 16, 245–276.
Ševčenko, I. 2011. *Chronographiae quae Theophanis continuati nomine fertur liber quo Vita Basilii imperatoris amplectitur*. Berlin.
Ševčenko, N. 1994. 'The Limburg Staurothek and its Relics.' In Θυμίαμα στη μνήμη της Λασκαρίνας Μπούρα. Vol. 1. Athens. 289–95.
Shannon-Henderson, K. E. 2019. *Religion and Memory in Tacitus' Annals*. Oxford.
Shea, G. W. 1973. 'Myth and Religion in an Early Christian Epic.' *Medieval Studies* 35, 118–28.
Shea, G. W. 1998. *The Iohannis or de Bellis Libycis of Flavius Cresconius Corippus*. Studies in Classics, 7. Lewiston.
Sherwin-White, S. and A. Kuhrt 1993. *From Samarkhand to Sardis: A New Approach to the Seleucid Empire*. London.
Shivola, J. and T. Engberg-Pederson (eds) 1998. *The Emotions in Hellenistic Philosophy*. Dordrecht.
Shotter, D. C. A. 1968. 'Tacitus, Tiberius and Germanicus.' *Historia* 17, 194–214.
Sidwell, B. and D. Dzino (eds) 2010. *Studies in Emotion and Power in the Late Roman Word: Papers in Honour of Ron Newbold*. Piscataway.
Siewert, P. 1982. *Die Trityyen Attikas und die Heeresreform des Kleisthenes*. Munich.
Signes Codoñer, J. 2003. 'Prokops *Anecdota* und Justinians Nachfolge.' *JÖB* 53, 47–82.
Sima Guang 1956. *Zizhi tongjian*. Beijing.
Singor, H. W. 1991. 'Nine against Troy: On Epic ΦΑΛΛΑΓΓΕΣ, ΠΡΟΜΑΧΟΙ, and an Old Structure in the Story of the Iliad.' *Mnemos* 44, 17–62.

Singor, H. W. 2000. 'The Military Side of the Peisistratean Tyranny.' In H. Sancisi-Weerdenburg (ed.) *Peisistratos and the Tyranny: A Reappraisal of the Evidence*. Amsterdam. 107–29.

Singor, H. W. 2009. 'War and International Relations.' In K. A. Raaflaub and H. van Wees (eds) *The Blackwell Companion to Archaic Greece*. London. 585–603.

Slings, S. R. (ed.) 1994. *Plato's Apology of Socrates: A Literary and Philosophical Study with a Running Commentary*. Leiden.

Smith, C. J. 1998. 'Onasander on How to Be a General.' In M. Austin, J. D. Harries and C. J. Smith (eds) *Modus Operandi: Essays in Honour of Geoffrey Rickman*. London. 151–66.

Smith, R. 1999. 'Telling Tales: Ammianus' Narrative of the Persian Expedition of Julian.' In J. W. Drijvers and D. Hunt (eds) *The Late Roman World and its Historian*. London. 89–104.

Smith, R. 2003. 'What Happened to the Ancient Libyans? Chasing Sources across the Sahara from Herodotus to Ibn Khaldun.' *Journal of World History* 14, 459–500.

Smith, W. (ed.) 1849. *Dictionary of Greek and Roman Biography and Mythology*. 3 vols. London.

Snell, B. (ed.) 1971. *Tragicorum graecorum fragmenta* [Ion of Chios]. Göttingen

Sommer, M. 2009. *Die Arminiusschlacht: Spurensuche im Teutoburger Wald*. Stuttgart.

Sørensen, A. D. 2016. *Plato on Democracy and Political Technē*. Leiden.

Sørensen, A. D. 2018. 'Political Office and the Rule of Law in Plato's *Statesman*.' *Polis: The Journal for Ancient Greek Political Thought* 35, 401–17.

Soultanian, G. 2009. *The History of Bishop Sebēos: Redefining a Seventh-Century Voice from Armenia*. London.

Spatharakis, I. 1976. *The Portrait in Byzantine Illuminated Manuscripts*. Leiden.

Stefou, K. 2018. *Socrates on the Life of Philosophical Inquiry: A Companion to Plato's Laches*. Cham.

Stephenson, P. 2005. 'The Tomb of Basil II.' In L. Hoffmann (ed.) *Zwischen Polis, Provinz und Peripherie: Beiträge zur byzantinischen Geschichte und Kultur*. Wiesbaden. 227–38.

Stephenson, P. 2012. 'Religious Services for Byzantine Soldiers and the Possibility of Martyrdom, c.400–c.1000.' In S. H. Hashmi (ed.) *Just Wars, Holy Wars, and Jihads: Christian, Jewish and Muslim Encounters and Exchanges*. Oxford. 25–46.

Stewart, D. J. 1968. 'Sallust and *Fortuna*.' *History and Theory* 7, 298–317.

Stewart, M. E. 2014. 'Contests of *Andreia* in Procopius' *Gothic Wars*.' Παρεκβολαι 4, 21–54.

Stewart, M. E. 2015. 'The *Andreios* Eunuch-Commander Narses: Sign of a Decoupling of Martial Virtues and Hegemonic Masculinity in the Early Byzantine Empire?' *Cerae* 2, 1–25.

Stewart, M. E. 2016a. *The Soldier's Life: Martial Virtues and Manly Romanitas in the Early Byzantine Empire*. Leeds.
Stewart, M. E. 2016b. 'The Soldier's Life: Early Byzantine Masculinity and the Manliness of War.' *Byzantina Symmeikta* 26, 11–44.
Stewart, M. E. 2017a. 'Breaking Down Barriers: Eunuchs in Italy and North Africa, 400–625.' In A. Brown and B. Neil (eds) *Byzantine Culture in Translation*. Leiden. 33–54.
Stewart, M. E. 2017b. 'The Dangers of the Soft Life: Manly and Unmanly Romans in Procopius' *Gothic War*.' *JLA* 10, 473–502.
Stiewe, K. 1976. 'Wahrheit und Rhetorik in Caesar's *Bellum Gallicum*.' *WJA* 2, 149–63.
Stouraitis, I. 2011. 'Jihād and Crusade: Byzantine Positions towards the Notions of "Holy War".' *Byzantina Symmeikta* 21, 11–63.
Stouraitis, I. 2014. 'Roman Identity in Byzantium: A Critical Approach.' *BZ* 107, 175–220.
Strano, G. 2013. 'Valore militare e cultura religiosa nella formazione del perfetto generale bizantino.' In A. Vaccaro (ed.) *Storia, religione e società tra Oriente e Occidente (secoli IX–XIX)*. Lecce. 175–88.
Strootman, R. 2014. *Courts and Elites in the Hellenistic Empires: The Near East after the Achaemenids, c. 330 to 30 BCE*. Edinburgh.
Strootman, R. 2017. *The Birdcage of the Muses: Patronage of the Arts and Sciences at the Ptolemaic Imperial Court, 305–222 BCE*. Leuven.
Sullivan, D. F. 2000. *Siegecraft: Two Tenth-Century Instructional Manuals by 'Heron of Byzantium'*. Washington, DC.
Sullivan, D. F. 2010. 'Byzantine Military Manuals. Perceptions, Practice and Pedagogy.' In P. Stephenson (ed.) *The Byzantine World*. London. 149–61.
Sullivan, D. F. 2018. *The Rise and Fall of Nikephoros II Phokas: Five Contemporary Texts in Annotated Translations*. Leiden.
Sumner, G. V. 1970. 'The Truth about Velleius Paterculus: Prolegomena.' *Harvard Studies in Classical Philology* 74, 257–97.
Suolahti, J. 1955. *The Junior Officers of the Roman Army in the Republican Period*. Helsinki.
Sutherland, C. H. V. 1984. *The Roman Imperial Coinage*. Rev. edn. Vol. 1. London.
Swain, S. C. R. 1989. 'Plutarch's *De Fortuna Romanorum*.' *CQ* 39, 504–16.
Swan, P. M. 2004. *The Augustan Succession: An Historical Commentary on Cassius Dio's Roman History Books 55–56 (9 BC–AD 14)*. Oxford.
Swift, L. A. 2012. 'Archilochus the "Anti-Hero"? Heroism, Flight and Values in Homer and the New Archilochus Fragments (P. Oxy LXIX 4708).' *JHS* 132, 139–55.

Swift, L. A. 2015. 'Lyric Visions of Epic Combat: The Spectacle of War in Archaic Personal Song.' In A. Bakogianni and V. M. Hope (eds) *War as Spectacle: Ancient and Modern Perspectives on the Display of Armed Conflict*. London.

Swift, L. A. 2019. *Archilochus: The Poems: Introduction, Text, Translation, and Commentary*. Oxford.

Syme, R. 1958. *Tacitus*. Vol. 2. Oxford.

Tafazzoli, A. 2000. *Sasanian Society: I. Warriors, II. Scribes, III. Dehqāns*. New York.

Talbot, A.-M. and D. F. Sullivan 2005. *The History of Leo the Deacon: Byzantine Military Expansion in the Tenth Century*. Washington, DC.

Talib, A. 2013 'Topoi and Topography in the Histories of al-Ḥīra.' In P. Wood (ed.) *History and Identity in the Late Antique Near East*. Oxford. 123–48.

Tappan, E. 1931. 'Julius Caesar's Luck.' *CJ* 27, 3–14.

Taragna, A. M. 2004. 'Λόγος e Πόλεμος: Eloquenza e persuasione nei trattati bizantini di arte militare.' In T. Creazzo and G. Strano (eds) *Atti del VI Congresso Nazionale dell'Associazione Italiana di Studi Bizantini, Catania-Messina, 2–5 ottobre 2000*. Special number of *Siculorum Gymnasium* n.s. 57. Catania. 797–810.

Taylor, M. 2013. *Antiochus the Great*. Barnsley.

Taylor, M. 2014. 'Roman Infantry Tactics in the Mid-Republic.' *Hist.* 63, 301–22.

Taylor, M. 2014/15. 'Visual Evidence for Roman Infantry Tactics.' *MAAR* 59/60, 103–20.

Taylor, M. 2018. 'The Election of Centurions during the Republican Period.' *Anc. Soc.* 48, 147–67.

Taylor, M. 2019. 'Reconstructing the Battle of Zama.' *CJ* 114, 310–29.

Theotokis, G. 2018. *Byzantine Military Tactics in Syria and Mesopotamia in the 10th Century: A Comparative Approach*. Edinburgh.

Thomson R. W., J. Howard-Johnston and T. Greenwood. 1999. *The Armenian History Attributed to Sebeos, Part 1: Translation and Notes*. Liverpool.

Thurn, H. 1973. *Ioannis Scylitzae Synopsis Historiarum*. Corpus Fontium Historiae Byzantinae, 5. Berlin.

Timpe, D. 1968. *Der Triumph des Germanicus: Untersuchungen zu den Feldzügen der Jahre 14–16 n. Chr. in Germanien*. Bonn.

Timpe, D. 1970. *Arminius-Studien*. Heidelberg.

Timpe, D. 2012. 'Die "Varusschlacht" in ihren Kontexten: Eine kritische Nachlese zum Bimillennium 2009.' *Historische Zeitschrift* 294, 593–652.

Tod, M. N. 1946. *A Selection of Greek Historical Inscriptions to the End of the Fifth Century BC*. Vol. 1. Oxford.

Tomlinson, R. A. 1972. *Argos and the Argolid: From the End of the Bronze Age to the Roman Occupation*. London.

Tomlinson, R. A. 2009. 'War and International Relations.' In K.A. Raaflaub and H. van Wees (eds) *A Companion to Archaic Greece*. Malden. 585–603.

Tommasi Moreschini, C. O. 2001. *Flavii Cresconii Corippi Iohannidos Liber III*. Florence.

Tommasi Moreschini, C. O. 2002. 'Realtà della storia e retorica dell' impero nella Iohannis di Corippo.' *Athenaeum* 90, 161–85.

Tönnies, B. 1992. 'Die Ausgrabungen in Kalkriese und Tac. *Ann.* 1,60,3: Eine Lösung für die Varusschlachtfrage in Sicht?' *Hermes* 120, 461–5.

Tougher, S. 1997. *The Reign of Leo VI (886–912): Politics and People*. Leiden.

Tougher, S. 1998. 'The Imperial Thought-World of Leo VI: The Non-Campaigning Emperor of the Ninth Century.' In L. Brubaker (ed.) *Byzantium in the Ninth Century: Dead or Alive?* Aldershot. 51–60.

Tougher, S. 2008. *The Eunuch in Byzantine History and Society*. London.

Tougher, S. 2013. 'Imperial Families: The Case of the Macedonians (867–1056).' In L. Brubaker and S. Tougher (eds) *Approaches to the Byzantine Family*. Farnham. 303–26.

Tougher, S. 2018. 'Byzantine Court Eunuchs and the Macedonian Dynasty (867–1056): Family, Power and Gender.' In A. Höfert, M. M. Mesley and S. Tolino (eds) *Celibate and Childless Men in Power: Ruling Eunuchs and Bishops in the Pre-Modern World*. London. 229–45.

Tougher, S. 2021. *The Roman Castrati: Eunuchs in the Roman Empire*. London.

Travis, D. S. 2017. 'Saving Samuel Huntington and the Need for Pragmatic Civil–Military Relations.' *Armed Forces and Society* 43, 395–414.

Treadgold, W. T. 1995. *Byzantium and its Army, 284–1081*. Stanford.

Treadgold, W. T. 2007. *The Early Byzantine Historians*. Basingstoke.

Treadgold, W. T. 2016. 'The Unwritten Rules for Writing Byzantine History.' In S. Marjanović-Dušanić (ed.) *Proceedings of the 23rd International Congress of Byzantine Studies: Plenary Papers*. Belgrade. 277–92.

Tret'yakova, N. E. 2019. 'Иоанн Троглита: Полководец Юстиниана' ['John Troglita: The General of Justinian']. *НАУЧНЫЕ ВЕДОМОСТИ. Серия: История. Политология* 46.1, 37–45.

Trombley, F. R. and S. Tougher 2019. 'The Emperor at War: Duties and Ideals.' In S. Tougher (ed.) *The Emperor in the Byzantine World*. London. 179–95.

Trundle, M. 2001. 'The Spartan Revolution: Hoplite Warfare in the Late Archaic Period.' *War and Society* 19, 1–17.

Trundle, M. 2010. 'Light Troops in Classical Athens.' In D. M. Pritchard (ed.) *War, Democracy and Culture in Classical Athens*. Cambridge. 139–60.

Tsougkarakis, D. 1996. *Κεκαυμένος, Στρατηγικόν*. Athens.

Tsybyshev, M. A. 1903. *Маврикий, Тактика и Стратегия: Первоисточник* сочинений о военном искусстве императора Льва Философа и Н. Макиавелли. St Petersburg.

Tuplin, C. 2018. 'Plato, Xenophon and Persia.' In G. Danzig, D. Johnson and D. Morrison (eds) *Plato and Xenophon: Comparative Studies*. Leiden. 576–611.

Turner, B. 2018. 'Imperial Reactions to Military Failure in the Julio-Claudian Era.' In J. H. Clark and B. Turner (eds) *Brill's Companion to Military Defeat in Ancient Mediterranean Society*. Leiden. 262–83.

Turquois, E. 2015. 'Technical Writing, Genre and Aesthetic in Procopius.' In G. Greatrex and H. Elton (eds) *Shifting Genres in Late Antiquity*. Farnham. 219–31.

Turtledove, H. 2009. *Give Me Back My Legions! A Novel of Ancient Rome*. New York.

Twitchett, D. 1992. *The Writing of Official History Under the T'ang*. Cambridge.

Tyler-Smith, S. 2000. 'Coinage in the Name of Yazdgerd III (AD 632–651) and the Arab Conquest of Iran.' *The Numismatic Chronicle* 160, 135–70.

Ulrich, B. 2011. 'Oman and Bahrain in Late Antiquity: The Sasanians' Arabian Periphery.' *Proceedings of the Seminar for Arabian Studies* 41, 377–86.

Ure, P. N. 1951. *Justinian and his Age*. Harmondsworth.

Van Dieten, J.-L. 1975. *Nicetae Choniatae Historia*. Corpus Fontium Historiae Byzantinae, 11. Berlin.

Van Effenterre, H. 1976. 'Clisthène et les mesures de mobilisation.' *Rev. Ét. Grec.* 89, 1–17.

Van Nuffelen, P. 2017. 'The Wor(l)ds of Procopius.' In C. Lillington-Martin and E. Turquois (eds) *Procopius of Caesarea: Literary and Historical Interpretations*. London. 40–56.

van Wees, H. 1986. 'Leaders of Men? Military Organisation in the *Iliad*.' *CQ* 36, 285–303.

van Wees, H. 1988. 'Kings in Combat: Battles and Heroes in the Iliad.' *CQ* 38, 1–24.

van Wees, H. 1996. 'Heroes, Knights and Nutters: Warrior Mentality in Homer.' In A. B. Lloyd (ed.) *Battle in Antiquity*. London. 1–86.

van Wees, H. 1997. 'Homeric Warfare.' In I. Morris and B. B. Powell (eds) *A New Companion to Homer*. Leiden. 668–93.

van Wees, H. 2000. 'The Development of the Hoplite Phalanx: Iconography and Reality in the Seventh Century.' In H. van Wees (ed.) *War and Violence in Ancient Greece*. London. 125–66.

van Wees, H. 2004. *Greek Warfare: Myths and Realities*. London.

van Wees, H. 2006. '"The Oath of the Sworn Bands": The Acharnae Stela, the Oath of Plataea and Archaic Spartan Warfare.' In A. Luther, M. Meier and L. Thommen (eds) *Das Frühe Sparta*. Stuttgart. 125–64.

van Wees, H. 2011. 'Defeat and Destruction: The Ethics of Ancient Greek Warfare.' In M. Linder and S. Tausend (eds) *'Böser Krieg': Exzessive Gewalt in der Antiken Kriegsführung und Strategien zu deren Vermeidung*. Graz. 69–110.
van Wees, H. 2013. *Ships and Silver, Taxes and Tribute: A Fiscal History of Archaic Athens*. London.
van Wees, H. 2018. 'Citizens and Soldiers in Archaic Athens.' In A. Duplouy and R. W. Brock (eds) *Defining Citizenship in Archaic Greece*. Oxford. 103–43.
van Wees, H. 2019. 'Thermopylae: Herodotus versus the Legend.' In L. W. van Gils, I. R. F. de Jong and C. H. M. Kroon (eds) *Textual Strategies in Ancient War Narrative: Thermopylae, Cannae and Beyond*. Leiden. 19–53.
Van Wickevoort-Crommelin, B. 1999. 'P. Quinctilius Varus: Das Bild des Verlierers.' *Osnabrücker Online-Beiträge zu den Altertumswissenschaften* 2, 1–10.
Vári, R. 1898. *Bölcs Leó császárnak 'A hadi taktikáról' szóló munkája*. Értekezések a történeti tudományok köréből, XVII.10. Budapest.
Vári, R. 1908. 'Zum historischen Exzerptenwerke des Konstantinos Porphyrogennetos.' *BZ* 17, 75–85.
Vári, R. 1917–22. *Leonis imperatoris Tactica*. Sylloge Tacticorum Graecorum, 3. 2 vols. Budapest.
Vernant, J.-P. (ed.) 1968. *Problèmes de la guerre en Grèce ancienne*. Paris.
Vervaet, F. 2014. *The High Command in the Roman Republic: The Principle of the Summum Imperium Auspiciumque from 509 to 19 BCE*. Stuttgart.
Virgilio, B. 2003. *Lancia, diadema, e porpora: Il re e la regalità ellenistica*. 2nd ed. Pisa and Rome.
Volk, K. 2009. *Manilius and his Intellectual Background*. Oxford.
Walbank, F. W. 1940. *Philip V*. Cambridge.
Walbank, F. W. 1957. *A Historical Commentary on Polybius*. Vol. 1. Oxford.
Walbank, F. W. 1972. *Polybius*. Berkeley.
Walbank, F. W. 2002. 'Polybius as a Military Expert.' In P. R. Hill (ed.) *Polybius to Vegetius: Essays on the Roman Army and Hadrian's Wall Presented to Brian Dobson*. Durham. 19–30.
Walser, G. 1951. *Rom, das Reich und die fremden Völker in der Geschichtsschreibung der frühen Kaiserzeit*. Baden.
Walser, G. 1995. 'Zu Caesars Tendenz in der geographischen Beschreibung Galliens.' *Klio* 77, 217–23.
Walter, C. 2003. *The Warrior Saints in Byzantine Art and Tradition*. Aldershot.
Wander, S. H. 2012. *The Joshua Roll*. Wiesbaden.
Wang Pu 1990. *Tang hui yao*. Beijing.
Wang Shounan 1968. *Tangdai fanzhen yu zhongyang guanxi zhi yanjiu*. Taiwan.
Ward, G. A. 2018. '"By Any Other Name": Disgrace, Defeat, and the Loss of

Legionary History.' In J. H. Clark and B. Turner (eds) *Brill's Companion to Military Defeat in Ancient Mediterranean Society*. Leiden. 284–308.

Warde Fowler, W. 1903. 'Caesar's Conception of *Fortuna*.' *CR* 17, 153–6.

Wardle, D. 2009. 'Caesar and Religion.' In M. Griffin (ed.) *A Companion to Julius Caesar*. Chichester. 100–11.

Wei Zheng 1973. *Sui shu*. Beijing.

Weinstock, S. 1971. *Divus Julius*. Oxford.

Welch, K. 1998. 'Caesar and his Officers in the Gallic War Commentaries.' In K. Welch and A. Powell (eds) *Julius Caesar as Artful Reporter: The War Commentaries as Political Instruments*. Swansea. 85–110.

Welch, K. and A. Powell (eds) 1998. *Julius Caesar as Artful Reporter: The War Commentaries as Political Instruments*. Swansea.

Wells, P. S. 2003. *The Battle that Stopped Rome: Emperor Augustus, Arminius, and the Slaughter of the Legions in the Teutoburg Forest*. New York.

West, M. L. 1974. *Studies in Greek Elegy and Iambus*. Berlin.

West, M. L. 2013. *The Epic Cycle: A Commentary on the Lost Troy Epics*. Oxford.

Whately, C. 2013. 'War in Late Antiquity: Secondary Works, Literary Sources and Material Evidence.' In A. Sarantis and N. Christie (eds) *War and Warfare in Late Antiquity: Current Perspectives*. Leiden. 101–52.

Whately, C. 2015a. 'The Genre and Purpose of Military Manuals in Late Antiquity.' In G. Greatrex and H. Elton (eds) with L. McMahon. *Shifting Genres in Late Antiquity*. Farnham. 249–61.

Whately, C. 2015b. 'Speech, adlocutio: Late Empire.' In Y. Le Bohec et al. (eds) *The Encyclopedia of the Roman Army*. Malden.

Whately, C. 2016. *Battles and Generals: Combat, Culture, and Didacticism in Procopius' Wars*. Leiden.

Whately, C. (forthcoming). 'Ammianus' Art of Generalship: How an Emperor Should Perform in Combat.'

Wheeler, E. L. 1978. 'The Occasion of Arrian's *Tactica*.' *GRBS* 19, 351–65.

Wheeler, E. L. 1983. 'The *hoplomachoi* and Vegetius' Spartan Drillmasters.' *Chiron* 13, 1–20.

Wheeler, E. L. 1988. *Stratagem and the Vocabulary of Military Trickery*. Leiden.

Wheeler, E. L. 1991. 'The General as Hoplite.' In V. D. Hanson (ed.) *Hoplites: The Classical Greek Battle Experience*. London. 121–70.

Wheeler, E. L. 2007. 'Battle: Land Battles.' In P. Sabin, H. Van Wees and M. Whitby (eds) *The Cambridge History of Greek and Roman Warfare, I: Greece, the Hellenistic World and the Rise of Rome*. Cambridge. 186–223.

Wheeler, E. L. 2010. 'Polyaenus: *Scriptor Militaris*.' In K. Brodersen (ed.), *Polyainos: Neue Studien/Polyaenus: New Studies*. Berlin. 7–54.

Wheeler, E. L. 2012. 'Notes on a Stratagem of Iphicrates in Polyaenus and Leo Tactica.' *Electrum* 19, 157–63.
Whitby, Mary 1998. 'Defender of the Cross: George of Pisidia on the Emperor Heraclius and his Deputies.' In M. Whitby (ed.) *The Propaganda of Power: The Role of Panegyric in Late Antiquity*. Leiden. 247–73.
Whitby, M. 2007. 'War.' In P. Sabin, H. Van Wees and M. Whitby (eds) *The Cambridge History of Greek and Roman Warfare, 2: From the Late Republic to the Late Empire*. Cambridge. 310–42.
Whitby, M. 2011. 'Army and Society in the Late Roman World: A Context for Decline?' In P. Erdkamp (ed.) *A Companion to the Roman Army*. Malden. 515–31.
Whitby, M. 2017. 'The Greatness of Procopius.' In C. Lillington-Martin and E. Turquois (eds) *Procopius of Caesarea: Literary and Historical Interpretations*. London. 26–39.
Whitby, M. and M. Whitby 1988. *The History of Theophylact Simocatta: An English Translation with Introduction and Notes*. Oxford.
Whitehead, D. 1990. *Aineias the Tactician: How to Survive Under Siege*. Oxford.
Whitehead, D. 2010. *Apollodorus Mechanicus: Siege-Matters (Πολιορκητικά): Translated with Introduction and Commentary*. Stuttgart.
Whitehead, D. 2016. *Philo Mechanicus: On Sieges: Translated with Introduction and Commentary*. Frankfurt.
Whittaker, C. R. 1969–1970. *Herodian: History of the Empire*. 2 vols. Cambridge, MA.
Whittow, M. 1996. *The Making of Orthodox Byzantium, 600–1025*. Basingstoke.
Wiegels, R. 2011. 'Zur literarischen Überlieferung der Varusschlacht: Eine überflüssige Re-tractio?' In S. Burmeister and N. Müller-Scheeßel (eds) *Fluchtpunkt Geschichte: Archäologie und Geschichtswissenschaft im Dialog*. Münster. 93–130.
Williams, A. V. 1990. *The Pahlavi Rivāyat Accompanying the Dādestān ī Dēnīg*. Copenhagen.
Williams, C. 2010. *Roman Homosexuality*. 2nd edn. Oxford.
Williams, K. F. 2009. 'Tacitus' Germanicus and the Principate.' *Latomus* 68, 117–30.
Williams, M. F. 1998. *Ethics in Thucydides: The Ancient Simplicity*. New York.
Wilson, N. G. 1983. *Scholars of Byzantium*. London.
Winkler, M. M. 2016. *Arminius the Liberator: Myth and Ideology*. Oxford.
Wirth, P. 1999. *Eustathii Thessalonicensis opera minora (magnam partem inedita)*. Berlin.
Wolters, R. 2008. *Die Schlacht im Teutoburger Wald: Arminius, Varus und das römische Germanien*. Munich.
Wood, P. J. 2011. 'Being Roman in Procopius' Vandal Wars.' *Byz* 81, 424–47.

Woodman, A. J. 1977. *Velleius Paterculus: The Tiberian Narrative (2.94–131)*. Cambridge.
Woodman, A. J. 1979. 'Self-Imitation and the Substance of History: Tacitus, *Annals* 1.61–5 and *Histories* 2.70, 5.14–15.' In D. West and A. J. Woodman (eds) *Creative Imitation and Latin Literature*. Cambridge. 143–56.
Woodman, A. J. 1998. *Tacitus Reviewed*. Oxford.
Woods, D. 2007. 'Jews, Rats and the Battle of Yarmūk.' In A. Lewin and P. Pellegrini (eds) *The Late Roman Army in the Near East from Diocletian to the Arab Conquest*. Oxford. 367–76.
Wörrle, M. 1975. 'Antiochos I, Achaios der Ältere und die Galater.' *Chiron* 5, 59–87.
Wu Jiulong et al. (eds) 1990. *Sunzi jiaoshi*. Beijing.
Zakeri, M. 1995. *Sāsānid Soldiers in Early Muslim Society: The Origins of 'Ayyārān and Futuwwa*. Wiesbaden.
Zali, V. 2016. 'Divine *Phthonos*, and the Wheel of Fortune: The Reception of Herodotean Theology in Early and Middle Byzantine Historiography.' In A. Ellis (ed.) *God in History: Reading and Rewriting Herodotean Theology from Plutarch to the Renaissance*. *Histos* supplements, 4. Newcastle-upon-Tyne. 85–126.
Zarini, V. 2003. *Rhétorique, poétique, spiritualité: La technique épique de Corippe dans la Johannide*. Turnhout.
Zhang Guogang 1987. *Tangdai fanzhen yanjiu*. Changsha.
Zuckerman, C. 1990. 'The Compendium of Syrianus Magister.' *JÖB* 40, 209–24.
Zuckerman, C. 1994. 'Chapitres peu connus de l'*Apparatus Bellicus*.' *TM* 12, 359–89.
Zur-Lauben, Baron de B. F. 1757. *Le général d'armée par Onosander*. Paris.

Index

ab epistulis Graecis, 146
Abolqasem Ferdowsi, 211
Abritus, 2, 139–41, 143–6, 148
Abydos, 172, 265 n. 5
Acanthus, 38
Achaemenid, 78, 84 n. 64, 85, 85 n. 68, 86, 214 n. 36, 215 n. 37
Achaemenids, 83, 92
Achaeus (the Elder), 72, 72 n. 18
Achaeus (the Younger), 85
Achilles, 2, 9–10, 11 n. 17, 12, 12 n. 19, 22 n. 50, 55, 152, 152 n. 10, 163, 297, 303
Acton, Lord John, 65, 65 n. 33
Ad Decimum, 176, 179–80, 182 n. 83, 183
Adrianople (Battle of), 152, 154–6, 156 n. 48, 157, 159
Aediles, 91
Aelian, 243, 243 n. 5, 247, 253, 253 n. 48, 254 n. 51, 255, 263, 263 n. 91, 288
 Taktikē Theoria, 243, 251, 253, 259, 263, 267
Aemilius Paullus, L., (cos. 219 BC) 4, 92, 96, 151 n. 7
Aemilius Paullus, L., (cos. 182 BC) 4, 89, 93, 95. 95 n. 40 and 44, 294
Aeneas, 189
Aeneas ('Tacticus'), 3, 27–8, 28 n. 66, 247, 252, 294
Aeschylus, 44, 45 n. 21, 49, 49 n. 35
Agesilaus, 3, 3 n. 8
Agathias, 167, 277, 310, 313318
 Histories, 167, 167 n. 19, 277 n. 75–6
Akragas, 45
Alamanni, 154 n. 33, 155, 155 n. 40, 157, 277
al-Balādhurī 209, 217 n. 48, 222, 222 n. 70
Albanian, 209, 216–17, 217 n. 45, n. 48, 218

Albinovanus Pedo, 123, 123 n. 33
Alcibiades, 55–7, 57 n. 11
Alexander of Sardis, 68, 68 n. 5, 71 n. 13, 72–3, 73 n. 20, 74–5, 77–8, 78 n. 41, 81–2, 82 n. 53
Alexander the Great, 2–3,43 n. 17, 70, 72, 74, 83–5, 87, 148, 151, 159, 225, 287 n. 11, 299 n. 78, 306
Alexandria, 81
Alexios I Komnenos, 286, 293 n. 41
al-Ḥīrah, 208
al-Mughīra b. Zurāra, 215
al-Qa'qā, 221
al-Qādessiyah (Battle of), 207, 207 n. 4, 208–9, 212–15, 25 n. 39, 216–19, 219 n. 54, 221–3
al-Ṭabarī, 212, 214, 214 n. 32, 215, 215 n. 39, 221, 221 n. 66, 222 n. 67
al-Yarmūk (Battle of), 207, 207 n. 4–5, 208 n. 6, 210 n.15, 217, 217 n. 48, 218–20, 222–3
Amida, 158–9
Aminias, 160
Ammatas, 176
Ammianus Marcellinus, 148, 151–2, 152 n. 9, n. 11–12, 153–5, 154 n. 36, 155 n. 43, 156, 156 n. 44, n. 45, 157, 157 n. 50, 158, 158 n. 55, 159–60, 160 n. 66, 161–3
 Res Gestae, 151–3, 153 n. 14, 154–6, 160
Amphipolis, 55
Amphissa, 42
An Lushan, 228, 230, 230 n. 22, 231 n. 22, 239
andreia, 36, 51, 287 n. 11
Andronikos Doukas, 268
Anatolia, 72–3, 81
Anonymous Dialogue on Political Science, 167
Anopaea, 42
Antalas, 192–3, 193 n. 29, 30 32

Anthemius, 170
Antioch, 208, 278–9, 279 n.86
Antiochus I, 72, 75–7, 79, 83
Antiochus II, 73, 73 n. 20, 75
Antiochus III, 40 n. 10, 69, 69 n. 6, 70, 70 n. 9, 71 n. 12, 85, 87, 90
Antiochus Hierax, 78
Antonia Castra, 193, 193 n. 29, 195 , 197, 200, 202 n. 76
Antonina, 173, 185 n. 95
antoniniani, 142
Apama, 76, 76 n. 33
Apollo, 42, 83,
Apollodorus, 247, 263, 263 n. 91
  Poliorketika, 243, 263
Arabian Desert, 208
Arabian Peninsula, 212
Arabs, 5, 207 n. 4, 211–12, 215–16, 218, 222, 222 n. 69, 223, 257
Archelaus, 174
Areobindus, 192, 204 n. 88
Argives, 30–1, 31 n. 73, 32, 42
Aristides, 3, 50, 58
Aristotle, 4, 88
  Eudemian Ethics, 164
Armenian, 209, 215–16, 216 n. 43, 217, 217 n. 44, 46, 218–19, 219 n. 54, 220, 220 n. 59–60, 223
Armenians, 209, 218 n. 48, 219
Arminius, 117, 120, 120 n. 22, 121, 125, 125 n. 40, 126, 130, 132, 132 n. 75, 133, 133 n. 78, 134, 134 n. 80–1, 137
Arsaces, 136
Arsacid, 216
Artabanes, 192, 204 n. 88
Artabanus, 165 n. 7
Artemisium, 37 n. 3, 39
Arzanene, 250
asbārān, 214
Asclepiodotus, 252
Asia Minor, 72–3 n.19, 77–81 n. 51, 287 n. 12, 297–8
Aspasius of Ravenna, 146
Astrices, 197, 202, 202 n. 76
Athamanians, 93
Athena Pronaea, 44
Athenian Democracy, 57, 57 n. 11, 59
Athenians, 6, 21, 24–5 n. 59, 26, 26 n. 60, 28–9, 29 n. 71, 32 n. 75, 38 n. 5, 43, 43 n. 18, 44 n. 20, 55–8 n. 15, 59–60, 60 n. 17–18, 86, 147–8, 175 n. 62, 183 n. 85
Athens, 3, 6, 17, 23, 23 n. 51–2, 24, 26–7, 27 n. 63, 28–9, 33 n. 79, 37, 37 n. 2, 39 n. 8, 42–3, 47, 47 n. 29, 50, 50 n. 35–6, 51, 56–7, 59–60 n. 18–19, 87, 150, 238
Atilius Regulus, M., (cos. 267 BC) 96

Attalus, 73
Attica, 25 n. 58, 29, 29 n. 71, 36–7, 42 n. 15, 60, 60 n. 17
Aufidius Bassus, 123, 123 n. 33
Augustus, 1–2, 4, 107 n. 48, 118, 120, 124, 124 n. 38, 128 n. 53, 131, 131 n. 69, 135, 155, 221 n. 64, 262
  Res Gestae, 128 n. 53
Aurelian, 140, 150
Aurelius Scaurus, M., (cos. suff. 108 BC) 136
Aurelius Victor, 144, 148
Autonous, 42
Avars, 302

Babylon, 74
Bacchylides, 44
Bactria, 76 n. 33, 78, 87
Balaclava (Battle of), 51
Balkans, 142, 301
Bardas Phokas, 270
Bargylia, 75
Bar-Kochva, Bezalel, 68, 68 n. 4, 70, 70 n. 10–11
barritus, 154
Basil I, 262, 262 n. 89, 265, 269, 272, 273, 274, 275, 282–3 n. 102
Basil II, 265, 267, 274–5, 275 n. 65, 67, 276, 278–9, 282–3
Basil Lekapenos, 5, 254, 276, 278–83
Basiliscus, 171, 174, 177, 184
Batavi, 135
Black Sea, 84
Bei, 231
Beijing, 230
Beli Lom (River), 149
Belisarius, 5, 156 n. 47, 166, 166 n. 11, 168–72, 172 n. 46, 173, 173 n. 52, 174–82, 182 n. 83, 183, 183 n. 84, 184–5, 185 n. 94–5, 186–8, 188 n. 5, n. 9, 190–1, 197, 203–4, 262, 266, 266 n. 12, 276, 298, 300–1
beneficiarius consularis, 142
Berbers, 192
Beroia, 141, 144
Bezina, 196
Bianzhou, 231, 231 n. 24, 232, 239–40
Billows, Richard, 72–3, 73 n. 19, 75 n. 30, 81 n. 51
Bin-Ning, 238
Bithynia, 296
Bo, 230
Boeotia, 36
Boeotian League, 37, 37 n. 2
Bohai Gulf, 230
Bosporus, 263
Britannia, 244, 246
Bructeri, 127–8
Bulgaria, 141, 264, 269, 274, 279, 285

Bulla (Plain of), 177–8
Busra, 208
Busta Gallorum (Battle of), 168
Byzacena, 203
Byzantine Empire, 4–5, 192, 196, 206, 212, 216–17 n. 44, 219, 264, 266, 268, 278
Byzantium, 5, 165 n. 5, 185, 220 n. 60, 242–3, 261–5, 267, 270, 276 n. 69–70, 282, 284–5 n. 4, 287 n. 12, 288, 288 n. 21, 289

Cacus, 129
Caecilides, 195 n. 46, 196 n.54, 202
Caecilius Metellus Caprarius, C., (cos. 113 BC) 136
Caecina Severus, A., (cos. 1 BC) 124, 124 n. 36, 131–3
Caesar *see* Julius Caesar, C. (cos. 59 BC)
Callimachus, 160
Callincium (Battle of), 168
Cambyses, 58
Cameron, Alan, 191, 191 n. 22
Cameron, Averil, 165 n. 8, 172, 172 n. 45, 177 n. 70, 179 n. 75, 183 n. 86, 184 n. 92, 185 n. 96, 188 n. 5, 189 n. 13–14, 190 n. 17 and 19, 191 n. 21, 196 n. 47, 201 n. 70, 204 n. 83–4, 205 n. 89, 209 n. 10
Cang, 230–1
Cannae, 4, 92, 92 n. 27, 151 n. 7
Capdetrey, Laurent, 68, 68 n. 4, 71–2, 72 n. 15–17, 78, 80
Caput Vada, 174
Caracalla, 146
Carcasan, 203
Caria, 75
Carnuntum, 142
Carsana, Chiara, 69 n. 6, 70, 70 n. 9, 74, 74 n. 27, 75 n. 29
Carthage, 88, 93, 159, 170–1, 173–4, 177–9, 189, 189 n. 13, 190 n. 17, 191–3, 195, 197
Carthaginians, 179, 280
Caspian Sea, 79, 82–4, 84 n. 63
Cassius Dio, 117–18, 121–2, 122 n. 28, 123, 128, 128 n. 54, 131, 135, 153
Cassius Longinus, L., (cos. 107 BC) 136
Caucasus, 216, 218 n. 50, 220, 224
Cestius, 118
Chandragupta Maurya, 74, 77, 77 n. 37, 82–3
Chang-an, 228, 236, 238, 2238 n. 48
Chaniotis, Angelos, 68, 68 n. 3, 70 n. 7, 73 n. 22
Chatti, 128, 134, 134 n. 84, 135
Chauci, 128
Chengde, 233–4, 234 n. 35, 236, 239
Chengdu, 229
Chesnut, Glenn, 292, 292 n. 37
chiliarchoi, 70, 90, 90 n. 19

Chiron, 297, 303
Chonodomarius, 155
Christendom, 262
Ci, 231
Cillium, 199
Cimbri, 96–7, 136
Civilis *see* Julius Civilis, C.
clades Caeciniana, 132
clades Quinctilii Vari, 123 n. 32
clades Variana, 123–4, 127–9
Claudius, 128, 137
Claudius Mamertinus, 160
Claudius Marcellus, C., (cos. 50 BC) 97
Claudius Marcellus, M., (cos. 222 BC) 96
Clausewitz *see* Von Clausewitz
Cniva, 141, 143–4, 149
Comentiolus, 301–2
comitia tributa, 89
consilium, 95, 109, 118, 120, 122, 122 n. 30, 297 n. 70, 299, 302
Constans II, 218
Constantine I (the Great), 2, 4, 131, 131 n. 68, 266, 266 n. 9, 275
Constantine VII, 251, 254, 265, 269–71, 271 n. 46, 272, 273, 273 n. 56, 274, 278–83, 297 n. 70
Constantine VIII, 265, 279, 283 n. 102
Constantine IX (Monomachos), 265, 265 n. 6
Constantine Doukas, 268
Constantine Gongylios, 277, 280 n. 92
Constantine (son of Basil I), 272–3, 273 n. 56, 274, 283 n. 102
Constantinople, 164, 171, 175, 184, 192–3 n. 29, 195, 252, 262, 266, 273, 275, 279, 294, 304
Constantius II, 4, 152, 156 n. 48, 160–1
Continuator of Theophanes, 262 n. 88–9, 279 n. 86, 296 n. 63, 297–8, 303
Corippus, Flavius Cresconius, 185, 187 n. 3, 188–9 n. 13–14, 190, 190 n. 17, n. 19, 191–3 n. 29–31, 194, 194 n. 40, 195, 195 n. 46, 196, 196 n. 47, 197–200, 200 n. 67, 201, 201 n. 71, 202–3, 203 n. 81
Iohannis (*De Bellis Libycis*), 188 n. 4, 189
Cornelius Scipio Calvus, Cn., (cos. 222 BC) 96
Cornelius Scipio, L. (cos. 190 BC), 87, 87 n. 7
Cornelius Scipio, P. (cos. 218 BC), 96
Cornelius Scipio Aemilianus, P. (cos. 147 BC), 95 n. 40 and 44, 159
Cornelius Scipio Africanus, P. (cos. 205 BC), 4, 92, 92 n. 27, 93, 95, 95 n. 40, 96, 198 n. 60, 221 n. 64, 287 n. 11, 305 n. 101
Cornelius Sulla, L. (cos. 88 BC), 97, 100, 100 n. 7, 101, 152 n. 7, 157 n. 50
Corsica, 204
Coutzinas, 196, 196 n. 55, 197, 197 n. 57, 199
Crimea, 51

Critias, 57, 57 n. 11
Crosby, Daniel, 4, 116, 117 n. 7
Ctesiphon, 162, 208, 211
Culham, Phyllis, 98 n. 3, 101 n. 16, 107 n. 46, 114 n. 78, 153, 153 n. 26
cursus honorum, 89–90, 20 n. 20, 91
Cybele, 142
Cynaegirus, 160
Cynoscephalae, 87
Cyprian, 145, 145 n. 20
Cyrus the Great, 57–8, 58 n. 14

D'Agostini, Monica, 68 n. 5, 73 n. 20, 75 n. 30, 78, 78 n. 39, n. 41, 80 n. 50, 85 n. 66
Danube (River), 140
David Komnenos, 303–4
De, 230–1
De Caesaribus, 148
Decius, C. Messius Quintus Traianus, 2, 4, 139–50
Deimachos, 77, 77 n. 37
Deinomenid, 45
De Jonge, Pieter, 161
Delium, 55
Delphi, 42–5 n. 23, 48–9
De Marre, Martine, 5, 187, 189 n. 14
Demetrius Poliorcetes, 77, 79
Demodamas (son of Aristeides), 73, 73 n. 22, 74, 74 n. 24, 76, 76 n. 33, 77, 79, 82–3, 82 n. 59, 84
demos, 32 n. 75, 74
Demosthenes, 8–9, 9 n. 12
Dexippus, P. Herennius, 139–44, 144 n. 18, 145–50
    Scythian Affairs (*Skythika*), 139
    Chronicle, 140, 142
Dezong, 232–3, 236, 238, 238 n. 48
Didyma, 73 n. 22, 74, 74 n. 24, 76, 76 n. 32, 83
Dionysius I of Syracuse, 3
Dionysius of Halicarnassus, 155, 155 n. 36
Dionysus, 83
domi militiaeque, 69
Domitian, 134 n. 85, 137
Doriscus, 38
Dreyer, Boris, 69 n. 6, 70 n. 8, 74, 74 n. 28
Drusus Caesar, 120, 123 n. 32, 130 n. 66, 131, 134, 136–7 n. 88
Dryanovets, 141–2, 149
dux limitis, 141
dux Mesopotamiae, 187
Dzanev, Georgi, 141

Eastern Wei, 226, 226 n. 5
Egypt, 3 n. 8, 10, 223
Elbe (River), 137

Engels, David, 68 n. 4, 69 n. 6, 70, 70 n. 8
Ephialtes, 60 n. 19
Ephialtes of Trachis, 39
Ephors, 25 n. 59, 32, 32 n. 75
Ephorus, 36 n. 1, 44
Epic of Digenis, 286
Euboea, 37
Eudocia, 170
Eurybiades, 39, 50
Eustathios of Thessalonike (Eustathios of Thessaloniki), 284 n. 1, 287 n. 11–12, 289 n. 24, 290, 290 n. 27, 293 n. 41, 297 n. 67, 303–4, 304 n. 96–7
    The Capture of Thessalonike, 304 n. 96–7
Eutropius, 148, 276
Excerpta de legationibus gentium ad Romanos, 140
Excerpta de Sententiis, 140
Excerpta de Strategmatis, 140, 143

Farrukhzād, 211 n. 20, 212
Fields of Cato, 193, 202
Flaminius (Nepos), C. (cos. 223 BC), 4, 96, 122
Flavus, 133
Florentius, 156
Florus, 117, 120–1, 121 n. 24–5, 122 n. 28, 123, 131, 135
Fortuna (also *fortuna*), 98, 98 n. 3, 99–100, 100 n. 6–9, n. 11, 101, 101 n. 14, 102, 102 n. 21, 103, 103 n. 23–4, 104, 104 n. 30–3, 105, 105 n. 37, n. 40, 106, 106 n. 40, n. 45, 107, 107 n. 46–7, n. 50, 108–9, 109 n. 57–8, 110, 110 n. 61–2, 111–12, 112 n. 70, n. 72–3, 113, 113 n. 74–5, 114, 114 n. 78, 115, 196 n. 47
Forum Thembronios, 139–40
Fronimuth, 199
Frontinus, Sex. Iulius, 27, 28 n. 65, 246
    Strategemata, 246
Fufeng, 229

Gabinius Secundus, P., 128
Galatian, 78
Gantharith, 192
Garsoïan, Nina, 217 n. 44–5, 219, 219 n. 55, 220 n. 60
Gao Wei, 228, 228 n. 9, 238
Gallic 1, 108–10, 110 n. 61, 111, 130 n. 68, 136
Gaul 1, 97, 98, 100, 1000 n. 7, 107, 136, 150, 159
Gauls, 108–9, 109 n. 58, 110, 110 n. 62, 111, 111 n. 68, 136
Geiseric, 170 n. 32–3, 171, 171 n. 40, 175, 178, 182
Geisirith, 199
Gelimer, 170 n. 33
Gens Quinctilia, 120

George (Georgios) Akropolites, 294–5 n. 53
George of Cyprus, 303 n. 93
George Maniaces (Maniakes), 287, 297
George of Pisidia, 208–9 n. 13
Gepids, 169
Germani, 111, 113, 137 n. 88
Germania, 117–20, 119 n. 18, 122–3 n. 32, 124–5, 128, 128 n. 55, 130 n. 66, 131, 133–5, 135 n. 87, 136, 136 n. 88, 137, 137 n. 91, 138
Germanicus (Caesar), 117, 123–5 n. 39, 126–7, 127 n. 48, 128–9, 129 n. 59, n. 61, 130, 130 n. 66, 131 n. 68, 132–4, 134 n. 84–5, 135–7, 136 n. 88
Germans, 118, 120–1, 125, 125 n. 39, 126, 129–30, 133, 134, 136–7, 154, 162
Germanus, 187, 191, 204, 204 n. 88
Gibamundus, 176
Godas, 178, 181
Golan Heights, 207
Gordian III, 140–1
Goths, 140, 144–6, 150, 157, 159, 168–9, 172 n. 49, 173 n. 53, 175 n. 64, 183, 277
Graff, David, 5, 225, 287 n. 12
Grainger, John, 67 n. 1, 68 n. 5, 71 n. 12, 73 n. 22, 74, 74 n. 25–7, 79 n. 44–5, 81 n. 51, 87 n. 6
Gratian, 157–8
Grumbates, 158–9
Grusková, Jana, 141 n. 5, 143, 143 n. 14–15, 144 n. 16–17, 145 n. 19, n. 21, 147 n. 25, 150 n. 31

Habicht, Christian, 74, 74 n. 28
Hades, 54–5, 271
Hadrian, 262–3
Haemisos, 144
Haldon, John, 218 n. 51, 243 n. 5, 255 n. 61, 256 n. 65, 260 n. 82, 263 n. 93, 266 n. 13, 267, 267 n. 15, n. 17–19, 269 n. 28, n. 30–3, 35, 36, 38, 270 n. 39–40, 272 n. 50–1, 273 n. 59, 274 n. 62–3, 284, 284 n. 2, 288 n. 20–1, 292 n. 40, 293, 293 n. 43–5, 297 n. 70
Hamilcar Barca, 88
Hannibal, 88 n. 11, 92, 122, 122 n. 42
Hasdrubal, 88
Hector, 2, 11–12, 14, 160
Helladius, 49
Hellas, 36, 46
Hellenic League, 36–7, 37 n. 2, 42 n. 14, 48, 51
Hellenistic period, 7, 70, 74, 80, 85 n. 67, 221 n. 66
Hellespont, 38, 42 n. 15, 172
Helvetii, 104, 106
Henan, 231
Heng-Ji, 234

Heraclea Pontica, 79
Heracleius *comes rei militaris* 171
Heraclidae, 36
Heraclius, 5, 206 n. 2, 208, 208 n. 6, 209 n. 13, 217 n. 48, 218, 218 n. 52, 219, 265–6
Hercules (Herakles), 129, 211
Herennius Etruscus, 148
Herod, 136
Herodotus, 8–9 n. 12, 24–5 n. 58, 27, 27 n. 63, 28, 28 n. 69, 29–31, 31 n. 72, 32, 33 n. 78–9, 36, 36 n. 1, 37–8, 38 n. 5, 39, 39 n. 6, n. 8, 40, 40 n. 10–11, 41, 41 n. 12, 42, 42 n. 15, 43–4, 44 n. 19, 45, 45 n. 21, n. 23, 46, 48, 48 n. 31, 49, 51, 60 n. 17, 165 n. 7, 172 n. 43, 183 n. 87
Herodian, 296, 296 n. 61
Heruli, 147
Hesychius of Miletus, 247
  Onomatologos, 247
Hieron, 45, 50, 50 n. 35
Hilderic, 165 n. 7, 170, 170 n. 33
Hindu Kush, 84
hipparchoi, 70
Hippias, 26, 29 n. 71, 33 n. 79, 45
Hoffman, Dietrich, 157, 157 n. 53
Homer, 6–7, 7 n. 5, 9–10, 13 n. 24–5, 14 n. 29, 15 n. 31–2, 19, 19 n. 40, 26, 53–4, 297
  Iliad, 2, 6 n.1, 7, 11, 13, 13 n. 23–4, 14, 14 n. 27, 15, 20, 22, 22 n. 50, 54, 198 n. 60
  Odyssey, 6 n. 1, 10–11, 54, 198 n. 60
Homeric epics, 7, 19 n. 40, 53
Honorius, 4, 169
Hoplites, 32, 38, 52, 56, 59, 280
Hostilianus, 142
Huan (River), 227, 233
Huazhou, 226, 231
hubris, 41, 48
Huguan Pass, 233
Hunneric, 165 n. 8, 17
Huns, 172, 176, 179, 276

Iaudas, 192, 196, 196 n. 55
Iaxartes (River), 83, 83 n. 59
Ibn A ☒tham, 220, 220 n. 61
Idistaviso, 130
Ifisdaias, 196, 196 n. 55, 197, 199
imperator, 90
imperium, 91–3, 122 n. 30, 137 n. 91
India, 77, 79 n. 49, 82–3, 220 n. 60
Indus (Treaty of), 82, 82 n. 55
Ipsus (Battle of), 79
Israel, 208
Iranic-Saka, 211, 211 n. 21
Issac Komnenos, 296
Isthmus, 36
Iunci, 198–9, 202

Jabala ibn al-Ayham al-Ghassānī, 222, 222 n. 70, 223, 223 n. 71, 224
Janniard, Sylvain, 161, 161 n. 70–1
Jerusalem, 170, 304
John the Armenian, 176, 182
John the Cappadocian, 165
John Doukas, 262
John II Komnenos, 286 n. 10, 287 n. 11
John Kourkouas, 262
John the Lydian, 247
John Skylitzes, 262 n. 89, 279 n. 86, 296, 296 n. 63–5
John Troglita, 5, 187, 191, 201
John Tzimiskes, 262, 262 n. 89, 270, 274, 276, 278–9, 282
Jordan, 208
Jordan (River), 207
Jordanes, 143–5, 148–9, 187 n. 1, 188 n. 4, 204 n. 82
    Getica, 140–1
Joseph Bringas, 276–7, 279, 279 n. 82, 281
Josephus, 123, 152 n. 8, 153
Juanšēr, 217–18, 224
Judhâm, 222
Jugurtha, 97, 101 n. 15
Julian, 2–4, 152, 155–6, 156 n. 48, 157, 157 n. 50, 158, 158 n. 55, 159–61, 161 n. 72, 162–3, 234 n. 35
Julius Caesar. C. (cos. 59 BC), 1–3, 97, 98 n. 2–3, 99, 99 n. 4–5, 100, 100 n. 6–7, n. 9, n. 11, 101, 101 n. 13–16, 102–3, 103 n. 23–5, 104, 104 n. 30–2, 105, 105 n. 40, 106, 106 n. 40, 107, 107 n. 46, n. 50–1, 108, 108 n. 53, 109, 109 n. 58, 110, 110 n. 61–2, 111, 111 n. 67–9, 112, 112 n. 73, 113–14, 114 n. 78, 115, 127 n. 49, 152 n. 7, 153, 201, 201 n. 72, 262, 296 n. 66, 298–9
    Bellum Gallicum, 98, 98 n. 3, 99–104, 106–7, 107 n. 50, 108, 112, 112 n. 73, 114
Julius Caesar, C. (Caligula), 136
Julius Civilis, C., 135
Jullien, François, 287, 287 n. 12
Justinian I, 4, 164–5, 165 n. 7–8, 166, 170 n. 33, 175 n. 60, 178, 187, 189 n. 14, 191–2, 204, 266, 266 n. 10, n. 12

Kagan, Donald, 7 n. 6, 153, 153 n. 18–19, n. 24, 154, 154 n. 32, n. 34, 156 n. 45
Kaldellis, Anthony, 164 n. 3, 165 n. 4, n. 7, 166 n. 10, 168 n. 26, 171 n. 38, 172 n. 44, 174 n. 57–8, 177 n. 70, 178 n. 73–4, 179 n. 78, 180 n. 79, 183 n. 84, n. 86, 184, 184 n. 92–3, 185 n. 95, 189 n. 12–13, 196 n. 47, 264 n. 1, 268 n. 26, 275 n. 67, 279 n. 86, 286 n. 6, 287 n. 12, 288 n. 21,
289 n. 23, 292 n. 38–40, 295 n. 54, 300 n. 87–8, 304 n. 98
Kalkriese, 116, 116 n. 2
Keegan, John, 151, 151 n. 5, 152, 152 n. 10, 153, 153 n. 20, 163, 163 n. 80, 225 n. 1
Khālid ibn al-Walīd, 208, 220–2, 224
Khorasani, 213
Khosrow, 208, 215 n. 37
Khusro II, 206
Koestermann, Erich, 125, 125 n. 41, 129 n. 59, 132 n. 73, 133 n. 78
Kosmin, Paul, 74 n. 26, 78, 78 n. 42–3, 79, 79 n. 44, n. 46–7, n. 49, 80–1, 81 n. 51, 82 n. 52, n. 54–7, 83, 83 n. 58, n. 60–1, 84, 84 n. 62–4
Krallis, Dimitris, 4–5, 173 n. 55, 177 n. 69–70, 267 n. 20, 284, 286 n. 6, 288 n. 21, 289 n. 25, 292 n. 32, 293 n. 44, 303 n. 94, 304 n. 98, 305 n. 101
Kraut, Richard, 53, 53 n. 5, 326
Kucewicz, Cezary, 2, 6, 12 n. 21, 22 n. 50, 23 n. 52, 24 n. 53, 25 n. 59, 29 n. 70
Kučma, Vladimir, 248, 248 n. 26–7, 249 n. 33, 250 n. 37

Laches, 56
Laguatan, 189, 192, 199, 205
Lakhm, 222
Laodice (wife of Antiochus II), 73, 73 n. 20
Laodice (wife of Antiochus III), 71 n. 12
Laodicea on the Lycus, 72, 72 n. 18
Laribus, 197, 199
Lariscus, 202
Lee, Doug, 168 n. 22, 191 n. 22, 201, 201 n. 74
Legio I Italica, 142
Legio IV Flavia Firma, 141
Legio VII Claudia, 142
Legio IX Claudia, 142
Legio XIII Gemina, 142
Legio XIV Gemina, 142
Lendon, Jon (Ted), 7 n. 3–4, 11 n. 16, 13, 13 n. 26, 103 n. 27, 104 n. 31, 151 n. 4, 152, 152 n. 8–9, 154 n. 27, 155 n. 42, 157, 160 n. 66, 162 n. 72, n. 74
Leo I, 170
Leo VI, 4, 251, 252, 253, 259, 265, 265 n. 7, 266, 267, 268, 269, 272, 273–4, 288 n. 19, 292, 292 n. 35, 300, 300 n. 82
    Taktika, 255–8, 259, 267, 273, 288, 292, 297, 300
Leo the Deacon, 276–7
Leo Katakylas/Katakalon, 272
Leonidas I, 36–8, 38 n. 5, 40–2, 42 n. 14, 43, 46, 50–1
Levant, 208, 218 n. 52, 219

lex Villia Annalis, 90
Li Chong, 226–7
Li Longji (Xuanzong), 228
Li Mi, 227
Li Wanrong, 239
Li Weiyue, 233
Libanius, 155, 155 n. 36, 156, 160
libertas, 136, 136 n. 88, 137 n. 91
Libya, 165–6, 178, 193 n. 29
Libyans, 173–4, 174 n. 58, 175, 175 n. 60, 177, 184, 204 n. 84
Licinius Crassus, M. (cos. 70 BC), 128 n. 53, 131 n. 69, 136
Liguria, 93
Ligustinus, Sp., 93
Linming, 233, 239 n. 52
Livy, 89 n. 18, 90 n. 19, 100 n. 11, 107 n. 47, 123, 123 n. 32, 129, 172 n. 43, 221 n. 64, 294, 294 n. 50
Locrians, 38 n. 5, 45 n. 22
Locris, 38
Loewe, Michael, 238, 238 n. 47
Lucian, 154, 154 n. 36, 155
  How to Write History, 155
Lucius Verus, 263
Luo (River), 227
Lycia, 244
Lydia, 92

Ma Sui, 233–4
Macameus, 160
McAuley, Alex, 3, 67–8 n. 5,72 n. 18, 73 n. 20, 78 n. 41, 81 n. 51
MacDonald, Eve, 5, 206
Macedonia, 86, 93, 144
Macedonians, 74, 74 n. 28, 280 n. 92
Magnesia, 80
Magnesia (Battle of), 87, 87 n. 3
magister militum Africae, 187, 192
Maiozamalcha, 160, 160 n. 66
Majorian, 170, 170 n. 36
Malians, 38 n. 5, 39 n. 8
Malis, 38
Mallius Maximus, Cn. (cos. 105 BC), 136
Mammes (Battle of), 168
Mangshan, 227
Manilius, M., 118, 118 n. 9
  Astronomica, 118, 118 n. 9
Manuel I Komnenos, 286, 286 n. 8–9, 287 n. 11, 290, 290 n. 27, 293 n. 41, 297
Manzikert (Battle of), 290
Marathon (Battle of), 29, 29 n. 71, 30, 38 n. 5, 42, 45 n. 21, n. 23, 47, 49, 49 n. 35, 50, 50 n. 35, 60 n. 18
Marcianopolis, 139, 143, 145

Marcomanni, 126, 133
Marcus Aurelius, 2, 4, 263
Mardonius, 86–7
margazān, 213
Marius C. (cos. 107 BC), 4, 96–7, 97 n. 46, 100, 100 n. 7, 109 n. 58, 127 n. 49, 136–7
Maroboduus, 125, 133
Marsi, 128
Marta, 199
Martin, Gunther, 140, 140 n. 2, n. 4, 141, 141 n. 5, 143, 143 n. 14–15, 144 n. 16–18, 145 n. 19, n. 21, 146, 146 n. 23, 147, 147 n. 25–6, 149, 149 n. 31–2
Massinissa, 198 n. 60
Massagetae (Huns), 176
Matthews, John 152 n. 11, 153, 153 n. 22, 154 n. 32, 155 n. 41
Maurus, 16
Maurice, 4, 161, 165 n. 4, 167, 190, 190 n. 18, n. 20, 193 n. 35, 194 n. 36, n. 41, 196, 199 n. 64, 201 n. 69–70, 202 n. 78, 247–8, 248 n. 29, 249, 249 n. 30–2, 250, 250 n. 35, 251 n. 39, 253, 253 n. 48, 252 n. 44, 253, 254 n. 51, 255–6, 256 n. 66, 259–61, 265, 267, 267 n. 15, 287, 295 n. 54
  Strategikon, 161, 167, 190 n. 20, 247, 267, 272 n. 50, 287
Maximinus Thrax, 4, 142, 266 n. 9, 296
Mazzucchi, Carlo, 252 n. 43, 253 n. 49, 254, 254 n. 54–5, 280 n. 91, 281 n. 96
Mecella, Laura, 140. 140 n. 2, n. 4, 141, 141 n. 15, 144 n. 18, 146–7, 147 n. 26, 148–50 n. 32, 242 n. 2, 257 n. 71, n. 73, 258 n. 74
Medic Wars, 160
Mediceo-Laurentianus, 251
Megara, 26, 49
Megarians, 27–8
Megasthenes, 74, 74 n. 26, 76–7, 77 n. 37, 79, 79 n. 49, 82, 82 n. 54, 83–4, 310
  Indica, 74, 82, 82 n. 54
Megistias, 43, 43 n. 18, 45, 45 n. 22, n. 24, 48, 48 n. 31
Mercurium, 171
Merv, 208 n. 8, 213, 214 n. 34
Messenian helots, 47
Michael III, 265, 297, 304
Michael IV, 265, 265 n. 6
Michael V, 265, 265 n. 6
Michael VI Stratiotikos, 296, 296 n. 65
Michael Attaleiates, 286, 290, 298, 302
  History, 286, 290, 302
Michael Botaneiates, 302
Milesians, 76
Military tribune, 89, 89 n. 14, n. 18, 90, 90 n. 18–19, 91, 93–4, 299, 301–2

358 | INDEX

Miletus, 73, 76, 79
Ming, 231
Mithridates VI, 97
Moesia Inferior, 141–43, 149
Moesia Superior, 142
Moesians, 140
Moore, Rosemary, 9 n. 11, 10 n. 14, 16 n. 33, 299, 299 n. 78–9
Moors, 169, 169 n. 28, 174 n. 58, 185, 193 n. 29
Mount Athos, 38
Mount Callidromus, 42
Mount Haemus, 141, 143, 145
Mount Papua, 182
Mount Parnassus, 43
Movsēs Daskhurants'i, 216 n. 44, 217

Naarmalcha (River), 162
nauarchoi, 70, 71 n. 12
naukraroi, 23, 25 n. 59
Naudé, Charles, 154, 154 n. 35
neglegentia, 118, 118 n. 12–13
Nero, 137, 137 n. 88
Nerva, 137
Neville, Leonora, 185, 186, 186 n. 97, 286 n. 11
New Carthage, 93, 95
Nicaea, 296
Nikephoros Ouranos, 257–8 n. 74, 259, 266
    Taktika, 257, 259, 266
Nikephoros Phokas, 268–9
Nikephoros II Phokas, 268, 270, 274, 276, 278, 279, 280, 282
Nikephoros III Botaneiates, 290–1, 302, 304
Niketas Choniates, 286
Nicias, 3, 43 n. 18, 52
Nicopolis (Nicopol), 140–3, 145–6
Nikolov, Nikolay, 141
Nile (River), 10
Nipperdey, Karl, 130, 130 n. 63
Nisaea, 27–8, 33
nobiles, 96
Nolan, David, 1, 98, 100 n. 11, 102 n. 17, 105 n. 36, n. 38, 106 n. 43–4
Northern Qi, 228
Northern Zhou, 226
novus homo, 96
Numidia, 96, 169 n. 28, 177, 182, 192, 203

Octavian *see* Augustus
Octodurus, 103, 105–6
Odysseus, 3, 9–10, 10 n. 15, 15 n. 31, 33, 54, 152, 152 n. 10, 160, 198 n. 60
Oescus (Pleven), 141, 143, 145
O'Gorman, Ellen, 116 n. 4, 130, 130 n. 65
oikoumene, 80, 84
Olympia, 38 n. 5

Olympiad, 140
Onasander, 244–9, 249 n. 31, 250–1, 251 n. 39, 253–6, 256 n. 65–6, 257 n. 73, 258–9, 261, 267, 288
    Strategikos, 244–61, 267
Osenets, 142
Ostrogotha, 143, 148
Ostrogoths, 276
Ovid, 137

Pacorus, 136
Pahlavi Rivāyat, 213, 213 n. 29
Pannonia Superior, 142
Papirius Carbo, Cn. (cos. 113 BC), 136, 136 n. 88
parakoimomenos, 254, 270, 278–9, 282–3
Parmenio, 87
Parthians, 128 n. 53, 136
Pataliputra, 77, 77 n. 37
pater familias, 170
patricius, 204, 204 n. 82
Patrocles 74, 74 n. 25–6, 76–9, 79 n. 44, 82–4
    Periplus, 83–4, 84 n. 62
Patroclus 54
Pausanias, 20 n. 43, 25 n. 58, 31 n. 73, 46, 46 n. 25
Pausanias (Regent of Sparta), 46–9
Pax Augusta, 244
Peleus, 297, 303
Peloponnese, 26, 38 n. 5
Peloponnesian War, 8, 8 n. 10, 9, 27, 37 n. 2, 44 n. 19, 55–6, 58 n. 15, 225
Pericles, 3, 8 n. 10, 58, 58 n. 15, 59, 59 n. 15, 60, 60 n. 19, 87–8, 189 n. 12, 204
Persian Empire, 38 n. 5, 51, 58, 225
Persian Wars, 8, 8 n. 10, 33 n. 78, 41–2, 44 n. 19, 45 n. 21, 49, 51, 60, 60 n.18, 206 n. 2
Persians, 5–6, 29 n. 71, 36–7, 37 n. 2, 38–41, 41 n. 12, 42 n. 14–15, 43, 43 n. 17, 44–5 n. 24, 47, 51, 57, 161–2, 175, 175 n. 64, 212, 275
Philip ('governor of Macedonian and Thracian cities'), 144
Philip II, 3, 3 n. 9, 86, 299 n. 78
Philip V, 87, 87 n. 5, 95
Philippopolis (Plovdiv), 139–41, 143–50
Philetaerus, 73
Philostratus, 146
Phocians, 38–40 n. 10
Phocion, 88
Phocis, 38
Phoenix, 297, 303
Phylacus, 42
Pindar, 44
Pirisabora, 158–60
Plataea, 24 n. 56, 33 n. 79, 37, 37 n. 2–3, 38 n. 5, 46, 48–50 n. 35, 60 n. 18, 86, 86 n. 1
Plato, 4, 52, 52 n. 1, 53–4, 54 n. 7, 55–7 n. 11, 58,

58 n. 13–14, 59–60, 60 n. 18, 61, 61 n. 24, 62–6, 244, 249 n. 31
Apology, 54, 56
Euthydemus, 61
Gorgias, 59
Ion, 7 n. 5, 53, 59
Laches, 52
Laws, 52–3, 57, 59–64
Meno, 58
Republic, 54, 61–4
Statesman, 60–1
Symposium, 55–6
Pliny the Elder, 79, 79 n. 46, 83, 83 n. 59, 101 n. 13, 123, 123 n. 33
Plutarch, 6, 31 n. 73, 40 n. 10, 47 n. 27, 50 n. 36, 52 n. 1, 60 n. 18, 77, 101 n. 13, 104 n. 29
polis, 23–5, 25 n. 59, 39 n. 8, 47 n. 27, 85
Polyaenus, 26, 31 n. 73, 78, 78 n. 41, 243, 243 n. 5, 259–61, 263
  Strategemata (*Strategika*), 243, 263, 267
Polybius (Polybios), 8–9, 9 n. 12, 70–1 n. 12, 95 n. 44, 107, 107 n. 51, 114 n. 78, 153, 159, 287 n. 12, 289, 292, 294 n. 48, 303, 305
Pompeius Magnus, Cn. (Pompey the Great, cos. 70 BC), 89, 89 n. 15, 97, 97 n. 47, 99–100 n. 7–8, n. 11
Pomponius, P., 128
Porcius Cato, M. (Cato the Elder, cos. 195 BC), 40 n. 10, 42, 90, 94–5
Porcius Cato, M. (Cato the Younger), 97, 104 n. 29
Porphyry, 73 n. 20, 78, 78 n. 39 and 41
Postumus, 150
Potidaea, 55
Potter, David, 2, 97 n. 48, 139, 141 n. 6, 142 n. 11–12, 148 n. 27, 149 n. 30
Praetor (praetorship), 87, 91, 91 n. 25, 93
Praetorian prefect, 165, 173
praetorium, 95
Priscus, L., 144, 146
Procopius (also Prokopios), 152 n. 10, 155, 156 n. 47, 161, 164, 164 n. 2, 165, 165 n. 5, n. 7, 166, 166 n. 11, n. 15, 167–8, 168 n. 26, 169–70, 170 n. 32–3, n. 36, 171–2, 172 n. 46–7, n. 49, 173, 173 n. 50, 174, 174 n. 57–8, 175, 175 n. 60, n. 62, 176, 176 n. 66, 177, 177 n. 70, 178–9, 179 n. 75–6, 180–1, 181 n. 80, 182, 182 n. 81, n. 83, 183, 183 n. 85, n. 87, 184–5, 185 n. 94–5, 186, 187 n. 1, 188, 188d n. 4–5, n. 9, 189, 189 n. 11–13, 190–1, 193 n. 29, 194, 194 n. 38–9, 195 n. 42, 197–9, 203, 203 n. 81, 204, 204 n. 82, n. 84, 266 n. 12, 292, 298, 300
  de bellis (*Wars*), 188–9
prorogatio, 86

provincia, 89
proxenos, 76, 76 n. 35
Psellos, Michael, 262, 262 n. 88, 263, 263 n. 90, 287 n. 18, 291, 291 n. 32, 292
Pseudo-Hermogenes, 155. 155 n. 37
Pourshariati, Parvaneh, 206 n. 2, 207 n. 5, 211 n. 20, 213 n. 26, 214, 214 n. 33, 222 n. 68
Putzintulus, 197 n. 56, 199
Pydna (Battle of), 4, 95
Pythia, 42

quaestor (also quaestors), 90–1, 93–4
quaestorship, 90, 90 n. 21
Quellenforschungen, 246
Quinctilius Varus, P. (cos. 13 BC), 4, 116, 116 n. 3, 117, 117 n. 7, n. 8, 118–19, 119 n. 18, 120, 120 n. 22, 121–2, 122 n. 28, 123, 123 n. 32, n. 34, 124–5, 125 n. 40, 126–7, 127 n. 48–9, 128, 128 n. 54–5, 129–33, 133 n. 77–8, 134, 134 n. 80–1, 135–8, 138 n. 92
Quinctius Flamininus, T. (cos. 198 BC), 87, 87 n. 5, 93

Radoslavova, Galena, 141
Rance, Philip, 4, 167 n. 16, 176 n. 67, 90, 90 n. 18, n. 20, 199 n. 64, 201 n. 69, 203 n. 79, 242, 242 n. 2–3, 243 n.5, 244 n. 6, 245 n. 10, 246 n. 15, 247 n. 19, n. 21–2, 248 n. 25, n. 28, 249 n. 30, n. 33, 250 n. 34, n. 36, 251 n. 41, 252 n. 42–6, 253 n. 47–50, 254 n. 51–52 and 54, 255 n. 58, n. 60–1, 256 n. 65, 257 n. 71, n. 73, 258 n. 74, n. 77, 259 n. 79, 260 n. 80–1, 261 n. 83, n. 86, 262 n. 87, 263 n. 93, 267 n. 15, n. 19, 281, 281 n. 96, 287 n. 13, 288 n. 19, 294 n. 47
Rashidun Caliphate (Caliphs), 206, 207 n. 4, 210 n. 15, 215 n. 39
Razgrad (Abritus), 141, 145
Rhine (River), 104, 113, 126, 131, 135, 137
Rhomaioi, 243, 262–3, 288–9
Richardot, Philippe, 187 n. 3, 193 n. 28, 196 n. 55, 200 n. 68, 202, 202 n. 75 and 77
Ricinarius, 198, 201–2
Rigault, Nicolas, 247, 247 n. 23
Rockwell, Nicholas, 4, 52
Roman Republic, 4, 67, 86, 93, 221 n. 64
Romanos I Lekapenos, 265–6, 278
Romanos II, 265, 269, 271–2, 274, 276, 281–3
Romanos III Argyrus, 262, 265, 265 n. 6
Romanos IV Diogenes, 290–1, 297–9, 304–5
Rome, 5, 91, 93–4, 96, 105 n. 40, 129, 134 n. 81, 137, 142, 145, 152 n. 7, 170, 170 n. 32, 178, 183, 206 n. 2, 245, 262, 274–5, 275 n. 67, 299 n. 78

Ross, Alan, 137 n. 89, 151, 152 n. 12, 153,
    153 n. 21, n. 23, 154 n. 29–30, 155 n. 36, 156,
    156 n. 45, 157 n. 50, 161, 161 n. 68, 164 n. 3,
    175 n. 65, 279 n. 85
Rostam b. Farrokh-Hormozd, 211, 211 n. 16,
    n. 20, 212, 212 n. 22, n. 24, 213, 213 n. 26,
    214, 214 n. 32–3, 215–17, 222–4
Rouveret, Agnès, 134, 134 n. 85
Rus, 278–9

Sabbah, Guy, 153, 153 n. 25, 156, 156 n. 48
Sabinus *see* Titurius Sabinus
Sa'd ibn Abī Waqqās, 208
Saint Sergius of Rusafa, 209 n. 13, 222 n. 67
Salamis, 27–8, 28 n. 66, 37, 37 n. 3, 39, 45 n. 21, 56
Sallust, 96, 96 n. 45, 101 n. 15, 104 n. 31,
    109 n. 58, 114, 221 n. 64
Sallustius, 159
Samaras, Thanassis, 63, 63 n. 28, 64,
    64 n. 29–31
Samnites, 136
Sardinia, 171, 173–4, 178, 181, 204
Sardis, 71 n. 12, 78, 81, 87
Sassanids, 187
Saturn (Temple of), 130
Savalli-Lestrade, Ivana, 71, 71 n. 14, 73 n. 22
Sayf al-Dawla, 270
Scalae Veteres, 191
Schofield, Malcom, 62, 62 n. 25, 63, 63 n. 27
Scipio Aemilianus *see* Cornelius Scipio
    Aemilianus, P. (cos. 147 BC)
Scythians, 140, 143, 275, 278, 288 n. 19
Sebēos, 214 n. 34, 215, 215 n. 38, 216 n. 43–4,
    219 219 n. 54, n. 58, 220, 220 n. 59, 222,
    222 n. 68
Second Sophistic, 246
Segestes, 121, 125, 125 n. 40, 126–7, 132
Segimerus, 132–3
Seidman, Jessica, 116 n. 4, 130, 130 n. 62
Seleucus I, 69–70, 74, 76–80, 82–3
Seleucus II, 78 n. 41
Seleucus IV, 70
Sempronius Gracchus, Ti. (cos. 215 BC), 96
Sempronius Gracchus, Ti. (cos. 177 BC), 93
Seneca, 118, 118 n. 13
Sergius, 188 n. 5, 192, 204, 204 n. 88
'Serpent Column', 48
Servilius Caepio, Q. (cos. 106 BC), 136
Servilius Geminus, Cn. (cos. 217 BC), 96
servitus, 136
Shahnameh (Šah-nāma) 211, 211 n. 18–19, 212,
    212 n. 23, 213
shophets, 88
Sibyrtius, 79–80

Sicily, 46, 50, 50 n. 35, 87, 91, 173, 173 n. 53,
    183 n. 85, 188 n. 9, 191, 223
Simon, 136
Simonides (of Ceos), 44–5, 45 n. 21–2, 46–7,
    49–50, 49 n. 35, 50 n. 56, 51
Sinduit, 197 n. 56, 199, 199 n. 63
Singidunum, 142
Skylitzes *see* John Scylitzes (Skylitzes)
Smbat Bagratuni, 219, 219 n. 58, 220 n. 59
Smith, Rowland, 159, 159 n. 61, 160, 160 n. 62–3,
    n. 65, 187 n. 3
Socrates, 53–7, 57 n. 11, 58–9, 62–3, 65–6
Socrates Scholasticus (Sokrates Scholastikos), 292
Sogdiana, 76 n. 33, 78
Solomon, 168, 168 n. 26, 187–8, 188 n. 5,
    189 n. 12, 191–2, 199–200 n. 67, 204,
    204 n. 88, 205
Sophanes, 160
Spain, 1, 91, 93, 96–7, 223
Sparta, 3, 23 n. 51, 26, 30, 32–3 n. 78, 36–7,
    37 n. 2, 38 n. 5, 43, 46, 46 n. 25, 47, 51
Spartacus, 97
Spartan, 1, 10, 18, 20, 20 n. 43, 21, 21 n. 45,
    22, 24, 24 n. 55–6, 25, 25 n. 58–9, 26–27,
    30–2 n. 75, 34, 40, 43–4 n. 19, 46, 50–1 n. 37,
    168 n. 21
Spartans, 18, 20, 25 n. 58, 30, 32–3 n. 79, 36, 38,
    38 n. 5, 39 n. 8, 41, 41 n. 12, 43, 43 n. 18,
    44 n. 19, 45, 45 n. 22, 46, 48
Spartiates, 38 n. 5, 39, 45 n. 24, 50–1 n. 37
Spercheius (River), 40, 45, 45 n. 24
Spirit of Wisdom, 206
Stephenson, Paul, 196, 196 n. 51, 203 n. 81,
    275 n. 66, n. 68
Stertinius, L., 127, 127 n. 50, 132, 132 n. 74
Stewart, Michael, 5, 164, 168 n. 26, 183 n. 89,
    185 n. 95, 215 n. 37, 218 n. 49, 219 n. 57,
    266 n. 12, 276 n. 70, 285 n. 5
Stotzas, 191
Strabo, 73 n. 21, 74 n. 26, 77, 77 n. 37, 79 n. 44,
    118
Strasbourg (Battle of Strasburg, Argentoratum),
    152, 154–6, 156 n. 48, 157–8, 158 n. 55, 160
Strategikon see Maurice *Strategikon*
strategoi, 9, 17–18, 24–6, 32 n. 75, 70, 72, 87
strategos, 17–18, 22, 27, 27 n. 63, 70, 70 n. 7, n. 11,
    71, 71 n. 12–13, 270, 280, 290
Strootman, Rolf, 68, 68 n. 4, 77 n. 38, 84 n. 65,
    85 n. 67
Smyrna, 80, 80 n. 50, 81
Suda, 244, 244 n. 6, 247
Suetonius, 101, 118
    Augustus, 118 n. 11
    Tiberius, 118
    Caligula, 118 n. 61

Sui dynasty, 226–7
Sulpicius, Galba, Ser. 103, 103 n. 27–8
Sunzi, *Art of War (Sunzi bingfa)*, 225–6
Syllectus, 174
Sylloge Tacticorum, 252, 252 n. 44, 257, 259–61, 266–7 n. 14
Syncellus, George, 140–1
synedron, 74
Syracusans, 44 n. 20
Syracuse, 3, 43 n. 18, 45, 50, 50 n. 35–6, 173
Syria, 81 n. 51, 117 n. 8, 119, 119 n. 18, 136, 142, 208, 218, 218 n. 52, 222–3, 268, 273
Syriac, 209
Syrian, 40 n. 10, 81, 93, 175 n. 60
Syrianus (Syrianos), 294, 297

Tacitus, Cornelius, 116–17, 121, 123, 123 n. 33, 124–7, 127 n. 48, 128–31, 130 n. 68, 132–4, 134 n. 85, 135–8
 Germania, 137, 137 n. 91
 Historiae, 135–6
 Annales, 124–7, 135–6
Taihang Mountains, 233
Taiyuan, 228
Tang dynasty, 5, 227, 232, 235–6
Tarsus, 269
Taylor, Michael, 4, 86, 87 n. 6, 92 n. 26–7
Tebesta, 192
temeritas, 118, 118 n. 12
Terentius Varro, C. (cos. 216 BC), 92
Teutoburg Forest, 4, 116, 116 n. 2, 117–19, 123 n. 32, 124–9, 131, 131 n. 70, 132–5
Teutones, 96–7
Theban, 3, 22 n. 50, 37 n. 2, 38 n. 5, 40, 49 n. 33
Thebes, 3, 28, 37 n. 2, 38, 38 n. 5, 47 n. 29
Themistocles, 3, 41, 50, 50 n. 36, 58–60, 60 n. 17–18
Theodore Laskaris, 294
Theodore Prodromos, 286 n. 10
Theodore Trithurious, 218 n. 52
Theophanes, 218 n. 52, 221 n. 65, 304 n. 99
Theophilos, 297, 304
Theophylact Simocatta (Theophylactos Simokattes), 301, 301 n. 90, 302, 302 n. 91–2
Therma, 38
Thermopylae (Thermopylai), 2, 36–7, 37 n. 3, 38, 38 n. 5, 39, 39 n. 6, n. 8, 41, 41 n. 12, 42, 42 n. 14, 43, 43 n. 18, 44, 44 n. 19, 45, 45 n. 21, 46–7, 47 n. 29, 49–50, 49 n. 35, 51, 51 n. 37, 60 n. 18, 150
Thespiae, 38, 38 n. 5
Thespian(s), 40, 45 n. 22
Thessalian, 33 n. 79, 160
Thessalonike (Thessaloniki), 242, 303
Thessaly, 36, 38

Third Macedonian War, 93
Thirteenth Sibylline Book, 142
Thirty Tyrants, 56–7, 57 n. 11
Thomas (the Slav), 296
Thrace, 6, 21, 38, 43 n. 17, 86, 144, 278
Thracian(s), 17 n. 34, 26 n. 61, 29, 140, 144–8
Thucydides, 43 n. 18, 44, 44 n. 19, 48–9, 58, 60 n. 19, 153, 166, 166 n. 13, 167 n. 17, 168, 168 n. 21, 172 n. 45, 175 n. 61–2, 183 n. 85, 189 n. 12, 195 n. 42, 225, 245
Tian Chengsi, 230, 230 n. 17, 231–2, 235, 237
Tian Xu, 237, 237 n. 44, 239
Tian Yue, 227–8, 230, 230 n. 17, 231–2, 232 n. 31, 233–4, 234 n. 35, 235, 235 n. 40, 237–9, 239 n. 52, 241
Tiberius, 118–20, 120 n. 22, 124, 128 n. 54, 130–1, 131 n. 69
Tiberius (Nero, Tac. *Germ.* 37), 136
Tiberius (Byzantine emperor), 266 n. 8
Tigris (River), 71 n. 12, 208
Tissaphernes, 92, 92 n. 30
Titurius Sabinus, 98 n. 2, 104, 104 n. 33, 105–6, 106 n. 44, 108–9, 109 n. 56
Titus, 152, 170
Totila, 168, 172 n. 49
Trachis, 39, 39 n. 8, 42
Trajan, 2, 136–7, 262–3
Trasimene Lake (Battle of), 4, 122
Trebia River (Battle of), 92
Trebonianus Gallus, C. Vibius, 140–3, 148
triarii, 92
Tribunes of the plebs, 91, 91 n. 23
tribunus militum, 90 n. 19; *see also* military tribune
Tricamerum, 179, 181, 184
triplex acies, 91–2
Tripolis, 171
Tripolitania, 192, 203
Tripolitanian, 192
Triremes, 39, 59
Tullius Cicero, M. (cos. 63 BC), 97, 100–1, 101 n. 15, 114
Tullius Cicero, Q, 105, 113, 113 n. 77
Tunis, 92, 92 n. 27
Turnus, 203
Tyche, 1, 114, 114 n. 78, 176–7 n. 70, 184, 186, 195 n. 47, 261, 289–92, 299, 305
Tyron, 75
Tzazo, 178–9, 181, 181 n. 80, 182

Ubii, 132
Umar, 207, 222 n. 68

Vadomarius, 157
Vahān, 218, 218 n. 51–2, 219. 219 n. 54, 220, 223

362 | INDEX

Valens, 4, 152–3 n. 14, 154, 156 n. 48, 157–8, 158 n. 55, 159
Valentinian I, 4, 154, 154 n. 33,
Valentinian III, 169–70, 170 n. 32, 178
Vandalic, 171–3 n. 54, 175, 175 n. 60, 185, 187–9 n. 11
Vandals, 140, 164–5, 169, 169 n. 28, 170–1, 173–4, 174 n. 58, 175, 175 n. 62, n. 64, 176–83, 183 n. 85, 184–5, 185 n. 94, 186, 191, 204–5
Van Nuffelen, Peter, 172 n. 46, 184, 184 n. 91, 185 n. 96
Varaz-Grigor, 217
Vegetius, 161, 166 n. 16, 190, 196 n. 49, 246, 294
 Epitoma rei militaris, 246
Velleius Paterculus, 117, 119, 119 n. 17, 120–1, 121 n. 26, 122 n. 28, 123, 125, 131, 135
Ventidius Bassus, P. (cos. suff. 43 BC), 136
Veranius, Q. (cos. AD 49), 244, 246, 263
Vercingetorix, 100, 109, 109 n. 58, n. 60, 110, 110 n. 60
Vergil (Virgil), 129, 294, 294 n. 50–1
Vespasian, 136
Vienna palimpsest, 139–40, 143–4, 147
Viminacium, 142
Virgilio, Biagio, 78, 78 n. 40
Viridovix, 108
Visigoths, 169
Völkerwanderung, 96
Voltaire, 289 n. 22
Voltairian, 288
Volusianus, 140
Von Clausewitz, Carl, 305

Wander, Steven, 270 n. 41, 278 n. 81, 279 n. 85–6, 280 n. 90, 281, 281 n. 93, n. 95–6, 282 n. 99, n. 101
Wang Shichong, 227, 227 n. 7
Wang Xiong, 226–7, 226 n. 5
Wei-Bo, 227, 230–4 n. 35, 235 n. 40, 236, 236 n. 43, 237–8
Weizhou, 227–8, 230, 230 n. 20, 233–4, 234 n. 35, 236–7
Weser (River), 133
Western Wei, 226
West Point, 86
Wey, 231, 231 n. 23
Whately, Conor, 4, 151, 152 n. 10, 155 n. 38, 156 n. 47, 157 n. 49, 161 n. 69, 164 n. 3, 166 n. 11–13, n. 15, 167 n. 16, 171 n. 38, 41, 172 n. 43, 173 n. 52, 176 n. 68, 179 n. 78, 188 n. 5–6, n. 8, 189 n. 10–11, n. 14, 190 n. 20, 196 n. 48, 198 n. 59, 259 n. 79
Wheeler, Everett, 7 n. 3–4, 9, 9 n. 12–14, 11 n. 16, 14 n. 28, 15 n. 31, 16 n. 33, 17 n. 35, 18 n. 38, 19 n. 39, 21, 21 n. 44, 23 n. 51, 151 n. 7, 152 n. 10, 158 n. 56, 159 n. 59, 243 n. 5, 249 n. 31, 260 n. 82, 263 n. 92–3
Wood, Philip, 171 n. 38, 172 n. 45 and 48, 174 n. 56–7, 175 n. 64, 184 n. 92, 188 n. 5, 201 n. 70, 204 n. 84
Woodman, Anthony, 120 n. 22, 129, 129 n. 59–60
Wu, 225

Xenophon, 3, 15 n. 31, 21 n. 45, 58 n. 14, 153, 245
 Cyropaedia, 250
Xerxes, 37, 39–40, 40 n. 10–11, 41–2 n. 14, 47, 47 n. 29, 48, 50 n. 35, 86, 165 n. 7, 172 n. 43
Xiang, 231
Xiang-Wey, 231
Xingzhou, 233
Xuanwu, 240
Xuanzong *see* Li Longji
Xue Song, 231

Yazdgerd III, 208, 208 n. 7–8, 211, 213, 214 n. 34, 215
Ye, 228
Yellow River, 230–1
Ying, 230–1
Youzhou, 236

Zacharias, 175 n. 60
Zama, 4, 92, 92 n. 27
Zeuxis, 87, 87 n. 3
Zhang (River), 233
Zhaoyi, 233, 239
Zhou dynasty, 225
Zhu Ci, 236
Zhu Tao, 236–7
Zi-Qing, 234
Zoe, 265, 265 n. 6
Zonaras, *Epitome of the Histories*, 141
Zoroastrian, 206, 209, 211, 213, 216 n. 41, 217, 222
Zosimus, *New History* 141

EU representative:
Easy Access System Europe
Mustamäe tee 50, 10621 Tallinn, Estonia
Gpsr.requests@easproject.com